ESSENTIALS OF MARKETING

FRANCES BRASSINGTON AND STEPHEN PETTITT

ESSENTIALS OF MARKETING
Brassington and Pettitt

FT Prentice Hall
FINANCIAL TIMES

An imprint of **Pearson Education**
Harlow, England • London • New York • Boston • San Francisco • Toronto • Sydney • Singapore • Hong Kong
Tokyo • Seoul • Taipei • New Delhi • Cape Town • Madrid • Mexico City • Amsterdam • Munich • Paris • Milan

Pearson Education Limited
Edinburgh Gate
Harlow
Essex CM20 2JE
England

and Associated Companies throughout the world

Visit us on the World Wide Web at:
www.pearsoned.co.uk

———————————

First published 2005

ISBN-10: 0-273-68785-9
ISBN-13: 978-0-273-68785-6

British Library Cataloguing-in-Publication Data
A catalogue record for this book is available from the British Library

Library of Congress Cataloging-in-Publication Data
Brassington, Frances.
    Essentials of marketing / Frances Brassington, Stephen Pettitt.
        p. cm
    Includes bibliographical references and index.
    ISBN 0-273-68785-9
    1. Marketing. I. Petitt, Stephen. II. Title.

    HF5415.B6336 2005
    658.8--dc22   2004047193

10 9 8 7 6 5 4 3 2
09 08 07 06 05

Typeset in 9.5/11.5 pt ITC Century Book by 30
Printed and bound by Mateu Chromo

The publisher's policy is to use paper manufactured from sustainable forests.

ESSENTIALS OF MARKETING

Visit the Essentials of Marketing Companion Website at **www.booksites.net/brassington** to find valuable student learning material including:

- Multiple choice questions to help test your learning
- Annotated links to relevant sites on the web
- An online glossary to explain key terms

Essentials of Marketing - Microsoft Internet Explorer

File   Edit   View   Favorites   Tools   Help

Address http://www.booksites.net/brassington   ▾ ➔ Go

PEARSON Education

ESSENTIALS OF MARKETING · · ·

FRANCES BRASSINGTON AND STEPHEN PETTITT

Home | Select Resource | Welcome ▾   Site Search: [   ] Go ❓

Welcome to the Companion Website for Essentials of Marketing.

ESSENTIALS OF MARKETING

Select the sections below, or use the drop-down menu above to navigate through the website. Use the 'Syllabus Manager' button within the sections to create and post your personalised online syllabus.

About the Book

Contains information on what you will find on this website, along with specific details about the book and its author.

Student Resources

A multitude of helpful resources to further increase your knowledge. Each chapter contains multiple choice questions to help test your understanding and annotated links to relevant sites on the Internet. There is also a comprehensive online glossary to explain key terms.

Lecturer Resources

Useful resources that can save you time and help to enhance your students' learning experience. Please note that these resources, including Instructor's Resource Manual and PowerPoint slides, are password protected and access is only given to verified lecturers. To apply for a password, use our password registration form. Your Pearson Education representative will then contact you to provide you with a password.

Copyright © 1995-2004, Pearson Education, Inc. | **Legal and Privacy Terms**

Done   🔒 Internet

contents

Preface   ix
Guided tour of the book   x
Guided tour of the website   xii
About the authors   xiii
Acknowledgements   xiv
Publisher's acknowledgements   xv

Chapter 1
Marketing dynamics   1

Learning objectives   1
Introduction   1

Marketing defined   2
   What marketing means   2
   The development of marketing   7
   Buisness orientations   7

The marketing concept in the organisation   15
   The external organisational environment   15
   The internal organisational environment   16
   Marketing as an integrative business function   17

Marketing management responsibilities   19
   Identifying customer needs   19
   Satisfying customer needs   20
   Strategic vision   24

Marketing scope   25
   Consumer goods   26
   B2B goods   26
   Service goods   26
   Non-profit marketing   26
   Small business marketing   27
   International marketing   27
   e-marketing   27

Chapter summary   28
Questions for review and discussion   28
Case study 1.1: lastminute.com: inspiration and
   solutions   29
References for chapter 1   31

Chapter 2
The European marketing
environment   33

Learning objectives   33
Introduction   33

The nature of the European marketing
   environment   34

Elements of the marketing environment   34
   Environmental scanning   35

The sociocultural environment   36
   The demographic environment   37
   Sociocultural influences   39

The technological environment   45
   Materials, components and products   46
   Production processes   46
   Administration and distribution   47
   Marketing and customers   47

The economic and competitive environment   48
   The macroeconomic environment   48
   The microeconomic environment   51

The political and regulatory environment   54
   National and local government   54
   The European Union   57
   Regulatory bodies   58
   Influences on the political and regulatory
      environment   61

Chapter summary   62
Questions for review and discussion   62
Case study 2.1: A Friend in need is a Friend
   indeed   63
References for chapter 2   64

Chapter 3
Buyer behaviour   66

Learning objectives   66
Introduction   66

The decision-making process   66
   Problem recognition   67
   Information search   68
   Information evaluation   69
   Decision   70
   Post-purchase evaluation   71

Buying situations   72
   Routine problem solving   72
   Limited problem solving   73
   Extended problem solving   74
   The significance of buying situations   74

Environmental influences   74
   Sociocultural influences   74
   Technological influences   75
   Economic and competitive influences   76
   Political and regulatory influences   76

Psychological influences: the individual 77
  Personality 77
  Perception 77
  Learning 78
  Motivation 79
  Attitudes 81
Sociocultural influences: the group 83
  Social class 83
  Culture and subculture 84
  Reference groups 87
  Family 88
Defining B2B marketing 91
B2B customers 92
Characteristics of B2B markets 93
  Nature of demand 93
  Structure of demand 93
  Buying process complexity 94
Buying decision-making process 96
  Precipitation 97
  Product specification 98
  Supplier selection 98
  Commitment 99
The buying centre 99
  Users 100
  Influencers 100
  Deciders 100
  Buyers 100
  Gatekeepers 101
Buying criteria 102
  Economic influences 102
  Non-economic influences 103
Chapter summary 103
Questions for review and discussion 104
Case study 3.1: Breezing out for a night on the
  tiles 104
References for chapter 3 106

Chapter 4
Segmenting markets 108

Learning objectives 108
Introduction 108
The concept of segmentation 109
Segmenting B2B markets 110
  Macro segmentation bases 110
  Micro segmentation bases 111
Segmenting consumer markets 112
  Geographic segmentation 112
  Demographic segmentation 113
  Geodemographic segmentation 113
  Psychographic segmentation 117
  Behaviour segmentation 119
  Multi-variable segmentation 122

Implementation of segmentation 123
  Targeting 123
Benefits of segmentation 127
  The customer 127
  The marketing mix 127
  The competition 127
Dangers of segmentation 127
Criteria for successful segmentation 128
  Distinctiveness 128
  Tangibility 128
  Accessibility 128
  Defendability 129
  B2B markets 129
Chapter summary 129
Questions for review and discussion 130
Case study 4.1: The pink pound 131
References for chapter 4 132

Chapter 5
**Marketing information and
research** 134

Learning objectives 134
Introduction 134
Marketing research: definition and role 135
  Defining marketing research 135
  The role of marketing research 136
Types of research 137
  The origins of research data 138
  Continuous research 139
Marketing information systems 141
  Sources of marketing information 142
Decision support systems 144
The marketing research process 144
  Problem definition 145
  Research objectives 145
  Planning the research 146
  Data collection 147
Secondary research 148
  Sources of secondary data 148
Primary research 149
  Research methods 149
  Sampling 157
Questionnaire design 159
  Conduct the research 163
  Analyse and interpret the information 165
  Prepare and present report 165
  Research evaluation 166
Ethics in marketing research 166
Chapter summary 168
Questions for review and discussion 168

Case study 5.1: Gathering information on an up-and-coming market   169
References for chapter 5   170

Chapter 6
Product   172

Learning objectives   172
Introduction   172
Anatomy of a product   173
  Product classification   174
  Understanding the product range   177
Branding   179
  The meaning of branding   180
  The benefits of branding   181
  Types of brands   183
Product management and strategy   184
  Creating the brand   184
  Developing the brand   191
  The product life cycle   195
  The diffusion of innovation   201
  Positioning and repositioning products   203
  Product management and organisation   206
  European product strategy   206
Chapter summary   207
Questions for review and discussion   208
Case study 6.1: Is small still beautiful second time around?   209
References for chapter 6   210

Chapter 7
Price   212

Learning objectives   212
Introduction   212
The role and perception of price   213
  The customer's perspective   213
  The seller's perspective   215
External influences on the pricing decision   217
  Customers and consumers   218
  Demand and price elasticity   218
  Channels of distribution   221
  Competitors   222
  Political and regulatory framework   223
Internal influences on the pricing decision   224
  Organisational objectives   224
  Marketing objectives   225
  Costs   226
The process of price setting   227
  Pricing objectives   228
  Demand assessment   230
  Pricing policies and strategies   230

  Setting the price range   234
  Pricing tactics and adjustments   238
Chapter summary   239
Questions for review and discussion   240
Case study 7.1: Kitting out the fans   240
References for chapter 7   241

Chapter 8
Place   243

Learning objectives   243
Introduction   243
Channel structures   244
  Consumer goods   244
  B2B goods   246
Rationale for using intermediaries   249
  Transactional value   250
  Logistical value   251
  Facilitating value   253
Types of intermediary   254
  Distributors and dealers   254
  Agents and brokers   254
  Wholesalers   255
  Franchisees   255
  Retailers   255
Channel strategy   265
  Channel structures   266
  Market coverage   268
  Influences on channel strategy   270
  Selecting a channel member   272
Chapter summary   274
Questions for review and discussion   275
Case study 8.1: Sweet harmony in the distribution channel   276
References for chapter 8   277

Chapter 9
Promotion: integrated marketing communications   279

Learning objectives   279
Introduction   279
Communications planning model   280
  Situation analysis (1): the target market   281
  Situation analysis (2): the product   287
  The product life cycle stage   288
  Situation analysis (3): the environment   290
  Objectives   293
  Strategies   294
  Budgeting   296
  Implementation and evaluation   299
Communications planning model: review   300

Chapter summary 300
Questions for review and discussion 301
Case study 9.1: Xbox: the mean green machine 301
References for chapter 9 303

Chapter 10
Promotion: advertising and personal selling 304

Learning objectives 304
Introduction 304

The role of advertising 305
Within the promotional mix 305
Within the marketing mix 307

Formulating the advertising message 308
Message 308
Creative appeals 310

Advertising media 312
Some definitions 313
Broadcast media 314
Cinema 315
Print media 315
Outdoor and ambient media 316

Using advertising agencies 318
Relative size of agency and client 318
Location and accessibility 318
Type of help required 319
Specialism 319
Track record 319
*Compatibility, empathy and personal
chemistry* 319
Business ability 319
The client–agency relationship 319

Developing an advertising campaign 320
Deciding on campaign responsibilities 320
Selecting the target audience 321
Campaign objectives 321
Campaign budgets 321
Media selection and planning 322
Advertising development and testing 322
Implementation and scheduling 323
Campaign evaluation 324

Personal selling: definition, role and tasks 324
Advantages of personal selling 325
Tasks of personal selling 327

The personal selling process 331
Prospecting 331
Preparation and planning 332
Initiating contact 332
The sales presentation 333
Follow-up and account management 335

Sales management 335
Planning and strategy 335
Recruitment and selection 336
Training 337
Motivation and compensation 338
Performance evaluation 339

Chapter summary 339
Questions for review and discussion 340
Case study 10.1: Driving a sober message
home 341
References for chapter 10 343

Chapter 11
Promotion: other tools of marketing communication 345

Learning objectives 345
Introduction 345

Sales promotion 346
Sales promotion: definition and role 346
Methods of sales promotion to consumers 353
*Methods of sales promotion to the retail
trade* 359
Sales promotion in B2B markets 361

Direct marketing 361
Direct marketing: definition and role 361
Techniques of direct marketing 364
Database creation and management 370

Trade shows and exhibitions 372

Public relations 373
Public relations: definitions and role 373
Techniques in public relations 375

Sponsorship 377
Sponsorship: definition and role 377
Types of sponsorship 378

Cause-related marketing 381

Chapter summary 382
Questions for review and discussion 383
Case study 11.1: Pennies off the price or points on
the plastic? 384
References for chapter 11 386

Chapter 12
Marketing management, planning and control 388

Learning objectives 388
Introduction 388

**The role and importance of marketing planning
and strategy** 389

Definitions   390
Influences on planning and strategy   393
Types of plan   395

The marketing planning process   397
Corporate objectives and values   398
The marketing audit   399
SWOT analysis   408
Marketing objectives   410
Marketing strategies   411
Intensive growth   412
Marketing programmes   419
Marketing budgets   419
Marketing controls and evaluation   419

Organising marketing activities   420
Organisational alternatives   420

Controlling marketing activities   423
Marketing control process   423

Chapter summary   424
Questions for review and discussion   424
Case study 12.1: Stopping the bottom falling out of
   the jeans market   425
References for chapter 12   426

Chapter 13
Services and non-profit marketing   428

Learning objectives   428
Introduction   428

Perspectives on services markets   429
Classifying services   429
Special characteristics of service markets   429

Services marketing management   436
Services marketing strategy   436

Interactive marketing: service quality   443
Internal marketing: training and productivity   446

Non-profit marketing   451
Classifying non-profit organisations   452
Marketing implications   456
Chapter summary   458
Questions for review and discussion   459
Case study 13.1: Full Stop   459
References for chapter 13   461

Chapter 14
e-marketing and new media   463

Learning objectives   463
Introduction   463

Internet marketing   465
The nature of Internet marketing   465
The website   467
Consumer Internet penetration and spending   468
B2B Internet spending   469
The marketing uses of a website   471
Broadband   478
The future of Internet marketing?   479

Marketing and new media   479
E-mail marketing   480
Wireless marketing   484
iTV marketing   488

Chapter summary   490
Questions for review and discussion   491
Case study 14.1: From dotcom to dotbomb to
   dotboom?   492
References for chapter 14   493

Index   496
Index of company names   508

Companion Website resources

Visit the Companion Website at **www.booksites.net/brassington**

For Students
■ Mulitple choice questions to help test your learning
■ Annotated links to relevant sites on the web
■ An online glossary to explain key terms

For lecturers
■ Complete, downloadable Instructor's Manual
■ PowerPoint slides that can be downloaded and used as OHTs

Also: This website has a Syllabus and Profile Manager, online help, search functions, and email results functions.

preface

Essentials of Marketing is a response to your request for an efficient, concise, no-nonsense book that will fit easily into your accelerated introductory courses.

This project is born out of the success of our *Principles of Marketing* text and contains all the essential ingredients that students need to understand in an introductory course.

Like *Principles of Marketing*, our essentials text brings together theory and practice. It covers a wide range of applications, industries and markets, exploring the way marketers must respond to those situations that demand an innovative response.

■ Distinctive features

Written in a lively, elegant style, *Essentials of Marketing* features the following:

- Up-to-date vignettes and examples from a range of industries, organisations and countries.
- 'Corporate Social Responsibility in Action' vignettes highlighting recent corporate scandals and focusing on ethical issues.
- End-of-chapter questions to reinforce understanding.
- Real-world case studies designed for discussion drawn from a range of small, medium and large-sized companies.
- Vibrant and fresh text design and imagery offers a wide and provocative range of real-world marketing campaigns.

guided tour of the book

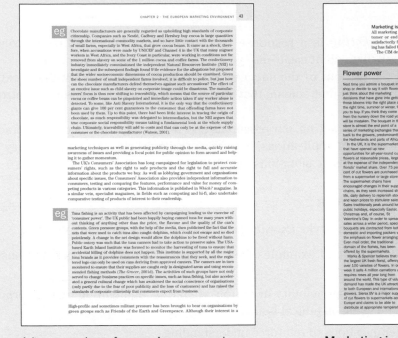

A large number of **examples** are used throughout the text providing engaging illustrations of marketing from a wide variety of industries and countries.

Marketing in action vignettes provide sustained coverage of the practical applications and implications of marketing in the real world.

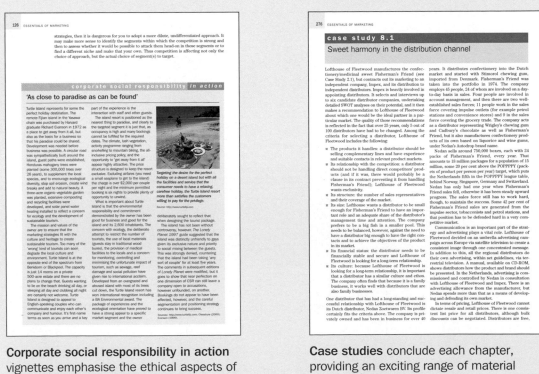

Corporate social responsibility in action vignettes emphasise the ethical aspects of marketing decisions and practice.

Case studies conclude each chapter, providing an exciting range of material for seminar or private study.

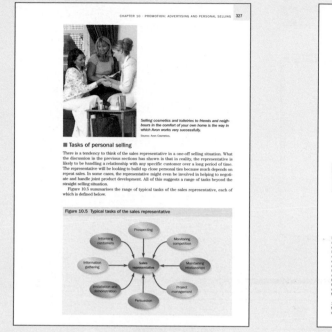

Clear, cogent, four-colour **diagrams** visually enhance important concepts.

Engaging **end-of-chapter questions** reinforce learning.

A **summary** at the end of each chapter serves as a useful learning tool for key concepts learnt in that chapter.

guided tour of the website

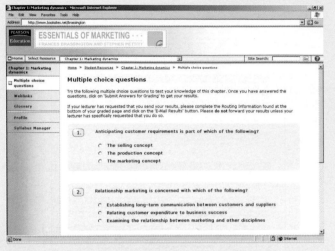

Multiple choice questions

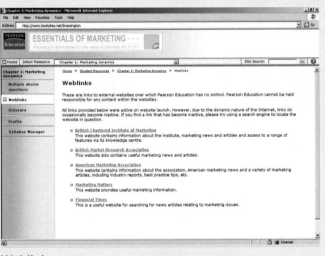

Weblinks

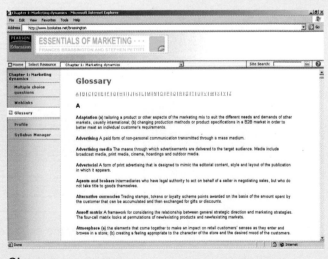

Glossary

about the authors

Stephen Pettitt is Deputy Vice Chancellor at the University of Luton. Previously he was the Pro Vice Chancellor and Dean of Luton Business School and before that, Director of Corporate Affairs at the University of Teesside. He has had, therefore, the opportunity to practise and plan marketing as well as being a marketing educator. He also worked at the University of Limerick in Ireland for four years as a Lecturer in Marketing and was the Managing Director of The Marketing Centre for Small Business, a campus company specialising in research and consultancy for the small business sector.

He worked initially in various sales and marketing management posts for Olivetti, Plessey and SKF before taking up a career in higher education. He holds a bachelor's degree in geography and an MBA and PhD from Cranfield. In addition to a wide experience in marketing education at all levels, he has undertaken numerous in-company training, research and consultancy assignments. He has lectured in marketing and entrepreneurship in France, Poland, Bulgaria, Slovakia, South Africa, Switzerland, the USA and Kenya. He has published over 30 papers and articles along with major studies in tourism innovation strategies, large buyer–small firm seller relationships and small firm development.

Frances Brassington is a Senior Lecturer in Retail Management and Marketing at Oxford Brookes University. She graduated from the University of Bradford Management Centre with a BSc (Hons) in business studies and a PhD, and her first teaching position was at the University of Teesside. She has taught marketing at all levels and on a wide range of undergraduate marketing modules and programmes and has supervised a number of PhD research students. Her own research interests include international services and retail management and the use of project-based learning in marketing education. She has also designed and delivered marketing programmes for managers and academics in Poland and Bulgaria and has given guest lectures in China and South Africa.

acknowledgements

We would like to thank all our friends and colleagues at Buckinghamshire Chilterns University College, the University of Luton and Oxford Brookes University for their constructive encouragement, support and unfailing good humour. We extend grateful thanks, yet again, to all those companies which have opened their doors to us and allowed us to write about them. Special thanks go to:

Lars Becker and Annabel Brog: Flytxt.
Tony and Duncan Lofthouse: Joint Managing Directors, Lofthouse of Fleetwood Ltd.
Rien van Ruremonde: Managing Director, Nedan Zoetwaren BV.
Gary Stevens and Nik Margolis: Inbox.

We would like to offer general thanks to all those other individuals and organisations who directly and indirectly helped to create the examples, case studies and vignettes.

We would also like to thank all those at Pearson Education who have helped deliver 'Baby B&P'. In particular, we would like to thank Thomas Sigel (Senior Acquisitions Editor), Natasha Dupont (Senior Editor), Peter Hooper (Editorial Assistant), Colin Reed (Senior Designer), Adam Renvoize (Senior Designer), Bridget Allen (Pre-press Manager) and Stuart Hay (Textbook Development Manager). We would also like to thank the unsung heroes behind the scenes: Philip Tye (freelance copy editor), Jonathon Price (freelance proofreader), David Barraclough (freelance indexer), Sue Williams (freelance picture researcher) and all of those involved in design, production, marketing and sales who have made this book the polished, professional package that it is.

And last, but by no means least, we thank all our friends and family. The last year has not been easy, and we have come to value their love and support more than ever.

publisher's acknowledgements

Table 2.1 Adapted from Table 1103, pp. 268–269, from *European Marketing Data and Statistics 2001, 36th Edition*, Euromonitor plc (2001); Table 3.2 reprinted with permission from *Journal of Marketing Research*, published by the American Marketing Association, Wells, W.D., and Gubar, R.G. (1966, Vol. 3, Nov), '*Life Cycle Concepts in Marketing Research*', pp. 355–363; Table 4.2 adapted from data from '*www.uk.Experian.com*' and '*www.micromarketing-online.com*', Copyright © 2001 Experian Limited; Figure 5.3 adapted from figure from *Marketing Research: Measurement and Method*, Macmillan, NY, (Tull, D.S., and Hawkins, D.I., 1990), Copyright © 1990 Pearson Education, Inc. Figure 8.3 reprinted and adapted from figure 7-2, p. 262 with the permission of The Free Press, a division of Simon & Schuster Adult Publishing Group, from *Diffusion of Innovations*, Fourth Edition, by Everett M. Rogers. Copyright © 1995 Everett M. Rogers. Copyright © 1962, 1971, 1983 by The Free Press, all rights reserved; Table 7.1 adapted from information from 'www.kitbag.com' website, accessed on 30 November 2001, Copyright © 2001 Kitbag.com Ltd; Figure 8.11 adapted from Figure 3.2, p.74 from *The Strategy of Distribution Management*, Heinemann Professional, The Marketing Series, (Christopher, M., 1990), Copyright © 1990 Professor Martin Christopher, reproduced by kind permission; Figure 9.2 adapted from figure of communications planning flow from Michael L. Rothschild, *Marketing Communications: From Fundamentals to Strategies*, D.C. Heath & Company, Copyright © 1987 D.C. Heath and Company. By permission of Houghton Mifflin Company; Table 9.2 from table from *The Marketing Communications Process*, McGraw-Hill, (Delozier, M.W., 1975), Copyright © 1975 The Estate of the late Professor M. Wayne DeLozier; Table 11.1 adapted from information from '*UK Direct Mail Volumes*' from website http://www.dmis.co.uk/keystats/keystats.html, Direct Mail Information Service, reproduced by kind permission of the Direct Mail Information Service (DMIS); Figure 12.7 adapted and reprinted by permission of *Harvard Business Review*. Exhibit I on p. 114 from '*Strategies of Diversification*' by Ansoff, H.I. Issue No. 25 (5), Sept/Oct 1957, pp. 113–25, Copyright © 1957 by the Harvard Business School Publishing Corporation; all rights reserved; Table 14.2 adapted from *Integrated Marketing Communications*, Financial Times Prentice-Hall, (Pickton, D. and Broderick, A., 2001), Copyright © 2001 David Pickton and Amanda Broderick, reprinted by permission of Pearson Education Limited; Figure 14.2 from '*Precision E-mail marketing*', in *Direct Marketing*, November 2001, pp. 56–60, Hoke Communications, Inc., (Rizzi, J. 2001), reprinted with permission from Direct Marketing Magazine, November 2001, pp. 56–60, 224, 7th Street, Garden City, NY 11530, tel: +1 (516) 746-6700, e-mail: dmmagazine@aol.com, Copyright © 2002 by e-Dialog, Inc.

Photographs: Age Concern UK p.309; Avon Cosmetics p.327; BAE systems p.95; Bailey's p.137; p.464; B&Q p.265; Bosch p.186; Botton Village/Camphill Village Trust Ltd p.285; Circular Distributions Ltd p.355; Club 18–30; Coors Brewers/BD London C&G p.69; Department for Transport p.341, p.342; Experian p.116; FBS Cars p.392; Flora London Marathon p.378; Florette p.253; Flytxt.com p.487; Foyles p.11; GlaxoSmithKline p.293; Gossard p.114; Great Ormond Street Hospital Children's Charity p.454; IKEA p.251; Jarvis Hotels p.447; KEF Audio (UK) p.226; Kelly Weedon Shute Ltd p.63; Kookai/CLM/BBDO p.317; Lastminute.com p.30; Lever Fabergé/Advertising Archives p.179; Lazenby's Sausages/ Northern Profile p.217; Linn Products Ltd p.391; Marks & Spencer p.6; Nationwide Building Society p.155; Odeon Cinemas/Red Consultancy p.431; Olympus UK Ltd p.215; Precious Woods p.41; Reckitt Benkiser plc p.193; Slendertone p.366; T&T Beverages Ltd p.289; Texaco HACL & Partners p.358; Tesco Stores Ltd p.384; Teuscher Chocolates p.409; Turtle Island, Fiji p.126; Whitworth Foods p.231; Yomega Corporation p.201.

In some instances, we have been unable to trace the owners of copyright material and we would appreciate any information that would enable us to do so.

chapter 1

marketing dynamics

LEARNING OBJECTIVES

This chapter will help you to:

1 define what marketing is;

2 trace the development of marketing as a way of doing business and consider the ways in which marketing is changing;

3 appreciate the importance and contribution of marketing as both a business function and an interface between the organisation and its customers; and

4 understand the scope of tasks undertaken in marketing, and the range of different organisational situations in which marketing is applied.

Introduction

You will have some sort of idea of what marketing is, since you are, after all, exposed to marketing in some form every day. Every time you buy or use a product, go window shopping, see an advertising hoarding, watch an advertisement, listen to friends telling you about a wonderful new product they've tried, or even when you surf the Internet to research a market, company or product for an assignment, you are reaping the benefits (or being a victim) of marketing activities. When marketing's outputs are so familiar, it is easy to take it for granted and to judge and define it too narrowly by what you see of it close to home. It is a mistake, however, to dismiss marketing as 'just advertising' or 'just selling' or 'making people buy things they don't really want'.

What this book wants to show you is that marketing does, in fact, cover a very wide range of absolutely essential business activities that bring you the products you *do* want, when you want them, where you want them, but at prices you can afford, and with all the information you need to make informed and satisfying consumer choices. And that's only what marketing does for you! Widen your thinking to include what marketing can similarly do for organisations purchasing goods and services from other organisations, and you can begin to see why it is a mistake to be too cynical about professionally practised marketing. None of this is easy. The outputs of marketing, such as the packaging, the advertisements, the glossy brochures, the all-singing, all-dancing websites, the enticing retail outlets and the incredible bargain value prices, look slick and polished, but a great deal of management planning, analysis and decision-making has gone on behind the scenes in order to bring all this to you. By the time you have finished this book, you should appreciate the whole range of marketing activities, and the difficulties of managing them.

eg The UK market for breakfast cereal is worth around £1bn and is the largest in Europe. Constant innovation and good marketing have helped Kellogg to achieve 43 per cent market share through a wide range of products targeting different consumer tastes and encouraging consumers to snack on cereals throughout the day. Kellogg's owns 6 out of the top 10 best-selling brands. The strong brand images of Rice Krispies, Frosties and Coco Pops are clearly targeted at the children's market, while Healthwise, All Bran and Optima meet the growing demand for healthy adult breakfasts. Advertising (particularly through characters such as Tony the Tiger) and promotions (such as in-pack gifts) aimed at children helped to differentiate the products, reinforce brand image and build customer loyalty. Children have a huge influence: 60 per cent of housewives with children agreed that they buy the cereals their children like and 20 per cent agree that they buy cereals featuring free gifts or special offers that their children want. Premium prices have also reinforced Kellogg's quality image. Thanks to competitors, however, continuing success is not necessarily guaranteed. Supermarket own-brand products, for instance, positioned close to the market leaders and accounting for about 25 per cent of the market, have made cereals more of a commodity purchase, undermining premium prices and brand images. To stay ahead, Kellogg has had to plan its product management, communications and pricing strategies carefully with a programme of new product launches to keep consumers interested; a high advertising spend to reinforce the Kellogg image; and price cuts and price-based promotional offers to close the pricing gap between Kellogg brands and supermarket own-brands (Brabbs, 2000; Mintel, 1999).

Before launching further into detailed descriptions, explanations and analyses of the operational tasks that make up the marketing function, however, it is important to lay a few foundations about what marketing really is, and to give you a more detailed overview of why it is so essential and precisely what it involves in practice.

This chapter defines and explores marketing as a philosophy of doing business which puts the customer first, and therefore casts the marketing department in the role of 'communicator' between the organisation and the outside world. Marketers have to tackle a surprisingly wide range of tasks on a daily basis to fulfil that function (hence the thickness of this book), and these too are defined. After you have read this section, marketing should mean a lot more to you than 'advertising', and you will appreciate that 'making people buy things they don't want' is the one thing that successful marketers do not do.

Marketing defined

This section is going to explore what marketing is and its evolution. First, we shall look at currently accepted definitions of marketing, then at the history behind those definitions. Linked with that history are the various business orientations outlined on pp. 7–10. These show how marketing is as much a philosophy of doing business as a business function in its own right. It is important to get this concept well established before moving on to the next section where we discuss philosophy and function in the context of the organisation.

■ What marketing means

Here are two popular and widely accepted definitions of marketing. The first is the definition preferred by the UK's Chartered Institute of Marketing (CIM), while the second is that offered by the American Marketing Association (AMA):

> *Marketing is the management process responsible for identifying, anticipating, and satisfying customer requirements profitably.*   (CIM, 2001)

> *Marketing is the process of planning and executing the conception, pricing, promotion and distribution of ideas, goods and services to create exchange and satisfy individual and organisational objectives.*   (AMA, 1985)

Both definitions make a good attempt at capturing concisely what is actually a wide and complex subject. Although they have a lot in common, each says something important that the other does not emphasise.

Both agree on the following points.

Marketing is a management process
Marketing has just as much legitimacy as any other business function, and involves just as much management skill. It requires planning and analysis, resource allocation, control and investment in terms of money, appropriately skilled people and physical resources. It also, of course, requires implementation, monitoring and evaluation. As with any other management activity, it can be carried out efficiently and successfully – or it can be done poorly, resulting in failure.

Marketing is about giving customers what they want

All marketing activities should be geared towards this. It implies a focus towards the customer or end consumer of the product or service. If 'customer requirements' are not satisfactorily fulfilled, or if customers do not obtain what they want and need, then marketing has failed both the customer and the organisation.

The CIM definition adds a couple of extra insights.

---

marketing *in action*

Flower power

Next time you admire a bouquet in a shop or decide to say it with flowers, just think about the marketing decisions that have gone into getting those blooms into the right place at the right time, summer or winter, for you to buy. If you think they come from the nursery down the road you will be mistaken. The bouquet in the store is almost the end point of a series of marketing exchanges that go back to the growers, predominantly in the Netherlands and parts of Africa.

In the UK, it is the supermarkets that have opened up new opportunities for all-year-round cut flowers at reasonable prices, largely at the expense of the independent florists' market share. Over 75 per cent of cut flowers are purchased from a supermarket or large store. The supermarket chains have encouraged changes in their supply chains, as they seek increased shelf-life, daily delivery to replenish stocks, and keen prices to stimulate sales. Sales traditionally peak around key public holidays, especially Easter, Christmas and, of course, St Valentine's Day. In order to spread sales across a wider period, special bouquets are contracted from both domestic and importing packers with the emphasis on flower arranging. Even mail order, the traditional domain of the florists, has been offered by the supermarkets.

Marks & Spencer believes that it is the largest UK fresh florist, offering over 100 varieties of flowers. In one week it sells 4 million carnations and requires roses all year long from around the world. This type of volume demand has made the UK attractive to both European and international growers. Sierex BV is a major supplier of cut flowers to supermarkets across Europe and claims to be able to distribute at appropriate temperatures and in hydro-packs throughout Europe within 24 hours. It buys from the large auction halls in the Netherlands, where 60 per cent of the world's cut flowers are sold, and also has direct contracts with growers both in the Netherlands and outside Europe. Each year, Sierex assembles 26 million mono and mixed bouquets. The supermarket determines the exact mix to suit its target groups and local tastes. The added value played by Sierex is in careful buying, rapid processing, creative packaging and product display combined with value for money. Chains such as Casino, Promodès and Migros are major customers and the UK is now a prime market for development. In order to meet UK supermarket demand, it has introduced daily deliveries and uses North Sea ferries especially equipped with temperature-controlled facilities.

The growth in year-round cut flower sales in Europe has brought a much needed cash earner for parts of Africa. Zimbabwe and Kenya, for example, can now pick, package, label and price so that products can soon be on the shelves after a 12-hour flight. For Kenya, cut flowers are now the fourth biggest export earner and it has developed prime markets in the Netherlands, UK, Germany and Switzerland, making use of tariff-free exporting for this product category. This market employs over 1 million people in Kenya and brings in $40m. for the rural economy. Tesco has been instrumental in setting ethical as well as quality and processing standards for the industry through its dealings with the growers' associations. Issues such as above-average wage levels, clothing, nutrition and healthcare for workers are to the fore as well as environmental issues and pest control practices.

The situation in Malawi, however, is more problematic. Despite the high

Marks & Spencer offers a range of cut flowers and plants in its stores to encourage its customers to think about 'saying it with flowers'.
Source: Marks & Spencer.

value-added and labour-intensive opportunities for cut flowers, part of the sector has been temporarily shut down due to poor management, escalating freight costs (denied by Air Malawi), and high financing costs. Fresh red roses originally for the Netherlands and South Africa remain uncut, resulting in a loss of over 700 jobs and $28m. to the economy. However, the success in other African countries clearly indicates that globalisation of production is now possible even where fast delivery is required. Transport costs of less than 5 per cent of the total cost of the flowers favour companies with a favourable growing environment and to some extent this has been at the expense of European growers. With limited capacity and volumes and higher cost structures, they cannot easily compete nor meet the supermarkets' demand for bulk, year-round supply contracts.

Sources: The Grocer (1998); Foottit (2000); *Marketing Week* (2001); Mhone (2000); Van Heck (2000); http://www.sierex.nl

Marketing identifies and anticipates customer requirements

This phrase has a subtle edge to it that does not come through strongly in the AMA definition. It is saying that the marketer creates some sort of offering only after researching the market and pinpointing exactly what the customer will want. The AMA definition is ambiguous because it begins with the 'planning' process, which may or may not be done with reference to the customer.

Marketing fulfils customer requirements profitably

This pragmatic phrase warns the marketer against getting too carried away with the altruism of satisfying the customer! In the real world, an organisation cannot please all of the people all of the time, and sometimes even marketers have to make compromises. The marketer has to work within the resource capabilities of the organisation, and specifically work within the agreed budgets and performance targets set for the marketing function. Nevertheless, profitability can still be questionable. Marketing practice and, in part, marketing thinking, is now accepted within many non-profit organisations, from schools and universities to hospitals, voluntary organisations and activist groups such as Greenpeace and Friends of the Earth. Each must manage its dealings with its various publics and user groups and manage them efficiently and effectively, but not for profit. That important context aside, most commercial companies exist to make profits, and thus profitability is a legitimate concern. Even so, some organisations would occasionally accept the need to make a loss on a particular product or sector of a market in order to achieve wider strategic objectives. As long as those losses are planned and controlled, and in the longer run provide some other benefit to the organisation, then they are bearable. In general terms, however, if an organisation is consistently failing to make profits, then it will not survive, and thus marketing has a responsibility to sustain and increase profits.

The AMA definition goes further.

Marketing offers and exchanges ideas, goods and services

This statement is close to the CIM's 'profitably', but a little more subtle. The idea of marketing as an exchange process is an important one, and was first proposed by Alderson (1957). The basic idea is that I've got something you want, you've got something I want, so let's do a deal. For the most part, the exchange is a simple one. The organisation offers a product or service, and the customer offers a sum of money in return for it. Pepsi offers you a can of cola and you offer payment; you sign a contract to offer your services as an employee and the organisation pays you a salary; the hospital offers to provide health care and the individual, through taxes or insurance premiums, offers to fund it. A range of further examples is shown diagramatically in Figure 1.1.

What all these examples have in common is the assumption that both parties value what the other has to offer. If they didn't, they would not be obliged to enter into the bargain. It is up to the marketer to make sure that customers value what the organisation is offering so highly that they are prepared to give the organisation what it wants in return. Whether the marketer is offering a product, a service or an idea (such as the environmental causes 'sold' by Greenpeace), the essence of the exchange is mutual value. From mutual value can come satisfaction and possible repeat purchases.

Pricing, promotion and distribution of ideas, goods and services

In saying that marketing involves the conception, pricing, promotion and distribution of ideas, goods and services, the AMA definition is a little more specific in describing the ways in which marketers can stimulate exchanges. It suggests a proactive seller as well as a willing buyer. By designing products, setting sensible, acceptable and justifiable prices, creating awareness and preferences, and ensuring availability and service, the marketer can influence the volume of exchanges. Marketing can be seen, therefore, as a demand management activity on the part of the selling organisation.

Both the CIM and the AMA definitions of marketing, despite their popular usage, are increasingly being criticised as failing to reflect the role and reality of marketing for the twenty-first century. Some criticism concerns the increasing importance of the globalisation of business and the focus on customer retention, relationship building and maintenance that characterises many markets (Christopher et al., 1991; Grönroos, 1997).

Figure 1.1 Exchange transactions

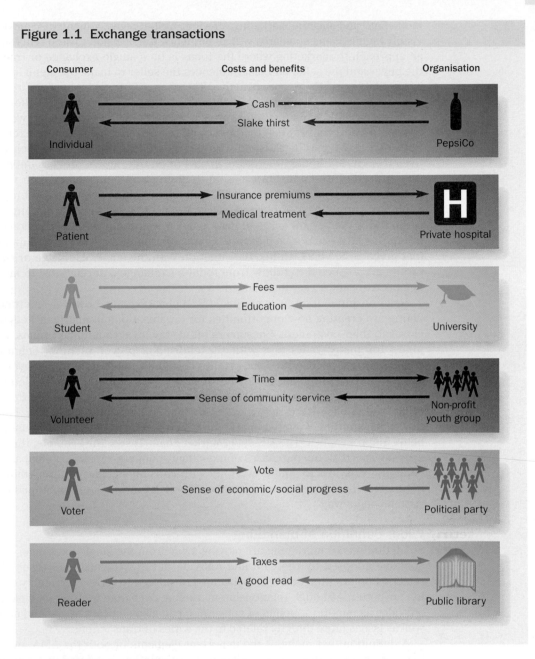

Relationship marketing

The traditional definitions of marketing tend to reflect a view that the transaction between buyer and seller is primarily seller oriented, that each exchange is totally discrete, and thus lacking any of the personal and emotional overtones that emerge in a long-term relationship made up of a series of exchanges between the same buyer and seller. In B2B markets in particular, each of these exchanges could involve a complex web of interactions between the staff of both organisations, each seeking to work together for their mutual benefit against a history of previous exchanges. Dwyer *et al.* (1987), Gummesson (1987) and Turnbull and Valla (1986) particularly highlight the importance of enduring buyer–seller relationships as a major influence on decision-making in international B2B markets.

In some circumstances, however, the traditional non-relationship view is perfectly appropriate. A traveller on an unknown road passing through a foreign country may stop at a wayside café, never visited before and never to be visited again. The decision to purchase is thus going to be influenced by the ease of parking, the decor and the ambience rather than by any feeling of trust or commitment to the patron. The decision, in short, is based on the immediate and specific marketing offering. Well-lit signs, a menu in your own language and visibly high hygiene standards will all influence the decision to stop. This scenario describes an approach to marketing where the focus is on a single exchange or transaction between the buyer and the seller and that influences the seller to make the menu look good, the parking available and the decor attractive. The chances of you becoming a regular customer in this instance are, of course, unlikely unless you are a frequent traveller on that route. In contrast, a relationship-focused approach to marketing describes a network of communications and contacts between the buyer and the seller and a series of exchanges over time. Both parties have to be satisfied with the relationship and achieve their respective objectives from it. Marketing, therefore, is part of an interactive process between people, over time, of which relationship creation, building and management are vital cornerstones (Grönroos, 1997; Sheth *et al.*, 1988). Individual exchanges between buyer and seller are important and influenced by previous experiences, good and bad, but any seller that is concerned with the one-off sale and the immediate gain may find that the longer-term interests of both parties are not well served. Companies such as Volvo have supplier relationships that go back 50 years. Unlike the situation with the single exchange or transaction where profits are expected to follow from today's exchanges, in relationship marketing the time perspective can be very long indeed.

Relationship marketing is not just a B2B phenomenon, however. Internet and direct marketing are creating new opportunities for organisations in mass markets to become much closer to their customers. Consumers often stay loyal to familiar brands, retailers and suppliers for many years and with the enormous power of new technology, individual consumers can be identified and profiles developed, whether through loyalty schemes, monitoring Internet shopping behaviour or other ways of capturing detailed information (see Chapter 5). It is now possible to track the purchase behaviour of individual shoppers and to create a database for directly targeted communication (see Chapter 11), and with such power it would be a foolish marketer who did not try to maintain customer loyalty and hence improve sales. The UK supermarket chain Tesco, for example, through its Clubcard scheme can track the purchases of individual shoppers, creating a database that allows it to communicate directly and powerfully with consumers. Thus 30-something males who are not buying their fair share of wine should watch out for the promotional mailshot that will soon be on its way!

Wider definition of marketing

So, definitions of marketing are moving away from the single exchange, seller-focused perspective adopted by the CIM and AMA definitions towards more socially relevant and relationship-oriented definitions that are considered to reflect the reality of modern marketing far better. Although relationship marketing over time focuses on customers' needs and attitudes as important points of concern, it can also embrace social and ethical concerns as well as issues more directly related to the series of transactions.

A definition that includes the important elements of both the AMA and CIM definitions, but still embraces the evolving relationship orientation, is offered by Grönroos (1997):

> *Marketing is to establish, maintain and enhance relationships with customers and other partners, at a profit, so that the objectives of the parties involved are met. This is achieved by mutual exchange and fulfillment of promises.*

Such relationships are usually, but not necessarily always, long-term. Some could be little more than a single episode but others could be very enduring. This definition still reflects a managerial orientation towards marketing, but emphasises the mutually active role that both partners in the exchange play. It does not list the activities that marketers undertake, but instead is more concerned with the partnership idea, the concept that marketing is about doing something *with* someone, not doing something *to* them. Of course, not all transactions between buyers and sellers can be considered to be part of a relationship, especially where the purchase does not involve much risk or commitment from the purchaser and thus there is little to gain from entering a relationship (Berry, 1983). This was clearly shown in the wayside café example cited earlier. Overall, however, marketing is increasingly about relationships in both B2B and consumer markets.

The idea of fulfilling promises is also an important one, as marketing is all about making promises to potential buyers. If the buyer decides, after the event, that the seller did not live up to those promises, the chances are that they will never buy again from that seller. If, on the other hand, the buyer decides that the seller has fulfilled their promises, then the seeds of trust are sown, and the buyer may be prepared to begin a long-term relationship with the seller.

Between them, therefore, the three definitions offered say just about everything there is to say about the substance and basic philosophy of marketing. Few would argue with any of that now, but marketing has not always been so readily accepted in that form, as the next two subsections show.

■ The development of marketing

The basic idea of marketing as an exchange process has its roots in very ancient history, when people began to produce crops or goods surplus to their own requirements and then to barter them for other things they wanted. Elements of marketing, particularly selling and advertising, have been around as long as trade itself, but it took the industrial revolution, the development of mass production techniques and the separation of buyers and sellers to sow the seeds of what we recognise as marketing today.

In the early days, the late nineteenth and early twentieth centuries, goods were sufficiently scarce and competition sufficiently underdeveloped that producers did not really need marketing. They could easily sell whatever they produced ('the production era' in which a 'production orientation' was adopted). As markets and technology developed, competition became more serious and companies began to produce more than they could easily sell. This led to 'the sales era', lasting into the 1950s and 1960s, in which organisations developed increasingly large and increasingly pushy sales forces, and more aggressive advertising approaches (the 'selling orientation').

It was not really until the 1960s and 1970s that marketing generally moved away from a heavy emphasis on post-production selling and advertising to become a more comprehensive and integrated field, earning its place as a major influence on corporate strategy ('marketing orientation'). This meant that organisations began to move away from a 'sell what we can make' type of thinking, in which 'marketing' was at best a peripheral activity, towards a 'find out what the customer wants and then we'll make it' type of market-driven philosophy. Customers took their rightful place at the centre of the organisation's universe. This finally culminated, in the 1980s, in the wide acceptance of marketing as a strategic concept, and yet there is still room for further development of the marketing concept, as new applications and contexts emerge.

Historically, marketing has not developed uniformly across all markets or products. Retailers, along with many consumer goods organisations, have been at the forefront of implementing the marketing concept. Benetton, for instance, has developed a strong, unique, international product and retail store image, but within the basic formula is prepared to adapt its merchandising and pricing strategies to suit the demands of different geographic markets. The financial services industry, however, has only very recently truly embraced a marketing orientation, some 10 years or more behind most consumer goods. Knights *et al.* (1994), reviewing the development of a marketing orientation within the UK financial services industry, imply that the transition from a selling to a marketing orientation was 'recent and rapid'. They cite research by Clarke *et al.* (1988) showing that the retail banks were exceptionally early, compared with the rest of the sector, in becoming completely marketing driven. The rest have since followed.

■ Business orientations

We discuss below the more precise definitions of the alternative approaches to doing business that were outlined above. We then describe the characteristic management thinking behind them, and show how they are used today. Table 1.1 further summarises this information.

Table 1.1 Marketing history and business orientations – a summary

Orientation	Focus	Characteristics and aims	Eavesdropping	Main era (generalised)		
				USA	Western Europe	Eastern Europe
Production	Manufacturing	• Increase production • Cost reduction and control • Make profit through volume	'Any colour you want – as long as it's black'	Up to 1940s	Up to 1950s	Late 1980s
Product	Goods	• Quality is all that matters • Improve quality levels • Make profit through volume	'Just look at the quality of the paintwork'	Up to 1940s	Up to 1960s	Largely omitted
Selling	Selling what's produced – seller's needs	• Aggressive sales and promotion • Profit through quick turnover of high volume	'You're not keen on the black? What if I throw in a free sun-roof?'	1940–1950s	1950–1960s	Early 1990s
Marketing	Defining what customers want – buyer's needs	• Integrated marketing • Defining needs in advance of production • Profit through customer satisfaction and loyalty	'Let's find out if they want it in black, and if they would pay a bit more for it'	1960s onwards	1970s onwards	mid-1990s onwards

Production orientation

The emphasis with a production orientation is on making products that are affordable and available, and thus the prime task of management is to ensure that the organisation is as efficient as possible in production and distribution techniques. The main assumption is that the market is completely price sensitive, which means that customers are only interested in price as the differentiating factor between competing products and will buy the cheapest. Customers are thus knowledgeable about relative prices, and if the organisation wants to bring prices down, then it must tightly control costs. This is the philosophy of the production era, and was predominant in Central and Eastern Europe in the early stages of the new market economies. Apart from that, it may be a legitimate approach, in the short term, where demand outstrips supply, and companies can put all their effort into improving production and increasing supply and worry about the niceties of marketing later.

A variation on that situation happens when a product is really too expensive for the market, and therefore the means have to be found to bring costs, and thus prices, down. This decision, however, is as likely to be marketing as production driven, and may involve technologically complex, totally new products that neither the producer nor the customer is sure of. Thus DVD players, videos, camcorders and home computers were all launched on to unsuspecting markets with limited supply and high prices, but the manufacturers envisaged that with extensive marketing and the benefits gained from progressing along the production and technology learning curve, high-volume markets could be opened up for lower-priced, more reliable products.

Product orientation

The product orientation assumes that consumers are primarily interested in the product itself, and buy on the basis of quality. Since consumers want the highest level of quality for their money, the organisation must work to increase and improve its quality levels. At first glance, this may seem like a reasonable proposition, but the problem is the assumption that

eg A modern form of production orientation can occur when an organisation becomes too focused on pursuing a low-cost strategy in order to achieve economies of scale, and loses sight of the real customer need. Tetra Pak, one of the market leaders in carton manufacture, ran into problems in the 1990s by concentrating on the interests of its direct customers rather than those of the end user. The focus was on production efficiency, i.e. how many cartons could be filled per hour, rather than on the problems of actually using a carton. Despite making nearly 90 billion cartons each year, the Swedish company did not fully address the problem that some of the cartons were difficult to open and tended to spill their contents rather easily all over the floor. It clearly had the know-how to solve the problem, but in the pursuit of a low-cost operator position, allowed its rival from Norway, Elo Pak, to develop a pack with a proper spout and a plastic cap that was more in tune with customer needs. It was also Elo Pak that pioneered the use of plasma technology for barrier coating to improve the range of uses for cartons and the life of the liquids they contained (Mans, 2000). This underlines the need to talk to end users constantly and to be prepared to consider their needs as well as the direct customer, i.e. the carton fillers. Tetra Pak has now realised that consumers want convenient packaging and have redesigned packs to be easier to handle and pour from with more user-friendly openings (http://www.tetrapak.com).

consumers *want this product*. Consumers do not want products, they want solutions to problems, and if the organisation's product does not solve a problem, they will not buy it, however high the quality level is. An organisation may well produce the best ever record player, but the majority of consumers would rather buy a cheap CD player. In short, customer needs rather than the product should be the focus.

In a review of the history of marketing thinking in China, Deng and Dart (1999) considered the market orientation of traditional state enterprises. From 1949 until economic reform began in 1979, Chinese organisations were part of a very rigid, planned economy. During that time denying marketing was a fundamental part of the political belief system and with a low GDP per capita and widespread scarcity of consumer goods, there was little, if any, incentive for the development of marketing activities (Gordon, 1991). The focus was on manufacturing output and all major marketing decisions such as product range, pricing, and selection of distribution channels were controlled by government. The state set production targets for each enterprise, distributed their products, assigned personnel, allocated supplies and equipment, retained all profit and covered all losses (Zhuang and Whitehill, 1989; Gordon, 1991). The priority was production and virtually any product would do.

Since the reforms and the opening up of the economy, most enterprises, even if state-owned, now have to make marketing decisions as they are no longer allocated production inputs, nor are their outputs assigned to prearranged buyers. Price controls have been relaxed and distribution lists from the state ended. However, the transition process is not yet complete: many state-owned enterprises are being subsidised to retain employment levels; government power is still great, as the Internet café owners recently found when they were shut down overnight; and the distribution infrastructure is still not very efficient. As consumer awareness and purchasing power increase, however, Chinese enterprises will have to become more marketing oriented to survive.

Sales orientation

The basis for the sales orientation way of thinking is that consumers are inherently reluctant to purchase, and need every encouragement to purchase sufficient quantities to satisfy the organisation's needs. This leads to a heavy emphasis on personal selling and other sales-stimulating devices because products 'are sold, not bought', and thus the organisation puts its effort into building strong sales departments, with the focus very much on the needs of the seller, rather than on those of the buyer. Home improvement organisations, selling, for example, double glazing and cavity wall insulation, have tended to operate like this, as has the timeshare industry.

Schultz and Good (2000) proposed that a sales orientation can also emerge from commission-based reward and remuneration packages for sales people, even though the seller might actually want longer-term customer relationships to be established. When the pressure is on to make a sale and to achieve target sales volumes there is a danger that the sales person will focus on the one-off sale rather than the long-term relationship. There is a tension between the need to spend time on relationships and the urge to move on to the next sale.

Marketing orientation

The organisation that develops and performs its production and marketing activities with the needs of the buyer driving it all, and with the satisfaction of that buyer as the main aim, is marketing oriented. The motivation is to 'find wants and fill them' rather than 'create products and sell them'. The assumption is that customers are not necessarily price driven, but are looking for the total offering that best fits their needs, and therefore the organisation has to define those needs and develop appropriate offerings. This is not just about the core product itself, but also about pricing, access to information, availability and peripheral benefits and services that add value to the product. Not all customers, however, necessarily want exactly the same things. They can be grouped according to common needs and wants, and the organisation can produce a specifically targeted marketing package that best suits the needs of one group, thus increasing the chances of satisfying that group and retaining its loyalty.

A marketing orientation is far more, however, than simply matching products and services to customers. It has to emerge from an organisational philosophy, an approach to doing business that naturally places customers and their needs at the heart of what the organisation does. Not all organisations do this to the same extent, although many are trying to move towards it.

Henderson (1998), however, urges caution in assuming that a marketing orientation is a guarantee of success in achieving above average performance. There are many internal and external factors at work in determining success, of which effective marketing thinking is but one. If marketing dominates the rest of the organisation it can help to diminish key competencies in other areas such as manufacturing productivity or technological innovation. Furthermore, the marketing department approach to organising the marketing function can isolate marketing from design, production, deliveries, technical service, complaints handling, invoicing and other customer-related activities. As a consequence, the rest of the organisation could be alienated from marketing, making the coordination of customer and market-oriented activities across the organisation more difficult (Piercy, 1992). This underlines the importance of Narver and Slater's (1990) three key factors that help the marketing function to achieve above average performance:

■ *Interfunctional orientation* enabling cooperation between the management functions to create superior value;
■ *Competitor orientation* to retain an edge; and finally
■ *Customer orientation*.

Having established the importance of the marketing concept to an organisation, the chapter now turns to the issue of developing marketing thinking and practice across the organisation.

The battle of Charing Cross Road

At 113–119 Charing Cross Road, Foyles, one of the oldest comprehensive bookshops in London, is limbering up after a long, self-imposed rest to take on the 'newcomers' such as Borders (often trading under the *Books* name in the UK), a leading global retailer from the United States, which has a store at 120 Charing Cross Road. It is a battle of retail formats that will also be fought alongside the threat from the increasing number of online booksellers such as Amazon.

Foyles was founded by a book lover at the turn of the twentieth century and became a leading bookstore in London. Before his death in 1963 William Foyle passed the business over to Christina, his daughter, and that is when the rot started. She stubbornly refused to change almost anything. At the time of the changeover, Foyles was *the* bookstore with five floors loaded with books and 30 miles of shelving. It carried a vast stock to cater for most tastes in a relaxed browser-friendly environment. However, other than the titles, little else changed. The philosophy was that a 'good book will sell itself'. Christina had a passion for books but not for the customers buying them nor staff selling them. Computers and electronic tills were resisted, resulting in customers having to queue twice with dockets just to buy one book. If customers wanted to buy from more than one department, they had to go through separate transactions in each department. The shelves became shabby and the shop in need of some tender loving care. Wages were low and sales staff had no proper employment contracts. The business stood still while others entered the market.

At 120 Charing Cross Road, things were rather different in Borders' new store. The retail marketing formula was applied on a global scale, with the customer at the heart of the

The shop itself is undergoing a massive £2 million refurbishment programme – with new bookshelves, carpets, lighting and air-conditioning. The in-store signage is being completely overhauled.

Source: Foyles.

business. Starting as a small retailer, the company expanded to over 290 stores in the United States, 32 stores in the UK and outlets in Australia, New Zealand and Singapore. It also has control of Waldenbooks in the USA with over 900 stores. It uses category management techniques to build stocks and collections based on customers' needs. One of the seven categories adopted, for example, is children's books. Stores are carefully planned in terms of size and location to exploit fully local market potential, but the range of book titles stocked is largely standardised. The priority at the moment is opening 'superstores', which are much larger than existing stores in the chain. Aisles are wide, stock is clearly laid out, and if shoppers cannot find their desired book on the shelves in the store, by using 'title sleuth' they may find it among the 700,000 titles held at a fulfilment centre. Special order sales have increased by 30 per cent since the introduction of the service in all stores. There is a café operation in all stores along with comfortable chairs so that shoppers can relax and read a little before making a purchase. Relationship marketing through the website and magazine *Inside Borders*, in-store merchandising and retail branding do the rest. Sales are now around $3.3bn of which about $219m. comes from the international operation which is the priority for further growth. As sales volume increases, the retailer's buying power also increases and the scope of the retail brand can be extended, for example to include an e-commerce facility co-branded with Amazon.

Meanwhile, under new management after Christina's death, Foyles is

enjoying its freedom from the shackles that have held it back since the 1960s. The tills have been computerised, staff (a high percentage of whom are graduates) have been given contracts and provided with customer service training. The dockets and the double queuing have gone. There is now a busy online ordering service. The 33 different departments offering 4 million books across 630,000 titles still remain, however. Sales are already increasing: up 24 per cent in the first four months of 2001 when the market was growing by just 6 per cent, but the new management team knows that there is still a long way to go and it is still a challenge to find the book you really want across so many departments. However, a new information point has been provided on the ground floor before the customer starts exploring any of the other floors. Foyles still wants to be a bookshop for book lovers and feedback from customers is that it should retain the feel of a 'real' bookshop rather than creating a supermarket-style experience. Finding the balance between modernity and tradition will be a challenge, as Foyles would not wish to lose existing customers in the pursuit of new ones. At least the customer is now coming back into focus, however. Some argue that it is the last proper comprehensive bookshop left in London capable of providing a quality browsing and shopping experience. For book lovers, the hunt and the impulse are both powerful forces.

And who will be the eventual winner? Visit Charing Cross Road and judge for yourself; after all it is your spending power that both are after.

Sources: Davies (2001); http://www.foyles.co.uk; http://www.bordersstores.com

Emergent marketing philosophies

The marketing concept and the philosophy of a marketing orientation continue to evolve. In increasingly competitive global markets consisting of increasingly demanding customers, organisations are continually striving to find more effective ways of attracting and retaining customers, and sometimes that could mean refining further exactly what marketing means.

Corporate social responsibility: societal and ethical marketing. Corporate social responsibility (CSR) suggests that organisations should not only consider their customers and their profitability, but also the good of the wider communities, local and global, within which they exist. As Smith and Higgins (2000) put it, consumers now are not only looking for environmentally sensitive and ethically considerate products, but also for businesses to demonstrate a wider set of ethical commitments to society: '[A business] must, as should we all, become a "good citizen".' Carroll (1999) provides an excellent review of the history and evolution of the CSR concept, but it is his own 1991 paper which provides the basis for the most succinct definition of CSR which will underpin the coverage of CSR in this book:

> . . . *four kinds of social responsibilities constitute total CSR: economic, legal, ethical and philanthropic. . . . [B]usiness should not fulfil these in sequential fashion but . . . each is to be fulfilled at all times. . . . The CSR firm should strive to make a profit, obey the law, be ethical, and be a good corporate citizen.*
>
> (Carroll, 1991, pp. 40–3, as summarised by Carroll, 1999)

Marketing within a CSR context is concerned with ensuring that organisations handle marketing responsibly, and in a way that contributes to the well-being of society. Consumers have become increasingly aware of the social and ethical issues involved in marketing, such as the ethics of marketing to children, fair trade with Third World suppliers, the ecological impact of business, and the extent of good 'corporate citizenship' displayed by companies, for example. Companies looking to establish a reputable and trustworthy image as a foundation for building long-term relationships with their customers thus need to consider the philosophy of CSR seriously if they are to meet their customers' wider expectations, and create and maintain competitive advantage (Balestrini, 2001). Indeed, some companies, such as Body Shop, have adopted a very proactive approach to societal marketing and have made CSR a central pillar of their whole business philosophy (see Hartman and Beck-Dudley, 1999 for a detailed discussion of marketing ethics within Body Shop International).

The implications of CSR for marketing is clearly shown by a UK report, *Who Are the Ethical Consumers?*, by journalist Roger Cowe and The Co-operative Bank's head of corporate affairs, Simon Williams (as quoted by Mason, 2000). The report says that 'caring' consumers cross most sociopolitical boundaries, and are not defined by party politics, social class, age or gender. Furthermore, the potential for ethical products and services in the UK could be as high as 30 per cent of consumer markets. This report also researched consumer behaviour with regard to ethical issues. While most consumers had done the obvious things (for example 73 per cent of respondents had recycled materials/waste at least once during the previous 12 months), significant numbers had also done things much closer to the marketer's heart: 52 per cent had recommended companies because of their responsible reputation; 51 per cent had chosen a product or service because of a company's responsible reputation; perhaps more seriously, 44 per cent had avoided a product or service because of a company's behaviour; and 29 per cent had bought primarily for ethical reasons (as reported by Mason, 2000). The ethical bandwagon is gaining momentum.

CSR is rapidly changing from being a 'would like' to a 'must have' feature of business. Although at the time of writing businesses are under no obligation to report on their CSR activities in the UK, many already do – about 80 per cent of the FTSE 100 companies in the UK provide information about their environmental and/or social performance (Gray, 2001) – and it is likely that pressure for transparency on CSR will only increase. The latest buzzword in corporate accountability is '360 degree reporting' which acknowledges the need to produce annual reports that take a much more holistic view of a company's activities to meet the information needs of pressure groups, those looking for ethical investments, and the wider audience interested in CSR, rather than just shareholders and traditional bankers. Companies in potentially sensitive sectors such as utilities and transport, have begun to produce separate reports on their CSR performance, for example utility company Kelda Group's *Environment and Community Report* and water company Severn Trent's *Stewardship Report*, and London Transport's *Environmental Performance Report* (Buxton, 2000).

Towards 'sustainable marketing'. Inextricably tied in with the concept and best practice of CSR in its widest sense is the idea of sustainable development. Sustainability was defined in the Brundtland Report of 1987 as:

> *development that meets the needs of the present without compromising the ability of future generations to meet their own needs.*   (WCED, 1987)

Sustainability is not just concerned with environmental and ecological issues, as important as these are, but also with the social, economic and cultural development of society. The

eg Severn Trent plc, based in the UK Midlands, has a turnover of some £1.6 bn and employs over 14,000 people across the UK, USA, and Europe. Severn Trent takes CSR very seriously. As an environmental services company, concerned with water treatment, waste disposal and utilities, it has always been focused on 'green' issues, but its commitment to CSR goes much further than that. In its 2001 Stewardship Report 'The Environment is Our Business', Robert Walker, the Group Chief Executive, said, 'Business cannot operate in isolation from society. Our responsibilities are not limited to our customers and shareholders but extend to a wider group of stakeholders, each of whom expects us to be ever more accountable and transparent in the way we do business. . . . Sustainable development encompasses economic and social issues as well as environmental considerations. We wholeheartedly embrace the concept of Corporate Social Responsibility and are playing an active role in the World Business Council for Sustainable Development' (Severn Trent, 2001, p. 1). The Stewardship Report thus covers many areas of CSR, not only relating to the Group's approach to the protection of the natural environment, biodiversity, and the efficient use of natural resources within its operations, but also its role within society and local communities, its perceived CSR leadership role among its suppliers and customers in improving the performance of the entire supply chain, and its internal application of ethical principles in its HRM policies, for example. A particularly interesting section of the report is headed 'Governance for Sustainability' which explains how the organisational structure facilitates the integration of CSR throughout the Group and its operations. It also summarises the Group's business principles which include concepts such as 'corporate citizenship', 'integrity', 'respect for local cultures', 'lawfulness' and 'shared values', very much in line with Carroll's (1999) ideas of CSR mentioned earlier.

wider 'softer agenda' includes, therefore, the fair distribution of economic benefits, human rights, community involvement and product responsibility. This is taken seriously by business. Echoing the sentiments expressed in the Severn Trent example above, Jurgen Strube, the chairman of BASF, the large German chemical company, said that sustainable development in the areas of the economy, ecology and society will be the key to the success in the twenty-first century (as reported by Challener, 2001). Society cannot continue to enjoy economic growth without reference to the consequences for environmental protection and social stability (*OECD Observer*, 2001).

In the light of the whole CSR/sustainability debate, sustainable marketing is likely to become the next stage in the conceptual development of marketing as it focuses on some of the significant long-term challenges facing society in the twenty-first century. The challenge to marketing thinking is to broaden the concept of exchange to incorporate the longer-term needs of society at large rather than the short-term pursuit of individual gratification and consumption. It is not about marketers revising strategies to exploit new societal opportunities, it is about what society can afford to allow marketers to exploit and over what timescale. This sounds very idealistic: in a competitive world in which the customer is free to choose and, moreover, in which business operates on the principle of meeting customers' needs and wants, it sometimes requires courage for a business to change those principles if those changes precede customer concern and government legislation. Consumers within society will have to travel up a learning curve and that process is only just beginning.

We would, therefore, like to define sustainable marketing as:

the establishment, maintenance and enhancement of customer relationships so that the objectives of the parties involved are met without compromising the ability of future generations to achieve their own objectives.

In short, consumers today, whatever the market imperative, cannot be allowed to destroy the opportunities for society tomorrow by taking out more than is being put back in. This not only embraces environmental and ecological issues but also the social and cultural consequences of a consumer society that equates 'more' with 'better'.

How does all this impact on the marketing process? The internalisation of costs (making the polluters pay), green taxes, legislation, support for cleaner technology, redesigned products to minimise resources and waste streams, reverse distribution channels to receive products for recycling and consumer education on sustainability are all an essential part of a new marketing agenda for the twenty-first century. To some it is not a choice, but a mandate that cannot be ignored (Fuller, 1999). Ecological and environmental agendas to date have had an impact on marketing strategy, but it has been patchy. The old adage 'reduce, recycle and reuse' has for example influenced the type of packaging materials used to ensure recyclability. Clothing manufacturers have produced plastic outdoor clothing that can be recycled; glue manufacturers have reduced the toxic emissions from their products; car manufacturers, in accordance with the EU's End-of-Life Vehicle Directive, now have to consider the recycling or other means of disposal of old cars. However, research often indicates that consumers given a free choice are reluctant to pay more for environmentally friendly products such as organic food and many find it hard to establish the link between their individual buying decision and its global impact. It will require a societal balance and adjustment period, but evidence is mounting that if change does not take place, the negative long-term impact on the environment and society could be irreversible.

corporate social responsibility *in action*

'An untouchable icon'?

Many in Europe and North America consider whale watching to be great fun and worth travelling thousands of miles for. It is a business worth over $1bn a year. To many Japanese, the whale is more of a luxury item on the menu to be enjoyed at the finest restaurants. The problem is that in 1987 the international community, through the International Whaling Commission (IWC), agreed that the whale was an endangered species that required protection from over-fishing and thus commercial whaling, other than for research purposes, was banned, a decision that still stands. The stage was set for a debate that goes to the core of the sustainable marketing concept: is it appropriate for the wider international community to deny the whale-eating nations of Japan and, to a lesser extent, Norway and Iceland, the right to catch a creature in international waters as a part of their traditional diet?

Japan is a seafood rather than cattle culture and the whale has for thousands of years been used as a source of animal protein. Because of the degree of urbanisation and the limited amount of agricultural land, Japan is only 41 per cent self-sufficient for food, compared with 139 per cent in France and 97 per cent in Germany, so it is natural for the nation to look to the seas. The Japanese Fishery Agency (JFA) feels that sustainable whaling should be allowed, arguing that other fish stocks are being destroyed by an abundance of some species of whales, such as

the minke which has recovered in numbers to over 1 million. Indeed, the head of the JFA called the minke whale the 'cockroach of the ocean'. In order to meet customer demand, therefore, the JFA wants a new scheme of conservative quotas and a move from preservation to regulation. There is some support for this position from some other countries who see it as a concession for ensuring greater international cooperation rather than risking alienating a few nations which then pursue other paths.

Meanwhile, the Japanese have still been able to catch whales for 'scientific research' purposes. When one ship returned home with 158 whales caught over three months, 70 more than the previous year and including 8 sperm whales, it was almost a hero's welcome. The JFA congratulated the work of the fleet and vowed to protect its activities. Meanwhile, a special dinner of whale meat was organised. In the name of research, Japan still catches around 500 whales each year and it has been estimated that, despite official denial, 2,500 tonnes of whale meat reaches the market each year with a value of £22m. According to the JFA, the Japanese culture views wastage as unethical and immoral so it is legitimate for the research by-product (whale meat) to be distributed. Therefore the research institutes sell to the government to recoup the research subsidies and the meat is then sold on to the local governments who in turn sell to the fish markets.

The only local government that does not buy whale meat is in Okinawa, as they prefer dolphins.

There is, however, an alternative view of the whaling industry. Even at consumer level some doubt has been placed on just how important the whale is to the mainstream Japanese diet and there is even some embarrassment over the condemnation of Japan's whaling operations. Greenpeace went further and stated that 'this is a lucrative commercial operation subsidised by the government to sustain the market for whale meat even though most Japanese are indifferent' (as quoted by http://www.greenpeace.org.uk). A survey conducted by the Japanese Prime Minister's Office found that 77 per cent of Japanese support regulated whaling but a poll by MORI in 1999 found that 61 per cent of those questioned had not eaten whale meat since childhood and only 1 per cent said they ate whale meat at least once per month.

Counter-arguments have been presented by such bodies as the International Fund for Animal Welfare (IFAW). They include highlighting how commercial fishing stocks worldwide have been depleted by over-commercialisation rather than by whales, as the Japanese argue, and how Japan has abused the concession for scientific whaling research not only in terms of quantity, but also when some protected whale meat, such as from the humpback, blue and fin whales, has found its way into the marketplace. IFAW claims that Japan has refused proposals for a DNA monitoring scheme which would enable easier checking of whether catches are within regulations. Meanwhile, a moratorium on commercial whaling is still in force. Some go further and believe on moral grounds that whales should not be killed for any purpose and the regulatory bodies are still not convinced that enough evidence has been accumulated to support the Japanese claim that renewed catching of some species should now be permitted for commercial reasons as stocks have recovered.

To the Japanese, or at least to its fishing industry, whaling has become a symbol of virility and pride that should be respected by the world in the same way that other societies' food culture is respected. They do not wish to have different cultural norms imposed upon them. To many people, however, whaling has become symbolic of the need to protect the environment and many other species in the same way that in the 1970s a focus on whaling led to far greater concern for the oceans, rainforests and wildlife. So, is it satisfied consumers and regulated whale meat today, and hope that the future will look after itself, or should the IWC continue to take a strong stand?

Sources: The Economist (2000, 2001); Morishta and O'Regan (2001); Suhre (1999); Watts (2001).

The marketing concept in the organisation

What does the philosophy of marketing as a way of doing business mean to a real organisation? In this section we explore the practicalities of implementing the marketing concept, showing just how fundamentally marketing can influence the structure and management of the whole organisation. First, we look at the complexity of the organisational environment, and then think about how marketing can help to manage and make sense of the relationship between the organisation and the outside world. Second, we examine the relationship between marketing and the internal world of the organisation, looking, for example, at the potential conflicts between marketing and other business functions. To bring the external and the internal environments together, this section is summarised by looking at marketing as an interface, i.e. as a linking mechanism between the organisation and various external elements.

■ The external organisational environment

Figure 1.2 summarises the complexity of the external world in which an organisation has to operate. There are many people, groups, elements and forces that have the power to influence, directly or indirectly, the way in which the organisation conducts its business. The

Figure 1.2 The organisation's environment

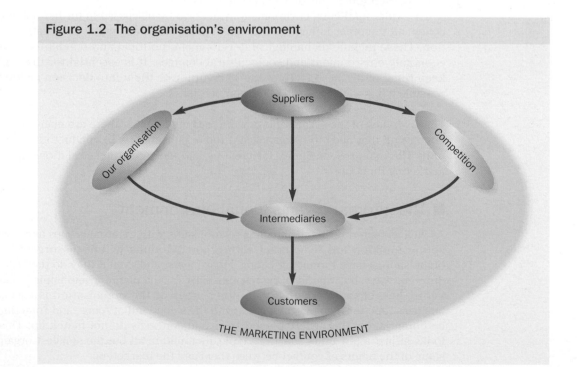

organisational environment includes both the immediate operating environment and the broader issues and trends that affect business in the longer term.

Current and potential customers

Customers are obviously vital to the continued health of the organisation. It is essential, therefore, that it is able to locate customers, find out what they want and then communicate its promises to them. Those promises have to be delivered (i.e. the right product at the right time at the right price in the right place) and followed up to ensure that customers are satisfied.

Competitors

Competitors, however, make the organisation's liaison with customer groups a little more difficult, since by definition they are largely pursuing the same set of customers. Customers will make comparisons between different offerings, and will listen to competitors' messages. The organisation, therefore, has not only to monitor what its competitors are actually doing now, but also to try to anticipate what they will do in the future in order to develop countermeasures in advance. European giants Nestlé and Unilever, for example, compete fiercely with each other in several fast-moving consumer goods (FMCG) markets.

Intermediaries

Intermediaries often provide invaluable services in getting goods from manufacturers to the end buyer. Without the cooperation of a network of wholesalers and/or retailers, many manufacturers would have immense problems in getting their goods to the end customer at the right time in the right place. The organisation must, therefore, think carefully about how best to distribute goods, and build appropriate relationships with intermediaries. Again, this is an area in which competition can interfere, and organisations cannot always obtain access to the channels of distribution that they want, or trade on the terms that they want.

Suppliers

Another crucial link in the chain is the supplier. Losing a key supplier of components or raw materials can mean that production flow is interrupted, or that a lower-quality or more expensive substitution has to be made. This means that there is a danger that the organisation will fail in its promises to the customer, for example by not providing the right product at the right time at the right price. Choice of suppliers, negotiation of terms and relationship building therefore all become important tasks.

The wider marketing environment, which will be discussed in further detail in Chapter 2, covers all the other influences that might provide opportunities or threats to the organisation. These include technological development, political and regulatory constraints, the economic environment and sociocultural changes. It is essential for the organisation to keep track of all these factors, and to incorporate them into decision-making as early as possible if it is to keep ahead of the competition.

This overview of the organisation's world has implied that there are many relationships that matter and that need to be managed if the organisation is to conduct its business successfully. The main responsibility for creating and managing these relationships lies with the marketing function.

■ The internal organisational environment

As well as fostering and maintaining relationships with external groups and forces, the marketing function has to interact with other functions within the organisation. Not all organisations have formal marketing departments, and even if they do they can be set up in different ways, but wherever the responsibility for the planning and implementation of marketing lies, close interaction with other areas of the organisation is essential. Not all business functions, however, operate with the same kind of focus, and sometimes there can be potential conflict where perspectives and concerns do not match up. This subsection looks at just a few other functions typically found in all but the smallest organisations and some of the points of conflict between them and the marketers.

Finance

The finance function, for example, sets budgets, perhaps early in the financial year, and expects other functions to stick to them. It wants hard evidence to justify expenditure, and it usually wants pricing to cover costs and to contribute towards profit. Marketing, on the other hand, tends to want the flexibility to act intuitively, according to fast-changing needs. Marketing also takes a longer, strategic view of pricing, and may be prepared to make a short-term financial loss in order to develop the market or to further wider strategic objectives.

In terms of accounting and credit, i.e. where finance comes into contact with customers, the finance function would want pricing and procedures to be as standardised as possible, for administrative ease. An accountant would want to impose tough credit terms and short credit periods, preferably only dealing with customers with proven credit records. Marketing, however, would again want some flexibility to allow credit terms to be used as part of a negotiation procedure, and to use pricing discounts as a marketing tool.

Purchasing

The purchasing function can also become somewhat bureaucratic, with too high a priority given to price. A focus on economical purchase quantities, standardisation and the price of materials, along with the desire to purchase as infrequently as possible, can all reduce the flexibility and responsiveness of the organisation. Marketing prefers to think of the quality of the components and raw materials rather than the price, and to go for non-standard parts, to increase its ability to differentiate its product from that of the competition. To be fair to purchasing, this is a somewhat traditional view. The rise of relationship marketing (pp. 5–6) and the increasing acceptance of just-in-time (JIT) systems (Chapter 8) mean that marketing and purchasing are now working more closely than ever in building long-term, flexible, cooperative relationships with suppliers.

Production

Production has perhaps the greatest potential to clash with marketing. It may be in production's interests to operate long, large production runs with as few variations on the basic product as possible, and with changes to the product as infrequently as possible, at least where mass production is concerned. This also means that production would prefer to deal with standard, rather than customised, orders. If new products are necessary, then the longer the lead time they are given to get production up to speed and running consistently, the better. Marketing has a greater sense of urgency and a greater demand for flexibility. Marketing may look for short production runs of many varied models in order to serve a range of needs in the market. Similarly, changes to the product may be frequent in order to keep the market interested. Marketing, particularly when serving B2B customers, may also be concerned with customisation as a means of better meeting the buyer's needs.

Research and development and engineering

Like production, research and development (R&D) and engineering prefer long lead times. If they are to develop a new product from scratch, then the longer they have to do it, the better. The problem is, however, that marketing will want the new product available as soon as possible, for fear of the competition launching their versions first. Being first into a market can allow the organisation to establish market share and customer loyalty, and to set prices freely, before the effects of competition make customers harder to gain and lead to downward pressure on prices. There is also the danger that R&D and engineering may become focused on the product for the product's sake, and lose sight of what the eventual customer is looking for. Marketing, in contrast, will be concentrating on the benefits and selling points of the product rather than purely on its functionality.

■ Marketing as an integrative business function

The previous subsection took a pretty negative view, highlighting the potential for conflict and clashes of culture between marketing and other internal functions. It need not necessarily be like that, and this subsection will seek to redress the balance a little, by showing how marketing can work with other functions. Many successful organisations such as Sony,

Nestlé and Unilever ensure that all functions within their organisation are focused on their customers. These organisations have embraced a marketing philosophy that permeates the whole enterprise and places the customer firmly at the centre of their universe.

What must be remembered is that organisations do not exist for their own sake. They exist primarily to serve the needs of the purchasers and users of their goods and services. If they cannot successfully sell their goods and services, if they cannot create and hold customers (or clients, or passengers, or patients or whoever), then they undermine their reason for existing. All functions within an organisation, whether they have direct contact with customers or not, contribute in some way towards that fundamental purpose. Finance, for example, helps the organisation to be more cost effective; personnel helps to recruit appropriate staff and make sure they are properly trained and remunerated so that they are more productive or serve the customer better; R&D provides better products; and production obviously churns out the product to the required quality and quantity specifications to meet market needs.

All of these functions and tasks are interdependent, i.e. none of them can exist without the others, and none of them has any purpose without customers and markets to serve. Marketing can help to supply all of those functions with the information they need to fulfil their specific tasks better, within a market-oriented framework. Those interdependencies, and the role of marketing in bringing functions together and emphasising the customer focus, are summarised in a simplified example in Figure 1.3.

Although the lists of items in the boxes in Figure 1.3 are far from comprehensive, they do show clearly how marketing can act as a kind of buffer or filter, both collecting information from the outside world then distributing it within the organisation, and presenting the combined efforts of the various internal functions to the external world. Taking, for example, two core issues from the 'customers' box:

Current product needs. To satisfy current needs, production has to know how much is required, when and to what quality specification. Production, perhaps with the help of the purchasing function, has to have access to the right raw materials or components at the right price. Keeping current products within an acceptable price band for the customer involves production, purchasing, finance and perhaps even R&D. A sales function might take orders from customers and make sure that the right quantity of goods is dispatched quickly to the right place. Marketing brings in those customers, monitoring their satisfaction levels, and brings any problems to the attention of the relevant functions as soon as possible so that they can be rectified with the minimum of disruption.

Future needs. Marketing, perhaps with the help of R&D, needs to monitor what is happening now and to try to predict what needs to happen in the future. This can be through talking to customers and finding out how their needs are evolving, or working out how new technology can be commercially exploited, or through monitoring competitors' activities and thinking about how they can be imitated, adapted or improved upon. Inevitably, there is a planning lead time, so marketing needs to bring in ideas early, then work with other functions to turn them into reality at the right time. Finance may have to sanction investment in a new product; R&D might have to refine the product or its technology; production may have to invest in new plant, machinery or manufacturing techniques; purchasing may have to start looking for new suppliers; and personnel may have to recruit new staff to help with the development, manufacture or sales of the new product.

When R&D and marketing do share common goals and objectives, it can be a very powerful combination. Marketing can feed ideas from the market that can stimulate innovation, while R&D can work closely with marketing to find and refine commercial applications for its apparently pointless discoveries.

These examples show briefly how marketing can be the eyes and ears of the organisation, and can provide the inputs and support to help each function to do its job more efficiently. Provided that all employees remember that they are ultimately there to serve the customers' needs, then the truly marketing-oriented organisation has no problem in accepting marketing as an interface between the internal and external worlds, and involving marketing in the day-to-day operation of its functions.

Figure 1.3 Marketing as an interface

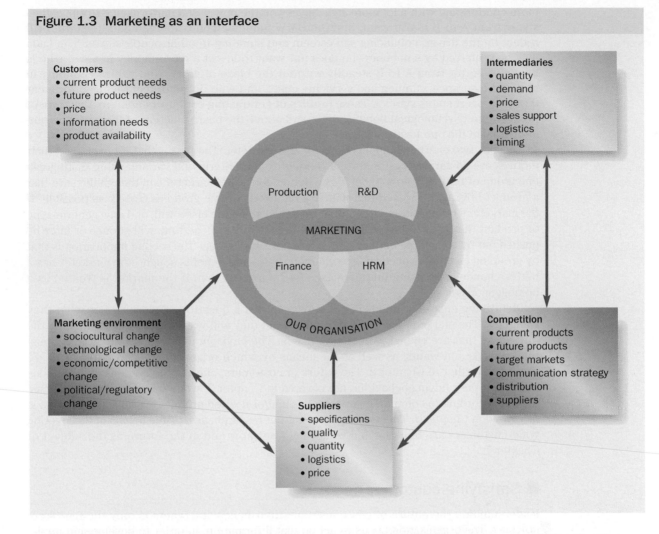

Marketing management responsibilities

This section outlines specifically what marketing does, and identifies where each of the areas is dealt with in this book.

All of marketing's tasks boil down to one of two things: identifying or satisfying customer needs in such a way as to achieve the organisation's objectives for profitability, survival or growth.

■ Identifying customer needs

Implicit in this is the idea of identifying the customer. The development of mass markets, more aggressive international competition and the increasing sophistication of the customer have taught marketers that it is unrealistic to expect to be able to satisfy all of the people all of the time. Customers have become more demanding, largely, it must be said, as a result of marketers' efforts, and want products that not only fulfil a basic functional purpose, but also provide positive benefits, sometimes of a psychological nature.

The basic functional purpose of a product, in fact, is often irrelevant as a choice criterion between competing brands – all fridges keep food cold, all brands of cola slake thirst, all cars move people from A to B, regardless of which organisation supplies them. The crucial questions for the customer are how does it fulfil its function, and what extra does it do for me in the process? Thus the choice of a BMW over a Lada may be made because the purchaser feels that the BMW is a better designed and engineered car, gets you from A to B in more comfort and with a lot more style, gives you the power and performance to zip aggressively from A to B if you want, and the BMW name is well respected and its status will reflect on the driver, enhancing self-esteem and standing in other people's eyes. The Lada may be preferred by someone who does not want to invest a lot of money in a car, who is happy to potter from A to B steadily without the blaze of glory, who values economy in terms of insurance, running and servicing costs, and who does not feel the need for a car that is an overt status symbol. These profiles of contrasting car buyers point to a mixture of product and psychological benefits, over and above the basic function of the cars, that are influential in the purchasing decision.

This has two enormous implications for the marketer. The first is that if buyers and their motives are so varied, it is important to identify the criteria and variables that distinguish one group of buyers from another. Once that is done, the marketer can then make sure that a product offering is created that matches the needs of one group as closely as possible. If the marketer's organisation does not do this, then someone else's will, and any 'generic' type of product that tries to please most of the people most of the time will sooner or later be pushed out by something better tailored to a narrower group. The second implication is that by grouping customers according to characteristics and benefits sought, the marketer has a better chance of spotting lucrative gaps in the market than if the market is treated as a homogeneous mass.

Identifying customer needs is not, however, just a question of working out what they want now. The marketer has to try to predict what they will want tomorrow, and identify the influences that are changing customer needs. The environmental factors that affect customer needs and wants, as well as the means by which organisations can fulfil them, are discussed further in Chapter 2. The nature of customers, and the motivations and attitudes that affect their buying behaviour, are covered in Chapter 3, while the idea of grouping customers according to common characteristics and/or desired product features and benefits is discussed in Chapter 4. The techniques of market research, as a prime means of discovering what customers are thinking and what they want now and in the future, is the subject of Chapter 5.

■ Satisfying customer needs

Understanding the nature of customers and their needs and wants is only the first step, however. The organisation needs to act on that information, in order to develop and implement marketing activities that actually deliver something of value to the customer. The means by which such ideas are turned into reality is the marketing mix. Figure 1.4 summarises the areas of responsibility within each element of the mix.

The concept of the marketing mix as the combination of the major tools of marketing was first developed by Borden in the 1950s (Borden, 1964), and the mnemonic '4Ps' (product, price, promotion and place) describing those tools was coined by McCarthy (1960). The marketing mix creates an offering for the customer. The use of the words *mix* and *combination* are important here, because successful marketing relies as much on interaction and synergy between marketing mix elements as it does on good decisions within those elements themselves. Häagen Dazs ice cream, for example, is a perfectly good, quality product, but its phenomenal success only came after an innovative and daring advertising campaign that emphasised certain adult-oriented product benefits. A good product with bad communication will not work, and similarly a bad product with the glossiest advertising will not work either. This is because the elements of the marketing mix all depend on each other, and if they are not consistent with each other in what they are saying about the product, then the customer, who is not stupid, will reject it all.

We now look more closely at each element of the marketing mix.

Product

This area, discussed in Chapter 6, covers everything to do with the creation, development and management of products. It is about not only what to make, but when to make it, how to make it, and how to ensure that it has a long and profitable life.

Figure 1.4 The marketing mix

Price
- Costs
- Profitability
- Value for money
- Competitiveness
- Incentives

Product
- New product development
- Product management
- Product features/benefits
- Branding
- Packaging
- After-sales service

Place
- Access to target market
- Channel structure
- Channel management
- Retailer image
- Logistics

Promotion
- Developing promotional mixes
- Advertising management
- Sales promotion management
- Sales management
- Public relations management
- Direct marketing

Furthermore, a product is not just a physical thing. In marketing terms, it includes peripheral but important elements, such as after-sales service, guarantees, installation and fitting – anything that helps to distinguish the product from its competition and make the customer more likely to buy it.

Particularly with fast-moving consumer goods (FMCG), part of a product's attractiveness is, of course, its brand imagery and its packaging. Both of these are likely to emphasise the psychological benefits offered by the product. With B2B purchases, however, the emphasis is more likely to be on fitness for functional purpose, quality and peripheral services (technical support, delivery, customisation, etc.). As well as featuring in the product chapters, echoes of these concerns will come through strongly in the chapters on buyer behaviour and segmentation (Chapters 3 and 4).

Although much of the emphasis is on physical products, it must also be remembered that service markets are an increasingly important growth area of many European economies. The product chapters do cover some aspects of services, but the main discussion of the service product is in Chapter 13, which deals with services marketing.

Price

Price is not perhaps as clear-cut as it might seem at first glance, since price is not necessarily a straightforward calculation of costs and profit margins. As Chapter 7 will show, price has to reflect issues of buyer behaviour, because people judge 'value' in terms of their perceptions of what they are getting for their money, what else they could have had for that money and how much that money meant to them in the first place.

Pricing also has a strategic dimension, in that it gives messages to all sorts of people in the market. Customers, for example, may use price as an indicator of quality and desirability for a particular product, and thus price can reinforce or destroy the work of other elements of the marketing mix. Competitors, on the other hand, may see price as a challenge, because if an organisation prices its products very low it may be signalling its intention to start a price war to the death, whereas very high (premium) prices may signal that there are high profits to be made or that there is room for a competitor to undercut and take market share away.

Overall, price is a very flexible element of the marketing mix, being very easy to tinker with. It is also, however, a dangerous element to play around with, because of its very direct link with revenues and profits, unless management think very carefully and clearly about how they are using it. The focus of the pricing chapter, therefore, is on the factors that influence price setting, the short-term tactical uses of pricing in various kinds of market and the strategic implications of a variety of pricing policies.

Place

Place is a very dynamic and fast-moving area of marketing. It covers a wide variety of fascinating topics largely concerned with the movement of goods from A to B and what happens at the point of sale. Chapter 8 therefore looks at the structure of channels of distribution, from mail order companies that deal direct with the end consumer, to long and complex chains that involve goods passing between several intermediaries before they get to a retailer. The chapter explores the range of different intermediaries, and the roles they play in getting goods to the right place at the right time for the end buyer, as well as the physical distribution issues involved in making it all happen.

For consumer goods, the most visible player in the channel of distribution is the retailer. Manufacturers and consumers alike have to put a lot of trust in the retailer to do justice to the product, to maintain stocks, and to provide a satisfying purchasing experience. Retailers face many of the same marketing decisions as other types of organisation, and use the same marketing mix tools, but with a slightly different perspective. They also face unique marketing problems, for example store location, layout and the creation of store image and atmosphere. Retailing has therefore been given a strong emphasis in this chapter.

Promotion

Chapters 9–11 are basically about communication, which is often seen as the most glamorous and sexy end of marketing. This does not mean, however, that marketing communication is purely an 'artistic' endeavour, or that it can be used to wallpaper over cracks in the rest of the marketing mix. Communication, because it is so pervasive and high profile, can certainly make or break a marketing mix, and thus it needs wise and constant analysis, planning and management.

These chapters look at the whole range of marketing communication techniques, not just advertising, but also sales promotions, personal selling, public relations and direct marketing. The activities undertaken within each area, the objectives each can best achieve, their relative strengths and weaknesses, and the kinds of management and planning processes that have to support them are discussed. To put all that into perspective, however, Chapter 9 first looks at the promotional mix as a whole, thinking about the factors that will influence the relative emphasis put on each individual communications area.

That, then, is the traditional 4Ps approach to marketing that has served very well for many years. More recently, however, it has become apparent that the 4Ps as they stand are not always sufficient. In the services sector in particular, they cannot fully describe the marketing activities that are going on, and so an extended marketing mix, the 7Ps, was proposed by Booms and Bitner (1981), adding people, processes and physical evidence to the traditional 4Ps.

People

Services often depend on people to perform them, creating and delivering the product as the customer waits. A customer's satisfaction with hairdressing and dentistry services, for example, has as much to do with the quality and nature of the interaction between the customer and the service provider as with the end result. If the customer feels comfortable with a particular service provider, trusts them and has a rapport with them, that is a relationship that a competitor would find hard to break into. Even where the service is not quite so personal, sullen assistance in a shop or a fast-food outlet, for example, does not encourage the customer to come back for more. Thus people add value and a dimension to the marketing package way beyond the basic product offering.

Processes

Manufacturing processes, once they are set up, are consistent and predictable and can be left to the production management team, and since they go on out of sight of the customer, any mistakes can be weeded out before distribution. Services, however, are 'manufactured' and consumed live, on the spot, and because they do involve people and the performance of their skills, consistency can be rather more difficult than with normal manufacturing. The marketer, therefore, has to think carefully about how the service is delivered, and what quality controls can be built in so that the customer can be confident that they know what to expect each time they consume the service product. This applies, for example, to banks and other retailers of financial services, fast-food outlets, hairdressers and other personal service providers, and even to professionals such as solicitors and management consultants.

Process can also involve queuing mechanisms, preventing waiting customers from getting so impatient that they leave without purchase; processing customer details and payment; as well as ensuring the high professional quality of whatever service they are buying.

Physical evidence

This final area is of particular relevance to retailers (of any type of product), or those who maintain premises from which a service is sold or delivered. It singles out some of the factors already mentioned when talking about retailers within the place element of the traditional 4Ps approach, such as atmosphere, ambience, image and design of premises. In other service situations, physical evidence would relate to the aircraft in which you fly, the hotel in which you stay, the stadium in which you watch the big match, or the lecture theatre in which you learn.

Other than in the services arena, the 4Ps are still widely accepted as defining the marketing mix. It has never been suggested, however, that the same mix is applicable in all situations or even for the same organisation at different times, so the task of the marketing manager is to review and change the mix to suit emerging circumstances. The marketing mix is simply therefore a set of categories of marketing variables that has become standard in marketing education and is the foundation for the structure of this book. As you read the chapters on the four elements of the marketing mix, look to see where aspects of people, process and physical evidence are being incorporated or implied within that traditional structure. Relationship marketing, in any type of market for any type of product, is increasingly throwing the emphasis on adding value to products through service. Inevitably, the extra 3Ps are going to impinge on that, and will be reflected in discussing applications of the original 4Ps.

The particular combination of the 4Ps used by any one organisation needs to give it competitive edge, or differential advantage. This means that the marketer is creating something unique, that the potential customer will recognise and value, that distinguishes one organisation's products from another's. In highly competitive, crowded markets, this is absolutely essential for drawing customers towards your product. The edge or advantage may be created mainly through one element of the mix, or through a combination of them. A product may have a combination of high quality and good value (price and product) that a competitor cannot match; an organisation may have established a 24-hour telephone ordering and home delivery service (place) that cannot easily be imitated; an effective and unique communications campaign combined with an excellent product living up to all its promises (promotion and product) can make an organisation's offering stand out above the crowd.

Nederman: creating a better workplace

Nederman is not a name that many readers will be familiar with, but it is typical of many engineering companies that have adopted marketing principles in order to build international business in B2B markets. Based in Helsingborg, Sweden, it is a medium-sized company with a turnover of SKr693m. in 2000. The underlying theme for the company is 'improving your workspace' and it has built a successful international business helping customers to solve their workstation problems. This is achieved by removing air pollution, reducing noise levels, screening out unwanted light, and making a workstation easier to operate in through greater efficiency in providing liquids, power, light, lifting equipment, etc. In short, the company provides a total solution for a workstation environment tailored to meet the customer's requirements.

At the heart of the marketing proposition is the ability to solve customers' problems. Nederman has to listen to the customer then design, manufacture and install solutions either for individual workstations or across a factory area. To be innovative Nederman has to invest in R&D to ensure that its products are at the cutting edge in design and performance. This requires a commitment to R&D and the sourcing of components that meet the specifications required. It is vital that Nederman is then able to listen to its

customers and tailor solutions to meet the need. For that reason it must have direct contact both before and after the sale has been made, and if sales agents are used in less important markets, they must be fully trained and skilled in matching customer needs with system solutions. Technical support is available to help in that task, although as in many other B2B markets, the sales person with appropriate technical knowledge and support is at the forefront of the promotional effort. Nederman has 11 sales subsidiaries in its main markets, such as Germany, Spain, the UK and USA, from which the sales teams operate.

The approach to customers is made either by responding to enquiries generated by advertising in trade publications, directory listings, web and print-based media, or by participation in trade fairs throughout the main markets. There is always the opportunity for repeat business, thus the importance of satisfied customers. Contact can also be initiated by the sales team, and this is sometimes achieved by offering a free health and safety assessment examining such matters as risk assessment, safety standards, signage, work practice, etc. Experience has indicated that this can often lead to the opportunity to open dialogue about production system improvement. Most of the sales subsidiaries have installed 'working environments' that visitors can inspect to compare with the systems currently used.

An experience with Hamlin Electronics is indicative of the sales and marketing challenge facing Nederman. When Hamlin decided to become involved in developing sensors for air bags destined for the motor industry, it needed new workstations to extract fumes from gluing, printing and varnishing processes. Nederman was approached along with other potential suppliers to consider the specification options prior to a detailed quote. Quotations were prepared on the proposed systems and presentations and site visits to other users were organised so that the buyer could be assured of the benefits of the Nederman offering. Although some time elapsed before the evaluation was complete, Nederman was awarded the contract, but that was not the end of the process, as installing and operationalising the workstations is also an important part of creating a satisfied customer. During all that time and subsequently 'a very good relationship was established with Nederman's contract engineers so that the installation was completed to a high standard. To date we have a maintenance-free system and all the units are popular with the operators who use them on a daily basis,' said the engineer at Hamlin. This forms the basis of further referrals and repeat business.

Source: http://www.nederman.com

■ Strategic vision

It is clear that individual marketing activities must be looked at within the context of a coherent and consistent marketing mix, but achieving that mix has to be an outcome of a wider framework of strategic marketing planning, implementation and control. Chapter 12 looks at these wider issues.

Strategy is concerned with looking into the future and developing and implementing the plans that will drive the organisation in the desired direction. Implicit in that is the need for strategy to inform (and be informed by) marketing. Strategic marketing thinking also needs a certain amount of unblinkered creativity, and can only be really successful if the marketer thinks not in terms of product, but rather in terms of benefits or solutions delivered to the customer. The organisation that answers the question 'What business are you in?' with the reply 'We are in the business of making gloss paint' is in danger of becoming too inwardly focused on the product itself and improving its manufacture (the production orientation). A more correct reply would have been: 'We are in the business of helping people to create beautiful rooms' (the identification of customer needs). The cosmetics executive who said that in the factory they made cosmetics but in the chemist's shop they sold hope, and the power tool manufacturer who said that they did not make drills, they made quarter-inch holes, were both underlining a more creative, outward-looking, problem-solving way of marketing thinking. Products are bought by customers to solve problems, and if the product does not solve the problem, or if something else solves it better, then the customer will turn away.

The organisation that cannot see this and defines itself in product rather than market terms could be said to be suffering from *marketing myopia*, a term coined by Levitt (1960). Such an organisation may well be missing out on significant marketing opportunities, and thus may leave itself open to new or more innovative competitors which more closely match customer needs. A classic example of this is slide rule manufacturers. Their definition of the business they were in was 'making slide rules'. Perhaps if they had defined their business as 'taking the pain out of calculation' they would still exist today and be manufacturing electronic calculators. Green (1995) discusses how the pharmaceutical companies are thinking about what business they are in. The realisation that patients are buying 'good health' rather than 'drugs' is broadening the horizons of companies such as Sandoz in Switzerland, GlaxoSmithKline in the UK and Merck in the USA, all of which have diversified into areas of health care other than R&D of drugs. GlaxoSmithKline in particular wants to spread its efforts across what it sees as the four core elements of health care: prevention, diagnosis, treatment and cure.

Therefore the distinction between the product and the problem it solves matters, because marketing strategy is about managing the organisation's activities within the real world in which it has to survive. In that turbulent and dynamically changing world, a marketing mix that works today may not work tomorrow. If your organisation is too product focused to remember to monitor how customer needs and wants are changing, then it will get left behind by competitors who do have their fingers on the customer's pulse. If your organisation forgets why it is making a particular product and why the consumer buys it, how can it develop marketing strategies that strike a chord with the customers and defend against the competition?

Think about a drill manufacturer that is product focused and invests vast amounts of time and money in developing a better version of the traditional electric drill. How do you think it would feel if a competitor then launched a hand-held, cordless, laser gun that could instantly zap quarter-inch holes (controllably) through any material with no physical effort on the part of the operator, and with no mess because it vaporises the residue? The laser company was thinking ahead, looking at the consumer's problem, looking at the weaknesses in the currently available solutions, and developing a marketing package that would deliver a better solution.

What we are saying here is that it is not enough to formulate a cosy marketing mix that suits the product and is entirely consistent with itself. That marketing mix is only working properly if it has been thought through with due respect to the external environment within which it is to be implemented. As well as justifying the existence of that marketing mix in the light of current internal and external influences, the strategic marketer has to go further by justifying how that mix helps to achieve wider corporate objectives; explaining how it is helping to propel the organisation in its longer-term desired direction; and finally, how it contributes to achieving competitive edge.

Ultimately, competitive edge is the name of the game. If marketers can create and sustain competitive edge, by thinking creatively and strategically about the internal and external marketing environments, then they are well on the way to implementing the marketing concept and fulfilling all the promise of the definitions of marketing with which this chapter began.

Marketing scope

Marketing plays a part in a wide range of organisations and applications. Some of these are discussed specifically in Chapters 13 and 14 and elsewhere in this book, while others are implicit throughout the text.

■ Consumer goods

The consumer goods field, because it involves potentially large and lucrative markets of so many individuals, has embraced marketing wholeheartedly, and indeed has been at the root of the development and testing of many marketing theories and concepts. Consumer goods and markets will be a major focus of this text, but certainly not to the exclusion of anything else. Since we are all consumers, it is easy to relate our own experience to the theories and concepts presented here, but it is equally important to try to understand the wider applications.

■ B2B goods

B2B or industrial goods ultimately end up serving consumers in some way, directly or indirectly. The cleaned wool that the woolcomber sells to the spinner to make into yarn to sell to the weaver to make into cloth eventually ends up in the shops as clothing; the rubber that Dunlop, Goodyear or Firestone buys to make into tyres to sell to car manufacturers ends up being bought by consumers; the steel girders sold by Corus to a civil engineering contractor for a new bridge end up serving the needs of individuals. If these organisations are going to continue to feed the voracious appetite of consumer markets successfully (the right product in the right place at the right time at the right price – remember?), then they also have to manage their relationships with other organisations, in a marketing-oriented way. A study by Avlonitis *et al.* (1997) found that companies in B2B markets that had developed a marketing orientation were a lot more successful than those that had not. The buying of goods, raw materials and components by organisations is a crucial influence on what can be promised and offered, especially in terms of price, place and product, to the next buyer down the line. If these interorganisational relationships fail, then ultimately the consumer, who props up the whole chain, loses out, which is not in the interests of any organisation, however far removed from the end consumer. As Chapter 3 in particular will show, the concerns and emphases in B2B markets are rather different from those of consumer markets, and thus need to be addressed specifically.

■ Service goods

Service goods, to be discussed in Chapter 13, include personal services (hairdressing, other beauty treatments or medical services, for example) and professional skills (accountancy, management consultancy or legal advice, for example), and are found in all sorts of markets, whether consumer or B2B. As already mentioned on pp. 22–3, services have differentiated themselves somewhat from the traditional approach to marketing because of their particular characteristics. These require an extended marketing mix, and cause different kinds of management headaches from physical products. Many marketing managers concerned with physical products are finding that service elements are becoming increasingly important to augment their products and to differentiate them further from the competition. This means that some of the concepts and concerns of services marketing are spreading far wider than their own relatively narrow field, and this is reflected throughout this book. In between the two extremes of a largely service product (a haircut, for instance) and a largely physical product (a machine tool, for instance), are products that have significant elements of both. A fast-food outlet, for example, is selling physical products, burger, fries and a coke, and that is primarily what the customer is there for. Service elements, such as speed and friendliness of service, atmosphere and ambience, are nevertheless inextricably linked with those physical products to create an overall package of satisfaction (or otherwise) in the customer's mind. This mixture of physical and service products is common throughout the retail trade, and thus services marketing not only features in its own chapter, but also permeates the chapter dealing with distribution (Chapter 8).

■ Non-profit marketing

Non-profit marketing is an area that increasingly asserted itself in the economic and political climate of the 1980s and 1990s. Hospitals, schools, universities, the arts and charities are all having to compete within their own sectors to obtain, protect and justify their funding and even their existence. The environment within which such organisations exist is increasingly subject to market forces, and altruism is no longer enough. This means that non-profit organisations need to think not only about efficiency and cost effectiveness, but also about their market orientation – defining what their 'customers' need and want and how they can provide it better than their rivals.

Chapter 13 looks in more detail at the particular marketing problems and situations facing non-profit organisations.

eg International charity Oxfam (http://www.oxfam.org.uk) believes that it is necessary to boost contributions from its trading operation in order to supplement the funds raised from donations and legacies. In 1999–2000, donations raised nearly £49.7m. – 80 per cent of its income (excluding grants) – and the retail stores added a further £8.8m. contribution after expenses. The first store in the UK was opened in Huddersfield in 1975 as a point for recycling unwanted clothes. In 1985 it opened the first clearance store to sell lines unwanted by other stores and in 1986 launched its first second-hand furniture store. Specialist lines have followed, again around the second-hand theme, including wedding outfits, retro party outfits, toys, electrical goods and books. From 850 stores it sells 27 million items, generating around £43m. in sales. The problem for the stores is tackling the negative public image that it sells second-hand cast-offs of dubious quality. Recent efforts have included using supermodels to emphasise style as well as value for money from the stores but this met with only limited success. In a 2001 trading review it was decided to allow a lot more freedom to the local store managers to build stock and to respond to local conditions. It remains to be seen whether this will enhance the overall image or just reinforce stereotypes. Operating local stores gives market presence and raises marginal income, but it could also have an impact on potential donors if the association with the stores creates an image of Oxfam as a worthwhile, but somewhat downmarket cause. The impression would be very wrong given the range of environmental, human rights and poverty issues it tackles, but a problem for many marketers is that people have the right to believe whatever they want, and that can be positive or negative!

■ Small business marketing

Many of the marketing theories and concepts laid out in this book have been developed with respect to larger organisations, relatively rich in marketing expertise, management skills and resources. Many small businesses, however, simply cannot live up to this. They often have only one or two managers who have to carry out a variety of managerial and operational functions and who often have very limited financial resources for investment in researching new markets and developing new products ahead of the rest. Throughout this book we therefore include examples that show more pragmatically how marketing theories and practice can be adapted to serve the needs of the small business.

■ International marketing

International marketing is a well-established field, and with the opening up of Europe as well as the technological improvements that mean it is now easier and cheaper to transfer goods around the world, it has become an increasingly important area of marketing theory and practice. Throughout the book, examples will be found of organisations dealing with issues of market entry strategy and the development and/or adaptation of marketing mixes for different geographic markets, all providing an interesting perspective on marketing decision-making.

■ e-marketing

The development, strategic integration and implementation of e-marketing techniques, along with the adoption of new marketing communications media, has been a rapid and startling phenomenon of the late 1990s and early 2000s. These techniques and media have pushed the boundaries of creativity as well as extending organisations' abilities to develop one-to-one relationships with consumers through better targeted and customised interactive communication. Again, this is an area that is given its own chapter, Chapter 14, to show how it has permeated all aspects of marketing decision-making.

Chapter summary

■ Marketing is about exchange processes, i.e. identifying what potential customers need and want now, or what they are likely to want in the future, and then offering them something that will fulfil those needs and wants. You thus offer them something that they value and, in return, they offer you something that you value, usually money. Most (but not all) organisations are in business to make profits, and so it is important that customers' needs and wants are fulfilled cost-effectively, efficiently and profitably. This implies that the marketing function has to be properly planned, managed and controlled.

■ Marketing in some shape or form has been around for a very long time, but it was during the course of the twentieth century that it made its most rapid developments and consolidated itself as an important business function and as a philosophy of doing business. By the late 1990s, all types of organisations in the USA and Western Europe had adopted a marketing orientation and were looking for ways to become even more customer focused, for example through relationship marketing.

■ The marketing orientation has been a necessary response to an increasingly dynamic and difficult world. Externally, the organisation has to take into account the needs, demands and influences of several different groups such as customers, competitors, suppliers and intermediaries, who all exist within a dynamic business environment. Internally, the organisation has to coordinate the efforts of different functions, acting as an interface between them and the customer. When the whole organisation accepts that the customer is absolutely paramount and that all functions within the organisation contribute towards customer satisfaction, then a marketing philosophy has been adopted.

■ Marketing's main tasks, therefore, are centred around identifying and satisfying customers' needs and wants, in order to offer something to the market that has a *competitive edge* or *differential advantage*, making it more attractive than the competing product(s). These tasks are achieved through the use of the *marketing mix*, a combination of elements that actually create the offering. For most physical goods, the marketing mix consists of four elements: product, price, place and promotion. For service-based products, the mix can be extended to seven elements with the addition of people, processes and physical evidence. The marketer has to ensure that the marketing mix meets the customer's needs and wants, and that all its elements are consistent with each other, otherwise customers will turn away and competitors will exploit the weakness. Additionally, the marketer has to ensure that the marketing mix fits in with the strategic vision of the organisation, that it is contributing to the achievement of longer-term objectives, or that it is helping to drive the organisation in the desired future direction. These marketing principles are generally applicable to any kind of organisation operating in any kind of market. But whatever the application, the basic philosophy remains: if marketers can deliver the right product in the right place at the right time at the right price, then they are making a crucial contribution towards creating satisfied customers and successful, efficient and profitable organisations.

questions for *review and discussion*

1.1 What is meant by the description of marketing as 'an exchange process'?

1.2 Distinguish between the four main business orientations.

1.3 What is competitive edge and why is it so important?

1.4 Why is the question 'What business are we in?' so important? How might

  (a) a fast-food retailer,
  (b) a national airline,
  (c) a car manufacturer, and
  (d) a hairdresser

answer that question if they were properly marketing oriented?

1.5 Choose a product that you have purchased recently and show how the elements of the marketing mix came together to create the overall offering.

1.6 Choose three different products within the same market and explain how each one is trying to gain a competitive edge over the others.

case study 1.1

lastminute.com: inspiration and solutions

lastminute.com is Europe's number one Internet travel website. The company was set up in 1998 with the mission statement:

lastminute.com encourages spontaneous, romantic and sometimes adventurous behaviour by offering people the chance to live their dreams at unbeatable prices!

These dreams do not only concern travel, however. lastminute.com sells three main groups of products and services:

- *Travel:* holidays, flights, hotels, etc.
- *Retail:* gifts (chocolates, gourmet foods, lingerie, adult fun items, etc.) and experiences (e.g. what about a bungee-jumping experience as a gift for your loved one?).
- *Leisure:* tickets for the theatre, concerts or sports events; eating in and eating out (through lastminute.com you can book a restaurant or order a meal to be delivered to your home).

In the early days, there was inevitably something of a product orientation to the company, as it sought to source and sell whatever products it could. As its brand name and reputation have developed, however, it has been possible to develop more of a marketing orientation as partnerships have evolved with suppliers who have come to recognise the potential of lastminute.com as a distribution channel and thus are negotiating more strategically about the most appropriate deals and offerings to place with lastminute.com. The company sees itself as an agent, putting last-minute buyers in touch with last-minute sellers. It is a 'lifestyle' retailer, for cash-rich, time-poor consumers, offering good value rather than being purely a 'bargain basement' store. The focus is on value and service, rather than on price. 'Inspiration and solutions' is a good summary of lastminute.com's core service:

- *Inspiration:* 'It's my friend's birthday. I know that I need a gift, but I don't know what I want'. lastminute.com can offer a variety of suggestions for gifts and experiences.

- *Solutions:* 'I know what I need and what I want: I want an economy class flight from Heathrow to New York next Friday'. lastminute.com can show available flights and prices to allow the customer to choose which they want.

In the view of Carl Lyons, the marketing director,

people love the idea of lastminute.com. It evokes a positive image of a shortcut to good times with their friends.

The product portfolio has evolved over time as the company strives to be able to offer the customer everything for the perfect experience. The latest addition to the product portfolio, for example, is the ability to book a taxi through lastminute.com. Thus the customer planning a special night out with friends can search for, check availability, and make bookings at a theatre and a restaurant, and even take care of transportation too in one easy and convenient transaction. Before a new product or service can be added, however, the company needs to be sure that the customer is ready for it, that it has a clear role within the cohesive set of offerings that lastminute.com makes, that suppliers are willing and able to deliver the promises that lastminute.com makes on their behalf, and that the technical capability is there to allow the transaction and/or the service delivery to take place successfully.

The structure of the company in the UK is similar to that of many others. There are the traditional departments, such as marketing, human resources and finance, as well as departments that reflect the high-tech retail focus of the business: a technical department to develop, maintain and manage the Internet infrastructure that allows communication and transactions to take place between the company and its customers; three supply managers whose departments source the products and services that lastminute.com sells; and a business development department that manages strategic issues, for example creating and managing partnerships with other companies. Recently, lastminute.com entered into a partnership with Granada Media, for instance, in order to generate awareness and traffic from complementary media. The marketing department consists of 13 people who undertake the complete range of well-integrated marketing activities, both online and offline. Although the marketing department can be thought of as being at the hub of the organisation, there is a spirit of mutual support and interdependence between the various departments.

Given the interactivity involved in Internet retailing generally, the kinds of products and services that the site is selling, and the 'last minute' focus, it is perhaps not surprising that timing is a key issue in lastminute.com's day-to-day marketing. Advertising within the website changes throughout the day to reflect deadlines for products and the customer's changing needs. Thus, for example, in terms of 'eating in' and 'eating out', in the morning the emphasis will be on lunchtime restaurant bookings, whereas in the afternoon, the focus will shift to evening bookings and there will perhaps be more emphasis on family-oriented eating in or out. The marketing department has also recognised that not all customers are willing and/or able to buy through the same platforms all the time. Thus the marketers have worked closely with the technical department to ensure that transactions can be made by phone, through digital interactive television, and via WAP phones as well as over the web from a PC. This is an important element of ensuring that customers can access lastminute.com's services whenever they want and in a way that is most convenient or acceptable to them.

Another very important and dynamic element of lastminute.com's marketing offering is its weekly newsletter distributed via e-mail to over 3.5 million people. The company sees the newsletter, in conjunction with other relationship marketing techniques, as a very cost-effective and quick way of achieving a number of objectives:

- building and maintaining brand awareness and loyalty among customers through frequent communication;
- building and communicating brand personality through the design and 'tone of voice' of the newsletter;
- emphasising the breadth of products and services offered – a customer might, for example, have only purchased a package holiday previously through lastminute.com and thus the newsletter can introduce them to the gifts and broader leisure products and services on offer;
- stimulating demand in terms of both planned and impulse purchases.

The content and distribution of the newsletter are based on the customer database, which allows the company to target individual customers based on their past purchasing history. This is important because it means that the customer is more likely to see some relevance or interest in the newsletter rather than dismissing it as junk e-mail and using anti-spam filtering to prevent it.

The customer database is seen as a powerful weapon for competitive advantage because of its size and sophistication. The database has grown organically over the course of three years (which is a long time in dotcom terms!) and because of the established brand name of lastminute.com, the company finds it relatively easy to continue to recruit new customers to the database. Newer competitors find it more difficult because consumers have become more wary about volunteering personal details to companies they do not know very well. The strong brand name and established reputation of lastminute.com also stimulates less formal, but nevertheless invaluable, marketing benefits such as word-of-mouth recommendation between friends which helps to generate new customers.

Market research is not always easy in the dotcom sector. When lastminute.com was set up, it was something of a pioneer so it was difficult to quantify exactly the market potential. Additionally, there was a lack of established sources of secondary research. In most mature industries, there are good quality, established, standard sources of market information, but in emerging industries, this is not necessarily the case.

Initially trading on last-minute flights and holidays, lastminute.com now offers a wide variety of products on the Internet for those whose time is precious and whose lifestyles require immediate satisfaction.

Source: lastminute.com

Now that the market is beginning to mature, research data are starting to be collated. lastminute.com itself, however, undertakes its own ongoing research programme through its continuous 'user monitor' survey. A percentage of visitors to the website are encouraged to fill in an online feedback form giving their views on everything from prices and product offerings to their expectations of what the site should offer. The company is very responsive to the views expressed in this way, and this has contributed to the rapid evolution of the site in terms of both what it offers and how it is offered and delivered.

The company is confident about its future:

There has already been a shakeout in this market. The barriers to entry are low, but the barriers to success are high. We have an established customer base; we have good supplier relationships; we have the technical know-how. We have travelled a long way up the learning curve. The key to the future will be continuing to serve customers' evolving needs, being quick/first with new offerings, and being consistently true to the brand. Marketing is marketing. It's easy to drape new

media in magic but it comes down to whether it's a good business or not.

Sources: with grateful thanks to Carl Lyons, UK Marketing Director, lastminute.com; http://www.lastminute.com; Rosier (2000).

Questions

1 Explain how and why lastminute.com's business orientation has evolved since its launch.

2 Divide lastminute.com's marketing activities into the 4Ps and explain how they fit together to create a consistent marketing mix. How might the other 3Ps of the services marketing mix fit in?

3 From the supplier's point of view, what are the advantages and disadvantages of selling travel and leisure services through an Internet-based intermediary such as lastminute.com?

4 'The barriers to entry are low, but the barriers to success are high.' What do you think Carl Lyons meant by this and to what extent and why do you believe it to be true?

References for chapter 1

Alderson, W. (1957), *Marketing Behaviour and Executive Action: A Functionalist Approach to Marketing*, Homewood, Irwin.

AMA (1985), 'AMA Board Approves New Marketing Definition', *Marketing News*, 1 March, p. 1.

Avlonitis, G. *et al.* (1997), 'Marketing Orientation and Company Performance: Industrial vs Consumer Goods Companies', *Industrial Marketing Management*, 26 (5), pp. 385–402.

Balestrini, P. (2001), 'Amidst the Digital Economy, Philanthropy in Business as a Source of Competitive Advantage', *Journal of International Marketing and Marketing Research*, 26 (1), pp. 13–34.

Berry, L. (1983), 'Relationship Marketing', in *Emerging Perspectives of Services Marketing*, L. Berry *et al.* (eds), American Marketing Association.

Booms, B. and Bitner, M. (1981), 'Marketing Strategies and Organisation Structures for Service Firms', in *Marketing of Services*, J. Donnelly and W. George (eds), American Marketing Association.

Borden, N. (1964), 'The Concept of the Marketing Mix', *Journal of Advertising Research*, June, pp. 2–7.

Brabbs, C. (2000), 'Kellogg "Luxury" Cereal Targets Career Women', *Marketing*, 14 September, p. 4.

Buxton, P. (2000), 'Companies with a Social Conscience', *Marketing*, 27 April, pp. 33–4.

Carroll, A. (1991), 'The Pyramid of Corporate Social Responsibility: Toward the Moral Management of Organizational Stakeholders', *Business Horizons*, 34 (July/August), pp. 39–48.

Carroll, A. (1999), 'Corporate Social Responsibility', *Business and Society*, 38 (3), pp. 268–95.

Challener, C. (2001), 'Sustainable Development at a Crossroads', *Chemical Market Reporter*, 16 July, pp. 3–4.

Christopher, M., Payne, A. and Ballantyne, D. (1991), *Relationship Marketing: Bringing Quality, Customer Service and Marketing Together*, London: Butterworth.

CIM (2001), accessed via http://www.cim.co.uk

Clarke, P. *et al.* (1988), 'The Genesis of Strategic Marketing Control in British Retail Banking', *International Journal of Bank Marketing*, 6 (2), pp. 5–19.

Davies, J. (2001), 'The Chaos Christina Left Behind', *The Times (2)*, 31 July, pp. 4–5.

Deng, S. and Dart, J. (1999), 'The Market Orientation of Chinese Enterprises during a Time of Transition', *European Journal of Marketing*, 33 (5), pp. 631–54.

Dwyer, F., Shurr, P. and Oh, S. (1987), 'Developing Buyer and Seller Relationships', *Journal of Marketing*, 51 (2), pp. 11–27.

The Economist (2000), 'The Politics of Whaling', *The Economist*, 9 September, p. 42.

The Economist (2001), 'For Watching or Eating?', *The Economist*, 28 July, p. 58.

Foottit, C. (2000), 'Kenya: Flower Industry Blooming', *African Business*, July/August, p. 36.

Fuller, D. (1999), *Sustainable Marketing: Managerial-Ecological Issues*, Sage Publications.

Gordon, M. (1991), 'Market Socialism in China', Working Paper, University of Toronto.

Gray, R. (2001), 'Responsibility up the Agenda', *Marketing*, 3 May, p. 39.

Green, D. (1995), 'Healthcare Vies with Research', *Financial Times*, 25 April 1995, p. 34.

The Grocer (1998), 'Dutch Exporter Going Flat out to Grow in Britain', *The Grocer*, 24 January, p. 40.

Grönroos, C. (1997), 'From Marketing Mix to Relationship Marketing – towards a Paradigm Shift in Marketing', *Management Decision*, 35 (4), pp. 322–39.

Gummesson, E. (1987), 'The New Marketing: Developing Long-term Interactive Relationships', *Long Range Planning*, 20 (4), pp. 10–20.

Hartman, C. and Beck-Dudley, C. (1999), 'Marketing Strategies and the Search for Virtue: A Case Analysis of the Body Shop International', *Journal of Business Ethics*, 20 (3), pp. 249–63.

Henderson, S. (1998), 'No Such Thing as Market Orientation – a Call for No More Papers', *Management Decision*, 36 (9), pp. 598–609.

Knights, D. *et al.* (1994), 'The Consumer Rules? An Examination of the Rhetoric and "Reality" of Marketing in Financial Services', *European Journal of Marketing*, 28 (3), pp. 42–54.

Levitt, T. (1960), 'Marketing Myopia', *Harvard Business Review*, July/August, pp. 45–56.

McCarthy, E. (1960), *Basic Marketing*, Homewood: Irwin.

Mans, J. (2000), 'The European View of Future Packaging', *Dairy Foods*, 101 (6), pp. 42–3.

Marketing Week (2001), 'Fresh Cut Flowers', *Marketing Week*, 22 March, pp. 34–5.

Mason, T. (2000), 'The Importance of Being Ethical', *Marketing*, 26 October, p. 27.

Mhone, C. (2000), 'Malawi: Fading Flowers', *African Business*, December, p. 46.

Mintel (1999), 'Breakfast Cereals, 1/12/99', accessed via http://sinatra2.mintel.com, October 2001.

Morishta, J. and O'Regan, F. (2001), 'Whaling: Should Japan be Allowed to Continue?', *The Ecologist*, July/August, pp. 18–21.

Narver, J. and Slater, S. (1990), 'The Effect of a Market Orientation on Business Profitability', *Journal of Marketing*, 54 (4), pp. 20–35.

OECD Observer (2001), 'Rising to the Global Development Challenges', Issue 226/7 (Summer), p. 41.

Piercy, N. (1992), *Marketing-led Strategic Change*, Oxford: Butterworth-Heinemann.

Rosier, B. (2000), 'The Long Game', *Marketing*, 31 August, p. 16.

Schultz, R. and Good, D. (2000), 'Impact of the Consideration of Future Sales Consequences and Customer-oriented Selling on Long-term Buyer–Seller Relationships', *The Journal of Business and Industrial Marketing*, 15 (4), pp. 200–15.

Severn Trent (2001), 'Stewardship Report 2001: The Environment is Our Business', accessed via http://www.severn-trent.com/reports/fin/steward2001/pdf/stewardship_report.pdf, August 2001.

Sheth, J., Gardner, D. and Garrett, D. (1988), *Marketing Theory: Evolution and Evaluation*, New York: Wiley.

Smith, W. and Higgins, M. (2000), 'Cause-related Marketing: Ethics and the Ecstatic', *Business and Society*, 39 (3), pp. 304–22.

Suhre, S. (1999), 'Misguided Morality: The Repercussions of the International Whaling Commission's Shift From a Policy of Regulation to One of Preservation', *Georgetown International Environment Law Review*, 12 (1), pp. 305–29.

Turnbull, P. and Valla, J. (1986), *Strategies for International Industrial Marketing*, Croom Helm.

Van Heck, E. (2000), 'The Cutting Edge in Auctions', *Harvard Business Review*, March/April, pp. 18–19.

Watts, J. (2001), 'Japanese Laud Whaling Haul', *The Guardian*, 8 August.

WCED (1987), *Our Common Future*, Oxford: Oxford University Press.

Zhuang, S. and Whitehill, A. (1989), 'Will China Adopt Western Management Practices?', *Business Horizons*, 32 (2), pp. 58–64.

chapter 2

the european marketing environment

LEARNING OBJECTIVES

This chapter will help you to:

1 understand the importance of the external environment to marketing decision-making;

2 assess the role and importance of scanning the environment as a means of early identification of opportunities and threats;

3 appreciate the evolving and diverse nature of the European marketing environment;

4 define the broad categories of factors that affect the marketing environment; and

5 understand the influences at work within each of those categories and their implications for marketing.

Introduction

Marketing, by its very nature, is an outward-looking discipline. As the interface between the organisation and the outside world, it has to balance internal capabilities and resources with the opportunities offered externally. Chapter 1 has already shown, however, that the outside world can be a complex and difficult place to understand. Although the definition and understanding of the customer's needs and wants are at the heart of the marketing philosophy, there are many factors influencing how those customer needs evolve, and affecting or constraining the organisation's ability to meet those needs in a competitive environment. Thus in order to reach an adequate understanding of the customer's future needs and to develop marketing mixes that will satisfy the customer, the marketer has to be able to analyse the external environment and clarify which influences and their implications are most important.

This chapter will dissect the external environment and look closely at the variety of factors and influences that help to shape the direction of marketing thinking. First, the chapter clarifies the nature of the external environment, underlining why it needs to be understood, and what opportunities that understanding offers to the marketer.

Although the environment consists of a wide variety of factors and influences, it is possible to group them under four broad headings: sociocultural, technological, economic and competitive, and political and regulatory influences. Each will be examined in turn, discussing the various issues they cover and their implications for marketing decision-making.

eg Food processors such as Nestlé must keep a close watch on trends in the marketing environment if they are to remain competitive and within the law. It is not an easy environment. Over the past few years the consumer has had to cope with the implications of BSE/CJD ('mad cow' disease and its human form), the effect of foot and mouth disease on meat stocks and prices, acceptance of GM (genetically modified) foodstuffs and other scares such as salmonella in eggs and powdered baby milk. All of this starts to raise issues about the integrity of the European food chain and the wisdom of high-intensity farming. The paradox is that at a time when most Europeans are spoilt for choice and generally enjoy very high quality foods, there is growing concern over production methods, animal welfare, environmental impact and the impact on public health of chemicals and additives. Whether the European food chain is safe, sustainable and ethical still seems debatable. The Swedish and British attitudes to food processing make an interesting comparison. In Sweden the consumer tends to pay more for food, to cover the higher costs of less intensive farming methods, improved animal welfare and tighter voluntary and legislated welfare controls. It is claimed that consumers are better educated about food and are prepared to pay more for home produced products. In the UK, the market is very price competitive and consumers seek to spend less on food. There are concerns about animal welfare and the intensity of

▶

farming, but often the connection is not made with supermarket prices. To many urban dwellers, eggs come from supermarkets, milk from cartons and beefburgers from McDonald's and that is that. Research by Taylor Nelson Sofres suggests that less than 30 per cent of shoppers actually check food labels for the calorie, preservative and additive content, let alone worry about the farming method: as long as it is perceived as 'safe', many don't care. This means that many farmers are now in a trap. The consumer will not pay more for the food; retailers and processors want cheaper supplies, and yet the demand for sustainable and environmentally friendly farming methods grows. At the same time, trade restrictions are being slowly lifted across the EU, and thus cheap supplies are coming in from developing countries with far fewer regulatory and welfare pressures on food processing, which is all very nice for the retailers and the consumers, but not so good for European food producers. And then there is the CAP reform programme . . . but more about that later (*The Grocer*, 2000b; Hunt, 2001).

The nature of the European marketing environment

This section will first define the broad groupings of environmental influences, and then go on to look at the technique of environmental scanning as a means of identifying the threats and opportunities that will affect marketing planning and implementation within the organisation.

■ Elements of the marketing environment

Figure 2.1 shows the elements of the external environment in relation to the organisation and its immediate surroundings. As the figure shows, the elements can be divided into four main groupings, known by the acronym **STEP**: **S**ociocultural, **T**echnological, **E**conomic and competitive, and **P**olitical and regulatory environments.

Sociocultural environment

The sociocultural environment is of particular concern to marketers as it has a direct effect on their understanding of customers and what drives them. Not only does it address the demographic structure of markets, but it also looks at the way in which attitudes and opinions are being formed and how they are evolving. A general increase in health consciousness, for instance, has stimulated the launch of a wide variety of products with low levels of fat and sugar, fewer artificial ingredients and no additives.

Technological environment

Technological innovation and technological improvement have had a profound effect in all areas of marketing. Computer technology, for instance, has revolutionised product design, quality control, materials and inventory management, the production of advertising and other promotional materials, and the management and analysis of customer information. The Internet has opened up new channels of communication and distribution. Technology also affects the development of new processes and materials, as well as the invention of completely new products or applications.

Economic and competitive environment

The economic and competitive environment covers both macro- and microeconomic conditions which affect the structure of competition in a market, the cost and availability of money for marketing investment in stock and new products, for example, and the economic conditions affecting a customer's propensity to buy.

Political and regulatory environment

The political and regulatory environment covers the external forces controlled by governments, both national and European, local authorities, or other trade or activity oriented regulatory bodies. Some of the rules and regulations developed and implemented by bodies

Figure 2.1 Elements of the external environment

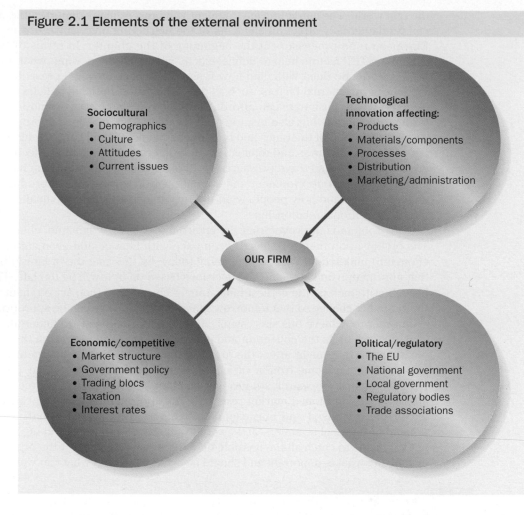

Sociocultural
- Demographics
- Culture
- Attitudes
- Current issues

Technological innovation affecting:
- Products
- Materials/components
- Processes
- Distribution
- Marketing/administration

OUR FIRM

Economic/competitive
- Market structure
- Government policy
- Trading blocs
- Taxation
- Interest rates

Political/regulatory
- The EU
- National government
- Local government
- Regulatory bodies
- Trade associations

under this heading have the force of law, while others are voluntary, such as advertising codes of practice.

Each of the STEP areas will be looked at in more detail on pp. 36 *et seq*. There is, of course, much interdependence between them. Rules and regulations concerning 'green' aspects of products, for example, are a result of sociocultural influences pressurising the legislators and regulators. Certain issues, therefore, such as international, ethical and green issues, will crop up with slightly different perspectives in the discussion of each STEP element.

eg Across Europe, voluntary agreements have been widely used in many industrial sectors. This involves the regulators, usually government, and regulatees working together to produce agreed standards and codes of practice to ensure progress in a less formal but more cooperative manner than outright legislation. In Germany the agreement on Global Warming Prevention was signed by the Ministry of Industry and Environment as well as 19 industry and trade associations. This committed members to reduce the level of CO_2 emissions by 2005 according to a trade association target. No targets are set at company level but as a result of the voluntary agreement, no energy taxes were introduced as originally planned (Delmas and Terlaak, 2001).

■ Environmental scanning

Even a brief discussion of the STEP factors begins to show just how important the marketing environment is: since marketing is all about looking outwards and meeting the customer's needs and wants, the organisation has to take into account what is happening in the real world. The marketing environment will present many opportunities and threats that can fundamentally affect all elements of the marketing mix, as we saw in the case of the European food processors at the beginning of the chapter. In terms of the product, for example, STEP factors help to define exactly what customers want, what it is possible (and legal) to provide them with, and how it should be packaged and presented. Pricing is also influenced by external factors, such as the competition's pricing policies, government taxation and what consumers can afford. STEP factors also affect promotion, constraining it through regulation, but also inspiring the creativity that develops appropriate messages to capture the mood of the times and the target audience. Finally, the strength of relationships between manufacturers and retailers or other intermediaries is also affected by the external environment. Competitive pressures at all levels of the distribution channel; technology encouraging joint development and commitment in terms of both products and logistics; shifts in where and how people want to buy: all help to shape the quality and direction of interorganisational relationships.

The problem is, however, that the environment is very dynamic, changing all the time. The organisation therefore has to keep pace with change and even anticipate it. It is not enough to understand what is happening today: by the time the organisation has acted on that information and implemented decisions based on it, it will be too late. The organisation has either to pick up the earliest indicators of change and then act on them very quickly, or try to predict change so that tomorrow's marketing offerings can be appropriately planned.

In order to achieve this successfully, the organisation needs to undertake environmental scanning, which is the collection and evaluation of information from the wider marketing environment that might affect the organisation and its strategic marketing activities. Such information may come from a variety of sources, such as experience, personal contacts, published market research studies, government statistics, trade sources or even through specially commissioned market research. The approach to scanning can vary from being extremely organised and purposeful to being random and informal. As Aguilar (1967) pointed out, formal scanning can be very expensive and time consuming as it has to cast its net very wide to catch all the possible influences that might affect the organisation. The key is knowing what is important and should be acted upon, and what can wait.

eg There is a great deal of skill and perceptiveness involved in assessing the significance of any piece of information and whether it should be acted upon. Volvo, for example, failed to pick up the early signs indicating the emergence of markets for 'people carriers' and four-wheel drive vehicles, and thus missed out on the growth stages of both markets. Organisations that supply components to the motor industry also have to be alert to changing tastes and trends, in order to plan production. Motor industry analysts predicted that air bags would not be as readily accepted by motorists in Europe as they were in the United States. What actually happened was that motorists quickly warmed to the idea and began to demand air bags as standard. The motor manufacturers were caught somewhat unprepared, and consequently put a lot of pressure on suppliers to fulfil demand immediately.

Environmental scanning is therefore an important task, but often a difficult one, particularly in terms of interpretation and implementation of the information gained. The following looks in more detail at each of the STEP factors, and gives a further indication of the range and complexity of the influences and information that can affect the marketing activities of the organisation.

The sociocultural environment

It is absolutely essential for organisations serving consumer markets, directly or indirectly, to understand the sociocultural environment, since these factors fundamentally influence the customer's needs and wants. Many of the factors discussed here will be looked at again in Chapters 3 and 4, and so this is a brief overview of the demographic and sociocultural influences on marketing thinking and activities.

■ The demographic environment

Demographics is the study of the measurable aspects of population structures and profiles, including factors such as age, size, gender, race, occupation and location. As the birth rate fluctuates and as life expectancy increases, the breakdown of the population changes, creating challenges and opportunities for marketers, particularly if that information is taken in conjunction with data on family structure and income.

One demographic group of great interest to marketers is what is known as the 'grey market', consisting of the over-55 age group which represents around one-quarter of the population of most EU countries (Euromonitor, 2001). Their numbers are increasing, and because of better health care and financial planning, a significant proportion are able to indulge in high levels of leisure-oriented consumption, especially as they are likely to have paid off any mortgage or similar long-term debt, and are not likely to have dependent children. 'Generational marketing', for organisations seeking to appeal to this target age group, requires a fundamentally different perspective on the part of advertisers, according to Shannon (1998). Attitudes are changing. For example, research into the over-50s in Germany revealed that rather than thrift and self-denial, the growing emphasis is on enjoyment through consumption. To communicate effectively to this age group, the focus now has to reflect attitude and lifestyle rather than reinforcing an age-based stereotype.

eg Saga Holidays also found that it had to redefine its idea of the most appropriate market to target and its notions of what potential customers want. In the 1990s, Saga shifted its focus from the over-60 to over-50 age group and at the same time diversified from being purely a tour operator to using the brand name to launch publishing and financial services products for the same target market. However, it also found that age alone was not a good indicator of holiday preferences. Over 90 per cent of customers now want holidays abroad compared with 50 per cent 10 years ago. They also want anything but two weeks in Benidorm or beach resorts. River rafting, jungle trekking, mountain hiking and elephant safaris are on the agenda as the age group becomes more diverse in outlook and aspirations. In 1996, Saga purchased the cruise ship *Saga Rose*, the only cruise ship exclusively for the over-50s: children and students are definitely not welcome! In a market in which the number of over-60s will grow by 20 per cent in 10 years' time, according to Henley Forecasting, and in which the over-50s are generally wealthier and have more leisure time, the future looks promising for Saga, but the formula remains the same: worry-free, well-organised and well-designed services for the 'mature in years, but young at heart' (Chesshyre, 2001; http://www.holidays.saga.co.uk).

Clearly, the size of a household combined with its income is also going to be a fundamental determinant of its needs and wants, and its ability to fulfil them. Data from Euromonitor (2001) suggest that most European countries are experiencing a pattern of decline in the average household size. Again, marketers need to be mindful of these changes and to adapt their offerings accordingly. A significant increase in the proportion of single-person households will affect a whole range of marketing offerings, for example solo holidays, smaller apartments, pack sizes and advertising approaches and family stereotypes.

What is also important is the level of disposable income available (i.e. what is left after taxes have been paid), and the choices the household makes about saving and/or spending it. Table 2.1 shows how the spending of disposable income varies across Europe.

Clearly, housing is a fundamental cost, but the proportion of income it takes varies widely across Europe, with the Greeks and Portuguese spending the lowest percentage on housing. Looking at the food column, however, it is in the less affluent economies, such as those of Greece and Portugal, that people are spending relatively more on food as a percentage of their total expenditure. In some of the other categories, the Irish spend a higher proportion than anyone else on tobacco while the Dutch spend more on health care; the Germans like their home comforts, with a higher than average spend on household fuels and household goods and services; the Spanish obviously like eating out while the Finns seem to enjoy their alcohol! Of course, patterns of expenditure will be dictated to some extent by national income levels and relative prices.

Table 2.1 Consumer expenditure by object, 1999 (% analysis)

Percentage of total

	Food	Alcoholic drinks	Non-alcoholic drinks	Tobacco	Clothing	Footwear	Housing	Household fuels	Household goods and services	Health	Transport	Communications	Leisure/ education	Hotels/ restaurants	Others
Austria	12.3	1.5	0.9	1.7	6.0	1.1	16.9	4.1	7.9	6.0	13.3	2.3	8.4	12.0	5.8
Belgium	13.4	2.7	1.2	1.5	5.3	0.6	15.9	3.9	11.4	11.1	11.7	1.1	5.2	6.3	8.7
Denmark	12.2	2.6	1.2	2.3	4.2	1.0	20.4	6.3	6.0	3.0	14.6	1.6	10.7	5.5	8.5
Finland	12.4	3.7	0.8	1.8	3.8	0.7	21.5	4.1	4.6	3.4	13.6	2.6	10.6	7.2	9.1
France	13.7	2.7	0.6	1.5	4.2	1.0	18.9	3.3	6.5	9.8	13.9	1.7	5.9	7.0	9.2
Germany	13.0	1.1	1.4	0.6	3.7	1.0	22.6	6.4	14.2	2.5	13.6	2.0	8.9	5.2	3.8
Greece	19.0	0.4	0.6	2.5	7.8	2.1	8.3	3.5	7.3	7.0	13.1	3.0	7.1	8.9	9.3
Ireland	14.1	2.4	1.2	3.7	5.6	1.0	11.2	3.6	7.3	4.0	12.5	2.0	11.1	11.9	8.4
Italy	14.3	0.8	1.0	1.8	7.4	2.1	16.8	3.4	9.4	3.3	12.8	2.6	7.9	8.7	7.7
Luxembourg	n/a	n/a	n/a	n/a	n/a	n/a	n/a	n/a	n/a	n/a	n/a	n/a	n/a	n/a	n/a
Netherlands	10.7	1.4	0.5	1.4	4.4	0.8	18.5	3.1	7.0	12.5	11.4	2.1	10.1	5.5	10.8
Portugal	23.3	1.9	0.4	1.6	6.5	2.0	8.7	1.9	7.3	5.7	14.8	1.9	8.3	10.3	5.4
Spain	15.6	0.9	0.4	1.6	4.5	2.5	10.7	3.1	6.5	5.5	14.0	1.6	8.2	17.4	7.3
Sweden	12.2	2.4	0.8	1.6	4.3	0.8	26.7	6.0	4.7	2.4	12.9	2.9	9.9	5.0	7.4
UK	10.4	2.3	0.8	2.3	5.3	0.9	15.2	2.8	9.6	1.3	15.1	2.1	11.9	11.5	8.7

Source: Euromonitor (2001, Table 1103, pp. 268–9).

Such spending patterns are not fixed: they will vary not only because of changes in the demographic and economic structure of the household, but also because of sociocultural influences, discussed in the next subsection. A further factor which cuts across both demographic and sociocultural issues is employment patterns, specifically the number of working women in a community and the rate of unemployment. This influences not only household income, but also shopping and consumption patterns.

■ Sociocultural influences

Demographic information only paints a very broad picture of what is happening. If the marketer wants a really three-dimensional feel, then some analysis of sociocultural factors is essential. These factors involve much more qualitative assessment, can be much harder to measure and interpret than the hard facts of demographics and may be subject to unpredictable change, but the effort is worthwhile for a truly marketing oriented organisation.

One thing that does evolve over time is people's lifestyle expectations. Products that at one time were considered upmarket luxuries, such as televisions and fridges, are now considered to be necessities. Turning a luxury into a necessity obviously broadens the potential market, and widens the marketer's scope for creating a variety of products and offerings to suit a spectrum of income levels and usage needs. Televisions, for example, come in a variety of shapes, sizes and prices, from the pocket-sized portable to the cheap, small set that will do for the children's bedroom, to the very large, technically advanced, state-of-the-art status symbol with plasma screen and digital connectivity. This variety has the bonus of encouraging households to own more than one set, further fuelling the volume of the market, particularly as improvements in technology and production processes along with economies of scale further reduce prices.

Broadening tastes and demands are another sociocultural influence, partly fuelled by the marketers themselves, and partly emanating from consumers. Marketers, by constant innovation and through their marketing communications, encourage consumers to become bored with the same old standard, familiar products and thus to demand more convenience, variety and variation.

eg Deli counter sales are falling all across Europe and in the United States. It has been suggested that the younger generation prefers to pay for pre-packed foods as it is more convenient and there is no need for counter queuing. Time is becoming increasingly precious to many consumers and queuing can be a real turn-off. Madrange, the French cooked meat and charcuterie producer, is attempting to address the loss of supermarket sales by introducing 'deli express' which means pre-slicing popular meats and cheeses and wrapping them in deli packaging, branded as 'Ultra fresh' so they can be sold in the 'ready to go' section of the deli counter. It looks like a deli package but has product information, weight and price displayed. It is hoped that the pre-packed option will become attractive to shoppers, combining the deli choice and freshness with the speed and convenience of self-selection. It will also clear some space on the deli counter to offer more exotic premium and regional speciality items which are still popular with shoppers (Hardcastle, 2001).

Fashions and fads are also linked with consumer boredom and a desire for new stimulation. The clothing market in particular has an interest in making consumers sufficiently discontented with the perfectly serviceable clothes already in the wardrobe that they go out to buy new ones every season. For some consumers, it is important for their social integration and their status to be seen to have the latest products and the latest fashions, whether it be in clothing, music or alcoholic drinks. Nevertheless, linking a product with fashion may create marketing problems. Fashions, by definition, are short-lived, and as soon as they become widespread, the fashion leaders are moving on to something new and different. Marketers therefore have to reap rewards while they can, or find a means of shifting the product away from its fashionable associations.

More deeply ingrained in society than the fripperies of fashion are underlying attitudes. These change much more slowly than fashion trends and are much more difficult for the

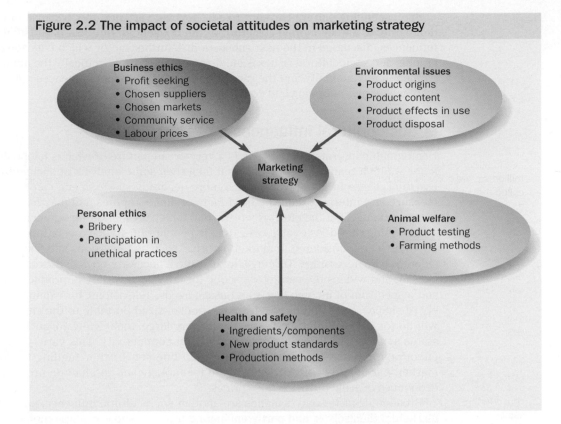

Figure 2.2 The impact of societal attitudes on marketing strategy

marketer to influence. It is more likely, in fact, that the marketer will assess existing or emerging attitudes and then adapt or develop to fit them. As can be seen in Figure 2.2, there are a number of areas in which changes in societal attitudes have influenced marketing approaches. Each is discussed below.

Environmental issues

Environmental issues have been of major concern in recent years, and this area has caused consumers to think more critically about the origins, content and manufacturing processes of the products they buy. Consumers, for example, want products made with the minimum of pollution and are looking for the reassurance, where applicable, that they come from renewable resources. Many paper products now carry notices stating that they are made of wood from managed forests that are replanted after harvesting. In the same spirit, consumers are also demanding that unnecessary packaging is eliminated and that packaging should be recyclable.

corporate social responsibility *in action*

Saving the trees to preserve the woods

Precious Woods Holding Ltd is proud of its record in sustainable logging in tropical regions. The Swiss-owned company was founded in 1994 to show that commercial logging and sustainability could go together. Other loggers have followed, such as Gethal, adopting a planned forest management approach to ensure that rainforest is protected despite commercial interest. Forest management means undertaking proper timber inventories (location, species, measurement), harvesting plans and long harvesting cycles. This is backed up by certification and labelling which clearly communicates to consumers that responsible logging has taken place. The formation of the Forest Stewardship Council (FSC) was regarded even by pressure groups such as Greenpeace as a vital step in making the industry more responsible. Achieving FSC certification means that demanding social, economic and environmental standards have been met. Thus

Precious Woods manages selective logging over a 25-year cycle and always seeks to preserve watercourses and to avoid soil erosion. Part of the deal also includes the principles that 25 per cent of the forest area remain permanently protected and that no pesticides or chemicals should be used.

The Amazon rainforest is one of the last frontiers on earth. Covering 2.3 million square miles, it has been called the earth's lungs as massive amounts of carbon dioxide are absorbed from the atmosphere each year and converted back into oxygen. However, land clearance, often by burning, and indiscriminate logging has meant that 40 per cent of the forest has already been destroyed and the destruction rate is 5,792 square miles of virgin forest destroyed each year. So what has all this to do with marketing and the consumer? It is demand for tropical wood that sets a chain of activities going that can be traced back to the forest. Wood consumption is closely related to per capita income: the higher the income the higher the wood consumption so the more trees get cut.

There are two diametrically opposed views over the future of the rainforest. The FSC scheme founded in 1993 enabled the environmentalists to negotiate with, rather than protest against, the commercial loggers. Certification and well-managed forests gave the loggers a way of continuing operations with far less pressure from the WWF, Greenpeace and Friends of the Earth. Ecological management, community involvement and good employment practice are all part of the guidelines. In the past, tropical timber markets in Europe and the USA were closed by the boycotting

For Precious Woods Amazon principles of sustainable forest management are paramount in the design of its forest management plan. Here an inventory of the trees is carefully made before decisions are made as to which ones to harvest.

Source: Precious Woods Holding Ltd.

campaigns in the 1990s, but the FSC scheme may allow them to reopen and thus stimulate more sustainable forest management in Brazil. The FSC labelling scheme operates worldwide and enables 'ethical buying' to take place, according to the loggers.

The alternative view, expressed by Laschefski and Freris (2001), questions the whole basis of continued logging before the rainforest has recovered from the ravages of the past 30 years. To them, the FSC has given an unwarranted legitimacy to logging under the ecologically sensitive label that allows commercial loggers to continue. At present, 96 per cent of certified forests are owned by either industrial-scale loggers or

governments. However, by shifting the ethical buying responsibility to the consumer, it assumes that the buyer in Germany or the UK is conscious of green products, values the FSC scheme and is prepared to pay a little more rather than buy wood that may have been logged outside FSC guidelines. They argue that the FSC marketing certification legitimises logging when the priority should be preservation and reforestation. Many of these views are strongly contested by Precious Woods.

The issue really comes back to the consumer in developed and developing countries. Pressure will grow in future years for Brazil to export more. The destruction of forests in SE Asia, the emergence of strong timber demand to fuel growth in China, along with the insatiable appetite for quality wood in Europe and North America, will create increasing pressure on the loggers to consume more forests even though it would be on a managed basis. Meanwhile, illegal logging still goes on. Forest clearance also continues both for fuel and land as in Brazil 85 per cent of timber is cut for the domestic market that cares little for certification, given how low per capita income is. The WWF, in alliance with the World Bank, aims to increase the number of hectares of certified forest covered by the FSC worldwide from 25 million to 200 million by 2005. However, will a marketing solution through the FSC really save the 'lungs of the earth' before it is too late? Should it be allowed to legitimise the continued logging of the rainforest? Will you look for the FSC label the next time you buy wood products?

Sources: Laschefski and Freris (2001); http://www.disasterrelief.org; http://preciouswoods.ch

Animal welfare

The issue of animal welfare is linked with environmental concerns, and shows itself in a number of ways. Product testing on animals has become increasingly unacceptable to a large number of vocal consumers, and thus there has been a proliferation of cosmetics and toiletries, for example, which proclaim that they have not been tested on animals. Cosmetics retailer, The Body Shop, has, for example, been at the forefront of positioning itself overtly on this issue, reassuring concerned customers about its own products and publicising the worst excesses of animal testing.

Another area of animal welfare which has captured the public imagination is that of intensive farm production methods. Public outcry against battery egg production, for example, opened new marketing opportunities for free range eggs, since consumers wanted the alternative and were prepared to pay for it. Similarly, outdoor-reared pork and organic beef are starting to appear in supermarkets. Pressure groups are becoming more adept at using advertising and promotional techniques to activate public opinion.

Health concerns

Health consciousness has played a major role in the thinking behind consumer markets. The tobacco market has been particularly hard hit by increased awareness of the risks of smoking, and pressure from health lobbyists and the public has led to increased regulation of that industry. Food products have also been reappraised in the light of health concerns, with more natural ingredients, fewer artificial additives, less salt and less sugar content demanded. Linked with this, the market for low calorie products has also expanded, serving a market that wants to enjoy tasty food in quantity, but lose weight or at least feel that they are eating healthily.

> **eg** Corned beef may improve the fertility of men, so food company Princes claims, after a study revealed that vitamin B3 and zinc, both in corned beef, were linked to fertility. The company hopes to compile a series of case studies to show how it worked in practice and advertisements are scheduled to appear in lifestyle magazines such as *Loaded* and *FHM* highlighting the benefits and showing exciting recipes for corned beef (*The Grocer*, 2000a). You have been warned!

Health concerns also led to a boom in products and services linked with fitness. Health clubs, aerobics classes, exercise videos, sportswear of all kinds and trainers are just some of the things that profited from the fitness boom.

Personal ethics

Apart from concern about the environment, animal welfare and health, all of which might be seen as ethical issues, there has been a subtle shift in people's attitudes to what is acceptable in other areas of their lives. In Western societies, a manageable level of personal debt is now considered normal. Hire purchase agreements, various types of loans and credit cards provide means of achieving a desirable lifestyle now and paying for it later. Previous generations might have been more inclined to take the view that if you want something, you save up for it and buy it outright when you can afford it. Consumers today are also more inclined towards self-indulgence and gratification, without too much guilt, through their consumption. This, it must be said, is openly encouraged by marketers, who want us to believe that we as individuals are special enough to deserve only the best. Indeed, a study by Dittmar and Pepper (1994) showed that adolescents, regardless of their own social background, generally formed better impressions of people who own rather than lack expensive possessions. In other words, materialism seems to play a big part in influencing perceptions and attitudes towards others.

Business ethics

Encouraged by various pressure groups and inquisitive media, consumers now want to see greater levels of corporate responsibility, and more transparency in terms of the openness of companies. Bad publicity about employee relations, environmental records, marketing practices or customer care and welfare now has the potential to move consumers to vote with their pockets and shun an organisation and its products. McDonald's, for example, felt sufficiently concerned about stories circulating about its beef and about its record in the South American rainforests to invest in a considerable marketing communications campaign to re-establish its reputation. The Body Shop again features business ethics strongly in its marketing, emphasising, for example, its 'trade not aid' policy with developing countries and native tribes.

Consumerism and consumer forces

Many of the influences discussed above might never have taken hold and become significant had it not been for the efforts of organised groups. They themselves often use eg Chocolate manufacturers are generally regarded as upholding high standards of corporate citizenship. Companies such as Nestlé, Cadbury and Hershey buy cocoa in large quantities through the international commodity markets, and so have little contact with the thousands of small farms, especially in West Africa, that grow cocoa beans. It came as a shock, therefore, when accusations were made by UNICEF and Channel 4 in the UK that many migrant workers in West Africa, and the Ivory Coast in particular, were working in conditions not far removed from slavery on some of the 1 million cocoa and coffee farms. The confectionery industry immediately commissioned the independent Natural Resources Institute (NRI) to investigate and the subsequent findings found little evidence for the allegations but proposed that the wider socioeconomic dimensions of cocoa production should be examined. Given the sheer number of small independent farms involved, it is difficult to police, but just how can the chocolate manufacturers defend themselves against such accusations? The effect of an emotive issue such as child slavery on corporate image could be disastrous. The manufacturers' focus is thus now shifting to *traceability*, which means that the source of particular cocoa or coffee beans can be pinpointed and immediate action taken if any worker abuse is detected. To some, like Anti Slavery International, it is the only way that the confectionery giants can give 100 per cent guarantees to the consumer that offending farms have not been used by them. Up to this point, there had been little interest in tracing the origin of chocolate, as much responsibility was delegated to intermediaries, but the NRI argues that true corporate social responsibility means taking a fundamental look at the whole supply chain. Ultimately, traceability will add to costs and that can only be at the expense of the consumer or the chocolate manufacturer (Watson, 2001).

marketing techniques as well as generating publicity through the media, quickly raising awareness of issues and providing a focal point for public opinion to form around and helping it to gather momentum.

The UK's Consumers' Association has long campaigned for legislation to protect consumers' rights, such as the right to safe products and the right to full and accurate information about the products we buy. As well as lobbying government and organisations about specific issues, the Consumers' Association also provides independent information to consumers, testing and comparing the features, performance and value for money of competing products in various categories. This information is published in *Which?* magazine. In a similar vein, specialist magazines, in fields such as computing and hi-fi, also undertake comparative testing of products of interest to their readership.

eg Tuna fishing is an activity that has been affected by campaigning leading to the exercise of 'consumer power'. The UK public had been happily buying canned tuna for many years without thinking of anything other than the price, the flavour and the quality of the can's contents. Green pressure groups, with the help of the media, then publicised the fact that the nets that were used to catch tuna also caught dolphins, which could not escape and so died pointlessly. A change in the net design would allow the dolphins to be freed without harm. Public outcry was such that the tuna canners had to take action to preserve sales. The USA-based Earth Island Institute was formed to monitor the harvesting of tuna to ensure that accidental killing of dolphins does not happen. This institute is supported by all the major tuna brands as it provides consumers with the reassurances that they seek, and the registered logo can only be used on cans deriving from approved canners. The canners are in turn monitored to ensure that their supplies are caught only in designated areas and using recommended fishing methods (*The Grocer*, 2001d). The activities of such groups have not only served to change business practices on specific issues, such as tuna fishing, but also accelerated a general cultural change which has awakened the social conscience of organisations (only partly due to the fear of poor publicity and the loss of customers) and has raised the standards of corporate citizenship that consumers expect from business.

High-profile and sometimes militant pressure has been brought to bear on organisations by green groups such as Friends of the Earth and Greenpeace. Although their interest is a wider, altruistic concern with ecology rather than consumer rights, they recognise that corporate practices that are harmful to the environment, wildlife and ecology can be partly discouraged by 'bottom-up' pressure. This means raising awareness, changing attitudes and altering purchasing habits among organisations' core customers.

Consumers have also been encouraged to think about their personal health as well as that of the planet. Sometimes sponsored by government (for example through the UK government's Department of Health) and sometimes through independent groups with a specific interest such as Action on Smoking and Health (ASH) or the British Heart Foundation, the public are urged to change their lifestyles and diets. Once it is generally known and accepted that too much of this, that or the other is unhealthy, food manufacturers are anxious to jump on the bandwagon and provide products to suit the emerging demand.

eg Awareness that full fat milk is high in cholesterol has been responsible for a significant shift towards semi-skimmed milk which retains most of the vitamin and mineral content but cuts down the fat. Sometimes, a health issue does not even need the support of an organised group to capture the public imagination. A flurry of media coverage about research findings which indicated that eating sugar can actually help weight loss had many of us reaching hopefully for the biscuit tin, purely on medical grounds, of course.

Pressure groups and consumer bodies are not just there to criticise organisations, of course. They also encourage and endorse good practice, and such an endorsement can be very valuable to the organisation that earns it. A consumer who is inexperienced in buying a particular type of product, or for whom that purchase represents a substantial investment, may well look for independent expert advice, and thus the manufacturer whose product is cited as *Which?* magazine's best buy in that category has a head start over the competition. Organisations may also commission product tests from independent bodies such as the Consumers' Association or the Good Housekeeping Institute as a means of verifying their product claims and adding the bonus of 'independent expert opinion' to their marketing.

marketing *in action*

More legroom please!

Those of you who have travelled economy class on a long-haul flight will know exactly what it feels like to be cramped into a seat that restricts leg movement, to be unable to eat without your elbow nudging the passenger next to you, and to find that just when you decide to stretch your legs in the cabin, the 'fasten seat belts' sign lights up with a merry little ding! In pursuit of keeping fares down and revenues up, the airlines have long been criticised for cramming as many seats into economy class as possible, which is only comfortable for those passengers of lower than average height and weight. That might now have to change because of DVT (deep vein thrombosis). A thrombosis or blood clot can form in the deep veins of the legs when the body is immobilised for long periods. The symptoms, cramp, shortness of breath

and stiffness, could be an early indication of trouble. If the clot breaks free and reaches the lungs it can be fatal. Research from the Nippon Medical School in Japan indicated that 100–125 people were treated for DVT after long-haul flights at Tokyo's Narita airport between 1992 and 2000, of whom 25 died.

Scientific research is, in fact, divided over the link between DVT and long-haul airline travel. A Dutch study of 800 passengers found no link with DVT, whereas a Norwegian study suggested that 1 in 10 suffer. A study conducted at Honolulu International Airport over 6 years found only 44 cases of DVT of which only 7 were not associated with prior risk factors. More extensive research is now under way in Australia into 10,000 medical records as, given Australia's geographical remoteness, Australian travellers have

a keener interest than most in the health aspects of long-haul flying. An investigation in the UK conducted by the House of Lords Select Committee on Science and Technology: Air Travel and Health, however, was more definitive and called for major changes in the regulations relating to the health of passengers, including a call for the airlines to take responsibility for providing adequate information to warn passengers of the risks from DVT.

The airlines are in a difficult position. Accept responsibility and a flood of expensive legal claims would follow. The first test case has already been filed in Australia after a passenger died following an Australia to London flight. Central to the case will be whether adequate information and warning were given to passengers before the flight. The lawyer claims that the airlines were aware of the problem 5 years previously but failed to take action to inform the public. It is further claimed that there are 100 people who have lost relatives or who have themselves suffered from DVT. Virgin, American Airlines and Qantas have all received notice of possible legal action. In addition to legal claims, there would be pressure to redesign cabins to provide more legroom and thus carry fewer passengers at a time when the numbers flying are growing. However, not to accept responsibility and to deny any link could be regarded by some as socially irresponsible, and if a link is proven scientifically, the longer-term legal claims and public condemnation would be very damaging.

There are steps that airlines can take to reduce risks, even though they do not accept that DVT is any greater a problem in air travel than in any other form of transportation. At the very least, passengers can be informed of the need to exercise, drink plenty of water and avoid alcohol on long-haul flights. Already some are giving such advice either in seat pockets or with ticketing, although it is not always easy to undertake exercises on a crowded jet. Singapore Airlines is calling for a more standardised approach by the airlines, rather than each doing their own thing, and for groups of airlines jointly to commission more research (Fiorino, 2001). Emirates has gone further by being first to provide an exercise device, the Airogym, for passengers which allows exercises in a seated position. The product claims are that it increases blood flow through veins by 50 per cent through the use of an inflatable footpad for pumping leg muscles.

Legislation may eventually follow if the link is established. Airlines still claim that the risks are very small for healthy people and, according to some, are in a state of denial. However, if there is stricter control on legroom and seat dimensions, compulsory health warnings and records kept for three months to enable 'traceback' in the event of problems, DVT scares could become a thing of the past. The Federal Air Surgeon's Medical Bulletin in the USA, although stopping short of specifying a direct link is clear about what is now needed:

It is only a matter of time before the aviation medical community and the air carriers themselves will be called upon to significantly increase their activity in dealing directly with medical issues associated with air travel and to direct educational efforts on the flying public (as quoted by Jordan, 2001).

Unfortunately, one way or the other it is the passenger who will end up paying.

Sources: *Asian Business* (2001); Durham (2001); Ecklof *et al.* (1996); Fiorino (2001); Jordan (2001); Kite and Bird (2000); *The Times* (2000); Webster (2001).

The technological environment

In an increasingly dynamic world, where the creation, launch and maintenance of a new product are more expensive and difficult than ever, no organisation can afford to ignore the technological environment and its trends. The costs and the risks involved can be very high, since there is no guarantee that an R&D project will be successful in delivering a solution that can be commercially implemented. Nevertheless, many organisations feel the need to invest in R&D, recognising that they will get left behind if they do not, and are optimistic that they will come up with something with an unbeatable differential advantage that will make it all worthwhile. Even if your organisation does not have the inclination or resources to adopt or adapt new technology, understanding it is important because competitors will exploit it sooner or later, with implications for your product and its marketing.

eg IBM takes R&D very seriously in its desire to be at the head of the innovation curve and to remain competitive. It has learned that lesson the hard way, though. Originally, the world ran on IBM mainframes and databases but the trend towards smaller networked computers meant that competitors took market share away from IBM. In the 1990s IBM sought to regain a dominant position in a fast-moving technologically based industry. The search for technological leadership means developing an understanding of how the market is moving and spotting the areas that are likely to offer opportunities. Although there are many R&D projects running within IBM and the total spend is something like $4,345m. (IBM, 2001a), there are three priority strategic research areas (IBM, 2001b):

■ *E-business and online technologies*: this research is examining the human resource and systems implications of the information economy that is developing as a result of the growth of the Internet. Such an economy is thought to be based on agents buying, analysing and selling information about the vast number of transactions that will be conducted over the web.

■ *Pervasive computing*: with the growth of home-based systems, the research examines the next major wave of product opportunities that will provide interconnected smart devices called 'portable personality'. This will mean that individuals will have the power of a PC in hand-held, credit-card sized devices or in other mobile spaces from watches to cars.

■ *Deep computing*: this area is targeting research into marrying computers with human intelligence. By using specialised software, advanced maths and hardware complex problems can be solved to far higher degrees of realism than is now possible.

To get the best out of the commercial exploitation of technology, R&D and marketers have to work closely together. R&D can provide the technical know-how, problem-solving skills and creativity, while the marketer can help guide and refine that process through research or knowledge of what the market needs and wants, or through finding ways of creating a market position for a completely innovative product. A lot of this comes back to the question 'What business are we in?' Any organisations holding the attitude that they exist to solve customers' problems and that they have to strive constantly to find better solutions through higher-quality, lower-cost or more user-friendly product packages will be active participants in, and observers of, the technological environment. A striking example of this is the Italian firm Olivetti, which began by making manual typewriters, then moved into computers as it saw the likely takeover of the word processor as a means of producing business documentation.

The technological environment is a fast-changing one, with far-reaching effects on organisations and their products. Technological advances can affect many aspects of business and some of these areas will now be looked at briefly, to give just a flavour of the immense impact that technology has had on marketing practice.

■ Materials, components and products

Consumers tend to take products, and the materials and components that go into them, for granted as long as they work and live up to the marketers' promises. Technology does, however, improve and increase the benefits that consumers derive from products, and raise expectations about what a product should be. Some technological applications are invisible to the consumer, affecting raw materials and components hidden within an existing product, for example car engines which produce less harmful emissions, while others create completely new products, for example DVD players that offer 'record' as well as 'playback' functions.

One innovation that has revolutionised many product markets is the microchip. Not only are microchips the heart and soul of our home computers, but they also program our washing machines, DVD players and video recorders, among many things. The incorporation of microchips into products has increased their reliability, their efficiency in operation and the range of sophisticated functions that they can perform, all very cost-effectively. This in turn has raised consumers' expectations of what products can do, and revised their attitudes towards cost, quality and value for money.

Technology is not just about the physical product itself. It can also affect its packaging. Lightweight plastics and glass, recycled and recyclable materials and cans that incorporate a device to give canned beer the character and quality of draught are examples of packaging innovations that have helped to make products more appealing, enhance their image or keep their cost down.

■ Production processes

The fulfilment of marketing promises can be helped or hindered by what happens in the production process. More efficient production can, for instance, increase the volume of product available, thus potentially meeting a bigger demand, or it can reduce the cost of the product, thus giving more scope to the pricing decision. Production can also contribute to better and more consistent product quality, again increasing customer satisfaction. Here are some examples where technology has influenced production processes and indirectly affected marketing activities.

Computer-aided design (CAD) and computer-aided manufacturing (CAM) systems have revolutionised product design/formulation, testing and production. In terms of design, technology allows ideas to be visualised, tested and accepted/rejected much more quickly than if paper plans and calculations had to be updated. Similarly, computer-controlled production systems can undertake tasks faster than human operatives, with more consistency and fewer errors. When this is all integrated with sophisticated quality assurance and control techniques, the outcome for the customer is that products get to the market more quickly, and in a more refined state, and may be cheaper and more reliable.

Materials handling and waste minimisation are also of concern for efficient, cost-effective production management. Stocks of materials need to be closely monitored; in a large operation, the location of materials needs to be planned so that they can be accessed quickly and spend the minimum amount of time being transported around the site; the packaging and bundling of materials need to be planned to balance out the sometimes conflicting concerns of adequately protecting and identifying the goods, and making sure that they can be unwrapped and put into the production line quickly. Computerised planning models and advances in packaging technology can both help to increase efficiency in these areas.

■ Administration and distribution

There is little point in using technology to streamline the production of goods if the support systems are inefficient or if distribution causes a bottleneck between factory and customer. Distribution has benefited from technology, as has materials handling, through systems for locating and tracking goods in and out. Integrated ordering and dispatch functions mean theoretically that as soon as an order is entered into the computer, goods availability can be checked and the warehouse can get on with the job of fulfilling it, while the computer handles all the paperwork, printing off packing slips and invoices, for example, and updating customer records. All of this speeds up the sending of orders to customers and reduces labour involvement, costs and risks of errors.

Telecommunications linking into computer systems can extend the administration efficiencies even further. Large retail chains, for example, can be linked with their major suppliers, so that as the retailer's stocks reduce, an order can be sent from computer to computer. Similarly, large organisations with sites and depots spread over a wide geographic area can use such technology to link sites, managing and tracking the flow of goods.

■ Marketing and customers

Much of the technology discussed above has implied benefits for the customer, in producing the right product at the right time in the right place at the right price, but technology also plays a part in the marketing processes that form the interface between buyer and seller. Increased and cheaper computer power, which means that large, complex sets of data can be input and analysed quickly and easily, has benefited both market research data collection and analysis, and relationship marketing initiatives, establishing and maintaining a one-to-one dialogue between buyer and seller. Organisations such as Heinz see this as an exciting development in consumer marketing, and it is only possible because of database technology that permits the storage, retrieval and maintenance of detailed profiles of many thousands, or even hundreds of thousands, of customers. The technology also allows the creation of tailored, personalised marketing offers to be made to subsets of those customers as appropriate.

Advertising media too have improved and proliferated through technology. The Internet, interactive television and text messaging have become alternative media for many organisations. These media not only allow them to disseminate information about their products, services, news and corporate philosophy, but also to set up interactive dialogue with customers and potential customers. A website can be an exciting communications medium as it can feature sound and video clips and, if the site is well structured, visitors can select the topics that interest them. Also, the information can be updated easily and regularly. In addition, both the Internet and interactive digital television allow potential customers to browse through product information, check availability and place an order, all in the comfort of their own armchairs.

Another area that can also be enhanced through computer technology is sales force support. Supplying a sales representative with a laptop computer can give access to current information about products, their availability and prices; it can store customer profiles and relevant information; the representative can update records and write reports while the information is still fresh in the mind; and it can store appropriate graphics to enhance a sales presentation. All of this is easily portable and accessible whether the representative is working in Scotland or Greece.

The economic and competitive environment

The effects of the economic and competitive environment are felt by organisations and consumers alike, and it has a profound effect on their behaviour. In the next few pages we look first at the macroeconomic environment, which provides the overall backdrop against which marketing activities take place. As well as issues of national interest, such as the effects of government economic policy on commerce, we cover the influence of international trading blocs and trade agreements. All of these things may provide opportunities or threats for an individual organisation. We then turn to the microeconomic environment. This is rather closer to home for the organisation, looking at the extent to which different market structures constrain or widen the organisation's freedom of action in its marketing activities and its ability to influence the nature of the market.

■ The macroeconomic environment

Figure 2.3 shows the basic economic concept of the circular flow of goods and income that makes a market economy go round. Marketing, as an exchange process and indeed as a force that actively encourages more exchanges, is an essential fuel to keep that flow going. The world is not, however, a closed, self-sustaining loop such as that depicted in Figure 2.3. Its operation is severely affected by the macroeconomic influences generated by government economic policy and by membership of international trading blocs and trade agreements.

Figure 2.3 Macroeconomic influences on the circular flow of goods and income

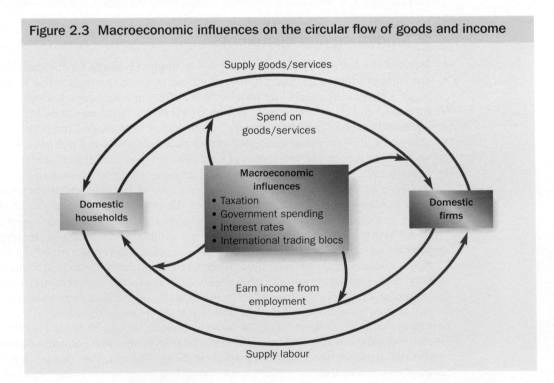

Governments can develop and implement policies in relation to several macroeconomic influences, which in turn affect markets, organisations and customers. Just a few of these are discussed below.

Taxation and government spending

Taxes may be direct or indirect. Direct taxation, such as income tax and national insurance contributions, reduces the amount of money, or disposable income, that a household has available to spend on the goods and services that organisations provide. Indirect taxation, such as purchase tax or value added tax (VAT), is collected for the government by the seller, who is obliged to add a percentage to the basic price of the product. Thus a PC sold in the UK may be advertised with two prices: a basic price of £999, then £1,174 including VAT.

Some products, such as alcohol, tobacco and petrol, have duty imposed on them, again collected by the seller. Both VAT and duties serve to increase the prices of products for the customer, and marketers need to think about the effect of the tax-inclusive price on the customer's attitude and buying habits. When rates of duty increase, marketers sometimes choose to absorb some of the increase themselves to keep prices competitive, rather than pass on the entire rise to the buyer.

Rates of VAT and duties vary across Europe and despite 30 years of trying, there is still no significant progress in persuading member states to move to a common VAT system based upon harmonised rates and structures (*Business Europe*, 2000). The problems faced by brewers because of the higher excise duties on alcohol and tobacco imposed in the UK compared with France has caused a significant amount of smuggling and reselling. Customs and Excise estimate that 20 per cent of the UK's £84bn annual tobacco turnover is made up of illegal imports, costing the Treasury £3.8bn in lost duty. Similarly, the Brewers and Licensed Retailers' Association estimates that a staggering 79 per cent of all beer brought into the UK every day is resold illegally (Thornton, 2001). It is one thing to put a crate of wine in the car boot, but quite another to load up a van with alcohol for resale with no declaration and no paperwork. The brewers want UK duty reduced so that it is in line with French rates, thus making the 'unofficial' market unprofitable.

A further challenge has come from the increased use of e-commerce, as this tends to bypass traditional VAT collection methods for international sales. For example, the UK has vetoed legislation that would have made non-EU competitors e-tailing digitalised products such as music, games and software downloaded from the net to EU consumers, liable for VAT. This would have levelled the playing field with EU marketers who are having to apply VAT. This veto was in line with the US policy of a moratorium on taxation on any goods sold over the net (*International Tax Review*, 2001).

Using the money they 'earn' from taxes, governments, like any other organisations, are purchasers of goods and services, but on a grand scale. They invest in defence industries, road building and other civil engineering projects, social and health services and many other areas. Such large purchasing power can be used to stimulate or depress economic development, but if a government decides as a matter of policy to cut back on its spending, industry can be very badly hit. Defence, for example, is an area which many governments are reviewing in the aftermath of the ending of the 'cold war'.

eg The shipbuilding industry in the UK barely survives and is a shadow of its former glory in days of Empire. When the Ministry of Defence decided to award the £130m. contract for the refit of *HMS Illustrious* to Babcock Rosyth Defence in Fife, it was not only guaranteeing nearly 1,000 jobs for a further 18 months, but also enabling suppliers to benefit from the subcontract work generated. This order, along with a £75m. contract to refit 23 Royal Navy frigates, has helped to sustain the yard for the foreseeable future (*Professional Engineering*, 2001).

The cost of money

Government economic policy affects interest rates, which have an impact on both consumers and business. For many consumers, the most serious effect of a rise in interest rates is on their monthly mortgage repayments. Paying £20 or more per month extra to the mortgage lender means that there is that much less cash available for buying other things, and across the country retail sales can be significantly reduced. Interest rate rises can also affect the attractiveness of credit to the consumer, either when buying large expensive items through instalments, or when using credit cards. A consumer thinking about buying a brand new car, for example, may need a loan, and will look at the repayment levels, determined by interest rates, when deciding how expensive a model can be afforded. To try to reduce this potential barrier to purchasing, many car dealers have entered into arrangements with credit companies to offer 0 per cent financing deals to car buyers.

A country's exchange rate is rather like the price of a share for a company; it is a sign of confidence in the continued prosperity, or otherwise, of an individual nation. Fluctuating exchange rates between different currencies can have a major impact on the prosperity of companies and individual consumers. If a currency is strong, imports become cheaper which is good news for businesses and consumers, but exports become more expensive which is bad news for manufacturers. The strength of sterling in the period after the launch of the euro was blamed by some for precipitating a manufacturing recession in the UK as prices in the prime continental markets become less competitive.

eg It is best to book early any planned flight to South Africa from Europe. A shortfall of 4,500 seats a week has been estimated during the peak summer period, largely due to carriers such as Austrian Airlines, Alitalia and Sabena stopping services. In 1997, there were 74 airlines flying to South Africa but by 2001 there were just 52. The reason was the slump in the value of the rand against the US dollar so that a ticket from South Africa to Europe would have become unaffordable to many South Africans, unless the airlines were prepared to absorb some of the currency loss. At a time when the euro has also been weak against the dollar, with a 20 per cent reduction in value, fuel and airport charges transacted in dollars have become even more expensive, so some airlines have given up on the routes. Others have allocated a share of seats for local customers paying in rand, thus making the shortage worse. Demand is being kept artificially high because of the failure to pass on the full costs to the customer. However, the loss to some airlines has meant opportunities for others. BA, KLM, Iberia and Olympic are taking up some of the slots that have become vacant and trust that they can fly through the currency turbulence (Innocenti, 2001).

International trading blocs

Governments also negotiate membership of international trading blocs, and the scope, terms and conditions of international trade agreements. Membership of the EU, for example, and particularly the advent of the single European market (SEM), has had a profound effect on the wider commercial dealings of organisations operating within the EU, as well as on the economic and competitive environment. Organisations which exist in countries outside the EU have found it increasingly difficult to sell into the EU, since there are now many more EU-based potential suppliers for purchasers to turn to, and also the logistics of purchasing within the EU are easier.

eg The EU provides duty-free access to its markets for 48 of the world's poorest and least developed economies. The import of cut flowers from Africa considered in Chapter 1 is part of this arrangement. However, extending the scheme to what are perceived as more sensitive products is causing some concern for the competitiveness of both home producers and their existing suppliers. Particular concern has been expressed over sugar, bananas and rice, for example. France and some of the southern European EU member states are especially concerned about the impact of imports on home produced sugar and rice. It will not be until 2009 that full liberalisation of trade will have occurred on sugar and rice and there is to be a review in 2005 to ensure that non-treaty state produce is not finding its way into the EU market via the poorer nations. Even then, tariff-free quotas will be set based upon normal production to ensure fair play. Currently tariff barriers on this produce keeps prices high and supplies limited. These will be progressively dismantled in the period up to 2009 (*The Grocer*, 2000c, 2001b, c).

The EU is not, however, the only major European international trading bloc. The European Free Trade Association (EFTA) was formed originally in 1959 by Austria, Denmark, Norway, Sweden, Switzerland and the UK, and was later expanded to include Finland, Iceland and Liechtenstein. Its philosophy was simply to make trade between the member states easier. Since several EFTA members subsequently became members of the EU, and as the prospect of the SEM raised the perceived barriers to entry to EU markets for non-EU organisations, the remaining EFTA countries (except Switzerland) became involved in the idea of the European Economic Area (EEA), formalised by treaty in 1993. Although not full members of the EU, EEA countries now share some of the benefits of the SEM, and certainly face fewer barriers to trade within the EU than they would otherwise have encountered. Participation in the EEA acted as a stepping stone for Austria and Sweden, who subsequently became full EU members. Similar cooperation and association agreements were made with the former communist states of Central and Eastern Europe, with the aim of helping to stimulate their economics as they prepared themselves for accession to the EU.

Beyond the confines of formalised trading blocs, business is often affected by the existence of trade agreements. Some of these are protectionist, in that they are trying to cushion domestic producers from the effects of an influx of imports, while others are trying to liberalise trade between nations. For many years, for example, the UK's textile industry benefited from the multi fibre arrangement (MFA), which protected jobs and businesses by basically restricting the imports of low-priced clothing from various Far Eastern countries. Similarly, Japan agreed to implement voluntary export restraint (VER) with regard to its car industry's sales to Western Europe and the USA. This helped to protect domestic car producers and jobs by imposing quotas on Japanese imports. One way of overcoming the restrictions of this VER was international direct investment, i.e. setting up factories within the EU (taking full advantage, by the way, of various EU investment incentives) to produce cars with sufficient local content to be labelled 'European'. Thus those people owning either a Nissan (built in Washington, Tyne and Wear), a Honda (built in Swindon) or a Toyota (built in Derby), for example, are technically driving a British car. From their British manufacturing bases, the companies can legitimately export, without quota constraints, to the rest of the EU under the terms of the SEM.

eg Earlier, the issue of EU trade agreements was mentioned. Bananas are not grown in Europe, but there is still a quota tariff system in place, largely to serve the interests of the traditional suppliers from the Caribbean where there are many ex-colonial ties and perceived responsibilities. Any system that opens up Europe to allcomers would have a major effect on the banana industry in many Caribbean countries and could result in severe social and economic problems. However, protection for the Caribbean means restrictions for other producers. Chiquita Brands, a US company, is struggling because of the restrictions on the quantity of bananas it can supply the EU. Since 1993, when import controls were introduced, the company's share of EU markets has declined from 40 to 20 per cent. Such controls have been criticised by the WTO for unfairly protecting the EU's own producers and importers and indirectly inflating the price we pay for bananas (*The Grocer*, 2001a, b).

The protectionist stance of agreements like the MFA is, however, being overshadowed by wider moves towards trade liberalisation, through the General Agreement on Tariffs and Trade (GATT), for example. The broad aim of GATT is to get rid of export subsidies and import tariffs (effectively taxes on imports that push their prices up to make them less competitive compared with the domestically produced equivalent product) to make international trade a great deal fairer. This means that negotiated VERs, which do not depend on tariffs to control imports, are becoming an increasingly important tool.

■ The microeconomic environment

The general discussion in Chapter 1 of what marketing is, and its main tools, did not pay particular attention to the structure of markets. It is nevertheless important to think about market structures, because these will influence what sort of competition the organisation is up against, what scope the organisation has to manipulate the 4Ps and how broad an impact the organisation's marketing activities could have on the market as a whole.

Market structures can be defined in four broad categories, based on the number and size of competitors in the market.

Monopoly

Technically, a monopoly exists where one supplier has sole control over a market, and there is no competition. The lack of competition may be because the monopolist is state owned and/or has a statutory right to be the sole supplier to the market. Traditionally in the EU, this applied to public utilities, such as gas, water, electricity, telephone and postal services, and some key industries such as the railways, steel and coal. Government policy in member states over the past 20 years, however, was to privatise and open up some of these industries to competition, with the idea that if they were exposed to market forces and were answerable to shareholders, they would operate more efficiently and cost-effectively. Manufacturing, banking, transportation, energy and public utilities have all been privatised in a significant number of countries. More recently, the telecommunications industry has the been the focus of attention. Privatisation in telecoms reflects the changing competitive structure facing the industry that organisations must operate within. With the internationalisation of telecoms, global competitiveness has increased while the pace of technological development requires significant investment to keep up to date.

eg The EU has also taken an interest in some state-owned monopolies. In Sweden, as in other Scandinavian countries, there is a state monopoly for retailing alcohol. The EU rejected the Swedish government's claim that it was better able to control retail sales and thus restrict the potential for Swedes to consume too much liquor. The EU considered that Systembolaget's state monopoly to sell wine, spirits and strong beer was a disproportionate measure for preventing alcohol abuse, and that the protected arrangement contravened the EU ruling on the free flow of goods. The grocery trade, for example, was not able to sell in competition with Systembolaget. In addition, Sweden, as part of its EU accession in 1995, negotiated a special five-year arrangement that restricted the amount of alcohol that could be brought into the country by returning Swedish travellers. The EU is reluctant to renew the agreement. Part of the argument is that the government wants to protect its people from the worst excesses of alcohol by restricting purchases and keeping prices high. There have also been complaints of long queues, poor service and restricted opening times in the state-owned retail alcohol outlets, which further frustrates the consumer. Over 61 per cent of Swedes want the import ban lifted. By comparison, the Germans drink more alcohol per year with no restrictions but the Swedish government wants to hold out as long as possible with over 5 per cent of its tax revenues coming from the monopoly retail chain (*The Economist*, 2000).

In practice, although the privatised companies have restructured themselves internally and revised their business philosophies to suit their new status, they still face limited competition as yet. This is mainly because of the barriers to entry faced by potential competitors, such as the massive capital investment required, or the monopolist's domination of essential resources or infrastructure.

The implication of all this is that a true monopoly is hard to find in a modern market economy, although several near-monopolies are operating. In the UK, a monopoly is deemed to exist where an organisation or a group of collaborating organisations control 25 per cent of a market. Where this occurs, or where a proposed or threatened takeover raises the possibility of its happening, the Competition Commission may undertake an inquiry to establish whether the situation is operating in the public interest and whether there is any unfair competition involved.

This discussion so far has been rather parochial in that it has concentrated on national or regional monopolies. In global markets, however, it is even more difficult, if not impossible, to establish and sustain a monopoly.

As a final thought, the concept of monopoly depends on how 'market' is defined. While it is true that currently SNCF, for example, holds a monopoly on passenger rail travel in

France, it does not have a monopoly on moving people from Paris to Lyon. To travellers, rail is only one option, and they might also consider travelling to their destinations by air, by coach or by car. In that sense, the traveller's perception of rail, in terms of its cost, reliability and convenience, is developed in a very competitive context.

Oligopoly

Well-developed market economies are far more likely to see the emergence of oligopolies than monopolies. In an oligopoly, a small number of firms account for a very large share of the market, and a number of the privatised ex-monopolies discussed above are moving into this category. The oligopoly creates a certain amount of interdependence between the key players, each of which is large enough for its actions to have a big impact on the market and on the behaviour of its competitors. This certainly occurs in large-scale, worldwide industrial markets, such as chemicals, oil and pharmaceuticals, because the amount of capital investment required, the levels of production needed to achieve economies of scale and the geographic dispersion of large customers demanding large quantities make this the most efficient way for these markets to be structured.

Other consumer oligopolies are less visible to the casual observer. In the supermarket, the shopper may see a wide variety of brands of clothes-washing detergents, and thus imagine that there is healthy, widespread competition in that sector. Most brands are, however, owned and managed by either Procter & Gamble (P&G) (Ariel, Daz, Bold, etc.) or Unilever (Persil, Radion, Surf, etc.), and the proliferation of brands is more to do with fragmented demand and the creation of discrete segments (see Chapter 4) than the fragmentation of supply. Again, the supermarkets are the biggest threat to this oligopoly, with their own-brands, such as retailer Sainsbury's own brand Novon.

eg Petrol retailing in the UK has largely been concentrated in the hands of a few companies, such as Shell, BP and Esso. This has periodically given rise to accusations of collusion, specifically in terms of 'price fixing', which would not be allowed in either UK or EU law. In reality, the organisations within the oligopoly watch each other keenly for signals, and when one makes a price move, the others tend to follow very quickly, because this is a price-sensitive market. It may appear to be orchestrated, but the important thing to emphasise is that each organisation makes its decision independently, on the basis of its analysis of what it sees happening in the market. The petrol oligopoly in the UK became somewhat wider after the entry of the supermarket chains into this market. Between 1996 and 1998, 2,600 petrol stations had closed and the supermarket's market share was thought to have reached over 20 per cent by 2000 in volume terms (Patten, 2000). Although the oil companies are fighting back with loyalty schemes and price promotions to match the supermarkets, the damage has been done now that market share has been surrendered.

In marketing terms, it is nevertheless still very difficult for a new brand from a new competitor to enter an oligopolistic market, other than in a small niche. This is because the oligopolists have spent many years and vast amounts of marketing money establishing their brands and shares. The threat from a supermarket's own-brand is more serious, however, because of the retailer's inherent control over a major channel of distribution which none of the other oligopolists can afford to lose. All of this really leaves only very small gaps in the market for the smaller competitor, such as that filled by products such as Ark and Ecover, two detergent brands that positioned themselves as more environmentally friendly than anything else available, appealing to the 'dark green' consumer.

Oligopolists therefore spend their time watching each other, and developing their marketing strategies and tactics on the basis of what the other main players are doing or are likely to do. If, for example, Unilever launches a new brand, or implements a major new marketing communications strategy, P&G would prefer to anticipate it, thus either pre-empting Unilever or at least having a calculated response ready when needed. From P&G's point of view this is essential, even if it is only to maintain the delicate status quo of the two companies' relative market shares.

Monopolistic and perfect competition

Good marketing practice and the emphasis on differential advantage have created a market structure that might seem a little paradoxical at first sight: monopolistic competition. The idea is that although there are many competitors in the market (with the emphasis on smaller competitors without enough individual influence to create either an oligopoly or a monopoly, as discussed above), each has a product sufficiently differentiated from the rest to create its own monopoly, because to the customer it is unique, or at least any potential substitutes are considered to be inferior. The concept forms the basis of much of the rest of this book.

Perfect competition is at the opposite end of the spectrum from monopoly, and is about as likely to be found in practice. It involves many small producers, all supplying identical products that can be directly substituted for each other. No producer has the power to influence or determine price, and the market consists of many small buyers, who similarly cannot influence the market individually. There are no barriers to market entry or exit, and all buyers and sellers have complete information about what is happening in the market. All of this is clearly unrealistic. The influence of marketing concepts on even the smallest organisations, along with the development of powerful buyers and sellers in all kinds of markets, consumer and B2B, mean that these conditions cannot hold, and some kind of monopolistic competition or oligopoly soon emerges.

> **eg** Farm produce, such as vegetables, is often cited as an example of near perfect competition. While it is true that the market does consist of many small suppliers, i.e. individual farms, the nature of the buyer is more complex, ranging from a family buying a few kilos of carrots from a farm shop, to the fruit and vegetable wholesalers and supermarket chains that buy such quantities that they can influence price and other supply variables. Even the product itself can be differentiated, for example organic and non-organic, or class I and class II quality. The farmer can also differentiate the offering through grading and packaging the produce to suit the retail customer. Even carrots, therefore, can be seen to be moving towards monopolistic competition.

The political and regulatory environment

Organisations have to exist in and operate according to the laws of the societies within which they do business, and thus in addition to the more general laws of contract and commerce, products have to conform to safety laws; manufacturing processes are subject to pollution controls; copyright and patents protect innovation; and retailers' opening hours are restricted in Germany, for example, by the *Ladenschlussgesetz*, and in the UK by the Sunday trading laws. We look below at the role and influence of national governments and the European Parliament in making rules that have a direct effect on the marketing mix.

Regulation is not only defined through legislation from national governments or the European Parliament, however. Organisations are also subject to rules passed by regulatory bodies, some of which have statutory powers delegated to them from government, while others are voluntary groupings, such as trade associations, with codes of practice to which the organisation chooses to adhere. We examine the nature and influence of such bodies on pp. 58 *et seq*. Inevitably, governments and other regulatory bodies are influenced in their policy making by other sources, such as lobbyists and pressure groups, and on p. 61 we take a wider view of the influences that drive the legislators and rule makers towards their policies.

■ National and local government

The obvious responsibility of national governments is to determine and maintain the legislative framework within which organisations do business. This will cover areas such as contract law, consumer protection, financial legislation, competition and trading practices, for example. There are variations in approaches across Europe but increasingly, as

European integration proceeds and the internal market is fully liberalised, national governments are working within EU guidelines and directives, with the longer-term aim of achieving consistency across member states.

Within the UK, although Parliament passes legislation and puts it on the statute books, the responsibility for implementing and enforcing it is often delegated to specialist bodies, such as the Office of Fair Trading (OFT), the Competition Commission, or the Independent Television Commission (ITC). The role of such bodies is discussed further on pp. 58 *et seq*.

As well as the legislation they pass that affects the day-to-day business practices of organisations, governments can also have profound effects on the competitive environment. The widespread privatisation of publicly owned utilities and other state-controlled national industries in the 1980s and 1990s, as has already been discussed, presented opportunities for new competitors to enter these markets, as well as profoundly changing the culture and business orientation of the newly privatised companies themselves.

marketing *in action*

Putting a CAP on it: the EU Common Agricultural Policy

Over 46 per cent of the EU's budget goes on subsidising agriculture. The Common Agricultural Policy (CAP) is a system designed to protect farmers in the various member states through guaranteed prices, quotas and subsidies. By protecting farming, rural jobs are protected and rural development made more feasible. However, there is a price: the OECD notes that in 1999 the EU was paying out an average subsidy of $17,000 to every full-time farmer in the EU, compared with an average of $11,000 in countries belonging to the OECD. Such a level of support does not come free, as in order to protect the farmers the average family in the EU pays around $1,200 a year more for food than if they were paying market-based world food prices (*The Economist*, 2001a). In addition, food processors seeking to export are placed at a competitive disadvantage due to higher raw material prices.

As might be expected, the CAP system is increasingly coming under strain. Although progress has been made in cutting subsidies, there is still a long way to go. Ironically, the BSE crisis could be a further cause of more rapid change. The cost of 'emergency measures' to deal with it, through the purchase and slaughter of cattle, has so far been almost €1bn ($918m.), out of a total farm budget of €42.8bn for 2001. If the budget ceiling is fixed, any long-term pressure on beef farmers from foot and mouth disease or BSE could mean reducing subsidies

elsewhere. Declining beef sales, as consumers decide to switch to other meats, would only make matters worse because if prices fall, the EU is required to buy beef at up to 60 per cent of the previous EU support price. Environmental issues are also coming to the fore as some politicians believe that subsidies should be used to encourage green rather than wasteful farming. Farmers would have to meet social and ecological criteria before handouts were given.

The 2.2 million olive producers in Europe are typical beneficiaries of the CAP system in practice. The subsidy is based upon production, so the more you produce the more subsidy you receive. The consequences are predictable. In Spain, olive production is booming and even after a belated attempt to restrict the planting of new trees, 2.5 per cent of the entire EU budget now goes on supporting olive growers. With the subsidy based on delivery to the olive mills rather than on the number of trees, the number of olive trees in Spain is expected to increase from 300 to 340 million and there are another 500 million trees around the rest of Europe. Europe is now well on the way to an olive oil lake, as there are only so many olives the EU consumer can eat at one sitting and only so much olive oil that can be used for cooking. Producing more to feed a lake of unwanted oil highlights the worst excesses of CAP and for that reason politicians are coming under increased pressure to

undertake significant reform. At least cereal and beef subsidies are unrelated to production or are designed to encourage non-production (*The Economist*, 2001b).

Even in the case of olives, there are environmental issues associated with the subsidy method adopted. Intensive production has led to soil erosion, forest clearance and water shortages. Thus under the environmental protection programme run by the EU, efforts are being funded to combat the impact of intensive farming on the marshland in the Doñana national park in Andalusia. Only the politicians can end the waste. A recent report from the World Wide Fund for Nature suggests linking subsidies to the amount of land under production rather than the amount produced, to take the emphasis away from intensive farming. However, the olive oil farmers from Spain, Greece, Italy and Portugal are a very effective lobbying group in Brussels and with $2bn a year in handouts there is a strong incentive to retain the status quo. It has been estimated that Spanish olive growers receive half their income from Brussels. With the three-year extension to the current EU's CAP regime, the lake will continue to get bigger (*The Economist*, 2001a).

Perhaps the cynical joke made at the founding of the EU that 'German industry would pay for French farmers' should now be 'European industry would pay for French, Spanish and

▶

Greek farmers' as it is closer to the truth, due to a failure to address the underlying issues. The normal rules of supply and demand are effectively

discarded under CAP and prices are not allowed to fall to anywhere near the market level. Whether for milk, olives, wheat or beef there is a price

that the consumer must pay until EU farm ministers are prepared to contemplate radical reform.

Sources: The Economist (2001a, b).

Local government also carries some responsibility for implementing and enforcing laws made at a national level. In Germany, local government has responsibility for implementing pollution and noise control legislation. In the UK, local trading standards officers may well be the first to investigate claims of shady or illegal business practices. Christmas often heralds a flurry of warnings from trading standards officers about dangerous toys, usually cheap imports from the Far East, that do not conform to EU safety standards. Officers can prosecute the retailer and prevent further sales of the offending goods, but by then, significant numbers of the product may already have been sold. Trading Standards offices play an important role in ensuring consumer safety and that fair trading and quality standards are maintained. They are provided by over 200 local authorities in the UK.

eg Trading standards officers also look into allegations of short weights and measures. In 1995, for example, they were asked by the angling fraternity in the north-east of England to investigate the practice of selling maggots by the pint. Although officers found that the number and weight of maggots to the pint varied significantly from retailer to retailer, they decided that this was tolerable because of the wriggly nature of the merchandise and, in any case, since this was a long-established method of selling maggots they would not intervene further. It is up to the individual angler to choose a maggot supplier with care! More recently, just what constitutes a pint of beer has been under consideration. It is all about liquid, gas and froth: get the mix wrong and it's a short measure! A pint of beer has been determined to be a pint of liquid which can include the liquid in the head of the froth, but not the gas in the head. Pint pullers must ensure 100 per cent liquid with no measure below 95 per cent. New legislation is being introduced under the Weights and Measures Act and trading standards officers will be watching to ensure compliance.

Local authorities in the UK also have responsibility for granting planning permission. For businesses, this means that if they want to build a factory or supermarket, or change the usage of a commercial building, then the local authority has to vet the plans and grant permission before anything can be done. Local authorities are under particular pressure from small retailers who are worried about the major shift towards out-of-town superstore shopping. The argument is that town centres and small local businesses are dying because people would rather go to the out-of-town retail park or shopping mall. This means that local authorities are increasingly reluctant to grant planning permission for further out-of-town developments, seriously affecting the growth plans of many large retailers.

eg Throughout the 1990s, supermarkets were criticised by some for changing the face of the high street by attracting shoppers to out-of-town hypermarkets, superstores and malls. A number of countries including France and the UK introduced tough planning regimes to limit growth. Now, supermarkets are starting to play a part in urban renewal schemes using brown-field sites largely as a response to the ease and favour given to planning permission for redeveloping sites (Bedington, 2001). The former gas works at Beckton is being transformed by Tesco into a 109,000 ft^2 store. Similarly, the redevelopment of a rundown shopping centre in Seacroft, Leeds, and the planned conversion of a derelict railway yard in Leyton by ASDA are all helping to play a leading role in urban regeneration schemes.

Although the EU is making considerable progress towards eliminating national regulations that are contrary to fair and free trade, the scale of the task is great. National environmental laws in Germany and Denmark, for example, have been criticised as favouring local rather than international suppliers. The extent to which regulations affect business, therefore, varies between countries and industries. There is a slow move towards standardisation, which generally means that the advanced industrialised northern European nations are tending to deregulate, whereas the southern nations are tending to tighten up controls. Moves towards deregulation have been accompanied by increased self-regulation within industries.

■ The European Union

It is unfortunate that the pronouncements from Brussels that make the headlines tend to be the offbeat or trivial ones, such as the proposal to regulate the curve on a cucumber, the redesignation of the carrot as a fruit to allow the Portuguese to carry on their trade in carrot jam, and questions as to whether Cheddar cheese and Swiss rolls can continue to bear those names if they are not made in those places. Despite these delightful eccentricities, the EU works hard towards ensuring free trade and fair competition across member states' boundaries.

The SEM, which officially came into being on 1 January 1993, was the culmination of many years of work in breaking down trade barriers and harmonising legislation across the member states. One area that directly affects marketing is the abolition of frontier controls, so that goods can be transferred from state to state, or carried in transit through states, without lots of paperwork and customs checks. Additionally, road haulage has been freed from restrictions and quotas so that a haulier with a licence to operate in one EU member state can operate in any other. Further European integration is sought through EMU (European Monetary Union) and the introduction of the euro as a replacement for national currencies. This has made cross-border price comparisons a lot easier for customers and created more transparent pan-European competition. The euro has also eliminated problems caused by fluctuating exchange rates, thus reducing the costs of the cross-border movement of goods and encouraging more imports and exports between the countries of the EU.

In terms of products themselves, a set of European standards have been implemented through a series of directives, ensuring common criteria for safety, public health and environmental protection. Any product adhering to these directives and to the laws of its own country of origin will be acceptable in any member state. Look for the stylised CE symbol on products as the sign that they do conform to European standards.

In other areas of marketing, harmonisation of regulations and codes of practice across member states has not been so easy. Over the next few years, the EU intends to bring a series of separate legislation together into an overarching EU Communications Act, which would be wide-ranging in terms of promotional and media types, including press and TV, direct marketing and sales promotion, online marketing and e-commerce (Simms, 2001). The problem with marketing communications is that the European law makers have to reconcile commercial freedom with consumer protection across all member states, each with its own customs, laws, codes and practices. Sometimes, best practice is followed and harmonisation across all states can be achieved but in other cases, the law of the country in which a transaction originates applies, by mutual recognition. There are wide variations in best practice across Europe, so finding a common approach will be difficult. The threats are, however, real for UK advertisers. Sweden, despite an initial rebuff, would still like to see a blanket ban across Europe on television advertising to children and the advertising of alcohol. Other lobbies exist to constrain advertising on 'unhealthy foods', financial services, and even cars (Smith, 2001).

eg   Defining just what chocolate actually is or is not has caused controversy in Europe among both politicians and chocolate manufacturers. The argument has been going on for nearly 30 years, since the UK and Ireland joined the EU with chocolate that included cheaper vegetable fats rather than a higher proportion of cocoa fats. The chocolate wars have been fought between an alliance of France and Belgium and a number of others against the UK, Ireland and five other states. An EU directive favouring one side over the other would create an unfair competitive advantage and would be a far cry from a single European market in chocolate. In 1997, the European Parliament ruled in favour of the France–Belgium alliance, overturning a previous compromise EU directive. This meant that the term 'milk chocolate' could not be used by the UK and the other states on its side. That meant that products from the UK and Ireland and some other member states would have to be renamed 'chocolate with milk and non-cocoa vegetable fats' or at least 'milk chocolate with high milk content'. Product labels would also need to show clearly that the product contains vegetable fats. That was not acceptable to the UK chocolate producers and a further compromise was realised in 2000 with directive 2000/36 which agreed to two definitions of chocolate: 'milk chocolate' and 'family milk chocolate', the latter replacing the 'milk chocolate with high milk content' designation for the UK and Irish markets. All this goes to show how a desire to create a common internal market and to establish pan-European rules for the manufacture, composition, labelling and packaging of a product such as chocolate, can run into bureau-cratic nightmares (Bremner, 1997; Tucker, 1997; http://www.europa.eu.int).

Direct marketing is a relatively new area which has great potential for the marketing of goods across Europe, and yet here too, a variety of national codes are in operation. In the UK, for example, 'cold calling' telephone selling (i.e. an organisation phoning a consumer for sales purposes without the consumer's prior permission) is permitted, but in Germany it is almost totally banned. Data protection laws (i.e. what information organisations are permitted to hold on databases and what they are allowed to do with it) and regulations on list broking (i.e. the sale of lists of names and addresses to other organisations) also vary widely across the EU. The relevant EU directives include the Data Protection Directive, the Distance Selling Directive and the Integrated Digital Services Network Directive.

■ Regulatory bodies

Within the UK, there are many regulatory bodies with greater or lesser powers of regulation over marketing practice. Quasi-governmental bodies such as the Office of Fair Trading (OFT) and the Competition Commission have had statutory duties and powers delegated to them directly by government to ensure the maintenance of free and fair commerce.

The OFT in the UK aims to ensure that markets are working effectively. This is achieved by ensuring that competition and consumer protection laws and guidelines are followed in the public interest. It is the OFT that refers mergers to the Competition Commission. Being accountable to Parliament for its performance, it is able to play a powerful role in shaping an organisation's marketing behaviour. Recent activities have included an inquiry into motorway catering facilities, where they found that value for money is generally poor but that it does not arise from anti-competitive practice; a report on the funeral industry (OFT, 2001) which called for better prior information for the bereaved on funeral charges and choices, and the successful achievement of the ability to apply through the courts for 'Stop Now' orders designed to curb the excesses of rogue traders. The latter can be especially important to stop the sale of defective goods and breaches in advertising or credit rules. Further examples can be found on the official website, http://www.oft.gov.uk.

Slightly more remote from central government, quasi-autonomous non-governmental organisations (quangos) have a specific remit and can act much more quickly than a government department. Quangos such as Oftel, Ofgem and Ofwat, for instance, exist to regulate the privatised telephone, gas and electricity, and water industries respectively in the UK. The prime aim for the quangos is to protect consumer interests by ensuring appropriate levels of competition. The scope of the work of quangos is clearly extensive and offers necessary protection for the consumer in markets that have been privatised. Suppliers in the industry must also consider the likely public and legislative impact of acting outside the public interest in the development of their marketing strategy and its implementation.

Voluntary codes of practice emerge from associations and trade bodies, with which their members agree to comply. The Advertising Standards Authority (ASA), for example, oversees the British Codes of Advertising and Sales Promotion Practice which were merged in 1995 into one comprehensive set of rules covering print, cinema, video, posters and leaflet media. The philosophy of the ASA is that advertisements should be:

■ Legal, decent, honest and truthful.
■ Prepared with a sense of responsibility to consumers and society.
■ In line with the principles of fair competition accepted in business.

The ASA is not a statutory body, and can only *request* an advertiser to amend or withdraw an advertisement that is in breach of the code. Of the 30 million advertisements placed each year, the ASA believes that 97 per cent of print advertisements and 98 per cent of posters adhere to the code. However, if the ASA's Council of 12 people decides that an advertisement contravenes the code, then it does have remedies other than persuasion. It can *request* media owners to refuse to accept or repeat the offending advertisement, generate adverse publicity, and/or *recommend* that the OFT should take proceedings to apply for a legal injunction to prevent publication.

Most advertisers conform to requests from the ASA to withdraw an advertisement and some avoid any possible problems by voluntarily using the pre-publication vetting service. However, the ASA can now ask for vetting for up to two years if a particular advertiser has proven troublesome in the past. Previously, offending campaigns attracted a lot of publicity because of their sensational nature. Then, when the ASA makes a ruling, further publicity is generated, for instance through opinion articles in newspapers discussing advertising standards which include a picture of an offending advertisement so that the readers know what sort of thing they're talking about. Indirectly, therefore, in some cases, ASA involvement rather defeats its own objectives.

eg Club 18–30 in the 1990s and more recently FCUK have become very adept at testing the frontiers of what is deemed acceptable by the ASA. An example of an adjudication by the ASA involved a poster campaign developed by Saatchi & Saatchi for the holiday firm Club 18–30. Copylines such as 'Beaver España', 'Discover Your Erogenous Zones', and 'It's Not Just Sex, Sex, Sex', drew a significant number of complaints which were upheld. The ASA told Club 18–30 to withdraw the advertisements straight away, since their sexual overtones might be considered offensive. In more recent years Club 18–30 has amended its execution of campaigns. It is still 'fun in the sun', but well within ASA guidelines. Nevertheless an enormous amount of publicity was achieved before the more raunchy posters were withdrawn. To some extent, history is now repeating itself with the continued controversy over the FCUK posters (see p. 87).

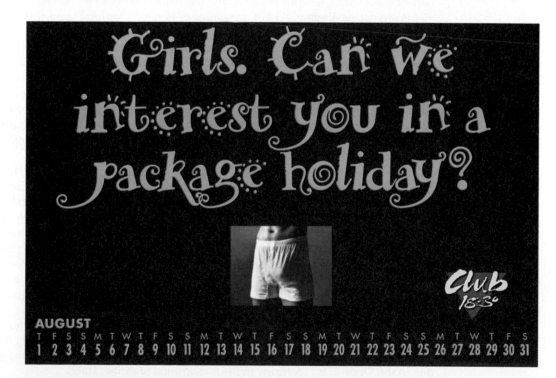

By the time the ASA required the withdrawal of a provocative poster campaign by Club 18–30, the company had already benefited from enormous publicity!

Source: Club 18–30/Saatchi and Saatchi.

With the development of the SEM and transnational advertising campaigns, marketers not only need to consider national laws, but also self-regulatory rules and systems across the member states. The European Advertising Standards Alliance (EASA) represents the various advertising regulatory bodies, such as the ASA, across Europe. Although it has no direct powers it can intervene on behalf of complainants by asking the various national regulators to act. For example, when a Luxembourgois consumer complained about a French chewing gum manufacturer's health claims, the case was referred back to the French for investigation and action.

eg The ASA takes a close interest in the claims made in advertisements. Danone ran into trouble with the ASA when it claimed that the calcium in a bottle of its Danone Activ was equivalent to the calcium in two glasses of milk. The National Dairy Council took offence at the claim as Danone only used a 250 ml glass of liquid which was well below the normal-sized glass. The ASA upheld the claim and Danone was told to use 'commonly accepted glass sizes in future' and to amend its promotional material accordingly (*The Grocer*, 2001e). The ASA is especially mindful of the claims made in the genetically modified (GM) and organic food areas. Iceland also fell foul of the ASA over using misleading and exaggerated claims regarding GM food. The company had for some time taken a strong position on offering organic ranges and non-GM food, but saying in an instore leaflet, for example, that there may have been 'mistakes in genetic engineering', and that a GM bacterium 'may have caused the deaths of 37 people in the US' went too far, according to the ASA (Jardine, 2000). According to the ASA, Iceland had taken the science that was available a little too far, and retailers should avoid using scaremongering tactics to get their message across to consumers.

The Independent Television Commission (ITC) looks after terrestrial television advertising, while the Radio Authority (RA) supervises radio advertising. These two organisations are statutory bodies and carry a great deal of weight, since they have the power to issue and control broadcasting licences, and compliance with the advertising codes of practice is effectively part of the licence. As with the ASA, the television advertising code ensures that advertisements are not misleading, do not encourage or condone harmful behaviour and do not cause widespread or exceptional offence. The frequency and duration of advertising breaks are restricted and it is the ITC that ensures that there is a distinct break between programmes and advertisements. Pharmaceuticals, alcohol, tobacco and diet products, to name but a few, are subject to tight restrictions under the code of practice and in addition EU directives specify what is and is not allowed. All of this means that although the basic philosophy of the ITC and RA is the same as that of the ASA, their concerns are a little wider, covering the timing of advertisements, making sure that the advertisements are suitably differentiated from the programmes, protecting children from unsuitable advertising, prohibiting political advertising and regulating programme sponsorship, among other things.

There are no hard and fast rules about how far an advertiser can go before running foul of regulatory bodies and this becomes even more complex once you start advertising across European boundaries. A naked couple can kiss in a shower in an advertisement for condoms, but a woman's naked buttocks on a poster are 'unnecessarily shocking' in the words of the ASA. Whether an advertisement causes complaints depends on the medium, the product and the audience likely to see it, so an advertisement that is 'slightly sexist' is fine in men's publications but would be banned in more family-oriented media. Posters, because of their size and unrestricted viewing, can be especially difficult. Mentioning religion or race can be a real minefield, especially if the advertisement focuses on a particular icon or leader. For example, the ASA upheld complaints against an advertisement for the Rey & Co. stationery brand headlined 'Jesus, he loves me', but did not ban a similar advertisement saying, 'Behold! The King of Paper is born'. The direct reference to Jesus made the difference. For Diesel, the 'nuns in jeans' advertisement was banned, not because of the nuns but due to the Virgin Mary featuring in the background (Jardine, 1999).

The Institute of Sales Promotion (ISP), the Institute of Practitioners in Advertising (IPA), the Institute of Public Relations (IPR) and the Direct Marketing Association (DMA) are effectively trade associations. All these areas are, of course, subject to prevailing commercial legislation generally, but, in addition, these particular bodies provide detailed voluntary codes of practice setting industry standards for fair dealing with customers. They are not statutory bodies, and only have jurisdiction over their members, with the ultimate sanction of suspending or expelling organisations that breach the code of practice. All of the bodies mentioned here represent organisations with interests in various areas of marketing communications, but trade associations can exist in any industry with similar objectives of regulating the professional practice of their members. There are, for example, the Fencing Contractors' Association, the Glass and Glazing Federation, the Association of British Insurers, the British Association of Landscape Industries, and the National House Builders' Confederation, to name but a few! As well as regulating business practice, such bodies can also provide other services for members, such as legal indemnities and representation, training and professional development services, and acting as the voice of the industry to government and the media.

■ Influences on the political and regulatory environment

The political and regulatory environment is clearly influenced by sociocultural factors, and particularly the pressure of public opinion, the media and pressure groups. Greenpeace and Friends of the Earth, for example, have educated consumers to become more aware of the content, origins and after-effects of the products they buy and use, and this led to the phasing out of chlorofluorocarbons (CFCs) as an aerosol propellant and as a refrigerant. The green movement has also spurred the drafting of regulations on the acceptable emissions from car exhausts, which has had a major impact on the product development plans of motor manufacturers for the next few years. Similarly, the consumer movement, through organisations such as the Consumers' Association, has also played an important role in promoting the rights of the consumer and thus in driving the regulators and legislators towards laws and codes of practice regarding product safety, selling techniques and marketing communications, for instance.

Not all pressure on legislators and regulators originates from pressure groups or consumer-based organisations, of course. Trade associations or groupings lobby the legislators to try to influence regulation in their members' favour. Sometimes, the lobbying is designed to slow the pace of change, influence the nature of any planned legislation, and to delay legislation perceived as potentially harmful to the industry's interests. In the case of tobacco, for instance, government must balance public health concerns against the employment and export potential from manufacturers. It is important, therefore, for the marketer to read the changing political environment, within Europe, in export markets and from international organisations such as the WTO and OECD who are influential in guiding change. Most industries face new legislation that affects them one way or another during the course of a year and an early appreciation gives companies more time to exploit an opportunity or to counter a threat. However, it could take between three and five years for legislation to come into effect in Europe, so a longer-term perspective must be taken (Smith, 2001). A failure to get involved early on in lobbying and putting across arguments can have knock-on effects down the line with policies that constrain marketing activity too much without enabling a more open internal market. Some policies could even favour particular member states who have lobbied harder. The directives on online trading and e-commerce, for example, are topical within the EU, so Internet marketers cannot afford to miss out on discussions concerning the legislative framework.

Tracking the legislative process can be a long and tortuous process. The Commission in Strasbourg frames EU legislation which is then debated and amended by the European Parliament before the legislation is endorsed by the Council of Ministers and then implemented through European directives. Even then it is not over, as individual member states may have to pass legislation to implement it at a local level (Simms, 2001). The greater the understanding of the EU and national political processes, the more an organisation can move with change rather than risk being left behind.

Chapter summary

■ This chapter has explored the importance of the external marketing environment as an influence on the way in which organisations do business and make their decisions. Ways in which customers, markets, competitors, technology and regulation are changing are all important pointers to future strategy. Thus failure to understand the environment fully could mean missing out on opportunities or ignoring threats which in turn could lead to lost revenue or, more seriously, loss of competitive advantage.

■ Using environmental scanning, a technique for monitoring and evaluating information, organisations can understand their environment more thoroughly, pick up early signs of emerging trends, and thus plan their future activities appropriately. Such information may come from secondary sources, such as trade publications or published research data, or an organisation can commission research to increase their knowledge of the environment. Care must be taken, however, to ensure that all appropriate sources are constantly monitored (but avoiding information overload), and that internal mechanisms exist for disseminating information and acting on it.

■ The main framework for the chapter is the categorisation of the marketing environment into STEP factors: sociocultural, technological, economic/competitive and political/regulatory.

■ The first of the STEP factors is the sociocultural environment. This deals with 'hard' information, such as demographic trends, and with less tangible issues, such as changing tastes, attitudes and cultures. Knowledge of demographic trends gives the marketer a basic feel for how broad market segments are likely to change in the future. To gain the fullest picture, however, the marketer needs to combine demographic information with 'softer' data on how attitudes are changing.

■ The second STEP factor is technology. An organisation's technological advances may arise from the exploitation of breakthroughs from other organisations, or may be the result of long-term investment in R&D in-house to solve a specific problem. Either way, technology can present the opportunity to create a clear differential advantage that cannot be easily copied by the competition.

■ The economic and competitive environment constitutes the third STEP factor, and can be further divided into macro- and microeconomic environments. The macroeconomic environment analyses the effects of the broader economic picture, looking at issues such as taxation, government spending and interest rates. It also takes account of the threats, opportunities and barriers arising from membership of international trading blocs. The microeconomic environment is a little closer to the individual organisation, and is concerned with the structure of the market(s) in which it operates.

■ The final STEP factor is the political and regulatory environment. Laws, regulations and codes of practice emanate from national governments, the EU, local government, statutory bodies and trade associations to affect the way in which organisations do business. Consumer groups and other pressure groups, such as those representing the ecological movement, health issues and animal rights, are active in trying to persuade government to deregulate or legislate, or to influence the scope and content of new legislation.

questions for *review and discussion*

2.1 What is environmental scanning, why is it important, and what are the potential problems of implementing it?

2.2 Differentiate between the macro- and microeconomic environments.

2.3 What sources of published demographic data are available in your own university or college library?

2.4 Find and discuss examples of products that are particularly vulnerable to changing consumer tastes.

2.5 What are the differences between the ASA and the ITC? Find and discuss recent examples of adjudications by these two bodies (or equivalent regulatory bodies in your own country). Do you agree with their judgement?

2.6 Using Figure 2.1 as a framework, choose a product and list under each of the STEP factors the relevant influences that have helped to make that product what it is.

case study 2.1

A Friend in need is a Friend indeed

Lofthouse of Fleetwood Ltd is a family-owned company based on the coast in the north-west of England. The company began in 1865 when a Fleetwood pharmacist, James Lofthouse, developed a warming lozenge for trawlermen to suck while at sea. That lozenge, branded as Fisherman's Friend, grew from its small beginnings into what is now a global business. Billions of Fisherman's Friend lozenges are sold every year in over 100 different countries. The main ingredients, including menthol, eucalyptus oil and capsicum tincture, make the lozenge a hot prospect and it is endorsed by medical authorities as an excellent means of clearing bronchial congestion. Although purely medicated confectionery, Fisherman's Friend holds ISO 2002 accreditation.

Because of its heritage, Fisherman's Friend is perceived in the UK as a 'semi-medicated' product, positioned alongside Tunes and Hall's Mentholyptus cough sweets. In overseas markets, however, where the product has no historical roots, Fisherman's Friend is positioned and accepted as 'adult confectionery'. The UK perceptions are reinforced by the retail trade which, in some cases, still sees Fisherman's Friend as a winter product and so does not give it optimum shelf space in the summer months. It is true to say that in past years, sales have experienced peaks and troughs and this is still the case in the UK. In newer markets, where the brand is treated purely as confectionery, there is much less seasonality and the product retains its normal shelf position throughout the year.

Another problem in the UK market for a brand trading on a heritage established over 130 or more

years is that many of its loyal customers are from older age groups. The company wants to target a younger market but has found it hard to change the heritage perceptions and create a 'cool' image. The perceptions among the young are still that it is 'the sort of product Granny buys', that 'it'll blow your head off' and that 'I haven't tried it and I know I won't like it'. Despite innovative advertising, those perceptions and the view of Fisherman's Friend being a medicinal product that 'I'll only take as a last resort' still persist. Efforts have been made to get the product sampled by younger consumers. It has been included, for example, in student welcome packs on university and college campuses. Nevertheless, there is still the reaction 'I've tried it once and I didn't like it' to be overcome.

To extend the brand, over 15 years or so from the mid-1980s, variants on the Original Extra Strong Fisherman's Friend brand were introduced. The first was an aniseed flavoured Fisherman's Friend. This has a milder flavour than the original and is targeted at the younger audience which dislikes the strong flavour of the original. A mint flavour was then developed in order to move the brand further towards the mainstream confectionery sector. Other products have been developed to meet the needs of export markets. The Norwegian market, for example, is very health conscious and wanted a sugar-free version. This caused some manufacturing problems for the company, however. The traditional method of making a hard lozenge did not work well with sugar substitutes as they absorbed too much moisture from the air and turned the lozenges very soggy very quickly. Thus a new method was introduced which compresses dry powders into hard tablets. This is very similar to the way in which the pharmaceutical industry makes aspirin tablets, for instance. The investment in the new method proved to be well worthwhile. Original, mint and lemon sugar-free Fisherman's Friends have all proved successful, not only in Scandinavia but also in the UK and other markets.

The company feels that research is an important basis for the strategic thinking that has driven these developments of the brand. Research has shown, for example, that there are different flavour preferences in different countries and the company exploits this information. Fruit flavours are preferred in southern European markets, such as Greece, Italy and Spain, where citrus fruits are grown, while northern Europe and Scandinavia prefer the non-fruit flavours. In

Medicine or sweetie? In any event, brace yourself!

Source: Kelly Weedon Shute Ltd.

France and the Far East, consumers have a milder palate, preferring the newer flavours that are less hot than the original Fisherman's Friend. Focus groups are also used as part of the market research effort to test advertising awareness and recall, and price perceptions. Blind tastings have also provided feedback which has allowed the company to identify the potential of new flavour variants.

In all its markets, including the UK, the company uses independent distributors to sell and distribute the product. Lofthouse of Fleetwood has no sales force of its own. 'Our forte is manufacturing quality products. It's what we enjoy and it's what we do best,' said Duncan Lofthouse, a director of the company. The company does not consider sales, marketing and logistics to be its strengths, and so it contracts out those activities. Nevertheless, the company still involves itself in the major decision-making. Its in-house technical and planning department designs the packaging, and the company retains control over its own brand. The company tries to keep a consistent brand image in all its markets, but some adaptation to suit local needs is necessary. For humid markets, such as those in the Far East, the brand's packaging has had to be adapted to include a foil lining to preserve the product and prevent it from going soggy. This gives it the same three-year shelf life as the paper packs have in other markets. Otherwise, the packaging is almost identical in all markets. The Fisherman's Friend brand name is in English on the front of all packs, but the back of the pack varies from market to market. The brand name can be represented in the local script (for example, in China, Thailand and Greece) and the local labelling regulations fulfilled.

Lofthouse of Fleetwood liaises closely with the specialist companies it works with. For example, it has worked for 26 years with an independent sales and marketing company, Impex Management Company Ltd, which represents only Fisherman's Friend. The relationship involves mutual respect and mutual dependency and works well. Impex and Lofthouse of Fleetwood sit down together to discuss the direction of Fisherman's Friend and the business's objectives and five-year plan.

Source: With grateful thanks to Tony and Duncan Lofthouse.

Questions

1 Summarise the STEP factors that might have affected Lofthouse of Fleetwood's marketing decisions.

2 Why is market research so important to this company?

3 Why should Lofthouse of Fleetwood want to reach a younger market? What is it doing and what more could it do to reach this audience?

4 Lofthouse of Fleetwood contracts its marketing activities to an independent company, Impex, so that it can focus on manufacturing. Does this make Lofthouse of Fleetwood a production or product-oriented company?

References for chapter 2

Aguilar, F.J. (1967), *Scanning the Business Environment*, Macmillan.

Asian Business (2001), 'Exercise on Emirates', *Asian Business*, June, p. 34.

Bedington, E. (2001), 'The Regeneration Game', *The Grocer*, 19 May, pp. 36–8.

Bremner, C. (1997), 'All Because the Belgians Do Not Like Milk Tray', *The Times*, 24 October, p. 5.

Business Europe (2000), 'A New Strategy on VAT', *Business Europe*, 3 July, p. 7.

Chesshyre, T. (2001), 'Over 50 But Not Up the Creek', *The Times*, 5 May.

Delmas, M. and Terlaak, A. (2001), 'A Framework for Analyzing Environmental Voluntary Agreements', *California Management Review*, 43 (3), pp. 44–63.

Dittmar, H. and Pepper, L. (1994), 'To Have is to Be: Materialism and Person Perception in Working Class and Middle Class British Adolescents', *Journal of Economic Psychology*, 15 (2), pp. 233–51.

Durham, M. (2001), 'Australia Launches DVT Investigation', *The Independent*, 9 August.

Ecklof, B. *et al.* (1996), 'Venous Thromboembolism in Association with Prolonged Air Travel', *Dermatologic Surgery*, 22 (July), pp. 637–41.

The Economist (2000), 'Europe: Sweden Bottles Up', *The Economist*, 26 February, p. 62.

The Economist (2001a), 'From Bad to Worse, Down on the Farm', *The Economist*, 3 March, pp. 45–6.

The Economist (2001b), 'Glut, Fraud and Eco-damage', *The Economist*, 30 June, pp. 46–7.

Euromonitor (2001), *European Marketing Data and Statistics 2001*, Euromonitor, 36th edn.

Fiorino, F. (2001), 'Anxious Passengers Seek Answers on DVT Risk', *Aviation Week and Space Technology*, 29 January, pp. 50–1.

The Grocer (2000a), 'Corned Beef Boosts Your Sperm Count', *The Grocer*, 9 September.

The Grocer (2000b), 'The Food Agenda, Let it Be Real', *The Grocer*, 11 November.

The Grocer (2000c), 'Brussels Report: EU Blocking Trade Tactics', *The Grocer*, 2 December.

The Grocer (2001a), 'Bananas: Hanging in the Balance', *The Grocer*, 20 January.

The Grocer (2001b), 'US: Chiquita Poised to Slip on Bananas', *The Grocer*, 27 January.

The Grocer (2001c), 'Sugar, Rice, Bananas: New Treaty will Liberate Imports', *The Grocer*, 10 March.

The Grocer (2001d), 'Reassuring Consumers', *The Grocer*, 5 May, p. 23.

The Grocer (2001e), 'Danone: Calcium Claim is Misleading', *The Grocer*, 12 May.

Hardcastle, S. (2001), 'Deli and Food to Go', *The Grocer*, 26 May, pp. 49–50.

Hunt, J. (2001), 'The Good Life', *The Grocer*, 7 April, pp. 32–4.

IBM (2001a), accessed via http://www.ibm.com/annualreport/2000/, October 2001.

IBM (2001b), accessed via http://www.research.ibm.com, October 2001.

Innocenti, N. (2001), 'Open Skies or Empty Skies for South Africa', *Financial Times*, 6 August, accessed via http://www.FT.com

International Tax Review (2001), 'UK Delays EU Web Tax Law', *International Tax Review*, June, p. 5.

Jardine, A. (1999), 'How Far Can You Go Before an Ad is Banned?', *Marketing*, 8 April, p. 14.

Jardine, A. (2000), 'ASA Slams Iceland Over GM Ad Claims', *Marketing*, 11 May, p. 1.

Jordan, J. (2001), 'Medical Risks Associated with Air Travel', accessed via http://www.caami.jccbi.gov, June 2001.

Kite, M. and Bird, S. (2000), 'Airlines Urged to Offer Passengers "Long Leg Class"', *The Times*, 23 November.

Laschefski, K. and Freris, N. (2001), 'Saving the Wood', *The Ecologist*, July/August, pp. 40–3.

OFT (2001), 'A Report of the OFT Enquiry into the Funeral Industry', accessed via http://www.oft.gov.uk, July 2001.

Patten, S. (2000), 'Supermarkets the Catalyst for Fuel Retailing Revolution', *The Times*, 13 September, p. 27.

Professional Engineering (2001), '£160m Orders Shore Up Two Ailing Shipbuilders', *Professional Engineering*, 13 June, p. 4.

Shannon, J. (1998), 'Seniors Convert to Consumerism', *Marketing Week*, 10 September, p. 22.

Simms, J. (2001), 'EU Rules, OK?', *Marketing*, 25 January, pp. 23–5.

Smith, C. (2001), 'Think Long Term or be Left Behind by EU Legislation', *Marketing*, 25 January, p. 19.

Thornton, P. (2001), 'Smugglers May Come to Aid of Chancellor's Growth Forecast', *The Independent*, 29 August, p. 11.

The Times (2000), 'Airlines Neglect Passengers' Health', *The Times*, 22 November.

Tucker, E. (1997), 'MEPs Reject Chocolate Compromise', *Financial Times*, 24 October, p. 20.

Watson, E. (2001), 'Blind Tasting', *The Grocer*, 9 June, pp. 38–9.

Webster, B. (2001), 'BA Faces Claim For "Failing to Warn" Health Danger', *The Times*, 31 July.

buyer behaviour

This chapter will help you to:

1 understand the decision-making processes that customers go through as they make a purchase;

2 appreciate how those processes differ between different buying situations;

3 understand the influences that affect decision-making, whether environmental, psychological or sociocultural, and appreciate the implications of those processes and influences for marketing strategies;

4 understand the nature and structure of B2B buying and the differences between B2B and consumer buying; and

5 analyse the B2B buying process and the factors that influence its outcomes.

Introduction

In contrast to Chapter 2, which looked at the broad backdrop against which marketers have to do business, this chapter focuses closely on the consumers and B2B customers, who are at the centre of many a marketer's universe. While the customer is part of the marketing environment, and is shaped to some extent by the influences already discussed in Chapter 2, it is also very important to understand the more personal and specific influences affecting customers and the nature of the decision-making processes through which they go. This chapter, therefore, begins by looking at consumers as buyers and analysing the factors, both internal and external, that determine how and why they make their choices. The later part of the chapter examines B2B buyer behaviour. Having considered some of the differences between consumers and B2B customers in terms of how and why they purchase goods and services, we shall then analyse the B2B buying process and the pressures that shape the decisions that are made within an organisational context.

The decision-making process

Figure 3.1 offers a deceptively simple model of consumer buyer behaviour, presented as a logical flow of activities, working through from problem recognition to purchase to post-purchase evaluation. This section of the chapter deals with this core process.

eg You would be very interested in understanding consumer marketing if you made yogurt, a rapidly growing and dynamic product category worth $1.2bn in the UK. The yogurt market is characterised by a variety of different products meeting different customer needs and usage occasions. It reflects many of the significant lifestyle trends in the food market such as increasing convenience, concern with healthy eating and a desire for value for money. Müller, the leading brand with 36 per cent of the market, has a record of innovation in providing brands to meet these different needs. The core market is met by Corners, the leading yogurt for family consumption. Müllerlight is aimed at the health-conscious by offering a virtually fat-free yogurt that has been actively promoted through sports, health clubs and to women who want to eat more healthily. At the other end of the market are products for those who don't care about the calorie count. The thicker and creamier, the better for self-indulgence. Other sectors include organic yogurts and children's products. Understanding the eating occasion, therefore, and the importance of different consumer preferences has been a powerful influence on product development and promotion in this category (Hardcastle, 2001).

Figure 3.1 The consumer buying decision-making process and its influencing factors

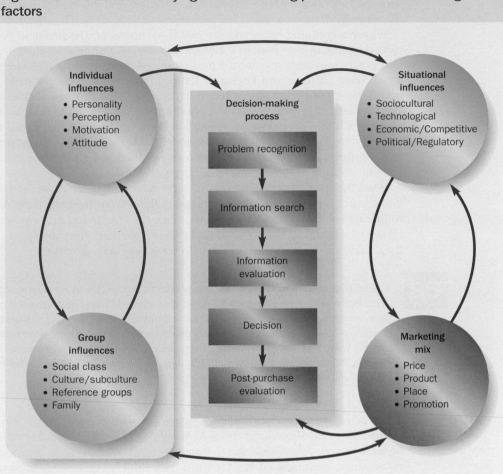

The decision-making process is affected by a number of other more complex influences, as can be seen in Figure 3.1. Some of these influences relate to the wider marketing environment in which the decision is being made (see pp. 74–6). Others, however, relate to the individual purchaser and therefore pp. 77–83 will consider those influences emanating from within the individual such as personality, attitudes and learning. Similarly, pp. 83–91 will look at how the individual's decisions are affected by their social context, especially family and cultural groupings.

There have been many attempts to create models of consumer decision-making of greater or lesser complexity and detail that try to capture the richness of the experience. The Engel, Blackwell and Miniard (1990) model presented here, although concise and simple in its outline, provides a framework that still allows us to consider, through discussion, many of the more complex elements. It traces the progress of a purchasing event stage by stage from the buyer's point of view, including the definition of likely information needs and a discussion of the level of rationality and analytical behaviour leading to the eventual decision.

We now look at each stage in turn.

■ Problem recognition

In trying to rationalise the decision-making process, this is a good place to begin. After all, if you are not aware that you have a 'problem', how can you decide to purchase something to solve it? More functional purchases, such as replenishing stocks of washing powder or petrol, may be initiated by a casual glance at current stock levels. Other purchases may be triggered by a definable event. If, for example, the exhaust falls off your car, you will soon become aware of the nature of the problem and the kind of purchase that will provide the remedy.

Where psychological needs are involved, however, the problem recognition may be a slow dawning or may lead to a sudden impulse, when the consumer, realising that the current position or feeling is not the desired one, decides to do something to change it through a purchase (Bruner and Pomazal, 1988). Imagine, for instance, that you are wandering round the supermarket after a tough day at work. You're tired, listless and a bit depressed. You've filled your trolley with the potatoes, bread and milk you intended to buy, but you also slip a bar of chocolate (or worse!) in there on the basis that it will cheer you up as you drive home. The 'problem' here is less definable, based on a vague psychological feeling, and it follows that the solution is also less definable – it could be chocolate, cream buns, wine or clothing, whatever takes the purchaser's fancy.

What the examples given so far do have in common, however, is that the impetus to go into a purchasing decision-making routine comes from the consumer. As will be seen in the following sections, marketers can then use the marketing mix elements to influence the choice of solution. It is also possible, however, for marketers to trigger the process by using the marketing mix to bring a problem to the consumer's attention.

eg The manufacturers of Radion laundry products ran an advertising campaign in the UK featuring a housewife who suddenly realised that even though the shirt she was ironing had just been washed, there was still a sweaty smell clinging to its armpits. Radion, of course, has the power to eliminate this in the wash. Housewives across the country supposedly became racked with fear and guilt, asking themselves: 'Do I have this problem? Should I switch to Radion?' A problem had been created in the consumer's mind, and a decision-making process initiated, largely through the marketer's efforts.

There is, of course, a significant difference between being aware of a need or problem and being able to do something about it. Many needs are latent and remain unfulfilled, either because consumers decide not to do anything about it now, or because they are unable to do anything. We might all feel the need for a three-week holiday in some exotic part of the world, but we must not only be willing, but also financially able, to disappear over the horizon. Problem recognition, if it is to lead anywhere, therefore requires both the willingness and the ability to fulfil the emerging need.

■ Information search

Defining the problem is one thing, but defining and implementing the solution is something else. The questions to be answered include what kind of purchase will solve the problem, where and how it can be obtained, what information is needed to arrive at a decision and where that information is available. In some cases, consumers will actively search out relevant information with a view to using it in making a decision, but they can also acquire information passively, storing it away until it is needed. Daily, consumers are exposed to a wide range of media all designed to influence awareness and recall of particular products and services. Thus they 'know' that Radion eliminates sweaty smells before they get anywhere near a conscious choice of laundry product in the supermarket. When they do get to the point of purchasing, the manufacturers hope that they will recall that knowledge and use it in making the brand choice.

Similarly, the Cheltenham & Gloucester mortgage advertisement is designed to appeal to someone who is already considering house purchase. It is hardly likely to inspire consumers to move house, but it could be useful if consumers are worried about finding the right mortgage for their circumstances before they start looking seriously. In some cases, a consumer might not be planning to move immediately, but the C&G would hope that they will recall the advertisement when the time does come.

Not all external sources of information are controlled by the marketer – don't forget the power of word of mouth as a marketing tool. Friends, family and colleagues, for example, may all give advice, whether based on experience, knowledge or opinion, to the would-be decision maker in this phase. People are more likely to trust information given through word of mouth, because the source is generally assumed to be unbiased and trustworthy, and the information itself often derives from first-hand experience.

In other situations, the consumer might seek out information from the Internet, specialist publications, retailers or even from marketing literature. For example, when buying a car, potential buyers will probably visit competing dealerships to talk to sales staff, look closely at the merchandise and collect brochures. Additionally, they might consult what they consider to be unbiased expert sources of advice such as *What Car?* magazine, and begin to take more notice of car advertisements in all media.

Hauser *et al.* (1993) emphasise the fact that time pressure can interfere with the information search. They found that consumers spend less time searching for different sources as pressure increases. At the other end of the spectrum, however, information overload may cause problems for the potential purchaser. There is evidence to suggest that consumers cannot cope with too much information at product level (Keller and Staelin, 1987). Thus the greater the relevance of the information to consumers, such as describing the key benefits and applications of the product, the easier it is for them to assimilate and process that information as part of their decision-making. In other words, more detailed and more extensive information may actually lead to poorer buying decisions!

■ Information evaluation

On what criteria do you evaluate the information gathered? If you are looking for a new car exhaust system, an online search could generate over 1,000 entries to sift through and even

The information search is made easy with freefone and online access.

Source: C&G.

a typical *Yellow Pages* could provide up to 10 pages of entries featuring over 100 potential outlets within reasonable travelling distance. If you have had no previous experience of any of them, then you have to find a means of differentiating between them. You are unlikely to investigate all of them, since that would take too long, and so you may draw up a shortlist on the basis of those with the biggest feature entries in *Yellow Pages*, those whose names pop up first in an Internet search, or those who also advertise prominently in the local press or on television. Location may also be an important factor; some outlets are closer to home or work than others.

In contrast, looking for chocolate in a supermarket, your information evaluation is likely to be less time consuming and less systematic. Faced with a set of brands of chocolate that are known and liked, the evaluation is cursory: 'What do I feel like eating?' The nearest to systematic thinking might be (in desperation) the evaluation of which one really represents the most chocolate for the price. Of course, if a new brand has appeared on the chocolate shelf, then that might break the habitual, unconscious grabbing at the familiar wrapper, and make a consumer stop and look closely to evaluate what the new product has to offer in comparison with the old ones.

What has been happening to varying degrees in the above examples is that the consumer has started to narrow down from a wide list of potential options to an evoked set (Howard and Sheth, 1969), a final shortlist for serious appraisal. Being a part of the consumer's evoked set, and staying there, is clearly important to the marketer, although it is not always easy. To make a choice from within the evoked set, the consumer needs either a formal or an informal means of selecting from the small number of choices available. This, therefore, implies some definition of evaluative or choice criteria.

Again, marketers will be trying to influence this stage. This can be done, for example, through their communications campaigns which may implant images of products in the consumer's mind so that they seem familiar (and therefore less threatening) at the point of sale. They may also stress particular product attributes, both to increase the importance of that attribute in the consumer's mind, i.e. to make sure that the attribute is number one on the list of evaluative criteria, and to ensure that the consumer believes that a particular brand is unsurpassed in terms of that attribute. Point-of-sale material can also reinforce these things, for example through displays, leaflets, the wording on packaging and on-pack promotions.

Generally, therefore, what is happening is that without necessarily being conscious of it, the potential buyer is constructing a list of performance criteria, then assessing each supplier or available brand against it. This assessment can be based on objective criteria, related to the attributes of the product and its use (price, specification, service, etc.), or subjective criteria such as status, fit with self-image or trust of the supplier.

To make the decision easier, the consumer often adopts mental 'rules of thumb' that cut corners and lead to a faster decision. The consumer is especially prepared to compromise on the quality and thoroughness of assessment when the problem-solving situation is less risky and complicated. They may focus on brand preferences, store choice, pricing, promotion or packaging, and will serve to limit the size of the evoked set and to eliminate some of the options.

■ Decision

The decision may be a natural outcome of the evaluation stage, if one of the options is noticeably more impressive on all the important criteria than the rest. If the choice is not as clear-cut as this, the consumer may have to prioritise the criteria further, perhaps deciding that price or convenience is the one overriding factor. In the car exhaust example, the decision-making is a conscious act, whereas with the impulse purchase of chocolate, the decision may be made almost unconsciously.

In any case, at this stage the consumer must finalise the proposed deal, and this may take place in a retail store, over the telephone, by mail or in the consumer's own home. In the supermarket, finalising the deal may be as simple as putting the bar of chocolate into the trolley with the rest of the shopping and then paying for it at the checkout. With more complex purchases, however, the consumer may have the discretion to negotiate the fine details of cash or credit, any trade-in, order quantity and delivery dates, for example. If the outcome of the negotiation is not satisfactory, then the consumer may regretfully decide not to go ahead with the purchase after all, or go to another supplier – you cannot be certain of your customer until they have either handed over their money or signed the contract!

Suppliers can, of course, make it easy or difficult for potential customers to make their purchases. Lack of sales assistants on the shopfloor, long queues or bureaucratic purchasing procedures may all tax the patience of consumers, giving them time either to decide to shop elsewhere or not to bother buying at all. Even if they do persist and make the purchase (eventually), their impression of the supplier's service and efficiency is going to be damaged and this may influence their repeat purchasing behaviour negatively.

eg   Vending machines make it easy for the consumer to make a decision and take action almost immediately, as long as they have some loose change in their pockets. Despite the sometimes infuriating ability of machines to gobble up coins faster than they are able to dispense goods, the vending industry in the UK alone is worth £2.5bn of which £1bn is generated from refreshment sales. Where impulse purchases are important, such as the confectionery sector in which up to 70 per cent of sales are impulse-led, what is presented, the familiarity of the brand names, and how they are presented can be vital to the sale, thus the growth of chilled and glass-fronted cabinets. New target sectors are being attacked by vending operators to make it easier for you to part with your money whenever and wherever you want. Vending machines for ping-pong balls and swimming hats are popping up in sports centres and you can now buy that desperately needed computer disk from machines in many educational establishments (http://www.ukvending.co.uk).

■ Post-purchase evaluation

The consumer's involvement with the product does not finish when cash changes hands, nor should the marketer's involvement with the consumer. Whatever the purchase, there is likely to be some level of post-purchase evaluation to assess whether the product or its supplier lived up to the expectations raised in the earlier stages of the process. Particularly if the decision process has been difficult, or if the consumer has invested a lot of time, effort and money in it, then there may be doubt as to whether the right decision has actually been made. This is what Festinger (1957) labelled cognitive dissonance, meaning that consumers are 'psychologically uncomfortable', trying to balance the choice made against the doubts still held about it. Such dissonance may be aggravated where consumers are exposed to marketing communication that sings the praises of the features and benefits of the rejected alternatives. Generally speaking, the more alternatives that have been rejected, and the more comparatively attractive those alternatives appear to be, the greater the dissonance. Conversely, the more similar to the chosen product the rejected alternatives are, the less the dissonance. It is also likely that dissonance will occur with more significant purchases, such as extended problem-solving items like cars and houses, because the buyer is far more likely to review and assess the decision consciously afterwards.

Clearly, such psychological discomfort is not pleasant and the consumer will work towards reducing it, perhaps by trying to filter out the messages that undermine the choice made (for example advertising for a product that was a rejected alternative) and paying extra attention to supportive messages (for example advertising for the chosen alternative). This all underlines the need for post-purchase reassurance, whether through advertising, after-sales follow-up calls and even the tone of an instruction manual ('Congratulations on choosing the Acme Home Nuclear Reactor Kit, we know it will give you many years' faithful service . . .'). Consumers like to be reminded and reassured that they have made a wise choice, that they have made the best choice for them. From the marketer's point of view, as well as offering post-purchase reassurance, they can minimise the risk of dissonance by making sure that at the information search and evaluation stages potential buyers gain a realistic picture of the product, its capabilities and its characteristics.

Thus the post-purchase evaluation stage is important for a number of reasons. Primarily, it will affect whether the consumer ever buys this product again. If expectations have not been met, then the product may not even make the shortlist next time. If, on the other hand, expectations have been met or even exceeded, then a strong possibility of lasting loyalty has been created. The next shortlist may be a shortlist of one!

eg Consumer post-purchase evaluation is personal and subjective and can sometimes even lead to an exaggerated perception of a product's benefits. Household antibacterial sprays and germ killers, for example, appear to get things clean, fresh and sparkling. Their advertising and packaging present a confident, no-nonsense image, they promise protection and the total annihilation of dirt and bugs, and their contents often smell strong and powerful. All of these pre- and post-purchase messages, influences and experiences lead some consumers to think that such cleaning products are an adequate substitute for good general kitchen hygiene. Thus 20 per cent of consumers do not change their dishcloths regularly and over 65 per cent do not wash their hands before preparing food. Some experts have criticised manufacturers for lulling them into a false sense of security. Perhaps, the experts say, consumer education should be a much higher priority so that the limits of such products and their proper role within good hygiene practice are better understood (Mintel, 2000b; Norton, 1997).

Monitoring of post-purchase feelings is an important task of marketing, not only to identify areas in which the product (or its associated marketing mix) falls short of expectations, but also to identify any unexpectedly pleasant surprises the purchaser may have had. The product may, for instance, have strengths that are being undersold. This is a natural part of the cycle of product and service development, improvement and evolution.

There are some points to note about the process as presented here. First, the consumer may choose to end the process at any stage. Perhaps the information search reveals that there is no obvious acceptable solution to the problem, or the information evaluation demonstrates that the cost of solving the problem is too high. It is, of course, the marketer's job to sustain the consumer's interest throughout this process and to prevent them from opting out of it. Second, the process does not necessarily have to run from stage 1 to stage 5 in an unbroken flow. The consumer may backtrack at any point to an earlier stage and reiterate the process. Even on the verge of a decision, it may be felt necessary to go back and get more information, just to make sure. Finally, the time taken over the process may vary enormously, depending on the nature of the purchase and the nature of the purchaser. Many months of agonising may go into making an expensive, important purchase, while only a few seconds may be invested in choosing a bar of chocolate. The next section looks more closely at this issue.

Buying situations

In the discussion of the decision-making process, it has been made clear that both the flow and the formality of the process, and the emphasis that is put on each stage, will vary from situation to situation. Some of these variations are to do with the particular environment relevant to the transaction (see pp. 74–76 *et seq.*), while others emanate from the consumer (pp. 77–83 *et seq.*) or from the consumer's immediate social surroundings (pp. 83–91 *et seq.*). The current section, however, will look more closely at the effect of the type of *purchasing situation* on the extent and formality of the decision-making process.

■ Routine problem solving

As the heading of this section implies, a routine problem-solving purchasing situation is one that the consumer is likely to experience on a regular basis. Most grocery shopping falls into this category, where particular brands are purchased habitually without recourse to any lengthy decision-making process. There is virtually no information search and evaluation, and the buying decision is made simultaneously with (if not in advance of) the problem recognition stage. This explains why many FMCG manufacturers spend so much time and effort trying to generate such loyalty and why it is so difficult for new products to break into an established market.

As well as building regular shopping habits, i.e. brand loyalty, the manufacturer is also trying to capitalise on impulse purchasing of many products within this category. While toothpaste and beans can be the objective of a planned shopping trip ('When I go to the supermarket, I need to get . . .'), some other products may be purchased as the result of a sudden impulse. The impulse may be triggered, as mentioned in the previous section, by a realisation of need or by external stimuli, for example eye-catching packaging attracting the shopper's attention. Whatever the trigger, there is no conscious preplanning or information search, but a sudden surge of desire that can only be fulfilled by a purchase that the shopper may or may not later regret.

eg Elior, the French catering company, has built a solid business on serving routine but last-minute purchases. It runs commercial concession catering operations at airports, motorway service areas, railway stations and even museums, all under contract with the infrastructure providers. In France, it is market leader in many categories and now further expansion is planned in the UK and Spain with the Netherlands, Italy and Belgium also on the agenda for market development. In the UK it has teamed up with Hachette to run multi-service stores on 40 railway station forecourts in the south of England, selling train tickets, food, coffee, snacks, magazines and newspapers (Bruce, 2001). The experience from France and elsewhere is that travellers, having purchased their tickets, are vulnerable to a host of other items if they are effectively displayed and even to the smell of fresh coffee. Research suggests that by raising the quality of ambient stimuli, impulse buying can be stimulated (Matilla and Wirtz, 2001).

The items that fall into the routine problem-solving category do tend to be low-risk, low-priced, frequently purchased products. The consumer is happy that a particular brand satisfies their requirements, and there is not enough benefit to be gained from switching brands to make the effort of information search and evaluation of alternatives worthwhile. These so-called low-involvement purchases simply do not carry enough risk, whether measured in terms of financial loss, personal disappointment or damage to social status, for the consumer to get excited about the importance of 'making the right decision'.

■ Limited problem solving

Limited problem solving is a little more interesting for the consumer. This is a buying situation that occurs less frequently and probably involves more deliberate decision-making than routine problems do. The goods will be moderately expensive (in the eyes of the individual consumer) and perhaps will be expected to last a long time. Thus the risks inherent in a 'wrong' decision are that much higher. There will, therefore, be some element of information search and evaluation, but this is still unlikely to absorb too much time and effort.

An example of this could be a consumer's purchase of a new piece of hi-fi equipment. If it is some years since they last bought one, they might feel that they need to update their knowledge of who makes what, who sells what, and the price brackets in this market. The information search is likely to include talking to any friends with recent hi-fi buying experience, and a trip round locally accessible electrical goods retailers. To this particular consumer, this is an important decision, but not a crucial one. If they make a 'wrong' choice (as defined in the post-purchase evaluation stage), they will be disappointed, but will feel that they have spent too much money to allow them simply to discard the offending product. Having said that, provided that the hi-fi fulfils its primary function of producing music on demand, they can learn to live with it and the damage is limited.

Limited problem solving is also likely to occur in the choice of service products. In purchasing a holiday or choosing a dentist (word-of-mouth recommendation?) the consumer has one chance to make the right choice. Once you are on the plane or in the dentist's chair, it is too late and the wrong choice could turn out to be expensive and painful. The necessity to get it right first time is thus likely to lead to a conscious and detailed information search, perhaps even going as far as extended problem solving, to which we now turn.

■ Extended problem solving

Extended problem solving represents a much more serious investment of money, time and effort from the consumer and, consequently, a much higher risk. Purchases of major capital items such as houses or cars fall into this category. These purchases occur extremely infrequently for most people and, given that they often require some kind of a loan, involve a serious long-term commitment. This means that the purchaser is motivated to gather as much information as possible, and to think quite consciously and systematically about what the decision-making criteria should be. That is not to say that the final decision will necessarily be made on purely functional, conscious or rational grounds. If, for example, two different makes of car have similar technical specifications, price, delivery and after-sales service terms, then final differentiation may be in terms of: 'which one will most impress the neighbours?'

■ The significance of buying situations

So what? Why categorise purchases in this way? After all, one consumer's limited problem-solving situation may be another's extended problem. This matters because it may add another dimension to help marketers develop more efficient and appropriate marketing strategies. If a significant group of potential buyers can be defined who clearly regard the purchase of a hi-fi as a limited problem-solving situation, then that has implications for the manufacturers in terms of both how and what to communicate, and where and how to distribute. If consumers are thought to regard a product as a limited problem-solving purchase, then perhaps the marketer will prefer to distribute it through specialist outlets, where the potential buyer can get expert advice, and can spend time making detailed product comparisons. Communication may contain a lot of factual information about technical specifications and product features (i.e. what the product can do), as well as selling product benefits (i.e. what all that means to you). In contrast, the same product as a routine problem-solving exercise may be distributed as widely as possible, to ensure availability, regardless of retailer specialism or expertise, and the communication might centre on product image and benefits, ignoring the detailed information.

Environmental influences

This section is about the wider context in which the decision-making is taking place. All of these environmental influences have already been covered in some depth in Chapter 2, so their treatment here will be brief. What is important is to recognise that decision-making is not completely divorced from the environment in which it is happening, whether the consumer is conscious of it or not.

■ Sociocultural influences

There are many pressures in this category and pp. 83 *et seq.* look at them more closely. Individuals are influenced both by current trends in society as a whole and by a need to conform with the norms of the various social groups to which they belong, as well as to enhance their status within those groups.

In wider society, for example, there has been a move in recent years towards demanding more environmentally friendly products, and many consumers who are not necessarily 'deep green' have allowed this to influence their decision-making, looking more favourably on CFC-free, recycled, non-GM or non-animal-tested products. Examples of social group pressures can be seen in children's markets. Many parents feel unfairly pressured into buying particular goods or brands because the children's friends all have them. There is a fear of the child being marginalised or bullied because they don't possess the 'right' things, whether those are trainers, mountain bikes or computer games.

■ Technological influences

Technology affects many aspects of consumer decision-making. Database technology, for example, as discussed in Chapter 11, allows organisations to create (almost) personal relationships with customers. At its extreme, this means that consumers receive better-tailored personalised offerings, and thus that their expectations are raised in terms of the quality of the product, communication and service.

marketing *in action*

e-woman

The role of women in society and their participation in business and domestic decision-making have changed radically since the 1970s. This is of great interest to marketers as they now find that women have more influence and more spending power. Faith Popcorn is a US futurologist who advises multinational companies on consumer trends and in her view, by 2010, every significant product or service category will be dominated by the companies that succeed in marketing effectively to women. She points to the fact that already in the USA, women make or influence 80 per cent of all consumer, health-care and vehicle purchases, and more than half of all electronic purchases. Similar things are happening in the UK. More women than ever in the UK are earning more than £25,000 and female unemployment is less than half that of men. Building careers also means that women are having babies later in life and thus in the meantime have more confidence and more disposable income to spend on themselves as well as on their families.

Popcorn also argues that women process information differently, yet this does not seem to feature prominently in companies' marketing strategies. This could explain why marketers are finding the gap between what they think they know and actual buying behaviour getting bigger. One area in which they are starting to understand the female psyche better, however, is in Internet marketing. There appear to be distinct differences in the ways in which men and women use the Internet. This is certainly a significant area, well worth understanding: NOP estimates that the UK has nearly 8 million female online users while Jupiter MMXI reports that 42 per cent of UK Internet users are

female. Sun Microsystems has found that, in contrast to men, women tend to visit a limited number of sites but demonstrate a high degree of loyalty. Marketing Director, Louise Proddow said:

The average female surfer goes on-line seven times a week for an average of 54 minutes. Thirty per cent will visit only one or two sites; another 30 per cent will visit only three or four. In view of this, the power of the brand is important (as quoted by Marsh, 2001).

Women also tend to use the Internet for practical reasons, so travel, education and shopping sites feature strongly in their surfing habits. The most popular activity, however, is using the Internet as a communications tool, so chat rooms and e-mail are also well patronised.

Agency Lowe Digital, which monitors women's online usage has similarly found that women use the Internet with a specific purpose in mind, for instance to search for product information. Joy Taylor, Head of e-strategy, said,

Women's purchases online will exceed those of men in the next few years but they will only purchase on sites that give them all the information they need and with which they have a comfort level. Important factors in establishing such a comfort level are prompt replies to specific questions, an easy return policy and clear navigation (as quoted by Marsh, 2001).

iVillage.co.uk is a site designed for women as somewhere they can go to find information and advice. One of the partners behind iVillage.co.uk is Tesco which has promoted the site heavily

both on its own tesco.com website and through in-store promotions centred around women's and family issues. The involvement of Tesco, the UK's biggest retailer with a largely female clientele, is an important element of the site's 'comfort level' and the sense of community created by the chatty and friendly approach helps to create regular repeat visitors. Similarly, handbag.com, another women's portal with which Boots (another female-oriented trusted brand name) is involved, has been able to establish an online community, capitalising successfully on the way women use the Internet. Its Marketing Director said,

Community is important. Discussion boards are among our most popular areas and the people using them are among the most regular visitors to the site. It seems women put more value on user opinions than on the experts. Our brand awareness campaign has tended to highlight our content whether it be how to find the right car, fashion tips, or getting back on your feet after a break-up (as quoted by Marsh, 2001).

Given the increasing importance of women's spending power and influence over buying decisions, sites such as iVillage.co.uk and handbag.com represent a real opportunity for advertisers to reach this key audience and communicate with it in a female-friendly environment and in terms that the audience can comfortably relate to. If Faith Popcorn is to be believed, no company that wants to be dominant in its product or service sector can afford to miss out on this opportunity.

Sources: Marsh (2001); Mazur (2001).

In its wider sense, technology applied to product development and innovation has created whole categories of fast evolving, increasingly cheap consumer 'toys' such as videos, hi-fi formats, camcorders and computer games. Many of these products used to be extended problem-solving goods, but they have moved rapidly towards the limited problem-solving area. As they have become cheaper and more widely available, the amount of risk inherent in the purchase reduces for the consumer, who does not, therefore, need to spend quite so much time searching for and evaluating alternative options.

■ Economic and competitive influences

The 1990s saw recession and economic hardship across Europe and this inevitably affected consumers' attitudes, as well as their ability and willingness to spend. With uncertainty about employment prospects, many consumers postponed purchasing decisions, adjusted their decision-making criteria or cut out certain types of spending altogether. Price, value for money and a conscious assessment of the need to buy become prevalent influences in such circumstances.

Retailers, in turn, had to respond to the slowdown in trade caused by the economic environment. Money-off sales became prevalent in the high street throughout the year, not just in the traditional post-Christmas period. While this did stimulate sales in the short term, it had one unfortunate effect for retailers. Consumers began to see the lower sale price as 'normal' and resented paying full prices, preferring to wait for the next sale that they were confident would come along soon.

In terms of competition, very few purchases, mainly low-involvement decisions, are made without any consideration of the competition. The definition of what constitutes competition, however, is in the mind of the consumer. The supplier of car exhaust systems can be fairly sure that the competition consists of other exhaust dealers and garages. The supplier of chocolate, however, may be in competition not only with other chocolate suppliers but also with cream buns, biscuits and potato crisps. The consumer's consideration of the competition, however it is defined, may be extensive, formal and time consuming, or it may be a cursory glance across the supermarket shelf, just to check. Competitors are vying for the consumer's attention through their packaging, their promotional mix and their mailshots, as well as trying to influence or interrupt the decision-making process. This proliferation of products and communication can either confuse the consumer, leading to brand switching and even less rational decision-making, or provide the consumer with the information and comparators to allow more discerning decision-making.

■ Political and regulatory influences

Political and regulatory influences, emanating either from the EU or from national bodies, can also affect the consumer. Legislation on minimum levels of product safety and performance, for example, means that the consumer does not need to spend time getting technical information, worrying about analysing it and comparing competing products on those criteria. Legislation and regulation, whether they relate to product descriptions, consumer rights or advertising, also reduce the inherent risks of making a decision. This takes some of the pressure off the customer, leading to better-informed and easier decisions and less risk of post-purchase dissonance.

This discussion of the STEP factors is not exhaustive, but simply acts as a reminder that an individual makes decisions within a wider context, created either by society's own dynamics or by the efforts of the market. Having set that context, it is now appropriate to look more closely at the particular influences, internal and external, that affect the individual's buying behaviour and decision-making.

Psychological influences: the individual

Although marketers try to define groups of potential customers with common attributes or interests, as a useful unit for the formulation of marketing strategies, it should not be forgotten that such groups or market segments are still made up of individuals who are different from each other. This section, therefore, looks at aspects that will affect an individual's perceptions and handling of the decision-making process, such as personality, perception, learning, motivation and the impact of attitudes.

■ Personality

Personality, consisting of all the features, traits, behaviours and experiences that make each of us distinctive and unique, is a very extensive and deep area of study. Our personalities lie at the heart of all our behaviour as consumers, and thus marketers try to define the particular personality traits or characteristics prevalent among a target group of consumers, which can then be reflected in the product itself and the marketing effort around it.

In the mid- to late 1980s, advertising in particular was full of images reflecting the personality traits associated with successful lifestyle stereotypes such as the 'yuppie'. Independent, level-headed, ruthless, ambitious, self-centred, materialistic traits were seen as positive characteristics, and thus marketers were anxious to have them associated with users of their products. The 1990s saw a softening of this approach, featuring images oriented more towards caring, concern, family and sharing as the route to self-fulfilment.

With high-involvement products, where there is a strong emotional and psychological link between the product and the consumer, it is relatively easy to see how personality might affect choice and decision-making. In choosing clothing, for instance, an extrovert self-confident achiever with an extravagant streak might select something deliberately avant-garde, stylishly daring, vibrantly coloured and expensive, as a personality statement. A quiet, insecure character, with underdeveloped social skills, might prefer to wear something more sober, more conservative, with less attention-seeking potential.

Overall, however, the link between personality and purchasing, and thus the ability to predict purchasing patterns from personality traits, is at best tenuous. Chisnall (1985) takes the line that personality may influence the decision to buy a certain product type, but not the final brand choice.

■ Perception

Perception represents the way in which individuals analyse, interpret and make sense of incoming information, and is affected by personality, experience and mood. No two people will interpret the same stimulus (whether it is a product's packaging, taste, smell, texture or its promotional messages) in exactly the same way. Even the same individual might perceive the stimulus differently at different times. For example, seeing an advertisement for food when you are hungry is more likely to produce a positive response than seeing the same advertisement just after a heavy meal. Immediate needs are affecting the interpretation of the message. Alternatively, relaxing at home on a Sunday afternoon, an individual is more likely to spend time reading a detailed and lengthy print advertisement than they would if they were flicking through the same magazine during a short coffee break in the working day. Naturally, marketers hope that their messages reach target audiences when they are relaxed, at leisure and at ease with the world, because then the individual is more likely to place a positive interpretation on the message and is less likely to be distracted by other pressures and needs.

Selective attention

Consumers do not pay attention to everything that is going on at once. Attention filters allow the unconscious selection of what incoming information to concentrate on. In daily life we filter out the irrelevant background noise: the hum of the computer, the birds in the garden, the cars in the street, the footsteps in the corridor. As consumers we filter out the irrelevant marketing messages. In reading the newspaper, for instance, a split-second glance spots an advertisement, decides that it is irrelevant and allows the eye to read around it.

This means that marketers have to overcome these filters, either by creating messages that we will decide are relevant or by building attention-grabbing devices into the message. A print advertisement, for example, might use its position on the page, intense colour or startling images to draw the eye, and more importantly the brain, to it.

Selective perception

The problems do not stop once the marketer has got the consumer's attention, since people are infinitely creative in interpreting information in ways that suit them. It is less threatening to interpret things so that they fit nicely and consistently with whatever you already think and feel than to cope with the discomfort of clashes and inconsistency.

One way of creating this consistency or harmony is to allow perception to be coloured by previous experience and existing attitudes. A particularly bad experience with an organisation's offering creates a prejudice that may never be overcome. Whatever positive messages that organisation transmits, the consumer will always be thinking 'Yes, but . . .'. Similarly, a negative attitude towards a subject will make the consumer interpret messages differently. For example, someone who is deeply opposed to nuclear power will try to read between the lines of the industry's advertising and PR, looking for cover-ups and counter-arguments. This can distort the intended message and even reinforce the negative feelings. Conversely, a good experience makes it a lot easier to form positive perceptions. The good experience from the past creates a solid foundation from which to look for the best in the new experience.

Selective retention

Not all stimuli that make it through the attention filters and the machinery of perception and understanding are remembered. Many stimuli are only transitory, hence one of the reasons for the repetition of advertising: if you did not notice it or remember it the first time round, you might pick it up on subsequent occasions. Jogging the memory, by repeating messages or by producing familiar stimuli that the consumer can recognise (such as brand names, packaging design, logos or colour schemes), is therefore an important marketing task to reduce the reliance on the consumer's memory.

People have the capacity to remember what they want to remember and to filter out anything else. The reasons for retaining a particular message may be because it touched them emotionally, or it was of immediate relevance, or it was especially entertaining, or it reinforced previously held views. The reasons are many, but the consumer is under no obligation to remember anything.

■ Learning

Perception and memory are closely linked with learning. Marketers want consumers to learn from marketing materials, so that they know which product to buy and why, and to learn from experience of the product, so that they will buy it again and pass on the message to others.

Learning has been defined by Hilgard and Marquis (1961) as:

> . . . the more or less permanent change in behaviour which occurs as a result of practice.

This implies, from a marketing perspective, that the objective must not only be for the consumer to learn something, but also for them to remember what has been learned and to act on it. Therefore advertising materials, for instance, are carefully designed to maximise the learning opportunity. A 30-second television advertisement selling car insurance over the phone repeats the freephone number four times and has it written across the bottom of the screen so that the viewer is likely to remember it. Demonstrating a product benefit in an advertisement also helps consumers to learn what they are supposed to notice about the product when they use it. Showing a product in a particular usage context, or associating it with certain types of people or situations, gives the consumer guidelines about what attitudes to develop towards the product.

Humour, and other methods of provoking an emotional response to an advertisement, can also help a message to stick because the recipient immediately becomes more involved in the process. Similarly, associating a product with something familiar that itself evokes certain emotions can allow those feelings to be transferred to the product. Thus the advertisements for Andrex that feature puppies have helped the British public to learn to think of toilet paper as warm, soft, cuddly and harmless rather than embarrassing.

■ Motivation

One definition of marketing puts the emphasis on the satisfaction of customers' needs and wants, but what triggers those needs and wants, and what drives consumers towards their fulfilment? Motives for action, the driving forces, are complex and changeable and can be difficult to research, since individuals themselves often cannot define why they act the way they do, and at different times, different motivations might take priority and have more influence over the individual's behaviour.

Maslow's (1954) *hierarchy of needs* has long been used as a framework for classifying basic motivations. Five groups of needs, as shown in Figure 3.2, are stacked one on top of another and form a progression. Having achieved satisfaction on the lowest level, the individual can progress to strive to achieve the goals of the next level up. This model does have a certain logic behind it, and the idea, for instance, that true self-actualisation can only grow from solid foundations of security and social acceptance seems reasonable. However, the model was developed in the context of US capitalist culture, where achievement and self-actualisation are often ends in themselves. It is questionable how far these motives can be extended to other cultural contexts.

Examples of consumer behaviour and marketing activity can be found to fit all five levels.

Physiological needs

Basic feelings such as hunger and thirst can be potent driving forces. After a strenuous game of squash, the immediate craving for liquid overrides normal considerations of brand

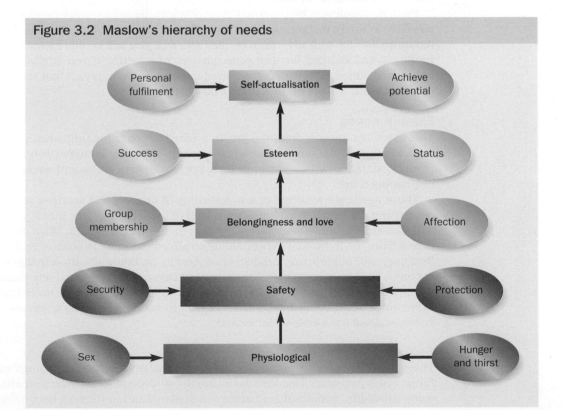

Figure 3.2 Maslow's hierarchy of needs

preference. If the sports centre shop only has one type of soft drink in stock, then it will do. Similarly, seasoned shoppers are well aware of the dangers of visiting a supermarket when they are hungry: so much more seems to go into the trolley.

Marketers can capitalise on such feelings. The soft drink manufacturer can ensure that the sports centre stocks that brand and that the product image reflects refreshment and thirst-quenching properties. The food manufacturer can advertise at a time of day when the audience is likely to be feeling hungry so that they are more likely to pay attention to the message and remember it.

Safety needs

Once the individual has taken care of the basic necessities of life: food, drink and warmth, the need for self-protection and long-term survival emerges. In modern Western societies this may be interpreted as the desire for a secure home, protected against intrusion and other dangers (floods and fire, for example). It might also cover the desire for health care, insurance services and consumer protection legislation.

The car market in particular has focused on safety needs as a marketing platform. Driving is an inherently dangerous activity, so the manufacturers try to reassure us that their cars are as safe as possible. Various manufacturers have featured side impact bars, air bags and/or anti-lock braking systems in their advertising, showing how these either protect you or help to prevent accidents.

Safety needs in terms of health protection feature strongly in the marketing strategies of products such as bleaches and toilet cleaners. The kind of approach used often appeals to the mother who takes responsibility for safeguarding the health and well-being of the whole family. The threat from bacteria can be eliminated by choosing the right cleanser.

Belongingness and love needs

This is about emotional security, wanting to feel accepted and valued by those closest to you. Marketers again play on this need through the portrayal of the family in particular. Over many years, advertising told women that they would be better appreciated and loved as wives and mothers if they did their washing in Persil, cooked with Oxo or fed their husbands cornflakes for breakfast.

Fear of loneliness or personal rejection can be a powerful motivator and features strongly in many marketing campaigns. Toiletries such as deodorants, toothpastes and mouthwashes have all advertised on the basis that you will be more lovable if you use these products, and showing the dire consequences of rejection if you don't. Even anti-smoking campaigns aimed at teenagers have tried this approach, implying that the smell of tobacco on your breath will put off prospective boy/girlfriends.

Esteem needs

This extends outwards from the previous stage to cover the individual's need for success, status and good opinion within wider society. This may include professional status and respect, standing within social groups, such as sports clubs and societies, or 'what the neighbours think'.

These needs are reflected in a wide variety of product and services marketing. Most car advertising, for example, contains some kind of message implying that if you drive this car it will somehow enhance your status and gain the respect of others. More overtly, esteem can derive from the individual's sheer ability to afford the most expensive and exclusive items. Perfumes and other luxury products play heavily on the implication that you are a discerning and elite buyer, a cut above the rest, and that using these products makes a statement about who you are and the status you hold. Brand names such as Rolls-Royce, Gucci and Rolex have acquired such a cachet that simply saying 'she owns a genuine Rolex' speaks volumes about a person's social status.

Self-actualisation needs

This is the ultimate goal, the achievement of complete satisfaction through successfully fulfilling one's potential. That may mean anything, depending on who you are and what you want out of life. Some will only achieve self-actualisation through becoming the head of a multinational organisation, while others will find it through the successful raising of a happy and healthy family. This is a difficult stage for the marketer to handle, because it is so individual, and thus the hope is that by fulfilling the other needs discussed above, the marketer can help to propel the individual towards self-actualisation. Only the individual can tell, however, when this stage has been reached.

Generally in Western economies the fulfilment of the very basic needs can be taken for granted, however. Real physiological hunger, thirst and lack of safety do not exist for most people. Manufacturers of food products, for instance, cannot therefore assume that just because their product alleviates hunger it will be purchased and accepted. Any one of hundreds of food brands can do that, and thus the consumer is looking to see how a particular product can fulfil a higher-order need, such as love or esteem. Consequently, foods are often marketed on the basis that your family will enjoy it and love you more for providing it (Oxo, for example) or because your dinner party guests will be impressed (Viennetta or After Eights, for example). The emphasis, therefore, is largely on the higher-order needs (belongingness and love, esteem and self-actualisation).

■ Attitudes

As implied at p. 78 above, an attitude is a stance that an individual takes on a subject that predisposes him/her to react in a certain way to that subject. More formally, an attitude has been defined by Hilgard *et al.* (1975) as:

> . . . *an orientation towards or away from some object, concept or situation and a readiness to respond in a predetermined manner to these related objects, concepts or situations.*

Thus in marketing terms, consumers can develop attitudes to any kind of product or service, or indeed to any aspect of the marketing mix, and these attitudes will affect behaviour. All of this implies that attitudes play an important part in influencing consumer judgement, whether through perception, evaluation, information processing or decision-making. Attitudes play a key role in shaping learning and while they are fluid, evolving over time, they are nevertheless often difficult to change.

Williams (1981), in summarising the literature, describes attitudes as having three different components.

Cognitive
Cognitive attitudes relate to beliefs or disbeliefs, thus: 'I believe that margarine is healthier than butter.' This is a component that the marketer can work on through fairly straightforward advertising. Repeating the message that your product is healthy, or that it represents the best value for money, may well establish an initial belief in those qualities.

Affective
Affective attitudes relate to feelings of a positive or negative nature, involving some emotional content, thus: 'I *like* this product' or 'This product makes me *feel* . . .'. Again, advertising can help the marketer to signal to the consumer why they should like it, or how they should feel when they use it. For some consumers, of course, affective attitudes can overcome cognitive ones. For example, I may believe that margarine is healthier than butter, but I buy butter because I like the taste better. Similarly, I believe that snacking on chocolate is 'bad', but it cheers me up so I do it anyway.

Conative
Conative attitudes relate to the link with behaviour, thus attitude x is considered likely to lead to behaviour y. This is the hardest one for marketers to predict or control, because so many things can prevent behaviour from taking place, even if the cognitive and affective attitudes are positive: 'I believe that BMWs are excellent quality, reliable cars, and I feel that owning one would enhance my status and provide me with many hours of pleasurable driving, but I simply cannot afford it,' or it may even be that 'Audi made me a better offer'.

It is this last link between attitude and behaviour that is of most interest to marketers. Fishbein (1975) developed a model based on the proposition that in order to predict a specific behaviour, such as a brand purchase, it is important to measure the individual's attitude towards performing that behaviour, rather than just the attitude towards the product in question. This fits with the BMW example above, where the most important thing is not the attitude to the car itself, but the attitude towards *purchasing* the car. As long as the attitude to purchasing is negative, the marketer still has work to do.

Attitudes can thus involve feelings (positive or negative), knowledge (complete or partial) and beliefs. A particular female consumer might believe that she is overweight. She knows that cream cakes are fattening, but she likes them. All these things come together to form her attitude towards cream cakes (wicked, but seductive) and her behaviour when confronted by one (five minutes wrestling with her conscience before giving in completely and buying two, knowing that she will regret it later). An advertising campaign for cream cakes, centred around the slogan 'naughty but nice', capitalised brilliantly on what is a common attitude, almost legitimising the guilt and establishing an empathy with the hopeless addict. The really admirable thing about that campaign was that the advertiser did not even attempt to overturn the attitude.

It is possible, but very difficult, to change attitudes, particularly when they are well established and deeply ingrained. The nuclear industry, for example, has been trying to overcome hostile and suspicious attitudes with an integrated campaign of advertising, PR and site visits (http://www.bnfl.co.uk). Many people have indeed been responsive to this openness, and have been prepared to revise attitudes to a greater or lesser extent. There will, however, always be a hard core who will remain entrenched and interpret any 'positive' messages in a negative way.

There is a difference between attitudes that relate to an organisation's philosophy, business ethics or market and those that centre around experience of an organisation's specific product or service. An organisation that has a bad reputation for its employment practices, its environmental record or its dealings with suspect foreign regimes will have created negative attitudes that will be extremely difficult to overturn. Similarly, companies operating in certain markets, such as nuclear power, tobacco and alcohol, will never redeem themselves in the eyes of significant groups of the public. People care too much about such things to be easily persuaded to change their outlook. In contrast, negative feelings about a specific product or brand are more amenable to change through skilful marketing.

eg

Skoda is a remarkable example of how negative attitudes can be tackled head-on with some success. Surely we all remember a few Skoda jokes from over 10 years ago, for example, 'why does the Skoda have a heated rear window? To keep your hands warm while you push it'. The communist era in Czechoslovakia meant that the Skoda had become cheap and cheerful but with a terrible reputation matched only by Lada's.

In 1991, VW took over Skoda and after investment in retooling, building a quality culture, using components in common with VW brands, and a fresh approach to design, Skoda products improved beyond recognition (Mudd, 2000; Kimberley, 2001). The trouble is that consumers were slow to believe it. In the UK, Skoda found that offering a quality product was not enough and sales development was disappointing. Not to be beaten, rather than adopting a eurobland advertising approach for the new Fabia supermini, with a focus on benefits, styling and features, the UK operation decided to tackle the problem by addressing the negative attitudes head-on. The television advertisements featured a car transporter delivery to a Skoda garage. When the unloading was about to begin, the transporter driver changed his mind and drove off – after all such great cars couldn't be destined for a Skoda dealership (they were!). In a similar vein, an apologetic car worker refuses to accept that the Skoda marque could possibly belong on such a stylish car (it was a Skoda). The overall theme was we've changed the car, now can you change your mind? The self-deprecating humour meant that the advertisement stood out (Simms, 2001).

There is still a long way to go. Negative attitudes are hard to shake off. By the end of the Fabia campaign, however, the number of people who would not buy a Skoda in the UK dropped from 60 to 42 per cent and sales had risen by one-third. In 2001, the campaign was a Marketing Society award winner (*Marketing*, 2001b).

As the cream cake example quoted earlier shows, defining attitudes can provide valuable insights into target groups of customers and give a basis for communication with them. Measuring feelings, beliefs and knowledge about an organisation's products and those of its competitors is an essential part of market research (see Chapter 5), leading to a more effective and appealing marketing mix.

In summary, the individual is a complex entity, under pressure to take in, analyse and remember many marketing messages in addition to the other burdens of daily life. Marketers need to understand how individuals think and why they respond in particular ways, if they are going to develop marketing offerings that cut through defence mechanisms and create loyal customers. Individuals' behaviour, however, is not only shaped in accordance with their personalities, abilities, analytical skills, etc., as discussed above, but also affected by wider considerations, such as the sociocultural influences that will be discussed next.

Sociocultural influences: the group

Individuals have membership of many social groups, whether these are formally recognised social units such as the family, or informal intangible groupings such as reference groups (see pp. 87 *et seq.*). Inevitably, purchasing decisions will be affected by group membership, as these sociocultural influences may help the individual to:

1 differentiate between essential and non-essential purchases;
2 prioritise purchases where resources are limited;
3 define the meaning of the product and its benefits in the context of their own lives; and thus to
4 foresee the post-purchase implications of this decision.

All of these things imply that the individual's decision has as much to do with 'What other people will think' and 'How I will look if I buy this' as with the intrinsic benefits of the product itself. Marketers have, of course, capitalised on this natural wish to express oneself and gain social acceptance through one's consumption habits, both as a basis for psychographic or lifestyle segmentation (which will be discussed later on pp. 117 *et seq.*) and for many years as a basis of fear appeals in advertising.

The following subsections look more closely at some of these sociocultural influences.

■ Social class

Social class is a form of stratification that attempts to structure and divide a society. Some argue that egalitarianism has become far more pronounced in the modern Europe, making any attempts at social distinction ill-founded, if not meaningless. Nevertheless, today social class is established largely according to occupation, and for many years, British marketers have used the grading system outlined in Table 3.1. It has been widely used to group consumers, whether for research or for analysing media readership.

eg The growth of the 'middle class' in the UK will probably mean the end of the official six-class structure adopted since 1921, as shown in Table 3.1. Government statistics suggest that half the UK population are now in the middle class and thus the old groupings are too broad and no longer meaningful. The new 'official' social classification introduced in 1998 has 17 categories, based not only on occupation (as in the old system) but also on the size of an individual's employing organisation and the type of contract, fringe benefits and job security that individual enjoys. It also takes into account how much the employer values that individual. These extra factors make a big difference. Looking only at occupation and income, the top social groups earn twice as much as the bottom ones. Accounting for the extra factors, however, makes the top groups seven times more affluent.

Table 3.1 UK socio-economic groupings

% of population	Group	Social status	Occupation of head of household
3	A	Upper middle	Higher managerial, administrative or professional
14	B	Middle	Intermediate managerial, administrative or professional
27	C1	Lower middle	Supervisory or clerical, junior managerial, administrative or professional
25	C2	Skilled working	Skilled manual workers
19	D	Working	Semi-skilled and unskilled manual workers
12	E	Those at lowest level of subsistence	State pensioners or widows, casual or lowest-grade workers

This is perhaps a much more realistic way of defining socioeconomic groups. Under the new scheme, those who acquire 'better' status include large-company managers, teachers, policemen and nurses. Those who slide down the scale, however, include shop assistants, plumbers and traffic wardens. For the marketer, the new system creates smaller, more clearly defined and currently relevant groups for targeting purposes. It still does not, however, get into the mind of consumers or explain their buying behaviour. Does all of this matter? Perhaps it does, as long as the top groups are up to seven times more affluent than the bottom ones (Henderson, 1997; Norton, 1998).

However, fundamental problems can be found in attempting to link consumer behaviour with social class. The usefulness of such systems is limited. They rely on the occupation of the head of the household (more correctly called the main income earner), but fail to put that into the context of the rest of the household. Dual income households are becoming increasingly common, with the second income having a profound effect on the buying behaviour of both parties, yet most of these systems fail to recognise this. They tell very little about the consumption patterns or attitudes that are of such great use to the marketer. The disposable income of a C2 class household may be just as high as that of an A or B household, and they may have certain upmarket tastes in common. Furthermore, two households in the A or B categories could easily behave very differently. One household might consider status symbols to be important and indulge in conspicuous consumption, whereas the other might have rejected materialistic values and be seeking a cleaner, less cluttered lifestyle. These contrasting outlooks on life make an enormous difference to buying behaviour and choices, hence the necessity for psychographic segmentation (see pp. 117 et seq.) to provide marketers with more meaningful frameworks for grouping customers.

■ Culture and subculture

Culture can be described as the personality of the society within which an individual lives. It manifests itself through the built environment, art, language, literature, music and the products that society consumes, as well as through its prevalent beliefs, value systems and government. As summarised by Chisnall (1985), culture is the total way of life of a society, passed on from generation to generation, deriving from a group of people sharing and transmitting beliefs, values, attitudes and forms of behaviour that are common to that society and considered worthy of retention. Breaking that definition down further, Figure 3.3 shows diagrammatically the influences that create culture.

Cultural differences show themselves in very different ways. Although eating, for example, is a basic natural instinct, what we eat and when is heavily influenced by the culture in which we are brought up. Thus in Spain it is normal to begin lunch at 4 p.m. and then have dinner after 10 p.m., while in Poland most restaurants would be closing down at those times. Similarly, lunch in Central Europe would almost certainly include sauerkraut, but little fish compared with the wide variety offered on a typical Spanish menu. Even the propensity for eating out may be a cultural factor.

Of course, culture goes much further in prescribing and describing the values and beliefs of a society. It influences shopping hours, with many Mediterranean supermarkets open for far longer hours in the evening than some of their northern European counterparts; the beliefs associated with advertising messages and symbols; the lifestyles of the inhabitants; and the products that are more or less acceptable and available in that culture, for example try purchasing an electric kettle in Spain or Italy.

Culture is thus very important for the marketer to understand, first because marketing can only exist within a culture that is prepared to allow it and support it, and second, it has to act within boundaries set by society and culture. Over the past 20 years or so, for example, it has become more and more socially unacceptable in Europe for organisations to use animals for testing cosmetics. Society has informally rewritten one of the rules and marketers have had to respond. Changing attitudes to tobacco, alcohol and marketing to children are also examples of areas within which cultural change is altering organisations' approaches to business. In the UK, for instance, food marketers have been criticised for aiming too much advertising of products such as sweets, soft drinks, sugary cereals, crisps and fast foods at children. These kinds of product are thought to be of dubious nutritional value, if consumed in excess, and are also thought to be contributing to an increase in dental decay and obesity among children.

Figure 3.3 Influences on culture

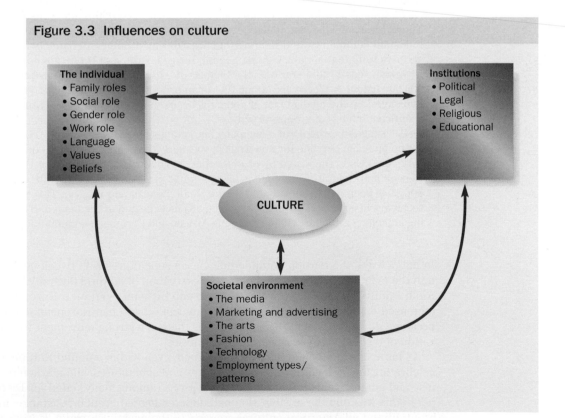

Any culture can be divided into a number of subcultures, each with its own specific characteristics, yet existing within the whole. It depends on the onlooker's perspective just how detailed a division is required. An American exporter might say that Europe represents a culture (as distinct from the US culture), with British, French, German and other national subcultures existing within it. Dealing with the home market, however, a German marketer would define Germany, or increasingly the German-speaking territories of Europe, as the dominant culture, with significant subcultures held within it. These subcultures could be based on ethnic origin (Turkish, Polish, Asian or whatever), religious beliefs, or more lifestyle-oriented groupings, defined by the values and attitudes held. Language may also be an important determinant of subculture. In Switzerland, for example, the three main languages reflect different customs, architecture and even external orientations. The Ticino region (Italian speaking) probably identifies itself more closely with Milan than Zurich or Basle as a point of cultural reference.

eg It has been argued that companies are ignoring the full potential of ethnic community groups in the UK by not addressing them properly. Ethnic communities account for nearly 5.5 per cent of the UK population and are growing by 2 or 3 per cent per year, yet do not appear to be well targeted by companies. It is an important omission: the Commission for Racial Equality (CRE) estimates that by 2020, ethnic communities will account for 10 per cent of the UK population and their spending power is estimated to be around £15bn. Research has shown that only 20 per cent of companies think that they target ethnic communities effectively, and 29 per cent are prepared to admit that they do not attempt to reach them at all. Some 25 per cent do not seek feedback from ethnic minorities in focus group research.

Nevertheless, there are advantages to be gained from acknowledging and addressing the specific needs and cultural influences on ethnic groups. It is a complex task. The Asian community, for example, is not in itself homogeneous. There are wide differences in language, religion, country of origin and attitudes. This is reflected in the proliferation of specialist media serving the Asian market. It is targeted by 15 digital TV channels. The four biggest (Zee, Sony, B4U and StarTV) have access to nearly 300,000 Asian households in the UK. There are specialist channels, such as Prime TV, serving the 40,000 households of the Pakistani community, and Reminiscent TV, offering a range of channels for its 15,000 subscribers from the Punjabi, Gujarati, Tamil, Bengali, Urdu and Hindu communities. There are five main Asian radio stations, the biggest of which, Sunrise Radio in London, has about 300,000 listeners. There are about 100 Asian press titles, 20 per cent of which are in Asian languages. So the media exist, if companies can come up with the right messages, to reach significant ethnic subgroups directly.

BT is a good example of a company marketing successfully to ethnic communities. It has set up an Asian helpline for non-English speakers to call for information on BT products and services. This is supported by product-specific advertising targeting the Punjabi, Pakistani, Bengali and Gujarati communities using a range of Asian print and radio media. Advertising copy has been written in Gujarati, Urdu, Hindi, Bengali and English. This led to the helpline receiving 1,000 calls per week, twice as many as expected at the launch. BT is also considering launching a similar scheme targeting African and Caribbean communities (Curtis, 2001).

In many ways, the tension within ethnic-based subcultures is between cultural assimilation into the main, dominant culture and the preservation of cultural diversity in language, dress, food, family behaviour, etc. This tension can be seen even on a European scale, where increased emphasis on travel, rapid communication and pan-European marketing is slowly breaking down barriers at the same time as there is a strong movement towards the preservation of distinct national and regional identities.

As far as the immediate future is concerned, even within a united Europe, people are still celebrating and defending their own cultures and subcultures, and marketers need to recognise and empathise with this. One of the reasons (among many) cited for Disneyland Paris's poor start was that the organisation had underestimated French resistance, in particular, to an undiluted all-American cultural concept in the heart of Europe. Europeans are happy, and indeed eager, to experience Disney on US soil as part of 'the American experience', but cannot accept it, it would appear, within their own culture (http://www.disney.go.com).

Subculture need not only be an ethnic phenomenon, however. The existence of a youth subculture, spanning international boundaries, is widely accepted by marketers, and media such as MTV that reach right across Europe allow marketers to communicate efficiently and cost-effectively with that subculture. Brands such as Coca-Cola, Pepsi and Pepe Jeans can create messages that capitalise on the common concerns, interests and attitudes that define this subculture. The core messages strike at something different from, and perhaps deeper than, national or ethnic culture, and thus may have pan-European currency without necessarily becoming bland in the process. That is not to say that all 16–25-year-olds across Europe should be stereotyped as belonging to a homogeneous 'yoof market'. What it does say is that there are certain attitudes and feelings with which this age group are likely to sympathise, and that these can therefore be used as a foundation for more targeted communication that manages to celebrate both commonalities and differences.

eg Some advertising agencies deliberately try to appeal to 15–25-year-olds with themes that some seniors could find offensive and shocking. French Connection UK, or FCUK for short, has been an outstanding success in the clothing retail sector at the same time that Marks & Spencer has been under strain. Although the marketing offering has to be right, the full-frontal use of the FCUK acronym means any advertising, especially on posters, is likely to get noticed. Since 1997, FCUK has had a few run-ins with the ASA, with some of its advertisements approved and some condemned. Poster themes such as 'fcuk fashion', 'fcuk advertising' met with disapproval, while T-shirts with such themes as 'French Connection me' and 'my place now' along with the FCUK trademark slipped through. To French Connection, it is all meant to be a bit of fun, worth a smile. It could be claimed it was pure coincidence, but the reader is left in no doubt as to the innuendo and FCUK has effectively taken ownership of the f-word (Broadbent, 2001).

The most recent campaign theme, however, met with particular disapproval. Fcukinkybugger.com generated 132 complaints despite being shown on only 13 road sites in London. Of particular concern was the danger of the poster being misread by children. The poster was, therefore, deemed offensive and furthermore, it was decided that for a period of two years, all FCUK posters should be pre-vetted for taste (*Marketing*, 2001a). To French Connection, however, its campaigns simply reflect the mood of the target audience rather than the attitudes and values of the wider population.

■ Reference groups

Reference groups are any groups, whether formally or informally constituted, to which an individual either belongs or aspires to belong, for example professional bodies, social or hobby-oriented societies, or informal, vaguely defined lifestyle groups ('I want to be a yuppie'). There are three main types of reference group, each of which affects buying behaviour, and these are discussed in turn below.

Membership groups

These are the groups to which the individual already belongs. These groups provide parameters within which individuals make purchasing decisions, whether they are conscious of it or not. In buying clothing, for example, the purchaser might think about the occasion for which it is going to be worn and consider whether a particular item is 'suitable'. There is great concern here about what other people will think.

Buying clothes for work is severely limited by the norms and expectations imposed by colleagues (a membership group) and bosses (an aspirant group?), as well as by the practicalities of the workplace. Similarly, choosing clothes for a party will be influenced by the predicted impact on the social group who will be present: whether they will be impressed; whether the wearer will fit in; whether the wearer will seem to be overdressed or underdressed; or whether anyone else is likely to turn up in the same outfit.

Thus the influence of membership groups on buying behaviour is to set standards to which individuals can conform, thus consolidating their position as group members. Of course, some individuals with a strong sense of opinion leadership will seek to extend those standards by exceeding them and challenging the norms with the expectation that others will follow.

Aspirant groups

These are the groups to which the individual would like to belong, and some of these aspirations are more realistic than others. An amateur athlete or musician might aspire to professional status in their dreams, even if they have little talent. An independent professional single female might aspire to become a full-time housewife with a husband and three children; the housewife might aspire to the career and independent lifestyle. A young, junior manager might aspire to the middle management ranks.

People's desire for change, development and growth in their lives is natural, and marketers frequently exploit this in the positioning of their products and the subtle promises they make. Bird's Eye frozen meals will not stop you being a bored housewife, but will give you a little more independence to 'be yourself'; buying Nike, Reebok or Adidas sports gear will not make you into Ronaldo, Beckham or Figo, but you can feel a little closer to them.

The existence of aspirant groups, therefore, attracts consumers towards products that are strongly associated with those groups and will either make it appear that the buyer actually belongs to the group or signal the individual's aspirations to the wider world.

Dissociative groups

These are groups to which the individual does not want to belong or to be seen to belong. A supporter of the England soccer team would not wish to be associated with its notorious hooligan element, for example. Someone who had a violent aversion to 'yuppies' and their values might avoid buying products that are closely associated with them, through fear of being thought to belong to that group. An upmarket shopper might prefer not to be seen in a discount store such as Aldi or Netto just in case anyone thinks they are penny pinching.

Clearly, these dissociations are closely related to the positive influences of both membership and aspirational groups. They are simply the other side of the coin, an attempt to draw closer to the 'desirable' groups, while differentiating oneself from the 'undesirable'.

■ Family

The family, whether two parent or single parent, nuclear or extended, with or without dependent children, remains a key influence on the buying behaviour of individuals. The needs of the family affect what can be afforded, where the spending priorities lie and how a purchasing decision is made. All of this evolves as the family matures and moves through the various stages of its life cycle. Over time, the structure of a family changes, for example as children grow older and eventually leave home, or as events break up families or create new ones. This means that a family's resources and needs also change over time, and that the marketer must understand and respond to these changes.

Traditionally, marketers have looked to the family life cycle as proposed by Wells and Gubar (1966), and shown in Table 3.2. Over the years, however, this has become less and less appropriate, as it reflects a path through life that is becoming less common in the West. It does not, for example, allow for single-parent families, created either voluntarily or through divorce, or for remarriage after divorce which may create new families with children coming together from previous marriages, and/or second families. Other trends too undermine the assumptions of the traditional model of the family life cycle. According to Lightfoot and Wavell (1995), estimates from the Office of Population Censuses and Surveys (OPCS) in the UK forecast that 20 per cent of women born in the 1960s, 1970s and 1980s may never have children. Those who do currently elect to have children are tending to leave childbearing until later in their lives, so that they can establish their careers first. At the other end of the spectrum, the number of single, teenage mothers has increased alarmingly in the UK to 3 per cent of girls aged 15–19, the highest figure in the EU.

All of these trends have major implications for consumers' needs and wants at various stages in their lives, as well as for their disposable incomes. The marketer cannot make trite assumptions based on traditional stereotypes of the nuclear family, and something more

Table 3.2 The family lifecycle

Stage	Title	Characteristics
1	Bachelor	Young, single, not living at home
2	Newly married	Young, no children
3	Full nest I	Youngest child under 6
4	Full nest II	Youngest child 6 or over
5	Full nest III	Older, married with dependent children
6	Empty nest I	Older married, no children living at home
7	Empty nest II	Older married, retired, no children living at home
8	Solitary survivor I	In labour force
9	Solitary survivor II	Retired

Source: Wells and Gubar (1966).

complex than the Wells and Gubar model is needed to reflect properly the various routes that people's lives can now take. Figure 3.4 offers a revised family life cycle for the way people live today.

Regardless of the structure of the family unit, members of a household can participate in each other's purchasing decision-making. In some cases, members may be making decisions that affect the whole family, and thus Figure 3.5 shows how a family can act as a decision-making unit where individual members play different roles in reaching the final decision. The roles that any one member takes on will vary from purchase to purchase, as will the length, complexity and formality of the process. The obvious manifestation of the family decision-making unit is in the ordinary week-to-week grocery shopping. The main shopper is not acting as an individual, pleasing only themselves by their choices, but is reflecting the tastes and requirements of a group of people. In a stereotypical family, Mother may be the ultimate decider and purchaser in the supermarket, but the rest of the family may have

Figure 3.4 A modern family lifecycle model

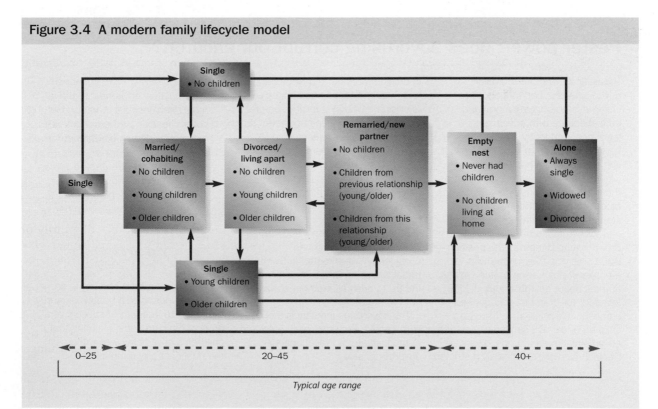

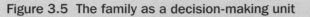
Figure 3.5 The family as a decision-making unit

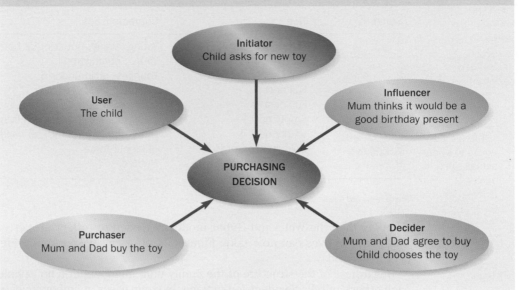

acted as initiators ('When you go shopping, will you get me some . . .?' or 'Do you know that we've run out of . . .?' or 'Can we try that new brand of . . .?') or influencers ('If you buy THAT, don't expect ME to eat it'), either before the shopping trip or at the point of sale.

The buying roles may be undertaken by different family members for different purchases at different times. Thus in the example of purchasing a bicycle, a child may well be the user and influencer, but the parents may be the principal deciders and buyers.

corporate social responsibility *in action*

Pester power: does advertising corrupt our children?

The issue of whether television advertising is a 'bad influence' on children is an ongoing moral and ethical debate with advertisers, legislators and lobby groups often having very different points of view. It is a debate which has become more urgent and more heated, however, as the advertising industry across Europe faces moves to harmonise and standardise regulations across all EU member states in the 2002 Broadcasting Directive. The position in 2001 was very fragmented with member states having a wide variety of rules about advertising to children. Sweden, for example, had banned all domestic television advertising to children under 12; similarly, television advertising aimed at under-12s was illegal in Norway, and heavily restricted

in Belgium, Ireland, the Netherlands and Austria. Greece had banned all television advertising for toys before 10 p.m. Italy and Denmark were considering their positions. The UK was not heavily regulated although advertisers were not supposed to encourage children to pester their parents to get them things (but then a clever advertiser can find indirect ways of generating desire . . .). Fear that regulations on children's advertising were going to be tightened considerably were rooted in Sweden's threat to use its 2001 Presidency of the EU to push all member states to opt for a total ban.

The advertising industry is feeling a bit paranoid. Rupert Howell, president of the Institute of Practitioners in Advertising, said,

The EU is having more impact on the regulatory environment and is more interventionist than our own government. . . . Advertising is very high profile and an easy target for anyone wanting to score some quick points. We are also up against pressure groups and single issue fanatics. They work hard to attack us, so we have to work even harder to protect our interests. If we don't, we will be hit with more restrictions – it's easy, gesture politics (as quoted by Curtis, 2000).

Those against a total ban argue on moral grounds, that a ban would curb their right to freedom of speech, and on economic grounds, claiming that if children's advertising was withdrawn, the quality of programming would deteriorate through lack of funding, choice would be restricted, and the price of children's products would go up. In terms of morality versus economics, the cynics argue that while many of the regulations around the EU have been enforced in the name of ethics, in reality, they are simply designed to protect domestic business interests and stifle competition.

The pro-advertising lobby also points to evidence that there is actually little difference in the perceived effects of pester power in Sweden (with a total ban in place) and Spain (without). Research by NOP found that pester power was a bigger problem in Sweden than in Spain. An additional finding, that in-store promotions were seen as more of a problem in Sweden than in Spain gives more ammunition to the pro-advertisers. They argue that if television advertising is banned, then marketers will find other ways of communicating with children, through in-store promotions, for instance, where kids can get their hands on toys and games and be subjected to a much more interactive, hard sell than a 30-second television advertisement could ever hope to achieve. One consultant said,

Activity will be more visible, more interactive, more colourful and noisier as brands try to encourage pester power. POP [point of purchase promotions] will have to be more interesting because it will have to sell harder against more competition (as quoted by Anderson, 1999).

Nevertheless, there are also those who feel that POP activity is actually a more responsible choice because parents are likely to be there as gatekeepers and they can see exactly what the toy is, assess how their child plays with it and then make an informed purchasing decision. This view, perhaps naïvely, does tend to assume that a child will take 'no' for an answer, and fails to take into account the sheer erosion of adult resolve that a determined child can achieve with persistent pester power.

Evidence does exist that television does have a marked effect on pester power. A UK study looking at children's viewing of advertisements for toys and games in the run-up to Christmas found that prolonged exposure to adverts in November and December dramatically increased children's demands, as expressed in their letters to Santa Claus. Those who were exposed to the most advertising asked for far more branded toys. A similar study in Sweden, where advertisers are banned from marketing at children under 12, found that they wanted significantly fewer toys than UK children did. There is some good news for UK parents, though: children who watched television with a parent were far less demanding. Watching with a parent seemed to make children less vulnerable because an adult could help to teach them the difference between adverts and programmes. One of the researchers made the point that,

A society which exposes young children to many thousands of adverts every year also has a duty to educate those children in consumer literacy and critical viewing (as quoted by *The Daily Telegraph*, 2001).

The critical role that parents must play is endorsed by Adrian Furnham, Professor of Psychology at University College London. His extensive studies have concluded that the cause of pester power is not advertising but 'irresponsible parenting'. In his view, parents need to adopt an 'authoritarian' approach, where rules are established, expectations are managed and decisions are explained, all with the child's point of view kept in mind.

Sources: Anderson (1999); Curtis (2000); *The Daily Telegraph* (2001); *Evening Standard* (2000); Oaff (2001).

Children are an important target group for the marketer, partly because of their ability to pester their parents and influence family purchasing, and partly because of the marketer's desire to create brand loyalty as early as possible in consumers' lives. For instance, Kellogg's gave away 800,000 sample packs of Choco Krispies, while McDonald's provides free meal vouchers to be used as prizes by schools. Not surprisingly, many teachers, parents and consumer groups are concerned that the young and vulnerable may be exposed to unreasonable marketing pressures.

Defining B2B marketing

So far, this chapter has looked exclusively at consumer buyer behaviour. We now turn our attention to organisational buyer behaviour, or B2B marketing. This is the management process responsible for the facilitation of exchange between producers of goods and services and their organisational customers. This might involve, for example, a clothing manufacturer selling uniforms to the army, a component manufacturer selling microchips to IBM, an advertising agency selling its expertise to Kellogg, Kellogg selling its breakfast cereals to a large supermarket chain, or a university selling short management training courses to local firms. Whatever the type of product or organisation, the focus is the same, centred on the exchange, the flow of goods and services that enable other organisations to operate, produce, add value and/or resell.

B2B marketing and purchasing are a complex and risky business. An organisation may buy many thousands of products and services, costing anything from a few pennies to many millions of pounds per item. The risks are high in these markets where a bad decision, even on a minor component, can bring manufacturing to a halt or cause entire production runs to be scrapped as substandard.

There are several differences between B2B and consumer marketing, as Table 3.3 shows. If a consumer goes to the supermarket and finds that their preferred brand of baked beans is not there, then it is disappointing, but not a disaster. The consumer can easily substitute an alternative brand, or go to another supermarket, or the family can have something else for lunch. If, however, a supplier fails to deliver as promised on a component, then the purchasing organisation has a big problem, especially if there are no easily accessible alternative sources of supply, and runs the risk of letting its own customers down with all the commercial damage that implies. Any failure by any link in this chain has a severe impact on the others.

Table 3.3 Differences between B2B and consumer marketing

B2B customers often/usually . . .	Consumer customers often/usually . . .
• purchase goods and services that meet specific business needs	• purchase goods and services to meet individual or family needs
• need emphasis on economic benefits	• need emphasis on psychological benefits
• use formalised, lengthy purchasing policies and processes	• buy on impulse or with minimal processes
• involve large groups in purchasing decisions	• purchase as individuals or as a family unit
• buy large quantities and buy infrequently	• buy small quantities and buy frequently
• want a customised product package	• are content with a standardised product package targeted at a specific market segment
• experience major problems if supply fails	
• find switching to another supplier difficult	• experience minor irritation if supply fails
• negotiate on price	• find switching to another supplier easy
• purchase direct from suppliers	• accept the stated price
• justify an emphasis on personal selling	• purchase from intermediaries
	• justify an emphasis on mass media communication

Thus the links have to be forged carefully, and relationships managed over time to minimise the potential problems or to diagnose them early enough for action to be taken.

B2B customers

While many B2B buying situations involve a profit-making organisation doing business with other similarly oriented concerns, there are, nevertheless, other kinds of organisation that have different philosophies and approaches to purchasing. Overall, there are three main classes: commercial enterprises, government bodies and institutions, each of which represents a lot of buying power.

Commercial enterprises consist of profit-making organisations that produce and/or resell goods and services for a profit. Some are *users* who purchase goods and services to facilitate their own production, although the item purchased does not enter directly into the finished product. Examples of this are CAD/CAM systems, office equipment and management consultancy services. In contrast, *original equipment manufacturers* (OEMs) incorporate their purchases into their own product, as a car manufacturer does with electrical components, fabrics, plastics, paint, tyres, etc. *Resellers*, such as retailers, purchase goods for resale, usually making no physical changes to them and thus the value added stems largely from service elements. Government bodies are also very large, important purchasers of goods and services. This group of B2B buyers includes both local and national government, as well as European Commission purchasing. The range of purchasing is wide, from office supplies to public buildings, from army bootlaces to battleships, from airline tickets to motorways, from refuse collection to management consultancy. Finally, institutions include (largely) non-profit-making organisations such as universities, churches and independent schools. These institutions may have an element of government funding, but in purchasing terms they are autonomous. They are likely to follow some of the same procedures as government bodies, but with a greater degree of flexibility of choice.

Characteristics of B2B markets

The differences between consumer and B2B markets do not lie so much in the products themselves as in the context in which those products are exchanged, that is, the use of the marketing mix and the interaction between buyer and seller. The same model of personal computer, for example, can be bought as a one-off by an individual for private use, or in bulk to equip an entire office. The basic product is identical in specification but the ways in which it is bought and sold will differ.

The following paragraphs look at some of the characteristics of B2B markets that generate these different approaches.

■ Nature of demand

Derived demand

All demand in B2B markets is derived demand – derived from some kind of consumer demand. So, for example, washing machine manufacturers demand electric motors from an engineering factory, and that is a B2B market. The numbers of electric motors demanded, however, depend on predictions of future consumer demand for washing machines. If, as has happened, there is a recession and consumers stop buying the end product, then demand for the component parts of it will also dry up.

Joint demand

It is also important to note that B2B is often joint demand. That is, it is often closely linked with demand for other B2B products. For example, demand for casings for computers is linked with the availability of disk drives. If there are problems or delays with the supply of disk drives, then the firm assembling the computer might have to stop buying casings temporarily. This emphasises that there is often a need to plan and coordinate production schedules between the buyer and a number of suppliers, not just one.

Inelastic demand

Elasticity of demand refers to the extent to which the quantity of a product demanded changes when its price changes. Elastic demand, therefore, means that there is a great deal of price sensitivity in the market. A small increase in price will lead to a relatively large decrease in demand. Conversely, inelastic demand means that an increase in price will make no difference to the quantity demanded. A car battery, for instance, is just one component of a car. A fall in the price of batteries is not going to have an impact on the quantity of cars demanded, and the car manufacturer will demand neither more nor fewer batteries than before the price change.

■ Structure of demand

One of the characteristics of consumer markets is that for the most part they comprise many potential buyers spread over a wide geographic area, that is, they are diffuse, mass markets. Think of the market for fast food, for example, which McDonald's has shown to have worldwide appeal to many millions of customers. B2B markets, in contrast, differ in both respects.

Industrial concentration

B2B markets tend to have a small number of easily identifiable customers, so that it is relatively easy to define who is or is not a potential customer. McDonald's can persuade non-customers to try its product and become customers; in that sense, the boundaries of the market are fuzzy and malleable, whereas a manufacturer of kilns to the brick and roofing tile industry would have problems in trying to extend its customer base beyond very specific types of customer.

Considerable knowledge, experience and trust can build up between buyers and suppliers. Where there is a finite number of known customers, most organisations in the trade know what the others are doing, and although negotiations may be private, the outcomes are very public.

Geographic concentration

Some industries have a strong geographic bias. Such geographic concentration might develop because of resource availability (both raw materials and labour), available infrastructure or national and EU government incentives. Traditionally, heavy industry and large mass producers, such as shipbuilders, the coal and steel industries and the motor industry, have acted as catalysts for the development of a range of allied suppliers. More recently, airports and seaports have given impetus to organisations concerned with freight storage, movement, insurance and other related services.

Kista, just north of Stockholm, has been described as 'Mobile Valley' because it has the second most important geographic concentration in the world of R&D in mobiles and broadband technology. With a well-educated population and the highest mobile and Internet per capita use in the world, the local conditions have been favourable for more modern forms of concentration. International companies such as IBM, Intel, Motorola, Nokia and Siemens have set up competence and research centres in the area which in turn has spawned many smaller niche suppliers and producers. The net effect is a technically highly skilled workforce that favours innovation (Brown-Humes, 2000). Similarly in Germany, the Baden-Württemberg region has developed many science parks and high technology research centres based on what is claimed to be the highest geographic concentration of scientists in Europe. From a traditional manufacturing base, the region now has thriving export businesses, at a rate well above that of many other German *Länder* (Barber, 2000). This new form of geographic concentration provides obvious opportunities for a range of service providers, whether software specialists or marketing consultants!

■ Buying process complexity

Consumers purchase primarily for themselves and their families. For the most part, these are relatively low-risk, low-involvement decisions that are made quickly, although there may be some economic and psychological influences affecting or constraining them. In contrast, B2B purchasers are always buying on behalf of other people (i.e. the organisation), which implies certain differences from the consumer situation. These differences give rise to much more complexity in the buying process, and the marketer must appreciate them when designing strategies for encouraging trial and reordering. The various dimensions of complexity are as follows.

B2B purchasing policy

Certain systems and procedures for purchasing are likely to be imposed on the B2B buyer. There may be guidelines on favoured suppliers, or rules on single/multiple sourcing or on the number of quotes required for comparison before a decision can be sanctioned. Further restraints might also be imposed relating to how much an individual is allowed to spend under particular budget headings on behalf of the organisation before a second or more senior signature is required. In addition to the formal requirements associated with purchasing, guidelines are often produced on ethical codes of practice. These do not just cover the obvious concerns of remaining within the law and not abusing authority for personal gain, but also address issues such as confidentiality, business gifts and hospitality, fair competition and the declaration of vested interests.

eg The new purchasing manager at the NSPCC, the UK's leading charity concerned with child protection, decided that changes were needed in purchasing policies and procedures. Charities have to be especially mindful how they spend money as any public criticism could affect fund-raising. Each year, the NSPCC raises £75m. from donations and legacies and from that, legitimate expenses, such as administration, must be deducted. The old system devolved purchasing to all the regional offices and teams resulting in a multitude of contracts and suppliers as often local managers preferred to buy locally. For office stationery alone, it had 160 different suppliers!

The new policies and procedures centralised purchasing to achieve both cost savings and greater efficiency. It was estimated that previously it had cost around £60 to raise an order so any move to reduce the number of suppliers by awarding national contracts was bound to reduce costs. This was just the start. There is now a move to a greater use of e-procurement systems for routine purchasing and the system adopted enables orders with approved suppliers to be both placed and tracked by any of the regional offices. The overall aim is to reduce purchasing costs by 10 per cent and that means a lot more money available for the core work of the NSPCC (Riley, 2001).

Professional purchasing

The risk and accountability aspects of B2B purchasing mean that it needs to be done professionally. Much negotiation is required where complex customised technical products are concerned and, even for small components used in manufacturing, defining the terms of supply so that they are consistent and compatible with production requirements (for example performance specification, delivery schedules and quality standards) is a significant job. Most consumer purchasing does not involve so great a degree of flexibility: the product is standard and on the shop shelf, with clearly defined price, usage and function; take it or leave it.

Group decision-making

The need for full information, adherence to procedures and accountability tends to lead towards groups rather than individuals being responsible for purchasing decisions (Johnson and Bonoma, 1981). While there are group influences in consumer buying, for example the family unit, they are likely to be less formally constituted than in the B2B purchasing situation. It is rare, other than in the smallest organisations or for the most minor purchases, to find individuals given absolute autonomy in organisational spending.

In supplying components for these British-built fighter aircraft, suppliers have to be as innovative and as technologically advanced as BAE Systems.

Source: BAE Systems.

Purchase significance

The complexity of the process is also dictated by the importance of the purchase and the level of experience the organisation has of that buying situation (Robinson *et al.*, 1967).

For instance, in the case of a routine rebuy, the organisation has bought this product before and has already established suppliers. These products may be relatively low-risk, frequently purchased, inexpensive supplies such as office stationery or utilities (water, electricity, gas, etc.). The decision-making process here is likely to involve very few people and be more a matter of paperwork than anything else. Increasingly, these types of purchase form part of computer-based automatic reordering systems from approved suppliers. A blanket contract may cover a specific period and a schedule of deliveries over that time is agreed. Bearings for the car and electrical motor industries are sold in this way. The schedule may be regarded as definite and binding for one month ahead, for example, but as provisional for the following three months. Precise dates and quantities can then be adjusted and agreed month by month nearer the time. Increasingly, with JIT systems, schedules may even be day- or hour-specific!

A modified rebuy implies that there is some experience of buying this product, but there is also a need to review current practice. Perhaps there have been significant technological developments since the organisation last purchased this item, or a feeling that the current supplier is not the best, or a desire to renegotiate the parameters of the purchase. An example of this is the purchase of a fleet of cars, where new models and price changes make review necessary, as does the fierce competition between suppliers who will therefore be prepared to negotiate hard for the business. The decision-making here will be a longer, more formal and involved process, but with the benefit of drawing on past experience.

New task purchasing is the most complex category. The organisation has no previous experience of this kind of purchase, and therefore needs a great deal of information and wide participation in the process, especially where it involves a high-risk or high-cost product. One example of this might be the sourcing of raw materials for a completely new product. This represents a big opportunity for a supplier, as it could lead to regular future business (i.e. routine or modified rebuys). It is a big decision for the purchaser who will want to take the time and effort to make sure it is the right one. Another situation, which happens less frequently in an organisation's life, is the commissioning of new plant or buildings. This too involves a detailed, many-faceted decision-making process with wide involvement from both internal members of staff and external consultants, and high levels of negotiation.

Laws and regulations

As we saw in Chapter 2, regulations affect all areas of business, but in B2B markets, some regulations specifically influence the sourcing of products and services. An obvious example would be the sourcing of goods from nations under various international trade sanctions, such as Iraq in the 1990s. More specifically, governments may seek to regulate sourcing within certain industrial sectors, such as utilities.

Buying decision-making process

It is just as important for marketers to understand the processes that make up the buying decision in B2B markets as it is in consumer markets. The formulation of marketing strategies that will succeed in implementation depends on this understanding. The processes involved are similar to those presented in the model of consumer decision-making described earlier, in that information search, analysis, choice and post-purchase evaluation also exist here, but the interaction of human and organisational elements makes the B2B model more complex.

There are many models of organisational decision-making behaviour, with different levels of detail, for example Sheth (1973), Webster and Wind (1972) and Robinson *et al.* (1967). How the model is formulated depends on the type of organisations and products involved; the level of their experience in purchasing; organisational purchasing policies; the individuals involved; and the formal and informal influences on marketing. Figure 3.6 shows two models of organisational decision-making and, on the basis of these, the following subsections discuss the constituent stages.

■ Precipitation

Clearly, the start of the process has to be the realisation that there is a need, a problem that a purchase can solve. The stimulation could be internal and entirely routine: it is the time of year to renew the photocopier maintenance contract. It could be a planned new buy precipitated, for example, by the implementation of expansion plans or the imminent production of a new product. It could also be something more sudden and dramatic than that, such as the failure of a piece of plant or machinery, or a lack of stock.

External influences can also stimulate a need. If the competition has invested in new technology, then other organisations will have to consider their response. Attending trade exhibitions, talking to visiting sales representatives or reading the trade press might also generate awareness of opportunities, whether based on new technology, cost reduction or

Figure 3.6 Models of organisational buying decision-making

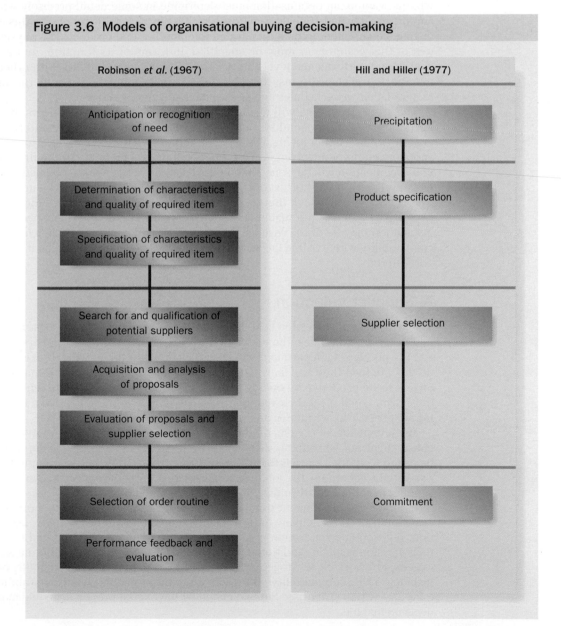

quality improvements, which would stimulate the buying process. Changes in the wider business environment can also trigger a need. The privatisation of electricity supply in the UK created a competitive market for supplying large industrial users. Organisations such as Ford, Tesco and Abbey National have appointed energy buyers with responsibility for undertaking a modified rebuy review of the electricity supply market. The energy buyers ensure that what was always considered a routine repurchase in the past can now be bought with the most advantageous long-term supply contracts from the most appropriate supplier. Thus changes in the energy environment have precipitated changes in purchasing decisions and processes.

Not all needs can or will be fulfilled and it is possible for the decision-making process to stop here, or be postponed until the organisational or environmental conditions are better. Nevertheless, some opportunities will be followed through and these move on to the next stage, product specification.

■ Product specification

Unlike a consumer, for whom half the fun of shopping is often not quite knowing exactly what is wanted, an organisation must determine in some detail precisely what is required, and the greater the strategic significance of the purchase, the more true this is. Think about buying a component to be incorporated into another end product. The physical characteristics of that component must be specified, in terms of its function, its design, expected quality and performance levels, its relationship and compatibility with other components, but there are also the less tangible but no less important considerations of quantity required, delivery schedules and service back-up, among others.

These specifications will need the combined expertise of engineers, production managers, purchasing specialists and marketers (representing the interests of the end customer), balancing ideals against cost and practicality. Even external consultants and suppliers could be involved in particularly complex situations. In the first instance, a general specification will be issued to potential suppliers, but a more detailed one would follow later, perhaps after a shortlist of two or three suppliers has been drawn up.

It is also worthwhile at this stage to define the criteria or priorities for choice. It may not necessarily be cost. If a machine has suddenly broken down, then speed of delivery and installation may be of the essence. In the case of new technology, the choice may hinge on compatibility with existing facilities, the future prospects for upgrading it or the service support offered.

■ Supplier selection

The next stage involves the search for a suitable supplier who can best meet all the specified criteria. Sometimes, the inclination to search for potential suppliers can be quite low, and the purchasing department will keep files on who can do what. If existing suppliers can do the job, then they are likely to be favoured. On other occasions, it may be necessary for buyers to be proactive by openly seeking new suppliers and encouraging quotations from those who could meet their requirements. Nevertheless, there is often a bias towards existing suppliers who are known and trusted.

Much depends, of course, on the nature of the purchasing task. A low-risk, frequent purchase might not warrant an extensive search effort, and an existing supplier might simply be asked to tender a price for resupply. One or two other known suppliers might also be requested to quote for the job, just as a checking procedure to make sure that the existing supplier is not taking advantage of the established relationship.

In a high-risk, infrequent purchase (i.e. the new task situation), a more serious, lengthy selection procedure is likely to be implemented. There will be complex discussion, negotiation, revision and reiteration at a high level with a number of potential suppliers before a final decision is made. Additional problems may be caused where different suppliers will be expected to work closely together, such as on the building of a new manufacturing plant, for instance. Their compatibility with each other, their reliability and their ability to complete their part within strict time limits dictated by the overall project schedule may all affect the decision-making.

eg   Kruidvat, with over 500 drugstores in the Netherlands and Belgium, wanted to improve its store security and cut wastage by the installation of EAS (electronic article surveillance). This involved detailed discussions with potential suppliers to assess alternative systems and eventually Meto, a leading European supplier based in Germany, was selected. Various systems were compared but the Meto system is expected to reduce pilfering considerably when all 25 million product items are tagged. Of particular importance to Kruidvat was the need to protect small cosmetic items that can come in various shapes. If this could be overcome it would be possible to change the store layout and allow greater use of self-service. The selected supplier had to be able to provide protection for the complete range and meet the specification to provide label and tag formats that could be incorporated into manufacturers' production lines and labelling for cost-effective protection. Linked to the labelling, Meto had to provide a security system to detect theft without causing embarrassment to genuine shoppers. Although there were many months of negotiation, the supply partnerships were formed, including the cosmetic suppliers, to allow Kruidvat to strengthen security, benefiting all players (http://www.meto.com).

■ Commitment

The decision has been made, the contract signed, the order and delivery schedules set. The process does not, however, end here. The situation has to be monitored as it unfolds, in case there are problems with the supplier. Is the supplier fulfilling promises? Is the purchased item living up to expectations? Are deliveries turning up on time? Some buyers adopt formal appraisal procedures for their suppliers, covering key elements of performance. The results of this appraisal will be discussed with the supplier concerned in the interests of improving their performance and allowing the existing buyer–seller relationship to be maintained.

In concluding this discussion of the buying process as a whole, we can say that the Hill and Hiller (1977) model has provided a useful framework for discussing the complexities and influences on B2B buying. It is difficult, however, to generalise about such a process, especially where technical and commercial complexity exists. Stages may be compressed or merge into each other, depending on circumstances; the process may end at any stage; there may have to be reiteration: for example if negotiations with a chosen supplier break down at a late stage the search process may have to begin again.

The buying centre

A potential supplier attempting to gain an order from a purchasing firm needs to know just who is involved in the decision-making process, at what point in the process each person is most influential and how they all interact with each other. Then, the supplier's marketers can deal most effectively with the situation, utilising both the group and individual dynamics to the best of their advantage, for example tailoring specific communication packages to appeal at the right time to the right people, and getting a range of feedback from within the purchasing organisation to allow a comprehensive product offering to be designed.

Clearly, the amount of time and effort the supplier is prepared to devote to this will vary with the importance and complexity of the order. A routine rebuy may consist of a telephone conversation between two individuals to confirm the availability of the product and the fine detail of the transaction in terms of exact price and delivery. A new task situation, however, with the promise of either a large contract or substantial future business, provides much more scope and incentive for the supplier to research and influence the buying decision. This section, therefore, looks at the different roles that can be played by individuals within the buying organisation, and how they interact to form a buying centre or decision-making unit (DMU).

Table 3.4 compares buying centres in consumer and B2B markets, indicating the membership, the roles they play and the functional areas that may be involved.

Table 3.4 Comparison of DMUs in consumer and B2B markets

Consumer	Example	B2B	Example
Initiator	Child pesters parents for a new bike.	User	Machine breaks down; the operator reports it, thus initiating the process. May also be asked to help with specs for replacement.
Influencer	Mother thinks about it and says, 'Well, perhaps he has grown out of the old one.'	Influencer	User may influence; may also involve R&D staff, accountants, suppliers, sales reps, external consultants.
Decider	Father agrees and they all go to Toys 'Я' Us where the final decision is the child's, but under restraints imposed by parents' credit card limit.	Decider	May be a senior manager with either an active or a passive role in the whole process. May also be the buyer and/or influencer.
Purchaser	Parents pay the bill.	Buyer	Handles the search for and negotiations with suppliers.
User	The child.	Gatekeeper	Secretarial staff preventing influencers reaching the decision maker; R&D staff withholding information.

■ Users

Users are the people who will use the end product, for example an operator who will use production machinery, or a secretary who will use a word processor. These people may trigger the purchasing process through reporting a need, and may also be consulted in setting the specifications for whatever is to be bought.

■ Influencers

Influencers can affect the outcome of the decision-making process through their influence on others. Influence could stem formally from expertise, for example the advice of an accountant on the return on investment from a piece of capital machinery or that of an engineer on a supplier's technical capability, or it could be an informal, personal influence. Their prime role is in specification, information gathering and assessment.

■ Deciders

Deciders have the formal or informal authority to make the decision. For routine rebuys, this may be the purchasing officer or someone in a functional role, but organisational structures may dictate that the final decision rests with top management, who are fed information and recommendations from below. The decider's role and level of involvement, therefore, will vary widely, depending on individual circumstances.

■ Buyers

Buyers have the authority to select and negotiate with suppliers. Buyers with different levels of seniority may exist to handle different types of transaction, for example a routine rebuy could be handled by a relatively junior clerical worker, whereas the high-cost, high-risk new buy might require a senior purchasing manager of many years' experience. Where devolved budgeting exists, the buyer may not belong to a formal purchasing department at all, but be someone who also has a functional role such as R&D or marketing.

■ Gatekeepers

Gatekeepers have some control over the decision-making process, in that they can control the flow of information by denying access to key members of the buying centre. For example, a secretary or purchasing manager may prevent a sales representative from talking directly to an executive, or intercept brochures and mailshots and throw them in the wastepaper basket before they reach the decision maker. Technical staff can also act as gatekeepers in the way in which they choose to gather, present and interpret information to other members of the buying centre.

The buying centre can be fluid and dynamic, evolving to meet the changing demands of the unfolding situation; it can be either formally constituted (for a major capital project, for instance) or loosely informal (a chance chat over coffee in the canteen between the purchasing manager and an R&D scientist); it can consist of two or three or many people. In other words, it is what it needs to be to do the job in hand.

When analysing the make-up of the buying centre, we should look not only at the allocation of roles between the different functional areas of the organisation, but also at the seniority of the members. Higher expenditure levels or purchases that have a critical impact on the organisation may involve much more senior management. Of course, input from the lower levels of the hierarchy will help to shape the decision, but the eventual authority may rest at board level. Thus, for example, a bank's decision to introduce a new account control system may be taken at a very senior level.

Also, an individual's contribution to it may not be limited to one role. In a small business, the owner/manager may be influencer and buyer as well as decider. Similarly, in a larger organisation, where routine rebuys are concerned, the buyer may also be the decider, with very little call for influencers. Whatever the structure, however fluid the buying centre is, it is still important for the aspiring supplier to attempt to identify the pattern within the target organisation in order to create effective communication links.

Having thus established decision-making structures, the next step is to examine the criteria applied during the process.

marketing *in action*

Nokia's global sourcing

Nokia is one of the market leaders in mobile phone development and manufacture. It uses 250 million components every day which are purchased from some 400 subcontractors and supply partners. The purchasing challenge for the company is to ensure that supplies can be regularly adjusted to meet growing demand from its production facilities spread across 10 countries. It must also be sure that suppliers are capable of producing components that are in line with expected technological advances in a market in which innovation is used to gain competitive advantage.

Given the worldwide scale of production and the need sometimes to adjust product specifications to meet local requirements, purchasing has been divided into two different organisations. First, *local procurement* deals with day-to-day purchasing for

the factories. Its primary role is not to source components, but to ensure that adequate supplies of components are available for production. *Global sourcing* is the other organisation. This actually sources materials, negotiates prices and terms, makes delivery arrangements, establishes quality procedures and sets supplier performance standards for appraisal. There is a close link between global sourcing and the R&D and manufacturing experts to ensure that the right technology is available and that it will continue into the future.

Nokia operates on formal contracts with suppliers, specifying prices, quality, quantities, etc. Suppliers are expected to meet these standards and are monitored at a local level to ensure that they comply. By aggregating demand from each of the production units, Nokia is able to get

better terms from suppliers because of the scale of the contracts. It insists, however, that a supplier should offer only one collection point in the world from which components can be collected, regardless of where they were produced. It is up to the supplier to handle its own logistics to ensure that the various products arrive in time at that collection point. Nokia then arranges for carriers to handle the transport, customs, etc. to ensure that components arrive on time at Nokia's own plants. This arrangement simplifies the ordering procedures for Nokia's local procurement teams.

Quality monitoring of components is critical so that Nokia can ensure that its own products meet standards. Targets are set for failure rates and robustness, for example, and the company asks each supplier to present its plan for meeting those

▶

targets over the lifespan of the contract. Nokia has to be convinced, as it does not inspect goods on arrival. It expects suppliers to take care of testing and to guarantee that they are meeting standards on a consistent basis. When problems do occur, they are normally identified at the local buying points, but it is the global sourcing operation that takes the necessary action with suppliers.

Nokia insists on each supplier nominating an account manager regarded as being responsible for the relationship between the companies on a global basis. The account manager is expected to be senior enough to be credible within Nokia and to carry influence within the supplier's top management if urgent action is required. By establishing clear lines of communication, issues such as annual purchasing agreements to cover forecasting, capacity planning and allocation can be fed through one point. It is then the responsibility of the account manager to link with the rest of the supplier's organisation to ensure that it all happens. It is the supplier's responsibility to adjust its own internal organisation to meet Nokia's requirements.

Although most of the collaboration is on commercial matters, in some areas closer technical cooperation is required. With 'application-specific integrated circuits' (purpose-designed complex microchips), for example, it is necessary for Nokia's engineers to work closely with the supplier's technical staff to create the most appropriate specification. The purchasing function's fear about such arrangements, however, is that it could become locked into a single supplier and this in turn could, it believes, jeopardise supply continuity, especially when the demand for a component is suddenly increased.

Nokia has refined its relationship approach to component suppliers over a number of years. It believes in partnership, openness and trust to ensure that it can plan its capacity and production schedules with a high degree of certainty that suppliers will not let it down. Nokia's faith in its suppliers is perhaps underlined by its stated plan during 2001 to double its outsourcing.

Sources: Kandell (2001); Serant (2001); Taimi (1996).

Buying criteria

In the previous sections, the emphasis in terms of decision-making has largely been on rational, functionally oriented criteria. These task-related or economic criteria are certainly important and reinforce the view of the organisation as a rational thinking entity. However, behind every job title lurks an individual whose motives and goals are not necessarily geared towards the greater good of the organisation. Such motives and goals may not form a direct, formally recognised part of the decision-making process, but nevertheless, they can certainly cause friction and influence the outcomes of it.

■ Economic influences

As has already been stressed, it is not always a matter of finding the lowest priced supplier. If the purchasing organisation can make the best use of increased reliability, superior performance, better customer service and other technical or logistical supports from its suppliers, then it can offer a better package to its own customers, with the rewards that brings. This route can also result in lower total costs, since it reduces production delays due to substandard components or delivery failures, and also improves the quality consistency of the purchaser's own end product, thus reducing the costs of handling complaints and replacing goods.

The main criteria are:

- Appropriate prices: the appropriate price is not necessarily the lowest, but one representing good value for money taking into account the whole service package on offer.
- Product specification: product specification involves finding the right product to meet the purchaser's specified needs, neither more nor less. There are, of course, various trade-offs between specification and price. The main point is the closeness of the match and the certainty that it will be maintained throughout the order cycle.
- Quality consistency: it is important to find a supplier with adequate quality controls to minimise defects so that the purchaser can use the product with confidence. This is especially true for JIT systems, where there is little room for failure.
- Supply reliability and continuity: the purchaser needs to be sure that adequate supplies of the product will be available as and when needed.
- Customer service: buyers require reassurance that the supplier is prepared to take responsibility for its product by providing fast and flexible back-up service in case of problems.

■ Non-economic influences

Powers (1991) summarises non-economic influences under four main headings:

■ Prestige: organisations, or more specifically the individuals who make up organisations, hanker after 'status'. So, for example, they may be prepared to spend a little more when the office accommodation is refurbished on better-quality furnishings, decor and facilities to impress, instil confidence or even intimidate visitors to the site.

■ Career security: few people involved in the decision-making process are truly objective about it; at the back of the mind there is always the question, 'What does this mean for my job?' First, there is the risk element. A problem may have two alternative solutions, one which is safe, predictable and unspectacular, and one which is high risk, but promises a high return. If the high-risk decision is made and it all goes wrong, what are the consequences? The individual may not want to be associated with such an outcome and thus will push for the safe route. Second, there is the awareness of how others are judging the individual's behaviour in the decision-making process: 'Am I prepared to go against the main body of opinion on a particular issue that I feel strongly about or will that brand me as a trouble-maker and jeopardise my promotion prospects?'

■ Friendship and social needs: needs such as friendship can be dangerous and can sometimes stray very close to ethical boundaries. It is necessary, however, to value trust, confidence and respect built on a personal level between individuals in the buying and selling organisations. It does help to reduce the perceived risk of the buyer–seller relationship.

■ Other personal needs: the individual's own personality and profile, such as demographic characteristics, attitudes and beliefs, coupled with factors like self-confidence and communication skills, can all shape the extent to which that individual is allowed to participate in and influence the outcome of the decision-making process.

A further dimension of non-economic forces is trust. Trust is the belief that another organisation will act in such a way that the outcomes will be beneficial to both parties and that it will not act in such a way as to bring about negative effects (Anderson and Narus, 1986). Trust can be built at an organisational level, but can also stem from a series of personal relationships between employees.

Chapter summary

This chapter has centred on consumer and B2B buying behaviour, in terms of both the processes through which potential buyers pass in deciding whether to make a purchase and which product to choose, and the factors that influence the decision-making itself.

■ The consumer decision-making process involves a number of stages: problem recognition, information search, information evaluation, decision and, finally, post-purchase evaluation.

■ The length of time taken over the process as a whole or over individual stages will vary according to the type of product purchased and the particular consumer concerned. An experienced buyer with past knowledge of the market making a low-risk, low-priced routine purchase will pass through the decision-making process very quickly, almost without realising that it has happened. This is a routine problem-solving situation. In contrast, a nervous buyer, lacking knowledge but facing the purchase of a one-off, high-risk, expensive purchase, will prolong the process and consciously seek and analyse information to aid the decision. This is extended problem solving.

■ Decision-making is influenced by many factors apart from the type of purchase. Some of these factors are external to the consumer, such as social, economic, legal and technological issues existing within the wider environment. Closer to home, the consumer influences the decision-making process through psychological factors. The type of personality involved; the individual's perceptions of the world and ability to interpret information; the ability to retain and learn from both experience and marketing communication; the driving motivations behind behaviour; and finally the individual's attitudes and beliefs all shape their responses to the marketing offering and ultimately their acceptance or rejection of it. In addition to that, the individual's choices and behaviour are affected by sociocultural influences defined by the groups to which the individual either belongs or wishes to belong.

One of the strongest group influences comes from the family, affecting decisions on what is purchased, how that decision is made and how the individual feels about that purchase.

■ B2B marketing is about exchanges between organisations, whether they are commercial enterprises, government bodies or institutions. B2B markets have a number of distinct characteristics, including the nature of demand (derived, joint and inelastic), the structure of demand (concentrated in size and in geography), the complexity of the buying process and the risks inherent in it. The decision-making process that B2B purchasers go through has elements in common with consumer decision-making, but is likely to be formalised, to take longer and to involve more people. It is likely to involve higher value, less frequently placed orders for products that are more likely to be customised than in consumer markets. Staff with various functional backgrounds will be involved in the process and form a buying centre. The membership of the buying centre, the roles played and who takes the lead may vary from transaction to transaction or even from stage to stage within a single process.

■ The stages in the decision-making process include: precipitation, product specification, supplier selection, and commitment to a long-term relationship. The decision-making process is affected not only by rational, measurable economic criteria (price, specification, quality, service, etc.), but also by non-economic influences (prestige, security, social needs, personality) emanating from the individuals involved.

questions for *review and discussion*

3.1 Why is post-purchase evaluation important for:

(a) the consumer; and
(b) the marketer?

3.2 How do perception, learning and attitudes affect consumer decision-making, and how can the marketer influence these processes?

3.3 Define the three main types of reference group. Within each type, think of examples that relate to you as a consumer, and analyse how this might affect your own buying behaviour.

3.4 What are the main differences between B2B and consumer buying behaviour?

3.5 Define the main economic and non-economic influences on B2B decision-making.

3.6 How might the roles undertaken by various members of a two-parent family vary between the buying decisions for:

(a) a house;
(b) something for tonight's dinner; and
(c) a birthday present for a 10-year-old child?

How would your answer change if it was a one-parent family?

case study 3.1

Breezing out for a night on the tiles

Since the 1990s, Bacardi-Martini has made a concerted effort to develop new products aimed at a younger market, taking advantage of the growing fashionability and popularity of premium pre-mixed spirit-based drinks among clubbers. In 1995, this sector was worth £20m. in the UK; by 1999 it had rocketed to £810m. and estimates for 2000 expected it to break the £1bn barrier (Mintel, 2000a). The most successful of these pre-packaged spirits (PPS) is Bacardi Breezer, a family of rum and fruit juice drinks (for example lime, lemon, peach, pineapple, watermelon, cranberry). Although launched in 1994, the Breezer brand really became well established in early 1999 when a £5.6m. advertising campaign targeting 18–24-year-olds assured us 'Bacardi Breezer: there's Latin spirit in everyone' (Cozens, 1999).

By mid-2000, the advertising spend was £14m. on what was described as an 'outwardly innocent, inwardly naughty' campaign. James Robinson, account executive on Bacardi at McCann's, was quoted by Brabbs (2000) as saying:

> *'The ads don't target people – they target a state of mind. Breezer represents a distinctive place in people's night out between beer and spirits – they're neither sober nor wasted on it – and that's what we tried to capture. We were seeking to dramatise the fun and mischievous side that Breezer brings out in you.'*

The campaign clearly captured the imagination as the brand was worth around £345m. in 2000, selling nearly 1 million bottles a day.

In summer 2000, the advertising was further reinforced by the investment of £1.5m. on the portable *Vivid* tent, 75 ft tall and the length and breadth of a football pitch, for use at events such as music festivals (*Marketing*, 2000). *Vivid* is entered via giant inflatable slides which take consumers to 'pleasure zones' including a glass dance floor made up of TV screens showing tropical fish, a 40 ft helter-skelter, an area with cushions and hammocks, and a games area with table football, air hockey and Quasar. There is also, of course, an ample bar area!

By November 2000, the company estimated that the 'Latin Spirit' campaign had doubled sales volumes of the brand which had become the UK's biggest selling pre-mixed spirit. Its market share by value was almost 40 per cent and it was available in 60 per cent of all UK on-trade outlets (the on-trade sells alcohol for consumption on the premises, for example pubs and clubs, while the off-trade, for example wine shops and supermarkets, sells it for consumption elsewhere) (Mason, 2000). A strong new development was introduced for the run-up to Christmas in the character of Tom the cat. Tom lives a normal pampered-puss existence with a sweet little old lady by day, but by night, he's a seasoned cat-about-town clubber, flirting with the girls, hanging round on the bar with the Breezer bottles, and grooving on the dance floor.

Bacardi Breezer also has a dedicated website (http://www.bacardi-breezer.co.uk) which has a strong clubbing theme. The web agency Loudcloud which designed the site said that 'The site will be pretty radical and out there' and that it would provide young adults with 'lunchtime escapism' from the daily routines of work (Chandiramani, 2001).

In an A C Nielson report published in March 2001, Bacardi Breezer featured at number 11 in the top 20 best-selling drink brands in pubs in England and Wales. With the exception of Strongbow cider at number 9, the top 10 consists of beers and lagers (Young, 2001). The pub and club on-trade is very important to Bacardi Breezer, accounting for 70 per cent of sales volumes. Some 73 per cent of 18–24-year-olds visit a pub or club at least once per week and they are looking for drinks that make fashion and lifestyle statements. Beverage Brands, another key player in the PPS sector said:

> *The highly experimental 18–35-year-olds are seeking more than just a drink, they are constantly looking for a new experience in their drinks repertoire* (as quoted by Mintel, 2000a).

The PPS brands seem to answer well to that need. The use of established 'pedigree' parent brand names such as Bacardi and Smirnoff help to create a quality image which is reinforced by the use of glass packaging. This is also perceived as 'female-friendly'. The brands and the bottles themselves have become fashion statements that drinkers are happy to be 'seen with'. Pubs and clubs like the PPS brands, not only because they are popular, but also because they are quick and easy to serve and they carry a high gross margin of 60–70 per cent, compared with 40 per cent for draught beers (Mintel, 2000a).

Sources: Brabbs (2000); Chandiramani (2001); Cozens (1999); *Marketing* (2000); Mason (2000); Mintel (2000a); Young (2001).

Questions

1 Give an overview of how the buying decision-making process might work for purchasing an alcoholic drink in a pub or club. How might that process differ if the consumer is buying drinks in a supermarket or off-licence?

2 What individual and group influences are likely to affect someone's choice of drink brand?

3 Explain the roles of the various marketing activities described in this case in influencing consumer behaviour.

4 Given the huge range of beers and lagers available and their dominance of the market, why do you think there is still room for products such as Bacardi Breezer?

References for chapter 3

Anderson, J. and Narus, J. (1986), 'Towards a Better Understanding of Distribution Channel Working Relationships', in K. Backhaus and D. Wilson (eds), *Industrial Marketing: A German–American Perspective*, Springer-Verlag.

Anderson, P. (1999), 'Child's Play', *Marketing Week*, 9 September, pp. 39–42.

Barber, A. (2000), 'Mittelstand Still the Backbone', *FT Survey: Baden-Württemberg* in *Financial Times*, 28 May.

Brabbs, C. (2000), 'Bacardi Parties on with Newest Latin Spirit "Landlady" Ad', *Marketing*, 15 June, p. 24.

Broadbent, G. (2001), 'Design Choice: FCUK', *Marketing*, 10 May, p. 15.

Brown-Humes, C. (2000), 'Sweden: Sector Enters Sober Times', *Financial Times*, 4 December.

Bruce, A. (2001), 'Connex Stations Set for 40 Stores', *The Grocer*, 11 August, p. 5.

Bruner, G. and Pomazal, R. (1988), 'Problem Recognition: The Crucial First Stage of the Consumer Decision Process', *Journal of Consumer Marketing*, 5 (1), pp. 53–63.

Chandiramani, R. (2001), 'Bacardi Targets Young with Site Revamp', *Marketing*, 28 June, p.13.

Chisnall, P. (1985), *Marketing: A Behavioural Analysis*, McGraw-Hill.

Cozens, C. (1999), 'Latin Spirit Surfaces in Bacardi Breezer Spots', *Campaign*, 9 April, p. 6.

Curtis, J. (2000), 'Should These Ads be Banned?', *Marketing*, 23 March, pp. 28–9.

Curtis, J. (2001), 'Think Ethnic, Act Ethnic', *Marketing*, 5 July, pp. 24–5.

The Daily Telegraph (2001), 'British Psychological Society: TV Adverts Blamed for Children's Gift Greed', *The Daily Telegraph*, 30 March, p. 13.

Engel, J., Blackwell, R. and Miniard, P. (1990), *Consumer Behaviour*, Dryden.

Evening Standard (2000), 'No Fun for Kids as EU Plans Ads Clampdown', *Evening Standard*, 20 December, p. 31.

Festinger, L. (1957), *A Theory of Cognitive Dissonance*, Stanford University Press.

Fishbein, M. (1975), 'Attitude, Attitude Change and Behaviour: A Theoretical Overview', in P. Levine (ed.), *Attitude Research Bridges the Atlantic*, Chicago: American Marketing Association.

Hardcastle, S. (2001), 'Yogurts and Pot Desserts', *The Grocer*, 21 April, pp. 33–6.

Hauser, J. *et al.* (1993), 'How Consumers Allocate Their Time When Searching for Information', *Journal of Marketing Research*, November, pp. 452–66.

Henderson, M. (1997), 'Class Tightens its Grip on Britain', *The Times*, 15 December, p. 7.

Hilgard, E. and Marquis, D. (1961), *Conditioning and Learning*, Appleton Century Crofts.

Hilgard, E. *et al.* (1975), *Introduction to Psychology* (6th edn), Harcourt Brace Jovanovich.

Hill, R. and Hiller, T. (1977), *Organisational Buying Behaviour*, Macmillan.

Howard, J. and Sheth, J. (1969), *The Theory of Buyer Behaviour*, Wiley.

Johnson, W. and Bonoma, T. (1981), 'The Buying Centre: Structure and Interaction Patterns', *Journal of Marketing*, 45 (Summer), pp. 143–56.

Kandell, J. (2001), 'Finland is Now Nokialand', *Institutional Investor*, June, pp. 75–82.

Keller, K. and Staelin, R. (1987), 'Effects of Quality and Quantity of Information on Decision Effectiveness', *Journal of Consumer Research*, 14 (September), pp. 200–13.

Kimberley, W. (2001), 'Skoda: An Eastern Europe Success', *Automotive Manufacturing and Production*, June, pp. 26–8.

Lightfoot, L. and Wavell, S. (1995), 'Mum's Not the Word', *Sunday Times*, 16 April.

Marketing (2000), 'Bacardi Breezer to Lure Clubbers With "Dance" Tent', *Marketing*, 10 August, p. 4.

Marketing (2001a), 'All Outdoor Ads to be Vetted for "Taste" by CAP', *Marketing*, 5 April, p. 5.

Marketing (2001b), 'Brand Re-vitalisation of the Year', Supplement to *Marketing*, 12 June, p. 12.

Marsh, H. (2001), 'Why Women are Taking to the Net', *Marketing*, 21 June, pp. 33–4.

Maslow, A. (1954), *Motivation and Personality*, Harper and Row.

Mason, T. (2000), 'Breezer Unveils £4m Christmas Push', *Marketing*, 9 November, p. 7.

Matilla, A. and Wirtz, J. (2001), 'Congruency of Scent and Music as a Driver of In-store Evaluations and Behaviour', *Journal of Retailing*, 77 (2), pp. 273–89.

Mazur, L. (2001), 'Marketers Need to Find out What We Women Want', *Marketing*, 29 March, p. 18.

Mintel (2000a), 'Alcoholic RTDs', *Market Intelligence*, April.

Mintel (2000b), 'Household Cleaning Products, 25/5/00', accessed via http://sinatra2.mintel.com, October 2001.

Mudd, T. (2000), 'The Last Laugh', *Industry Week*, 18 September, pp. 38–44.

Norton, C. (1997), '"Dettox Generation" Fails Hygiene Test', *The Sunday Times*, 9 November, p. 10.

Norton, G. (1998), 'Upwardly Mobile Britain Splits into 17 New Classes', *The Sunday Times*, 13 September, p. 1.9.

Oaff, B. (2001), 'The Playground Market', *The Observer*, 29 April, p. 8.

Powers, T. (1991), *Modern Business Marketing: A Strategic Planning Approach to Business and Industrial Markets*, St Paul, Minn.: West.

Riley, H. (2001), 'Buying Better, Helping More', *Supply Management*, 10 May, pp. 32–3.

Robinson, P. *et al.* (1967), *Industrial Buying and Creative Marketing*, Allyn and Bacon.

Serant, C. (2001), 'SCI Lands Big Deal with Nokia', accessed via http://www.ebonline.com, September 2001.

Sheth, J. (1973), 'A Model of Industrial Buying Behaviour', *Journal of Marketing*, 37 (October), pp. 50–6.

Simms, J. (2001), 'Think Global, Act Local', *Campaign*, 29 March, pp. 24–5.

Taimi, K. (1996), 'The Face in the Supermarket Window', *European Purchasing and Materials Management*, No. 7, pp. 159–69.

Webster, F. and Wind, Y. (1972), *Organisational Buyer Behaviour*, Prentice Hall.

Wells, W. and Gubar, R. (1966), 'Life Cycle Concepts in Marketing Research', *Journal of Marketing Research*, 3 (November), pp. 355–63.

Williams, K.C. (1981), *Behavioural Aspects of Marketing*, Heinemann Professional Publishing.

Young, R. (2001), 'Cider Joins Favourite Pub Drinks', *The Times*, 27 March.

segmenting markets

LEARNING OBJECTIVES

This chapter will help you to:

1 explain how both B2B and consumer markets can be broken down into smaller, more manageable groups of similar customers;

2 understand the effects on the marketing mix of pursuing specific segments;

3 understand the potential benefits and risks of segmentation; and

4 appreciate the role of segmentation in strategic marketing thinking.

Introduction

Building on the understanding of buyer behaviour and decision-making processes outlined in the previous chapter, this chapter concerns a question that should be very close to any true marketer's heart: 'How do we define and profile our customer?' Until an answer is found, no meaningful marketing decisions of any kind can be made. It is not usually enough to define your customer as 'anyone who wants to buy our product' because this implies a product-oriented approach: the product comes first, the customer second. If marketing is everything we have claimed it to be, then the product is only a small part of a total integrated package offered to a customer. Potential customers must, therefore, be defined in terms of what they want, or will accept, in terms of price, what kind of distribution will be most convenient for them and through what communication channels they can best be reached, as well as what they want from the product itself.

Remember too that in a consumer-based society, possession of 'things' can take on a symbolic meaning. A person's possessions and consumption habits make a statement about the kind of person they are, or the kind of person they want you to think they are. The organisation that takes the trouble to understand this and produces a product that not only serves its functional purpose well, but also appears to reflect those less tangible properties of a product in the purchaser's eyes, will gain that purchaser's custom. Thus sport shoe manufacturers such as Reebok and Nike not only developed shoes for a wide range of specific sports (tennis, soccer, athletics, etc.), but also realised that a significant group of customers would never go near a sports facility and just wanted trainers as fashion statements. This meant that they served three distinctly different groups of customers: the professional/serious sports player, the amateur/casual sports player and the fashion victim. The R&D invested in state-of-the-art quality products, combined with the status connected with the first group and endorsement from leading sports icons, helped these companies to build an upmarket image that allowed them to exploit the fashion market to the full with premium-priced products. This in turn led to the expansion of product ranges to include branded sports and leisure clothing.

eg The business traveller is an important market segment for travel industry operators, such as airlines, hotel chains and car rental companies. Although business travellers expect better service, as frequent travellers they tend to spend more money, more often. This group of customers, therefore, differs significantly from leisure- and economy-class customers. Business travellers sometimes need to book at short notice, travel to tight schedules, travel frequently and could need to change arrangements at the last minute. Airlines have adapted their service provision to meet the needs of this group. Fast check-in facilities, first- or business-class travel options and lounges, special boarding arrangements and loyalty schemes are all important for attracting these customers. Airlines also advertise specifically to the business traveller and keep their pricing competitive within the business flyer segment on competitive routes such as London–Brussels. British Airways (BA) has extended its focus on business travellers beyond just pricing and service. It has introduced the 'flying bed' seating arrangement to enable the business-class traveller to get a good night's sleep as well as more legroom, more shoulder room, seat power, and the freedom to raid the galley whenever the traveller feels peckish. Although the price is higher, around $850 extra on the New York–London route, it is cheap compared with the risks business executives associate with making poor decisions through lack of a comfortable sleep. Already, 40 per cent of the 112 long-haul aircraft have been converted and the rest should be completed by 2003. BA claims to have improved sales by 8 per cent in the first full year of operation of the 'flying bed' service (Evans, 2001).

All this forms the basis of the concept of segmentation, first developed by Smith (1957). Segmentation can be viewed as the art of discerning and defining meaningful differences between groups of customers to form the foundations of a more focused marketing effort. The following section looks at this concept in a little more depth, while the rest of the chapter will examine how the concept can be implemented and its implications for the organisation.

The concept of segmentation

The introductory section of this chapter has presented the customer-oriented argument for the adoption of the segmentation concept. There is, however, also a practical rationale for adopting it. Mass production, mass communication, increasingly sophisticated technology and increasingly efficient global transportation have all helped in the creation of larger, more temptingly lucrative potential markets. Few organisations, however, have either the resources or the inclination to be a significant force within a loosely defined market. The sensible option, therefore, is to look more closely at the market and find ways of breaking it down into manageable parts, or groups of customers with similar characteristics, and then to concentrate effort on serving the needs of one or two groups really well, rather than trying to be all things to all people. This makes segmentation a proactive part of developing a marketing strategy and involves the application of techniques to identify these segments (Wind, 1978).

It may help you to understand this concept better if you think of an orange. It appears to be a single entity, yet when you peel off the skin you find that it is made up of a number of discrete segments, each of which happily exists within the whole. Eating an orange is much easier (and much less wasteful and messy) if you eat it systematically, segment by segment, rather than by attacking the whole fruit at once. Marketers, being creative people, have adopted this analogy and thus refer to the separate groups of customers that make up a market as market segments.

The analogy is misleading, however, in that each segment of an orange is more or less identical in size, shape and taste, whereas in a market, segments may be very different from each other in terms of size and character. To determine these things, each segment has its own distinct profile, defined in terms of a number of criteria, referred to as *bases* or *variables*, set by the marketer. The choice of appropriate criteria for subdividing the market is very important (Moriarty and Reibstein, 1986) and thus a significant proportion of this chapter is devoted to thinking about the bases upon which segments might be defined in both consumer and B2B markets. Leading on from this, there is also the question of influences that might affect an organisation's choice of segmentation variables. Then, once an organisation has defined its market segments, what is it supposed to do with the information? This too is addressed in this chapter.

B2B and consumer markets, in general, tend to be segmented differently and will, therefore, be discussed separately, beginning with B2B markets.

Segmenting B2B markets

One major feature of B2B segmentation is that it can focus on both the organisation and the individual buyers within it. Additionally, there is the need to reflect group buying, that is, the involvement of more than one person in the purchasing decision (Abratt, 1993). All of this can be compared with a family buying situation in a consumer market, but operating on a much larger scale, usually within a more formalised process.

Wind and Cardozo (1974) suggest that segmenting a B2B market can involve two stages:

1 *Identify subgroups* within the whole market that share common general characteristics. These are called macro segments and will be discussed further below.

2 *Select target segments* from within the macro segments based on differences in specific buying characteristics. These are called micro segments and are discussed on p. 111.

■ Macro segmentation bases

Macro segments are based on the characteristics of organisations and the broader purchasing context within which they operate. Defining a macro segment assumes that the organisations within it will exhibit similar patterns and needs, which will be reflected in similar buying behaviour and responses to marketing stimuli.

The bases used for macro segmentation tend to be observable or readily obtained from secondary information (i.e. published or existing sources) and can be grouped into two main categories, each of which will now be discussed.

Organisational characteristics

There are three organisational charactistics: size, location and usage rate.

1 *Size*. The size of an organisation will make a difference to the way in which it views its suppliers and goes about its purchasing. A large organisation, for instance, may well have many people involved in decision-making; its decision-making may be very complex and formalised (because of the risks and level of investment involved), and it may require special treatment in terms of service or technical cooperation. In contrast, a small organisation may operate on a more centralised decision-making structure, involving one or two people and with simpler buying routines.

eg Corporate banking hardly existed in Poland in the 1980s, but following economic reform, the number of companies in Poland grew from 500,000 in 1990 to over 3 million in 2001. As well as this increase in the potential corporate customer base, the banks have been privatised and many have been taken over or have gone into partnership with Western European and US banks. This has led to a much more marketing-oriented attitude within the Polish banks and has started the process of client segmentation. Small and medium-sized enterprises, defined as those with a turnover of between Z15 and Z250, have been targeted, initially for savings and loans products, but increasingly with cross-selling of factoring, leasing, trade finance and investment banking. This is changing the role of the banks from being simply lenders and deposit-takers to being financial advisers, and this has far-reaching implications for the type and level of communication required by existing and new customers. The next stage of development, Internet banking, is still some way off, however, because of the need to create a stronger and more secure IT infrastructure for Polish businesses (Smorszczewski, 2001).

2 *Location*. Organisations may focus their selling effort according to the geographic concentration of the industries they serve. Such specialisation is, however, slowly breaking down as the old, heavy, geographically based industries, such as shipbuilding, mining and chemical production, become less predominant. Additionally, there is the emergence of smaller more flexible manufacturers, geographically dispersed in new technology parks, industrial estates and enterprise zones. Nevertheless, there are still examples of geographic segmentation, such as that of computer hardware and software sales, or of the financial sector, which is concentrated in London, Frankfurt, Zurich and the major capi-

tals of the world. Organisations providing certain kinds of services might also look to geographic segments. A haulage company might specialise in certain routes and thus look for customers at specific points to make collection, delivery and capacity utilisation as efficient as possible.

3 *Usage rate.* The quantity of product purchased may be a legitimate means of categorising potential customers. A purchasing organisation defined as a 'heavy user' will have different needs from a 'light user', perhaps demanding (and deserving) different treatment in terms of special delivery or prices, for example. A supplier may define a threshold point, so that when a customer's usage rate rises above it, their status changes. The customer's account may be handed over to a more senior manager and the supplier may become more flexible in terms of cooperation, pricing and relationship building. It is generally a better investment to make concessions in order to cultivate a relationship with a single heavy user than to try to attract a number of light users, as implied in Chapter 3.

Product or service application

This second group of segmentation bases acknowledges that the same good can be used in many different ways. This approach looks for customer groupings, either within specific industries as defined by standard industrial classification (SIC) codes, each with its own requirements, or by defining a specific application and grouping customers around that.

The SIC code may help to identify sectors with a greater propensity to use particular products for particular applications. Glass, for example, has many industrial uses, ranging from packaging to architecture to the motor industry. Each of these application sectors behaves differently in terms of price sensitivity, ease of substitution, quality and performance requirements, for instance. Similarly, cash-and-carry wholesalers serve three broad segments: independent grocers, caterers and pubs. Each segment will purchase different types of goods, in different quantities and for different purposes.

The macro level is a useful starting point for defining some broad boundaries to markets and segments, but it is not sufficient in itself, even if such segmentation does happen too often in practice. Further customer-oriented analysis on the micro level is necessary.

■ Micro segmentation bases

Within a macro segment, a number of smaller micro segments may exist. To focus on these, the organisation needs to have a detailed understanding of individual members of the macro segment, in terms of their management philosophy, decision-making structures, purchasing policies and strategies, as well as their needs and wants. Such information can come from published sources, past experience of the potential buyer, sales force knowledge and experience, word of mouth within the industry, or at first hand from the potential buyer. An overview of common bases for micro segmentation is given in Table 4.1.

Gathering, collating and analysing such depth of information is, of course, a time-consuming and sometimes difficult task, and there is always the question of whether it is either feasible or worthwhile. However, there are benefits in defining such small segments (even segments of one!) if it enables fine tuning of the marketing offering to suit specific needs. Given the volumes of goods and levels of financial investment involved in some B2B markets, the effort is not wasted. An organisation that has a small number of very important

Table 4.1 Bases for micro segmentation in B2B markets

- Product
- Applications
- Technology
- Purchasing policies
- DMU structure
- Decision-making process
- Buyer–seller relationships

customers would almost certainly treat each as a segment of one, particularly in a market such as the supply of organisation-wide computer systems where individual customer needs vary so much. In contrast, in a market such as office stationery, where standard products are sold to perhaps thousands of B2B customers, any segmentation is likely to centre around groups aggregating many tens of customers on the macro level.

Segmenting consumer markets

Segmenting consumer markets does have some similarities with B2B segmentation, as this section indicates. The main difference is that consumer segments are usually very much larger in terms of the number of potential buyers, and it is much more difficult, therefore, to get close to the individual buyer. Consumer segmentation bases also put more emphasis on the buyer's lifestyle and context, because most consumer purchases fulfil higher-order needs (see, for example, Maslow's hierarchy of needs, discussed on pp. 79 *et seq.*) rather than simply functional ones. The danger is, however, that the more abstract the segments become, the less easily understood they may become by those designing marketing strategies (Wedel and Kamakura, 1999). Each of the commonly used bases is now discussed in turn.

■ Geographic segmentation

Geographic segmentation defines customers according to their location. This can often be a useful starting point. A small business, for example, particularly in the retail or service sector, operating on limited resources, may look initially for custom within its immediate locale. Even multinationals, such as Heinz, often tend to segment geographically by dividing their global organisation into operating units built around specific geographic markets.

In neither case, however, is this the end of the story. For the small business, simply being there on the High Street is not enough. It has to offer something further that a significant group of customers want, whether it is attractively low prices or a high level of customer service. The multinational organisation segments geographically, partly for the sake of creating a manageable organisational structure, and partly in recognition that on a global scale, geographic boundaries herald other, more significant differences in taste, culture, lifestyle and demand. The single European market (SEM) may have created a market of some 400 million potential customers, yet the first thing that most organisations are likely to do is to segment the SEM into its constituent nations.

> **eg** Take the marketing of an instant hot chocolate drink, made with boiling water. In the UK, virtually every household owns a kettle, and hot chocolate is viewed either as a bedtime drink or as a substitute through the day for tea or coffee. In France, however, kettles are not common, and hot chocolate is most often made with milk as a nourishing children's breakfast. Thus the benefits of speed, convenience and versatility that would impress the UK market would be less applicable in the French market. France would require a very different marketing strategy at best or, at worst, a completely different product.

Geographic segments are at least easy to define and measure, and information is often freely available from public sources. This kind of segmentation also has an operational advantage, particularly in developing efficient systems for distribution and customer contact, for example. However, in a marketing-oriented organisation, this is not sufficient. Douglas and Craig (1983), for example, emphasise the dangers of being too geographically focused and making assumptions about what customers in a region might have in common. Even within a small geographic area, there is a wide variety of needs and wants, and this method on its own tells you nothing about them. Heinz divides its global operation into geographically based subdivisions because it does recognise the effects of cultural diversity and believes in 'local marketing' as the best means of fully understanding and serving its various markets. It is also important to note that any organisation segmenting purely on geographic grounds would be vulnerable to competition coming in with a more customer-focused segmentation strategy.

■ Demographic segmentation

Demographic segmentation tells you a little more about the customer and the customer's household on measurable criteria that are largely descriptive, such as age, sex, race, income, occupation, socio-economic status and family structure.

Demographics might even extend into classifications of body size and shape! It has been suggested that any male with a waist over 102 cm or female with a waist over 88 cm should consider it a warning of obesity. That amounts to an awful lot of people, especially in the UK, Germany and the USA, where the working classes are relatively affluent (Stuttaford, 2001). Over 9 million people in the UK alone are classified as clinically obese and are at risk of weight-related illness. That could be good news for some pharmaceutical and diet food manufacturers, but it presents a challenge to some other business sectors. Clothing retailers such as High and Mighty and Evans primarily target larger men and women respectively. Other retailers have to get their mix of stock sizes right to meet demand. Marks & Spencer, for example, undertook a survey of 2,500 women and found that the average dress size is now a 14 whereas in 1980 it was a 12. Transport operators such as airlines and railways have even bigger problems. Economy-class seats on many aircraft are around 26 inches wide which is pretty cramped, even for those of us who are not built along the lines of a Sumo wrestler! The increasing size of travellers as well as the bad publicity about deep vein thrombosis being associated with sitting in cramped aircraft on long-haul flights is making airlines rethink their seating arrangements (Bale, 2001).

As with the geographic variable, demographics are relatively easy to define and measure, and the necessary information is often freely available from public sources. The main advantage, however, is that demographics offer a clear profile of the customer on criteria that can be worked into marketing strategies. For example, an age profile can provide a foundation for choice of advertising media and creative approach. Magazines, for instance, tend to have readerships that are clearly defined in terms of gender, age bands and socio-economic groups. The under-35 female reader, for example, is more likely to go for magazines such as *Marie Claire*, *Bella* and *Cosmopolitan* than the over-35s who are more likely to read *Prima*, *Good Housekeeping* and *Family Circle*.

On the negative side, demographics are purely descriptive and, used alone, assume that all people in the same demographic group have similar needs and wants. This is not necessarily true (just think about the variety of people you know within your own age group).

Additionally, as with the geographic method, it is still vulnerable to competition coming in with an even more customer-focused segmentation strategy. It is best used, then, for products that have a clear bias towards a particular demographic group. For instance, cosmetics are initially segmented into male/female; baby products are primarily aimed at females aged between 20 and 35; school fee endowment policies appeal to households within a higher income bracket at a particular stage of the family life cycle. In most of these cases, however, again as with the geographic method, the main use of demographic segmentation is as a foundation for other more customer-focused segmentation methods.

■ Geodemographic segmentation

Geodemographics can be defined as 'the analysis of people by where they live' (Sleight, 1997, p. 16) as it combines geographic information with demographic and sometimes even lifestyle data (see below) about neighbourhoods. This helps organisations to understand where their customers are, to develop more detailed profiles of how those customers live, and to locate and target similar potential customers elsewhere. A geodemographic system, therefore, will define types of neighbourhood and types of consumer within a neighbourhood according to their characteristics. Table 4.2 gives an example of how Experian's MOSAIC UK classification profiles one of its neighbourhood types. This Group E can be further split into subgroups: E28 Counter Cultural Mix; E29 City Adventurers; E30 New Urban Colonists; E31 Caring Professionals; E32 Dinky Developments; E33 Town Gown Transition and E34 University Challenge.

Go for bust: bra wars go high-tech

The British bra and lingerie company Gossard has found that a geographic approach to market segmentation can have some validity. The types of product that sell best in various countries are different, partly for the practical reason that women vary in average size across Europe, and partly because of cultural and lifestyle factors. While the British female figure averages around sizes 12–14, German women tend towards sizes 14–16 and the French towards 10–12. Italian women want to be seductive and thus buy a lot of basques; the Germans are practical and look for support and quality; the French want to be fashionable and impress other women; and the Scandinavians want natural fibres. This is, of course, a grossly generalised survey, but the basic trends are there and give Gossard a basis for developing appropriate new products and strategies for different markets.

Not all bra brands are constrained by geographic markets, however. The Wonderbra was designed to target younger women, aged between 18 and 35, wanting a fashionable, fun, sexy bra that allows them to make the most of their assets. This appeal was reinforced by advertising slogans such as 'Hello, Boys', 'Mind If I Bring a Couple of Friends?' and 'In Your Dreams' alongside scantily clad, beautiful models. It's not all about frills and lace, however. Many new developments aimed at stimulating the bra market are based on technology and engineering. The latest variation on Wonderbra, for example, is a 'variable cleavage' bra, equipped with pulleys to draw the breasts together. Meanwhile, Gossard has launched the Airotic, based on the same principle as a car air bag, which used valves to provide lift. Then there is the Bioform which replaces underwiring with a soft moulded core of plastic around a rigid ring. The Bioform, which starts at size 34C in the UK, is aimed specifically at big women who find normal, underwired bras painful. Another new launch is the Ultimo which has silicone-gel pads sewn into the cups as a safer alternative to implants.

So whatever you are looking for, whether it's frills, thrills or functionality, the right bra is out there somewhere.

Sources: Broadhead (1995); *The Economist* (2000).

Gossard designs different products for different European markets as both taste and average sizes differ across regional boundaries.

Source: Gossard.

Table 4.2 MOSAIC Group E: urban intelligence

- Nearly 1.9 million households, representing 7.19 per cent of all UK households
- Nearly 4 million people in this group
- Young, single and mostly well-educated
- Many people are still in further education, while others are making the transition from full-time student to full-time worker
- The majority live in small purpose-built flats or in rented accommodation
- Regular visitors to the cinema, concerts, exhibitions and the arts
- Like weekend and short breaks; particularly outdoor adventure holidays
- Enthusiastic consumers of all forms of media, in particular the broadsheet press, current affairs and environmental magazines
- Older and better-off members of the group shop at very specialist food stores. They are very aware of the relationship between food and health
- Prefer the inner areas of large provincial cities and inner London
- Preferred shopping channel is the Internet
- Enjoy living in a diverse, cosmopolitan and multicultural environment, and are liberal in their views
- Fashion is important to the more affluent members of the group

Source: Experian's Business Strategies Division.

A number of specialist companies, including Experian, offer geodemographic databases. Most of them are generally applicable to a range of consumer markets, although some are designed for specific industries, and others have developed a range of variations on the main database to suit different industries or geographic regions.

Geodemographic systems are increasingly becoming available as multimedia packages. MOSAIC UK is available on CD-ROM, giving the manager access to colour maps, spoken commentary on how to use the system, photographs and text. Experian and other providers are also working on customised geodemographic packages, tailored to suit a particular client's needs.

marketing *in action*

PRiZM: Pan European lifestyle segmentation

PRiZM is an example of Pan European lifestyle segmentation. This and other similar tools such as ACORN and MOSAIC work by characterising each postal unit as containing residents of a particular segment. Claritas, the vendor of PRiZM, suggests that PRiZM can be used for these aims by the marketer:

1 To assess market potential or demand for a given area.
2 Develop customer loyalty and value through identifying the most attractive customers.
3 Identify emerging niche markets.
4 Identify and target customers most likely to defect in order to reduce churn.
5 Target telemarketing activity by concentrating on the households with the greatest propensity to purchase.

The type of lifestyle information on which PRiZM is based is indicated by the fields available through the related Prospect Locator database. These data can be purchased for specific purposes. For example, a financial services provider could purchase the data on building insurance renewal month in order to target customers in the period before renewal using a direct mail or e-mail campaign. Examples of data within the Prospect Locator includes:

- Personal information such as age/gender and marital status.
- Household information such as home details, home occupancy, home improvements, building/contents insurance renewal month, MOSAIC and financial MOSAIC.

- Financial information such as mortgage information, investments and savings.
- Assurance information – health, life and pet insurance.
- Charitable concerns – type of charity supported and propensity to make donations.
- Travel – whether self-catering, typical destination, frequency.
- Utility bills – electricity, gas and telephone.
- Hi-tech goods – satellite TV, mobile, home computer and Internet access.
- Media – daily, Sunday newspaper, TV viewing, musical interests.
- Motor – annual mileage, car status, spend on next car, insurance.
- Sports interests – what sports participated in.

Source: Claritas Europe
claritaseurope@claritaseu.com

Such systems are invaluable to the marketer across all aspects of consumer marketing, for example in planning sampling areas for major market research studies, or assessing locations for new retail outlets, or finding appropriate areas for a direct mail campaign or door-to-door leaflet drop.

eg Door-to-door marketing has evolved still further in its ability to target individual homes. Blanket drops of product samples or sales literature have been used for some time by consumer goods marketers, but the increasing refinement of databases has led to more sophisticated targeting. Circular Distributors, a leading door-to-door drop company, has launched its *Personal Placement* service which can match a purchased or client-provided database with geodemographic neighbourhoods from ACORN and MOSAIC, etc. to identify those areas with a reasonable proportion of target households. Within each neighbourhood postcode there are around 2,500 homes, and there are 8,900 postcodes in the UK. By adopting a micro-targeting system, units as small as 700 households can be identified to reflect differences in housing types even within a neighbourhood. This, matched with mailing lists and databases, enables cost-effective, better targeted door-to-door delivery.

To build a database, a range of criteria can be used, for example how many kids, pets and cars; age profile; ownership of home computer, etc. An organisation, therefore, can target only those who fit a profile, to cut out waste. One client, for example, an ISP, wanted to target households with a CD-ROM and which currently use a PC. A database called *Computer Plan* contained details of 500,000 such users, providing a relevant and low cost means of direct marketing. A further list called *Posh Plan* is being produced to reach the most affluent households in the UK, enabling upmarket products and services to be better targeted. When L'Oréal Elvive wanted to test market a new shampoo in Italy, Circular Distributors targeted householders in the 35–54 age range with more than three adults in the nest. This was then overlaid with supermarket catchment areas to provide an indication of the penetration and acceptance of the dropped samples (Miller, 2001).

Experian's MOSAIC geodemographic system is available on CD-ROM, thus enhancing its user-friendliness and flexibility.

■ Psychographic segmentation

Psychographics, or lifestyle segmentation, is an altogether more difficult area to define, as it involves intangible variables such as the beliefs, attitudes and opinions of the potential customer. It has evolved in answer to some of the shortcomings of the methods described above as a means of getting further under the skin of the customer as a thinking being. The idea is that defining the lifestyle of the consumer allows the marketer to sell the product not on superficial, functional features, but on benefits that can be seen to enhance that lifestyle on a much more emotional level. The term lifestyle is used in its widest sense to cover not only demographic characteristics, but also attitudes to life, beliefs and aspirations.

Plummer (1974) was an early exponent of lifestyle segmentation, breaking it down into four main categories: activities, interests, opinions and demographics.

Activities

The activities category includes all the things people do in the course of their lives. It therefore covers work, shopping, holidays and social life. Within that, the marketer will be interested in people's hobbies and their preferred forms of entertainment, as well as sports interests, club memberships and their activities within the community (voluntary work, for instance).

Interests

Interests refer to what is important to the consumer and where their priorities lie. It may include the things very close to them, such as family, home and work, or their interest and involvement in the wider community. It may also include elements of leisure and recreation, and Plummer particularly mentions areas such as fashion, food and media.

Opinions

The category of opinions comes very close to the individual's innermost thoughts, by probing attitudes and feelings about such things as themselves, social and cultural issues and politics. Opinion may also be sought about other influences on society, such as education, economics and business. Closer to home for the marketer, this category will also investigate opinions about products and the individual's view of the future, indicating how their needs and wants are likely to change.

Demographics

Demographic descriptors have already been extensively covered, and this category includes the kinds of demographic elements you would expect, such as age, education, income and occupation, as well as family size, life-cycle stage and geographic location.

eg Javalqi and Dion (1999) found that the importance placed on financial choice criteria and the type of financial services for personal banking changed over the life cycle of the individual. The stages of the family life cycle were considered in Chapter 3 (see p. 88). Thus young single people rate such factors as location, service quality, credit facilities and a one-stop approach to banking, newly-weds rate the quality of financial and mortgage advice, while for empty nesters, the safety of accumulated funds and interest rates become more important. Although the results are not surprising, there are implications for the marketing programmes of financial service advisors. Given the considerable information that banks have collected on what and how we spend, an underlying life-cycle appreciation can be an important factor in shaping a direct marketing programme to existing and potential customers.

By researching each of these categories thoroughly and carefully, the marketer can build up a very detailed and three-dimensional picture of the consumer. Building such profiles over very large groups of individuals can then allow the marketer to aggregate people with significant similarities in their profiles into named lifestyle segments. As you might expect, because lifestyles are so complex and the number of contributory variables so large, there is no single universally applicable typology of psychographic segments. Indeed, many different typologies have emerged over the years, emphasising different aspects of lifestyle, striving to provide a set of lifestyle segments that are either generally useful or designed for a specific commercial application.

In the USA, for example, advertising agencies have found the Values And Life Style (VALS-2) typology, based on Mitchell (1983), particularly useful. The typology is based on the individual's *resources*, mainly income and education, and *self-orientation*, i.e. attitude towards oneself, one's aspirations and the things one does to communicate and achieve them. The segments that emerge include, for example, *Achievers*, who fall within the category of 'status oriented'. They have abundant resources and are career minded with a social life that revolves around work and family. They mind very much what other people think of them, and particularly crave the good opinion of those who they themselves admire. The implication is that Achievers have largely 'made it' in terms of material success, in contrast to *Strivers* (who are likely to be Achievers in the future) and *Strugglers* (who aspire to be Achievers, but may never make it). Both these segments are also status oriented, but are less well endowed with resources and still have some way to go.

Schoenwald (2001) highlighted some of the dangers in taking psychographic segmentation so far that the relationship between segment characteristics and brand performance becomes lost. Although it may be useful for identifying broad trends, segment boundaries can change as the market changes and some individuals may not fit categories easily or neatly, for example being conservative on financial issues yet highly progressive when it comes to embracing high technology. Schoenwald reminds us that segmentation is a marketing tool for defining markets better and must, therefore, be actionable and not confusing.

eg The 'grey market' or 'seniors market' is an important segment for travel companies as it represents a potentially affluent group with perhaps more time on their hands. As we saw in Chapter 2 (see p. 37), Saga holidays has built a business around the grey market. Shoemaker (2000), in a study of seniors in the USA, found three distinct lifestyle segments among mature holidaymakers that marketers could usefully address in different ways, underlining the point that defining a segment purely on age is too broad. Furthermore, he found that these segments were reasonably stable over time. The segments were:

■ *Escape and learn*: those who want to visit new places, have new experiences, and may be seeking spiritual and intellectual enrichment through visiting new destinations, historic places and participating in physical activities. The group tends to be in higher-income brackets and still employed.

■ *Retirees*: this is a less active group that favours a quieter time, often revisiting known and trusted destinations. The visit could be combined with visiting friends and relatives. Most are retired.

■ *Active storytellers*: this segment tends to be more sociable, spending time with family and friends or favouring group travel. They enjoy making new friends on a trip and often return enriched but more tired than before they set out. The group enjoy relating their experiences to others upon their return.

With the advent of the SEM, many organisations have been trying to produce lifestyle-based psychographic segment profiles that categorise the whole of Europe. One such study, carried out by Euro Panel and marketed in the UK by AGB Dialogue, was based on an exhaustive 150-page questionnaire administered across the EU, Switzerland and Scandinavia. The main research areas covered included demographic and economic factors, as well as attitudes, activities and feelings. Analysis of the questionnaire data allowed researchers to identify 16 lifestyle segments based on two main axes, innovation/conservatism and idealism/materialism. The results also identified 20 or so key questions that were crucial to matching a respondent with an appropriate segment. These key questions were then put to a further 20,000 respondents, which then allowed the definition of 16 segments, including for example Euro-Citizen, Euro-Gentry, Euro-Moralist, Euro-Vigilante, Euro-Romantic and Euro-Business.

Despite the extent and depth of research that has gone into defining typologies such as these, they are still of somewhat limited use. When it comes to applying this material in a commercial marketing context, the marketer still needs to understand the underlying national factors that affect the buying decisions for a particular product.

Nevertheless, there are compelling reasons for such methods of segmentation being worth considering and persevering with, despite their difficulties. Primarily, they can open the door to a better-tailored, more subtle offering to the customer on all aspects of the marketing mix. This in turn can create a strong emotional bond between customer and product, making it more difficult for competitors to steal customers. Euro-segmentation adds a further dimension, in that it has the potential to create much larger and more profitable segments, assuming that the logistics of distribution allow geographically dispersed members of the segment to be reached cost-effectively, and may thus create pan-European marketing opportunities.

The main problem, however, as we have seen, is that psychographic segments are very difficult and expensive to define and measure. Relevant information is much less likely to exist already in the public domain. It is also very easy to get the implementation wrong. For example, the organisation that tries to portray lifestyle elements within advertisements is depending on the audience's ability to interpret the symbols used in the desired way and to reach the desired conclusions from them. There are no guarantees of this, especially if the message is a complex one (more of this in Chapter 9). Additionally, the user of Euro-segments has to be very clear about allowing for national and cultural differences when trying to communicate on lifestyle elements.

In summary, psychographic segmentation works well in conjunction with demographic variables to refine further the offering to the customer, increasing its relevance and defendability against competition. It is also valuable for products that lean towards psychological rather than functional benefits for the customer, for instance perfumes, cars and clothing retailers. For such a product to succeed, the marketer needs to create an image that convinces consumers that the product can either enhance their current lifestyle or help them to achieve their aspirations.

■ Behaviour segmentation

All the categories of segmentation talked about so far are centred on the customer, leading to as detailed a profile of the individual as possible. Little mention has been made, however, of the individual's relationship with the product. This needs to be addressed, as it is quite possible that people with similar demographic and/or psychographic profiles may yet interact differently with the same product. Segmenting a market in these terms, therefore, is known as behaviour segmentation.

End use
What is the product to be used for? The answer to this question has great implications for the whole marketing approach. Think about soup, for instance. This is a very versatile product with a range of potential uses, and a wide variety of brands and product lines have been developed, each of which appeals to a different usage segment. A shopper may well buy two or three different brands of soup, simply because their needs change according to intended use, for example a dinner party or a snack meal. At this point, demographic and psychographic variables may become irrelevant (or at least secondary) if the practicalities of usage are so important to the customer. Table 4.3 defines some of the possible end uses of soup and gives examples of products available on the UK market to serve them.

Table 4.3 Usage segmentation in the soup market

Use	Brand examples
Dinner party starter	Baxter's Fresh soups; Covent Garden soups
Warming snack	Crosse & Blackwell's soups
Meal replacement	Heinz Wholesoups
Recipe ingredient	Campbell's Condensed soups
Easy office lunch	Batchelor's Cuppa Soups

Benefits sought

This variable can have more of a psychological slant than end usage and can link in very closely with both demographic and psychographic segments. In the case of a car, for example, the benefits sought may range from the practical ('reliable'; 'economic to run'; 'able to accommodate mum, dad, four kids, a granny, a wet dog and the remains of a picnic') to the more psychographically oriented ('environmentally friendly'; 'fast and mean'; 'overt status symbol'). Similarly, the benefits sought from a chilled ready meal might be 'ease of preparation', 'time saving', 'access to dishes I could not make myself', 'a reassuring standby in case I get home late one evening', and for the low-calorie and low-fat versions, 'a tasty and interesting variation on my diet!' It is not difficult to see how defining some of these *benefit segments* can also indicate the kinds of demographic or lifestyle descriptors that apply to people wanting those benefits.

eg McCain decided to rebrand its oven-ready chips range to fit with the 'surprisingly good for you' slogan. Rather than emphasising speed and convenience, the plan was to educate consumers and make them aware of the 'health benefits' of oven-ready chips. The 'only 5% fat' claim and other facts such as 'the high-fibre option' were designed to exploit growing consumer interest in health matters (*The Grocer*, 1998).

Usage rate

Not everyone who buys a particular product consumes it at the same rate. There will be heavy users, medium users and light users. Figure 4.1 shows the hypothetical categorisation of an organisation's customer base according to usage. In this case, 20 per cent of customers account for 60 per cent of the organisation's sales. This clearly raises questions for marketing strategies, for example should we put all our resources into defending our share of heavy users? Alternatives might be to make light users heavier; to target competitors' heavy users aggressively; or even to develop differentiated products for different usage rates (such as frequent-wash shampoo).

Again, this segmentation variable can best be used in conjunction with others to paint a much more three-dimensional picture of the target customer.

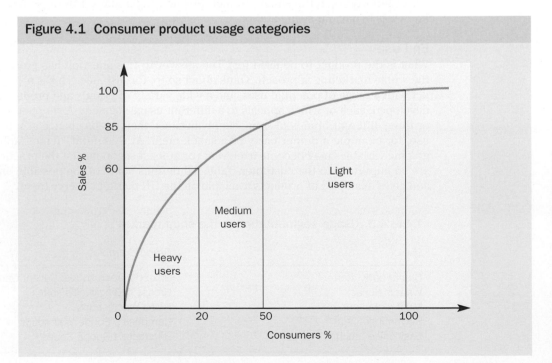

Figure 4.1 Consumer product usage categories

Loyalty

As with usage rate, loyalty could be a useful mechanism, not only for developing detail in the segment profile, but also for developing a better understanding of which segmentation variables are significant. For instance, a carefully thought-out market research exercise might help an organisation to profile 'loyal to us', 'loyal to them' and 'switchers', and then discover what other factors seem to differentiate between each of these groups. More specifically, Wind (1982) identified six loyalty segments as:

1 current loyal users who will continue to purchase the brand;
2 current customers who might switch brands or reduce consumption;
3 occasional users who might be persuaded to increase consumption with the right incentives;
4 occasional users who might decrease consumption because of competitors' offerings;
5 non-users who might buy the brand if it was modified;
6 non-users with strong negative attitudes that are unlikely to change.

What is certain is that brand loyalty can be a fragile thing, and is under increasing threat. This is partly as a result of the greater number of alternative brands available and incentives or promotions designed by competitors to undermine customer loyalty. The most serious threat in the UK, however, has come from supermarket own brands, many of which look uncannily like the equivalent manufacturer brands but undercut them on price. Consumers thus believe that the own brands are just as good, if not identical, and are thus prepared to switch to them and to be more price sensitive.

Assuming that loyalty does exist, even a simple combination of usage rate and loyalty begins to make a difference to the organisation's marketing strategy. If, for example, a large group of heavy users who are also brand switchers was identified, then there is much to be gained from investing resources in a tightly focused marketing mix designed to turn them into heavy users who are loyal to a particular company.

Attitude

Again, trespassing on the psychographic area, attitude looks at how the potential customer feels about the product (or the organisation). A set of customers who are already enthusiastic about a product, for example, require very different handling from a group who are downright hostile. A hostile group might need an opportunity to sample the product, along with an advertising campaign that addresses and answers the roots of their hostility. Attitude-based segments may be important in marketing charities or causes, or even in health education. Smokers who are hostile to the 'stop smoking' message will need different approaches from those who are amenable to the message and just need reassurance and practical support to put it into practice. Approaches aimed at the 'hostile' smoker have included fear ('look at these diseased lungs'), altruism ('what about your children?') and vanity (warning young women about the effect on their skin), but with little noticeable effect.

Buyer readiness stage

Buyer readiness can be a very valuable variable, particularly when one is thinking about the promotional mix. How close to purchasing is the potential customer? For example, at a very early stage the customer may not even be aware that the product exists, and therefore to get that customer moving closer to purchase, the organisation needs to generate *awareness* of the product. Then there is a need for information to stimulate *interest* in the product. The customer's ability to understand and interpret that information may lead to *desire* for the product, which in turn stimulates *action*: the purchase itself. Figure 4.2 summarises this progression.

Behavioural segmentation, therefore, examines closely the relationship between the potential customer and the product, and there are a number of dimensions on which this can be done. Its main achievement is to bring the relationship between customer and product into sharper focus, thus providing greater understanding of the customer's specific needs and wants, leading to a better defined marketing mix. Another advantage of this kind of segmentation approach is that it provides opportunities for tailored marketing strategies to target brand switchers or to increase usage rates. All these benefits do justify the use of behavioural segmentation, as long as it does not lead to the organisation becoming product centred to the neglect of the customer's needs. The customer must still come first.

Figure 4.2 The AIDA response hierarchy model

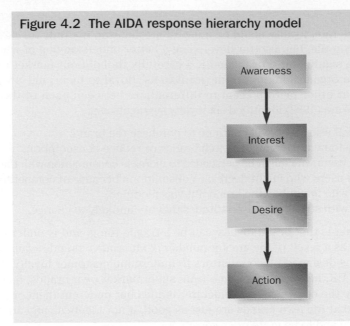

■ Multi-variable segmentation

As has been hinted throughout the previous sections, it is unlikely that any one segmentation variable will be used absolutely on its own. It is more common for marketers to use a multi-variable segmentation approach, defining a 'portfolio' of relevant segmentation variables, some of which will be prosaic and descriptive while others will tend towards the psychographic, depending on the product and market in question. The market for adult soft drinks includes age segmentation along with some usage considerations (for example as a substitute for wine as a meal accompaniment), some benefit segmentation (healthy, refreshing, relaxing), and lifestyle elements of health consciousness, sophisticated imagery and a desire for exotic ingredients. Similarly, the banking sector is moving from traditional segmentation based upon corporate and retail customers to approaches aimed at creating segments based upon combinations of customer attitudes towards bank services and expected benefits. Simply grouping customers according to demographic criteria failed to reflect their attitudes towards technology and their readiness to use it, which could be strategically important as Internet banking develops further (Machauer and Morgner, 2001).

The emergence of geodemographics in recent years, as discussed on pp. 113 *et seq.* above, is an indicator of the way in which segmentation is moving, that is, towards multi-variable systems incorporating psychographics, demographics and geographics. These things are now possible and affordable, as Chapter 5 will show, because of increasingly sophisticated data collection mechanisms, developments in database creation and maintenance (see Chapter 11) and cheaper, more accessible computing facilities. A properly managed database allows the marketer to go even further and to incorporate behavioural variables as the purchaser develops a trading history with a supplier. Thus the marketers are creeping ever closer to the individual consumer. The UK supermarkets that have developed and launched store loyalty cards that are swiped through the checkout so that the customer can accumulate points towards discounts, for example, are collecting incredibly detailed information about each individual shopper's profile. It tells them when we shop, how often, which branches of the store we tend to use, how much we spend per visit, the range of goods we buy, and the choices we make between own brands and manufacturers' brands. The supermarkets can use this information to help them define meaningful segments for their own customer base, to further develop and improve their overall marketing mix or to make individually tailored offers to specific customers.

Implementation of segmentation

This chapter so far has very freely used the phrase 'segmenting the market', but before segmentation can take place, there has to be some definition of the boundaries of that market. Any such definition really has to look at the world through the consumer's eyes, because the consumer makes decisions based on the evaluation of alternatives and substitutes. Thus a margarine manufacturer cannot restrict itself to thinking in terms of 'the margarine market', but has to take a wider view of 'the spreading-fats market' which will include butter and vegetable oil based products alongside margarine. This is because, generally speaking, all three of these product groups are contending for the same place on the nation's bread, and the consumer will develop attitudes and feelings towards a selection of brands across all three groups, perhaps through comparing price and product attributes (for example taste, spreadability, cooking versatility and health claims). This opens up a much wider competitive scene, as well as making the margarine manufacturer think more seriously about product positioning and about how and why consumers buy it.

This whole issue of market definition and its implications for segmentation comes back, yet again, to what should now be the familiar question of 'What business are we in?' It is a timely reminder that consumers basically buy solutions to problems, not products, and thus in defining market segments, the marketer should take into account any type of product that will provide a solution. Hence we are not in 'the margarine market', but in the 'lubricating bread' market, which brings us back full circle to the inclusion of butter and vegetable oil based spreads as direct competitors.

It is still not enough to have gone through the interesting exercise of segmenting a market, however it is defined. How is that information going to be used by the organisation to develop marketing strategies? One decision that must be made is how many segments within the market the organisation intends to target. We look first at targeting.

■ Targeting

There are three broad approaches available, summarised in Figure 4.3, and discussed in detail below.

Figure 4.3 Segmentation targeting strategies

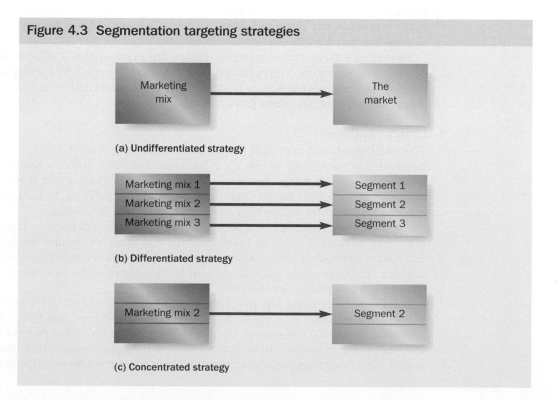

(a) Undifferentiated strategy

(b) Differentiated strategy

(c) Concentrated strategy

Concentrated

The concentrated approach is the most focused approach of the three, and involves specialising in serving one specific segment. This can lead to very detailed knowledge of the target segment's needs and wants, with the added benefit that the organisation is seen as a specialist, giving it an advantage over its more mass-market competitors. This, however, carries a risk of complacency, leaving the organisation vulnerable to competitive entry into the segment.

In terms of management, concentration is attractive because costs are kept down, as there is only one marketing mix to manage, and there is still the potential for economies of scale. Strategically, the concentration of resources into one segment may lead to a stronger, more defendable position than that achievable by competitors which are spreading their effort more thinly. However, being a niche specialist may make it more difficult for an organisation to diversify into other segments, whether through lack of experience and knowledge, or through problems of acceptance arising from being identified with the original niche.

The benefits also need to be weighed against the other potential risks. First, all the organisation's eggs are in one basket, and if that segment fails, then there is no fallback position. The second risk is that if competitors see a rival establishing and clearly succeeding in a segment like this, then they may try to take some of it.

Differentiated

As Figure 4.3 implies, a differentiated strategy involves the development of a number of individual marketing mixes, each of which serves a different segment. For example, Ford manufactures a range of cars, covering a number of different segments, from the Ka at the bottom end of the price range, generally intended for the younger female driver, to the Scorpio in the higher price bracket, intended for the status-seeking executive.

As with the concentrated strategy, this approach does allow the organisation to tailor its offerings to suit the individual segments, thus maintaining satisfaction. It also overcomes one of the problems of concentration by spreading risk across the market, so that if one segment declines, the organisation still has revenue from others.

To be implemented properly, this approach requires a detailed overview of the market and how it is developing, perhaps leading to the early detection of new opportunities or emerging segments. This knowledge is valuable for an organisation with a healthy curiosity about its environment, but is acquired at a cost (in terms of both finance and managerial time). It also leads to increased costs in trying to manage the marketing mixes for a number of products, with possible diseconomies of scale.

Overall, a differentiated strategy dilutes the organisation's efforts through the thin spreading of resources. The organisation must, therefore, be very careful not to overreach itself in the number of segments it attempts to cover. Nevertheless, it can help an organisation to survive in highly competitive markets.

Undifferentiated

The undifferentiated approach is the least demanding of the three approaches, in that it assumes that the market is one great homogeneous unit, with no significant differences between individuals within that market. Thus a single marketing mix is required that serves the needs of the entire market. The emphasis is likely, therefore, to be on developing mass communication, mass distribution and as wide an appeal as possible.

An undifferentiated approach does have some apparent advantages. It involves relatively low costs, as there is only one marketing mix that does not require the depth of research, fine tuning and updating that a concentrated or differentiated strategy would entail. It could also lead to the possible maximisation of economies of scale, because of having a single product in a potentially large market.

It is naive to hope that you can please everyone. What is likely to happen in reality is that some people will like your product offering more than others, and thus a segment (not of your own definition) will emerge by default. Because your product has not been tailored to that segment, it is unlikely to be exactly what that segment wants, and therefore any competitor who does target the segment more closely will attract those customers.

If an undifferentiated approach is possible at all, then it might best be suited for products with little psychological appeal. For example, petrol is essentially a very ordinary product that many of us purchase regularly but never even see (unless we are not very adept with a self-service pump). It makes the car go, regardless of whether it is a Rolls-Royce or a Lada and, traditionally, the only discriminating factor between brands has been price. Petrol retailers have now begun to create market segments, through the petrol itself (as with unleaded and petrols with extra additives); through the extended product (providing car washes, mini-supermarkets, etc.); and also through strong corporate images that create brands and engender loyalty. All of this is moving the petrol retailers away from undifferentiated strategies.

Quite apart from the advantages and disadvantages connected with each of the alternative approaches above, there are a number of factors influencing the choice of targeting strategy.

Marketing theory may well point to a particular strategy as being ideal, but if an organisation's resources cannot support and sustain that strategy, then an alternative must be found. A smaller organisation may, for example, need to adopt a concentrated strategy (perhaps based on a geographic segment in a consumer market, or on a specialist niche in a B2B market) to generate the growth required to allow a wider coverage of the market.

It is also important to make the choice of strategy in the context of the product itself. As has already been indicated, certain types of product lend themselves more readily to certain approaches, for example a product with many potential variations that involve a high level of psychological relationship with the customer (such as clothing or cosmetics) is better suited to a differentiated or concentrated approach. Other products with a more functional bias can be treated in a more undifferentiated way.

It must be reiterated, though, that undifferentiated approaches are becoming increasingly rare. Salt used to be held up to marketing students as the prime example of a commodity product sold in an undifferentiated way. Table 4.4 demonstrates how all that has changed.

Table 4.4 Differentiation in the salt market

- Table salt
- Cooking salt
- Sea salt
- Rock salt
- Alpine rock salt
- Iodised salt
- Low-sodium salt
- Garlic salt
- Celery salt

      et cetera!

The product's life-cycle stage (see Chapter 6 for a full definition of this concept) might also affect the choice of strategy. For example, an innovative new product, of which neither the industry nor the consumer has past experience, may first be marketed with an undifferentiated strategy in order to gain practical knowledge of the market's behaviour and reactions. It is very difficult to undertake meaningful market research in advance of launching such a new product, because the market may have problems conceptualising the product or putting it into context. It will be in the growth and maturity stages of the life cycle that differentiated strategies will emerge as competitors enter the market and organisations learn from experience.

That last comment is a reminder that strategic decisions cannot be taken in isolation from the activities of the competition. If competitors are clearly implementing differentiated strategies, then it is dangerous for you to adopt a more dilute, undifferentiated approach. It may make more sense to identify the segments within which the competition is strong and then to assess whether it would be possible to attack them head-on in those segments or to find a different niche and make that your own. Thus competition is affecting not only the choice of approach, but the actual choice of segment(s) to target.

corporate social responsibility *in action*

'As close to paradise as can be found'

Turtle Island represents for some the perfect holiday destination. The remote Fijian island in the Yasawa chain was purchased by Harvard graduate Richard Evanson in 1972 as a place to get away from it all, but also as the basis for a business so that his paradise could be shared. Development was needed before business was possible. A circular road was sympathetically built around the island, guest paths were established, Honduras mahogany trees were planted (some 300,000 trees over 26 years), to supplement the local species, and to encourage ecological diversity, stop soil erosion, create wind breaks and add to natural beauty. A three-acre organic vegetable garden was planted, extensive composting and recycling facilities were developed, and solar panel water heating installed to reflect a concern for ecology and the development of sustainable tourism.

The mission and values of the owner are to ensure that the marketing strategies fit with the culture and heritage to create sustainable tourism. Too many of the 'wrong' kind of tourists can soon degrade the local culture and environment. Turtle Island is at the opposite end of the spectrum from Benidorm or Blackpool. The capacity is just 14 rooms on a private 500-acre estate and there are no plans to change that. Guests wanting to lie on the beach drinking all day, or sleeping all day and clubbing all night are certainly not welcome. Turtle Island is designed to appeal to English-speaking couples who can communicate and enjoy each other's company and humour. It's first-name terms as soon as you arrive and a key

part of the experience is the interaction with staff and other guests.

The island resort is positioned as the nearest thing to paradise, and clearly to the targeted segment it is just that, as occupancy is high and many bookings cannot be fulfilled for the required dates. The climate, lush vegetation, activity programme ranging from snorkelling to mountain biking, the all-inclusive pricing policy, and the opportunity to 'get away from it all' appear highly attractive. The price structure is designed to keep the resort exclusive. Excluding airfares (you need a small seaplane to get to the island) the charge is over $2,000 per couple per night and the minimum permitted booking is six nights to provide plenty of opportunity to unwind.

What is important about Turtle Island is that the environmental responsibility and commitment demonstrated by the owner has been good for business and good for the island and its 2,600 inhabitants. The concern with ecology, the deliberate attempt to restrict the number of tourists, the use of local materials (guests stay in traditional wood bures), the provision of medical facilities to the locals and a concern for monitoring, controlling and minimising the unfortunate impact of tourism, such as sewage, reef damage and social pollution have given rise to international acclaim. Developed from an overgrazed and abused island with most of its trees cut down, the Turtle Island resort has won international recognition including a BA Environmental award. The package of experiences and the ecological orientation have proved to have a strong appeal to a specific market segment and the owner

Targeting the desire for the perfect holiday on a desert island but with all the facilities and service that the consumer needs to have a relaxing, carefree holiday, the Turtle Island resort more than satisfies the customers willing to pay for the privilege.

Source: http://www.turtlefiji.com

deliberately sought to reflect that when designing the tourist package.

The island has not been without controversy, however. *The Lonely Planet 1997* guide suggested that the island was distinctly unfriendly to gays given its exclusive nature and priority to social mixing between the guests. This was strongly denied, countering that the island had been taking 'any sort of couple' for at least five years. The comments in subsequent editions of *Lonely Planet* were modified, but it goes to show that near perfection on one dimension of CSR can still leave a company open to accusations, however unfounded, on another. Bookings do not appear to have been affected, however, and the careful segmentation and positioning strategy continues to bring success.

Sources: http://www.turtlefiji.com; Chesshyre (2000); Evanson (1999).

Benefits of segmentation

The previous sections of this chapter should at least have served to show that market segmentation is a complex and dangerous activity, in the sense that the process of choosing variables, their measurement and their implementation leaves plenty of scope for poor management and disappointment. Nevertheless, there are few, if any, markets in which segmentation has no role to play, and it is important to remember the potential benefits to be gained, whether looking at the customer, the marketing mix or the competition.

■ The customer

The obvious gain to customers is that they can find products that seem to fit more closely with what they want. These needs and wants, remember, are not only related to product function, but also to psychological fulfilment. Customers may feel that a particular supplier is more sympathetic towards them, or is speaking more directly to them, and therefore they will be more responsive and eventually more loyal to that supplier. The organisation that fails to segment deeply enough on significant criteria will lose custom to competitors that do.

■ The marketing mix

This is a timely reminder that the marketing mix should itself be a product of understanding the customer. Market segmentation helps the organisation to target its marketing mix more closely on the potential customer, and thus to meet the customer's needs and wants more exactly. Segmentation helps to define shopping habits (in terms of place, frequency and volume), price sensitivity, required product benefits and features, as well as laying the foundations for advertising and promotional decisions. The customer is at the core of all decisions relating to the 4Ps, and those decisions will be both easier to make and more consistent with each other if a clear and detailed definition of the target segments exists.

In the same vein, segmentation can also help the organisation to allocate its resources more efficiently. If a segment is well defined, then the organisation will have sufficient understanding to develop very precise marketing objectives and an accompanying strategy to achieve them, with a minimum of wastage. The organisation is doing neither more nor less than it needs to do in order to satisfy the customer's needs and wants.

This level of understanding of segments that exist in the market also forms a very sound foundation for strategic decisions. The organisation can prioritise across segments in line with its resources, objectives and desired position within the market.

■ The competition

Finally, the use of segmentation will help the organisation to achieve a better understanding of itself and the environment within which it exists. By looking outwards, to the customer, the organisation has to ask itself some very difficult questions about its capacity to serve that customer better than the competition. Also, by analysing the competitors' offerings in the context of the customer, the organisation should begin to appreciate the competition's real strengths and weaknesses, as well as identifying gaps in the market.

Dangers of segmentation

The benefits of segmentation need to be balanced against the dangers inherent in it. Some of these, such as the risks of poor definition and implementation of psychographic segmentation, have already been mentioned.

Jenkins and McDonald (1997) raise more fundamental concerns with market segmentation processes that are not grounded in the capabilities of the organisation. To them, there needs to be more focus on how organisations should segment their markets rather than a focus on how to segment using the range of variables mentioned earlier in this chapter. To decide on the 'should' means having an understanding of the organisation, its culture, its operating processes and structure which all influence the view of the market and how it could be segmented (Piercy and Morgan, 1993).

Other dangers are connected with the essence of segmentation: breaking markets down into ever smaller segments. Where should it stop? Catering for the differing needs of a large number of segments can lead to fragmentation of the market, with additional problems arising from the loss of economies of scale (through shorter production runs or loss of bulk purchasing discounts on raw materials, for instance), as mentioned on p. 124 above. Detail needs to be balanced against viability.

Within the market as a whole, if there are a number of organisations in direct competition for a number of segments, then the potential proliferation of brands may simply serve to confuse the customer. Imagine 5 competitors each trying to compete in 5 market segments. That gives the customer 25 brands to sort out. Even if customers can find their way through the maze of brands, the administration and marketing difficulties involved in getting those brands on to the supermarket shelves can be very costly.

Criteria for successful segmentation

Cutting through the detail of how to segment, and regardless of the complexities of segmentation in different types of market, are four absolute requirements for any successful segmentation exercise. Unless these four conditions prevail, the exercise will either look good on paper but be impossible to implement, or fail to deliver any marked strategic advantage.

■ Distinctiveness

Any segment defined has to be *distinctive*, that is, significantly different from any other segment. The basis of that difference depends on the type of product or the circumstances prevailing in the market at the time. It may be rooted in any of the segmentation variables discussed above, whether geographic, demographic or psychographic. Note too the use of the word *significant*. The choice of segmentation variables has to be relevant to the product in question.

Without a significant difference, segment boundaries become too blurred, and there is a risk that an organisation's offerings will not be sufficiently well tailored to attract the required customers.

■ Tangibility

It must be remembered that distinctiveness can be taken too far. Too much detail in segmentation, without sound commercial reasoning behind it, leads to fragmentation of effort and inefficiency. A defined segment must, therefore, be of a sufficient *size* to make its pursuit worthwhile. Again, the notion of size here is somewhat vague. For FMCG goods, viable size may entail many thousands of customers purchasing many tens of thousands of units, but in a B2B market, it may entail a handful of customers purchasing a handful of units.

Proving that a segment actually exists is also important. Analysis of a market may indicate that there is a gap that existing products do not appear to fill, whether defined in terms of the product itself or the customer profile. The next stage is to ask why that gap is there. Is it because no organisation has yet got round to filling it, or because the segment in that gap is too small to be commercially viable? Does that segment even exist, or are you segmenting in too much detail and creating opportunities on paper that will not work in practice?

■ Accessibility

As well as existing, a defined segment has to be *accessible*. The first aspect of this is connected with distribution. An organisation has to be able to find the means of delivering its goods and services to the customer, but this may not be so easy, for example, for a small organisation targeting a geographically spread segment with a low-priced infrequently purchased product. Issues of access may then become an extension of the segment profile, perhaps limiting the segment to those customers within a defined catchment area, or those who are prepared to order direct through particular media. Whatever the solution to problems of access, it does mean that the potential size of the segment has to be reassessed.

The second aspect of access is communication. Certain customers may be very difficult to make contact with, and if the promotional message cannot be communicated, then the chances of capturing those customers are much slimmer. Again, the segment profile may have to be extended to cover the media most likely to access those customers, and again, this will lead to a smaller segment.

■ Defendability

In talking about targeting strategies on pp. 123 *et seq.* above, one of the recurrent themes was that of the competition. Even with a concentrated strategy, targeting only one segment, there is a risk of competitors poaching customers. In defining and choosing segments, therefore, it is important to consider whether the organisation can develop a sufficiently strong differential advantage to defend its presence in that segment against competitive incursions.

■ B2B markets

Most of the above discussion has centred on consumer markets. With specific reference to B2B markets, Hlavacek and Ames (1986) propose a similar set of criteria for good segmentation practice. They suggest, for example, that each segment should be characterised by a common set of customer requirements, and that customer requirements and characteristics should be measurable. Segments should have identifiable competition, but be small enough to allow the supplier to reduce the competitive threat, or to build a defendable position against competition. In strategic terms, Hlavacek and Ames also propose that the members of a segment should have some logistical characteristic in common, for example that they are served by the same kind of distribution channel, or the same kind of sales effort. Finally, the critical success factors for each segment should be defined, and the supplier should ensure that it has the skills, assets and capabilities to meet the segment's needs, and to sustain that in the future.

Chapter summary

This chapter has focused on the complexities and methods involved in dividing markets into relevant, manageable and targetable segments in order to allow better-tailored offerings to be developed.

■ In B2B markets, segmentation techniques are divided into macro and micro variables or bases. Macro variables include both organisational characteristics, such as size, location and purchasing patterns, and product or service applications, defining the ways in which the product or service is used by the buyer. Micro segmentation variables lead to the definition, in some cases, of segments of one customer, and focus on the buyer's management philosophy, decision-making structures, purchasing policies and strategies, as well as needs and wants.

■ In consumer markets, five main categories of segmentation are defined: geographic, demographic, geodemographic, psychographic and behaviour based. Between them, they cover a full range of characteristics, whether descriptive, measurable, tangible or intangible, relating to the buyer, the buyer's lifestyle and the buyer's relationship with the product. In practice, a multi-variable approach to segmentation is likely to be implemented, defining a portfolio of relevant characteristics from all categories to suit the market under consideration.

- The implications of segmentation are wide reaching. It forms the basis for strategic thinking, in terms of the choice of segment(s) to target in order to achieve internal and competitive objectives. The possibilities range from a niche strategy, specialising in only one segment, to a differentiated strategy, targeting two or more segments with different marketing mixes. The undifferentiated strategy, hoping to cover the whole market with only one marketing mix, is becoming increasingly less appropriate as consumers become more demanding, and although it does appear to ease the managerial burden, it is very vulnerable to focused competition.

- Segmentation offers a number of benefits to both the consumer and the organisation. Consumers get an offering that is better tailored to their specific needs, as well as the satisfaction of feeling that the market is offering them a wider range of products to choose from. The organisation is more likely to engender customer loyalty because of the tailored offering, as well as the benefits of more efficient resource allocation and improved knowledge of the market. The organisation can also use its segmentation as a basis for building a strong competitive edge, by understanding its customers on a deeper psychological level and reflecting that in its marketing mix(es). This forms bonds between organisation/product and customer that are very difficult for competition to break. There are, however, dangers in segmentation, if it is not done well. Poor definition of segments, inappropriate choice of key variables or poor analysis and implementation of the outcomes of a segmentation exercise can all be disastrous. There is also the danger that if competing marketers become too enthusiastic in trying to 'outsegment' each other, the market will fragment to an unviable extent and consumers will become confused by the variety of choice open to them.

- On balance, segmentation is a good and necessary activity in any market, whether it is a mass FMCG market of international proportions, or a select B2B market involving two or three well-known customers. In either case, any segment defined has to be distinctive (i.e. features at least one characteristic pulling it away from the rest that can be used to create a focused marketing mix); tangible (i.e. commercially viable); accessible (i.e. both the product and the promotional mix can reach it) and finally, defendable (i.e. against competition).

questions for *review and discussion*

4.1 How might the market for personal computers, sold to B2B markets, be segmented?

4.2 Find examples of products that depend strongly on demographic segmentation, making sure that you find at least one example for each of the main demographic variables.

4.3 What is psychographic segmentation and why is it so difficult and so risky to do?

4.4 In what major way does behavioural segmentation differ from the other methods? Outline the variables that can be used in behavioural segmentation.

4.5 For each targeting strategy, find examples of organisations that use it. Discuss why you think they have chosen this strategy and how they implement it.

4.6 How can market segmentation influence decisions about the marketing mix?

The pink pound

It is very difficult to estimate the size of the gay market in the UK. Although gay culture has increasingly become part of the mainstream, with many more openly gay celebrities and gay themes and characters featuring regularly in television dramas and comedies, Mintel (2000a, b) has found that the gay market is largely a hidden population. Estimates of the size of the gay population vary between 3 and 15 per cent of the total population, but in Mintel's view it is likely to be towards the lower end of the scale overall with a higher concentration in urban areas. Estimates of its spending power also vary between £6bn and £8bn per annum.

There is some consensus on the characteristics of the gay market, however. Gay consumers are perceived to have a higher than average income, and almost 60 per cent of gay men are either single or not cohabiting. Those who are cohabiting are likely to be in dual-income households. In terms of spending patterns, therefore, the lack of dependants and responsibilities gives gay consumers more opportunities for lifestyle spending with a strong focus on leisure and socialising. *The Gay Times* has found that 80 per cent of its readership comes from the ABC1 socio-economic groups, compared with 43 per cent of the general population.

There is plenty of opportunity for reaching the gay market. Mintel's (2000b) survey found that 77 per cent had Internet access at home and/or at work which is much higher than the national average of 26 per cent. The Internet is important in that it allows gay people to build a stronger sense of community and it gives marketers a chance to locate and target the gay market efficiently and discreetly. The average household income of the gay Internet user is £42,500. There are many ISPs and portals set up specifically for online gays (see for example http://uk.gay.com, http://www.rainbownetwork.com or http://www.pinklinks.co.uk). These sites attract mainstream advertisers, such as Tesco Direct, Marks & Spencer Financial, Virgin, British Airways, First Direct and IBM as well as companies specifically targeting the gay community.

There are also print media. In the UK, Chronos Publishing produces four national gay publications: *Boyz* (a free weekly magazine aimed at the younger end of the gay market), *The Pink Paper* (weekly newspaper sold via mainstream newsagents), *Fluid Magazine* (monthly style and listings magazine), and *Homosex* (free monthly glossy magazine focusing on sex and relationships). The other major media owner is the Millivres-Prowler Group which owns *The Gay Times* as well as a number of gay shops called Prowler. *The Gay Times* is a monthly, glossy publication which is one of Europe's best-selling gay magazines. Newsagent WH Smith classifies *The Gay Times* as a Tier One magazine, i.e. it must be stocked in every branch. Although the circulation figures for gay publications are not as high as those of mainstream media – *The Gay Times*, for example, has a circulation of around 70,000 – they do deliver to a high-quality affluent audience.

Many mainstream companies have still not realised the potential of the gay market. Market research has found that 86 per cent of companies have not communicated specifically with gay audiences. Many companies say that they target all groups, not just niche markets, and besides that, they can reach the same audience through mainstream media. In their view, many gays' purchasing decisions are made using the same criteria as heterosexual consumers. Companies could, however, be missing out. A phenomenal 92 per cent of gay consumers surveyed said that they were more likely to favour companies that acknowledge and support gay people, and 88 per cent said that it is important to them that a company is gay-friendly.

There are some product and service sectors in which gay consumers are explicitly targeted. The development of 'gay villages', particularly in London, Brighton and Manchester, has in turn led to many overtly gay pubs, bars, restaurants, clubs and shops opening close to each other. This creates a focal point for gay communities and indeed, gay pubs and clubs are important social venues. Mintel (2000b) found that 90 per cent of gay respondents were pub visitors (compared with 69 per cent of the general population) and 81 per cent had visited a club (compared with less than 30 per cent of the general population). Interestingly, club visiting does not decline with age among the gay community as dramatically as it does among the general population.

According to Mintel (2000b), the five most important factors which contribute towards enjoyment of a gay venue were cited as:

- type of music (77 per cent)
- not intense or intimidating (75 per cent)
- have been before and liked it (68 per cent)
- spacious with seating areas (62 per cent)
- cheaper drinks and special offers (56 per cent).

▶

The majority of gay bars and pubs are run by independents, although some mainstream breweries have committed themselves to the gay market. Coors, for example, runs 28 gay pubs across the UK while Scottish & Newcastle runs a number of gay pubs, mainly in London (6 outlets) but with two in Manchester, purely due to their location on Canal Street at the heart of the 'gay village'. Some operators focus purely on the gay sector, such as the Manto Group (centred on Manchester) and Kudos Group (centred on London).

The holiday market too lends itself to gay targeting by both mainstream and specialised companies. There are many specialised gay tour operators and travel agents, although the majority of gay holiday-makers still use mainstream travel suppliers as long as they appear to be gay-friendly. Some companies and destinations are, however, perceived as homophobic, and these tend to be avoided. Sandals, for example, explicitly advertises its resorts as being for heterosexual couples only.

According to Mintel (2000a), respondents in its survey took an average of 2.07 holidays each per year, and 72 per cent of them had taken at least one holiday lasting a week or longer within the previous year. *The Gay Times* found that 41 per cent of its readership took two or more holidays per year. The beach/resort holiday destination is almost as popular with the gay community as with anyone else, but gay holidaymakers are more likely to take city-based holidays (23 per cent of Mintel's respondents) than the general population (9 per cent). Mintel (2000a) points

out that cities are more likely to have some form of gay infrastructure, in the form of bars and clubs, that would add value to a holiday.

Surprisingly, only 4 per cent of Mintel's respondents had been on a gay-themed holiday and only 3 per cent had booked their holiday using a gay travel agent or tour operator. Around 11 per cent had actually booked holidays over the Internet which is much higher than among the general population in which less than 2 per cent of holidays are booked on the Internet. Via the gay websites mentioned earlier, it is easy to find gay-oriented travel agencies. http://www.throb.co.uk, for example, offers holidays to popular gay or gay-friendly resorts in Spain and offers incentives to encourage booking over the Internet.

In summary, Mintel (2000a) says that gay holiday-makers want a more diverse array of gay travel products, targeting them with 'quality gay-friendly holidays, rather than gay-themed holidays'.

Sources: Fry (1998, 2000); Mintel (2000a, b).

Questions

1 To what extent does the gay segment conform to the criteria for successful segmentation?

2 What segmentation bases are relevant to the gay pub/club and holiday markets?

3 What are the risks and rewards for a mainstream company targeting the gay segment?

References for chapter 4

Abratt, R. (1993), 'Market Segmentation Practices of Industrial Marketers', *Industrial Marketing Management*, 22, pp. 79–84.

Bale, J. (2001), 'Seats Built for Those that Travel Light', *The Times*, 15 February.

Broadhead, S. (1995), 'European Cup Winners', *Sunday Express*, 7 May, p. 31.

Chesshyre, T. (2000), 'Gay Can Be Green in Fiji', *The Times*, 19 February.

Douglas, S. and Craig, C. (1983), *International Marketing Research*, Prentice-Hall.

The Economist (2000), 'Bra Wars', *The Economist*, 2 December, p. 64.

Evans, R. (2001), 'Luxury Liners', *Barrons*, 9 April, pp. 25–6.

Evanson, R. (1999), 'A Global Icon in Sustainable Tourism', paper presented at the 2nd Annual Samoan Tourism Convention, 24–25 February 1999.

Fry, A. (1998), 'Reaching the Pink Pound', *Marketing*, 4 September, pp. 23–6.

Fry, A. (2000), 'Profits in the Pink', *Marketing*, 23 November, pp. 41–2.

The Grocer (1998), 'Taking the Guilt out of Eating Chips', *The Grocer*, 24 October, p. 73.

Hlavacek, J.D. and Ames, B.C. (1986), 'Segmenting Industrial and High Tech Markets', *Journal of Business Strategy*, 7 (2), pp. 39–50.

Javalqi, R. and Dion, P. (1999), 'A Life-cycle Segmentation Approach to Marketing Financial Products and Services', *The Service Industries Journal*, 19 (3), pp. 74–96.

Jenkins, M. and McDonald, M. (1997), 'Market Segmentation: Organizational Archetypes and Research Agendas', *European Journal of Marketing*, 31 (1), pp. 17–32.

Machauer, A. and Morgner, S. (2001), 'Segmentation of Bank Customers by Expected Benefits and Attitudes', *The International Journal of Bank Marketing*, 19 (1), pp. 6–18.

Miller, R. (2001), 'Marketers Pinpoint Their Targets', *Marketing*, 18 January, pp. 40–1.

Mintel (2000a), 'The Gay Holiday Market, 8/11/00', accessed via http://sinatra2/mintel.com, October 2001.

Mintel (2000b), 'The Gay Entertainment Market, 12/12/00', accessed via http://sinatra2/mintel.com, October, 2001.

Mitchell, A. (1983), *The Nine American Lifestyles: Who Are We and Where Are We Going?*, Macmillan.

Moriarty, R. and Reibstein, D. (1986), 'Benefit Segmentation in Industrial Markets', *Journal of Business Research*, 14 (6), pp. 463–86.

Piercy, N. and Morgan, N. (1993), 'Strategic and Operational Market Segmentation: A Managerial Analysis', *Journal of Strategic Marketing*, 1, pp. 123–40.

Plummer, J.T. (1974), 'The Concept and Application of Lifestyle Segmentation', *Journal of Marketing*, 38 (Jan), pp. 33–7.

Schoenwald, M. (2001), 'Psychographic Segmentation: Used or Abused', *Brandweek*, 22 January, pp. 34–8.

Shoemaker, S. (2000), 'Segmenting the Travel Market: Ten Years Later', *Journal of Travel Research*, 39 (1), pp. 11–26.

Sleight, P. (1997), *Targeting Customers: How to Use Geodemographic and Lifestyle Data in Your Business*, 2nd edn, NTC Publications.

Smith, W. (1957), 'Product Differentiation and Market Segmentation as Alternative Marketing Strategies', *Journal of Marketing*, 21 (July).

Smorszczewski, C. (2001), 'Corporate Banking', *Euromoney: The 2001 Guide to Poland*, May, pp. 4–5.

Stuttaford, T. (2001), 'The Heart Bears the Ulitimate Burden', *The Times*, 15 February.

Wedel, M. and Kamakura, W. (1999), *Market Segmentation: Conceptual and Methodological Foundations*, Dordrecht: Kluwer Academic Publishers.

Wind, Y. (1978), 'Issues and Advances in Segmentation Research', *Journal of Marketing Research*, 15 (3), pp. 317–37.

Wind, Y. (1982), *Product Policy and Concepts, Methods and Strategy*, Addison-Wesley.

Wind, Y. and Cardozo, R. (1974), 'Industrial Marketing Segmentation', *Industrial Marketing Management*, 3 (March), pp. 153–66.

chapter 5

marketing information and research

This chapter will help you to:

1 recognise the importance of information to an organisation and the role information plays in effective marketing decision-making;

2 understand the role of a marketing information system and a decision support system, and develop an awareness of the various types of information available;

3 become familiar with the various steps involved in the marketing research process;

4 outline the sources of secondary and primary data, understand their role and the issues involved in their collection and analysis; and

5 appreciate some of the ethical concerns surrounding marketing research.

Introduction

To be an effective marketing-oriented organisation requires specialised and sophisticated approaches to identifying, assessing and satisfying market demands in a competitive environment. Particularly in global or international markets, each with subtly different needs and market characteristics, effective information is essential to help the organisation to make a better decision on the most appropriate market entry and competitive strategies. To support all this, the organisation also needs a properly designed and managed information system to enable timely and appropriate information to be available for the marketing decision maker. In the UK alone, organisations spend over £1bn a year on research and conduct over 15 million consumer interviews in the search for the 'right' answers (Forestier-Walker, 2000).

Every aspect of marketing considered in this book, including the definition of markets and market segments, the formulation of an integrated strategy based on the 4Ps and planning and control mechanisms, requires the collection and analysis of information. The better the planning, data collection, information management and analysis, the more reliable and useful the outputs become, and thus marketers are able to make decisions that are more likely to satisfy the needs and wants of selected market segments. The organisation that is prepared to contemplate making a significant change to its marketing effort, without first assessing likely market reaction, is running a very high risk of failure.

In general, gathering information on the actual or potential marketplace not only allows the organisation to monitor trends and issues concerning its current customers, but also helps it to identify and profile potential customers and new markets, and to keep track of its competition, their strategies, tactics and future plans. In this context, market research and information handling offer the organisation a foundation from which it can adjust to the changing environment in which it operates.

eg If you are a recent graduate or if you are about to graduate, then the market researchers are interested in you. The Abbey National, a financial services company, wanted to understand better the aspirations and lifestyles of a target group of customers that, if attracted early, could become long-term important customers. Through a research agency, Future Foundation, it surveyed 800 students in four UK universities and the results were compared with the actual life experiences of students who had graduated 10 years previously.

Students' dreams at graduation soon changed with reality. Out went the single, *Friends*-type lifestyle, with the aim of living in London, Sydney or New York, and in came the desire for a permanent relationship, probably one child and living close to one's home town. After 10 years, just 10 per cent were living the single lifestyle, over 70 per cent had become domesticated and most preferred to be in their home area. The urban lifestyle was still preferred to rural living, however, and the home-ownership vision, although strong, extended to purpose-built flats or semi-detached houses only. Immediately after graduation, over half of the former students found themselves living at their parents' home after being faced with the economic reality of student loans and the cost of housing, and 40 per cent did not want to pay for the privilege and couldn't wait to move out again. Most, especially males, tended to outstay their welcome.

Overall, the results confirm that students' ideals and lifestyle aspirations soon transform, turning them into more steady, family-oriented employees. According to Abbey National's research, facing so many significant life changes in a short period of time, graduates wanted a bank that could grow and change with them, rather than abandon them if the going got tough. This was becoming increasingly important as the graduates sought to repay their student debt. From such generalised research, Abbey National is better able to understand the lifestyle pressures facing the age group and the aspirations and motivations that could result in the need for financial services.

Source: http://www.futurefoundation.net

This chapter first considers the role of marketing research and discusses the structure of the marketing information system (MIS) as a means of collecting, analysing and disseminating timely, accurate and relevant data and information throughout the organisation. It then looks at the marketing research planning framework. The stages in designing and implementing a marketing research project are considered, from defining the problem to writing a brief and then executing the project and disseminating the findings. The chapter also looks in detail at sourcing and collecting secondary (or desk) research, from existing or published sources, and primary (or field research) derived from scratch through surveys, observation or experimentation for a specific purpose. The important aspects of designing samples and data collection instruments are explored, since however well managed the rest of the research process is, asking the wrong questions in the wrong way to the wrong people is a recipe for poor quality marketing information.

Finally, because marketing research is potentially such a complex process, with so much riding on its findings, and because organisations often delegate it to agencies, it is important that it is carried out professionally and ethically. There is, therefore, a section on ethical issues involved in marketing research on pp. 166 *et seq*.

Throughout this chapter, the terms client and researchers have been used. Client means the organisation that has commissioned the marketing research, whether from an external agency or from an in-house department. Researchers mean the individual or the team responsible for actually undertaking the research task, regardless of whether they are internal or external to the client organisation.

Marketing research: definition and role

Marketing research is at the heart of marketing decision-making and it is important to understand what it involves and its place within the organisation. This section thus discusses the meaning of marketing research and the role that it plays in helping managers to understand new or changing markets, competition, customers' and potential customers' needs and wants.

■ Defining marketing research

Marketing research is a critical input into marketing decisions and can be defined as:

> . . . *the function which links the consumer, customer, and public to the marketer through information – information used to identify and define marketing opportunities and problems; generate, refine, and evaluate marketing actions; monitor marketing performance; and improve understanding of marketing as a process. Marketing research specifies the information required*

to address those issues; designs the method for collecting information; manages and implements the data collection process; analyses the results; and communicates the findings and their implications.

(AMA definition as quoted by McDaniel and Gates, 1996)

Marketing research links the organisation with the environment in which it is operating and involves specifying the problem, gathering data, then analysing and interpreting those data to facilitate the decision-making process. Marketing research is an essential link between the outside world and the marketer through the information used to identify and define marketing opportunities and problems, generate, refine and evaluate marketing actions, monitor marketing performance and improve understanding of marketing as a process. Marketing research thus specifies the information required to address these issues and designs the methods for collecting the necessary data. It implements the research plan and then analyses and interprets the collected data. After that, the findings and their implications can be communicated.

■ The role of marketing research

The role of marketing research in consumer markets has become well established across the EU. It is particularly important for manufacturers, because of the way in which retailers and other intermediaries act as a buffer between manufacturers and their end consumers. If the manufacturer is not to become isolated from market trends and changing preferences, it is important that an accurate, reliable flow of information reaches the marketing decision maker. It might be very limiting if only feedback from the trade were used in making new product and marketing mix decisions.

Another factor facing the consumer goods marketer is the size of the customer base. With such a potentially large number of users and potential users, the onus is on the organisation to make sure that it generates a backward flow of communication from those customers. The potential size of consumer markets also opens up the prospect of adapting products and the general marketing offering to suit different target groups. Decisions on product range, packaging, pricing and promotion will all arise from a well-understood profile of the different types of need in the market. Think back to Chapter 4, where the links between market segments and marketing mixes were discussed in more detail. Marketing research is essential for ensuring that segments exist and that they are viable, and for establishing what they want and how to reach them. As markets become increasingly European and global in their scope, marketing research plays an even more crucial role in helping the organisation to Europeanise its marketing effort, and to decide when to standardise and when to vary its approaches as new markets are opened up.

In B2B markets, the role of marketing research is still very similar to that in consumer markets, in that it helps the organisation to understand the marketing environment better and to make better informed decisions about marketing strategies. Where the two types of market may differ is in the actual design and implementation of marketing research, because of some of the underlying factors peculiar to B2B markets, such as the smaller number of customers and the closer buyer–seller relationships, as introduced in Chapter 3. Despite any differences, the role of marketing research is still to provide an essential insight into opportunities, markets and customers.

eg Bailey's Irish Cream is often drunk at home by a loyal band of drinkers. Bailey's wanted the liqueur brand to have wider appeal, however, especially outside the home and among younger consumers. It decided to use market research to provide better insights into attitudes towards and perceptions of the brand. In one study, a group of consumers aged between 18 and 30 were asked to keep a record of their reactions to drinking Bailey's in situations when it would not normally be considered. These included drinking it at Sunday breakfast after a night out, at a funeral, and as a pick-me-up, and the reactions to each situation were recorded. A quantitative research questionnaire was also used, asking multiple choice questions on respondents' brand perceptions. Four group sessions with around six people in each were held and participants were asked what products they associated with Bailey's. The results of the research were perhaps somewhat sobering for the company: Bailey's is valued as part of a home-based, comfortable, relaxing experience rather than a social drink for a night out. It was thus going to be tough to reposition the product (Clarke, 2001)

In order to appeal to a wider group of drinkers, particularly the 18–30 age group, the makers of Bailey's Irish Cream have effectively transformed the brand into a more everyday and sociable offering. The global advertising campaign has been a key element in the process of changing its perception from an in-home special occasion drink to a mainstream spirit suitable for drinking out of home and more frequently. More information can be found on the global brand website at www. baileys.com

Source: Bailey's.

The need for marketing research sometimes arises because the organisation needs specific details about a target market, which is a well-defined, straightforward descriptive research task. Sometimes, though, the research need arises from a much broader question, such as why a new product is not achieving expected market share. The organisation may have a theory about the nature of the problem, but it is up to marketing research to establish whether any assumptions are correct and to check out other possibilities. In practice, most marketing researchers spend a fair proportion of their time on informal projects, undertaken in reaction to specific requests for marketing information. Often these projects lack the scientific rigour associated with the more formal definition of market research. However, problems of a more innovative and complex nature have to be solved through major, formal pieces of market research, simply because of the risks involved in going ahead without the fullest possible insights.

Types of research

So far, the discussion of marketing research has been very general and has not distinguished between different types of research. There are, however, three main types of research, each suitable as an approach to different kinds of problem.

The first type, exploratory research, is often undertaken in order to collect preliminary data to help clarify or identify a problem, rather than for generating problem solutions. Before preparing a major proposal, some exploratory work may be undertaken to establish the critical areas to be highlighted in the main body of the research. Whether primary or secondary sources of data are used, the purpose is to make an initial assessment of the nature of a marketing problem, so that more detailed research work can be planned appropriately.

An American manufacturer of high-pressure fire-fighting hose nozzles wanted to enter the European market with its most recent innovative design. Before it made a serious commitment to detailed market research across Europe to establish customer reaction and the market entry strategy, some exploratory research was undertaken. This made use of secondary data to establish who the competition would be, what the safety and product standards across Europe were and, not least, what the trends and profile of purchasing by the different fire-fighting authorities were. In addition, a small number of key interviews were held with purchasing bodies in Germany, France and the UK to establish the procedures for trial and adoption in those markets.

This provided a valuable insight into the characteristics of European markets and revealed that significant differences existed in what had been believed to be a relatively homogeneous market. In this case, exploratory research helped to identify the areas that the main survey would consider in more depth and ensured that the company's original assessments and expectations were tested before detailed surveys were designed.

The second type of research, descriptive research, aims to provide the marketer with a better understanding of a particular issue or problem. This can range from quite specific briefs, for example profiling the consumers of a particular brand, assessing the actual purchase and repurchase behaviour associated with that brand and the reasons behind the behaviour exhibited. Most research in this category tends to be of a large-scale survey type, designed to provide a means of better understanding of marketing problems through the presentation of both quantitative and qualitative data.

Finally, causal or predictive research is undertaken to test a cause-and-effect relationship so that reasonably accurate predictions about the probable outcome of particular actions can be made. The difficulty with this kind of research for the marketing manager is that to be confident that more of x does cause more of y, all the other variables that influence y must be held constant. The real-world laboratory is rarely so obliging, with competitors, retailers and other intermediaries, and the marketing environment generally, all acting independently, doing things that will change the background conditions. Thus researchers trying to establish, for instance, whether or not a promotional 10 per cent price reduction would increase sales volume by 15 per cent during a specified period are faced with the problem of ensuring that all the other variables that might influence sales volume are held constant during the research. Random sampling may help in this process, so that the 10 per cent offer would only be made in a random selection of stores, with the other stores offering normal terms. Any difference in the performance of the product in the two groups of stores is likely to have been caused by the special promotion, since both the 'normal' and the 'promotional' product have been subjected to identical environmental factors, impacting on all the stores, during the same period.

■ The origins of research data

There are two main types of data, which are generated by fundamentally different research approaches.

Qualitative research

Qualitative research involves the collection of data that are open to interpretation, for example people's opinions, where there is no intention of establishing statistical validity. This type of research is especially useful for investigating motivation, attitudes, beliefs and intentions. It is often based on very small-scale samples and, as a result, cannot be generalised in numerical terms. Although the results are often subjective, tentative and impressionistic, they can reflect the complexity that underlies consumer decision-making, capturing the richness and depth of how and why consumers act in the way they do. Quantitative techniques, despite their statistical rigour, are rarely able to capture the full complexity and the wealth of interrelationships associated with marketing activity. The real value in qualitative research, therefore, lies in helping marketers to understand not what people say, but what they mean (or think they mean), and a range of techniques have been developed to assist in that task such as:

- survey research/questionnaires
- focus groups
- in-depth interviews
- observational techniques
- experimentation.

All of these are discussed further on pp. 149 *et seq*.

Quantitative research

Quantitative research involves the collection of information that is quantifiable and is not open to the same level of interpretation as qualitative research. It includes data such as sales figures, market share, market size, consumer product returns or complaints, and demographic information (see pp. 113 *et seq*.) and can be collected through primary research, such as questionnaire-based surveys and interviews, or through secondary sources.

Quantitative research usually involves larger-scale surveys or research that enable a factual base to be developed with sufficient strength to allow statistically rigorous analysis. The success of quantitative research depends in part on establishing a representative sample that is large enough to allow researchers to be confident that the results can be generalised to apply to the wider population. It is then possible to specify that 'Forty-five per cent of the market think that . . . whereas 29 per cent believe . . .'. The research can be undertaken through telephone interviews, face-to-face interviews, or mail questionnaires (see pp. 153 *et seq*.), and can also utilise secondary data sources (see pp. 148 *et seq*.).

The Internet is now starting to revolutionise quantitative research. The early emphasis was on gaining cooperation online and structuring questions, but now the techniques used are becoming more sophisticated, interactive, usable over time and more directly linked to systems to integrate all data sources whether online or offline (James, 2001).

■ Continuous research

A large number of research projects are developed specifically to better understand and to overcome marketing problems as they are identified. On pp. 144 *et seq*. we trace the development of such projects from inception through to final evaluation. Some research, however, is conducted on a continuous basis for a subscription or agreement to purchase the updated findings. Usually offered by market research agencies, syndicated research provides much useful data on an ongoing basis. In the UK, retail purchases by consumers are tracked by A C Nielsen, while Target Group Index (TGI), produced by BMRB, plots the fortunes of some 5,000 brands. Similar services are available in all the main European markets. The quality of such research is very high, but the important advantage is shared cost, since Nielsen data, for example, are essential to any large multiple retailer or brand manufacturer and they will all buy the data. The cost to each organisation is still far, far less than that of doing or commissioning the research individually. The big disadvantage, of course, is that competitors also have access to exactly the same information.

There are a number of different approaches to generating continuous data.

Consumer panels

Market research companies recruit large numbers of households which are prepared to provide information on their actual buying and consumption patterns on a regular basis. The panel may be constituted to provide as wide a coverage of the population as possible, or it may be defined to home in on a particular segment. The make-up of a consumer panel can be quite specific. The Pre- and Post-Natal Survey (PNS), operated in the UK, runs a regular survey of 700 pregnant women and 600 mothers with babies up to six months old. For manufacturers of baby foods, nappies, toiletries and infant medicines, such inside information can be invaluable. Taylor Nelson Sofres Superpanel is the UK's leading continuous consumer panel and provides purchasing information on all main grocery markets. The panel was launched in 1991 and now consists of 15,000 households which are demographically and regionally balanced to offer a representative picture of the various sub-markets. Data are collected twice weekly through electronic terminals in the home, with purchases being recorded via home-scanning technology (http://www.tnsofres.com).

Data can be extracted from consumer panels in two main ways: home audits and omnibus surveys. Consumer panels enable buying profiles to be built up over time and provide much useful information for brand managers. Panel data are particularly useful for assessing consumer loyalty, brand switching and the frequency and quantities purchased.

Home audits. A home audit means monitoring and tracking the purchasing and consumption patterns of individual households. A C Nielsen Homescan has 126,000 households globally in 18 countries linked to in-home barcode scanners that record grocery purchases as well as collect answers to survey questions (http://www.acnielsen.com). Information is simply downloaded to the research company on a regular basis using a modem.

Television viewership panels are a very similar form of home audit, in that they involve the recruitment of households and the installation of in-home monitoring equipment. This time, the objective is to use the equipment to enable minute-by-minute recording of audience viewing by channel. From these data, organisations such as AGB and RSMB are able to provide detailed ratings for programmes and viewing patterns during commercial breaks, a critical factor in the sale of advertising time.

Omnibus surveys. An omnibus survey, as the term suggests, enables an organisation to participate in an existing research programme whenever it is felt appropriate. When an organisation wants to take part, it can add a few extra questions to the next round of questionnaires sent to the large number of respondents who are regularly contacted. The big advantage is cost, although normally the number of questions that can be asked on behalf of a specific organisation is very small. The speed with which answers are received is also an important factor.

There are three types of omnibus survey: those carried out face to face during an interviewer visit to the home, telephone surveys and finally Internet interviews. Face-to-face omnibuses tend to offer a larger sample size, often around 2,000 adults, and allow support material to be used. They are also better for exploring more complex or sensitive issues (for example health or finance-related questioning) than the other two methods. Telephone omnibuses offer a faster turnaround time (about 4–5 days quicker than a face-to-face survey), but the sample sizes tend to be smaller and the scope of questioning is more limited. Internet omnibuses are new and are now spreading after their introduction in the United States. They are all based on self-completion of questionnaires and the sample must be carefully controlled to avoid unwanted respondents. It is, however, a very quick way of accessing the views of the Internet population.

Taylor Nelson Sofres Consumer Omnibus has a number of options:

- *Capibus* is the UK's largest weekly omnibus offering a sample of 2,000 adults, interviewed face to face with full results within 10 days. Questions can be targeted and considerable information on the individual and household is collected.
- *PhoneBus* is run twice-weekly providing data from 2,000 UK adults interviewed by telephone. It offers a four-day turnaround so if the questions are submitted by 10 a.m. on Tuesday, responses in full tables are available by Friday lunchtime.
- *Ncompass* is Taylor Nelson Sofres' international omnibus, compiled through data collected by offices in over 80 countries. Results can be available within two weeks and if the Speedline is used, that can be reduced to just six days in the main European markets from a sample of 1,000 adults per country.

Other companies such as Access Omnibus Surveys and RSGB Omnibus also offer regular omnibus surveys in a similar manner, allowing considerable choice in selecting the most appropriate survey for the target audience.

The Internet is now starting to have a bigger impact on consumer panel research. Nielsen, for example, has a 9,000-strong panel of Internet users in the UK and 90,000 worldwide and this is growing at a rapid rate as part of audience measurement research (Gray, 2000b). Every time a page is visited, specialised software installed in participants' computers records the information for Nielsen. Some caution must, however, be exercised in the use of Internet research. MORI, after using e-mail in an IT survey panel, dropped it because of falling response rates and reverted to telephone interviews. Although the online panel was a lower cost to clients, this had to be related to its effectiveness in actually generating data (http://www.researchlive.com).

Retail audits

The retail audit concept is perhaps the easiest to implement, as it relies on trained auditors visiting selected retail stores and undertaking regular stock checks. Increasingly, the use of barcode scanning is providing even more up-to-date information on what is sold where and when. Changes in stock, both on the shelf and in the warehouse, indicate an accurate figure for actual sales to consumers by pack size. This information is especially useful for assessing brand shares, response to sales promotions and the amount of stock being held within the retail trade. Along with information on price levels, the brand manager has much useful information with which to make revised marketing mix decisions.

Marketing information systems

In order to serve the information needs of the organisation and to support decision-making, marketers need to focus not only on collecting data and information, but also on handling and managing issues of storage, access and dissemination (McLuhan, 2001b). There is little point in having a highly complex information system that cannot readily deliver what managers want, when they want it and how they want it. Any system must be responsive to the needs of the users.

A marketing information system (MIS) has been defined as:

> *an organised set of procedures and methods by which pertinent, timely and accurate information is continually gathered, sorted, analysed, evaluated, stored and distributed for use by marketing decision makers.*
>
> (Zikmund and d'Amico, 1993, p. 108)

Nowadays, most of these systems are data based and use high-powered computers. System requirements need to coordinate data collection and decision support, as shown in Figure 5.1. The MIS should be tailored to the specific requirements of the organisation. These will be influenced by the size of the organisation and the resources available as well as the specific needs of decision makers. While these needs are likely to be broadly similar between organisations, they will not be exactly the same and therefore the design of the systems and their sophistication will vary. What is important is that the information is managed in a way that facilitates the decision-making process, rather than just being a collection of data gathering dust.

eg   Haburi.com established an MIS to improve its tracking of web customers across Europe. The system was designed to identify 'value' customers, the group that buys most frequently, prefers premium brands, and makes the fewest returns. At the other end of the spectrum, another group of customers tends to shop for bargains only, seeks low-priced lines, and often returns goods. By tracking the former group, Haburi.com was able to maximise sales to customers within the group, improve conversion rates and service levels, and keep in touch with them better, using the software provided by SAS and Delano to analyse its transactional database (McLuhan, 2001b).

It can be seen from Figure 5.1 that an MIS provides a comprehensive framework for managing a potentially overwhelming flow of information. Along with generating huge amounts of data about their day-to-day activities (sales, customer details, incoming and outgoing orders, transactions, service requirements, etc.), organisations are usually in various stages of gathering other data about competitors, new product tests, improved service requirements and changing regulations, for example. Timeliness of information, whether it be for short- or long-term decision-making, is also of importance, as the provision of immediate feedback or projected trend details to decision makers can provide a competitive advantage in the marketplace.

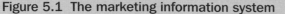

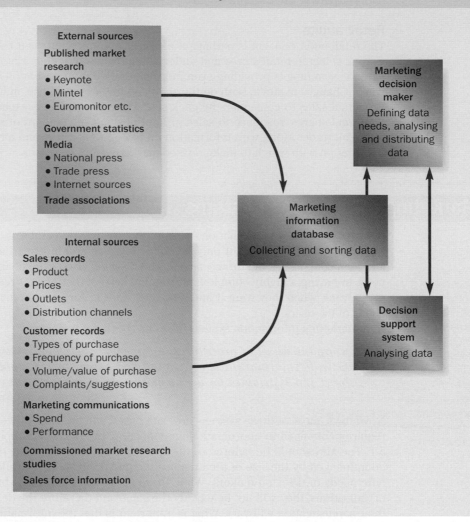

Figure 5.1 The marketing information system

The other requirement of information is that it should be appropriate to the needs of those using it. Organisations have to manage the information they have, identify what information they need, and present it in the form that the various decision makers require. Not all information that the organisation has is necessarily appropriate for all marketing decision makers. It is therefore important to identify the various needs of those decision makers and to ensure they are supplied with only the information that meets their needs. This facilitates decision-making and helps to avoid information overload.

■ Sources of marketing information

As indicated at the outset of this chapter and in Figure 5.1, there are two main sources of information for an MIS system, internal and external.

External sources

External sources are either ad hoc studies using secondary and primary research, or continuous data provided by the various syndicated and omnibus studies mentioned earlier. Information can come from sources such as customers, suppliers, channels of distribution, strategic alliance partners, independent third parties, commercial agencies, industry associations, CSO, Eurostat, etc., and sources like the Internet. The challenge for the marketing manager is to integrate the findings from analysis of data from these sources into the organisation to effect change.

Keeping an eye on mother

Lifestyle changes can be a good predictor of when consumers will be interested in certain goods and services. One company, Bounty, offers a worldwide target marketing service to help organisations seeking to market to such 'changers' exploit their opportunities. Pregnancy and birth is one such lifestyle change that represents enormous potential for marketers. Initial contact is made when the woman visits the obstetrician to confirm a pregnancy and she receives a pregnancy information pack containing a Bounty Pregnancy Guide. This way, Bounty reaches 92 per cent of expectant mothers. A questionnaire card inside the pack asking for the recipient's name, address and the expected date of the baby's birth can then be redeemed at any Mothercare retail store for a free Mother-to-Be gift pack, containing sample products and money-off vouchers. Johnson & Johnson and Procter & Gamble are both among the companies providing products in the pack. With a redemption rate of 80 per cent, a large database of expectant mothers is created.

After the birth, Bounty's *New Mother* programme kicks in. Within 72 hours of giving birth, 92 per cent of new mothers will be visited by one of the 280 Bounty ladies in the UK. Again a gift pack incentive is used, but during the bedside visit the mother's name and address are verified, further details recorded on other children and their ages, and the new mother is asked for her agreement to receive further mail samples and direct mail offers. The data collected at the time of the birth are used to update and enhance the pre-natal data that Bounty collected several months previously. In this way, a more complete profile of the consumer and the samples received can be built up on the database. Research indicates that new mothers often stay with the products they receive in hospital, so baby product suppliers are keen to work with Bounty in making the gift packs attractive and effective.

Bounty also seeks to maintain its relationship with the new mother. A card in the Bounty Young Family Guide within the gift pack asks for the mother's name and address, and the name and age of her new child, acting as another data capture mechanism. Completed cards can then be redeemed for a Progress pack within six months of the birth at Boots, the UK multiple retailer. Seventy per cent elect to trade the information card for the pack. Bounty, therefore, has at least three opportunities to capture data to expand, enhance and update its database.

Of course, all of this is not just done for the sake of gathering information. Bounty makes its mother-to-be and new mother lists available for rent to UK marketers, although it does seek to control usage to avoid claims of exploitation and damage to its relationships with doctors and hospitals. Before Bounty rents a list to a prospective mailer, it approves the mailing and checks the credentials of the mailer.

Source: Yorgey (2000).

Internal sources

Information also comes from sources within the organisation, including the internal record-keeping system (production, accounting, sales records, purchase details, etc.), marketing research, sales representatives' field reports, call details, customer enquiries and complaints, product returns, etc. All of this information, again, must be managed appropriately and distributed in a timely fashion if it is going to be used effectively to assist decision-making.

eg   The development of electronic point of sale (EPOS) technology has revolutionised the flow of information within retail operations, providing a base for fast and reliable information on emerging trends. Either by using a laser barcode scanner or by keying in a six-figure code, retailers can be right up to date in what is moving, where and what the immediate impact will be on stock levels. Retail managers can monitor movement on different product lines on a daily basis and adjust stock, orders and even in-store promotions, based on information either from individual stores or across all the branches. Tesco, with its Clubcard loyalty scheme, can track and record the purchasing and shopping habits of millions of individual customers, and tailor its marketing offerings, both locally and nationally, based on solid, internally generated information.

Clegg (2001) emphasised the importance not just of collecting externally generated marketing data but also of ensuring that there is effective communication within the organisation so that customer contact personnel in particular can contribute fully to building market research knowledge. If the marketing database is seen as being owned by the research department rather than being a knowledge reservoir for the whole organisation, it may not be so well informed of the experiences of customer-facing staff.

Organisations thus get everyday information, often as a matter of course, from a variety of sources that can influence their decision-making, but *intelligence* means developing a perspective on the information that provides a competitive edge, perhaps in new product opportunities or the opening up of a new market segment.

The main difficulty is information overload (Smith and Fletcher, 1999) where there is too much information and not enough intelligence. One study suggested that 49 per cent of managers surveyed cannot cope with the information they receive and another that organisations use as little as 20 per cent of their knowledge (Von Krogh *et al.*, 2000), meaning that a lot of perhaps useful intelligence is locked away or not evident to the decision maker. Collecting marketing information should not, therefore, be an end in itself but should be part of a valuable and usable knowledge management source that can be accessed upon demand in a meaningful and digestable form.

Sometimes environmental scanning can provide useful insights. By deliberately looking at the various influences on product markets, an organisation may spot early warning signs before the competitors are aware of them. This will help in the forward planning process and will be especially useful as an input to strategic development decisions.

Decision support systems

The availability and use of a range of computer-based decision support systems (DSS) are changing the way information is used and presented to decision makers, and the way in which they interpret it (Duan and Burrell, 1997). While an MIS organises and presents information, the DSS actually aids decision-making by allowing the marketer to manipulate information and explore 'What if . . .' type questions. A DSS usually comprises a software package designed for a personal computer, including statistical analysis tools, spreadsheets, databases and other programs that assist in gathering, analysing and interpreting information to facilitate marketing decision-making. By having the DSS connected to the MIS, marketers further enhance their ability to use the information available. Effectively, this brings the MIS to the desktop, and even to the personal laptop, with the appropriate connections, servers and modems. This can encourage wide use of information, although there may be some problems about restricting access to more sensitive areas and ensuring that the complexity can be handled from a systems perspective.

A DSS was developed, for example, to help decide the launch price of a new pharmaceutical product. The system enabled various marketing, sales force and pricing actions to be assessed to find the best price to charge. The system simulated market conditions as closely as possible to assess the impact of price on sales, share and profits over time (Rao, 2000).

The MIS or DSS will never replace decision makers, only help them. Marketing decisions still need the imagination and flair that can interpret 'hard' information and turn it into implementable tactics and strategies that will maintain competitive edge.

The marketing research process

When an organisation has decided to undertake a research project, it is important to make sure that it is planned and executed systematically and logically, so that the 'right' objectives are defined and achieved as quickly, efficiently and cost-effectively as possible. A general model of the marketing research process is presented here, which can be applied to a wide range of real situations with minor adaptations. Figure 5.2 shows the broad stages, and although it may suggest a logic and neatness that are rarely found in practice, it does at the very least offer a framework that can be tailored to meet different clients, situations and resources. Each stage in the process will now be discussed in turn.

■ Problem definition

Problem definition is the first and one of the most important stages in the research process, because it defines exactly what the project is about and as such influences how the subsequent stages are conducted, and ultimately the success of the project itself. The organisation sponsoring the research, whether it intends to use in-house researchers or an agency, needs to define precisely what the problem is and how that translates into research objectives. This may also lead to the identification of other concerns or problems that need to be included in the project. For example, if the fundamental problem has been defined as 'People are not buying our product', the organisation may feel that it should not only explore people's attitudes to the product itself, but also look at how they rate the product on other aspects of the marketing mix in comparison with the competition.

Once the broad nature of the problem has been established, the next stage involves more precise definition of objectives.

■ Research objectives

The tight specification of research objectives is important to ensure that the project is developed along the right lines. Usually, primary objectives need to be distinguished from secondary objectives. The primary objective for an electric components manufacturer seeking to enter the French market, for example, might be to establish the market potential for the products specified and to indicate appropriate market entry strategies. The secondary

Figure 5.2 The market research process

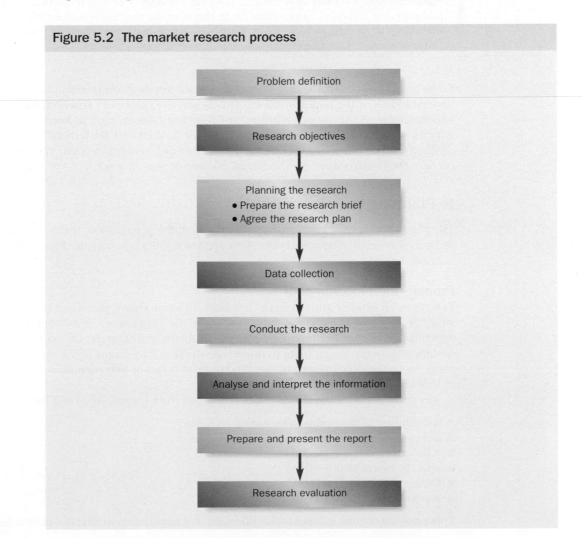

objectives tend to be more specific and comprehensive. For the components manufacturer they might include:

■ defining market trends and competitive structure over the past 5 years
■ profiling the existing main suppliers in terms of strengths and weaknesses (products, prices, distribution, branding, service, etc.)
■ identifying the main buyers of electrical components
■ identifying the main buying criteria when purchasing
■ surveying potential trade and end users for willingness to switch supply source.

The list above is not exhaustive, but the main point is that objectives clearly drive the whole research process, and should provide the necessary foundations for whatever management decisions will have to be taken at the end. In all cases, the research objectives need to be clearly and concisely stated in writing to ensure that the research brief can be adequately prepared.

eg   BT Cellnet wanted to know how families used mobile phones to stay in touch. The objective was specified as finding out the nature and purpose of the day-to-day interaction taking place over the phone between family, friends and work colleagues. The overall purpose was to enable better forecasts to be made of how new mobile communication forms are likely to be received. The study ran for over a year and involved an extensive survey of daily communications behaviour, including a one-day diary completed by 1,500 people covering communications activity at home and at work. The survey revealed the magnitude of both inbound and outbound communication in the morning and the practices adopted to cope, including a steady switch from telephone to e-mail for communication at work (http://www.futurefoundation.com).

To be successful at this stage, the project team needs good communication and a solid understanding of the issues involved. This is where exploratory research may be useful, in eliminating some of the possibilities or filling some basic gaps in knowledge and understanding. This could involve some preliminary discussions with distributors, experts or customers. The information collected, including any secondary data, can then be used to prepare the research brief for the formal commissioning of work.

■ Planning the research

The planning stage falls into two main parts: first, the preparation of the research brief, and second, agreeing the research plan. This applies equally whether the research is conducted in-house or not.

Prepare the research brief

The research brief originates from the client. In some cases, the client has a vague idea of what the problem is, but is not sure what the underlying causes or dynamics are. They thus rely heavily on researchers to specify the problem and then decide on the best research design, effectively asking them to undertake the first two stages of the research process. In many ways, the development of this kind of brief is rather like consultancy and may be part of that kind of overall process.

The main points of the research brief (adapted from Hague, 1992) will be:

■ a definition of the problem, including its history
■ a description of the product to be researched
■ a description of the market to be researched
■ specific research objectives
■ time and financial budget
■ reporting requirements.

This brief may be the subject of modification and negotiation during the meetings.

Agree the research plan

On the basis of the brief, a research plan needs to be agreed before the project begins. Not only is this important for cost and timing considerations, but it also ensures that the data generated will enable management decisions to be resolved without the need for further analysis. There is nothing worse than completing a major research project only to find that the results are at best of only partial use to managers!

The details of the research plan will vary according to the project, but ideally should contain:

- background information for the research
- research objectives (based on decisions that need to be made and the criteria to be used)
- research methods (secondary and/or primary)
- type of analysis to be employed
- degree of client involvement
- data ownership
- details of subcontractors (if any)
- level and timing of ongoing reporting
- format of final report
- timing and cost of research.

An organisation with a major research project may well ask a number of research agencies to tender for the business. Each agency will obviously propose different research plans. These need to be evaluated alongside the organisation's more usual buying criteria. The final decision by the clients should be based on confidence that the chosen agency can best meet its information needs through the research plan proposed, but within any constraints imposed.

■ Data collection

The first requirement in preparing the research plan is to identify clearly what additional data are needed and then to establish how they are to be collected. This may involve collecting both primary and secondary data, or just primary data.

Secondary research

Sometimes also referred to as *desk research*, secondary research consists of data and information that already exist and can be accessed by an organisation. Thus, for example, it would include published government statistics and published market research reports. Clearly, if secondary research is available that answers the question or solves the problem, then that is the quickest and most efficient way of gathering the necessary data. In many cases, however, secondary data may not be directly applicable, or may only give half the picture. The pursuit of secondary data should be exhaustive, as secondary data are usually far more cost-effective and quicker to collect than primary data. However, because secondary data were collected for another purpose they are not always in a form that is useful or appropriate, and thus they often have to be reanalysed to convert them into a form that can be used for a particular project. We will look in detail at secondary research below.

Primary research

Sometimes also called *field* research, primary research is undertaken by, or commissioned by, an organisation for a specific purpose. The required information does not already exist in any available form and so the research has to be undertaken from scratch. The advantage of primary research is that it is exactly tailored to the problem in hand, but it can be expensive and time consuming to undertake. We will look in detail at methods of primary research on pp. 149 *et seq.*

Once the researchers have recognised that information is needed that is not currently available, they must decide from what source they can most effectively get that information. It is well worth checking secondary data sources first to see what has already been done. Even if secondary data are available, or can be converted, they may still not be sufficient to meet all the researchers' needs, and thus a primary research study may still have to be developed to fill the gaps or further explore the issues. This means that a market research project will often incorporate both primary and secondary research, each complementing the other.

Secondary research

Secondary data can be either internal or external to the organisation. The former is considered to be part of the normal MIS, as outlined on pp. 141 *et seq*. The advantage of secondary research is that it can be much cheaper and quicker to access, and may provide information that the organisation would not otherwise have the time, resources or inclination to gather. External secondary data offer valuable information to researchers but of course, the major drawback with secondary data is that the information has been collected for purposes other than this particular research project, and may not be in a suitable or usable form. The organisation also needs to be careful that secondary data are current and that they are appropriate and applicable to the problem in hand.

Secondary data can play a variety of roles in the research process. Their main role is probably in providing background information on industries and markets, in terms of trends, dynamics and structure. Some of this information may be useful in its own right in informing management decision-making, although it is more likely to provide pointers for further primary research. It can also provide useful information that may assist in sample selection for surveys by indicating the main competitor and customer groups.

eg Sports Marketing Surveys was commissioned to assess the feasibility of building a new golf course in Surrey. Most of the research was drawn from existing data such as the population profile within a 30-minute drive time, a listing of existing and new courses planned, and a profile of potential competitors such as their green fees, joining fees and the length of course and waiting lists. From the secondary research, a demand model, and market analysis, a sensible financial analysis could be made dealing with different scenarios. Recommendations were also made on the level of fees and services expected (http://www.sportsmarketing surveys.com). The Early Learning Centre also uses secondary data when considering a new retail location. By using a GIS, birth data, father's occupation and mother's age, it can find appropriate locations near more affluent parents (Hayward, 2001).

■ Sources of secondary data

It would be impossible to list all potential sources of data, as the number of sources is vast and much will depend on the type of research project in question. A discussion with a business librarian will soon reveal how extensive such a list can be!

Using secondary data

Secondary data vary widely in terms of relevance and quality. Boyd *et al.* (1977) suggest four criteria for evaluating secondary data sources:

1 pertinency of the data;
2 who collects the data and why;
3 method of collecting data;
4 evidence of careful work.

Although secondary sources of data are widely used, the criteria above do suggest some potential problem areas. Often the data fail to get down to the micro level necessary to support management decisions. The focus is often at industry level rather than the sector or segment of particular interest, perhaps within a defined geographical area. Some data may have been collected to promote the well-being of the industry, rather than to provide wholly accurate figures, and sometimes they are not always accurate because of their source, their age or the way they were collected. However, for most surveys the sorting, sifting and analysis of secondary data are useful for purposes ranging from developing sample frames (see pp. 157 *et seq*.) to providing comprehensive insights into market size, structure and trends.

Online databases

Up until the 1990s most secondary data was print-based. Directories, both specialist and general, were essential tools for the market researcher. Although most directories are still in hard copy, most have been supplemented by CD-ROMs and by direct Internet access via websites. The key to the Internet is offering an effective search engine so that the drudgery can be taken out of searching for and sourcing information. In Internet versions, it is the relevance of the data to the task that is making them ever more attractive (Wilson, 2001).

Other market research databases are also going online. Euromonitor, through its Market Research Monitor, offers an online database available on subscription to cover 1,300 consumer market and retail briefings. It covers consumer market analysis from 52 countries, and market profiles from four major industrialised countries: the UK, France, Germany and the USA (Marshall, 2000; http://www.euromonitor.com). It pays, therefore, to explore thoroughly what is currently available before going out and generating more information at a far higher cost.

Primary research

Once the decision to use primary research has been made, researchers have to define what data need to be collected and how. This section looks specifically at 'how'. First, there is an overview of primary research methods. Whatever method is chosen as most appropriate to the client's information needs, researchers then have to think about defining a sample of individuals or organisations from the total population of interest (defined as a market segment or an industry, for instance). This topic is covered on pp. 157 *et seq*. Finally, of particular interest to those conducting surveys, pp. 159 *et seq*. look specifically at questionnaires.

eg
MRSL concentrates on undertaking regular research in the travel industry for airports and related service providers. It runs specialist teams at most of the UK's main airports focusing on issues such as:

- travel industry-related issues, e.g. satisfaction with travel agents, evaluation of potential new services, monitoring attitudes to companies/facilities/major events
- traveller-related issues, e.g. goods or services needed during stay, clarity and usefulness of information provision, activity patterns during stay
- airport-related issues, e.g. upmarket retailing, catering, new facility development
- airline-related issues, e.g. advertising, passenger satisfaction
- service-related issues, e.g. speed of connection, quality of handling.

Source: http://www.mrsl.co.uk

■ Research methods

The three most commonly used methods for collecting primary data are interviews and surveys, observation and experiments.

Interviews and surveys

Interviews and surveys involve the collection of data directly from individuals. This may be by direct face-to-face personal interview, either individually or in a group, by telephone or by a mail questionnaire. Each of these techniques, considered in turn below, has its own set of advantages and disadvantages, which are summarised in Table 5.1.

Personal interviews. A personal interview is a face-to-face meeting between an interviewer and a respondent. It may take place in the home, the office, the street, a shopping mall, or at any prearranged venue. In one extreme case, a holiday company decided to interview respondents who were at leisure on the beach. One can imagine the varied responses!

Table 5.1 Comparative performance of interview and survey techniques

	Personal interviews	Group interviews	Telephone survey	Mail survey
Cost per response	High	Fairly high	Low	Very low
Speed of data collection	Fast	Fast	Very fast	Slow
Quantity of data collectable	Large	Large	Moderate	Moderate
Ability to reach dispersed population	Low	Low	High	High
Likely response rate	High	Very high	Fairly high	Low
Potential for interviewer bias	High	Very high	Fairly high	None
Ability to probe	High	High	Fairly high	None
Ability to use visual aids	High	High	None	Fairly high
Flexibility of questioning	High	Very high	Fairly high	None
Ability to ask complex questions	High	High	Fairly high	Low
Ability to get truth on sensitive questions	Fairly low	Fairly high	Fairly high	High
Respondent anonymity	Possible	Fairly possible	None	None
Likely respondent cooperation	Good	Very good	Good	Poor
Potential for respondent misunderstanding	Low	Low	Fairly low	High

There are three broad types of personal interview:

(a) the in-depth, largely unstructured interview, taking almost a conversational form: this is very useful for exploring attitudinal and motivational issues. It could last for one or two hours and can range fairly freely over a number of relevant issues. There is often considerable scope for the interviewer to explore some topics in more depth if additional unforeseen themes emerge in the interview, and thus high-level interviewing skills are needed, along with a sound knowledge of the product-market concept being examined. However, the time taken to complete an interview, and the cost of each interview, make large-scale surveys of this nature prohibitively expensive. In B2B markets, they are often used on a small-scale basis to fill gaps left by other approaches such as mail or telephone surveys.

(b) the structured interview: this allows the interviewer far less flexibility to explore responses further and results in a more programmed, almost superficial interview. Little use is made of open-ended questions and the questionnaire is carefully designed for ease and speed of recording information and progress through the interview. The use of a standardised questionnaire means that the responses from a large number of individuals can be handled with considerable ease, as there is no need for further interpretation and analysis. The limitations stem mainly from the need to design and pilot the questionnaire very carefully to ensure that it meets the specification expected of it. We look more closely at some of these questionnaire issues on pp. 159 *et seq.*

(c) the semi-structured interview: this is a hybrid of the other two methods and is based around a programmed script, but the inclusion of some open-ended questions gives the interviewer scope to pursue certain issues more flexibly.

marketing *in action*

Category management

Category management (CM) is a partnership between a supplier or a small number of suppliers and a retailer. A category is a group of brands that have something in common that makes them complement each other, compete directly or act as substitutes for each other. Examples of categories might include breakfast cereals, dairy products, bagged snacks or hot beverages. It is not just FMCG products that have adopted category management techniques. Borders (see pp. 10–11) reorganised to emphasise category management for specialised categories of books, children's products, multimedia, gifts, stationery and the café (Mutter, 2001). Each category has its own sales and marketing team and different merchandising activities. The objective of CM is to streamline the number of brands offered in the store in a category and to manage logistics, space allocation on the shelf, pricing and promotions for the category as a whole to enhance sales and profits for both the retailer and the supplier. CM has not, however, been without its critics (Basuroy et al., 2001). It has been suggested that both consumers and brand owners lose out despite the fact that CM is claimed as a win–win situation as it eliminates the cost of inefficiency for all. They claimed that retailers win at the expense of the other two parties; the consumer pays higher prices and the supplier gets lower prices. Either way, the process is information hungry, as the whole business has to start to be managed by a good understanding of consumer impact and by facts rather than intuition in the supplier–retailer–consumer chain (Marsden, 2001).

Market research has a big role to play in developing and implementing CM effectively, but according to Reed (1998) it is a very different, more complex kind of research because it has to examine all the levels in the partnership. Before CM, retailers and major manufacturers tended to stick to their own areas and confine their research problem to those areas. Retailers thus mainly worried about how customers shop and manufacturers mainly worried about consumer behaviour connected with brands and brand image. Under CM, both sets of concerns come together and add a further dimension relating to how brands fit together and interact with each other within a category. Certainly, market research objectives that are to influence CM decisions have an impact on what kind of research is done. More research, for example, is likely to be carried out in the retail environment itself and

researchers will be looking for representative samples of category users rather than representative households (Reed, 1998). For market research companies, all this means bigger, more complex research studies, and the need to ensure that objectives are well defined and that findings are clearly communicated.

The Harris Research Centre undertook research for brand manufacturer Van den Bergh Foods to discover in detail how shoppers in store buy 'yellow fats' as part of a category management exercise. To answer the client's questions, this complex research involved (Qureshi and Baker, 1998):

- *36 hours of shopper observation using remote control video equipment*. This allowed researchers to see how shoppers naturally behaved at the fixture: how long they spent, how they reacted to point of sale material, what products they picked up, what they selected, etc.
- *1,200 entrance/exit interviews*. Entrance interviews establish what intentions shoppers have when starting the shopping trip, including whether they intend to buy a specific brand of yellow fat or just any brand, or whether they have no intention of buying at all. Exit interviews of the same consumers then record what actually happened, whether they bought what they planned or switched brands, or impulse purchased something that they had not intended to buy on entering the store.

- *1,300 shopper interviews at the fixture*. This allows researchers to probe the reasons that shoppers think they are behaving as they are, as it is happening. Thus the researcher can ask about price awareness, influences on selection, reasons for final selection, etc.
- *200 in-store, in-depth interviews*. This helps researchers to check out shopping routes around the store and to gain deeper insights into how shoppers behave in the store as a whole.
- *72 accompanied shopping interviews*. A researcher visits the shopper at home before a shopping trip and investigates pre-shopping behaviour and decisions. Then the researcher accompanies the shopper around the store and gathers information about issues connected with the retailer (e.g. branding of the store, colour schemes, layout, queuing, parking, fixtures, service), but putting the emphasis on their relationship with the category and how the shopper buys that category.

The results of all these primary research methods give Van den Bergh a detailed and three-dimensional view of not only how its brands fit into the consumer's life at home, but also their role and impact on the shopping trip, how its brands and the competitors' brands affect the consumer's decisions and behaviour at the fixture, and how those brands fit into the retailer's store.

Group interviews or focus groups. Group interviews are used to produce qualitative data that cannot be generalised to the wider population, but which can provide useful insights into underlying attitudes and behaviours relevant to the marketer. A group interview, often referred to as a focus group, normally involves between six and eight respondents considered to be representative of the target group being examined. The role of the interviewer is to introduce topics, encourage and clarify responses and generally guide proceedings in a manner that is effective without being intrusive (Witthaus, 1999).

In this kind of group situation, individuals can express their views either in response to directed questions or, preferably, in response to general discussion on the themes that have been introduced. Often, the interaction and dialogue between respondents are more revealing of opinions. So that participants will relax enough to open out like this, it is often helpful to select the group concerned to include people of a similar status. For example, a manufacturer of an innovative protective gum shield for sports persons organised different group interviews for sports players (users) and dentists (specifiers). Further subdivision could have been possible by type of sport, or to distinguish the casual player from the professional.

Primary data collection is a familiar sight in the majority of High Streets and shopping centres. The interviewer relies on interviewees being amenable and giving up some time.

Group interviews are especially useful where budgets are limited or if the research topic is not yet fully understood. If secondary data have clearly indicated in quantitative terms that there is a gap in the market, group interviews may be useful in providing some initial insights into why that gap exists, whether customers are willing to see it filled and with what. This could then provide the basis for more detailed and structured investigation. There are, of course, risks in the approach. Relying too much on direct responses from a small number of consumers can present an inaccurate picture and some see it as part of being customer focused rather than as a serious approach to market research due to its vulnerability to delivering 'what you want to hear' (Gofton, 2000). Then again, if between four and six different discussion groups have been held, some common patterns worth investigating further may begin to emerge.

Telephone interviews. Telephone interviews are primarily used as a means of reaching a large number of respondents relatively quickly and directly. It is far more difficult to ignore a telephone call than a mail survey, although the amount and complexity of information that can be gathered are often limited. In the absence of any visual prompts and with a maximum attention span of probably no more than 10 minutes, the design of the questionnaire needs to be given great care and piloting is essential to ensure that the information required is obtainable.

The range of applications is wide but the telephone is especially useful for usage and purchase surveys where market size, trends and competitive share are to be assessed. Other applications include assessing advertising and promotional impact, customer satisfaction studies and establishing a response to a very specific phenomenon, such as the launch of a new export assistance scheme. Kwik Fit Exhausts telephones its recent customers to establish the degree of satisfaction with their recent purchase.

The interviewing process itself is highly demanding, but the use of software packages can enable the interviewer to record the findings more effectively and formally and to steer through the questionnaire, using loops and routeing through, depending on the nature of the response. With the demand for such surveys, a number of agencies specialise in telephone research techniques.

eg   Telder, based in Utrecht in the Netherlands, offers a full range of market research services including telephone research. Although not a large company, it nevertheless has 70 interviewers per shift using CATI (computer-assisted telephone interviewing). Quality control is maintained by careful training and by listening to and observing interviews via the computer system as they are happening. This enables helpful feedback to be given to the interviewer (http://www.telder.com). Hermelin Research in Scandinavia has over 230 computerised interviewing stations at its CATI centres in Norrköping, Halden, Pori and Copenhagen. To the company the design of the computer support system is crucial in reflecting the aims of the research and giving clear guidelines to the interviewers. In the CATI forms, recording sounds for music surveys is possible, for example. Careful design also helps the structuring of the data once captured to provide the client with the insights required. The interviewers are again central to Hermelin. They need a basic knowledge of computers and are selected for different kinds of surveys in different areas depending on their level of education, age and experience for the project (http://www.hermelin.swe).

Mail questionnaires. This popular form of research involves sending a questionnaire through the post to the respondent for self-completion and return to the researchers. Questionnaires can, of course, also be handed out at the point of sale, or included in product packaging, for buyers to fill in at their own convenience and then post back to the researchers. Hotels and airlines assess their service provision through this special kind of mail survey, and many electrical goods manufacturers use them to investigate purchasing decisions.

While the mail survey has the advantage of wide coverage, the lack of control over response poses a major problem. Researchers cannot control who responds and when and the level of non-response can create difficulties. Response rates can drop to less than 10 per cent in some surveys, although the more pertinent the research topic to the respondent, and the more 'user friendly' the questionnaire, the higher the response rate. The variable cost of a 1,000 questionnaire postal survey is between £600 and £800. That excludes the cost of buying a mailing list or investment in specialised mail handling equipment. It is not the cost of the mailing that counts, however, but the cost per response gained when response rates can vary between 5 and 50 per cent (http://www.b2binternational.com). Offering an incentive can also work (Brennan *et al.*, 1991). In a survey of Irish hotel and guest house owners, the offer of free tickets to a local entertainment facility proved an attractive incentive. Other larger-scale consumer surveys promise to enter all respondents into a draw for a substantial prize.

Mail surveys are especially prevalent in B2B markets, where target respondents can be more easily identified from contacts or mailing lists. The process of mailing can also be readily implemented and controlled using the organisation's normal administrative and mailing infrastructure already set up for response logging, address label generation, folding and franking, etc. One way of trying to improve response rates for B2B mail surveys is to warn or notify the desired respondent in advance that the survey is on its way. Haggett and Mitchell (1994), reviewing the literature on prenotification, found that overall it increases response rates by around 6 per cent and on average reduces by 1 the number of days taken to respond. The telephone shows the best results, increasing responses by 16 per cent, while postcards only manage a 2.5 per cent improvement. There is, however, no evidence to suggest that the quality of the response is also improved.

There is no one best method to select from the group discussed above. Much will depend on the nature of the research brief, especially in the light of the resources available and the quality and quantity of information required for decision-making. Another factor that has become of significant concern is the cost of the research survey. Face-to-face interviews, especially if conducted on an in-depth basis, tend to be the most costly and time consuming, thus making this form of survey less attractive. Other survey techniques, such as group interviews, telephone surveys and mail questionnaires, all provide alternative, cheaper ways of gathering data. Each of them, however, also has its own set of limitations. Ultimately, the decision on choice of technique has to put aside absolute cost considerations and think in terms of finding the most cost-effective way of collecting those vital data.

Internet research

The growth in the use of the Internet is having a big impact on the market research industry and online research is now being increasingly used in preference to other research methods. Billings (2001) reported that electronic market research revenues in the USA in 2000 were £179m., up from £23m. in 1998. In Europe the market is worth £31m. (compared with £3m. in 1998), but that figure was expected to double within two years. By 2004, according to Poynter (2000), around 50 per cent of market research will be conducted over the Internet.

Internet usage rates will determine the speed and scope of Internet market research. In the UK, the figure is 45 per cent compared to 60 per cent in the USA, so obtaining a representative sample of the population is still highly problematic. It is fine if you want to research Internet users, but for more targeted or representative samples it has severe limitations. A range of techniques is being employed, however, including online focus groups, questionnaires, pop-up surveys and extended e-mail groups. Table 5.2 highlights the advantages and disadvantages of online research. The big attractions are the significantly reduced data collection costs and the speed of setting up and implementing research activities. As with any research technique, however, it is important to ensure that what comes back is reliable and useful. There is always a risk that 'cheap' will mean devaluing the quality of the research.

The market research company, Future Foundation, has used the Internet for qualitative research, including week-long e-mail groups, online moderated groups with panels and offline groups (Cornish, 2001; http://www.futurefoundation.net). Others are making full use of the power of the Internet to present media such as sounds, images and video clips or to use complex question routeings that are incompatible with the printed page or interview (Bolden *et al.*, 2000).

The law on data collection over the Internet is tightening. The UK's Data Protection Act 1998 prohibits the collection of data without consent, or for purposes not disclosed at the time. This means that the consumer must be made aware of any recording of websites browsed or online purchases in advance, allowing them to opt out if they want (Anstead, 2000). This

Table 5.2 Advantages and disadvantages of Internet research

	Type of online research	
	Quantitative	Qualitative
Benefits	Inexpensive compared with traditional research methodologies	Slightly faster and cheaper than traditional focus groups
	Fast turnaround	Avoids dominance by 'loud' personalities
	Automated data collection	More client control
	Can show graphics, sometimes video	Can show concepts or websites
	No interviewer bias in data	Easier to recruit respondents
	Data quality (logic checks and in-depth open-ended answers)	Can be coordinated internationally and allows for mixed nationalities
	Seamless international coordination	
Limitations	Respondent 'universe'	Lose non-verbal elements of traditional focus groups
	Sampling issues: narrow target audience; difficult to identify; understanding the sample	Less useful for emotive issues
		Online moderation requires new skills
	Often self-completion based, therefore potentially self-selecting	Some respondents can be hampered by slow typing speeds
	Technical problems	Technical problems
		Sampling issues: narrow target audience can be tricky to identify; can be difficult to understand the sample

Source: Alex Johnston, Technology and Communications Director for New Media Research International, as reported by Gray (2000b).

also applies to online research. In order to undertake a survey prior permission has to be obtained from respondents before a potentially unwanted e-mail is sent: it is essential that people agree in advance to their e-mail addresses being used for that purpose. Obtaining e-mail addresses and ensuring that the consumer is happy to be sent information is one thing, but per-suading people to e-mail back to verify their identity and signify their willingness to participate – a process known as closed-loop verification – is another (Billings, 2001). This is bad news from the researcher's point of view, because if a significant proportion of potential respondents opt out, it will reduce the representativeness of online research.

The Internet will increasingly become a useful way of researching customer behaviour, especially for online purchasing. It is also emerging as a complementary tool for collecting consumer research data alongside traditional methods. Although it may not replace these methods, its advantages of higher response rates, spontaneity, multimedia application and personalisation will help to improve the targeting of those harder-to-find groups.

Observational research

This method involves, as its name implies, the observation by trained observers of particu-lar individuals or groups, whether they are staff, consumers, potential consumers, members of the general public, children or whoever. The intention is to understand some aspect of their behaviour that will provide an insight into the problem that has been identified by the marketing research plan. For example, trials are often conducted with new products in which consumers are asked to use a particular product and are observed while they do so, thus giving information about design, utility, durability and other aspects, such as ease of use by different age groups, and whether people naturally use it in the intended way. This provides an opportunity to test the product and observe how it is used first hand.

eg   In 2001, Nationwide Building Society built a 'Usability Centre' in Swindon. Consumers are invited to evaluate all media through interaction; paper, web, voice, ATM and face-to-face in simulated environments. The centre has a fully working branch and a lounge with a televi-sion and sofa to recreate the customer's experience of the places in which they come into contact with information and equipment. This helps Nationwide to fully understand the actual interaction between consumers and the Society (Moeng, 2001). Tennents Caledonian Breweries preferred to observe the real thing in an attempt to understand how consumers behave in a bar towards premium draught beer. Researchers observed consumer behaviour in real bars, then introduced themselves and asked consumers why they had behaved that way (Miles, 2000).

'Making Nationwide easy to do business with.' By simulating the customer's experiences of their services in their usability centre, Nationwide can fully understand the interaction between customers and staff and improve them where necessary.

Source: Nationwide Building Society.

Another form of observational research that deliberately seeks feedback on employee performance is *mystery shopping*. This allows a researcher to go through the same experience as a normal customer, whether in a store, restaurant, plane or showroom. As far as the employees are concerned, they are just dealing with another customer and they are not aware that they are being closely observed. The 'shopper' is trained to ask certain questions and to measure performance on such things as service time, customer handling and question answering. The more objective the measures, the more valuable they are to marketing managers in ensuring that certain benchmark standards are being achieved. Mystery shopping is widely used by the larger retailers and service organisations to support staff training and help the organisation to understand the customer–service provider interface (Bromage, 2000).

The potential problems that can be experienced with interviews are also likely with observation where human observers are used. That is, the training and supervision of observers are of great importance and, since it is more subjective, the likelihood of misinterpretation is higher. On the other hand, mechanical observation tools may be used to overcome bias problems, such as supermarket scanners monitoring the purchases of particular consumers or groups of consumers, and the Nielsen people meters, used to monitor the viewing and listening habits of television watchers and radio listeners.

Other devices can be used to observe or monitor closely the physiological responses of individuals, such as their pupil dilation (using a tachistoscope) when watching advertisements, to indicate degree of interest. A galvanometer, which measures minute changes in perspiration, can also help to gauge a subject's interest in advertisements.

eg Specialised software is now available to enable real-time recording of consumer behaviour in a retail environment. A system developed by DMP DDB, Noldus and Tracksys created an improved method to introduce speed and rigour into the observational process. First, a store map is scanned into the PC and the relevant aisles, checkouts and other zones of interest are specified by the researcher. This map is then displayed during data collection on a mini-notebook PC with a touch screen. When an 'interesting' consumer enters the store, the researcher must first request permission to observe him/her as they are followed by camera through the store using the screen. Behavioural variables can also be recorded according to pre-selected categories, for example what products the consumer is looking at, picking up, placing in their basket, or returning to the shelf. Data files collected during the day can be e-mailed to a central database where detailed analyses of the data can be carried out. This includes the time spent in different areas of the store, the frequency of movement between the various zones of interest, and the number of times shoppers engaged in different behaviours, e.g. browsing, picking products up, talking to co-shoppers, asking for assistance. This data can be calculated per individual or across different groups of customers according to age, sex or other independent variables. By reducing the long and tedious hours of observing the observers' videos, conclusions can be drawn more quickly and effectively (http://www.noldus.com).

In some ways, observation is a more reliable predictor of behaviour than verbal assertions or intentions. Where interaction is not needed with the respondent, or where the respondent may be unable to recall the minutiae of their own behaviour, direct observation may be a valuable additional tool in the researcher's armoury. It is particularly informative when people are not aware that they are being observed and are thus acting totally naturally, rather than changing their behaviour or framing responses to suit what they think researchers want to see or hear.

Experimentation

The third method through which primary data can be collected is by conducting an experiment. This may involve the use of a laboratory (or other artificial environment), or the experiment may be set in its real-world situation, for example test marketing a product. In the experimental situation, researchers manipulate the independent variable(s), for example price, promotions or product position on a store shelf, and monitor the impact on the dependent variable, for example sales, to try to determine if any change in the dependent variable occurs. The important aspect of an experiment is to hold most of the independent variables constant (as well as other potentially confounding factors) while manipulating one independent variable and monitoring its impact on the dependent variable. This is usually possible in a laboratory, where control of the environment is within the power of researchers, but far less possible in a real-world situation where a myriad of external complications can occur that can confuse the results.

For example, a manufacturer may want to find out whether new packaging will increase sales of an existing product, before going to the expense of changing over to the new packaging. The manufacturer could conduct an experiment in a laboratory, perhaps by setting up a mock supermarket aisle, inviting consumers in and then observing whether their eyes were drawn to the new packaging, whether they picked it up, how long they looked at it and whether they eventually chose it in preference to the competition. The problem with this, however, is that it is still a very artificial situation, with no guarantees that it can replicate what would have happened in real life. Alternatively, therefore, the manufacturer could set up a field experiment, trialling the new packaging in real stores in one or more geographic regions and/or specific market segments and then monitoring the results.

Not all experimental research designs need to be highly structured, formal or set up for statistical validation purposes. For example, side-by-side experiments where shop A offers a different range or mix from shop B, which in all other respects is identical to shop A, can still reveal interesting insights into marketing problems, even though the rigour of more formal experimental designs is not present.

■ Sampling

Particularly in mass consumer markets, time and cost constraints mean that it is impractical to include every single target customer in whatever data-gathering method has been chosen. It is not necessary even to begin to try to do this, because a carefully chosen representative sample of the whole population (usually a target market) will be enough to give the researchers confidence that they are getting a true picture that can be generalised. In most cases, researchers are able to draw conclusions about the whole population (i.e. the group or target market) based on the study of a sample.

Figure 5.3, based on Tull and Hawkins (1990), shows the main stages in the sampling process. Each will be considered briefly in turn.

Figure 5.3 Stages in the sampling process

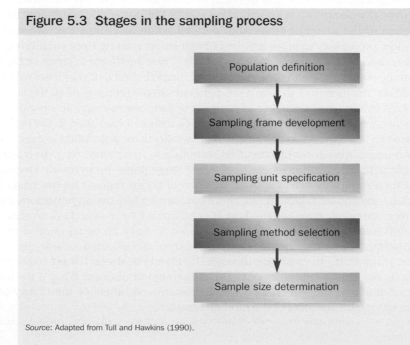

Source: Adapted from Tull and Hawkins (1990).

Population definition

The population to be surveyed will derive from the overall research objectives. Often this will be based on a target market or segment, but even then further definition based on markets, products or behaviours is unlikely to be necessary to create a tightly defined population.

Sampling frame

The sampling frame is the means of access to the population to be surveyed. It is basically a list from which individual names can be drawn. Registers of electors or lists of organisations compiled from directories such as *Kompass* and *Dun and Bradstreet* are examples of possible sampling frames. Internal customer records may also provide a sampling frame, although researchers need to be very sure that such records give a complete picture, and that there is no doubt that this is the required population for the study, rather than just a cheap, quick and easy way of generating an extensive list of names.

Sampling unit

The sampling unit is the actual individual from whom researchers want a response. In consumer markets, the sampling unit is usually the name attached to the address in the sampling frame. In B2B markets, however, this stage can be complex because organisations can have a number of individuals concerned with decision-making. It is very important to identify the right individual, as the responses of the purchasing manager in this case may be different from those of the managing director.

Sampling method selection

The next step in the process is to select the sample method, which is the means by which individual sample units and elements are selected from the larger sampling frame. The main and early decision is whether to use probability or non-probability sampling methods.

Probability sampling. Random, or *probability sampling*, where each member of the population has an equal or known chance of being selected for the sample, offers specified levels of confidence about the limits of accuracy of the results. So if a retailer wanted to do a survey to establish satisfaction levels with checkout services, it might decide to interview every thirtieth customer coming through the checkouts during research sessions held at different times of the week. At the end of the process, the retailer might be able to conclude that the findings were correct to the 95 per cent level of confidence – in other words there was only a 1 in 20 chance that the sample was biased or unrepresentative.

Stratified sampling is an important method of probability sampling, which involves the division of the sampling frame into defined strata or groups that are mutually exclusive. Random probability samples are then drawn independently from each group. This method is widely used in B2B markets, as they naturally divide into discrete layers or bands, reflecting for example company size, geographic location, market shares or purchase volumes. Researchers could decide, therefore, to take a 100 per cent sample (census) of all the larger firms (defined perhaps by turnover or number of employees) and then use random sampling with the rest. By effectively restructuring the sample frame in a manner best suited to the project, greater confidence can be enjoyed that the sample closely reflects the population in question.

An alternative form of stratified sampling is *area sampling*. In a survey of German builders' merchants, for example, the first stage might be to divide Germany into regions and then randomly select a small number of those regions as the basis for the sample. Within each chosen region, researchers randomly select the organisations for the sample.

With a random sampling method, it is important for researchers to ensure that the sampling frame used does enable each member to have an equal chance of being selected. Furthermore, actually obtaining responses from the selected sample can be quite difficult. What if the thirtieth customer through the checkout doesn't want to stop? What if there's nobody at home when the interviewer calls round or phones? What if the sampling frame is out of date and the selected consumer has moved house or died? Any of these circumstances violates the ideal of the random sample.

Non-random sampling. *Non-random samples* are much easier to identify than random samples because they are not based on the same strict selection requirements and allow researchers a little more flexibility. The results from these samples are not representative of the population being studied and may lack the statistical rigour generated by random sampling, but they are still often of considerable use to researchers. Two main non-random sampling methods may be used:

1 *Judgemental sampling.* This method is widely used in B2B market research. Sample units are selected deliberately by researchers, because they are felt to represent better sources of the required information. Given the concentrated nature of many industries, if a contracting company wanted to enter a new geographic market, for example, it would probably make sense to survey the larger users if that was the target segment of interest, rather than draw at random from all users, large and small. Of course, no inference could be drawn about the wider population from such a sample method.

2 *Quota sampling.* Quota samples are formed when researchers decide that a certain proportion of the total sample should be made up of respondents conforming to certain characteristics. It may be decided, for example, that for a particular study, the sample should consist of 400 non-working women aged between 25 and 35, 250 full-time working and 350 part-time working women in the same age group. This breakdown may reflect the actual structure of the market under consideration. Each interviewer is then told how many completed questionnaires to bring back within each quota category. The choice of respondents is not random, since the interviewer is actively looking for people who fulfil the quota definitions and, once the quota is full, will reject any further respondents in that category. The advantage of quota sampling is that it is quicker and cheaper to do than a full random sample would be, as no sample frame has to be devised and researchers do not have to worry whether the sampling frame is up to date or not. Furthermore, interviewers are not committed to following up specific respondents. Under a quota sample, if a particular respondent does not want to cooperate, then that's fine – the interviewer will look for another one.

Sample size

A final yet very important consideration in the sampling process is sample size. There is no point in spending more time and money pursuing any bigger sample than you have to. With random sampling based on statistical analysis, researchers can have confidence within prescribed limits that the sample elements are representative of the population being studied.

As one would expect, the higher the levels of confidence required, the greater the size of the sample needed. In Europe, surveys of consumer buying habits are often around 2,000 units, which would typically yield a 95 per cent confidence level that the sample reflects the characteristics of the population. In B2B markets, sample sizes of between 300 and 1,000 can be used to produce high levels of confidence. This would be especially true when suppliers operate within limited geographical areas (such as plumbers, or van hire firms), the value of sales is usually small (motor factors), and the buying organisations are also small (http://www.b2binternational.com).

■ Questionnaire design

The questionnaire is a commonly used research instrument for gathering and recording information from interviews, whether face-to-face, mail or telephone surveys. Researchers soon learn that the best planned surveys soon fall apart if the questionnaire is poorly designed and fails to gather the data originally anticipated. To minimise the risk of disappointment, there are several dimensions to consider in questionnaire design.

Objectives

The aim of a questionnaire is closely linked with the overall purpose of the research. It is tailor-made to meet the information requirements of the study and therefore lies at the heart of the research process. If the questionnaire is to fulfil its role properly as a means of data collection, then there are several areas that need to be analysed, as outlined in Table 5.3.

Table 5.3 The objectives of a questionnaire

Objective	Suggestions
To suit the nature of the target population	Pitch the questions in a way they can understand; ask questions they can be expected to be able to answer given their knowledge and experience.
To suit the research methods	For example, a telephone survey cannot use the kind of visual aids that a face-to-face interview can; a postal survey is less likely to get responses if it is lengthy or if it is probing feelings/attitudes.
To suit the research objectives	It must be designed appropriately to gather the right information for answering the research questions – no more, no less.
To collect the right kind of data	The quality and completeness of responses are important for a successful survey. There must also be the right depth of data, whether it is factual or probing attitudes, beliefs, opinions, motivations or feelings.
To aid data analysis	Ensure that it is as easy as possible to take the raw data from the questionnaires and input them accurately into any analytical framework/software package being used.
To minimise error and bias	Ensure that the questionnaire is 'tight' enough to allow it to be administered by any interviewer, to any respondent, at any time, in any location with consistency. Also ensure that questions cannot be misinterpreted or misunderstood.
To encourage accurate and full responses	Avoid leading or judgemental questions; ensure clarity in the way questions are asked; ensure that respondents feel at ease rather than threatened or intimidated by the questions.

Some thought also needs to be given to ensuring that the questionnaire will retain the interest of the respondent, so that full completion takes place. It is easy with self-administered questionnaires for the respondent to give up if the questionnaire becomes tedious, seems to be poorly explained, or is too long or complex. It is thus important to make sure that the questionnaire takes as little time as possible to complete. Research in the USA found that 20 per cent of consumers thought that questionnaires in general, including 30-minute telephone surveys, were too long (McDaniel *et al.*, 1985). According to Gander (1998), the 30-minute survey is still common, making the interviewer's job much more difficult.

Types of questions

There are two main types of question that can be asked in a questionnaire: open-ended questions and closed questions. The category of open-ended questions has many significant style variations within it, but they all allow considerable scope for the respondent to express views on the selected theme (and in some cases, on other themes!). Closed questions force the respondent to choose one or more responses from a number of possible replies provided in the questionnaire.

Open-ended questions. Questions such as 'In the buying of garden furniture, what factors do you find important?' or 'What do you think of the trend towards out-of-town shopping centres?' are open ended because they do not give a range of potential answers for the respondent to choose from. In both cases, interviewers could be faced with as many different answers as there are respondents. Using such questions can, therefore, be rewarding, because of the rich insights given in a relatively unrestrained manner. The difficulties, however, emerge in recording and analysing the responses, given their potential length and wide variations. Nevertheless, it has been argued that using open-ended questions can help to build the goodwill of the respondent through allowing an unrestricted response (Chisnall, 1986).

Closed questions. Closed questions fall into two broad groups, dichotomous and multiple-choice questions. *Dichotomous questions* allow only two choices, such as 'yes or no' or 'good or bad'. These questions are easy to ask and easy to answer. With careful pre-coding, it is also relatively easy to analyse responses and to use them for cross-tabulation with another variable, for example to find out whether those who say that they do use a product pay more attention to product-specific advertising than those who say that they do not use it.

Multiple-choice questions are a more sophisticated form of closed question, because they can present a list of possible answers for the respondent to choose from. This could be, for example, a list of alternative factors that might influence a purchasing decision (price, quality, availability, etc.), or it could reflect alternative levels of strength of feeling, degree of importance or other shades of variation in response to the variable under consideration.

These questions need to be designed carefully, to incorporate and group as wide a range of answers as possible, since restraining the amount of choice available creates a potential source of bias. The alternative responses need to reflect the likely range, without overlap or duplication, since this too may create bias. By offering an 'other, please specify' category, these questions provide some opportunity to collect responses that were not originally conceived (but that should have been identified in the pilot stage) or responses that do not fit neatly into the imposed structure. However, the advantage of multiple-choice questions is that again they are relatively straightforward to analyse, if pre-coding has been used.

Multiple choices can also be used to overcome some respondent sensitivities. If asked 'How old are you?' or 'What do you earn?' as open questions, many people may refuse to answer because the questions are too specific and personal. Phrasing the question as 'To which of these age groups do you belong, 17 or under, 18–24, 25–34, 35–44, 45 or over?' allows respondents to feel that they have not given quite so much away. The bands need to be defined to reflect the likely scope of responses from the target respondents, and to be easy for them to relate to. Professionals, for example, will be more likely to relate to bands based on annual salary than manual workers, who are more likely to know what their weekly wage is.

Rating scales are a form of multiple-choice question, widely used in attitude measurement, motivational research and in situations where a number of complex, interacting factors are likely to influence a situation. There are a number of scaling methods, including:

1 *Likert summated ratings*. A large number of statements, relevant to the research study, are built up from preliminary research and piloting. These statements are then given to respondents who are asked to respond on a five- or seven-point scale, for example 'strongly agree', 'agree', 'neither agree nor disagree', 'disagree' and 'strongly disagree'. The responses are scored from 5 (strongly agree) down to 1 (strongly disagree). The average score across all respondents can then be used to establish the general strength of attitude towards the variable under consideration. An examination of the pattern of individual responses may also reveal issues of interest to the marketer.

2 *Semantic differential scales*. These scales were developed to measure differences in the meaning of words or concepts. This method involves a bipolar five- or seven-point rating scale, with each extreme defined by carefully selected adjectives representing opposite extremes of feeling. A study of retail store atmosphere might offer a series of scales including 'warm–cold', 'friendly–unfriendly', or 'fashionable–unfashionable', for example. Once the scales have been defined, the product (or whatever) is rated on each of them to reveal a profile of the respondent's opinion. Such scales can also be used for measuring corporate image or advertising image and for comparing different brands. In the latter case, if two products are plotted at the same time on the same scales, significant differences may emerge, and help the marketer to understand better the relative positioning of products in consumers' minds.

Examples of both types of rating scale can be found in Figure 5.4.

Figure 5.4 Examples of rating scales

Likert scale

	Strongly agree	Agree	Neither agree nor disagree	Disagree	Strongly disagree
Safeway's prices are generally lower than those of other supermarkets					
Safeway's offers the widest range of groceries					
Safeway's staff are always friendly and helpful					
I never have to queue too long at the checkout					
Supermarket own-brands are just as good as manufacturers' brands					
Low prices are important to me in choosing a supermarket					
Supermarkets should provide more personal services					

Semantic differential scale

	1	2	3	4	5	6	7	
Modern								Old-fashioned
Friendly								Unfriendly
Attractive								Unattractive
Spacious								Crowded
High quality goods								Low quality goods
Wide choice of goods								Limited choice of goods
Convenient opening hours								Inconvenient opening hours
Tidy								Untidy
Short queues								Long queues
Low prices								High prices

The wording of questions. The success or failure of a questionnaire lies as much in the detail as in the grand scheme and design. This includes the detailed wording of questions so that the respondent fully understands what is required and accurate responses are encouraged. The next few paragraphs raise a number of pertinent issues.

It is always important to ensure that the *meaning of words and phrases* is fully understood by the respondent. Particular effort should be made to avoid the use of jargon and technical language that may be unfamiliar to the respondent.

Ambiguity can lead to misunderstandings and thus poor or inaccurate responses. A question such as 'Do you buy this product frequently, sometimes, seldom or never?' seems to be clear and unambiguous, but think about it for a minute. What does 'frequently' mean? To one respondent it might mean weekly, to another it might mean monthly. Researchers should therefore be as specific as possible.

A further source of ambiguity or confusion occurs when the respondent is asked to cope with too many concepts at once. Two questions should therefore never be *piggy-backed*, i.e. asked in one question, such as: 'How important is price to you, and how do you think we could improve on value for money?'

Leading questions may tempt the respondent to favour a particular answer. This is not, of course, the essence of good research. Thus asking 'Are you, or are you not, in favour of capital punishment?' is more balanced than 'Are you in favour of capital punishment?', which is edging the respondent towards 'Yes' as an answer.

Questions that are *too closed* are a kind of leading question that may also frustrate researchers. 'Is price an important factor in your purchase?' begs the answer 'Yes', but even if it was a balanced question, the responses tell very little. It does not indicate how important price is to the respondent or what other factors influence the purchase. An open-ended or multiple-choice question might tell much more.

Researchers need to be sympathetic to people's *sensitivity*. Some areas are highly personal, so building up slowly may be important and 'soft' rather than 'hard' words should be used, for example 'financial difficulties' rather than 'debt'. Of course, the more sensitive the information, the more likely the respondent is to refuse to answer, lie or even terminate the interview.

Coding and rules. It is more important to obtain accurate and pertinent information than to design a questionnaire that embraces everything but rarely gets completed. Hague (1992) proposes an *ideal length* for three different types of questionnaire:

- telephone interviews: 5–30 minutes;
- visit interviews: 30 minutes to 2 hours;
- self-completion: four sides of A4, 20–30 questions.

A street interview would need to be very much shorter than 30 minutes to retain interest and prevent irritation.

The *layout* of the questionnaire is especially important for self-administered questionnaires. A cramped page looks unappealing, as well as making it difficult to respond. The layout should assist the recording and coding of responses and ease of flow through the interview to maintain momentum. Most questionnaires are now designed with *data coding* and ease of analysis in mind. This means that all responses to closed questions and multiple choices need to be categorised before the questionnaire is released, and that the layout must also be user friendly for whoever has to transfer the data from the completed questionnaire into a database.

The *order of the questions* is important for respondents, as the more confusing the flow and the more jumping around they have to do, the less likely they are to see it through to completion.

Support materials and explanation can be very important. For a mail survey a covering letter can be reassuring and persuasive while, at an interview, the interviewer needs to gain the respondent's attention and interest in participation. Visual aids, such as packaging or stills from advertising, can also get respondents more involved, as well as prompting their memories.

Piloting

Whatever care has been taken in the design of the questionnaire, problems usually emerge as soon as the questionnaire is tried on innocent respondents. Piloting a questionnaire on a small-scale sample can help to iron out any 'bugs', so that it can be refined before the full survey goes ahead. Initially, a fresh eye from colleagues can eliminate the worst howlers, but for most projects, it is best to set aside time for a full field pilot. This would mean testing the questionnaire on a small sub-sample (who will usually not then participate in the main survey) to check its meaning, layout and structure and, furthermore, to check whether it yields the required data and whether it can be analysed in the intended manner.

■ Conduct the research

Once the research plan has been developed and the methods of collection and proposed analysis identified, it is necessary to go about conducting the research itself. This stage will vary according to the type of research. The demands of a consumer survey involving perhaps thousands of respondents over a wide geographic area are very different from those of a select number of interviews in depth.

Particularly in primary research, it is this part of the process that often presents the biggest problem, because the collection of the data should not be left to poorly trained or badly briefed field researchers. In recent years, however, considerable progress has been made in professionalising research interviewers, moving away from the rather clichéd image of housewives earning extra cash. Training is now widespread and more male interviewers have been recruited both to enable access to previously no-go areas, such as high-crime housing estates, and to handle situations where gender may matter during the interview (Gray, 2000a).

eg Recruiting market research interviewers is not an easy job. Staff have to be prepared to work afternoons and evenings to make sure that they get representative samples of all kinds of workers. They also have to be well organised and good at managing themselves and their time, especially if they are working out in the field rather than in a telephone interview call centre, for example. All researchers need a strong sense of responsibility and have to be prepared to take an ethical approach to what they do. Field researchers have to be tough, to cope with less cooperative interviewees or to deal with the stranger kinds of people one meets when spending a lot of time hanging around city streets with a clipboard.

Research companies take a great deal of care in recruiting and training researchers. Some companies undertake lengthy initial telephone screening, partly to give applicants a better idea of what the job entails and partly to help develop a profile of the candidate. Many companies then insist on a face-to-face interview to check a candidate's appearance (especially for field researchers), their interaction skills and their ability to deal with situations. This is important because staff are effectively representing the research company and its clients and they have to be able to develop a rapport with interviewees quickly, reassure them and hold their attention, often through a fairly long and detailed survey.

Research company Gallup maintains that only 1 out of 16 candidates makes it through its selection procedures, a clear indication that the company sees the quality of its staff as an important asset. Those recruiting interviewers for telephone research call centres are less concerned about the appearance of their staff but more concerned about their telephone voice and ability to establish rapport without the face-to-face contact. Some companies even recruit people with certain regional accents to help this process (Gander, 1998).

There are a number of areas, in any kind of face-to-face research, where careful attention to detail can pay dividends. The greater the need for the interviewer to depart from a carefully prepared script and modus operandi, the greater the skill involved and the higher the cost of the interview. This is particularly emphasised in the implementation role of the interviewer who conducts a group discussion or an in-depth interview. The dangers of interview bias are always present where the interviewer records what they think has been said or meant, not what has actually been said in response to a question. This sort of bias can be particularly pronounced where open-ended questions are being used. There are some situations where conducting field research is especially challenging, such as when particular targets or subjects need to be covered. The extremely affluent or poor, ethnic minorities, youth and corporate executives are often harder to reach than many target groups in the UK (Gray, 2000a). Community intermediaries are thus often used, for example, to reach target groups such as older Asian women and the Jamaican community and persuade them to participate in research.

New technology is making a big impact in the implementation of field research by assisting in the questioning and recording process. Computer-aided telephone interviewing (CATI) and computer-aided personal interviewing (CAPI) have revolutionised data collection techniques and are now widely used. CAPI means that each interviewer is provided with a laptop computer which has the questionnaire displayed on screen. The interviewer can then read out text from the screen and key in the responses. The pre-programmed questionnaire will automatically route the interviewer to different parts of the questionnaire as appropriate and will prompt the interviewer to clarify any illogical answers. It helps quality control by creating greater consistency in interviewer questioning and the recording of answers, and furthermore allows the interviewer to concentrate on building a rapport with the respondent to help prevent fatigue and loss of interest in more complex questionnaires. CATI provides similar technology for telephone interviewing and again allows for greater consistency in interviewing and the recording of information.

■ Analyse and interpret the information

While the quality of the research data is essential, it is the analysis of the data, i.e. turning raw data into useful information, that provides the most value to the organisation. It is on the basis of the reports prepared from the data analysis that significant managerial decisions are likely to be made. The use of sophisticated computer hardware and software packages provides a powerful means of processing large quantities of data relatively easily. CAPI and CATI, scanners that can read completed questionnaires, complex statistical analysis and data manipulation have improved the speed, accuracy and depth of the analysis itself. However, it is still the human element, the researcher's expertise in identifying a trend or relationship or some other nugget hidden within the results, that provides the key component for decision makers and transforms the data and techniques used into valuable information.

eg   Speed of analysis is often just as important as the depth of analysis in some situations. Some clients want information within days of starting a campaign rather than waiting until three weeks after it has finished. With time-sensitive products, such as video/DVD and CD releases, the sales data from the first few days is a good indicator of the success of the campaign. If adjustments have to be made to the campaign, they often have to happen in the first week (McLuhan, 2001a).

Some care needs to be exercised in the interpretation of quantitative data. Outputs of calculations should never overrule sound common sense in assessing the significance and relevance of the data generated. There is sometimes the danger of analysis paralysis, where the use of highly sophisticated techniques almost becomes an end in itself, rather than simply a means of identifying new relationships and providing significant new insights for management. While the old saying that trends, differences or relationships are only meaningful if they are obvious to even the untrained statistical eye may be going too far, it does highlight the danger of misinterpreting cause and effect and the differences between groups of consumers, arising from over-reliance on finely balanced statistics pursued by researchers.

Not all data are quantitative, of course. Qualitative data arising from in-depth interviews or group discussions pose a different kind of challenge to researchers. Whereas quantitative data have to prove their reliability when compared with the wider population, qualitative data can never be claimed to be representative of what a wider sample of respondents might indicate. The main task of qualitative data, therefore, is to present attitudes, feelings and motivations in some depth, whether or not they are representative of the wider population.

To handle qualitative data analysis, great care must be taken in the recording of information. Video or taped interviews are thus helpful in enabling classification and categorisation of the main points to be checked and explored in depth. Similarly, issue or content analysis enables particular themes to be explored across a range of interviews. For example, if researchers wanted to identify the barriers to exporting in small firms, they might define such themes as market entry, market knowledge, finance or using agents as indicative of the main barriers to be assessed. The data analysis might be supported by a range of quotations from the interviews. Because of the richness and complexity of this kind of data, skilled psychologists are often used to explore and explain much of what is said and, indeed, not said.

So although the risks of bias are great in qualitative analysis, both in data selection and analysis, and although the results can, in untrained hands, be rather subjective and conjectural, the advantage arises from the fresh insights and perspectives that more rigorous statistical techniques would simply not generate.

■ Prepare and present report

The information provided by researchers must be in a form that is useful to decision makers. Too often, research reports are written in highly technical language or research jargon that, to a layperson, is confusing or meaningless. Marketers who want to use these reports to make decisions need them to be easily understandable. A report that is too complex is all but useless. That is why the formal presentation of the report, whether written or verbal (which allows the client to ask questions and seek clarification of points made), should be given as much thought, care and attention as any previous stage in the research process. It also allows the results to be personalised for the receiving organisation which can improve the perceived credibility of the findings and thus increase willingness to take action (Schmalensee, 2001).

Although a verbal presentation can play an important part in sharing understanding, it is the report itself that has the power to influence thinking significantly. Arguments can be carefully presented, with data used appropriately in their support, and the detail surrounding the main findings can be displayed to increase the client's confidence that the research was well executed to plan. There are no standard report formats, as much will depend on the nature of the research task undertaken.

■ Research evaluation

Research projects rarely go completely to plan. Although greater care in conducting pilot studies and exploratory research will make it more likely that the actual outcomes will match those planned, problems may still emerge that will require careful consideration in weighing up the value of the project. Thoughtful analysis of the planning, conduct and outcomes of the project will also teach valuable lessons for the future to both clients and researchers.

This stage can involve a review of all aspects of the research plan described above. Any deviations need to be understood, both in terms of the current results and for designing future research. With regard to the research project undertaken, the most important point is whether the research actually provided a sufficient quality and quantity of information to assist management decision-making. Sometimes, the research objectives may have been ambiguous or poorly framed in the context of the marketing problem being addressed. Ultimately, it is the marketing manager who must take responsibility for ensuring that the objectives and research plan were compatible and reflected the requirements, although researchers can help in this task.

Ethics in marketing research

The ethical concerns surrounding market research have been the subject of an ongoing debate in the industry for a long time. Because much consumer research involves specific groups of consumers, including children and other groups that might be considered vulnerable, it is essential that the researchers' credibility is maintained and that the highest standards of professional practice are demonstrated, and so the industry has established a set of professional ethical guidelines. These include such matters as protecting the confidentiality of respondents or clients, not distorting or misrepresenting research findings (for example, two major newspapers could both claim to be the market leader by using readership figures gathered over different time spans and failing to mention the time period), using tricks to gain information from respondents, conducting an experiment and not telling those being studied, and using research as a guise for selling and sales lead building.

BMRA, the British Market Research Association, is a trade association representing the interests of market research companies and helping to regulate them. It requires its members to subscribe to a code of conduct and insists that its larger members are accredited by the Market Research Quality Standards Association (BMRA, 1998). Of course, not all providers of market research are committed to compliance and not all bad practice can be eliminated, but considerable progress is being made.

5.6 Design a c
types of q
The object
questionn
then make
questionna

case s
Gatherir

The condom ma
as a bit of an en
as deadly seriou
ted diseases or
manufacturers,
just like any oth
company, on sou
sumers and their
Condom purc
impulse buys. A
that travelling ab
often led to plan
report found that
day to be the m
while in the 48–
business trip m
larger group of p
women expectir
travelled with co
planned purcha
condom manufa
assured of a qual
buying at home.
Impulse or re
second group, wh
tinued sales. The
retailers that con
selected, preferab
priced to avoid ar
the checkout. Thi
in distribution pat
exclusively in ph
sells nearly 30 pe
value, while phar
hold a 25 per cent
per cent share) a
shampoos. This ex
women, and encou
as a normal part
ASDA believes tha

corporate social responsibility *in action*

Finding out what kids are up to

When market researchers have to investigate children's behaviour and motivation as consumers, they have to proceed with extreme caution. It is very easy to step over both the legal line and industry codes designed to protect children and young people from predatory practices. Nevertheless, marketers cannot afford to ignore the needs of a segment estimated to be worth £300bn. Market research is especially important among these 5–16-year-olds because they can change their minds and preferences frequently and not always with reason, and there is a real risk that today's best-selling product is tomorrow's uncool fad from the past. Thus implementing carefully designed research that generates reliable insights and data ethically and with due respect to both children and their parents is well worth the effort.

The Market Research Society (MRS) has issued strict guidelines for researchers. Measures such as obtaining parental consent for interviews with under 16s in the home and preventing interviewer and child being alone together help to protect the rights of children and ensure that they are not exploited. The MRS Code of Conduct also seeks to reassure parents and protect the researcher from unfortunate claims (Cowlett, 2001).

Researchers also have a responsibility to prepare valid reports for their clients. Children are not easy to engage in research unless considerable care is taken in selecting research methods, location, group and interviewer dynamics, and response mechanisms. Children are often eager to please, may be intimidated by adult interviewers and may not understand the concepts and language used in research. Creative ways of engaging children often have

to be employed, using pictures, toys, play and multimedia stimuli.

An interactive website (http://www.yorg.com) conducts online research through a network of schools. The website claims that the surveys are completed in school classes by 21,000 children aged between 6 and 16 over the course of the year. The children respond intuitively to specialist software with full teacher approval as part of an IT session, each child playing on a multimedia workstation. The researchers go on to say, 'We don't bore them with books of multiple choice answers that are worse than homework. Our research programme involves them completely by using technology they love and understand. These kids respond live, on screen and with their peers. They interact with our software online so that the data gets to you fast, making your planning work in kid's time, not past times. You experience the honesty of today's kids as they have fun learning about themselves. Enrol your brand and learn fast what kids are really saying when the adults get out of their way' (www.yorg.com).

Throughout the process, there is not a researcher in sight. Profiles are then developed for different children's segments so that eager marketers can understand the target market better. Boys aged between 10 and 12, for example, are described as 'Money Mercenaries' with the following sample descriptors:

- Turned on by money and the prospect of making money.
- Prime target for financial institutions – savings/earnings schemes rule!
- Explosive energy – often boisterous and impulse driven.

- Bicycles, blades and music accessories are status objects prized by peers.
- Sports and computer interests intensified. Computer magazines avidly read.
- Violent TV and videos rule! Combat sports are essential viewing. Schwarzenegger remains a hero. Soaps keenly watched. Collections are in the decline. Entertained by TV advertising but sceptical of hard sell.
- Big brand (global) preferences, particularly sports brands, which translate into fashion statements.
- Mothers still important as clothes suppliers, footwear excepted!
- Girls kept at some distance – tolerated.
- Risk takers with tobacco, alcohol, drugs (including solvent abuse) and gambling.

Such profiles are no doubt read avidly by marketers keen to keep up with events and to tap into the potential. It does, however, raise perhaps another more serious social question: to what extent do we want today's youth to be exposed to better informed and targeted marketing effort? Who should decide what is acceptable? Is it right to target sports and music-related merchandise at this age group? Is the marketing of violent television programmes and video games or overt appeals to materialism in the child's best interests? High degrees of professionalism and ethical standards are adopted by most market research companies and brand suppliers when children are involved, but that does not take away the need to question the societal impact of excessive exposure to naked commercialism. Does the profile above simply lead branded-goods thinking, or is it a product of previous marketing exposure?

Sources: Cowlett (2001); Flack (1999).

duce Condomania South Park Condoms in 1999, targeting the 16–25-year-old group, and distributing via stores such as Virgin Megastores, Top Man and Our Price.

■ *Condomi* claims to be Europe's largest manufacturer of condoms, making over 300 million a year. Condomi sells its Stimulation, Sensation, Premium and Supersafe variants in the UK through Boots, Superdrug and other chemists. It also targets the younger end of the market with its slogan, 'you don't have to carry the brand your Dad used'. Its website, available in five languages, includes online shopping, but also has pinups, news and magazine elements making it more of a lifestyle site than just a place to shop.

Government health campaign advertising worked well for the manufacturers in creating generic demand for the product. In 1984, only 31 per cent of males and 35 per cent of females said that they would use a condom the first time they had sex with someone, but by 2001, 87 per cent of people said they would not have sex with a new partner without using a condom (this figure falls to 70 per cent among the 16–20-year-old group, however). It is also easier now for manufacturers to advertise directly and more explicitly, although they still have to be careful not to offend people too much or else they will not listen to the message. All the major manufacturers link themselves with various safer sex organisations, government-sponsored health education programmes, and events. Durex supports National Condom Week in the UK, just one example of its global involvement in AIDS education and health-care issues. Condomania too has sponsored World Aids Day 2000 in conjunction with the Terrence Higgins Trust and donated 10 per cent of its December Internet sales to the Trust. Mates Healthcare contributed £1m. to the Virgin Healthcare Foundation and gave a grant of £21,000 to the Institute of Population Studies at Exeter University for a study into condom shapes.

Overall, however, developing new products in this market and getting the approach right is not always easy. Durex claims that it bases its product development on in-depth research into people's sexual habits and attitudes, developing brands to meet different consumer needs and preferences. Durex failed, however, with a new brand called Assure, targeted at young women. It was packaged in a pastel coloured unbranded box, to keep in a handbag. The target market turned out to be confident enough to buy the brand that suited them best, regardless of the discretion, or lack of it, in the packaging design. In contrast to the Durex approach, Mates focuses on size and comfort, supporting its range of different sized condoms with a 'size does matter' advertising campaign. The company claims that a pilot study indicated that men can tell the difference between shapes and sizes and that choosing the right condom makes a difference.

Sources: Bray (1997); Mintel (2001); http://www.durex.co.uk

Questions

1 Briefly outline the types of market research information that might be useful to a condom manufacturer.

2 What are the problems of undertaking primary consumer research for a product like this? How can these problems be overcome?

3 Thirty per cent of buyers still have some reservations about purchasing condoms. Suggest a programme of primary research that might tell the manufacturers why this is.

4 To what extent do you think it would be ethical for condom manufacturers to undertake a survey of 14–16-year-olds?

References for chapter 5

Anstead, M. (2000), 'Taking a Tough Line on Privacy', *Marketing*, 13 April, p. 31.

Basuroy, S., Mantrala, M. and Walters, R. (2001), 'The Impact of Category Management on Retailer Prices and Performance: Theory and Evidence', *Journal of Marketing*, 65 (4), pp. 16–32.

Billings, C. (2001), 'Researchers Try Electronic Route', *Marketing*, 29 March, pp. 27–8.

Boyd, H. *et al.* (1977), *Marketing Research*, 4th edn, Irwin.

BMRA (1998), 'BMRA – What Does BMRA Stand For?', advertisement in *Marketing Week*, 25 June, p. 50.

Bolden, R., Moscarola, J. and Baulac, Y. (2000), 'Interactive Research: How Internet Technology Could Revolutionise the Survey and Analysis Process', paper presented at The Honeymoon is Over! Survey Research on the Internet Conference, Imperial College, London, September.

Bray, L. (1997), 'Focus on Condoms', *The Grocer*, 15 February, pp. 49–50.

Brennan, M. *et al.* (1991), 'The Effects of Monetary Incentives on the Response Rate and Cost Effectiveness of a Mail Survey', *Journal of the Market Research Society*, 33 (3), pp. 229–41.

Bromage, N. (2000), 'Mystery Shopping', *Management Accounting*, April, p. 30.

Chisnall, P.M. (1986), *Marketing Research*, 3rd edn, McGraw-Hill.

Clarke, A. (2001), 'Research Takes an Inventive Approach', *Marketing*, 13 September, pp. 25–6.

Clegg, A. (2001), 'Talk among Yourselves', *Marketing Week*, 6 December, pp. 41–2.

Cornish, C. (2001), 'Experiences of Qualitative Research on the Internet', in Westlake, A., Sykes, W., Manners, T. and Rigg, M. (eds), *The Challenge of the Internet*, proceedings of the second ASC International Conference on Survey Research Methods.

Cowlett, M. (2001), 'Research Can be Child's Play', *Marketing*, 10 May, p. 35.

Duan, Y. and Burrell, P. (1997), 'Some Issues in Developing Expert Marketing Systems', *Journal of Business and Industrial Marketing*, 12 (2), pp. 149–62.

Flack, J. (1999), 'Child Minding', *Marketing Week*, 8 July, pp. 41–4.

Forestier-Walker, M. (2000), 'Research is Not a Substitute for Talent and Skills', *Marketing*, 29 November, p. 22.

Gander, P. (1998), 'Just the Job', *Marketing Week*, 25 June, pp. 51–4.

Gofton, K. (2000), 'Consult the Consumers', *Marketing*, 24 August, p. 33.

Gray, R. (2000a), 'How Research Has Narrowed Targets', *Marketing*, 10 February, pp. 31–2.

Gray, R. (2000b), 'The Relentless Rise of Online Research', *Marketing*, 18 May, p. 41.

Haggett, S. and Mitchell, V. (1994), 'Effect of Industrial Prenotification on Response Rate, Speed, Quality, Bias and Cost', *Industrial Marketing Management*, 23 (2), pp. 101–10.

Hague, P. (1992), *The Industrial Market Research Handbook*, 3rd edn, Kogan Page.

Hayward, C. (2001), 'The Child-catchers', *Marketing Week*, 18 October, pp. 45–6.

James, D. (2001), 'Quantitative Research', *Marketing News*, 1 January, p. 13.

McDaniel, C. and Gates, R. (1996), *Contemporary Marketing Research*, 3rd edn, West.

McDaniel, S. *et al.* (1985), 'The Threats to Marketing Research: an Empirical Reappraisal', *Journal of Marketing Research*, 22 (February), pp. 74–80.

McLuhan, R. (2001a), 'How to Aid Clients Using Technology', *Marketing*, 30 August, p. 48.

McLuhan, R. (2001b), 'How Data Can Help Target Customers', *Marketing*, 27 September, p. 25.

Marsden, A. (2001), 'Why Categories Can Breathe Life into Marketing', *Marketing*, 6 September, p. 22.

Marshall, J. (2000), 'Monitoring Market Research Online', *Information World Review*, October, p. 31.

Miles, L. (2000), 'A Watchful Eye on Consumer Habits', *Marketing*, 20 April, p. 35.

Mintel (2001), 'Contraceptives', 1 August, accessed via http://www.mintel.com

Moeng, S. (2001), 'At Home with Big Brother', *Financial World*, September, pp. 42–3.

Mutter, J. (2001), 'Borders Adopts Category Management', *Publishers Weekly*, 5 February, p. 10.

Poynter, R. (2000), 'Keynote: a Guide to Best Practice in Online Quantitative Research', paper presented at The Honeymoon is Over! Survey Research on the Internet Conference, Imperial College, London, September.

Qureshi, B. and Baker, J. (1998), 'Category Management and Efficient Consumer Response: the Role of Market Research', *Marketing and Research Today*, 26 (1), pp. 23–31.

Rao, S. (2000), 'A Marketing Decision Support System for Pricing New Pharmaceutical Products', *Marketing Research*, 12 (4), pp. 22–9.

Reed, D. (1998), 'Categorical Truths', *Marketing Week*, 25 June, pp. 45–9.

Schmalensee, D. (2001), 'Rules of Thumb for B2B Research', *Marketing Research*, 13 (3), pp. 28–33.

Smith, D. and Fletcher, J. (1999), 'Fitting Market and Competitive Intelligence into the Knowledge Management Jigsaw', *Marketing and Research Today*, 28 (3), pp. 128–37.

Tull, D.S. and Hawkins, D.T. (1990), *Marketing Research: Measurement and Method*, Macmillan.

Von Krogh, G., Ichijo, K. and Nonaka, I. (2000), *Enabling Knowledge Creation: How to Unlock the Mystery of Tacit Knowledge and Release the Power of Innovation*, New York: OUP.

Wilson, R. (2001), 'Search Engines', *Marketing Week*, 5 July, pp. 53–4.

Witthaus, M. (1999), 'Group Therapy', *Marketing Week*, 28 January, pp. 43–7.

Yorgey, L. (2000), 'Reaching Expectant and New Mums', *Target Marketing*, March, pp. 60–3.

Zikmund, W. G. and D'Amico, M. (1993), *Marketing*, West.

chapter 6

product

LEARNING OBJECTIVES

This chapter will help you to:

1 define and classify products and the key terms associated with them;

2 understand the nature, benefits and implementation of product and brand development;

3 understand the product life-cycle concept, its influence on marketing strategies and its limitations;

4 appreciate the importance of product positioning and how it both affects and is affected by marketing strategies;

5 define the role and responsibilities of the product or brand manager; and

6 outline the issues surrounding pan-European branding.

Introduction

The product is at the heart of the marketing exchange. Remember that customers buy products to solve problems or to enhance their lives and thus the marketer has to ensure that the product can fully satisfy the customer, not just in functional terms, but also in psychological terms. The product is important, therefore, because it is the ultimate test of whether the organisation has understood its customer's needs.

The example below raises a number of interesting questions about what makes a product and the importance of brand image and customer perceptions of it. To start the process of thinking about these issues, therefore, this chapter examines some fundamental concepts. The definition of product and ways of classifying products lead to some basic definitions of product ranges. Then, the underlying concepts, such as branding, packaging, design and quality, that give the product its character and essential appeal to the buyer will be examined along with issues relating to brand management.

An important concept linked with product and brand management is that of the product life cycle. This traces the life story of the product, helping managers to understand the pressures and opportunities affecting products as they mature. To create and sustain long-lived brands, the product range needs to be managed in sympathy with changes in the customer and competitive environment through the concept of product positioning and repositioning. This may involve changes in marketing strategies, including promotion, packaging, design or even in the target market profile. Every product has to be assessed and managed according to how the consumer perceives it in relation to the competition. This chapter then turns to the practical problems of managing these processes, presenting a brief overview

eg Perhaps the best-known product and brand name in the world is Coca-Cola. First trademarked in 1887, everything about the product such as the bottle shape, the colours and packaging design, and the logo design that has been developed from the word Coca-Cola, is instantly recognisable, distinctive, and familiar to almost everyone globally. As one of its advertising campaigns of the 1990s put it, 'If you don't know what it is, Welcome to Planet Earth' (Pavitt, 2001). In blind tasting, Coca-Cola may not score significantly better than its rivals in terms of taste and quality, but the strength of the brand name and the brand image have certainly helped it to maintain its market dominance. Product and branding concepts are not just linked with inanimate physical products, however. The pop music industry is very sophisticated in its use of marketing techniques to create products and brands out of artists and bands. Morgan (2001) claims that over a 17-year career, pop icon Madonna 'has achieved what every brand strives for: an enduring, unique, meaningful and relevant place in consumers' hearts and minds'. She goes on to suggest that Madonna's brand is expressed through three core values: provocativeness (demanding attention and generating positive and/or negative reactions to her messages), innovation (taking risks to allow the 'brand' to evolve) and reality ('striving for perfection but acknowledging imperfection').

of product management structures. Finally, the issues surrounding the development and management of pan-European brands will be considered.

Anatomy of a product

A formal definition of product may be that:

> *a product is a physical good, service, idea, person or place that is capable of offering tangible and intangible attributes that individuals or organisations regard as so necessary, worthwhile or satisfying that they are prepared to exchange money, patronage or some other unit of value in order to acquire it.*

A product is, therefore, a powerful and varied thing. The definition includes tangible products (tins of baked beans, aircraft engines), intangible products (services such as hairdressing or management consultancy) and ideas (public health messages, for instance). It even includes trade in people. For example, the creation and hard selling of pop groups and idols are less about music than about the promotion of a personality to which the target audience can relate. Does an Eminem fan buy his latest album for its intrinsic musical qualities or because of the Eminem name on the sleeve? Politicians too try to sell themselves as people with caring personalities in exchange for your vote at election time. Places are also saleable products. Holiday resorts and capital cities, for example, have long exploited their natural geographic or cultural advantages, building service industries that in some cases become essential to the local economy.

Whatever the product is, whether tangible, intangible or Eminem, it can always be broken down into bundles of benefits that mean different things to different buyers. Figure 6.1 shows the basic anatomy of a product as a series of four concentric rings representing the core product, the tangible product, the augmented product and finally the potential product.

The *core product* represents the heart of the product, the main reason for its existence and purchase. The core benefit of any product may be functional or psychological and its definition must provide something for the marketer to work on to develop a differential advantage. Any make of car will get the purchaser from A to B, but add on to that the required benefits of spaciousness, or fuel economy or status enhancement, and a definition of a core product to which a market segment will relate begins to emerge. The core benefit

Figure 6.1 The anatomy of a product

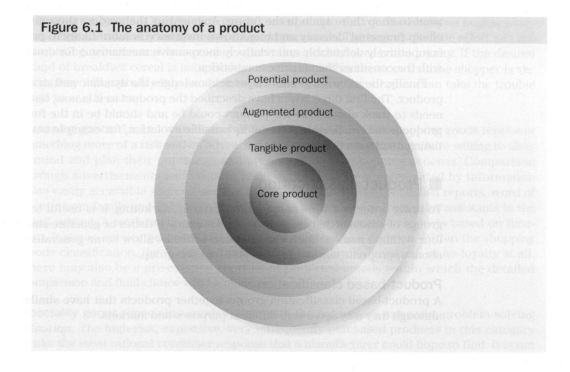

Potential product

Augmented product

Tangible product

Core product

Forget the £20 version of a toaster. If you want a Dualit toaster, they start at over £100 and go can go up to over £200. Each one is hand-built and they are made in limited quantities, despite increasing demand. The toaster does not pop up; it stops cooking when the timer tells it to and then keeps the toast warm until you throw a lever to get it out. It is designed to last, with cast aluminium ends, stainless steel bodywork and patented heating elements that can produce two, three, four or six variations. Although old-fashioned production methods are used, it offers state-of-the-art performance. You would have to shop around to find one, however. You have little chance of finding one in the High Street electrical stores, but you might strike lucky in selected stores such as John Lewis. Dualit prides itself in offering a 'shopping good' (Pearman, 2001; http://www.dualit.co.uk).

entirely rational, however. The psychological and emotive pull of a brand name like Porsche could still override objective assessment of information, leading to a biased, but happy, decision for the consumer. If you allow the inclusion in this category of products like designer perfumes, those that cost several hundred pounds for 50 ml and would be a once (or never) in a lifetime purchase for most consumers, then rationality goes right out of the window and the purchase is made entirely on the basis of the dream and the imagery woven around the product. The products in this category need very specialist retailing that will provide a high level of augmented product services, both before and after the sale. Limiting distribution to a small number of exclusive and well-monitored outlets not only protects the product from abuse (for example inappropriate display or sales advice), but also helps to enhance the product's special image and the status of the buyer.

Unsought goods. Within the unsought goods category, there are two types of situation. The first is the sudden emergency, such as the burst water pipe or the flat tyre. The organisation's job here is to ensure that the consumer either thinks of its name first or that it is the most accessible provider of the solution to the problem. The second unsought situation arises with the kinds of products that people would not normally buy without aggressive hard-selling techniques, such as timeshare properties and some home improvements.

User-based classification: B2B goods and services

This type of classification of B2B goods and services is linked closely with the discussion on p. 96, where the spectrum of buying situations from routine rebuy to new task purchasing was discussed. The novelty of the purchase influences the time, effort and human resources put into the purchasing decision. If that is then combined with the role and importance of the purchase within the production environment, it is possible to develop a classification system that is both widely applicable and indicative of particular marketing approaches.

Capital goods. Capital equipment consists of all the buildings and fixed equipment that have to be in place for production to happen. Such items tend to be infrequently purchased and, given that they are expected to support production over a long lifetime and that they can represent a substantial investment, they are usually regarded as a high-risk decision in the new task category. They thus tend to use extensive decision-making, involving a wide range of personnel from all levels of the organisation and perhaps independent external consultants as well. This category might also include government-funded capital projects such as the building of motorways, bridges, housing and public buildings like hospitals and theatres.

Accessory goods. Accessory goods are items that give peripheral support to the production process without direct involvement. Included in this group, therefore, will be items such as hand tools, fork-lift trucks, storage bins and any other portable or light equipment. Office equipment is also included here, such as word processors, desks, chairs and filing cabinets. Generally speaking, these items are not quite as expensive or as infrequently purchased as the capital goods. The risk factor is also lower. This suggests that the length and the degree of involvement in the purchasing process will be scaled down accordingly into something closer to the modified rebuy situation.

Raw materials. Raw materials arrive more or less in their natural state, having been processed only sufficiently to ensure their safe and economical transport to the factory. Thus iron ore is delivered to Corus; fish arrives at the Findus fish-finger factory; beans and tomatoes are delivered to Heinz; and fleeces arrive at the textile mill. The raw materials then go on to further processing within the purchaser's own production line. The challenge for the supplier of raw materials is how to distinguish its product from the competition's, given that there may be few specification differences between them. Often, the differentiating factors in the purchaser's mind relate to non-product features, such as service, handling convenience, trust and terms of payment, for example.

Semi-finished goods. Unlike raw materials, semi-finished goods have already been subject to a significant level of processing before arriving at the purchaser's factory. They still, however, need further processing before incorporation into the ultimate product. A clothing manufacturer, therefore, will purchase cloth (i.e. the product of spinning, weaving and dyeing processes), which still needs to be cut and sewn to create the ultimate product.

Components and parts. Components and parts are finished goods in their own right, which simply have to be incorporated into the assembly of the final product with no further processing. Car manufacturers, for example, buy in headlamp units, alarm systems and microchips as complete components or parts and then fit them to the cars on the assembly line.

If the components are buyer-specified, then the sales representative's main responsibility is to make sure that the right people are talking to each other to clarify the detail of the buyer's precise requirements. Even when the product has been agreed, there is still a need to maintain the relationship. In contrast, supplier-specified products demand clear appreciation of customer needs, carefully designed and priced products and effective selling and promotion to exploit the opportunities identified by market research.

Supplies and services. Finally, there are several categories of minor consumable items (as distinct from the accessory goods discussed above) and services that facilitate production and the smooth running of the organisation without any direct input.

Operating supplies are frequently purchased consumable items that do not end up in the finished product. In the office, this group mainly includes stationery items such as pens, paper and envelopes, as well as computer consumables such as printer toner or ink cartridges and floppy disks. Maintenance and repair services ensure that all the capital and accessory goods continue to operate smoothly and efficiently. This category can also include minor consumable items, such as cleaning materials, which assist in providing this service. Business services may well be a major category of purchases for an organisation, involving a great deal of expenditure and decision-making effort, since they involve the purchase of services like management consultancy, accounting and legal advice and advertising agency expertise. This takes the discussion back to new task purchasing and its associated problems of involvement and risk.

■ Understanding the product range

Most organisations offer a variety of different products and perhaps a number of variations of each individual product, designed to meet the needs of different market segments. Car companies clearly do this, producing different models of car to suit different price expectations, different power and performance requirements and different usage conditions, from the long-distance sales representative to the family wanting a car largely for short journeys in a busy suburban area.

To understand any product fully, it is essential to appreciate its position in the wider family of the organisation's products. The marketing literature uses a number of terms when talking about the product family that are easy to confuse because of their similarity. Here are some definitions that sort out the confusion and offer some insight into the complexity of the product family.

Product mix

The product mix is the total sum of all the products and variants offered by an organisation. A small company serving a specialist need may have a very small, tightly focused product mix. Van Dyck Belgian Chocolates, for example, offers boxed chocolates, chocolate bars, liqueur chocolates, fruit-flavoured chocolate, nut chocolates, etc. A large multinational supplier of FMCG goods, such as Nestlé, has a very large and varied product mix, from confectionery to coffee to canned goods.

Product line

To impose some order on to the product mix, it can be divided into a number of product lines. A product line is a group of products that are closely related to each other. This relationship may be production oriented, in that the products have similar production requirements or problems. Alternatively, the relationship may be market oriented, in that the products fulfil similar needs, or are sold to the same customer group or have similar product management requirements.

Product item

A product line consists of a number of product items. These are the individual products or brands, each with its own features, benefits, price, etc. In the FMCG area, therefore, if Heinz had a product line called table sauces, the product items within it might be tomato ketchup, salad cream, mayonnaise, reduced calorie mayonnaise, etc.

Product line length

The total number of items within the product line is the product line length. Bosch, for example, might have a product line of DIY power tools, as shown in Figure 6.2. Its equivalent industrial range of power tools would probably be even longer.

Product line depth

The number of different variants of each item within a product line defines its depth. A deep product line has many item variants. A deep line may be indicative of a differentiated market coverage strategy where a number of different segments are being served with tailored products. If we look again at the Bosch example in Figure 6.2, we can break hammer drills down into a number of variants, giving a depth of 10, each of which has different performance and application capabilities, as well as fitting into different price segments ranging from under £50 to over £120.

Similarly, in an FMCG market, the Lynx brand (known as Axe outside the UK) produced by Lever Fabergé offers great product line depth in male toiletries. Under the Lynx

Figure 6.2 Bosch DIY power tools product line

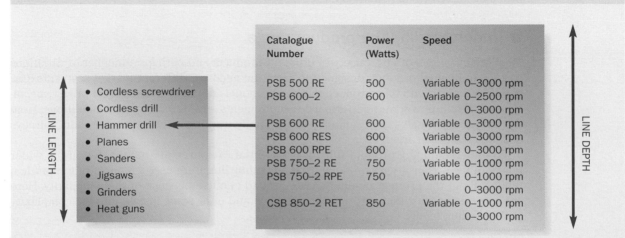

	Catalogue Number	Power (Watts)	Speed
• Cordless screwdriver	PSB 500 RE	500	Variable 0–3000 rpm
• Cordless drill	PSB 600–2	600	Variable 0–2500 rpm
• Hammer drill			0–3000 rpm
• Planes	PSB 600 RE	600	Variable 0–3000 rpm
• Sanders	PSB 600 RES	600	Variable 0–3000 rpm
• Jigsaws	PSB 600 RPE	600	Variable 0–3000 rpm
• Grinders	PSB 750–2 RE	750	Variable 0–1000 rpm
• Heat guns	PSB 750–2 RPE	750	Variable 0–1000 rpm
			0–3000 rpm
	CSB 850–2 RET	850	Variable 0–1000 rpm
			0–3000 rpm

LINE LENGTH   LINE DEPTH

umbrella, aftershave, shaving gel, shower gel, body spray, deodorant (in stick, roll-on and spray forms), shampoo and conditioner are offered in a variety of fragrances with suitably exotic and macho names such as Voodoo, Gravity, Africa, Phoenix, Apollo and Atlantis. This depth does not aim to cover different market segments, but does offer sufficient variation and choice to keep the target segment interested and loyal. The line includes all the basic male toiletry products so that the customer does not need to purchase anything from outside the line, and the variety of fragrances, with a new one introduced every year to keep the line fresh and interesting, allows the customer to experiment and have a change from time to time!

By continually adding alternative fragrances to the Lynx range, the male buyer tends to remain loyal to the overall brand and not look elsewhere for something new or different.

Source: The Advertising Archives. Reproduced with kind permission of Lever Faberge Limited.

Product mix width

The width of the product mix is defined by the number of product lines offered. Depending on how broadly or narrowly defined the product lines are, a wide mix might indicate an organisation with a diverse interest in a number of different markets, such as Nestlé.

Branding

Branding is an important element of the tangible product and, particularly in consumer markets, is a means of linking items within a product line or emphasising the individuality of product items. This points to the most important function of branding: the creation and communication of a three-dimensional character for a product that is not easily copied or damaged by competitors' efforts. The prosaic definition of brand, accepted by most marketers, is that it consists of any name, design, style, words or symbols, singly or in any combination that distinguish one product from another in the eyes of the customer. Brands are used by people to establish and reflect their status: we are often judged by the brands we select, the football teams we support, the television programmes we watch, the clothes we buy, the car marque we drive, where we eat and even what we eat. It is, therefore, perhaps of no great surprise that brands are often not about physical attributes but a set of values, a philosophy that can be matched with the consumer's own values and philosophy. Orange represents a bright future, Nike is about achievement ('just do it') and Avantis about life (Bunting, 2001).

■ The meaning of branding

The definition of brand provided above offered a variety of mechanisms through which branding could be developed, the most obvious of which are the name and the logo. As with the product mix jargon discussed in the previous section, you are likely to meet a number of terms in the course of your reading and it is important to differentiate between them.

Brand name

A brand name is any word or illustration that clearly distinguishes one seller's goods from another. It can take the form of words, such as Weetabix and Ferrero Rocher, or initials, such as AA. Numbers can be used to create an effective brand name, such as 7-Up. Brand names can also be enhanced by the use of an associated logo, such as the one used by Apple computers, to reinforce the name, or through the particular style in which the name is presented. The classic example of this is the Coca-Cola brand name, where the visual impact of the written name is so strong that the onlooker recognises the design rather than reads the words. Thus Coca-Cola is instantly identifiable whether the name is written in English, Russian, Chinese or Arabic because it always somehow *looks* the same.

Trade name

The trade name is the legal name of an organisation, which may or may not relate directly to the branding of its products. Some companies prefer to let the brands speak for themselves and do not give any prominence to the product's parentage. Washing powder brands produced by either Unilever or Procter & Gamble do not prominently display the company name, although it is shown on the back or side of the pack. Few consumers would realise that Persil, Surf and Radion come from the same stable. Similarly, RHM produces brands such as Paxo that have no obvious corporate identity.

Trade mark

A trade mark is a brand name, symbol or logo, which is registered and protected for the owner's sole use. To bring the UK into line with EU legislation, the Trade Marks Act 1994 allowed organisations to register smells, sounds, product shapes and packaging, as well as brand names and logos (Olsen, 2000). This means that the Coca-Cola bottle, the Toblerone bar and Heinz's tomato ketchup bottle are as protectable as their respective brand names. Advertising slogans, jingles and even movements or gestures associated with a brand can also be registered as trade marks. The Act prevents competitors from legally using any of these things in a way that may confuse or mislead buyers, and also makes the registration process and action over infringement much easier.

eg | There has been a long dispute between Arsenal FC and Matthew Reed, an Arsenal supporter who also sells Arsenal memorabilia such as scarves and hats from a stall in the front garden of a house near the ground. The merchandise was not just red and white, but bore the words 'Arsenal' and 'Gunners' as well as the distinctive badge. As far as Arsenal FC was concerned these were registered trade marks so it took Reed to court on the basis of trade mark infringement. It argued that purchasers might think that the merchandise sold by Reed was officially licensed. The stall, however, displayed a prominent disclaimer saying that the goods were not endorsed by Arsenal FC. Reed had also been selling from the site for 31 years so the judge ruled, surprisingly, that customer confusion was not likely and that badges were merely signs of support and loyalty, and so Reed could continue trading. Experts still believe, however, that it is a direct abuse of the legitimate Arsenal trade mark, since by using the trade mark Reed gained an advantage that he otherwise would not have had. The matter may now go to the European court as a test case (Rose, 2001).

Brand mark

The brand mark is specifically the element of the visual brand identity that does not consist of words, but of design and symbols. This would include things like McDonald's golden arches, Apple's computer symbol, or Audi's interlocking circles. These things are also protectable, as discussed under trade marks above.

■ The benefits of branding

Branding carries benefits for all parties involved in the exchange process and in theory at least makes it easier to buy or sell products. This section, summarised in Figure 6.3, looks at the benefits of branding from different perspectives, beginning with that of the buyer.

Consumer perspective

Branding is of particular value to the buyer in a complex and crowded marketplace. In a supermarket, for example, brand names and visual images make it easier to locate and identify required products. Strong branding can speak volumes about the function and character of the product and help consumers to judge whether it is their sort of product, delivering the functional and psychological benefits sought. This is especially true for a new, untried product. The branding can at least help the evaluation of product suitability, and if there is an element of corporate branding it can also offer reassurance about the product's quality pedigree.

This all aids in the shopping process and reduces some of its risks, but it goes further. Giving a product what amounts to a three-dimensional personality makes it easier for consumers to form attitudes and feelings about the product. It gets them sufficiently interested to want to be bothered to do that. This has the double effect of creating brand loyalty (the product as a trusted friend) and of creating something special in the consumer's mind that the competition would find difficult to touch.

This has led to brands being regarded as 'packaged meanings' that shoppers can identify with and that organisations are happy to engender. Being able to humanise products with characteristics such as being honest, friendly, trustworthy, fun or avant garde all helps to build stronger customer relationships and makes the product attributes almost secondary.

Manufacturer perspective

The manufacturer benefits, of course, from the relationship of the buyer with branding. The ease of identification of the product at the point of sale, the connotations of quality and

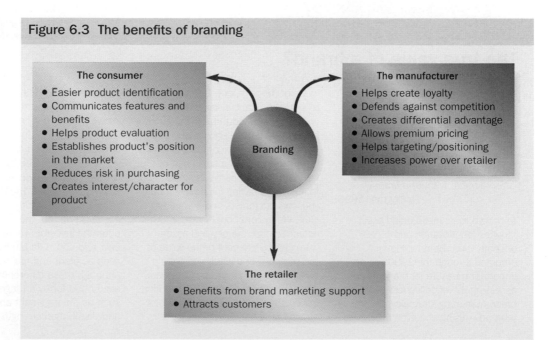

Figure 6.3 The benefits of branding

The consumer
- Easier product identification
- Communicates features and benefits
- Helps product evaluation
- Establishes product's position in the market
- Reduces risk in purchasing
- Creates interest/character for product

Branding

The manufacturer
- Helps create loyalty
- Defends against competition
- Creates differential advantage
- Allows premium pricing
- Helps targeting/positioning
- Increases power over retailer

The retailer
- Benefits from brand marketing support
- Attracts customers

familiarity and the creation of a three-dimensional product personality all help the manufacturer. The manufacturer's key interest is in the building of defendable brand loyalty to the point where the trust, liking and preference for the brand overcome any lingering price sensitivity, thus allowing a reasonable measure of premium pricing and the prevention of brand switching. Some of the best-known brands that have emerged over the past 50 years have become almost synonymous with the product sector: Kellogg's for cereal, Hoover for vacuum cleaners, Nike for sports shoes and Sony Walkman for the personal stereo market. Achieving such a 'generic brand' position creates considerable strength for the manufacturer in shaping marketing strategy, but it is no guarantee of continued success – ask Levi's or Marks & Spencer.

Other more subtle advantages of branding for the manufacturer are linked with segmentation and competitive positioning strategies. Different brands can be used by one organisation to target different segments. Because the different brands have clearly defined individual characteristics, the consumer does not necessarily link them and thus does not become confused about what the organisation stands for. Even where there is a strong corporate element to the branding, as with Ford cars, the individual models within the range are clearly seen as separate products, serving different market needs, with price differences justified in terms of design and technical specification. Consumers view this wide range of brands positively, as a way of offering as tailored a choice as possible within the confines of a mass market.

Strong branding is also important for providing competitive advantage, not just in terms of generating consumer loyalty, but also as a means of competing head-on, competing generally across the whole market in an almost undifferentiated way or finding a niche in which to dominate. Brand imagery can help to define the extent of competition or exaggerate the differentiating features that pull it away from the competition.

Retailer perspective

The retailer benefits from branding to a certain extent. Branded products are well supported by advertising and other marketing activities, and so the retailer has some assurance that they will sell. Branded products do draw customers into the store, but the disadvantage is that if a brand is unavailable in one store, then the shopper is likely to patronise another instead. The retailer may prefer the shopper to be less brand loyal and more store loyal! Supermarkets have always recognised the value and necessity of manufacturer-branded goods, but they have also looked for ways of reducing the power that this gives the brand owner. This issue will be looked at in detail in the next subsection.

marketing *in action*

The true value of a brand?

A brand asset has been defined as

a name and/or symbol used to uniquely identify the goods and services of a seller from those of its competitors, with a view to obtaining wealth in excess of that obtainable without a brand.
(Tollington, 1998).

To have a meaningful brand asset requires identification and quantification. Brand valuation emerged through the 1990s as an important measure for brand owners assessing the effectiveness of their brand marketing strategies, their long-term advertising and even the overall

worth of the company. Brands represent a financial value to a company reflected through the goodwill component of a balance sheet. The physical assets of a company often now only represent a small part of the value of that company: it is reputation that is worth paying for, as it can bring you loyal customers and committed staff. When Ford bought Jaguar it was estimated that the physical assets were just 16 per cent of the value of the company and when Vodafone bought Orange, physical assets were just 10 per cent of the value (Bunting, 2001). This reflects the real value of strong brand names.

Interbrand Newell & Sorrell, in research for trade magazine *Marketing Week*, plotted the growth in brand values for top US and UK companies between 1988 and 1998. Brand value was calculated by comparing market capitalisation with net tangible or physical assets. The difference between these two figures shows the goodwill gap, i.e. the extent to which potential investors value a company over and above its tangible assets such as plant and machinery. Although these differences can be accounted for by a range of factors, such as management ability, patents and distribution strength, research has found that a significant part of the difference can be accounted for by the worth of the brands. In the case of Coca-Cola the figure is 4,000 per cent of the tangible assets, Cadbury Schweppes is 33 per cent or £1.5bn and Scottish & Newcastle Breweries is 158 per cent.

A similar study by Interbrand and Citibank examining stock market performance found that those companies that were heavily branded tended to outperform the rest of companies in the FTSE 350 index by between 15 and 20 per cent over a 15-year period. Brand value clearly makes a difference to companies.

The history of brand valuation can be traced back to 1988 when Rank Hovis McDougall (RHM) successfully defended against a hostile takeover by

including the value of its brands in its balance sheet. Since then, organisations such as Burmah Castrol, Cadbury Schweppes, ICI and Disney have all used brand-valuation techniques for management and acquisition purposes. The value of brands to many companies has now become so important that it has been argued that the chief executive should ultimately be the brand manager and that all staff need to realise that they are in the front line of brand delivery. Such an approach is clearly demonstrated by Richard Branson at Virgin, where the strength of the Virgin brand name has successfully carried it into many sectors.

The recognition of brands as assets is likely to become more emphasised in future as finance directors and

accountants increasingly use brand-valuation techniques in balance sheets. In December 1998, the UK Accounting Standards Board recommended through Standards 10 and 11 that the value of acquired brands should be included in company accounts. Most brand valuations are, however, excluded from published balance sheets and are often only considered during mergers and acquisitions when they can be used to increase the asset base and force up the bidding price (Tollington, 2001). However, because of issues of the subjectivity and reliability of valuation measurement, the accounting profession still treats brand valuation with some caution.

Sources: Baird (1998); Bunting (2001); Butterfield (1998); Butterfield and Haigh (1998); Tollington (1998, 2001).

Lest this discussion should seem too enthusiastic about branding, we now turn to some of the disadvantages. Echoing one of the risks of segmentation (discussed in Chapter 4, pp. 127–8), there is the danger of proliferation if brands are created to serve every possible market niche. Retailers are under pressure to stock increasing numbers of lines within a product area, which means in turn that either less shelf space is devoted to each brand or retailers refuse to stock some brands. Both options are unpleasant for the manufacturer. The consumer may also begin to see too much choice and, at some point, there is a risk that the differences between brands become imperceptible to the consumer and confusion sets in.

■ Types of brands

The discussion so far has centred on the brands created and marketed by manufacturers and sold through retail outlets. An area of growing importance, however, is the brand created by a wholesaler or retailer for that organisation's sole use. This development has taken place partly because of conflicts and power struggles between manufacturers and retailers, and partly because the retailers also need to generate store loyalty in a highly competitive retail sector.

This section, therefore, distinguishes between the brands emanating from different types of organisation.

Manufacturer brands

Most manufacturers, particularly in the FMCG sector, are at arm's length from the end buyer and consumer of their product. The retail sector is in between and can make the difference between a product's success and failure through the way the product is displayed or made available to the public. The manufacturer can attempt to impose some control over this through trade promotions, but the manufacturer's best weapon is direct communication with the end buyer. Planting brand names and recognition of brand imagery in the consumer's mind through advertising or sales promotion gives the manufacturer a fighting chance of recognition and selection at the point of sale. Furthermore, the creation of a strong brand that has hard-core loyalty can tip the balance of power back in favour of the manufacturer, because any retailer not stocking that brand runs the risk of losing custom to its competitors.

Retailer and wholesaler brands

The growth of own-label brands (i.e. those manufactured by or on behalf of a retailer and bearing the retailer's name) or own-brands has become a major factor in retailing. Why do it? One possible problem a retailer has is that if a consumer is buying a recognised manufacturer's brand, then the source of that purchase is less relevant. A can of Heinz baked beans represents the same values whether it is purchased from a corner shop or from Harrod's. Retailers can differentiate from each other on the basis of price or service, but they are looking for more than that. The existence of a range of exclusive retailer brands that the consumer comes to value creates a physical reason for visiting that retailer and no other. These brands also serve the purpose of giving the consumer 'the retailer in a tin', where the product in the kitchen cupboard is a constant reminder of the retailer and embodies the retailer's values in a more tangible form, reinforcing loyalty and positive attitudes.

Other reasons include the fact that the retailer can earn a better margin on an own-brand and still sell it more cheaply than a manufacturer's brand. This is because the retailer's own-brand is sold on the back of the retailer's normal marketing activity and not with the massive advertising, promotion and selling costs that each manufacturer's brand has to bear.

The use of own-brand varies across different retailers. Some retailers, such as Kwik Save, use their own label to create a no-nonsense, no-frills, value-for-money, generic range. Others, such as Marks & Spencer, Sainsbury's and the Albert Heijn chain in the Netherlands, have created own-brands that are actually perceived as superior in quality to the manufacturer's offerings.

Given that own-label products seem to put so much power into the hands of the retailers, why do manufacturers cooperate in their production? For a manufacturer of second-string brands (i.e. not the biggest names in the market), it might be a good way of developing closer links with a retailer and earning some sort of protection for the manufacturer's brands. In return for the supply, at attractive prices, of own-brand products, the retailer might undertake to display the manufacturer's brands more favourably, or promise not to delist them, for example. The extra volume provides some predictability for the manufacturer and it also could help to achieve economies of scale of benefit to both parties. The danger, of course, is that of the manufacturer becoming too dependent on the retailer's own-brand business.

Product management and strategy

This chapter has already hinted at a number of important dimensions to be considered in developing and maintaining a branding strategy. Each one will now be treated separately.

■ Creating the brand

New product development

New product development (NPD) is important to organisations for many reasons, including the need to create and maintain competitive advantage through innovation and better serving the customer's changing needs and wants. Whether a product is a totally new innovation, an update of a familiar product or an imitation of a competitor's product, it needs careful planning and development to ensure that it meets customers' needs and wants, that it has a significant competitive advantage and that it is accepted within the marketplace. NPD can be a long and expensive process, with no guarantees that the resulting product will succeed, and therefore to minimise the risks, it needs careful and skilful management to ensure that the best ideas are successfully developed into commercially viable, potentially profitable products with a future.

Product design, quality and guarantees

Design. Design is an integral part of the product, affecting not only its overall aesthetic qualities but also its ergonomic properties (i.e. the ease and comfort with which it can be used) and even its components and materials. All of this together can enhance the product's visual appeal, its ability to fulfil its function and its reliability and lifespan.

eg   Video Net, a video on demand system, wanted an electric plug that could fit through a letter-box so that it could send its modem, complete with plug, through the post. It needed either a smaller plug or expensive couriers. The solution was a folding plug, designed by Rutland Gilts, that met both the strict British Standard 1363 and Vision Net's requirements. The design process took two years to fine-tune the 9 parts of the plug/adapter. Market research revealed that although people would not be prepared to pay any extra for the plug on its own, manufacturers of mobile phones, laptops and travel accessories were all very interested. The new European and UK plug is now being developed which will provide even more flexibility in use, and all because a company wanted to save on delivery costs! (Design Council, 2001a).

Design is increasingly being recognised as being more than just the shape and colour of new products. It also involves the process by which new products and service are produced to meet customer needs and bring creative ideas to reality (Design Council, 2001b). Research by the UK Design Council, however, has indicated that smaller companies are often far less design-oriented than larger ones and in some companies, design still plays only a small role in the marketing and product development process. Governments have, however, recognised the importance of design in helping industry to gain a sustainable competitive edge in global markets. Bodies such as the UK's Design Council, the Netherlands Design Institute and the French Agence pour la Promotion de la Création Industrielle promote and support good design practice. The EU also encourages design with initiatives such as the biannual European Community Design Prize aimed at small and medium-sized businesses.

Quality. Unlike design, quality is a very well-understood concept among managers. Many organisations now recognise the importance of quality and have adopted the philosophy of total quality management (TQM), which means that all employees take responsibility for building quality into whatever they do. TQM affects all aspects of the organisation's work, from materials handling to the production process, from the product itself to the administrative procedures that provide customer service. Marketers, of course, have a vested interest in all these manifestations of quality, because creating and holding on to customers means not only providing the quality of product that they want (and providing it consistently), but also supporting the product with quality administrative, technical and after-sales service.

Performance. Performance is about what the product can actually *do*. Thus with the Bosch hammer drills mentioned earlier (see Figure 6.2), a customer might perceive the more expensive model with a variable speed of 3,000 rpm as being of 'better quality' than a more basic lower-powered drill. The customer might have more difficulty judging between competing products, however. Black & Decker, for example, produces a range of hammer drills that are very similar to the Bosch ones, with minor variations in specification and price levels. If both the Bosch model and the equivalent Black & Decker model offer the same functions, features, benefits and pricing levels, the customer might have problems differentiating between them in terms of performance and will have to judge on other characteristics.

Durability. Some products are expected to have a longer lifespan than others and some customers are prepared to pay more for what they perceive to be a better-quality, more durable product. Thus the quality level built into the product needs to be suited to its expected life and projected usage. Thus a child's digital watch fitted into a plastic strap featuring a licensed character such as Barbie or Batman, retailing at around £5, is not expected to have the same durability or quality level as a Swiss Tissot retailing at £125. Disposable products in particular, such as razors, biros and cigarette lighters, need to be manufactured to a quality level that is high enough to allow them to perform the required function for the required number of uses or for the required time span, yet low enough to keep the price down to a level where the customer accepts the concept of frequent replacement.

Reliability and maintenance. Many customers are concerned about the probability of a product breaking down or otherwise failing, and about the ease and economy of repairs. As with durability, some customers will pay a price premium for what are perceived to be more reliable products or for the peace of mind offered by comprehensive after-sales support. These days most makes of car, for example, are pretty reliable if they are properly maintained and so car buyers may differentiate on the basis of the cost and ease of servicing and the cost and availability of spare parts.

Design and style. As mentioned earlier, the visual and ergonomic appeal of a product may influence perceptions of its quality. The sleek, stylish, aerodynamic lines of the Lamborghini contrast sharply with the functional boxiness of the Lada. Packaging design can also enhance quality perceptions.

eg England's Fly Fishers also used innovation in design and style to carve out a new market niche. The company designed an inflatable fishing jacket that not only matched those already on the market for style, but also had the added advantage of a life-saving device that gives automatic self-inflation and is self-righting. This means that the jacket will inflate even if the wearer is unconscious or unable to inflate an orthodox lifejacket and that the head will be kept above water. Just the thing for the unfortunate fisherman taking a premature dip, and not bad for sales either, as the company exports its goods throughout Europe and the Americas (Warman, 1997).

Corporate name and reputation. If, after all that, customers are still uncertain about the relative quality offerings of the alternative products under consideration, they may fall back on their perceptions of the organisation. Some may feel that Black & Decker is a well-established, familiar name, and if they have had other Black & Decker products that have served well in the past, then that might swing the quality decision in Black & Decker's favour. Others may decide in favour of Bosch because of its associations with high-quality German engineering.

Marketers recognise that quality in the marketplace is a matter of perception rather than technical specification. This is particularly true in consumer markets, where the potential customer may not have the expertise to judge quality objectively and will use all sorts of cues, such as price, packaging or comparison with competitors, to form an opinion about quality level.

The variety of different power tools that Bosch offers the consumer give them the possibility of choosing the right power tool that suits them when they undertake DIY jobs around the home.

Source: Bosch.

Guarantees. One way in which an organisation can emphasise its commitment to quality and its confidence in its own products and procedures is through the guarantees it offers. Although customers are protected under national and EU laws against misleading product claims and goods that are not fit for their intended purpose, many organisations choose to extend their responsibility beyond the legal minimum. Some will offer extended warranties. Others are less ambitious and simply offer 'no questions asked' refunds or replacements if the customer is unhappy with a product for any reason at all. Such schemes not only reflect

eg The growth of Internet shopping has highlighted the importance of guarantees. As you cannot feel, touch or see the product in advance, a full refund satisfaction guarantee can be a powerful part of the offer. It has been estimated that such a guarantee can increase catalogue response or web conversion by between 5 and 15 per cent (Baird, 2001). As a rule of thumb, cancellation rates under such schemes should be no higher than 7 per cent of gross sales, so estimates can be made of the cost of satisfaction guarantees against the expected returns. Lands' End, the clothing catalogue shopping firm, offered its German customers an unconditional, unlimited guarantee. The German courts, based on a 1932 statute, ruled that such a practice created unfair competition as it was not common practice in Germany. Lands' End turned it to its advantage in a European marketing campaign, however (Girard, 2000). In Germany, the advertisements featured black strokes over the wording of the guarantee with the words 'advertising not allowed by German courts'. In the UK, the advertisements called the guarantee 'so good, the Germans banned it'.

the organisation's confidence in its product and its commitment to customer service, but also reduce the risk to the customer in trying the product.

It may also be possible for the organisation to use its guarantees to create a differential advantage over its competitors. The danger is, however, that promises can be copied, and once similar guarantees have become widespread within a particular market or industry, they start to be seen as a normal part of the product package and their impact may be lost as customers look for other differentiating factors.

Naming, packaging and labelling the brand

Selecting a brand name. A brand name must be memorable, easy to pronounce and meaningful (whether in real or emotional terms). As manufacturers look increasingly towards wider European and international markets, there is a much greater need to check that a proposed name does not lead to unintended ridicule in a foreign language. Neither the French breakfast cereal Plopsies (chocolate-flavoured puffed rice) nor the gloriously evocative Slovakian pasta brand Kuk & Fuk are serious contenders for launch into an English-speaking market. From a linguistic point of view, care must be taken to avoid certain combinations of letters that are difficult to pronounce in some languages.

Language problems apart, the ability of a brand name to communicate something about the product's character or functional benefits could be important. Blackett (1985) suggests that approaches to this can vary, falling within a spectrum ranging from free-standing names, through associative names, to names that are baldly descriptive. This spectrum is shown with examples of actual brand names in Figure 6.4. Names that are totally free-standing are completely abstract and bear no relation to the product or its character. Kodak is a classic example of such a name. Associative names suggest some characteristic, image or benefit of the product, but often in an indirect way. Pledge (furniture polish), Elvive (shampoo) and Impulse (body spray) are all names that make some kind of statement about the product's positioning through the consumer's understanding of the word(s) used in the name. The extremely prosaic end of the spectrum is represented by descriptive names. Such names certainly tell you about what the product is, but they are neither imaginative nor easy to protect. Bitter Lemon, for example, began as a brand name and was so apt that it soon became a generic title for any old bottle of lemon-flavoured mixer. Somewhere between associative

Figure 6.4 The brand name spectrum

Descriptive	Associative	Freestanding
Bitter Lemon	Walkman	Kodak
Dairy Milk Chocolate	Natrel	Esso
Shredded Wheat	Burger King	Pantene
Liquorice All Sorts	Bold	Mars Bar
	Sensodyne	

and descriptive names come a group with names that are descriptive, but with a distinctive twist. Ex-Lax (laxative), Lucozade (fizzy glucose drink) and Bacofoil (aluminium cooking foil) are names that manage to describe without losing the individuality of the brand.

In summary, there are four 'rules' for good brand naming. As far as possible, they need to be:

1 *distinctive*, standing out from the competition while being appealing to the target market and appropriate to the character of the product;
2 *supportive* of the product's positioning with respect to its competitors (pp. 203 *et seq.* will discuss positioning in further detail), while remaining consistent with the organisation's overall branding policy;
3 *acceptable*, recognisable, pronounceable and memorisable, in other words user-friendly to the consumer; and finally,
4 *available*, registerable, protectable (i.e. yours and only yours).

With respect to this last point, it is important to ensure that the suggested brand name is not infringing the rights of existing brands. This is particularly difficult with international brands.

Packaging. Packaging is an important part of the product that not only serves a functional purpose, but also acts as a means of communicating product information and brand character. The packaging is often the consumer's first point of contact with the actual product and so it is essential to make it attractive and appropriate for both the product's and the customer's needs.

Packaging is any container or wrapping in which the product is offered for sale and can consist of a variety of materials such as glass, paper, metal or plastic, depending on what is to be contained. The choice of materials and the design of the packaging may have to take account of the texture, appearance and viscosity of the product, as well as its perishability. Dangerous products such as medicines or corrosive household cleaners need special attention. Other design issues might include the role of the packaging in keeping the product ready for use, the means of dispensing the product and the graphic design, presenting the brand imagery and the statutory and desired on-pack information.

eg Heinz (http://www.heinz.com) undertook a repackaging exercise to bring greater coherence to the appearance of its soups, pasta meals and beans. For convenience foods, packaging design has to be clear and distinctive to attract busy shoppers moving through supermarkets. Research had indicated to Heinz that shoppers were moving more quickly through aisles and spending less time on shopping. Although the traditional packaging colours for tomato soups and beans were retained, colour was used to emphasise the distinctiveness of other ranges. 'Big Soup' labels were, therefore, presented with a dark green background rather than red. Similarly, 'Chef's Specials' pasta meals, such as ravioli and macaroni cheese, appeared with a yellow background including the traditional Heinz keystone design, rather than in their original orange and bright green respectively (Smith, 1998).

Naturally, there is a cost involved in all of this. Although it can cost £100,000 to create a packaging design for an FMCG product, it seems a very reasonable sum compared with the £3m. or more that will be spent on the advertising to launch that same product. McKenzie (1997) found that the packaging design was becoming a vital element in developing a brand proposition to the consumer both in advertising and point-of-sale promotion. This could be the case both for a new product launch and for relaunching existing products that might be starting to look tired.

With the rise of the self-service ethos in consumer markets, packaging has indeed grown in importance. It has to communicate product information to help the consumer make a choice, to communicate brand image and positioning and, mostly, to attract attention at the point of sale and invite the consumer to explore the product further (Pieters and Warlops, 1999). Thus packaging is an important part of the overall product offering and has a number of marketing and technical dimensions, some of which are discussed below.

Functions of packaging. First among the functions of packaging are the practicalities. Packaging must be *functional*: it must protect the product in storage, in shipment and often in use. Other packaging functions centre on convenience for the consumer, both in terms of ease of access and ease of use. In the convenience food sector, ease of use has come with the development of packaging that can be placed straight inside a microwave oven and thus serves as a cooking utensil. This underlines the necessity for packaging materials, design and technology to develop in parallel with markets and emerging market needs. Consumer pressure for fewer preservatives and additives in food products has also encouraged the development of packaging that better preserves pack content. Products also need to be protected from tampering, and many jars or packages now have at least a visually prominent seal on the outer pack with the verbal warning that the product should not be used if the seal is damaged.

In addition to offering functional information about product identity and use, packaging also serves a *promotional* purpose. It needs to grab and hold the consumer's attention and involve them with the product. It has been suggested that packaging may be the biggest medium of communication for three reasons (Peters, 1994):

1   its extensive reach to nearly all purchasers of the category;
2   its presence at the crucial moment when the purchase decision is made; and
3   the high level of involvement of users who will actively scan packaging for information.

This involvement of the user makes the packaging an essential element in branding, both in the communication of brand values and as an essential part of the brand identity (Connolly and Davidson, 1996).

Packaging can also be used, for example, as a means of distributing coupons, for advertising other related products, announcing new products, presenting on-pack offers or distributing samples and gifts. A special can was developed for Lucozade Sport, for example, that allowed 'instant win' vouchers to be sealed into the packaging, separate from the liquid. There is more on all of this in Chapter 11.

> **eg** The added psychological value of the packaging is an absolutely essential part of some products. Perfumes, for example, rely heavily on their packaging to endorse the qualities of luxury, expense, exclusivity, mystery and self-indulgence that they try to represent. Champagne, a perfume by Yves St Laurent, comes in a crimson-lined gold box, which opens out like a kind of casket to reveal an elegant bottle representing a champagne cork, complete with gold wire. It is estimated that the packaging for such a product actually costs about 3 times as much as the content of the bottle itself. Closer to the mass market, Easter eggs are also an example of the packaging outshining the content. Novelty carton shapes, bright graphics, ribbons and bows are central to the purchasing decision and dull any natural inclination to compare the price with the actual chocolate content.

Packaging in the marketing mix. Packaging plays an important part in the marketing mix. This chapter has already outlined its functional importance, its communication possibilities and its crucial role as a first point of physical contact between the buyer and the product. Effective and thoughtful packaging is recognised as a means of increasing sales.

Even the choice of the range of pack sizes to offer the market can reinforce the objectives of the marketing mix. Trial-size packs, clearly labelled as such, help with new product launch (see also Chapter 11) by encouraging low-risk product trial. Small-sized packs of an established product may reinforce a commitment to a market segment comprising single-person households or infrequent users. Larger packs target family usage, heavy users generally or the cost-conscious segment who see the large pack as better value for money. The increase in out-of-town shopping by car means that consumers are far better able than ever before to buy large, bulky items. This trend has developed further into the demand for multiple packs. Pack sizes may also be closely linked with end-use segmentation (see pp. 119 *et seq.*). Ice cream can be packaged as either an individual treat, a family block or a party-sized tub. The consumer selects the appropriate size depending on the end use, but the choice must be there or else the consumer will turn to another brand.

Heinz (http://www.heinz.com) is a prime example of the monolithic approach. The Heinz brand is well respected and very strong, but individual Heinz products have little identity of their own. Brand names are descriptive and always include the word Heinz to link them, such as Heinz Cream of Tomato Soup, Heinz Baked Beans, Heinz Low Calorie Mayonnaise, etc. Even the label design of each product shows that it clearly belongs to the Heinz family, further drawing the products together. Such family unity creates a strong overall image and allows new products easy entry into the existing product lines (although it might take consumers a while to notice a new flavour of soup in among the rest). It is also possible to achieve economies of scale in communication, if desired, and distribution, through treating the family as a unit rather than as a number of independent products. The danger is, however, that if one product fails or gains a bad reputation, the rest may suffer with it.

A compromise between monolithic and discreet branding is an approach that allows individual brand images, but uses a corporate or family name as a prominent umbrella to endorse the product. Some organisations, such as Ford and Kellogg, use a *fixed endorsed* approach. Here, there is a rigid relationship between the company name and the brand, with a high degree of consistency between the presentation of different brands (but not as extreme as the Heinz approach). A *flexible endorsed* approach, such as that practised by Cadbury's, gives the brand more latitude to express its individuality. The company name may be more or less prominent, depending on how much independence the organisation wants the brand to have. These products seem to enjoy the best of both worlds. The family name gives the products and any new products a measure of credibility, yet the individuality of the products allows variety, imagination and creativity without being too stifled by the 'house style'. Marketing costs are, however, going to be higher because of the need to develop and launch individual identities for products and then to communicate both the family image and the individual brand images.

Product range and brand extension

A kind of flexible endorsement that does not involve the corporate name is where a brand name is developed to cover a limited number of products within a product line. Consumers may be more favourably inclined towards brands that are associated with known and trusted products (DelVecchio, 2000).

Reckitt and Benckiser, the Anglo-Dutch household group, established the Dettol brand name in 1933. The name was extended to include a whole range of clearly related products, such as Dettox, Dettol antibacterial soap, foam bath, antiseptic cream, pain relief spray and hand-wash in a mini-family, again capitalising on the established reputation of the 'parent' product.

Reckitt and Benckiser brands have gained worldwide sales so that few kitchen and bathroom cabinets are without at least one. Most of its brands, such as Lemsip, Disprin, Mr Sheen and Finish, are strong and thus a high proportion of sales come from products that are either number one or two in their categories. After the merger between Reckitt and Colman and Benckiser in 1999, the priority for the new group was to focus on five core categories: surface care, home care, dishwashing, health, and fabric care, and then to invest heavily in the family brand range in each category to retain a strong position. The review of branding policy that took place meant that Dettox was renamed to become a more direct member of the Dettol family, as the step from disinfectant to cleaning fluids is not that great. Traditionally, Dettox was for things and Dettol was for people, so the success of the name change will depend on how consumer perceptions adapt. If consumers cannot relate to Dettol rather than Dettox, even though the product itself remains the same, they will switch to competing brands. Dettol has already been extended into many areas and some argue that this could be one extension too many (Singh, 2001; Trefgarne, 2001).

Extending the brand range. This example raises the issue of brand extension. Dettol has been very successful in launching variants or new products. Such a policy is cost-efficient in that it saves the cost of developing totally new images and promoting and building them up from nothing. It has been argued, however, that the introduction of additional products to the brand family can dilute the strength of the brand (John *et al.*, 1998). As the number of products affiliated to a brand name increases, the original brand beliefs may become less focused. To some extent, Virgin has suffered from this. Extending the brand name from a successful airline to the more problematic rail service could damage the core brand reputation.

The strength of the Dettol brand has allowed numerous extensions.

Source: Reckitt Benkiser plc.

Brand extension does not only happen 'horizontally', as in the Dettol case. Brands can be extended upwards, downwards or in both directions. An upwards extension might involve introducing a higher-priced, higher-quality, more exclusive product, while a downwards extension might require a basic, no-frills product at a rock-bottom, mass-market price. In thinking about such an extension, the marketer needs to be sure that the gaps thus filled are worth filling. Will sufficient customers emerge to take up the new product? Will the trade accept it? Is it a significant profit opportunity? Will it simply cannibalise existing products? This last issue is particularly important; there is no point in extending a product range downwards if the main effect is to pull customers away from an existing mid-range product.

An upwards extension could create a product with higher margins (see Chapter 7) as well as enhancing the organisation's image. It also helps to build a kind of staircase for the customer to climb. As the customer becomes more affluent or as their needs and wants become more sophisticated, they can trade up to the next product in the range and still maintain their loyalty to one organisation.

eg   Pringle, a Scottish knitwear firm best known for its sweaters and golf sponsorship, tried to extend upwards into luxury goods, such as high-quality luggage and accessories. At the same time, it was also expanding sideways into non-knitwear clothing and its own retail outlets. This combination of upwards and sideways expansion did not work well. The Pringle brand name was appearing on too many items that were too far removed from its core image. This diluted the impact and exclusivity of the name and meant that customers did not perceive the luxury goods as being suitably classy or elite.

A downwards extension can be used to attack competitors operating at the volume end of the market. It can build a larger base of sales if a lower-priced product broadens the number of potential customers. Then, by introducing people to the bottom of the range product and forming some kind of relationship with them, it may be possible to get them to trade up, thus assisting sales of the mid-range product. This would be the ideal situation, but do remember the risks of cannibalisation if the bottom of the range product acts as a magnet to existing mid-range customers. There can be a risk of undermining brand equity by extensions at the bottom of the range. This can cause an overall loss of equity to the whole range that is greater than the incremental sales of the new products (Reibstein *et al.*, 1998).

Filling the product range. The option of filling the product range involves a very close examination of the current range, then creating new products to fill in any gaps between existing products. One way of filling out the range could be to increase the number of variants available. The product remains the same, but it has a range of different presentations. Thus a food product might be available in single-serving packs, family-sized packs or catering-sized freezer packs. Tomato ketchup is available in squeezy bottles as well as in glass ones.

eg Heinz has been very active in new product development in recent years, offering alternative packaging and new varieties around the traditional soup, baked beans and tomato sauce recipes. Chunky and Weightwatchers soups cater for very different usage segments from the standard soups and have proved to be highly successful. Heinz soup bars are now being evaluated, microwaveable soups are on offer, and the next stage could be soup from vending machines on garage forecourts. Best of all, green ketchup caught the buyer's imagination in the USA and should now be available in Europe. It tastes just the same as the red version, but offers a highly squeezable bottle and creates new fun opportunities for the under-12s (*The Grocer*, 2001a, b).

Filling the range can be a useful strategy for keeping the competition out, by offering the consumer some novelty and a more detailed range of products closer to their needs, and to add incrementally to profits at relatively low risk. The danger, however, is the risk of adding to costs, but with no overall increase in sales. This is the risk of cannibalisation, of fragmenting existing market share across too many similar products. There is the added irony that the consumer might well be indifferent to these variants, being perfectly satisfied with the original range.

Deleting products. The final stages of a product's life are often the hardest for management to contemplate. The decision to eliminate a poor seller that may be generating low or even negative profits is a tough one to make. The economic rationale for being ruthless is clear. A product making poor returns absorbs management time and can quickly drain resources if it is being kept alive by aggressive selling and promotion. There is, however, often a reluctance to take action. There are various reasons for this, some of which are purely personal or political. Managers often form emotional attachments to the products they have looked after: 'I introduced this product, I backed it and built my career on it.' If the offending product was launched more recently, then its deletion might be seen as an admission of failure on the part of its managers. They would, therefore, prefer to try just once more to turn the product round and to retain their reputations intact.

Other reasons for being reluctant to delete a product are based on a desire to offer as wide a range as possible, regardless of the additional costs incurred. While there is still some demand (however small) for a particular product, the organisation feels obliged to continue to provide it, as a service to its customers. Suddenly deleting that product might result in negative feelings for some customers. Car owners in particular become attached to certain models and react badly when a manufacturer decides to withdraw them from the available range.

All of this means that there is a need for a regular systematic review to identify the more marginal products, to assess their current contribution and to decide how they fit with future plans. If new life can be injected into a product, then all well and good, but if not, then the axe will have to fall and the product either phased out or dropped immediately.

eg Colman's French Mustard is no more. This was not strictly a commercial decision, as it was based on a ruling from the European Union. When the parent company, Unilever, bought a competitor, Amora Maille, in 2000, the EU ruled that Unilever had too high a market share and so Colman's French Mustard was deleted to reduce the alleged monopoly position. From now on, it will have to be mustard from Dijon or Bordeaux rather than Norwich. Unilever chose, however, not to sell the brand, contrary to the EU view, as it could have been a threat in the hands of a strong competitor. Instead, Unilever discontinued it to focus on better developing the Amora Maille brand name (Bridgett, 2001).

■ The product life cycle

The product life-cycle (PLC) concept reflects the theory that products, like people, live a life. They are born, they grow up, they mature and, eventually, they die. During its life, a product goes through many different experiences, achieving varying levels of success in the market. This naturally means that the product's marketing support needs also vary, depending on what is necessary both to secure the present and to work towards the future. Figure 6.5 shows the theoretical progress of a PLC, indicating the pattern of sales and profits earned. The diagram may be applied either to an individual product or brand (for example Kellogg's Cornflakes) or to a product class (breakfast cereals).

Figure 6.5 indicates that there are four main stages, introduction, growth, maturity and decline, and these are now discussed in turn along with their implications for marketing strategy.

Stage 1: introduction

At the very start of the product's life as it enters the market, sales will begin to build slowly and profit may be small (even negative). A slow build-up of sales reflects the lead time required for marketing efforts to take effect and for people to hear about the product and try it. Low profits are partly an effect of the low initial sales and partly a reflection of the possible need to recoup development and launch costs.

The marketer's main priority at this stage is to generate widespread awareness of the product among the target segment and to stimulate trial. If the product is truly innovative, there may be no competitors yet and so there is the added problem of building primary demand (i.e. demand for the class of product rather than simply demand for a specific brand) as a background to the actual brand choice.

There is also a need to gain distribution. With new FMCG goods, the retail trade may be hard to convince unless the product has a real USP (unique selling point), because of the pressure on shelf space and the proliferation of available brands. In parallel with that, there

Figure 6.5 The product life cycle

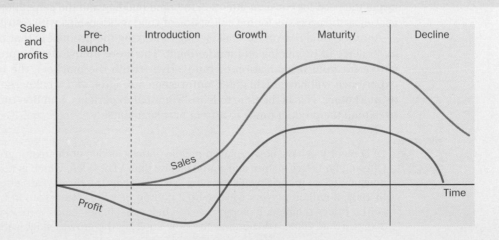

is still the task of generating awareness among consumers and moving them through towards a purchase. The decision on the product's price, whether to price high or low or whether to offer an introductory trial price, could be an important element in achieving that first purchase.

eg Microsoft's new operating system, Windows XP, was, according to the company, a highly successful launch, with 7 million licences shipped in the first two weeks after the official launch. Early retail sales were double those of any previous Windows version. Several trade pundits, however, believed that sustained sales would be slow as there was no 'killer' application for the new system, so consumers would wait until they purchased new machines before they bothered with XP (Darrow, 2001). It is one thing to be interested, but another to develop the motivation to buy. Despite a £136m. advertising spend in the USA, retail sales of XP dropped from 400,000 in the first month after launch to 250,000 in the second month whereas Windows 98 had sold 350,000 in its second month. Most copies of operating systems are sold as part of a new computer sale and 2001 was a sluggish market (Ayres, 2001).

Given the failure rate of new products and the importance of giving a product the best possible start in life, the introduction stage is likely to make heavy demands on marketing resources. This can be especially draining for a smaller organisation, but nevertheless is necessary if the product is to survive into the next stage: growth.

Stage 2: growth

In the growth stage, there is rapid increase in sales. One reason for this might be that word is getting around about the product and the rate of recruitment of new triers accelerates. Another reason is that the effects of repeat purchases are starting to be seen. There is some urgency at this stage to build as much brand preference and loyalty as possible. Competitors will now have had time to assess the product, its potential and its effect on the overall market, and will thus have decided their response. They may be modifying or improving their existing products or entering a new product of their own to the market. Whatever they do, they will deflect interest and attention away from the product and there is a risk that this will flatten the growth curve prematurely unless the company takes defensive steps.

Figure 6.5 shows that profits start to rise rapidly in this stage. This too might be affected by competitive pressure, if other organisations choose to compete on price, forcing margins down. Again, repeat purchases that build brand loyalty are the best defence in these circumstances.

Even though the product might seem to be still very young and only just starting to deliver its potential, towards the close of the growth stage might be a good time to think about product modifications or improvements to keep one step ahead of the competition. If the initial novelty of your product has worn off, buyers might be vulnerable to competitors' new products. This might also threaten the security of your distribution channels, as heavy competition for shelf space squeezes out weaker products perceived as heading nowhere. This all reinforces, yet again, the need for constant attention to brand building and the generation of consumer loyalty, as well as the necessity for the cultivation of good relationships with distributors.

Another good reason for considering modifying the product is that by now you have real experience of producing and marketing it. The more innovative the product (whether innovative for your organisation or innovative within the market), the more likely it is that experience will have highlighted unforeseen strengths and weaknesses in the product and its marketing. This is the time to learn from that experience and fine-tune the whole offering or extend the product range to attract new segments.

eg DVD recorders have now replaced mobile phones as one of the major growth product areas. Offering far better picture and sound quality than VHS video, which is now over 20 years old, consumers are increasingly switching systems. Over the three years after their introduction in 1998, 3 million players were sold, 2 million of which were sold in 2000 alone (Poulter, 2001). Prices tumbled, in some cases to below £100, and sales were expected to double in 2002 (Arthur, 2001). DVD brands are now entering the growth stage with everything to play for. At the start of 2002, while 90 per cent of UK homes had a video recorder, only 10 per cent already had DVD. As recordability becomes cheaper and as consumers become more willing to switch formats and dump their video collections, DVD will continue to grow. In 2001, however, 4 million video players were still sold which suggests that the changeover period could take several years yet, but as long as the growth continues, the consumer electronics companies will not complain.

At some point, the growth period comes to an end as the product begins to reach its peak and enters the next stage: maturity.

Stage 3: maturity

During the maturity stage, the product achieves as much as it is going to. The accelerated growth levels off, as everyone who is likely to be interested in the product should have tried it by now and a stable set of loyal repeat buyers should have emerged. The mobile phone market, for example, had achieved 70 per cent penetration in the UK by the end of 2001 and sales levelled off to upgrading and replacement rather than converting those harder-to-win customers. This is not a cause for complacency, however. There are few new customers available and even the laggards have purchased by now. This means that there is a high degree of customer understanding of the product and possibly of the market. They know what they want, and if your product starts to look dated or becomes unexciting compared with newer offerings from the competition, then they might well switch brands. Certainly, the smaller or more poorly positioned brands are going to be squeezed out. In these circumstances, the best hope is to consolidate the hard-core loyal buyers, encouraging heavier consumption from them. It may also be possible to convert some brand switchers into loyal customers through the use of sales promotions and advertising.

At this stage, there is likely to be heavy price competition and increased marketing expenditure from all competitors in order to retain brand loyalty. Much of this expenditure will be focused on marketing communication, but some may be channelled into minor product improvements to refresh the brand. Distribution channels may also need careful handling at this stage. Unless the product remains a steady seller, the retailer may be looking to delist it to make room on the shelves for younger products.

The sales curve has reached a plateau, as the market is saturated and largely stable. Any short-term gains will be offset by similar losses and profits may start to decline because of price competition pressure. It is thus very important to try, at least, to retain existing buyers. Sooner or later, however, the stability of the maturity phase will break, either through competitive pressure (they are better at poaching your customers than you are at poaching theirs) or through new developments in the market that make your product increasingly inappropriate, pushing the product into the decline stage.

eg It is possible for the marketer to take action to extend the maturity stage or even to stimulate new growth in the market. Scotch whisky is a mature product (in all senses of the phrase) in its biggest markets, the UK and France. This is partly because of the high level of competition in the market, over 2,000 brands, and partly because of the image of whisky as 'something your parents drink'. The potential to inject new life into the market has come from the trend in countries such as Portugal, Spain and Greece, where whisky is commonly drunk with water, ice or cola by the under-30 age group. If whisky manufacturers can successfully give their brands a more youthful emphasis and a more consistent European image, then they may be able to extend the life cycle still further.

Stage 4: decline

Once a product goes into decline for market-based reasons, it is almost impossible to stop it. The rate of decline can be controlled to some extent, but inevitably sales and profits will fall regardless of marketing effort.

Decline can often be environment related rather than a result of poor management decisions. Technological developments or changes in consumer tastes, for example, can lead to

Product failure. Some products never even achieve a growth stage: they fail. This may be because the product itself is badly thought through or because it never gained awareness or distribution. New food products from small manufacturers without the resources to create strong brands may fail because they simply cannot gain mass distribution from retailers unwilling to take risks with unknown producers or brands.

Revitalisation product. By updating a product, either through design or through a fresh marketing approach, new life can be injected to regenerate customer and retailer interest and loyalty. Tango, for example, was a standard, uninteresting fizzy orange drink until some surreal, controversial and imaginative advertising repositioned it as a trendy teenage drink. Hiam (1990) argued that many products can be revitalised and that 'maturity simply reflects saturation of a specific target market with a specific product form'. Generally it is argued that 'it is a myth that products have a predetermined life span'.

Product level, class, form and brand. As said at the beginning of this section, the PLC can operate on a number of different levels. It is important to distinguish between the PLCs of total industries (such as the motor industry), product classes (such as petrol-driven private vehicles), product forms (such as hatchback cars) and individual brands (such as the Fiat Uno).

Industries and product classes tend to have the longest PLCs, because they are an aggregate of the efforts of many organisations and many individual products over time. An industry, such as the motor industry, can be in an overall state of fairly steady maturity for many years even as individual product forms and brands come and go. In the motor industry, for example, the hatchback is probably a mature product form, while the people carrier is still in its growth stage. Although a number of hatchback 'brands' have come and gone, the number of people carrier 'brands' is still growing. At the same time, the earliest entrants in the European market are starting to reach maturity.

Despite its weaknesses, the PLC is a well-used concept. Product marketing strategies should, however, take into account other considerations as well as the PLC, as the next section shows.

The yo-yo craze: the fad that bounces back

Fads and crazes are especially challenging to marketers as it is very hard to predict whether they will take off, how fast and for how long they will last. If the predictions and timing are wrong, then the marketer risks either being too slow to benefit before the craze passes or being left with unsold stock. The trouble with fad products, however, is that traditional marketing rules do not apply. There is no point in building for the long term if there is not going to be one and thus being flexible enough to capitalise quickly on a craze is critical.

Fad products often crop up in the toy market which, in the UK alone, is worth around £800m. per year. The yo-yo is a craze toy with a different kind of product life cycle because it keeps coming back!

Popular for short periods in the 1960s, 1970s and 1980s, sales suddenly burst into life yet again in 1998. In 1997, the UK's largest independent toy retail chain, The Entertainer Group, hardly sold a yo-yo. In the first quarter of 1998, however, sales went up to between 3,000 and 4,000 yo-yos per week. By the end of the year the sales level had reached between 15,000 and 18,000 per week. The British Association of Toy Retailers estimated that sales nationally were approaching 150,000 per week and the yo-yo become the top-selling toy for pre-teen children. In an era of sophisticated computer games and in a market faced with an ever-increasing array of tempting toys, it was not a bad performance for a simple wheely thing on a piece of string.

So why did the yo-yo make a comeback? Some argue that the craze was fuelled by parents who saw it as a wholesome and nostalgic alternative to letting their kids gaze at a computer screen all day. A more likely explanation, however, is that marketers made the yo-yo a more acceptable play alternative by careful product development and a marketing campaign selling the yo-yo's benefits as an outdoor toy, emphasising its street credibility. Product improvements encouraged ease of use, for example the 'centrifugal clutch system' makes it easier to perform tricks, even for beginners. To encourage children to practise their skills and to reinforce brand awareness, yo-yo company

Yomega started a reward programme called 'Tricknology'. If children bought the yo-yos from accredited stores they could be tested to earn certificates at bronze, silver, gold and platinum levels.

Skills development was not the only attraction. Through design and colour, the yo-yos became fashion accessories rather than just toys and some kids even began collecting them! Although yo-yos can be purchased for as little as £1, the average sale value was between £8 and £15, with premium products costing up to £100. Children became brand conscious, looking for the 'coolest' names such as Yomega X-Brain and Pro Yo III, and perhaps the fact that some schools banned yo-yos from playgrounds only served to enhance the 'cool' factor.

The Rolls-Royce of yo-yos!
Source: Yomega Corporation Inc.

By the new millennium the craze was over. The shortages reported a few years previously were things of the past and the yo-yo had again become a niche product. Yomega still offers a

wide selection on its website of both classic and fashion accessory yo-yos. Yo-yo events are still held around the world but they are a shadow of the 1998 event in Japan, attended by 41,000 people. Membership is still promoted for the Yomega Yo-Yo Association where like-minded people can meet. Products are still available in some specialist retail stores, but the queues to buy them have gone. Roll on 2007. The product is mature, yet appears to reinvent itself on a cyclical basis before it slips into decline. As yo-yo means 'come back' in the Tagalog dialect of the Philippines, even though the late 1990s craze ended, the yo-yo is almost guaranteed to make another reappearance – eventually!

Sources: Gray (1998); Rigby (1998); Wright (1998); http://www.yomega.com

■ The diffusion of innovation

The product life cycle is clearly driven by changes in consumer behaviour as the new product becomes established. The rate at which the growth stage develops is linked in particular to the speed with which customers can be led through from awareness of the product to trial and eventual adoption of the product, in other words how fast the AIDA model (see Figure 4.2 on p. 122) works. The problem is, however, that not all customers move through it with equal speed and eagerness and some will adopt innovation more quickly than others. This has led to the concept of the diffusion of innovation (Rogers, 1962), which looks at the rate at which innovation spreads across a market as a whole. Effectively, it allows the grouping or classification of customers depending on their speed of adoption into one of five adopter categories, as shown in Figure 6.7.

Figure 6.7 Diffusion of innovation: adopter categories

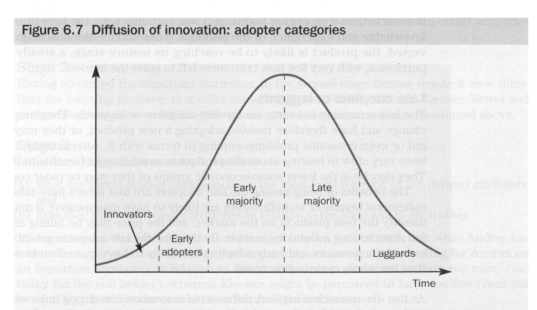

Source: Based on Rogers (1962). Reprinted and adapted from figure 7–2, p. 262 with the permission of The Free Press, a division of Simon & Schuster Adult Publishing Group, from *Diffusion of Innovations*, Fourth Edition, by Everett M. Rogers. Copyright © 1995 Everett M. Rogers. Copyright © 1962, 1971, 1983 by The Free Press. All rights reserved.

tion search. In B2B markets, they are more likely to relate to the final use of the product. An organisation's product mix, made up of individual product items, can be divided into product lines. These are groups of items that have some common link, either operational or marketing based. Product mix width is established by the number of product lines, while product line depth is defined according to the number of individual items within a line.

■ Branding is an important way of creating differentiated tangible products. It helps the manufacturer to establish loyalty through the three-dimensional character imposed on the product, as well as deflecting consumer attention away from price. Branding is carried out not only by manufacturers, but also by retailers who want to create a more tangible character for themselves, as well as wanting consumers consciously to prefer to shop at their outlets. Relevant issues concerning brand owners include the creation and design of products and their brand identities as expressed through the core and tangible product via elements such as naming, quality, packaging and labelling. The strategic management of product and brand ranges is also important.

■ The product life-cycle (PLC) concept is the foundation for the idea that products move through stages in their lives and that they may, therefore, have different marketing needs over time. The PLC suggests four stages: introduction, growth, maturity and decline. Inevitably, the PLC is a very general concept, perhaps too general to be of real use, and there are many practical problems in using it. For an organisation, product management is important not only for making sure that existing products live profitable and efficient lives, and that they are deleted at the most appropriate time, but also to enable it to plan for the future and the flow of new products, taking advantage of new technologies and other opportunities. This implies the need for a balanced portfolio of products: some still in development, some in the early stages of their lives, some more mature and some heading for decline.

■ One way of ensuring that products get the most out of their life cycles is to think about how they are positioned. This means defining what attributes or benefits are important to the market, then researching how your product, its competitors and a hypothetical ideal product are rated against those criteria, then analysing each brand's position in relation to the others and to the ideal. Perceptual mapping, using two or more dimensions, can help to visualise the state of the market. All of this can stimulate debate as to whether a product needs to be further differentiated from its competitors or brought closer to the market segment's ideal. Over a product's life cycle, repositioning may become necessary in response to the changing marketing and competitive environment.

■ In FMCG companies in particular, product or brand managers may be given the responsibility of looking after a particular product or group of products. Although a similar product management structure may be found in B2B markets, alternative options may be considered. Management responsibility may be divided by end user or on a geographic basis, again because the needs of different regions may differ. In either case, the organisation can develop managers with depth of expertise relating to a specific group of end users or a particular geographic market.

■ The creation of the SEM opened up opportunities for pan-European branding. For many smaller organisations, however, this is not a serious issue and they do not have the resources or the real desire to move beyond their own national boundaries. Organisations interested in pan-European branding need abundant resources, to be sure that they can deliver consistent quality in all aspects of the operations and marketing and that they are prepared to support the brand through a long lead time before the product begins to make a return on its investment.

questions for *review and discussion*

6.1 Choose three different brands of shampoo that you think incorporate different core products.

(a) Define the core product for each brand.
(b) How does the tangible product for each brand reflect the core product?

6.2 What is a speciality product and how might its marketing mix and the kind of buying behaviour associated with it differ from those found with other products?

6.3 Develop a weighted set of five or six criteria for 'good' labelling. Collect a number of competing brands of the same product and rate each of them against your criteria. Which brand comes out best? As a result of this exercise, would you adjust your weightings or change the criteria included?

6.4 Discuss the relationship between product adopter categories and the stages of the PLC. What are the implications for the marketer?

6.5 Choose a consumer product area (be very specific – for example, choose shampoo rather than haircare products) and list as many brands available within it as you can.

   (a) What stage in the PLC has each brand reached?

   (b) Does any one organisation own several of the brands and, if so, how are those brands distributed across the different PLC stages?

6.6 Define product positioning and summarise the reasons why it is important.

case study 6.1

Is small still beautiful second time around?

The original Mini became an icon for the 60s' generation, a triumph of its time for innovative style and mechanical engineering. Its owners included The Beatles, Mick Jagger, Peter Sellers and Twiggy and it played a star role with Michael Caine in the movie *The Italian Job*. As an aside, it also won the Monte Carlo rally three times. At its launch in 1959, however, its creators had no such pretensions or ambitions for the car. It was simply a response to the possibility of petrol rationing. Its fuel economy and a competitive price tag of £497 set it aside from the rest, and it became almost a generic name for small cars.

Although The Beatles' music and Mick Jagger all survived well beyond the swinging 60s, by 1972 fashions had changed and the Mini brand was in decline. It increasingly became a small-volume, niche car with a cult following reliving earlier times. An influx of competitive small cars, a shift in consumer preference for more space and comfort, and changing design appreciation meant that the Mini became stuck with being a likeable, but dated brand. Although the Mini was kept in production, the then owner BL (British Leyland) was looking for a replacement. Its efforts were not an unqualified success, however. The Mini Metro launched in the 1980s, again an economical, low-priced brand, was again soon left behind by later entrants in terms of quality, design and performance. To succeed in the small car segment requires production efficiency and volume sales along with some distinguishing features. The Metro did not survive the Mini and is best remembered as the car people learned to drive in after the British School of Motoring adopted the brand for its fleet in the 1980s.

In the 1990s, the Mini passed into BMW's hands and plans were laid for a new Mini. The brand name was considered so strong and evocative that it was capable of a renaissance. The challenge was to create a car that was readily identified with the old Mini and handled like a Mini, yet had twenty-first-century quality and comforts. It was described as a baby BMW at £10,300 for the entry-level Mini One and £11,600 for the sporty Mini Cooper. The new Mini retained its sense of fun, both in its looks and its heart. The Cooper S version had a 1.6-litre engine offering 130 bhp for those seeking the on-road experience of the original. BMW avoided making the same mistake as VW, however. When VW launched the new Beetle in 1999 it was priced at £15,000, well beyond the target market's price limit, especially for a two-car household. BMW had originally planned to launch the Mini at £14,000, but changed it to the more competitive £10,000, just a little higher than some of the popular alternatives.

So will the new or 'retro' Mini sell? The initial target markets are past Mini drivers and BMW owners seeking a second vehicle. The appeal could then broaden if the Mini becomes established as a powerful competitor to mass market cars such as the Renault Clio, Audi A2 and Mercedes A-class. The production target for 2001 was a modest 20,000 but in a full year, 100,000 will be nearer the expected number leaving the production line in Oxford. At the UK launch, it already had 6,000 advance orders, 2,500 in Britain alone, and prospective buyers soon had to join a six-month waiting list. Registrations in the first eight weeks were claimed to be double those of the Ford Puma in 1997 and more than 10 times the

chapter 7

price

LEARNING OBJECTIVES

This chapter will help you to:

1 define the meaning of price;

2 understand the different roles price can play for buyers and sellers and in different kinds of market;

3 appreciate the nature of the external factors that influence pricing decisions;

4 explore the internal organisational forces that influence pricing decisions; and

5 understand the managerial process that leads to price setting and the influences that affect its outcomes.

Introduction

At first glance, price might seem to be the least complicated and perhaps the least interesting element of the marketing mix, not having the tangibility of the product, the glamour of advertising or the atmosphere of retailing. It does, however, play a very important role in the lives of both marketers and customers, and deserves as much strategic consideration as any other marketing tool. Price not only directly generates the revenues that allow organisations to create and retain customers at a profit (in accordance with one of the definitions of marketing in Chapter 1), but can also be used as a communicator, as a bargaining tool and as a competitive weapon. The customer can use price as a means of comparing products, judging relative value for money or judging product quality.

Ultimately, the customer is being asked to accept the product offering and (usually) to hand money over in exchange for it. If the product has been carefully thought out with the customer's needs in mind, if the distribution channels chosen are convenient and appropriate to that customer, if the promotional mix has been sufficiently seductive, then there is a good chance that the customer will be willing to hand over some amount of money for the pleasure of owning that product. But even then, the price that is placed on the product is crucial: set too high a price, and the customer will reject the offering and all the good work done with the rest of the marketing mix is wasted; too low, and the customer is suspicious ('too good to be true'). What constitutes 'a high price' or 'a low price' depends on the buyer, and has to be put into the context of their perceptions of themselves, of the entire marketing package and of the competitors' offerings. Pricing has a spurious certainty about it because it involves numbers, but do not be misled by this; it is as emotive and as open to misinterpretation as any other marketing activity.

It is thus important for the marketer to understand the meaning of price from the customer's point of view, and to price products in accordance with the 'value' that the customer places on the benefits offered.

This chapter expands on these initial concepts of price. It will look further at what price is, and what it means to marketers and customers in various contexts. It will also examine more closely the role of price in the marketing mix, and how it interacts with other marketing activities. This sets the scene for a focus on some of the internal factors and external pressures that influence pricing thinking within an organisation. The final section of the chapter then draws all this together to give an overview of the managerial process that leads to decisions on pricing strategies and price setting.

eg You would think that in the rosy glow of satisfaction and pride at taking delivery of your nice new shiny car, the registration plate would be the last thing you would think about. You would also think that the registration plate itself would be a minimal part of the total cost of the car. For some people, however, a personalised registration plate is the ultimate status symbol, and it is worth paying a considerable sum of money to get the plate they want. Since 1989, the UK's Driver and Vehicle Licensing Agency (DVLA) has been developing a profitable business in personalised plates as a spin-off from its formal governmental licensing role.

Dealers have also sprung up, offering second-hand plates. The car buyer can, of course, just select from the limited range of registration numbers available from the car dealer at the time of the purchase as part of the purchase price of the car, but a designer registration from the DVLA will cost at least £499. Some particularly attractive registrations due for release in 2001 include MU51CAL, DE51RES and DE51GNS and these are expected to sell for up to £30,000 each at auction – nearly three times more expensive than the average family car. This all goes to show that from a consumer perspective, it is not the cost that matters, but the perceived value, and that is the first important lesson for marketers when setting prices (Arnold, 2001a).

The role and perception of price

Price is the value that is placed on something. What is someone prepared to give in order to gain something else? Usually, price is measured in money, as a convenient medium of exchange that allows prices to be set quite precisely. This is not necessarily always the case, however. Goods and services may be bartered ('I will help you with the marketing plan for your car repair business if you service my car for me'), or there may be circumstances where monetary exchange is not appropriate, for example at election time when politicians make promises in return for your vote. Any such transactions, even if they do not directly involve money, are exchange processes and thus can use marketing principles (go back to Chapter 1 for the discussion of marketing as an exchange process). Price is any common currency of value to both buyer and seller.

Even money-based pricing comes under many names, depending on the circumstances of its use: solicitors charge fees; landlords charge rent; bankers charge interest; railways charge fares; hotels charge a room rate; consultants charge retainers; agents charge commission; insurance companies charge premiums; and over bridges or through tunnels, tolls may be charged. Whatever the label, it is still a price for a good or a service, and the same principles apply.

Price does not necessarily mean the same things to different people, just because it is usually expressed as a number. You have to look beyond the price, at what it represents to both the buyer and the seller if you want to grasp its significance in any transaction. Buyer and seller may well have different perspectives on what price means. We now turn to that of the buyer.

■ The customer's perspective

From the buyer's perspective, price represents the value they attach to whatever is being exchanged. Up to the point of purchase, the marketer has been making promises to the potential buyer about what this product is and what it can do for that customer. The customer is going to weigh up those promises against the price and decide whether it is worth paying (Zeithaml, 1988).

In assessing price, the customer is looking specifically at the expected benefits of the product, as shown in Figure 7.1.

Functional benefits
Functional benefits relate to the design of the product and its ability to fulfil its desired function. For example, a washing machine's price might be judged on whether or not it can handle different washing temperatures, operate economically and dry as well as wash.

Not all products conform to the classic demand curve shown in Figure 7.3. Some products with a deep psychological relationship with the consumer, perhaps with a high status dimension, can show a reverse price–demand curve where the higher the price the higher the demand. As Figure 7.4 shows, as the price goes down from P1 to P2 and demand falls from Q1 to Q2, the product loses its mystique and demand falls. There is, however, still an upper threshold beyond which the good becomes too expensive for even a status-conscious market. Then as the price rises higher, beyond P3, a more normal relationship holds true in which higher price leads to lower demand. This creates a boomerang-shaped demand curve. Knowing at what point the curve begins to turn back on itself could be useful for a marketer wishing to skim the market. Price too high and you could have turned the corner, becoming too exclusive.

eg Fine fragrances, especially those with designer names, might display a boomerang demand curve. The fragrance houses have been careful to price them sufficiently highly to position them well away from ordinary toiletries. This means that fine fragrances appeal not only to a well-to-do segment who can easily afford this sort of product on a regular basis, but also to those who aspire to be part of this elite and are prepared to splash out what seems to them to be a large sum of money occasionally to bring themselves closer to a world of luxury and sophistication. In either case, the high price is part of the appeal and the excitement of the product. The higher the price, the bigger the thrill. If the price became too high, however, the aspiring segment would probably fall away and live out their fantasies with something more affordable. They might find £30 to £80 acceptable, but £70 to £120 might be perceived as too extravagant. Even the elite segment might have its upper threshold. If the price of designer-label fine fragrances becomes too high, then they might as well buy the designer's clothes instead if they want to flaunt their wealth and status!

Another dimension of the demand curve is that marketers can themselves seek to influence its shape. Figure 7.5 shows how the demand curve can be shifted upwards through marketing efforts. If the marketer can offer better value to the customer or change the customer's perceptions of the product, then a higher quantity will be demanded without any reduction in the price. It is valuable for the marketer to be able to find ways of using non-price-based mechanisms of responding to a competitor's price cut or seeking to improve demand, to avoid the kind of mutually damaging price wars that erode margins and profits. This may create a new demand curve, parallel to the old one, so that demand can be increased from Q1 to Q2 while retaining the price at P1.

Price elasticity of demand

It is also important for the marketer to have some understanding of the sensitivity of demand to price changes. This is shown by the steepness of the demand curve. A very steep

Figure 7.4 The boomerang demand curve

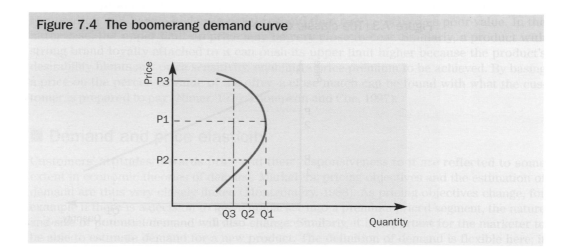

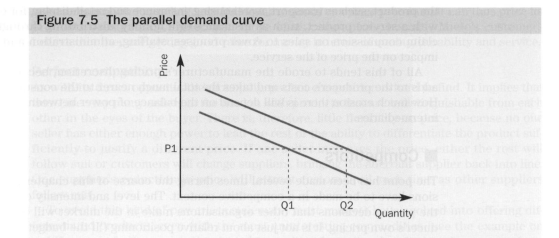

Figure 7.5 The parallel demand curve

demand curve shows a great deal of price sensitivity, in that a small change in price, all other things remaining equal, leads to a big change in demand. For some essential products, such as electricity, the demand curve is much more shallow; changes in price do not lead to big changes in demand. In this case, demand is said to be inelastic because it does not stretch a lot if pulled either way by price. The term 'price elasticity of demand' thus refers to the ratio of percentage change in quantity over percentage change in price:

$$\text{Price elasticity} = \frac{\% \text{ change in quantity demanded}}{\% \text{ change in price}}$$

Thus the higher the price elasticity of demand, the more sensitive the market. Goods like electricity will have a price elasticity much closer to zero than do goods like convenience foods. For most goods, as the quantity demanded usually falls if the price rises, price clasticity is often negative, but by convention, the minus sign is usually ignored.

It is important for the marketer to understand price elasticity and its causes, whether for an organisation's brand or within the market as a whole, as a basis for marketing mix decisions. There are a number of factors that will influence the price sensitivity (i.e. the price elasticity of demand) of customers. According to economic theory, the emergence of more, or closer, substitutes for a product will increase its price elasticity as buyers have the option of switching to the substitute as the price of the original product rises. From a marketing perspective, however, it does not seem quite so simple. The emergence of vegetable-based spreadable fats, for example, has offered consumers an alternative to butter and thus something with which to compare the price of butter. Further than that, however, it has completely changed the character of butter's demand curve from that of a necessity (a fairly flat straight line) to that of a luxury (more of a boomerang shape). Those who now choose to buy butter because of its superior taste or because of the status it bestows on the contents of the buyer's fridge will be no more price sensitive now than they ever were and, indeed, may even be less so.

As well as looking at the influence of substitutes on the shape and steepness of demand curves, it is also interesting to consider the relative importance of the purchase to the buyer. A purchase involving a relatively large cash outlay compared with the buyer's income will make that buyer more price sensitive. As discussed in Chapter 3, the more risky and infrequent the purchase, the more rational the buyer becomes, and more important the value for money aspects of the offering become. A rise in the price of cars, for example, might deter a potential buyer from replacing an old car.

■ Channels of distribution

An organisation's approach to pricing has also to take into account the needs and expectations of the other members of the distribution chain. Each of them will have a desired level of profit margin and a requirement to cover the costs associated with handling and reselling

Caught in the act!

Both Roche and BASF fell foul of the European Commission when the latter found that there had been a 9-year conspiracy to control prices in the vitamins market (Guerrera and Jennen, 2001). Both parties, along with a number of other companies, were accused of working together to ensure that prices of vitamin products were kept artificially high and that there was no excessive price competition to bring them down. The cartel was exposed in 1999 and investigation by the Commission resulted in fines of €462m. for Roche, as leader of the cartel (*Le Temps*, 2001), and €296m. for BASF (Court, 2001). Both organisations were expected to

appeal. The scale of the fines was more than double the previous record of ECU 270m. imposed on a shipping cartel, due to the extent of the price fixing, the length of time it had been operating and its being in a health-related market.

A similar probe took place in the United States where antitrust legislation tends to be tougher. Not only was Roche fined $500m., but a former executive was jailed for four months and fined $100,000 for playing an active part in the cartel's operation. The EU Commission is coming under increased pressure to take ever stronger measures against uncompetitive practices, regardless of the previous reputation of the

organisations being investigated. Both Roche and BASF are amongst Europe's largest and oldest drug companies. Aventis, the French drug company, escaped fines, however, as it 'co-operated with the enquiries and the Commission are keen to encourage whistleblowers so that other cartels can be exposed' (Court, 2001). In order to avoid a repeat of such incidents, Roche and a number of other companies now conduct training programmes for their staff on anti-competitive behaviour and have strengthened the internal audit function to root out such reputation-damaging practices.

Sources: Court (2001), Guerrera and Jennen (2001), *Le Temps* (2001).

Internal influences on the pricing decision

Pricing is, of course, also influenced by various internal factors. Pricing needs to reflect both corporate and marketing objectives, for example, as well as being consistent with the rest of the marketing mix. It is also important to remember, however, that pricing may also be related to costs, if the organisation is looking to generate an acceptable margin of profit. Figure 7.6 summarises the internal influences on price, and the rest of this section discusses each of them in further detail.

■ Organisational objectives

The area of organisational objectives is an internal influence, linked with corporate strategy. Marketing plans and objectives have to be set not only best to satisfy the customer's needs and wants, but also to reflect the aspirations of the organisation. These two aims should not be incompatible! Organisational objectives such as target volume sales, target value sales, target growth in various market segments and target profit figures can all be made more or less attainable through the deployment of the marketing mix and particularly through price.

Figure 7.6 Internal influences on the pricing decision

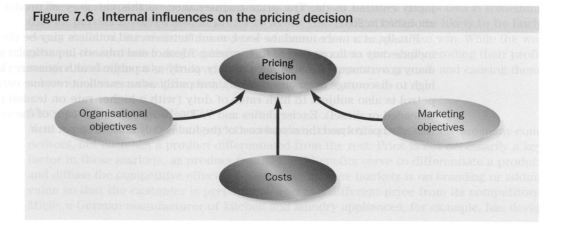

Corporate strategy is not simply concerned with quantifiable target setting. It is also concerned with the organisation's relative position in the market compared with the competition. Pricing may be used to help either to signal a desire for leadership (whether in terms of lowest cost or price, or superior quality) or to establish a clearly differentiated niche, which can then be emphasised and consolidated through the other elements of the marketing mix. In launching the Midnight Sun brand of butter on to the UK market, the Finnish company Valio used high-quality silver packaging as well as pricing the product to match the market leader, Lurpak, to communicate an upmarket image to the customer.

At the other end of the pricing spectrum, discount supermarket chains, such as Netto, Aldi, Lidl and Kwik Save, are trying to achieve objectives relating to price leadership in the market. Obviously, low pricing within their stores is their primary tool, but this can only be achieved through cost reduction (hence the minimalist retail environment and low levels of customer service) and accepting lower profit margins (1 per cent, compared with the industry average of between 5 and 8 per cent). Achieving all of this is also dependent on attracting many more customers through the doors to generate the higher volume of sales needed to make a reasonable profit. The higher volumes also give the discount retailer scope for negotiating more favourable terms with the manufacturers for bulk buying.

Organisational objectives can change over time as the organisation and its markets evolve. A new business, or a new entrant into a market, faces initial problems of survival. There is a need to generate orders to use excess capacity and to establish a foothold in the market. Relatively low pricing (at the sacrifice of profit margins rather than quality) is just one possible way of doing that. Once established, the organisation can begin to think in terms of target profits and building a competitive position, which may involve a revised approach to pricing. Using price as part of an integrated marketing mix, the organisation can aim to achieve market leadership in terms of whatever criteria are important. Once leadership is achieved, objectives have to be redefined to maintain and defend that leadership, thus keeping competition at arm's length.

Corporate objectives can also have both short- and long-term dimensions to them. In the short term, for example, a small business on the verge of collapse might use low price as a survival tactic to keep it afloat, even if its longer-term ambitions include quality leadership at a higher price.

■ Marketing objectives

As the previous subsection has implied, marketing and organisational objectives are very closely interrelated and influence each other to a great extent. The distinction, though, is that while organisational objectives relate primarily to the operation, the well-being and the personality of the organisation as a whole, marketing objectives are more closely focused on specific target markets and the position desired within them.

Marketing objectives are achieved through the use of the whole marketing mix, not just the price element, emphasising again the need for an integrated and harmonious marketing mix. An organisation may have a portfolio of products serving different segments, each of which requires a different approach to pricing. Such a differentiated strategy can be seen in telecommunications, with British Telecommunications developing a range of tariffs for both domestic and business users to suit different needs and priorities.

In that sense, it is no different from a car manufacturer making a cheap and cheerful $8,000 runabout model at one end of the range and a sleek, executive $40,000 status machine at the other. The key is to use the other elements of the marketing mix to support the price or to provide a rationale for it. The concept of the product portfolio and the management issues surrounding it are fully covered in Chapter 12.

Another product concept that might influence the pricing of a particular product over a period of time is the product life cycle (see pp. 195 et seq.). In the introductory stage, a lower price might be necessary as part of a marketing strategy to encourage trial. Advertising this as 'an introductory trial price' would be one way of preventing 'low price = low quality' judgements. As the product becomes established through the growth and early maturity stages, and gains loyal buyers, the organisation may feel confident enough to raise the price. As indicated earlier, this has to be done with due reference to the competitive sit-

Another aspect of the high or low price-setting decision is the likely impact on the competition. A high price might encourage them to enter the market too, as they see potentially high profit margins. The organisation launching the new product may not, however, have too much choice. Internal pressure to recoup development costs quickly may force a high price, or alternatively a price-sensitive market might simply reject a high price and force prices lower.

According to Monroe and Della Bitta (1978), much depends on how innovative the new product is. A new brand in a crowded market can be precise with its price positioning as there are many competitors to compare with, and both the price setter and the consumer can 'read' the price signals clearly. A completely unknown product, such as the very first domestic video recorder, has no such frame of reference. The price setter can work on three things. First, the prices of other domestic electrical goods might give clues as to the sort of prices consumers expect to pay. This is a tenuous link because this new product is so obviously different it may not be comparable, especially in the mind of an opinion-leading consumer. Second, market research may have been carried out to discover how enthusiastic consumers are about the new idea, and hypothetically what they would pay to possess it. Again, this may be misleading because the consumers have no experience of this product and may not themselves be able to foresee in theory how they would respond in practice. Third, the price setter can work on internal factors such as costs, breakeven analysis and return on investment. This serves as a starting point and experience and emerging competition will allow a more realistic price structure to evolve. It is a dangerous route, however. If that cost-based price turns out to be inappropriate, rescuing the product could be almost impossible, particularly if astute competitors are learning from your mistakes and launching realistically priced products themselves.

With all this in mind, the high or low entry price decision boils down to two alternative strategies, skimming or penetration, first proposed by Dean (1950).

Price skimming. In order to skim, prices are set high to attract the least price-sensitive market segments. Such pricing might appeal, for instance, to opinion leaders who want to be seen to be first with any new product regardless of the price, or to those who seek status and see high price as the mark of an exclusive product.

Skimming has a number of advantages. It allows the organisation to establish a quality brand image that could serve as a stepping stone to future development of lower-priced, more mass-market versions. If the product in question is a difficult one to produce, then pricing to keep the market small and exclusive can also give breathing space to gain learning experience on lower volumes while still marketing the product in a real market. The risk here, of course, is that high price raises high expectations, and if that learning experience does not go well, then the market will think that the product quality is too poor or inconsistent to justify the price, a bad reputation will stick and the future of the product becomes questionable. Finally, it is easier to reduce price than to raise it. If an initial high price does not generate the required response, it can be slowly lowered until an appropriate level is found.

eg High definition digital television sets were priced high when they were first launched but prices are now starting to drop in the USA and Europe. In 1998, a 60 inch projection unit would have cost around $8,000, but by 2001 it could be bought for around $3,000. The dramatic drop in price could be due to economies of scale, as the volume of sales has risen with consumers' growing appreciation of high definition picture quality for DVD usage. It could also be an outcome of the manufacturer's journey along a learning curve: as cumulative sales volumes build, the manufacturer gets more efficient at making the televisions and the manufacturing cost per unit falls. Finally, increasing competition could also have something to do with it, as potential buyers start to have more choice and can make price comparisons. Whatever the causes, the pioneering manufacturers are now able to lower prices and this in itself helps support further expansion in demand as more price-sensitive segments for home entertainment can be targeted (Heller, 2001).

Penetration pricing. In an attempt to gain as big a market share as possible in the shortest possible time, an organisation may price aggressively below existing competition, deliberately paring its margins for the sake of volume. This is *penetration pricing*. It may be a necessary strategy if cost structures are such that a very large volume of sales is required to break even or to achieve economies of scale in production or marketing terms. It is a risky strategy because it could establish a poor-quality brand image and also, if it does not work, it would be very difficult to raise the price.

It is, nevertheless, a legitimate strategy to seek to deny the competition volume share within the market. Penetration pricing of a new product, particularly in a market where product differentiation is difficult, reduces the attractiveness of market entry to competitors unless they can be sure that they can produce and market much more efficiently and on a tighter cost base. Penetration pricing is also useful in elastic demand situations where price is a critical factor for the buyer.

As emphasised above, the choice of launch price should take into account future plans for the pricing and positioning of the product. Some products can enter a market with a skimming price and retain it, particularly luxury goods that are well differentiated from each other and have an element of uniqueness about them. The Swiss company Bueche Girod, for example, advertised a 9 carat gold and diamond ladies' watch for £1,675 with a matching necklace for a further £2,975. In markets where a new product has a high level of technological innovation and customers have no benchmark against which to compare prices, the introductory price may skim, but this will give way to something more competitive as rival products enter the market, economies of scale are achieved and costs reduce with the learning curve. In contrast, penetration pricing at launch sets an aggressive, value for money stance that the manufacturer would find hard to break away from, regardless of what the competition do. This product will always have to be priced competitively.

Product mix pricing strategies

A product that is part of a product range cannot be priced in isolation from the rest of the range. The range has to be viewed as an entity, and different products serve different purposes that come together to benefit the whole. In seeking to serve the needs of a number of market segments and build a strong competitive defence across the market, one product may be allowed to earn a relatively low return while another is skimming.

Within an individual product line (see pp. 177 *et seq.* for the distinction between range and line), such as SLR cameras, each product within the line offers additional features and their pricing needs to be spaced out accordingly. Customers see the set of products within the line and relate the price steps with additional features, benefits or quality. This may also encourage consumers to trade up to a more expensive model in the line as they begin to indulge in a type of marginal analysis: 'For an extra £20 I can have a zoom facility as well. Seems like a better deal. . . .' The process may not be so rational. As discussed on p. 214, price may be used as an indicator of quality in the absence of other knowledge or indicators. Thus a buyer may find a model within the product line at (or slightly beyond) the preconceived spending limit and feel that the best possible quality purchase has been made, regardless of whether the product benefits and features are useful or appropriate.

Rather than presenting a predetermined collection of standard products with standard prices, some organisations prefer to offer a basic-priced product to which the consumer can then add extras, each of which adds to the overall price. The beauty of this is that the basic price seems very reasonable and affordable, and thus the consumer can easily get to the stage of wanting the product. Once that stage is reached, the odd few pounds here and there for extra features seem insignificant, even though the final total price may be somewhat higher than the consumer would have been comfortable with in the first place. At least the customer is getting a personally tailored purchase.

eg   Holiday packages prominently feature low prices on their brochures to attract attention and make themselves seem eminently affordable. Two weeks in the sun for only £99 per person soon increases to something closer to £300 when airport transfers and taxes are added, along with the supplements for a local departure, insurance, better-quality accommodation with a sea view, full board, and an August rather than May holiday. Buying a car is also a minefield of extras. Delivery charges, taxes, registration plates, metallic paint, sunroof, alarm system, central locking are among the items that may not necessarily be quoted in the advertised price.

The problem with any such approach is knowing what to leave out and what to include in the basic price. A basic price that does not include non-optional items such as tax is likely to lead to an unimpressed customer. There is also the danger that a competitor who comes in with an all-inclusive price may be seen as attractive by customers who feel that they have been deceived by overpriced extras that are actually essentials.

Managing price changes

Prices are rarely static for long periods. Competitive pressures may force prices down, either temporarily or permanently, or new market opportunities might increase the price premium on a product. The pressure of cost inflation means that the marketing manager has to decide whether to pass these cost increases on to customers through prices charged, and when. However, changing prices can have a serious effect on profit margins and on market stability. If the changes are too significant, whether on transatlantic air fares or the price of vegetables in the local market, it is almost inevitable that competitors will respond in some way. Price changes not only cause ripples through the market, but also have an impact on sales volume. Normally, it is likely that a price cut will increase volume, and it is sometimes a very fine calculation to predict whether the profit margin earned on the extra volume gained more than compensates for the lost margin caused by the price cut. At various times, an organisation might be faced with the prospect of initiating price changes, or of responding to competitors' price changes.

■ Setting the price range

Once the strategic direction of the pricing decision has been specified, a price range needs to be set within which the final detail of price can be established. A pricing method is needed that can generate purposeful and sound prices throughout the year. The method and its rigidity will obviously vary depending on whether the organisation is setting one-off prices for a few products or many prices for a large product range or is in a fast-moving retailing environment.

There are three main pricing methods, which take into account some of the key pricing issues already discussed. They are cost based, demand based and competition based. The organisation may adopt one main method of operation or use a flexible combination depending on circumstance. Each method will be discussed in turn, once the general principles of cost–volume–profit relationships have been established.

The cost–volume–profit relationship

The demand patterns discussed on pp. 218 *et seq.*, although established and understood in their own right, also need to be understood in the context of their relationship with costs, volume of production and profit. The marketer needs to understand how the organisation's costs behave under different conditions, internally and externally generated, in order to appreciate fully the implications of marketing decisions on the operation of the organisation. The marketer should understand the different types of costs and their contribution to the pricing decision. The four most important cost concepts are fixed costs, variable costs, marginal cost and total cost. These are now defined.

Fixed costs. Fixed costs are those that do not vary with output in the short term. This category thus includes management salaries, insurance, rent, buildings and machine maintenance, etc. Once output passes a certain threshold, however, extra production facilities might have to be brought on stream and so fixed costs will then show a step-like increase.

Variable costs. Variable costs are those that vary according to the quantity produced. These costs are incurred through raw materials, components, and direct labour used for assembly or manufacture. Variable costs can be expressed as a total or on a per unit basis.

Marginal cost. The change that occurs to total cost if one more unit is added to the production total is the marginal cost.

Total cost. Total cost is all the cost incurred by an organisation in manufacturing, marketing, administering and delivering the product to the customer. Total cost thus adds the fixed costs and the variable costs together.

Costs may not be the only factor involved in setting prices, but they are an important one. No organisation would wish to operate for very long at a level where its selling price was not completely recovering its costs and making some contribution towards profit.

Breakeven analysis. Breakeven analysis offers a simple, convenient approach to examining the cost–volume–profit relationship. It is a technique that shows the relationship between total revenue and total cost in order to determine the profitability of different levels of output. The breakeven point is the point at which total revenue and total cost are equal (i.e. no profit is made, nor are any losses incurred). Producing beyond this point generates increasing levels of profit.

Knowing how many units at any given price would have to be made and sold in order to break even is important, especially in new product and small business situations where an organisation has limited resources to fall back on if losses are incurred. Combining the breakeven analysis with known market and competitive conditions may make an organisation realise that it cannot compete unless it either reduces costs or develops a marketing strategy to increase volume sales.

Cost-based pricing methods

The emphasis in *cost-based* pricing methods is on the organisation's production and marketing costs. Analysis of these costs leads to an attempt to set a price that generates a sufficient profit. The obvious disadvantage is the lack of focus on the external situation. An organisation implementing such a method would need to be very sure of the market's response. It is, however, a simple method to use, drawing the sort of direct parallels between cost and price that make accountants very happy. There are some variations in cost-based pricing.

Mark-up. Especially in the retail sector, where it can be difficult to estimate demand patterns for each product line, percentage mark-up is used as a means of price setting. This means that the retailer starts with the price paid to the supplier for the goods and then adds a percentage to reach the retail price to the customer. In FMCG high-volume markets this can be as low as 8 per cent, whereas in low-volume fashion clothing markets it can be 200 per cent or more. Mark-ups may be standard across all retailers in a particular sector, although the smaller business may have to accept a lower mark-up to compete with the retail prices of bigger operators who can negotiate better cost prices from suppliers. A retailer such as Costco that deliberately violates the mark-up traditions of its sector can be seen as initiating an all-out price war.

Although this is basically a cost-based pricing method, it does not operate in isolation from external events. Retailers will be wary of implementing a mark-up that leads to a retail price way out of line with the competition, or that violates the consumer's expectations.

Cost-plus pricing. Cost-plus pricing involves adding a fixed percentage to production or construction costs. It is mainly used on large projects or for custom-built items where it is difficult to estimate costs in advance. The percentage will be agreed between buyer and seller in advance, and then just before, or after, the project's completion, buyer and seller agree the admissible costs and calculate the final price. It sounds straightforward enough, but in large, complex construction projects, it is not so easy to pin down precise costs. Problems arise where the seller is inflating prices and it can take some time for buyer and seller to negotiate a final settlement.

An industry operating on this kind of pricing method, using a standard percentage, is oriented less towards price competition, and more towards achieving competitiveness through cost efficiency.

Experience curve pricing. Over time, and as an organisation produces more units, its experience and learning lead to more efficiency. This can also apply in service situations (Chambers and Johnston, 2000). Cost savings of between 10 and 30 per cent per unit can be achieved each time the organisation doubles its experience.

Some organisations use this learning curve, essentially predicting how costs are going to change over time, as part of the price-planning process. Such planning means not only that the organisation is under pressure to build the volume in order to gain the experience benefits, but also that if it can gain a high market share early on in the product's life, it can achieve a strong competitive position because it gains the cost savings from learning sooner (Schmenner, 1990). It can thus withstand price competition.

Although the savings are made mainly in production, there is still a close link with the volume share and price-dominating strategies discussed earlier. Scanners and WAP phones are examples of products that are reducing their relative prices, partly because of the experience curve effect.

The problem with cost-based methods is that they are too internally focused. The price determined has to survive in a marketplace where customers and competitors have their own views of what pricing should be. An organisation's price may thus make perfect sense in cost terms and generate a respectable profit contribution, but be perceived as far too high or far too low by customers in comparison with the features and benefits offered. The price may also be way out of line compared with a competitor with a different kind of cost base.

Demand-based pricing

Demand-based pricing looks outwards from the production line and focuses on customers and their responsiveness to different price levels. Even this approach may not be enough on its own, but when it is linked with an appreciation of competition-based pricing, it provides a powerful market-oriented perspective that cost-based methods just do not provide.

At its simplest, demand-based pricing indicates that when demand is strong, the price goes up, and when it is weak, the price goes down. This can be seen in some service industries, for example, where demand fluctuates depending on time. Package holidays taken during school holidays at Christmas, Easter or in the summer when demand is high are more expensive than those taken at other times of the year when it is more difficult for families to get away. Similarly, holidays taken when weather conditions at the destination are less predictable or less pleasant are cheaper because there is less demand. Even within the course of a single day, travel prices can vary according to demand. Tickets on shuttle flights between Heathrow and UK regional airports vary in price depending on when the peak times for business travellers occur.

marketing *in action*

'A flight from Dublin to London? That will be £10, including tax'

At a time when over 100,000 jobs have been lost in the US airline industry and European airlines are suffering from changed travel patterns after 11 September 2001, the budget airlines such as Ryanair and easyJet have experienced a boom in ticket sales. British Airways and KLM have cut staff, Swissair has gone bankrupt and Sabena has filed for bankruptcy, routes have been cut, planes grounded and some other national airlines are teetering on the edge. The air passenger market is in turmoil and

the winners so far have been the low-cost, low-price operators.

Rather than cut capacity and staff, the low-cost airlines cut their fares even further to keep passengers flying. In one week alone in October 2001, Ryanair sold half a million tickets, double its previous best month, and easyJet sales rose 27 per cent in September 2001 compared with the previous year. The low-cost airlines better understood the psychology of potential travellers in the aftermath of September 11th. People just didn't

want to fly unless they had to, for example as business travellers. But as the price came down to unimaginably low levels, the temptation to go away for a long weekend or on a trip increases, especially if it is to what is perceived as a relatively safe destination. Having taken the decision to fly once, there is a good chance that they will fly again, thereby sustaining the loyalty and allowing new routes and services to be offered (Binyon, 2001). The budget airlines realised this early on and intensified price competition rather than pursuing the other options.

Admittedly, it is difficult for the big airlines to follow suit. They traditionally make their money from business class and transatlantic travel. Cutting prices in the former may have little impact as it is companies that pay for the tickets, while the loss of the profitable transatlantic trade has had a serious impact on already fragile margins. Lowering economy-class fares would perhaps make the larger airlines too vulnerable. However, September 11th probably only served to exaggerate and accelerate the effect of underlying problems in the industry that would have had to have been dealt with sooner or later anyway. The speed with which capacities were cut and redundancy programmes announced suggests that the industry had been in trouble for some time. For many years, the national airlines had been protected, subsidised and allowed to control key routes and key slots at the major airports. Many would have fallen by the wayside had free competition been allowed to operate, but national pride would have meant such bankruptcies or mergers were unthinkable.

Sources: Arnold (2001b), Binyon (2001).

There is an underlying assumption that an organisation operating such a flexible pricing policy has a good understanding of the nature and elasticity of demand in its market, as already outlined on pp. 218 *et seq*.

One form of demand-based pricing is psychological pricing. This is very much a customer-based pricing method, relying as it does on the consumer's emotive responses, subjective assessments and feelings towards specific purchases. Clearly, this is particularly applicable to products with a higher involvement focus, i.e. those that appeal more to psychological than to practical motives for purchase. Thus, for example, high prices for prestige goods help to reinforce the psychological sense of self-indulgence and pampering that is such an important part of the buying experience. At the other end of the scale, lots of big splashy '10 per cent off' or 'buy one get one free' offers scattered around a retail store on key items helps to create and reinforce a value for money image and the sense of getting a bargain.

Competition-based pricing

This chapter has frequently warned of the danger of setting prices without knowing what is happening in the market, particularly with respect to one's competitors. According to Lambin (1993), there are two aspects of competition that influence an organisation's pricing. The first is the structure of the market. Generally speaking, the greater the number of competitors, i.e. the closer to perfect competition the market comes, the less autonomy the organisation has in price setting. The second competitive factor is the product's perceived value in the market. In other words, the more differentiated an organisation's product is from the competition, the more autonomy the organisation has in pricing it, because buyers come to value its unique benefits.

eg · Internet service providers (ISPs) have adopted competition-based pricing. Most ISPs in the USA tend to adopt flat-rate plans which means that users pay the same amount regardless of usage. In Europe and Asia, the main form of competition-based pricing is the price per minute plan, where users pay according to the time they spend connected to the Internet. Although this is gradually changing towards the US model, pioneered by global operators such as AOL, variable rates do still apply. Despite aggressive competition for users, most competitors in Europe tend to try to offer the lowest price within a pricing plan rather than trying to offer more customised plans to suit the needs of different user groups (Altmann and Chu, 2001).

Most markets are becoming increasingly competitive, and a focus on competitive strategy in business planning emphasises the importance of understanding the role of price as a means of competing. An organisation that decides to become a cost leader in its market and to take a price-oriented approach to maintaining its position needs an especially efficient intelligence system to monitor its competitors. Levy (1994) looks at organisations that offer price guarantees in B2B markets. Any supplier promising to match the lowest price offered by any of its rivals needs to know as much as possible about those rivals and their cost and pricing structures in order to assess the likely cost of such a promise.

In consumer markets, market research can certainly help to provide intelligence, whether this means shopping audits to monitor the comparative retail prices of goods, or consumer surveys or focus groups to monitor price perceptions and evolving sensitivity relative to the rest of the marketing mix. Data gathering and analysis can be more difficult in B2B markets, because of the flexibility of pricing and the degree of customisation of marketing packages to an individual customer's needs in these markets. There is a heavy reliance on sales representatives' reports, information gained through informal networks within the industry and qualitative assessment of all those data.

Competitive analysis can focus on a number of levels, at one end of the spectrum involving a general overview of the market, and at the other end focusing on individual product lines or items. Whatever the market, whatever the focus of competitive analysis, the same decision has to be made: whether to price at the same level as the competition, or above or below them.

An organisation that has decided to be a price follower must, by definition, look to the market for guidance. The decision to position at the same level as the competition, or above or below them, requires information about what is happening in the market. This is pricing based on the 'going rate' for the product. Conventional pricing behaviour in the market is used as a reference point for comparing what is offered, and the price is varied from that. Each supplier to the market is thus acting as a marker for the others, taking into account relative positioning and relative offering. Effectively, pricing is based on collective wisdom, and certainly for the smaller business it is easier to do what everyone else does rather than pay for market research to prove what the price ought to be, and run the risk of getting it wrong. In a seaside resort, for example, a small bed and breakfast hotel is unlikely to price itself differently from the one next door, unless it can justify doing so by offering significantly better services. Within an accepted price range, however, any one organisation's move may not be seen as either significant or threatening by the rest.

The dangers of excessive price competition, both in terms of the cost to the competitors and the risk to a product's reputation, thus attracting the 'wrong' kind of customer, have already been indicated. But if neither the organisation nor the product has a particularly high reputation, or if the product has few differentiating features, then price competition may be the only avenue open unless there is a commitment to working on the product and the marketing mix as a whole.

■ Pricing tactics and adjustments

Pricing tactics and adjustments are concerned with the last steps towards arriving at the final price. There is no such thing as a fixed price; price can be varied to reflect specific customer needs, the market position within the channel of distribution or the economic aspects of the deal.

Particularly in B2B markets, *price structures* give guidelines to the sales representative to help in negotiating a final price with the customer. The concern is not only to avoid overcharging or inconsistent charging, but to set up a framework for pricing discretion that is linked with the significance of the customer or the purchase situation.

> **eg** At one extreme, price structure may involve a take it or leave it, single price policy such as IKEA operates. It offers no trade discount for organisational purchasers, seeing itself largely as a consumer-oriented retailer. Compare this with some industrial distributorships, which offer different levels of discount to different customers. Most try to find a middle ground, between consistent pricing and flexibility for certain key customers.

A variation on price structures, *special adjustments* to list or quoted prices can be made either for short-term promotional purposes or as part of a regular deal to reward a trade customer for services rendered. Discounts, for example, consist of reductions from the normal or list price as a reward for bulk purchases or the range of distribution services offered. The level and frequency of discounts will vary according to individual circumstances. Blois (1994) points out that most organisations offer discounts from list prices and that these discounts form an important part of pricing strategies.

There are examples of both types of discount in consumer and B2B markets. The promotional technique of 'buy two and get the third free' is effectively a bulk discount and is found on many products in many supermarkets. Similarly, a promotion that requires a consumer to collect tokens then send them off for a cash rebate is a form of cumulative discount. In B2B markets, a retailer may be offered a twelfth case of a product free if 11 are initially purchased (quantity discount), or a rebate on the number of cases of a product sold by the end of the trading period (cumulative discount).

Allowances are similar to discounts, but usually require the buyer to perform some additional service. A trade-in, for example, is a form of allowance that makes a transaction more complicated because it involves the exchange of a good as well as money for whatever is being purchased. It is a common practice in the car market, where consumers trade in their old cars as part exchange for a new one. The qualitative judgement of the value of the trade-in disguises the discount offered, and it is further complicated by the attitudes of the respective parties. A car that is an unreliable liability to the owner may have potential to a dealer with a particular customer in mind or a good eye for scrap. The owner thinks they are getting a good deal on the old car, while the dealer thinks they can actually recoup the trade-in value and make a bit more besides.

Finally, geographic adjustments are those made, especially in B2B markets, to reflect the costs of transport and insurance involved in getting the goods from buyer to seller. In consumer markets, they can be seen in the case of mail-order goods, which carry an extra charge for postage and packing. Zoned pricing relates price to the geographic distance between buyer and seller. A DIY warehouse, for example, might add a £5 delivery charge to any destination within 5 miles, £7.50 for up to 10 miles, £10 for up to 15 miles and so on, reflecting the extra time and petrol involved in delivering to more distant locations. Operating a single zone means that the delivery price is the same regardless of distance, as is the case with the domestic postal service, which charges on the weight of letters rather than the destination. The international mail service does, however, operate on a multiple-zone basis, dividing the world up into areas and pricing to reflect different transport costs.

Chapter summary

- Pricing is a broad area, defined as covering anything of value that is given in exchange for something else. 'Price' is a blanket term to cover a variety of labels and is a key element in the marketing exchange. Price is usually measured in money, but can also involve the bartering of goods and services.

- Price serves a number of purposes. It is a measure against which buyers can assess the product's promised features and benefits and then decide whether the functional, operational, financial or personal advantages of purchase are worthwhile or not. The seller faces the difficult job of setting the price in the context of the buyers' price perceptions and sensitivities. In a price-sensitive market, finding exactly the right price is essential if customers are to be attracted and retained. The seller also needs to remember that price may involve the buyer in more than the handing over of a sum of money. Associated costs of installation, training and disposal of old equipment, for example, are taken into account in assessing the price of a B2B purchase.

- The external influences influencing the pricing decision include customers, channels of distribution, competition and legal and regulatory constraints.

- Corporate and marketing objectives set the internal agenda in terms of what pricing is expected to achieve, both for the organisation as a whole and for the specific product. The organisation's costs relating to the development, manufacture and marketing of the product will also affect price.

- The process of price setting involves a great deal of research and managerial skill. The five stages of the process are setting pricing objectives; estimating demand; setting pricing policies and strategies; determining the price range; and finally, defining any pricing tactics and adjustments that may be necessary.

questions for *review and discussion*

7.1 Define price elasticity. Why is this an important concept for the marketer?

7.2 To what extent and why do you think that costs should influence pricing?

7.3 Define the various stages involved in price setting.

7.4 Find an example of a price-sensitive consumer market. Why do you think this market is price sensitive and is there anything that the manufacturers or retailers could do to make it less so?

7.5 Choose a consumer product and explain the role that pricing plays in its marketing mix and market positioning.

7.6 To what extent and why do you think that a marketing manager's pricing decision should be influenced by the competition's pricing?

case study 7.1

Kitting out the fans

Love it or hate it, Manchester United is big business. It is a worldwide brand name that generates a loyalty and affinity that enables the soccer club, like many others, to develop merchandise, media products and alliances with service providers on a scale not thought possible in the era before the English Premier League was established. Merchandising sales have been helped as soccer has repositioned itself from a working-class game, sometimes dominated by violent youth, to a family entertainment dominated by middle and higher earners. For many clubs, what happens on the pitch or terrace is just a small part of a powerful marketing organisation.

Manchester United can be considered a typical 'passion brand', characterised by a sometimes fanatical following and a strong sense of belonging that is far removed from the discerning and rational consumer. Its following spreads far wider than its Old Trafford ground and many supporters have never seen a live game. Even passion brands are not immune from criticism, however, and there is a risk of over-commercialisation, which can undermine the special relationship between the club and the consumer.

A major source of revenue is the sale of replica kit. The market for replica shirts alone is worth about £210m. per annum. Manchester United sells around 500,000 per year, Arsenal 350,000 and Tottenham Hotspur 250,000. Between 1993 and 2001, Manchester United introduced something around 20 new kits, and at around £40 per shirt, that represents a major investment for its keenest fans. One really dedicated fan even paid £4,600 for a second-hand Manchester United shirt, although admittedly it was the one worn by Ole Gunnar Solskjaer when he scored the injury-time winner against Bayern Munich in the 1999

Champion's League Final in Barcelona. The incentive for clubs to change kits is clear and does not necessarily relate to fashion or sponsorship: the absence of a new Manchester United strip in the 1997–98 season, however, meant a drop in merchandise sales of 16 per cent on the previous year's level.

Fans have long been grumbling about the high prices of replica kit and allegations of price-fixing have been rife. In 1999, the Football Association, the Premier League and the Scottish Football Association agreed to try to stop price-fixing for replica football kits, for instance stopping practices such as shops being threatened with not receiving supplies if they slash prices. Prices had been expected to drop by up to one-third – but it didn't happen. Table 7.1 shows 2001 prices for an adult replica shirt:

Table 7.1 Replica kit: adult shirt prices 2001

Selected Premiership clubs

Club	Price
Arsenal	£39.99
Chelsea	£39.99
Derby County	£39.99
Leeds United	£39.99
Manchester United	£48.00
Newcastle	£40.00
West Ham United	£39.99

Sources: online club shops and http://www.kitbag.com, accessed 30 November 2001.

According to Arkell (2001), the biggest winners are the manufacturers rather than the football clubs. If a shirt costs £40, about £20 goes to the manufacturer (yet it allegedly only costs about £7 to make one), about £13 goes to the retailer and £7 on tax, leaving a minimal amount for the club. The clubs gain from selling licences to the manufacturers in the first place and from royalties on each kit sold. The clubs also obviously earn more by cutting out the middleman and selling kit via their own retail stores and mail-order operations.

Nevertheless, as a result of years of criticism from fans that top clubs had been financially exploiting them, a charter, incorporated into the Premiership rules, came into force in the 2000–1 season covering a range of issues such as ticket prices, complaints handling and replica kit. In terms of replica kit, the charter states that they will have a minimum lifespan of two years and carry a sticker on them stating the launch date. Premiership clubs could, therefore, be fined for changing their kits too regularly or for failing to conduct research among fans on the design and number of new strips. The charter does not, however, deal with the issue of pricing replica kit.

In addition, the Competition Act came into force in 2000 which allows fines of up to 10 per cent of turnover to be imposed on companies proved to have been involved in price-fixing. In September 2001, OFT officials raided the British offices of sportswear retailers and manufacturers, including JJB Sports, Nike and Umbro, as part of a probe into price-fixing of replica sports kits. The OFT made it clear, however, that 'No assumption should be made at this stage that there has been an infringement of competition law. We will not be in a position to decide that until we have all the facts' (as quoted by Arkell, 2001).

It would appear that the worm has turned at last. Sales of replica football kits are falling, partly because of changing fashions (hardly a consideration for the die-hard fans, surely) and partly because of parents rebelling against the cost. A Mintel survey showed that 43 per cent of respondents with families felt that football clothing was too expensive. It is interesting to note that Manchester United has found that replica kit sales through its own outlets are holding up well, but sales through other retailers are declining.

As Fresco (2001) points out, many clubs are trying to protect their revenue by diversifying their range of merchandise. Now that we've told you about them, can you continue to live without Niall Quinn's Disco Pants CD (courtesy of Sunderland) or Norwich City knickers?

Sources: Arkell (2001), Chaudhary (2000), Farrell (1998), Fresco (2001), Mintel (2000), Mitchell (1998), Narain (2001).

Questions

1 Why is merchandise so important to a Premier League soccer club? Why do clubs go into retailing and mail-order when their core business is football?

2 What do you think are the internal factors influencing a club like Manchester United's pricing decision for replica kit?

3 What kind of factors are consumers taking into account when assessing the retail price of replica kit? Do you think they are sensitive to price or to the number of new kits that come out?

4 Why do you think the kit prices listed in the table above are so similar from club to club?

References for chapter 7

Altmann, J. and Chu, K. (2001), 'How to Charge for Network Services – Flat-rate or Usage-based?', *Computer Networks*, August, pp. 519–31.

Arkell, H. (2001), 'Raid on Replica Soccer Kit Companies as "Price-Fixing" is Probed', *Evening Standard*, 6 September, p. 18.

Arnold, M. (2001a), 'Will New Licence Plates Push Sales?', *Marketing*, 6 September, p. 19.

Arnold, M. (2001b), 'Airlines Fight to Survive Crisis', *Marketing*, 27 September, p. 27.

Baumol, W.J. (1965), *Economic Theory and Operations Analysis*, Prentice Hall.

Binyon, M. (2001), 'Airlines Must Cut Prices Not Jobs or Routes', *The Times*, 6 October, p. 22.

Blois, K. (1994), 'Discounts in Business Marketing Management', *Industrial Marketing Management*, 23 (2), pp. 93–100.

Chambers, S. and Johnston, R. (2000), 'Experience Curves in Services: Macro and Micro Level Approaches', *International Journal of Operations and Production Management*, 20 (7), pp. 842–59.

Chaudhary, V. (2000), 'Greedy Clubs are Called to Account: Premier Fans Promised New Deal over Ticket Prices and Replica Kits', *The Guardian*, 17 August, p. 1.32.

Court, M. (2001), 'EU Fines Vitamin Cartel £530m', *Financial Times*, 22 November.

Darwent, C. (1996), 'Bangers and Cash', *Management Today*, June, pp. 72–4.

Davies, K. (2001), 'Sausage King Launches Franchise Operation', *The Grocer*, 15 December, p. 20.

Dean, J. (1950), 'Pricing Policies for New Products', *Harvard Business Review*, 28 (November), pp. 45–53.

Diamantopoulos, A. and Mathews, B. (1995), *Making Pricing Decisions: A Study of Managerial Practice*, Chapman & Hall.

Erickson, G.M. and Johansson, J.K. (1985), 'The Role of Price in Multi-attribute Product Evaluations', *Journal of Consumer Research*, 12, pp. 195–9.

Farrell, S. (1998), 'Clubs Accused of Fixing Replica Soccer Kit Prices', *The Times*, 24 February, p. 6.

Fresco, A. (2001), 'Football Club Profits Hit as Fans Rip Off Replica Shirts', *The Times*, 3 April, p. 9.

The Grocer (2001a), 'Mackerel Price Up', *The Grocer*, 8 September, p. 27.

The Grocer (2001b), 'Manufacturers Urged to Sign Up as Sausages Get the Quality Mark', *The Grocer*, 27 October, p. 14.

The Grocer (2001c), 'See it in Store Says Asda: We Are 15% Better Value', *The Grocer*, 3 November, p. 6.

Guerrera, F. and Jennen, B. (2001), 'Vitamins Cartel Faces Euros 850m EU Fine', *Financial Times*, 21 November, p. 1.

Hardcastle, S. (2001), 'Grocer Focus: Pizza', *The Grocer*, 17 November, pp. 49–52.

Heller, L. (2001), 'Better Pricing, DVD Growth Keep HDTV Sales on the Rise', *DSN Retailing Today*, 5 November, p. 35.

Howard, C. and Herbig, P. (1996), 'Japanese Pricing Policies', *Journal of Consumer Marketing*, 13 (4), pp. 5–17.

Lambin, J. (1993), *Strategic Marketing: A European Approach*, McGraw-Hill.

Le Temps (2001), 'Amende recorde pour le cartel des vitamines, dirigé par Roche', *Le Temps*, 22 November.

Levy, D. (1994), 'Guaranteed Pricing in Industrial Purchases: Making Use of Markets in Contractual Relations', *Industrial Marketing Management*, 23 (4), pp. 307–13.

Mintel (2000), 'The Football Business', 8 November (accessed via http://www.mintel.com).

Mintel (2001a), 'Sausages and Meat Pies', 28 March (accessed via http://www.mintel.com).

Mintel (2001b), 'Pizza', 1 August (accessed via http://www.mintel.com).

Mitchell, A. (1998), 'Sky's the Limit for New Breed of Passion Brands', *Marketing Week*, 17 September, pp. 44–5.

Monroe, K. and Cox, J. (2001), 'Pricing Practices that Endanger Profits', *Marketing Management*, September/October, pp. 42–6.

Monroe, K. and Della Bitta, A. (1978), 'Models for Pricing Decisions', *Journal of Marketing Research*, 15 (August), pp. 413–28.

Montgomery, S. (1988), *Profitable Pricing Strategies*, McGraw-Hill.

Nagle, T. (1987), *The Strategy and Tactics of Pricing*, Prentice Hall.

Narain, J. (2001), 'United are Beaten at Home by Tesco Bonanza for Families as Supermarket Sells Replica Kit at Half Price', *Daily Mail*, 30 April, p. 23.

Nimer, D. (1975), 'Pricing the Profitable Sale Has a Lot to Do with Perception', *Sales Management*, 114 (19), pp. 13–14.

Perks, R. (1993), 'How to Win a Price War', *Investor's Chronicle*, 22 October, pp. 14–15.

Schmenner, R. (1990), *Production/Operations Management*, New York: Macmillan.

Thompson, K. and Coe, B. (1997), 'Gaining Sustainable Competitive Advantage through Strategic Pricing: Selecting a Perceived Value Price', *Pricing Strategy and Practice*, 5 (2), pp. 70–9.

Zeithaml, V.A. (1988), 'Consumer Perceptions of Price, Quality and Value', *Journal of Marketing*, 52 (July), pp. 2–22.

chapter 8

place

LEARNING OBJECTIVES

This chapter will help you to:

1 define what a channel of distribution is and understand the forms it can take in both consumer and B2B markets;

2 discuss the rationale for using intermediaries and their contribution to efficient and effective marketing efforts;

3 differentiate between types of intermediary and their roles; and

4 appreciate the factors influencing channel design, structure and strategy and the effect of conflict and cooperation within channels.

Introduction

Shopaholics of the world unite! Retailing is one of the highest-profile areas of marketing and, like advertising, has had a tremendous impact on society, culture and lifestyles. We often take for granted the availability of wide ranges of goods and know that if we search hard enough, we will find just what we are looking for. Some people, indeed, find that half the fun is in the searching rather than the ultimate purchase. Although to us as consumers retailing means fun, excitement and the opportunity to splash out vast quantities of cash (thanks to plastic cards!), it is a very serious business for the managers and organisations that make it happen. It is often the last stage in the channel of distribution before consumption, the final link in fulfilling the responsibility of a marketing-oriented supply chain to get the product to the customer in the right place at the right time. The retail store is thus at the end of an extremely efficient and sophisticated distribution system designed to move goods down the distribution channel from manufacturer to consumer. A retailer can be just one of the intermediaries whose role is to facilitate that movement of goods and to offer them at a time and place (and at a price) that are convenient and attractive to the end consumer.

In considering how and why goods get to consumers, the chapter begins with a definition of channels of distribution, highlighting the roles played by different types of intermediaries, and looks at the relative merits of using intermediaries compared with direct selling. Attention then turns to the strategic decision-making necessary to design and implement a channel strategy. Although channels of distribution are important economic structures, they are also social systems involving individuals and organisations. This chapter, therefore, also considers issues associated with the general conduct of the relationship.

eg   Safeway in the UK and Dutch retailer Ahold are both keen to change the nature of the shopping experience and to encourage shoppers to spend a little longer in store. At the first Safeway hypermarket in Plymstock, Devon, the idea of a 'hub' was created at the centre of the store. It is a café-style seating area where, with the fresh food counter on one side and the books and CDs displays on the other, shoppers can meet and relax and of course contemplate what extra little treats to buy. The idea is not new to supermarkets. Some of the Albert Heijn branches operated by Ahold feature 'circle stores' with a market area in the centre featuring a coffee shop, bakery, cooking school and freshly prepared food snacks. The ring of convenience products leads the shopper down 'themed streets' of other grocery products. Supermarkets are keen to encourage new ways of presenting themselves uniquely, other than on price. The greater the quality of the experience, the longer the stay for some shoppers and perhaps the greater the spend. This message has certainly been learnt by some book retailers who offer comfortable armchairs and free coffee to maximise browsing (Bedington, 2001b; *The Grocer*, 2001e; Hunt, 1998, 1999).

Channel structures

A marketing channel can be defined as the structure linking a group of individuals or organisations through which a product or service is made available to the consumer or industrial user. The degree of formality in the relationships between the channel members can vary significantly, from the highly organised arrangements in the distribution of FMCG products through supermarkets, to the more speculative and transient position of roadside sellers of fruit and vegetables.

eg　When Carrefour first decided to expand into China, it found that a number of factors influencing its retail and distribution strategy differed from those it experienced in its domestic market, France. Although the Chinese market is huge, with potentially 1.3 billion consumers, it is widely dispersed and the distances between major population centres can be vast. Given the poor transportation infrastructure, the notion of national buying and local distribution is not as feasible in China as it is in France. For some goods, Carrefour has had to select 3 different suppliers to provide the same product to its 27 hypermarkets spread across 15 Chinese cities. Even then, lorries are often delayed due to road congestion and at times some lorries have been 'lost' altogether. While a typical store in France might receive 8–10 lorries per day from a regional distribution centre, a Chinese branch might receive up to 300 deliveries per day direct from suppliers (although some deliveries are made by bicycle!).

Carrefour also found wide differences in income levels, local customs, food tastes, local bureaucracy and consumer demands between Chinese regions. In the larger cities such as Shanghai and Beijing, consumer tastes are adapting and becoming much more sensitive to Western food retail formats, which is not surprising, given that there are 25 hypermarkets in Shanghai alone. In some of the 34 provinces, however, the experience is much more limited. There is still a preference, for example, for fresh produce bought from street markets and as many households do not have freezers, it is rare to find demand for a wide range of frozen food. Unlike in France, the product assortment offered tends to vary by region and according to local circumstances. Despite the differences, Carrefour turns over $33.6m. a year from a typical store in China, about 60 per cent of the turnover of a similar sized store in France and despite the average spend being four times lower (Goldman, 2001; Hunt, 2001).

The route selected to move a product to market through different intermediaries is known as the *channel structure*. The chosen route varies according to whether the organisation is dealing with consumer or B2B goods. Even within these broad sectors, different products might require different distribution channels.

■ Consumer goods

The four most common channel structures in consumer markets are shown in Figure 8.1. As can be seen, each alternative involves a different number of intermediaries, and each is appropriate to different kinds of markets or selling situations. Each will now be discussed in turn.

Producer–consumer (direct supply)

In the producer–consumer direct supply channel, the manufacturer and consumer deal directly with each other. There are many variants on this theme. It could be a factory shop, a manufacturer's mail-order catalogue or website, or a pick-your-own fruit farm. Door-to-door selling, such as that practised by double-glazing companies, and party plan selling, such as Tupperware and Ann Summers parties, are all attempts by producers to eliminate intermediaries.

Producer–retailer–consumer (short channel)

This channel is the most popular with the larger retailers, since they can buy in large quantities, obtaining special prices and often with tailor-made stock-handling and delivery arrangements. This route is typically used by large supermarket chains and is most appropriate for large manufacturers and large retailers who deal in such huge quantities that a direct relationship is efficient.

Figure 8.1 Channel structures for consumer goods

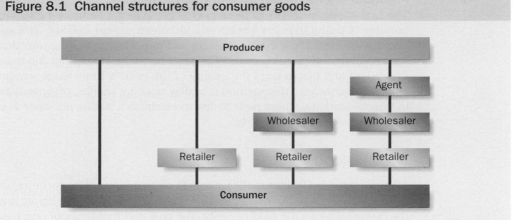

In the car trade, a local dealer usually deals directly with the manufacturer, because, unlike FMCG products, there is a need for significant support in the supply infrastructure and expertise in the sales and service process. This is an example of the grey area between retailing and distributorships, discussed on pp. 254 *et seq.*

Producer–wholesaler–retailer–consumer (long channel)

The advantage of adding a wholesaler level can be significant where small manufacturers and/or small retailers are involved. A small manufacturing organisation does not necessarily have the skills or resources to reach a wide range of retail customers and, similarly, the small corner shop does not have the resources to source relatively small quantities direct from many manufacturers. The wholesaler can provide a focal point for both sides, by buying in bulk from manufacturers, then splitting that bulk into manageable quantities for small retailers; bringing a wider assortment of goods together for the retailer under one roof; providing access to a wider range of retail customers for the small manufacturer; and similarly providing access to a wider range of manufacturers' goods for the small retailer. Effectively, the wholesaler is marketing on behalf of the manufacturer.

eg The independent grocery sector is serviced by a number of wholesalers and cash and carry providers. Nearly two-thirds of the trade is through cash and carries in which the retailer can be offered greater choice or more items than the delivered wholesaler handles (*The Grocer*, 1999a). The delivered sector is growing, however, and the major multiple-depot wholesalers are taking business from the smaller cash and carries and the unaffiliated groups.

Sugro UK, a Nantwich-based wholesale group that is part of a German-based parent company, is an amalgam of 79 wholesalers and cash and carry operators specialising mainly in confectionery, snacks and soft drinks. It services 43,000 outlets including CTN (confectionery, tobacco, news) stores, convenience stores, petrol forecourt stores and pubs. To provide the service, it has 350 field and telesales personnel and 450 delivery vehicles to negotiate and support sales. The whole international group handles 250,000 different products. The advantages for small independent retailers sourcing from the group are mainly linked with the group's centralised bulk buying from major manufacturers, the availability of Sugro own-brands on some lines, as well as an efficient and comprehensive stocking and delivery service. To be competitive itself, Sugro aims to provide a 'point of difference' for the retailer so that a win–win situation is created (http://www.sugro.co.uk).

The wholesaler can also act on behalf of relatively large manufacturers trying to sell large volumes of frequently reordered products to a wide retail network. Daily national newspapers, for example, are delivered from the presses to the wholesalers, which can then break bulk and assemble tailor-made orders involving many different titles for their own retail customers. This is far more efficient than each newspaper producer trying to deal direct with each small corner shop newsagent.

Producer–agent–wholesaler–retailer–consumer

This is the longest and most indirect channel. It might be used, for example, where a manufacturer is trying to enter a relatively unknown export market. The agent will be chosen because of local knowledge, contacts and expertise in selling into that country, and will earn commission on sales made. The problem is, however, that the manufacturer is totally dependent and has to trust the quality of the agent's knowledge, commitment and selling ability. Nevertheless, this method is widely used by smaller organisations trying to develop in remote markets, where their ability to establish a strong presence is constrained by lack of time, resources or knowledge.

■ B2B goods

As highlighted in Chapter 3, B2B products often involve close technical and commercial dialogue between buyer and seller, during which the product and its attributes are matched to the customer's specific requirements. The type and frequency of purchase, the quantity purchased and the importance of the product to the buyer all affect the type of channel structure commonly found in B2B markets. Office stationery, for example, is not a crucial purchase from the point of view of keeping production lines going and, as a routine repurchase, it is more likely to be distributed through specialist distributors or retailers such as Staples, Office World or Rymans. In contrast, crucial components that have to be integrated into a production line are likely to be delivered direct from supplier to buyer to specific deadlines. The variety of B2B distribution channels can be seen in Figure 8.2. Each type will now be discussed in turn.

Manufacturer–user

The direct channel is most appropriate where the goods being sold have a high unit cost and perhaps a high technical content. There is likely to be a small number of buyers who are perhaps confined to clearly defined geographical areas. To operate such a channel, the manufacturer must be prepared to build and manage a sales and distribution force that can negotiate sales, provide service and administer customer needs.

eg AB Konstruktions-Bakelit, one of Sweden's largest manufacturers of industrial plastic components, deals directly with customers such as Volvo, Saab and Alfa Laval. This is because of the need for considerable dialogue during the design and development stage to ensure a close fit between the customer's specification and components that are made to order. There would be a very high risk of misunderstanding if a third party were introduced.

Sales branches tend to be situated away from the manufacturer's head office in areas where demand is particularly high. They are a conveniently situated focal point for the area's sales force, providing them with products and support services so that they in turn can better meet their customers' needs more quickly. Sales branches may also sell products themselves directly to small retailers or wholesalers.

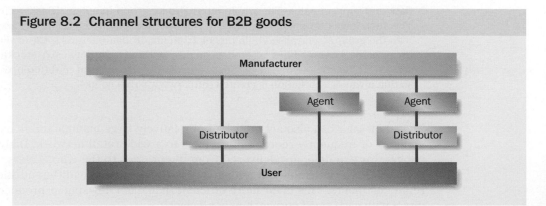

Figure 8.2 Channel structures for B2B goods

Sales offices do not carry stock, so, although they might take orders from local customers, they are only acting as agents and will pass the order on to head office. Again, they provide a locally convenient focus in busy areas.

Manufacturer–distributor–user

Less direct channels tend to be adopted as the number of customers grows, the size of customers reduces, and the number of intermediary functions also increases. Building materials, for example, are often sold to builders' merchants, who then sell to the building trade based on lower order quantities, and consequently with a greater range of stock availability but greater proximity to local need. The philosophy is similar to that of the short channel of distribution discussed in the consumer context on p. 244.

> This less direct type of structure can also apply to software products. Moser GmbH is one of the leading software houses in Germany and specialises in selling to trade and handicraft organisations. Although it had over 10,000 software installations in Germany and the Netherlands, it decided to seek expansion elsewhere in Europe. This was done by selling through other software and system houses which already had the sales and technical appreciation to generate sales for Moser.

Manufacturer–agent–user

Sometimes an agent is introduced to act on behalf of a group of manufacturers in dealing with users in situations where it would not be economically viable to create a direct selling effort, but where there is a need for selling expertise to generate and complete transactions.

> Teijo Pesukoneet from Nakkila in Finland specialises in technically advanced cleaning machines for metal components in enclosed cabinets. Although it has its own sales offices in Sweden and Norway, it operates through agents in other main European markets such as the UK and Germany. Agents are trained to handle technical queries and sales enquiries but relay orders to Finland for direct delivery.

Generally speaking, agents do not take title to goods, but may buy and sell, usually on a commission basis, on behalf of manufacturers and retailers. They facilitate an exchange process rather than participating fully in it. They tend to specialise in particular markets or product lines and are used because of their knowledge, or their superior purchasing or selling skills, or because of their well-established contacts within the market. The distinction between an agent and a broker is a fine one. Agents tend to be retained on a long-term basis to act on behalf of a client, and thus build up working rapport. A broker tends to be used on a one-off, temporary basis to fulfil a specific need or deal.

The main problem with agents is the amount of commission that has to be paid, as this can push selling costs up. This cost has to be looked at in context and with a sense of proportion. That commission is buying sales performance, market knowledge and a degree of flexibility that would take a lot of time and money to build for yourself, even if you wanted to do it. The alternative to using agents, therefore, may not be so effective or cost efficient.

Manufacturer–agent–distributor–user

A model comprising manufacturer–agent–distributor–user links is particularly useful in fast-moving export markets. The sales agent coordinates sales in a specified market, while the distributors provide inventory and fast restocking facilities close to the point of customer need. The comments on the longest channel of distribution in the consumer context (see p. 245) are also applicable here.

Increasingly, using multiple channels of distribution is becoming the rule rather than the exception (Frazier, 1999). Where there is choice, the retailer could have a virtual, web-based store as well as physical retail outlets. In global markets stronger branded manufacturers

South African oranges

The next time you tuck into a South African orange, stop to think of the many stages in the distribution channel through which the product has moved, from the South African orange growers to the local supermarket. Each year South Africa exports some 50 million cartons of oranges, with Western Europe consuming over 50 per cent of them. The industry is made up of 200 private farmers and 1,200 growers in cooperatives. Many growers and cooperatives pool their output for marketing and distribution purposes under the Capespan International selling operation (50 per cent owned by Fyffes). The challenge for Capespan has been to align its distribution strategy with increased international competition, greater customer sophistication and the demands of ever-powerful supermarket chains. Product freshness, variety, quality and supply must all meet customer demand and the product must move smoothly through the supply chain from grower to buyer.

The oranges move from the growers to the fruit-handling facilities run by Capespan near the major ports such as Durban, Cape Town and Port Elizabeth. Capespan purchases the oranges and then adds handling and transportation costs and a profit margin. The services provided include some initial de-greening, environmental control, labelling and packing, all before shipment. It also arranges shipment, increasingly in large bulk bins for ease of handling, from the ports. At this stage, data are collected on the fruit, size, type, quality grade, treatment and origin.

Another service that Capespan undertakes is to move the oranges to cold storage before they depart for Europe. Most of these processes are provided by Capespan subsidiaries: Fresh Produce Terminals provides cold storage and warehousing facilities, Cape Reefers provides shipping coordination and CSS Logistics, the clearing and forwarding documentation.

European ports such as Flushing, Sheerness and Tilbury have been selected as destinations. A partnership approach between Capespan and the port authorities has resulted in a specialist infrastructure for handling and storing palletised or binned oranges. In order to ensure that the right oranges arrive at the right EU port, data are sent to Capespan planners in Europe, who then decide which fruit should be unloaded at which port to meet local demand. On arrival, Capespan reinspects the produce. Where necessary, the cartons are labelled and quality control checks undertaken to ensure that the fruit is consistent with specific buyers' expectations. This all helps to preserve the reputation of the Capespan brand name, Outspan. There are plans to add more valuable services such as pre-packing, size grading and fruit preparation for fresh fruit salad. After processing, the oranges are ready either to enter the UK domestic distribution chain or to go for further storage. Because an electronic data system has been used, fruit that has ripened during transit is ready to leave port quickly in 'table-fresh' condition.

Shipment can be to external pre-packers contracted by the supermarkets or straight to the wholesale and supermarket distribution systems at regional or central warehouse collection points. These shipments fulfil orders placed either direct by the supermarkets or through selling agents dealing with Capespan in the UK. Some oranges go into the fruit and vegetable distribution chain and end up being sold in markets and through wholesalers dealing with specialist fruit and vegetable stores.

Capespan relies heavily on timely information produced at every step of the supply chain to manage the procurement, distribution, marketing and sales processes. Customised information systems and pallet tracking systems such as Paltrack are used for pallet tracking and stock control. Using data provided by the order and shipments, a decision support infrastructure ensures that information is generated to support Capespan's key decisions, such as destination priorities, and that information is also provided in the most useful form to suppliers. Capespan also uses web technology throughout the supply chain, such as its extranet (http://www.ourgrowers.co.za) which links Capespan with its growers/suppliers, allowing access to critical market information in real time from marketplaces around the world. Other Internet sites provide an encyclopaedia of information to customers and support grower/customer interaction.

Sources: Shapley (1998), http://www.capespan.com; http://www.networking.ibm.com

could adopt different methods to reach customers, depending upon local distribution structures. Using multiple channels enables more market segments to be reached and can increase penetration levels, but this must be weighed against lower levels of support from trade members who find themselves facing high degrees of intra-channel competition.

The type of structure adopted in a particular sector, whether B2B or consumer, will ultimately depend on the product and market characteristics that produce differing cost and servicing profiles. These issues will be further explored in the context of the main justification for using marketing intermediaries, described next.

Rationale for using intermediaries

Every transaction between a buyer and a seller costs money. There are delivery costs, order picking and packing costs, marketing costs, and almost certainly administrative costs associated with processing an order and receiving or making payment. The role of the intermediary is to increase the efficiency and reduce the costs of individual transactions. This can be clearly seen in Figure 8.3.

If 6 manufacturers wished to deal with 6 buyers, a total of 36 links would be necessary. All of these transaction links cost time and money to service, and require a certain level of administrative and marketing expertise. If volumes and profit margins are sufficient, then this may be a viable proposition. However, in many situations this would add considerably to the cost of the product. By using an intermediary, the number of links falls to just 12, and each buyer and each seller only needs to maintain and service one link. If this makes sense when considering only six potential buyers, just imagine how much more sensible it is with FMCG goods where there are millions of potential buyers! On economic grounds alone, the rationale for intermediaries in creating transaction efficiency is demonstrated.

However, there are other reasons for using intermediaries, because they add value for the manufacturer and customer alike. These value added services fall into three main groups (Webster, 1979), as shown in Figure 8.4.

Figure 8.3 The role of intermediaries

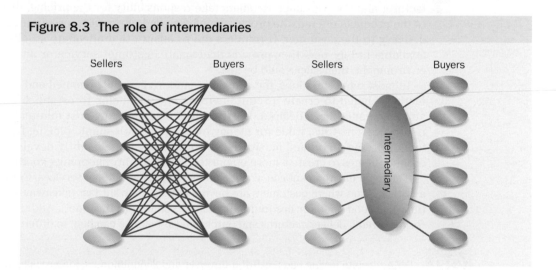

Figure 8.4 Value added services provided by intermediaries

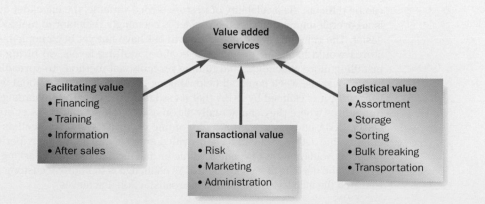

■ Transactional value

The role of intermediaries in creating transaction efficiency has already been highlighted. To perform this role adequately, the intermediary must assemble products that it believes its own target customers need and then market them effectively. The selection is extremely important, and requires careful purchasing in terms of type, quantity and cost to fit the intermediary's own product strategy.

Risk

Both wholesalers and retailers (but not agents) take title to goods and services, accepting legal responsibility for the product, including its storage, security and resale, and thus the risks move to the intermediary. Of course, it is in the manufacturer's interest to see the product moving through the distribution system in order to achieve sales and profit objectives. However, the risk of being lumbered with obsolete, damaged or slow-moving stock rests with the intermediary, not the manufacturer. This is a valuable service to that manufacturer.

Marketing

With the transfer of title and risk, the need to market effectively increases. Intermediaries may recruit and train their own sales forces to resell the products that they have assembled. This is another valuable service to the manufacturer, as it means that the product may have a greater chance of being brought to the attention of the prospective customer, especially in B2B markets. In consumer markets, retailers are an important interface between the manufacturer and the consumer. Retailers take responsibility for the pricing, display and control of the products offered, the processing of cash and/or credit transactions, and, if necessary, delivery to the customer. If retailers fail to ensure that adequate stocks of products are available to buy, or if they provide inadequate customer service or an unappealing retail environment, then sales could be lost.

In most retail situations, the consumer enters a carefully planned and controlled environment designed to create a retail environment that helps to establish and reinforce the ambience and image desired. In some, this may be a low-cost minimalist approach that reinforces a no-frills, value for money philosophy, with simple picking from racks and pallets or drums. In others, music, decor and display are all subtly developed and designed around themes to create a more upmarket, higher-quality shopping experience.

The retail environment can also include a range of additional services. Convenient parking is a critical issue where customers are buying in bulk, or want fast takeaway services (the 'drive-thru' fast food operator has found the logical solution to this one!). Additional services in the form of credit, delivery, returns and purchasing assistance can help to differentiate a retailer.

eg   IKEA, despite having had a €10.4bn turnover and 255 million customer visits in 2000, has been criticised over the level of customer service and advice it offers. It has achieved high degrees of consistency worldwide in its operations, with self-assembly, self-service, high-design merchandise that is affordable, especially for the first-time homeowner. The problem, however, can be seen (and experienced) by anyone visiting an IKEA store on a busy Saturday. Parking can be difficult, the availability of in-store advice variable, the checkout queues long and there is an overall impression that the retailer is seemingly reluctant to make the shopper's burden easier. The solutions are straightforward, but have not yet been implemented. Opening more stores would help, but primarily it is about staffing levels, so hiring more in-store staff, installing more checkouts, and finding promotional methods to spread shopper visits more evenly over the week could all help. Making the website transactional would also help a lot. Currently, it is claimed by IKEA that its strategies are 'geared towards generating customers into stores where they can actually sit on and touch products' (as quoted by Stewart-Allen, 2001). IKEA is, however, piloting an online ordering system as well as an e-mail customer enquiry line. Other retailers have provided an adequate shopping experience online and few people nowadays want to spend a whole or half day battling for a parking space, searching for trolleys and queuing at checkouts. IKEA's challenge is to improve customer service satisfaction to match the high levels of merchandise satisfaction it achieves.

Ikea shows its products in room settings so that customers can match their lifestyle aspirations to what is on offer.

Source: IKEA Ltd.

■ Logistical value

Assortment

A critical role for the intermediary is the assembly of an assortment of products from different sources that is compatible with the needs of the intermediary's own customers. This assortment can operate at product or brand level. A drinks wholesaler, for example, may offer a full range of merchandise from beer to cognac, but within each category considerable brand choice may also be offered. The benefit to the customer is the wide choice available from one source, supported perhaps by a competitive and comprehensive pre- and post-sales service. However, for other intermediaries the choice may be more limited. If one manufacturer occupies a dominant position, the choice of competing brands may be severely restricted to just complementary products. In many car dealerships, for example, only one manufacturer's new cars can be sold, although there might be more flexibility over second-hand cars.

Assortment strategy is a critical variable in a retailer's marketing strategy. The key is to build an assortment to reflect the needs of the target market. Within a particular product area or market, variety is ensured, as retailers seek to differentiate their offerings from those of their competitors, although increasingly this is becoming more difficult. In any assortment strategy there are risks in misjudging changes in customer fads or tastes. This is particularly noticeable in high fashion areas where even the sale rails do not move assortments that have been left behind.

eg Think about the variations between music stores in the High Street, for instance. Some retailers specialise in a particular style of music, going for depth without breadth, while others go for breadth of coverage without the depth, stocking the bestselling popular items from a variety of music styles, but not much more. Others have heavily diversified into videos and computer games. HMV in the UK, however, has chosen to maintain a tight focus on music, claiming that customers should be able to find any current recording that they want, at least within the largest of its 521 stores. Its computerised stock-control system means that HMV can assess demand and track the availability of the 270,000 releases current in the UK at any one time.

▶

HMV also has an online selling operation which allows customers to search for an album in various music categories, see a listing of tracks, check availability and in some cases listen to a sample track. This enables a wider group of customers to be reached and reduces the pressure on some of the smaller local stores where the range carried may be more limited (Finch, 2001b).

Wholesalers can play a major role in providing the wide assortment of goods required. While some retailers deal directly with manufacturers, others, particularly smaller stores, may prefer the convenience and accessibility of the wholesaler, especially where fast, responsive supply is assured. In the book trade, for example, it is difficult for a retailer to offer anything like the total number of titles available. Instead, the retailer acts as an order conduit, so that either the wholesaler or the publisher can service individual orders that have been consolidated into economic shipment sizes. The wholesaler can maintain a much wider range of products than is possible in all but the largest retail groups, and can provide efficient support activities for rapid stock replenishment.

Storage, sorting and bulk breaking

A further dimension of logistical value is the accumulation and storing of products at locations that are appropriate and convenient to the customer. The small manufacturer can make one large delivery of output to the wholesaler's warehouse, where it can be stored until a retailer wants it, and broken down into smaller lots as necessary. The hassles of transporting small quantities to many different locations, finding storage space and insuring the goods are taken away from the manufacturer.

Sorting is a very basic step in the logistical process, and means grouping many diverse products into more uniform, homogeneous groups. These groups may be based on product class and further subdivided by such factors as size, shape, weight and colour. This process may also add value by grading, which means inspecting, testing or judging products so that they can be placed into more homogeneous quality grades. These standards may be based on intermediary or industry predetermined standards. Large supermarket chains, for example, are particularly demanding about the standardisation of the fruit and vegetables that they retail. If you look at a carton of apples in a supermarket, you will see that they are all of a standard size, colour and quality. Mother Nature hasn't quite worked out how to ensure such uniformity, so the producers and wholesalers have to put effort into sorting out and grading the top quality produce for the High Street. The second-class produce ends up in less choosy retail outlets, while the most irregular specimens end up in soup, fruit juices and ready meals.

A further important role for the intermediary, as already implied, is bulk breaking, the division of large units into the smaller, more manageable quantities required by the next step in the chain. Whereas a builder's merchant may purchase sand by the lorry load, the small builder may purchase by the bagged pallet load, and the individual consumer by the individual bag. The value of bulk breaking is clear to the DIY enthusiast, who certainly would not wish to purchase by the pallet load. There is, of course, a price to pay for this convenience, and the consumer would expect to pay a higher price per bag purchased individually than the builder would pay per bag purchased by the pallet load.

Transportation

A final role is in actually transporting the product to the next point in the chain. Lorry loads may be made up of deliveries to several customers in the same area, thus maximising the payload, and with careful siting of warehouse facilities, minimising the distances the products have to travel. Again, this is more efficient than having each manufacturer sending out delivery vans to every customer throughout the country.

The provision of storage and transportation has become increasingly important with the widening distance, in terms of both geography and the length of distribution channels, between producer and consumer. Purchasing patterns increasingly include products sourced from wherever the best deal can be offered, whether local or international. As production becomes more concentrated into a relatively small number of larger operations, the need to move products over large distances increases. The distance can be even greater in the food-stuffs area, with the demand for exotic and fresh foods from elsewhere in Europe and well beyond. The availability of Chilean grapes in the UK supermarket in winter, for example, is the end point of a long series of distribution decisions including a number of intermediaries.

Retailers and wholesalers, by allowing larger shipments to be made and then breaking bulk, play an important role in establishing economies of scale in channels of physical distribution. Some wholesalers are themselves heavily involved in performing physical distribution roles such as inventory planning, packing, transportation and order processing in line with customer service objectives. This assists the manufacturer as well as the retailer. Often the wholesaler will incur costs in inward-bound transportation, maintain a safety stock buffer and absorb associated inventory and material handling expenses, all of which represent savings for the manufacturer.

eg

A walk around a market in a developing country reveals row upon row of sellers with small tables offering piles of undifferentiated home-grown carrots or turnips and little else, a far cry from town centre markets in the UK or France. By using intermediaries, farmers or market gardeners do not need to find their own markets. A fruit and vegetable wholesaler can accumulate small quantities of different products from specialist growers, sort them, and then make larger deliveries of assorted goods to the next point in the chain, thus gaining economies in transport costs.

Soleco is France's largest producer of pre-packed salads and fresh stir-fry and snack vegetables. Trading under the Florette and Manon brands, it enjoys a 42 per cent share of the French pre-packed salad market. To make the business a success, it had to invest in high levels of quality control, strict temperature control and specialist preparation machinery. It also needed regular supply. Not only has it contracted with 450 French growers, but about 15 per cent of its supply needs comes from Italy, Spain and Portugal. All crops are allocated batch numbers as part of an ISO 9001 system. Through such transparency, Soleco can assure the trade that the 'use by' date will never exceed seven days after processing, fewer on more fragile items such as lettuce. Soleco knows the field of origin, the variety, the date of harvesting, and the date and place of packaging to ensure that even when distribution lines are extended, freshness of the produce can be guaranteed (http://www.soleco.co.uk). All of this enables the consumer to enjoy top quality, fresh produce.

Appealing to the customer as a convenience product, Florette sells pre-packed salad leaves which come from a variety of suppliers.

Source: Florette.

■ Facilitating value

Financing

The intermediary also offers a range of other value added services either to the manufacturer or to the customer. Not only do intermediaries share the risks, as outlined above, they also provide a valuable financing benefit. The manufacturer only has to manage a small number of accounts (for example with two or three wholesalers rather than with 200 or more individual retailers) and can keep tighter control over credit periods, thus improving cash flow. As part of the service to the consumer, retailers may offer credit or other financial services such as credit card acceptance, easy payment terms and insurance. Manufacturers selling direct would not necessarily be interested in such financial services.

Information, training and after-sales service

Both retailers and wholesalers are part of the forward information flow that advises customers and persuades them to buy. Although in the supermarket environment the role of personal advice is minimal, many retailers, especially those in product lines such as clothing, hobbies, electrical goods and cars, are expected to assist the consumer directly in making a purchase decision and to advise on subsequent use. These are the kinds of goods that require limited or extended decision-making behaviour, as discussed on pp. 74 *et seq.* Manufacturers might well invest in training wholesale or retail staff in how to sell the benefits of their product ranges and provide after-sales service support.

Wholesalers are also important sources of advice for some retailers and users. The more specialised a wholesaler, the greater the opportunity for developing an in-depth market understanding, tracking new or declining products, analysing competitive actions, defining promotions needed and advising on best buys. This role may be especially valuable to the smaller retailer who has less direct access to quality information on broader trends in a specific market. Similarly, an industrial distributor may be expected to advise customers on applications and to assist in low-level technical problem solving.

Market information and feedback are precious commodities, as we saw in Chapter 5. The intermediary is much closer to the marketplace, and therefore alert to changes in consumer needs and competitive conditions. Passing on this information up the channel of distribution can enable manufacturers to modify their marketing strategies for the benefit of all parties. While there is no replacement for systematic, organised market research, information derived from sales contacts and meetings with intermediaries provides specific, often relevant intelligence. For the small manufacturer, with very limited market research resources, this can be particularly invaluable.

All the above functions need to be performed at some point within the marketing channel. The key decision concerns which member undertakes what role. This decision may be reached by negotiation, where the power in the channel is reasonably balanced, or by imposition, when either manufacturer or retailer dominates. Whatever the outcome, the compensation system in terms of margins needs to be designed to reflect the added value role performed.

Types of intermediary

As we have already seen, many marketing channels involve the physical movement of goods and the transfer of legal title to the goods to various types of intermediary. This section summarises the key characteristics of each of those types.

■ Distributors and dealers

Distributors and dealers are intermediaries who add value through special services associated with stocking or selling inventory, credit and after-sales service. Although these intermediaries are often used in B2B markets, they can also be found in direct dealing with consumers, for example computer or motor dealers. The term usually signifies a more structured and closer tie between the manufacturer and intermediary in order that the product may be delivered efficiently and with the appropriate level of expertise. Clearly, some retail outlets are also closely associated with dealerships and the distinction between them may be somewhat blurred.

■ Agents and brokers

Agents and brokers are intermediaries who have the legal authority to act on behalf of the manufacturer, although they do not take legal title to the goods or indeed handle the product directly in any way. They do, however, make the product more accessible to the customer and in some cases provide appropriate add-on benefits. Their prime function is to bring buyer and seller together. Universities often use agents to recruit students in overseas markets.

■ Wholesalers

Wholesalers do not normally deal with the end consumer but with other intermediaries, usually retailers. However, in some situations sales are made directly to the end user, especially in B2B markets, with no further resale taking place. An organisation may purchase its catering or cleaning supplies from a local cash and carry business that serves the retail trade. A wholesaler does take legal title to the goods as well as taking physical possession of them.

■ Franchisees

A franchisee holds a contract to supply and market a product or service to the design or blueprint of the franchisor (the owner or originator of the product or service). The franchise agreement covers not only the precise specification of the product or service, but also the selling and marketing aspects of the business. The uniformity of different branches of McDonald's is an indication of the level of detail covered by a franchise agreement. There are many products and services currently offered through franchise arrangements, especially in the retail and home services sector.

■ Retailers

Retailers sell direct to the consumer and may either purchase direct from the manufacturer or deal with a wholesaler, depending on purchasing power and volume. Retailers can be classified on a number of criteria, not all of which are immediately obvious to the average shopper. These are discussed in this section which will also help to shed further light on what retailers actually do and why they are important to both manufacturer and consumer.

Form of ownership

Retailing was for many years the realm of the small independent business. Some grew by adding more branches and some grew by acquisition, but it is only since the 1950s that the retail structure of the High Street has evolved significantly, favouring the larger organisation. Nevertheless, there are still several predominant forms of ownership to be found.

Independent. Still the most common form of ownership in terms of number of retail outlets is independent, with over 62 per cent of UK outlets falling into this category. In sales volume terms, however, this group accounts for less than 30 per cent. Marked variances exist between retail categories, with a significant role for the small independent in the drinks sector and in CTN (confectionery, tobacco and news) retailing. Typically, the independent retail outlet is managed by a sole trader or a family business. For the consumer, the main benefits are the personalised attention and flexibility that can be offered. These operations can be highly individualistic in terms of the variety and quality of merchandise stocked, ranging from very upmarket to bargain basement.

Although it may not be possible for the small independent to compete on price and breadth of range offered, the key is to complement the big multiples rather than to try to compete head-on. Howe (1992) is clear about forces that work against the small retailer, such as changing population patterns, the drift towards out of town shopping, supply and resource problems and the sheer scale and professionalism of the large multiple chains. To combat this, the small retailer thus needs to look for niches, specialised merchandise, flexible opening hours and special services and to make more effective use of suppliers. This boils down to sound management and marketing thinking.

eg Small village grocery shops are becoming an endangered species. Estimates have suggested that 300 close every year and that around one-third of all villages now have no local store. Turnover varies widely. Some smaller stores are hard pushed to generate $20,000 per week, but more favoured locations can easily double that. The Rural Shops Alliance estimates that there are only about 12,000 rural shops left; the rest have become victims of increased consumer mobility and the attraction of the supermarkets, some of which actually run weekly free bus services to their stores. The key to survival is diversification. Having the local Post Office franchise can be a big help, as it attracts people into the store, but it is also about offering fax and photocopying facilities, Internet access, lottery access, cash points, video hire, flexible opening hours and fresh local produce. Although shopping for convenience items or those forgotten on the main shopping trip provides basic turnover for the village store, what is really needed to increase the value and loyalty of customers is a change in the retailer's attitude and the creation of a service-oriented multi-activity centre appealing to the cross-section of the community that could create a captive audience (Gregory, 2001a, b).

Corporate chain. A corporate chain has multiple outlets under common ownership. The operation of the chain will reflect corporate strategy, and many will centralise decisions where economies of scale can be gained. The most obvious activity to be centralised is purchasing, so that volume discounts and greater power over suppliers can be gained. There are, of course, other benefits to be derived from a regional, national or even international presence in terms of image and brand building. Typical examples include Next and M&S. Some chains do allow a degree of discretion at a local level to reflect different operating environments, in terms of opening hours, merchandise or services provided, but the main strength comes from unity rather than diversity.

Contractual system. The linking of members of distribution channels through formal agreements rather than ownership (i.e. a contractual system) is included later in this chapter. For retail or wholesale sponsored cooperatives or franchises, the main benefit is the ability to draw from collective strength, whether in management, marketing or operational procedures. In some cases, the collective strength, as with franchises, can provide a valuable tool for promoting customer awareness and familiarity, leading in turn to retail loyalty. The trade-off for the franchisee is some loss of discretion, both operationally and strategically, but this may be countered by the benefits of unity. Franchising might also pass on the retailing risk to the franchisee. When Benetton's performance was poor in the US market, 300 stores closed, with all the losses borne by the franchisees rather than by Benetton (Davidson, 1993).

If the independent retailer wants to avoid the risks of franchising, yet wants to benefit from collective power, then affiliation to either a buying group or a voluntary chain might be the answer. Buying groups are usually found in food retailing and their purpose is to centralise the purchasing function and to achieve economies of scale on behalf of their members.

Level of service

The range and quality of services offered vary considerably from retailer to retailer. Some, such as department stores, offer gift-wrapping services, and some DIY stores offer home delivery, but in others most of the obligation for picking, assessing and taking the product home rests with the customer.

Three types of service level highlight the main options.

Full service. Stores such as Harrods provide the full range of customer services. This includes close personal attention on the shopfloor, a full range of account and delivery services, and a clear objective to treat each customer as a valued individual. Such high levels of service are reflected in the premium pricing policy adopted.

Limited service. The number of customers handled and the competitive prices that need to be charged prevent the implementation of the full range of services, but the services that are offered make purchasing easier. Credit, no-quibble returns, telephone orders and home delivery may be offered. This is a question of deciding what the target market 'must have' rather than what it 'would like', or defining what is essential for competitive edge. A retailer, such as Next, which claims to sell quality clothing at competitive prices, cannot offer too many extra services because that would increase the retailer's costs. They do, however, have to offer a limited range of services in order to remain competitive with similar retailers.

Self-service. In self-service stores, the customer performs many of the in-store functions, including picking goods, queuing at the checkout, paying by cash or perhaps credit card, and then struggling to the car park with a loaded trolley. Some food and discount stores operate in this mode, but the trend is towards offering more service to ease bottleneck points that are particularly frustrating to the customer. This could include the provision of more staff at the delicatessen counter, more checkouts to guarantee short queues, and assistance with packing.

Merchandise lines

Retailers can be distinguished by the merchandise they carry, assessed in terms of the breadth and depth of range.

Breadth of range. The breadth of range represents the variety of different product lines stocked. A department store will carry a wide variety of product lines, perhaps including electrical goods, household goods, designer clothing, hairdressing and even holidays.

eg A catalogue retail showroom (see pp. 262–3), such as Argos, is not expected to display its whole range of stock 'live' and is thus able to provide much greater breadth and depth of range than its department store rivals. It is limited only by its logistical systems and ability to update and replenish its in-store warehouses quickly. Argos has 475 stores. Despite the breadth of range it offers, it was felt that Argos was not capitalising on the increased demand for home-based PCs, so the new line was introduced at most of its stores. Also, as a means of reducing the complexity of the Argos offering for customers, a number of more focused catalogues have been introduced. One of these is Argos Additions, a clothing and home catalogue including brands such as Reebok, Levi's and Gossard. In addition, online shopping and ordering have been introduced that can involve secure payment, home delivery or showroom collection. The main problem for Argos is its image. Its stores look tired and a little downmarket; many people buy well-known brands from them, but few admit to it, although its shopping catalogue has massive penetration and sales have consistently grown. Argos has remained true to its strengths, providing convenience, availability and choice at low prices (Jardine, 2001; Kleinman, 2001).

Depth of range. The depth of range defines the amount of choice or assortment within a product line, on whatever dimensions are relevant to that kind of product. A music store stocking CDs, tapes, minidiscs and vinyl records could be said to have depth in its range. Similarly, a clothing store that stocks cashmere jumpers might be said to have a shallow range if the jumpers are available only in one style, or a deep range if they are available in five different styles. Introducing further assortment criteria, such as size range and colour, creates a very complex definition of depth. A specialty or niche retailer, such as Tie Rack, would be expected to provide depth in its product lines on a number of assortment criteria.

eg Hennes and Mauritz (H&M) is Sweden's fifth largest company and operates around 730 stores in 14 countries. It is still expanding in the UK, USA, Germany and Austria. It owns over a dozen own-labels covering men's, women's and children's clothing, casual and classic wear, and underwear and outerwear. These labels are targeted at specific segments in the 18–45 age range, for example Clothes is very trend conscious, Hennes is classic fashion and

Mama is the maternity range. The assortment is, however, varied by region to suit local demographics and tastes. Although it is a speciality retailer, concentrating on fashion, it provides a broad but shallow range, compared with other fashion retailers which specialise in just women's wear or jeans (narrow and deep). H&M is happy to offer low prices, reasonable quality and a wide range of fashionable clothing. To keep customers interested in its stores and to broaden the width of range further, new products designed by 70 in-house staff are introduced every day and no product is kept in the stores for longer than one month. That means some stores receive between two and four deliveries each day, and slower-moving items soon hit the mark-down racks. It also means an extensive logistics operation involving regional warehouses, with half supplied from within Europe and the rest from Asia. Most other fashion retailers tend to change ranges only two to four times a year (Scardino, 2001; Teather, 2001).

Operating methods

The area of operating methods has seen significant change, with the growth of alternatives to the traditional approach. Traditional store retailing, which itself includes a wide number of types of retailer, still predominates, however. These various types of store are considered in the next section. Non-store retailing, however, where the customer does not physically travel to visit the retailer, has become increasingly popular. This is partly because of changing customer attitudes, partly because of the drive upmarket made by the mail-order companies in particular, and partly because of technological advances in Internet retailing and logistics. The whole area of non-store shopping will be further discussed on pp. 263 *et seq*.

Store types

A walk down any High Street or a drive around the outskirts of any large town reveals a wide range of retailers of all shapes and sizes, enticing us in with what they hope are clearly differentiated marketing mixes. The following discussion groups retailers according to the type of retail operation that they run. Each type will be defined, and the role it plays within the retail sector will be discussed.

Department stores. Department stores usually occupy a prominent prime position within a town centre or a large out-of-town shopping mall. Most towns have one and some centres, such as London's Oxford Street, support several. Department stores are large and are organised into discrete departments consisting of related product lines, such as sports, ladies' fashions, toys, electrical goods, etc.

eg Royal Vendex KBB is the main non-food retail company in the Netherlands, with a portfolio of department stores and speciality stores. The company operates 27 well-known formats across more than 2,500 outlets in seven countries and generates total net sales of €4.6bn. Its department stores have three formats, Vroom & Dressman, Hema and Bijenkorf, each acting as separate business units, with different positioning strategies and customer profiles. The stores have own-label women's, babies' and children's clothing, personal care products, spectacles, shoes, home and interior decoration products, consumer and household electronics including computers, books, in-store catering services, external restaurants, bakery, Internet shopping services, and photo service. Although the combined sales of these stores is €990m., operating margins are between 4 and 6 per cent, reflecting the competitive markets in which department stores operate (http://www.vendexkbb.com).

To support the concept of providing everything that the customer could possibly want, department stores extend themselves into services as well as physical products, operating hairdressing and beauty parlours, restaurants and travel agencies. In some stores, individual departments are treated as business units in their own right. Taking that concept a little further, it is not surprising that concessions or 'stores within a store' have become common. With these, a manufacturer or another retail name purchases space within a department store, paying either a fixed rental per square metre or a percentage commission on turnover, to set up and operate a distinct trading area of its own. Jaeger, a classic fashion manufacturer and retailer, operates a number of its own stores throughout the UK, but also generates over one-third of its turnover from concessions within department stores such as House of Fraser.

The department store format is not without problems. In the UK, it is under threat from out-of-town shopping and the general growth of specialist retailers. There are also difficulties with the high cost of city-centre location and operation. The department stores' answer to these threats has been a concerted effort to improve their purchasing policies, to update their image and provide a higher-quality ambience through refurbishment of existing stores, and to locate new stores in out-of-town retail parks. John Lewis, for example, at the Bluewater shopping centre in Kent, boasts half a million product lines, 2,500 different types of furnishing fabric, 75 different ranges of carpet, 80 models of televisions, and for the connoisseur, over 150 types of light bulb.

Variety stores. Variety stores are smaller than department stores, and they stock a more limited number of ranges in greater depth. Stores such as BhS and Marks & Spencer in the UK, and Monoprix in France provide a great deal of choice within that limited definition, covering ladies' wear, menswear, children's clothing, sportswear, lingerie, etc. Most, however, carry additional ranges. BhS, for example, offers housewares and lighting while Marks & Spencer offers shoes, greeting cards, plants, and extensive and successful food halls within its stores.

Like department stores, the major variety stores such as Monoprix in France and Kaufhalle in Germany operate as national chains, maintaining a consistent image across the country, and some also operate internationally. Whatever the geographical coverage of the variety store chain, given the size of the stores, they need volume traffic (i.e. lots of customers) and thus to develop a mass-market appeal, offering quality merchandise at no more than mid-range price points. Variety stores tend to offer limited additional services, with a tendency towards self-service, and centralised cashier points. In that sense, they are something between a department store and a supermarket.

Supermarkets. Over the last few years, the supermarket has been accused of being the main culprit in changing the face of the High Street. The first generation of supermarkets, some 30 years ago, were relatively small, town-centre operations. As they expanded and cut their costs through self-service, bulk buying and heavy merchandising, they began to replace the small, traditional independent grocer. They expanded on to out-of-town sites, with easy free parking, and took the customers with them, thus (allegedly) threatening the health of the High Street.

The wheel then turned full circle. As planning regulations in the UK tightened, making it more difficult to develop new out-of-town superstores, retailers began looking at town-centre sites again. They developed new formats, such as Tesco Metro and Sainsbury's Local, for small stores carrying ready meals, basic staple grocery goods such as bread and milk, and lunchtime snacks aimed at shoppers and office workers.

The dominance of supermarkets is hardly surprising, because their size and operating structures mean that their labour costs can be 10–20 per cent lower than those of independent grocers, and their buying advantage 15 per cent better. This means that they can offer a significant price advantage. Additionally, they have made efficiency gains and increased their cost-effectiveness through their commitment to developing and implementing new technology in the areas of EPOS, shelf allocation models, forecasting and physical distribution management systems. The effective management of retail logistics has, therefore, become a major source of sustainable competitive advantage (Paché, 1998). Most supermarkets, however, work on high turnover and low operating margins.

Hypermarkets. The hypermarket is a natural extension of the supermarket. While the average supermarket covers up to 2,500 m^2, a superstore is between 2,500 and 5,000 m^2 and a hypermarket is anything over 5,000 m^2 (URPI, 1988). It provides even more choice and depth of range, but usually centres mainly around groceries. Examples of hypermarket operators are Intermarché and Carrefour in France, Tengelmann in Germany and ASDA in the UK. Because of their size, hypermarkets tend to occupy new sites on out-of-town retail parks. They need easy access and a large amount of space for parking, not only because of the volume of customers they have to attract, but also because their size means that customers will buy a great deal and will therefore need to be able to bring the car close to the store.

Obtaining planning permission is becoming increasingly difficult for new hypermarket locations anywhere in Europe, however. Nevertheless, a small number of developments are still taking place as part of new out-of-town shopping centres, with the hypermarket, such as Auchan, playing a central role. The Irish planning authorities have looked at the effects of hypermarket and superstore developments in other EU countries and concluded that they damage town centres, leading to the closure of small shops, and cause traffic congestion. As a result of this, the Irish government decided to introduce new planning guidelines designed to prevent further development of superstores and hypermarkets. The new guidelines mean that supermarket developments within the Dublin area will be limited to no more than $3,500 \text{ m}^2$ and, outside Dublin, to no more than $3,000 \text{ m}^2$ (*The Grocer*, 1999b).

The impact on the environment and town planning is, therefore, a far more important consideration than in the past in granting planning permission. Arrangements for the recycling of packaging, store architecture which blends in with surroundings, access arrangements, and the impact on retail diversity are now to the fore. The situation across Europe is little different from in the UK and Ireland. Spanish law favours small local stores with a surface area of below 300 m^2, and in Poland before planning permission is granted, the impact of the hypermarket on the employment structure in an area has to be specified (Auchan, 2001). In France, the birthplace of European hypermarkets, planning regulations have become more stringent in recent years for any developments over $1,000 \text{ m}^2$. This has slowed down the domestic expansion of hypermarkets and encouraged the likes of Auchan and Carrefour to expand internationally.

Out-of-town speciality stores. An out-of-town speciality store tends to specialise in one broad product group, for example furniture, carpets, DIY or electrical. It tends to operate on an out-of-town site, which is cheaper than a town-centre site and also offers good parking and general accessibility. It concentrates on discounted prices and promotional lines, thus emphasising price and value for money. A product sold in an out-of-town speciality store is likely to be cheaper than the same item sold through a town-centre speciality or department store.

The store itself can be single storey, with no windows. Some care is taken, however, over the attractiveness of the in-store displays and the layout. Depending on the kind of product area involved, the store may be self-service, or it may need to provide knowledgeable staff to help customers with choice and ordering processes. Recent years have seen efforts to improve the ambience of such stores and even greater care over their design.

Toys "Я" Us in particular has become known as a *category killer* because it offers so much choice and such low prices that other retailers cannot compete. Its large out-of-town sites mean that it is efficient in terms of its operating costs, and its global bulk buying means that it can source extremely cheaply. Shoppers wanting to buy a particular toy know that Toys "Я" Us will probably have it in stock, and shoppers who are unsure about what they want have a wonderful browsing opportunity. Additionally, the out-of-town sites are easily accessible and make transporting bulky items much easier. The small, independent toy retailer, in contrast, cannot match buying power, cost control, accessibility or choice and is likely to be driven out of business.

eg Even category killers are not immune from the need to change, however. Toys "Я" Us is currently going through a 'turnaround strategy' to strengthen the retailer after a few years of depressing results. There will be more attention paid to branding, sourcing exclusive merchandise, improving customer service, linking the toys format with Kids "Я" Us, and revamping the stores to attract parents and kids back there (Boyes, 2001; English, 2001; Prior, 2001).

Town-centre speciality stores. Like out-of-town speciality stores, town-centre speciality stores concentrate on a narrow product group as a means of building a differentiated offering. They are smaller than the out-of-town speciality stores, averaging about 250 m². Within this sector, however, there are retailers such as florists, lingerie retailers, bakeries and confectioners that operate in much smaller premises. Well-known names such as H&M (see pp. 257–8), Superdrug, Thorntons, Next and HMV all fit into this category and some, for example Dixon's, operate from both town-centre and out-of-town locations.

Most goods sold through these stores are comparison products, for which the fact of being displayed alongside similar items can be an advantage, as the customer wants to be able to examine and deliberate over a wider choice of alternatives before making a purchase decision. Given their central locations, and the need to build consumer traffic with competitive merchandise, the sector has seen the growth of multiple chains, serving clearly defined target market segments with clearly defined product mixes, such as most of the High Street fashion stores. To reinforce the concept of specialisation and differentiation, some, especially the clothing multiples, have developed their own-label brands.

eg A visit to Thorntons is strictly about self-indulgence or buying gifts. Its slogan, 'Chocolate Heaven Since 1911' captures the core values of the brand. It now has 500 company-owned or franchised confectionery shops throughout the UK and also sells by catalogue and online. The format is always the same, only the range stocked expands or contracts depending on the size and profile of each shop. It aims to be the finest sweetshop in town. Although the locations do vary from shopping malls to airports and railway stations, the retail formula normally specifies the products to promote by season, the required selling area, the type of window displays, and the serving arrangements (O'Grady, 2001; http://www.thorntons.co.uk).

Town-centre speciality stores are usually a mixture of browsing and self-service, but with personnel available to help if required. The creation of a retail atmosphere or ambience appropriate to the target market is very important, including for instance the use of window display and store layout. This allows the town-centre speciality store to feed off consumer traffic generated by larger stores, since passing shoppers are attracted in on impulse by what they see in the window or through the door. The multiples can use uniform formulae to replicate success over a wide area, but because of their buying power and expertise, they have taken a great deal of business away from small independents.

Convenience stores. Despite the decline of the small independent grocer in the UK, there is still a niche that can be filled by convenience stores. Operating mainly in the groceries, drink and CTN sectors, they open long hours, not just 9 a.m. until 6 p.m. The typical CTN is still the small independent corner shop that serves a local community with basic groceries, newspapers, confectionery and cigarettes, but the range has expanded to include books, stationery, video hire and greetings cards.

They fill a gap left by the supermarkets, which are fine for the weekly or monthly shopping trip, if the consumer can be bothered to drive out to one. The convenience stores, however, satisfy needs that arise in the mean time. If the consumer has run out of something, forgotten to get something at the supermarket, wants freshness, or finds six unexpected guests on the doorstep who want feeding, the local convenience store is invaluable. If the emergency happens outside normal shopping times, then the advantages of a local, late-night shop become obvious. Such benefits, however, do tend to come at a price premium. To try to become more price competitive, some 'open-all-hours' convenience stores operate as voluntary chains, such as Spar, Londis, Today's and Mace, in which the retailers retain their independence but benefit from bulk purchasing and centralised marketing activities. The priority for many CTNs is to keep trying new services and lines that might sell in the local community. A large number now have off-licences, fax facilities, and the provision of other outsourced services, including dry cleaning and shoe repairs. The National Lottery ticket terminals have provided a boost to income, while even sales of travel cards and phone cards have generated new streams of revenue.

Two more recent developments in convenience retailing are forecourt shops at petrol stations and computerised kiosks. Many petrol retailers, such as Jet and Shell, have developed their non-petrol retailing areas into attractive mini-supermarkets that pull in custom in their own right. In some cases, they are even attracting customers who go in to buy milk or bread and end up purchasing petrol as an afterthought. Offering a diversified portfolio of services can be a critical factor in the survival of some rural petrol stations, and fuel sales are expected to drop below 20 per cent of sales, on average, over the next few years.

In the UK, however, the big supermarket chains are muscling in on the convenience store sector by taking over chains of convenience stores and by entering into partnerships with petrol companies to operate forecourt shops.

Discount clubs. Discount clubs are rather like cash and carries for the general public, where they can buy in bulk at extremely competitive prices. Discount clubs do, however, have membership requirements, related to occupation and income.

eg Costco is a form of discount club for both traders and individual members. Operating from 13 UK warehouses and 360 more across seven countries, the principle is to stock a wide range of merchandise for small business owners. Products are packaged, displayed, and sold in bulk quantities in a no-frills, warehouse atmosphere on the original shipping pallets. The warehouses are self-service and the member's purchases are packed into empty product boxes. By stripping out the service and merchandising, the prices can be kept low. Individual members must meet certain qualifying criteria based on current or former occupation such as working in education or local government (*The Grocer*, 2001b; http://www.costco.co.uk).

The discount clubs achieve their low prices and competitive edge through minimal service and the negotiation of keen bulk deals with the major manufacturers, beyond anything offered to the established supermarkets. Added to this, they pare their margins to the bone, relying on volume turnover, and they purchase speculatively. For instance, they may purchase a one-off consignment of a manufacturer's surplus stock at a very low price, or they may buy stock cheaply from a bankrupt company. While this allows them to offer incredible bargains, they cannot guarantee consistency of supply, thus they may have a heap of televisions one week but once these have been sold, that is it, there are no more. The following week the same space in the store may be occupied by hi-fis. At least such a policy keeps customers coming back to see what new bargains there are.

Markets. Most towns have markets, as a last link with an ancient form of retailing. There are now different types of market, not only those selling different kinds of products but street markets, held on certain days only; permanent markets occupying dedicated sites under cover or in the open; farmers' markets selling fresh produce and preserves; and Sunday markets for more specialised products.

eg The value of the market stall as a first step on the retailing ladder is well understood. The management of the Gateshead Metro Centre, for example, not only rents out permanent retail space, but also hires out a number of mobile barrows, situated throughout the shopping centre, at relatively low rents. This gives a more lively, market type of character to the public areas, but, more importantly, gives an opening for small traders, or individuals with little cash but a lot of entrepreneurial flair, to test a retail concept and to begin developing a business. Many barrow retailers then build up sufficient confidence and resources to take on a permanent shop unit.

Catalogue showrooms. A fairly recent development, catalogue showrooms try to combine the benefits of a High Street presence with the best in logistics technology and physical distribution management. The central focus of the showroom is the catalogue, and many copies are displayed around the store as well as being available for the customer to take home for browsing. Some items are on live display, but this is by no means the whole product range.

The consumer selects from the catalogue, then goes to a checkout where an assistant inputs the order into the central computer. If the item is immediately available, the cashier takes payment. The consumer then joins a queue at a collection point, while the purchased product is brought round from the warehouse behind the scenes, usually very quickly.

A prime example of this type of operation is Argos, which carries a very wide range of household, electrical and leisure goods. It offers relatively competitive prices through bulk purchasing, and savings on operating costs, damage and pilfering (because of the limited displays).

Non-store retailing. A growing amount of selling to individual consumers is now taking place outside the traditional retailing structures. Non-store selling may involve personal selling (to be dealt with in Chapter 10), selling to the consumer at home through television, Internet or telephone links or, most impersonally, selling through vending machines.

marketing *in action*

Home delivery or 'drive thru' grocery shopping?

Not every shopper enjoys the 'fun' of shopping, especially when it involves a trip to the supermarket. It is this group, those who cannot, or prefer not to visit the supermarket, but who must buy, that has been the target of several attempts to develop home ordering and home delivery grocery services. The latest estimates, however, suggest that home shopping still only accounts for around 1 per cent of UK grocery sales.

The reasons why home shopping should be popular are clear: increasingly busy lives with extended working hours; the increasing number of people at work, especially women; the feeling that people have better things to do with their free time such as 'real' leisure pursuits; and growing acceptance of home delivery in a range of sectors such as books, pizza, flowers, etc. All of this, combined with the increasing use of the Internet, sets the scene for significant growth in home grocery shopping. The trouble is that the supermarket chains that have experimented with online grocery shopping have had variable results. Somerfield and Budgens closed down their home delivery operations in 2000 due to poor take-up. In contrast to that, Tesco and Sainsbury's are often quoted as the two most successful operators. The Sainsbury's 'To You' online home delivery business, however, is thought to have lost £29m. in just six months in 2001 and is thought to have cost £200m. overall in getting it launched. Its original idea

was to follow US practice, with central warehouses serving the online orders rather than adopting the Tesco model of picking from local store shelves. Sainsbury's now offers store picking alongside the central warehouse and has 40 stores offering the service, a number that is likely to expand.

Tesco.com has persevered with home shopping for five years and is starting to see results. Although the level of profit that has been made from this venture is unknown, its turnover has grown to over £300m. and it has 750,000 registered customers of whom 70,000 shop regularly. Tesco claims that it has opened up new market segments and attracted business away from Waitrose in the south and Sainsbury's in the north of the UK. Customers do not just order groceries; CDs, DVDs and wine are also popular. Perhaps what is more important is that while the typical shopper at Tesco spends under £25 per visit, the online shopper spends over £80 (presumably on the basis that if you are going to pay a £5 delivery fee, you might as well make it worthwhile). Tesco offers 40,000 products online and operates a fleet of 800 vans to ensure prompt delivery.

At present, the future is far from clear, however. Forrester Research has suggested that home shopping will account for 2 per cent of grocery turnover by the end of 2002, and Dresdner Kleinwort Benson has estimated that by 2008, 10 per cent of the UK food market sales with a

value of £14bn will be delivered to the home. This supports Tesco's belief that online shopping could be the biggest revolution in supermarket shopping since self-service was introduced. Independent research is less encouraging, however. An Institute of Grocery and Distribution survey has suggested that most consumers have little interest in buying groceries over the Internet: they prefer to choose food in-store, don't like paying online and enjoy the spontaneity and exploration of shopping. The level of understanding is also low, as they think that the product range will be limited with shorter shelf life and that they will lose out by having fewer price promotions.

Other retailers such as Waitrose and ASDA are thought to be considering expanding operations, despite the existing operators' variable results. Interestingly, in the USA, where home shopping began, a new scheme called 'On the Go' run by Shaw's, a Sainsbury subsidiary, proposes a hybrid model that offers the benefits of convenience without the prohibitive cost that faces most retailers trying to plan deliveries on a low delivery charge rate. For a flat rate fee of $4.95, customers can order from 20,000 lines on the multiple's website, pay by credit card and collect the assembled order from the store, rather like a 'drive-thru' arrangement at a fast food restaurant, without ever leaving the car. Now there's a thought.

Sources: Finch (2001a), *The Grocer*; (2001c, d; 2002), Ryle (2001).

In-home selling. The longest-established means of selling to the consumer at home is through door-to-door selling, where the representative calls at the house either trying to sell from a suitcase (brushes, for example), or trying to do some preliminary selling to pave the way for a more concerted effort later (with higher-cost items such as double glazing, burglar alarms and other home improvements). Cold calling (i.e. turning up unexpectedly and unannounced) is not a particularly efficient use of the representative's time, nor is it likely to evoke a positive response from the customer.

A more acceptable method of in-home selling that has really taken off is the party plan. Here, the organisation recruits ordinary consumers to act as agents and do the selling for them in a relaxed, sociable atmosphere. The agent, or a willing friend, will host a party at a house and provide light refreshments. Guests are invited to attend and during the course of the evening, when everyone is relaxed, the agent will demonstrate the goods and take orders.

Since the pioneering days of the Tupperware party, many other products have used the same sort of technique. Ann Summers, for instance, is an organisation that sells erotic lingerie and sex aids and toys through parties. The majority of the customers are women who would otherwise never dream of going into 'that kind of shop', let alone buying 'that kind of merchandise'. A party is an ideal way of selling those products to that particular target market, because the atmosphere is relaxed, the customer is among friends, and purchases can be made without embarrassment amidst lots of giggling. One of the best features of party selling is the ability to show and demonstrate the product. This kind of hands-on, interactive approach is a powerful way of involving the potential customer and thus getting them interested and in a mood to buy.

The main problem with party selling, however, is that it can be difficult to recruit agents, and their quality and selling abilities will be variable. Supporting and motivating a pyramid of agents and paying their commission can make selling costs very high.

Mail order and teleshopping. Mail order has a long history and traditionally consists of a printed catalogue from which customers select goods that are then delivered to the home, either through the postal service or via couriers. This form of selling has, however, developed and diversified over the years. Offers are now made through magazine or newspaper advertisements, as well as through the traditional catalogue, and database marketing now means that specially tailored offers can be made to individual customers. Orders no longer have to be mailed in by the customer, but can be telephoned, with payment being made immediately by credit card. The strength of mail order varies across Europe, but is generally stronger in northern Europe than in the south. It is strong in Germany through companies such as Otto Versand, Quelle and Nekermann.

Teleshopping represents a much wider range of activities. It includes shopping by telephone in response to television advertisements, whether on cable, satellite or terrestrial channels. Some cable and satellite operators run home-shopping channels, such as QVC, where the primary objective is to sell goods to viewers. Teleshopping also covers interactive shopping by computer, using mechanisms such as the French Minitel system or the Internet. The Internet in particular offers interesting opportunities to a variety of sellers, including established retailers. Many, such as Toys "Я" Us and Blackwell's Bookshop, have set up 'virtual' stores on Internet sites, so that a potential customer can browse through the merchandise, select items, pay by credit card and then wait for the goods to be delivered.

eg Many retailers are embracing e-commerce as a means of providing additional services to their customers. A website can provide information for customers in their own homes, perhaps on product availability, pricing, special offers or new products. The website can also educate customers, not only by establishing the company's policies on the environment or employee relations issues, for example, but also by giving them ideas about how to use products or about other products in the company's range. Online ordering then makes it very easy for customers to place an order, which can then be delivered to their homes. DIY chain B&Q's website (http://www.diy.com) incorporates an online ordering service aimed at the amateur DIY enthusiast. B&Q feels that with over 300 UK stores, its online service is not so much about extending its geographic reach as adding value for its customers through convenience, service and information.

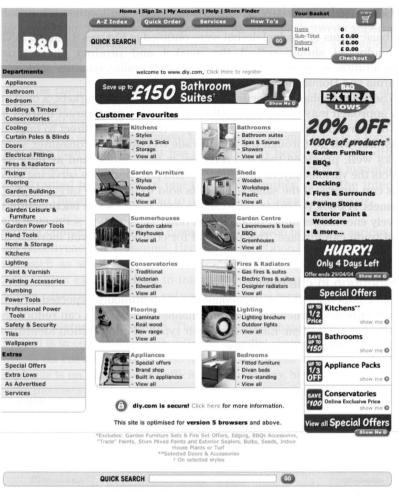

B&Q uses e-commerce as a new way of offering customers advice and guidance on its products.

Source: http://www.diy.com, B&Q plc.

Vending. Vending machines account for a very small percentage of retail sales, less than 1 per cent. They are mainly based in workplaces and public locations, for example offices, factories, staffrooms, bus and rail stations. They are best used for small, standard, low-priced, repeat purchase products, such as hot and cold drinks, cans of drink, chocolate and snacks, bank cash dispensers and postage stamps. They have the advantage of allowing customers to purchase at highly convenient locations, at any time of the day or night. Vending machines can also help to deliver the product in prime condition for consumption, for example the refrigerated machines that deliver a can of ice-cold Coke. A human retailer cannot always maintain those conditions.

Channel strategy

With the various added value roles implicit in the marketing channel, decisions need to be taken about the allocation and performance of these roles, the basis of remuneration within the system and the effectiveness of alternative configurations in enabling market penetration to be achieved competitively and efficiently. This is channel strategy.

Working patterns. The growth in the number of women working has had a profound effect on some distribution channels, making some channels more difficult to operate, such as door-to-door selling during the daytime, while home shopping and convenience shopping outside usual trading hours have become much more widely accepted.

European Union regulations. Generally speaking, manufacturers have the right to decide which intermediaries should or should not distribute their products. Both national and European regulatory bodies start to become interested, however, where exclusion of certain intermediaries might be seen as a deliberate attempt to distort competition or to achieve price-fixing. There has been, for example, a long-running legal debate over Levi Strauss's refusal to supply supermarket chains with jeans. The debate hinged on whether the refusal to supply was based on a legitimate concern over trade-mark protection and the quality of the retail premises and staff, or whether it was simply an attempt to prevent retail prices falling.

■ Selecting a channel member

The final phase of the channel design strategy is the selection of specific intermediaries. The selection decision tends to become more critical as the intensity of distribution itself becomes more selective or exclusive. In mass-distribution decisions, such as those concerning products like confectionery, any willing outlet will be considered. However, where a selective distribution approach is adopted, great care must be taken over the final selection of intermediary, as a poor decision may lead to strategic failure. For example, the selection of a wholesaler to allow entry into a new European market may be critical to the degree and speed of penetration achieved.

eg Klemm is part of the Ingersoll-Rand group and specialises in a range of German-built piling and drilling rigs for construction sites. Its channel approach is often to appoint sole distributors in target countries. Thus in the UK, Skelair handles all sales, while in the Netherlands, Drilcon has exclusive rights. Klemm seeks to develop a close and effective relationship with its distributors. Although individual domestic markets may be relatively small, the selling task is complex in defining machines for applications and good after-sales service is also crucial. This demands close technical support and a level of trust and confidence between manufacturer and distributor (http://www.klemm-bt.com).

In situations where organisations need to select intermediaries on a fairly frequent basis, it would be useful to select on the basis of predetermined criteria. Table 8.2 highlights a range of issues that should be examined as part of an appraisal process.

Table 8.2 Selection criteria for intermediaries

Strategic	Operational
• Expansion plans	• Local market knowledge
• Resource building	• Adequate premises/equipment
• Management quality/competence	• Stockholding policy
• Market coverage	• Customer convenience
• Partnership willingness	• Product knowledge
• Loyalty/cooperation	• Realistic credit/payment terms
	• Sales force capability
	• Efficient customer service

The relative importance of the various criteria will vary from sector to sector and indeed over time. Inevitably, there is still a need for management judgement and a trading of pros against cons, as the 'ideal' distributor that is both willing and able to proceed will rarely be found. Remember that intermediaries have the choice of whether or not they will sell the products offered. This luxury of choice is not just restricted to supermarkets and large multiple retailers. Travel agents can only stock a limited number of holidays, and are very careful about offering new packages from smaller tour operators. In some industrial distribution channels, the intermediary can decide whether or not to stock ancillary products around the main products that it sells on a dealership basis.

Conflict and cooperation

Most of this chapter so far has concentrated largely on economic issues involved in channel decisions. However, all channel decisions are ultimately made between people in organisations. There is, therefore, always the potential for disagreement over the many decisions, such as expected roles, allocation of effort, reward structures, product and marketing

---

corporate social responsibility *in action*

Buy local

The UK's Prince Charles warned supermarkets and consumers that the countryside's natural beauty could be at risk if shoppers fail to support local producers by buying more regional food and drink. If the agrifood sector could expand, then the sustainability of rural life could be enhanced and there would be less risk of rural areas disappearing under housing developments. Sustainable local foods, such as speciality farmhouse cheeses, distinctive apple varieties, and locally reared meat, can help reconnect consumers with farmers and give the public real choices about the food they eat, the way it is produced and its impact on the countryside, says the CPRE. This view is reflected in the Countryside Agency's *Local Products Programme* which aims to improve environmentally sound land management and to support rural communities. Its 'Eat the View' slogan was designed to increase consumers' awareness and strengthen their links with the economic vitality of the countryside. This means creating stronger consumer demand for certain products, and helping small and specialist producers to find markets in the face of increasing globalisation and the powerful forces of large retailers.

To be successful, any programme has to encourage more farmers, supermarkets, independent retailers and manufacturers to work together in a flexible, win–win manner. Altruism is not enough for supply chain cooperation: all parties need to achieve an outcome that is both sustainable and meets commercial criteria. The problem is that farmers and processors are often good at growing and processing but unskilled, badly informed and naive about downstream supply chain issues such as branding, marketing and service consistency. At the other end of the chain, there is also the problem of what can be done to encourage retailers, especially the large multiples, to operate on a local scale when their own systems are geared around national buying and national distribution systems and volume.

In fact, the supermarket chains have already realised the benefits of 'localness' by allowing some local produce from small suppliers on to their shelves. There is a perception among food shoppers that local food is more trustworthy and of better quality. Sainsbury's, for example, has a dedicated regional sourcing team to select locally produced foods from all parts of the UK. It stocks 2,480 regional lines in the areas of their origins and these are sourced from around 375, often small, regional suppliers. Somerfield works with 600 small businesses, generating £10m. of sales in 600 stores. It is also planning to hold roadshows to link retail buyers with local farmers.

There are strategic issues associated with how the multiples treat smaller suppliers, especially on pricing and supply continuity. More practical adjustments also need to be made. Getting delivery of produce from a small producer to a supermarket regional distribution depot can be a problem and supermarkets sometimes have to make special allowances by, for example, accepting shipment direct to stores. Cobblewood Mushrooms in Selby, Yorkshire, for example, provides fresh mushrooms to its local Safeway store every day. Often, however, the retailers prefer shipment to distribution centres, not the stores. Some suppliers have complained that the multiples are passing on the extra costs of distribution to producers by opening more depots and then expecting supply to each. Usually, retailers will not allow suppliers to recoup these costs through higher prices. Tesco has introduced a scheme where empty lorries returning from making deliveries to stores collect goods from some smaller suppliers to ease their problems of delivering to distribution centres.

Supermarkets dominate the grocery market, so any business needs to weigh the risks and problems of dealing with them against the restriction to potential by not doing so. A Code of Conduct is currently being considered by the food industry to improve and guide relationships between local suppliers and the supermarkets following a critical Competition Commission report. Should the supermarkets go further with supporting training, brand development and business improvement on the basis that stronger, committed local suppliers can mean better opportunities for local produce in the stores?

Sources: Bedall (2001a, b), Bedington (2001a), Competition Commission (2000), CPRE (2002), MLC Industry Strategy Ltd (2001), http://www.countryside.org.uk

strategies, that ensure that the system operates effectively. A channel is an interorganisational social system comprising members who are tied together by a belief that by working together (for the time being at least), they can improve the individual benefits gained. A climate of cooperation is perhaps the most desirable within a channel system. It does not just happen, however, but needs to be worked on and cultivated.

Good communication, in terms of amount, direction, medium and content, is also essential for closer cooperation in a channel (Mohr and Nevin, 1990). In a study of computer dealers, Mohr *et al.* (1999) found that effective communication led to greater satisfaction, stronger commitment and better coordination. The development of electronic sharing of data and intelligence is strengthening many channel relationships as technology helps all members to make better decisions in times of market uncertainty as well as reducing selling and coordination costs (Huber, 1990).

Some view conflict and cooperation as being at opposite ends of a continuum, while others view them as distinct concepts. Whatever the view, strong cooperation can lead to a feeling of satisfaction and partnership, one of give and take. Cooperation may lead to strong personal and organisational ties that are difficult for outsiders to break. However, not all cooperation need be voluntary. A weaker channel member may think it best to cooperate and comply with the wishes of a more powerful member, rather than risk retribution.

Conflict is a natural part of any social system. Conflict may exist where, for example, one channel member feels that another member is not dealing fairly with it, or that the system is not working sufficiently in its favour. There are numerous possible causes of conflict, some arising from poor understanding, others from a fundamental difference of opinion that goes to the heart of the relationship.

eg The danger of conflict in a channel is ever present. Sometimes disputes can become public and embarrassing to both sides. Landmark, a leading buying group in the UK, criticised drinks suppliers for not being supportive during a benzene contamination scare. Many of the suppliers, it was argued, were not prepared to cope with product recalls and gave poor and ineffective advice. With potentially 52 million cans to be removed from the shelves, it was a major headache for retailers to identify which products could have been affected (Dearden, 1998). Also in the grocery trade, cash and carry operator Bestway claimed that some suppliers were giving better terms and conditions to multiples and delivered to wholesalers rather than cash and carry operators. It considered such prices to be discriminatory and alleged that this made it more difficult to give its own retailers the best prices. The suppliers rejected this accusation and stated that it was caused by a confusion between normal and promotional prices (*The Grocer*, 1998).

Conflict needs to be spotted early and dealt with before it becomes too overt. This can be helped by regular meetings, frequent communication, and ensuring that all parties emerge satisfied from negotiations. It is critical that each channel member should fully understand their role and what is expected of them, and that this is agreed in advance. If conflict does become overt, communication, formation of channel committees, a fast arbitration service and top management commitment to resolution are all essential to prevent an irrevocable breakdown of the channel.

Chapter summary

■ The channel of distribution is the means through which products are moved from the manufacturer to the end consumer. The structure of channels can vary considerably depending on the type of market, the needs of the end customer and the type of product. Consumer goods might be supplied direct, but in mass markets for convenience goods, however, this might not be feasible and longer channels might be used. B2B markets are far more likely to involve direct supply from manufacturer to B2B buyer. Some B2B purchases, however, particularly routine repurchases of non-critical items such as office stationery, might be distributed in ways that are similar to those used in consumer markets, with various intermediaries involved.

- Intermediaries play an important role in increasing efficiency and reducing costs, reduce the manufacturer's risk, gather, store, sort and transport a wide range of goods, and ease cash flow for manufacturers and for customers. These functions are not all necessarily performed by the same member of the distribution channel and the decision as to who does what may be made by consensus or by the use of power in the channel. Distributors, agents and wholesalers tend to act as intermediaries in B2B markets or as an interface between manufacturers and retailers. Retailers tend to serve the needs of individual consumers and can be classified according to a number of criteria: form of ownership (independents, corporate chains or contractual systems), level of service (full or limited), merchandise lines (breadth and depth) and operating methods (type of store, whether department store, supermarket, variety store or other). Non-store retailing, closely linked with direct marketing, has also become increasingly popular and widespread. It includes in-home selling, parties, mail-order operations, teleshopping and vending machines.

- Channel design will be influenced by a number of factors, including organisational objectives, capabilities and resources. Market size might also constrain the choice of channel, as might the buying complexity associated with the product and the buying behaviour of the target market. The changing environment can also influence the choice of channel. Selecting specific intermediaries to join a channel can be difficult but this choice can be a critical success factor since, for example, the speed of entry and the degree of penetration into a new market can depend on the right choice of intermediary. Sometimes, however, the intermediary has the power to reject a manufacturer or a specific product. Vertical marketing systems (VMS) have evolved to create a channel that is more efficient and effective for all parties, ideally working towards the common good in a long-term relationship. Clearly, voluntary cooperation is the best way of achieving an effective and efficient channel. However, conflict might arise and, if it is not dealt with promptly and sensitively, might lead, sooner or later, to the dissolution of that channel. Manufacturers are not restricted to using only one channel. There are three broad levels of intensity of distribution, each implying a different set of channels and different types of intermediary: intensive distribution, selective distribution and exclusive distribution.

questions for *review and discussion*

8.1 What are the different types of intermediary that might be found in a distribution channel?

8.2 What are the five factors influencing channel strategy?

8.3 To what extent and why do you think that the creation of a VMS can improve the performance of a channel and its members?

8.4 What kind of market coverage strategy might be appropriate for:
(a) a bar of chocolate;
(b) a toothbrush;
(c) a home computer; and
(d) a marketing textbook; and why?

8.5 Using Table 8.2 on p. 272 as a starting point, develop lists of criteria that a manufacturer might use in defining:
(a) 'good' retailers; and
(b) 'good' wholesalers to recruit for consumer market channels.

8.6 In what ways and to what extent do you think that non-store retailing poses a threat to conventional retailers?

case study 8.1

Sweet harmony in the distribution channel

Lofthouse of Fleetwood manufactures the confectionery/medicinal sweet Fisherman's Friend (see Case Study 2.1), but contracts out its marketing to an independent company, Impex, and its distribution to independent distributors. Impex is heavily involved in appointing distributors. It selects and interviews up to six candidate distributor companies, undertaking detailed SWOT analyses on their potential, and it then makes a recommendation to Lofthouse of Fleetwood about which one would be the ideal partner in a particular market. The quality of those recommendations is reflected in the fact that over 25 years, only 5 out of 100 distributors have had to be changed. Among the criteria for selecting a distributor, Lofthouse of Fleetwood includes the following:

- The products it handles: a distributor should be selling complementary lines and have experience and suitable contacts in relevant product markets.
- Its relationship with the competition: a distributor should not be handling direct competitors' products (and if it was, there would probably be a clause in its contract preventing it from handling Fisherman's Friend); Lofthouse of Fleetwood wants exclusivity.
- Its structure: the number of sales representatives and their coverage of the market.
- Its size: Lofthouse wants a distributor to be small enough for Fisherman's Friend to have an important role and an adequate share of the distributor's management time and attention. The company prefers to be a big fish in a smaller pool. This needs to be balanced, however, against the need to have a distributor big enough to have the right contacts and to achieve the objectives of the product in its market.
- Its financial status: the distributor needs to be financially stable and secure and Lofthouse of Fleetwood is looking for a long-term relationship.
- Its culture: because Lofthouse of Fleetwood is looking for a long-term relationship, it is important that a distributor has a similar culture and ethos. The company often finds that because it is a family business, it works well with distributors that are also family businesses.

One distributor that has had a long-standing and successful relationship with Lofthouse of Fleetwood is its Dutch distributor, Nedan Zoetwaren BV. Its profile certainly fits the criteria above. The company is privately owned and has been in business for over 40 years. It distributes confectionery into the Dutch market and started with Stimorol chewing gum, imported from Denmark. Fisherman's Friend was taken into the portfolio in 1974. The company employs 45 people, 24 of whom are involved on a day-to-day basis in sales. Four people are involved in account management, and then there are two well-established sales forces; 11 people work in the sales force covering impulse outlets (for example petrol stations and convenience stores) and 9 in the sales force covering the grocery trade. The company acts as a distributor representing Wrigley's chewing gum and Cadbury's chocolate as well as Fisherman's Friend, but it also manufactures confectionery products of its own based on liquorice and wine gums, under Nedan's Autodrop brand name.

Nedan sells around 750,000 boxes, each with 24 packs of Fisherman's Friend, every year. That amounts to 18 million packages for a population of 15 million, some 20 per cent above the POPPPPY (packets of product per person per year) target, which puts the Netherlands fifth in the POPPPPY league table, behind Norway, Singapore, Germany and Switzerland. Nedan has only had one year when Fisherman's Friend sales fell, otherwise it has been steady upward progress. The sales force still has to work hard, though, to maintain the success. Some 42 per cent of Fisherman's Friend sales are generated from the impulse sector, tobacconists and petrol stations, and that position has to be defended hard in a very competitive market.

Communication is an important part of the strategy and advertising plays a vital role. Lofthouse of Fleetwood decided on an umbrella advertising campaign across Europe via satellite television to create a consistent image through one concentrated message. In addition to this, all the regional distributors do their own advertising, within set guidelines, via terrestrial television. A manual, available on CD-ROM, shows distributors how the product and brand should be presented. In the Netherlands, advertising is commissioned and controlled by Nedan in consultation with Lofthouse of Fleetwood and Impex. There is an advertising allowance from the manufacturer, but Nedan spends more than that as a means of developing and defending its own market.

In terms of pricing, Lofthouse of Fleetwood cannot dictate resale and retail prices. There is one consistent list price for all distributors, although bulk discounts can be negotiated. Distributors are free, however, to set resale prices according to conditions in their own local markets, although the company will advise a distributor if its prices seem to be too far out of line with those of other distributors. Retail buyers and buying groups, such as Carrefour, Ahold and Tesco, and particularly those operating right across Europe, know very well what prices are like in different European countries and will place their orders in the cheapest market. The advent of the euro, however, means greater price transparency, although there are still variations in VAT and sales tax rates in different countries which will cloud the issue somewhat. It is true to say, however, that the general increase in and ease of pan-European trade are encouraging more pricing consistency between European distributors who cannot work in total isolation from each other. Although they do have their own defined territories, any decisions distributors make on pricing, for instance, take into account what is happening in neighbouring and other markets. Nedan is confident that its pricing is comparable with that of other European distributors, however, and does not feel that its major customers, such as Ahold, could gain any advantage from shopping around. Pricing in euros emphasises the consistency.

As part of their contracts, distributors are expected to carry about one month's stock. In general terms, once a market is established, demand is fairly predictable, unless there is a flu epidemic or some other unpredictable effect. Nedan has never had any serious problems in replenishing its stocks from the UK. Nedan, in turn, receives orders electronically from its own customers and undertakes to deliver within 24 hours.

Although the Netherlands–UK ordering routine is very well established, occasional meetings, either in the UK or in the Netherlands, offer an opportunity to discuss any real or potential concerns at a senior level and help to cement the relationship further. Distributors are also encouraged to network with each other and exchange information so that they are more likely to work collaboratively than competitively and Nedan finds this a positive and useful experience. Distributors exchange ideas on how to

make cost savings and achieve economies of scale, for example. Lofthouse of Fleetwood facilitates this networking by organising two conferences per year, one in Europe and one in the Far East, so that distributors can meet with each other and with the company to discuss tactics.

The relationship between Lofthouse of Fleetwood and Nedan is built on mutual trust, cooperation and communication. Nedan feels that Lofthouse of Fleetwood strikes about the right balance between creating and maintaining a consistent brand image across its global markets while allowing local distributors sufficient autonomy to distribute and market the brand appropriately for their own environments. Lofthouse of Fleetwood brings its manufacturing expertise and strategic vision for the brand to the relationship as well as coordinating the cohesive network of distributors that allows best practice to be disseminated. The distributors themselves bring their local knowledge and contacts and their operational expertise in marketing and growing the brand to the benefit of all parties.

Sources: Adapted from interviews with Rien van Ruremonde, Managing Director of Nedan Zoetwaren BV and with Duncan and Tony Lofthouse, Joint Managing Directors of Lofthouse of Fleetwood Ltd. Our grateful thanks to all of them.

Questions

1 Summarise the reasons why Lofthouse of Fleetwood chooses to use distributors rather than dealing direct with the retail trade itself.

2 What kind of market coverage strategy would you expect to find in the confectionery market and why? What evidence is there in the case that Lofthouse of Fleetwood/Nedan conform to that strategy?

3 Outline the different issues and problems you think Nedan might face in dealing with large multiple supermarket chains and small convenience stores.

4 Why are trust and cooperation so critical in the relationship between Lofthouse of Fleetwood and Nedan? In what ways are trust and cooperation built and expressed in this relationship?

References for chapter 8

Auchan (2001), 'Hypermarkets Won't Be Built without Prior Employment Forecast', *Polish News Bulletin*, 14 December, (accessed via http://www.auchan.com).

Bedall, C. (2001a), 'Charles: Rural Beauty at Risk', *The Grocer*, 13 May, p. 10.

Bedall, C. (2001b), 'Charles Pushes Local Sourcing', *The Grocer*, 28 July, p. 13.

Bedington, E. (2001a), 'Little and Large', *The Grocer*, 24 March, pp. 38–40.

Bedington, E. (2001b), 'Living Up to the Hype', *The Grocer*, 15 December, pp. 36–8.

Boyes, S. (2001), 'Reinventing Toys "Я" Us', *Corporate Finance*, September, pp. 27–8.

Butaney, G. and Wortzel, L. (1988), 'Distribution Power versus Manufacturer Power: the Customer Role', *Journal of Marketing*, 52 (January), pp. 52–63.

Competition Commission (2000), *Supermarkets: A Report on the Supply of Groceries from Multiple Stores in the United Kingdom*, Competition Commission.

CPRE (2002), 'Sustainable Local Foods: Reconnecting Consumers, Farmers, Communities and the Countryside' (accessed via http://www.cpre.org.uk).

Davidson, H. (1993), 'Bubbling Benetton Beats Recession', *Sunday Times*, 4 April, pp. 3–11.

Dearden, A. (1998), 'Landmark Hits Out at Suppliers', *The Grocer*, 6 June, p. 11.

English, S. (2001), 'It's Not All Fun and Games as "Kid's Recession" Hits Toys "Я" Us Hard', *The Daily Telegraph*, 14 July, p. 27.

Finch, J. (2001a), 'Sainsbury Hits a 10-year Sales High', *The Guardian*, 22 November, p. 1.24.

Finch, J. (2001b), 'Sweet Music: Tills Start to Jingle at HMV', *The Guardian*, 8 December, p. 24.

Frazier, G. (1999), 'Organizing and Managing Channels of Distribution', *Journal of the Academy of Marketing Science*, 27 (2), pp. 226–40.

Frazier, G. and Lassar, W. (1996), 'Determinants of Distribution Intensity', *Journal of Marketing*, 60 (October), pp. 39–51.

Goldman, A. (2001), 'The Transfer of Retail Formats into Developing Economies: the Example of China', *Journal of Retailing*, 77 (2), pp. 221–42.

Gregory, H. (2001a), 'Country Ways', *The Grocer*, 31 March, pp. 36–8.

Gregory, H. (2001b), 'What it Takes', *The Grocer*, 24 November, pp. 26–8.

The Grocer (1998), 'Pervez Attacks Discriminatory Pricing', *The Grocer*, 1 August, p. 8.

The Grocer (1999a), 'Difficult Future Forecast for Cash and Carry Firms', *The Grocer*, 9 January, p. 12.

The Grocer (1999b), 'Irish Plan Crackdown on Major Superstores', *The Grocer*, 24 April, p. 11.

The Grocer (2001b), 'Costco Total is Now 13', *The Grocer*, 1 September, p. 8.

The Grocer (2001c), 'Consumers Fight Shy of On-line Groceries', *The Grocer*, 22 September, p. 12.

The Grocer (2001d), 'Shaw's Decides to Trial "More Viable" Net Shopping Service', *The Grocer*, 17 November, p. 16.

The Grocer (2001e), 'Safeway Creates Instore Theatre in the Round', *The Grocer*, 24 November, p. 6.

The Grocer (2002), 'Asda Ditches Depots in Online Arm Restructure', *The Grocer*, 5 January, p. 5.

Howe, W. (1992), *Retailing Management*, Macmillan.

Huber, G. (1990), 'A Theory of the Effects of Advanced Information Technologies on Organizational Design, Intelligence, and Decision Making', *Academy of Management Review*, 15 (1), pp. 47–72.

Hunt, J. (1998), 'Heijn Works to Fix New Concept', *The Grocer*, 12 September, p. 15.

Hunt, J. (1999), 'Going into Orbit', *The Grocer*, 9 January, p. 32.

Hunt, J. (2001), 'Orient Express', *The Grocer*, 12 May, pp. 36–7.

Jardine, A. (2001), 'Argos Diversifies to Update Image', *Marketing*, 5 August, p. 4.

Kleinman, M. (2001), 'Can Argos Hold on to a Position of Strength?', *Marketing*, 27 September, p. 13.

MLC Industry Strategy Ltd (2001), *Setting Up Initiatives for the Collaborative Marketing of Local/Regional Products: Best Practice Procedures*, MLC Industry Strategy Ltd.

Mohr, J., Fisher, R. and Nevin, J. (1999), 'Communicating for Better Channel Relationships', *Marketing Management*, 8 (2), pp. 38–45.

Mohr, J. and Nevin, J. (1990), 'Communication Strategies in Marketing Channels: a Theoretical Perspective', *Journal of Marketing*, 54 (October), pp. 36–51.

O'Grady, S. (2001), 'Sweet Smell May Be Thornton's Success', *The Independent*, 8 December, p. 5.

Paché, G. (1998), 'Logistics Outsourcing in Grocery Distribution: a European Perspective', *Logistics Information Management*, 11 (5), pp. 301–8.

Palamountain, J. (1955), *The Politics of Distribution*, Harvard University Press.

Prior, M. (2001), 'TRU's Eyler Touts Sound Growth Plan', *DSN Retailing Today*, 18 June, p. 3.46.

Rosenbloom, B. (1987), *Marketing Channels: A Management View*, Dryden.

Ryle, S. (2001), '@business: Delivering the Goods Brings Net Success', *The Observer*, 12 August, p. 6.

Scardino. E. (2001), 'H&M: Can it Adapt to America's Landscape?', *DSN Retailing Today*, 17 September, pp. A10–A11.

Shapley, D. (1998), 'The Cape Crusaders', *The Grocer*, 20 June, pp. 59–63.

Sharma, A. and Dominguez, L. (1992), 'Channel Evolution: a Framework for Analysis', *Journal of the Academy of Marketing Science*, 20 (Winter), pp. 1–16.

Stern, L., El-Ansary, A. and Coughlan, A. (1996), *Marketing Channels* (5th edn), Prentice Hall.

Stewart-Allen, A. (2001), 'Ikea Service Worst in its Own Backyard', *Marketing News*, 23 April, p. 11.

Teather, D. (2001), 'H&M Plans to Open 50 Fashion Stores', *The Guardian*, 22 June, p. 1.23.

URPI (1988), *List of UK Hypermarkets and Superstores*, Unit for Retail Planning Information.

Webster, F. (1979), *Industrial Marketing Strategy*, John Wiley & Sons.

promotion: integrated marketing communication

LEARNING OBJECTIVES

This chapter will help you to:

1 understand the importance of planned, integrated communication in a marketing context;

2 appreciate the variety and scope of marketing communication objectives;

3 explain the use of promotional tools in the communication process;

4 identify the factors and constraints influencing the mix of communications tools that an organisation uses; and

5 define the main methods by which communications budgets are set.

Introduction

The promotional mix is the direct way in which an organisation attempts to communicate with various target audiences. It consists of five main elements, as shown in Figure 9.1. Advertising represents non-personal, mass communication; personal selling is at the other extreme, covering face-to-face, personally tailored messages. Sales promotion involves tactical, short-term incentives that encourage a target audience to behave in a certain way. Public relations is about creating and maintaining good-quality relationships with many interested groups (for example the media, shareholders and trade unions), not just with customers. Finally, direct marketing involves creating one-to-one relationships with individual customers, often in mass markets, and might involve mailings, telephone selling or electronic media. Some might classify direct marketing activities as forms of advertising, sales promotion or even personal selling, but this text treats direct marketing as a separate element of the promotional mix while acknowledging that it 'borrows' from the other elements.

Ideally, the marketer would like to invest extensively in every element of the mix. In a world of finite resources, however, choices have to be made about which activities are going to work together most cost-effectively with the maximum synergy to achieve the communications objectives of the organisation within a defined budget. This chapter, along with the two that follow it, will aim to explain why such choices are made.

Figure 9.1 The elements of the promotional mix

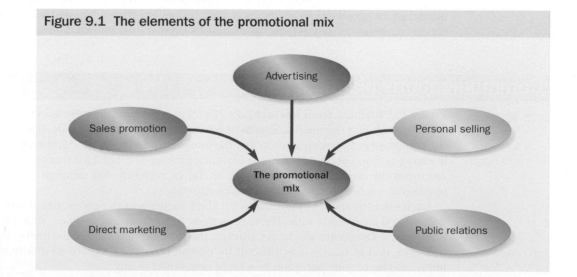

This chapter provides a general strategic overview by focusing on the integrated marketing communications planning process. Pickton and Broderick (2001, p. 67) define integrated marketing communication as

> . . . *a process which involves the management and organisation of all agents in the analysis, planning, implementation and control of all marketing communications contacts, media, messages and promotional tools focused at selected target audiences in such a way as to derive the greatest economy, efficiency, effectiveness, enhancement and coherence of marketing communications effort in achieving predetermined product and corporate marketing communications objectives.*

This definition emphasises the need to plan and manage the integrated marketing communications function carefully and strategically within the market context and using the full range of communications tools effectively and efficiently. This chapter, therefore, looks at some of the influences that shape an appropriate blend within the promotional mix, allowing the marketer to allocate communication resources most effectively.

eg Amazon.co.uk uses different elements of the promotional mix to communicate different messages to different audiences and to achieve different objectives. It often uses e-mail to communicate with its regular customers. Sometimes, it will send a personal message to tell the recipient about a new book or other merchandise that is relevant to them in the light of their past purchases. The message contains a hyperlink so that the recipient can easily visit the site to find out more and to pre-order the book before publication. E-mail is also used to offer or advertise incentives to customers. Virtual vouchers offering 'money off your next order' are sent to encourage customers to revisit the site and buy more merchandise. Personal messages are also used to inform the customer about a special offer that they can find on the site, for example three best-sellers for £10. Sometimes, though, Amazon wants to reach a wider audience, perhaps with the objective of attracting non-users to visit the site for the first time. Banner advertising on other websites generates awareness of Amazon, and its partnership with search engines, so that you can click on the Amazon logo to get details of books relevant to your search, also leads potential customers to the site. Mainstream media are used too. In March 2002, for example, Amazon placed an advertisement in *The Times* newspaper offering three CDs for £20 to entice people to visit the site to see what was on offer and perhaps to buy.

The main focus of the chapter is on developing a planning framework within which managerial decisions on communication activity can be made. Each stage in the planning flow is discussed in turn, with particular emphasis being given to relevant issues and the kind of integrated promotional mix that might subsequently be appropriate. It is becoming increasingly important for organisations to design and implement effective integrated marketing communications strategies as they expand their interests beyond their known domestic markets.

Communications planning model

Figure 9.2, adapted from Rothschild's (1987) communications decision sequence framework, includes all the main elements of marketing communications decision-making. Given the complexity of communication and the immense possibilities for getting some element of it wrong, a thorough and systematic planning process is crucial for minimising the risks. No organisation can afford either the financial or reputational damage caused by poorly planned or implemented communications campaigns.

Each element and its implications for the balancing of the promotional mix will now be defined and analysed in turn. The first element is the situation analysis, which has been split into three subsections: the target market, the product and the environment. Bear in mind, however, that in reality it is difficult to 'pigeon hole' things quite so neatly as this might imply, and there will, therefore, be a lot of cross-referencing.

Figure 9.2 The communications planning flow

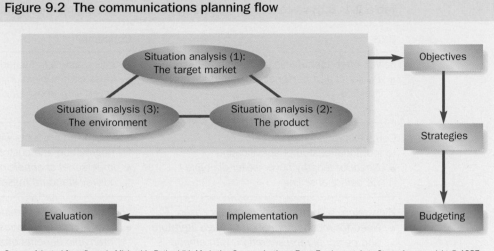

Source: Adapted from figure in Michael L. Rothschild, *Marketing Communications: From Fundamentals to Strategies*, copyright © 1987 D.C. Heath and Company. By permission of Houghton Mifflin Company.

■ Situation analysis (1): the target market

B2B or consumer market

The target market decision most likely to have an impact on the balancing of the overall promotional mix is whether the market is a consumer market or a B2B market. Recalling the comparison made in Chapter 3 between consumer and B2B markets, Table 9.1 summarises the impact of the main distinguishing features on the choice of promotional mix. The picture that emerges from this is that B2B markets are very much more dependent on the personal selling element, with advertising and sales promotion playing a strong supporting role.

The converse is generally true in consumer markets. A large number of customers each making relatively low-value, frequent purchases can be most efficiently contacted using mass media. Advertising, therefore, comes to the fore, with sales promotion a close second, while personal selling is almost redundant. Figure 9.3 shows this polarisation of B2B and consumer promotional mixes. This does, of course, represent sweeping generalisations

Figure 9.3 B2B vs consumer promotional mix

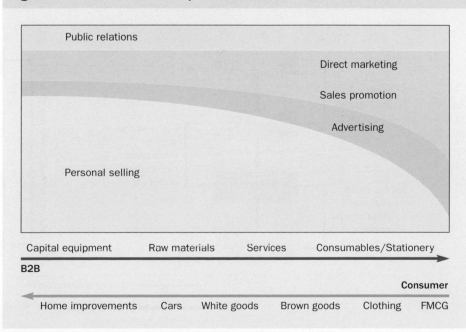

Table 9.1 B2B vs consumer marketing communications: characteristics and implications

B2B	Consumer
Fewer, often identifiable customers • *Personal and personalised communication feasible*	Usually mass, aggregated markets • *Mass communication, e.g. television advertising, most efficient and cost effective*
Complex products, often tailored to individual customer specification • *Need for lengthy buyer–seller dialogue via personal selling*	Standardised products with little scope for negotiation and customisation • *Impersonal channels of communication convey standard message*
High value, high-risk, infrequent purchases • *Need for much information through literature and personal representation, with emphasis on product performance and financial criteria*	Low value, low-risk, frequent purchases • *Less technical emphasis; status and other intangible benefits often stressed; incentives needed to build or break buying habits*
Rational decision-making process over time, with a buying centre taking responsibility • *Need to understand who plays what role and try to influence whole buying centre*	Short time scale, often impulse purchasing by an individual or family buying unit • *Need to understand who plays what role and to try to influence family*

about the nature of these markets, which need to be qualified. The product itself, for instance, will influence the shape of the mix, as will the nature of competitive and other environmental pressures. These will be addressed later (pp. 287 *et seq.* and 290 *et seq.*).

Push or pull strategy

Remember, however, that even consumer goods marketers are likely to have to consider B2B markets in dealing with channels of distribution. Figure 9.4 offers two strategies, push and pull, which emphasise different lines of communication (Oliver and Farris, 1989). With

Figure 9.4 Push–pull strategy

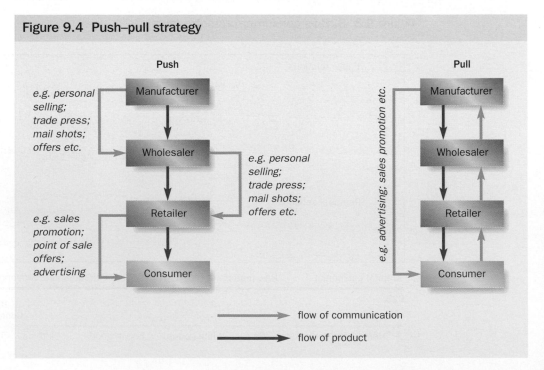

a push strategy, the manufacturer chooses to concentrate communications activity on the member of the distribution channel immediately below. This means that the wholesaler, in this example, has a warehouse full of product and thus an incentive to use communication to make a special effort to sell it quickly on to the retailer, who in turn promotes it to the end consumer. The product is thereby pushed down the distribution channel, with communication flowing from member to member in parallel with the product. There is little or no communication between manufacturer and consumer in this case.

In contrast, the pull strategy requires the manufacturer to create demand for the product through direct communication with the consumer. The retailers will perceive this demand and, in the interests of serving their customers' needs, will demand the product from their wholesaler, who will demand it from the manufacturer. This bottom-up approach pulls the product down the distribution channel, with communication flowing in the opposite direction from the product!

The reality is, of course, that manufacturers take a middle course, with some pull and some push to create more impetus for the product.

eg Pharmaceutical companies have to be very careful how they market prescription drugs. Although consumers are the end users of their products, it is doctors who do the prescribing and who are, therefore, the key decision makers. Companies effectively have to use push strategies to ensure that their products make it down the chain as far as the patient. There are, however, restrictions in the UK on what drugs companies can ethically do. Under government rules, companies dealing with the NHS can only offset a maximum of 7 per cent of their sales against marketing and promotion. Furthermore, promotional freebies given to individual doctors cannot be worth more than £5, thus branded pens, notepads and calendars are probably OK, but a meal out in a top restaurant with a sales representative isn't. In addition to advertising in medical journals, direct marketing and visits from sales representatives, an effective means of targeting doctors is through medical conferences, and many pharmaceutical companies spend a lot of money sponsoring conferences, exhibiting at them, and entertaining doctors. This is acceptable as long as the conference has clear educational content and any hospitality is 'secondary to the meeting, . . . appropriate and not out of proportion to the occasion'. Educational meetings focused on particular areas of medicine are very useful to the marketers as they help doctors to understand the relative performance of different drugs, and they hear it in detail from reputable colleagues rather than just from a sales representative making a quick visit to the surgery (Benady, D., 2002).

Buyer readiness of the target market

In terms of message formulation, a further tempering influence on communication with consumers will be the buyer readiness stage of the target market. It is most unlikely that a target market is going to undergo an instant conversion from total ignorance of a product's existence to queuing up at the checkout to buy it. Particularly in consumer markets, it is more likely that people will pass through a number of stages en route from initial awareness to desire for the product. A number of models have been proposed – for example Strong's (1925) AIDA model, which put various labels on these stages, as shown in Figure 9.5 – but broadly speaking, they all amount to the same sequence.

Cognitive. The cognitive stage involves sowing the seeds of a thought, i.e. catching the target market's attention and generating straightforward awareness of the product: 'Yes, I know this product exists.' As part of the launch of the Mini, for example, BMW used media advertising, PR and hospitality events to get the updated brand known and understood as being something different and special.

Affective. The affective stage involves creating or changing an attitude, i.e. giving the consumer sufficient information (whether factual or image based) to pass judgement on the product and to develop positive feelings towards it: 'I understand what this product can do for me, and I like the idea of it.'

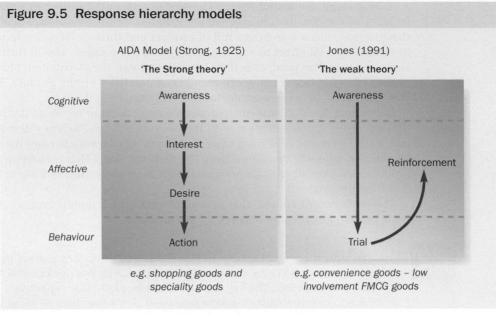

Figure 9.5 Response hierarchy models

e.g. shopping goods and speciality goods

e.g. convenience goods – low involvement FMCG goods

The 2001 UK general election threw up some worrying statistics. It was the lowest voter turnout overall since 1918 and only 39 per cent of 18–24-year-olds bothered to vote. The Electoral Commission, therefore, is looking at ways of overcoming young people's apathy towards voting. Part of the problem lies in the methods of voting available. For the general election in 2001, an individual could either have a postal vote or go to their local polling station to write a cross on a ballot paper. It seems as though that was just too much like hard work for many potential voters. More than half of 18–24-year-olds are in favour of telephone or Internet voting instead of the traditional methods. The other part of the problem is an education and communications issue. Young people are not interested in politics and don't see the point of voting. The Electoral Commission and the politicians are thus faced with the task of convincing young people that their votes can make a difference on the issues that matter to them.

Changing attitudes will begin in schools as social studies, including voting processes and the creation of legislation as part of the syllabus, becomes part of the national curriculum for 11–16-year-olds. For the current group of 18–24-year-olds, however, the May 2002 local elections were heralded by a radio and poster campaign on the theme of 'Votes are Power' to encourage them to turn out to vote. Overcoming such deep-seated apathy, however, is going to be a long-term task which will need all the tools and skills of the professional marketing communicators (Thurtle, 2002).

Behaviour. The behaviour stage involves precipitating action, i.e. where the strength of the positive attitudes generated in the affective stage leads the consumer to desire the product and to do something about acquiring it: 'I want this product and I'm going to go and buy it.' Many press advertisements incorporating a mail order facility are operating at this level.

The speed with which a target market passes through these stages depends on the kind of product, the target market involved and the marketing strategies adopted by the organisation. Nevertheless, each stage becomes increasingly more difficult to implement, since more is being asked of the consumer. Generating awareness, the first stage, is relatively easy as it involves little risk or commitment from the consumer, and may even operate unconsciously. The second stage needs some effort from consumers if it is to be successful, because they are being asked to assimilate information, process it and form an opinion. The third and final stage requires the most involvement – actually getting up and doing something, which is likely to involve paying out money!

Botton Village

Botton Village, one of eleven communities comprising the Camphill Village Trust, is described as a very special place where 135 people with special needs live in extended family settings in a community that utilises their skills in various craft and agricultural activities. There are 5 farms and many workshops on the site selling goods such as hand-crafted toys and organically grown farm produce. Situated in the North Yorkshire Moors national park, the community needs to raise sufficient funds from donors to supplement its income from the state and from its trading activities.

Fund raising is essential for supporting new projects and supplementing income. Open days and fairs are held during the year and a distribution system enables some of the produce, such as foods and toys, to be sold both through local retailers and internationally. It has a regular net surplus income of around £2.0m. per year raised largely through highly professional and targeted direct marketing. A single mailing can generate between £5,200 and £9,400 per thousand donors mailed in one segment. As a smaller charity, it is not easy for Botton Village to stand out against the better-known charities seeking donations. It has a very small marketing budget, no full- or part-time fund raisers and it needs external professional advice in developing campaigns.

The main problem facing any charity is the danger of donation fatigue or overload. Sometimes mailing lists are shared and special appeals can divert funds, an important obstacle if the donor has a finite limit to spend with

Photograph showing the activities at Botton which appears in promotional material gives donors an insight into the work they are supporting.

Source: Botton Village/Camphill Village Trust Ltd.

charities. It has been estimated that a charity donor can receive up to 12 appeals during a year. The Botton Village approach to mailing its 76,000 active donors is to maintain communication and nurture the relationship throughout the year, not just during a special appeal. After the first donation, a thank-you letter is sent within 48 hours, regardless of the size of donation. An early response is considered important for building the relationship and has been found to affect future giving. Donors also have a wide choice of options, including donation through the Gift Aid scheme, legacies, and a regular payment plan.

Four 'warm' mailings per year are sent out, linked with a newsletter that focuses on the people helped within the

community and outlines key activities and future events. It encourages donors to feel involved and to see tangible effects from their giving. The mailing letters are all personalised and vary in appeal depending on the donor plan adopted. All donations are logged on the database and if no further donations are received during the following year, the donor is sent a reminder. If further contact produces no results, the donor is placed in the group that receives only a Christmas card, before finally being dropped after a further two years. Botton is concerned not to be seen as intrusive in its mailings and so donors can opt out of regular communication at any time. Even though some switch to Christmas contact only, donations still run at a high level from this group.

The direct marketing group has been very successful and is now supported by the website. Botton can receive as high as a 50 per cent response rate from some mailings, whereas typical figures are 15 per cent for 'warm' mailings and less than 1 per cent for 'cold' mailings. Even when it shares lists with other charities, it can achieve response rates of around 5 per cent rather than the norm of 1 per cent. The first mailing is crucial and the specially developed pack focuses on the work of the community, its ideals and the lives of those that it is designed to help. By adopting a sensitive and caring approach along with professional marketing, Botton has achieved many of its targets for fund raising.

Sources: *Marketing Week* (1999); http://www.ukonline.co.uk/botton.village

The Strong (1925) theory of communication proposed these stages as forming a logical flow of events driven by marketing communication. Advertising, for example, creates the initial awareness, stimulates the interest and then the desire for the product, and only then does trial take place. In other words, the attitude and opinion are formed before the consumer ever gets near the product. There is, however, another school of thought that maintains that it does not always happen like that. The weak theory of communication (Jones, 1991) accepts that marketing communication can generate the awareness, but then the consumer might well try the product without having formed any particular attitude or opinion of it. Only then, after the purchase and product trial, does the marketing communication begin to contribute to attitude and opinion working alongside consumer experience of the product. This would make sense for low-involvement products, the frequently purchased boring goods about which it is difficult to get emotional, such as washing powder.

A consumer might see a television advertisement for a new brand of washing powder and then forget about it until the next trip to the supermarket. The consumer sees that new brand on the shelf and thinks, 'Oh yes, I saw an ad for that – I'll give it a try' and buys a packet. Having tried the product, the consumer might decide that it is quite good and then start to pay more attention to the advertising content as a way of legitimising and reinforcing that opinion.

Whatever the route through the response hierarchy, the unique characteristics of each stage imply that differing promotional mixes may be called for to maximise the creative benefits and cost-effectiveness of the different promotional tools. Figure 9.6 suggests that advertising is most appropriate at the earliest stage, given its capacity to reach large numbers of people relatively cheaply and quickly with a simple message. Sales promotions can also bring a product name to the fore and help in the affective stage: using a sample that has been delivered to the door certainly generates awareness and aids judgement and recognition of a product. Adding a coupon to the sample's packaging is also an incentive to move into the behaviour stage, buying a full-sized package.

Notice that in Figure 9.6 the role of advertising diminishes as the behaviour stage moves closer and personal selling comes to the fore. Advertising can only reiterate and reinforce what consumers already know about the product, and if this wasn't enough to stimulate action the last time they saw/heard it, it may not be so this time either. At this point, potential buyers may just need a last bit of persuasion to tip them over the edge into buying, and that last kick may be best delivered by a sales representative who can reiterate the product benefits, tailoring communication to suit the particular customer's needs and doubts in a two-way dialogue. With many FMCG products sold in supermarkets, however, this is not a feasible option, and the manufacturer relies on the packaging and, to some extent, the sales promotions to do the selling at the point of sale without human intervention. Many FMCG products, therefore, strive for distinctively coloured packaging that stands out on the supermarket shelf, commanding attention. This issue will be readdressed in the following subsection.

In reality, individuals within the target market may pass through the stages at different times or may take longer to pass from one stage to the next. This means that it may be necessary to develop an integrated promotional mix recognising that the various elements

Figure 9.6 Buyer readiness stages and the promotional mix

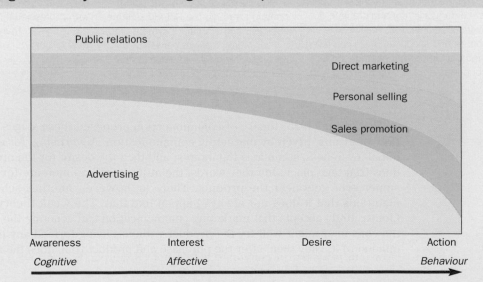

are appealing to sub-segments at different readiness stages, with imagery and content tailored accordingly. The implementation of the various elements may be almost simultaneous, with some fine-tuning of the campaign over the longer term.

Knowledge of the target market is an important foundation stone for all of the communication decisions that you are going to make. The more you know about the people you want to talk to, the more likely you are to create successful communication. This does not only mean having a clear demographic profile of the target market, but also having as much detail as possible about their attitudes, beliefs and aspirations, and about their shopping, viewing and reading habits. In addition it is important to understand their relationship with your product and their perceptions of it. This will be explained in relation to communication objectives on pp. 293 *et seq.*

This is a good time for you to look back at Chapter 4 and revise some of the methods of segmenting markets, whether consumer or B2B, since the criteria by which the target market is defined (including product-oriented criteria) may well have a strong influence not only on the broad issue of balancing the promotional mix, but also on the finer detail of media choice and creative content.

■ Situation analysis (2): the product

Inextricably linked with consideration of the target market is consideration of the *product* involved. This section will look again at the area of B2B and consumer products in the light of the influence of other product characteristics, and then explore the specific influence of the product life cycle on the promotional mix.

B2B and consumer products

It is simplistic in the extreme to define a product either as a B2B purchase, personal selling being the best way to sell it, or as a consumer product, which must be advertised. Other product characteristics or the buying habits associated with the product may make such a distinction meaningless.

eg An illustration of this 'grey area' is the sale of double glazing to domestic householders. Strictly speaking, this is a consumer market, in that the product is being purchased by individuals or families for private consumption. There are, however, a number of features suggesting that this particular product has more in common with typical B2B purchases than with other consumer goods. It is an expensive, infrequent purchase with a high level of technical personalisation required to match the product exactly with the customer's needs. It involves a fairly rational decision-making process that takes place over time, and there is a high demand for product information and negotiation before commitment to purchase is made. To the buyer, it is a high-risk purchase that may well involve several members of the family (effectively acting as a buying centre) and will almost certainly involve a great deal of persuasion, reassurance and dialogue from a sales representative.

All these product and customer-oriented characteristics completely override the superficial definition of a consumer product and point to a different kind of promotional mix. Advertising, along with website content, play a role in generating awareness of a double glazing company's existence and in laying the foundations for corporate and product image building. They also prepare the way for the sales representative, since a potential customer who has seen an advertisement for a sales representative's company or has read the information on the website will have an impression of what kind of company this is, and will feel less uneasy about the sales representative's credibility and trustworthiness. The personal selling element is, however, the most important and effective element of this mix because of the need for information, product tailoring and negotiation in the affective and behaviour stages. It is also cost-effective in relation to the likely value of a single order.

At one end of the consumer product spectrum, a frequently purchased, low-involvement, low unit price bar of chocolate would not, of course, warrant such an investment in personal selling to millions of end consumers, even if such an exercise were logistically possible. The marketing would be more likely to conform to the standard mix, emphasising mass communication through advertising.

eg   Another example chosen to illustrate the grey area between consumer and B2B markets is that of day-to-day consumable office supplies, such as pencils, pens and paperclips, for small businesses. This has more in common with the chocolate bar than the double glazing, although technically it is a B2B product, in that it is used to support the production of goods for resale. Compared with most B2B purchases, it is a routine rebuy, a low-priced, low-risk, low-involvement purchase, probably delegated to an individual who goes out to the nearest stationer's or office supplies retailer at lunchtime with the contents of the petty cash tin. It is simply not cost-effective to use personal selling of such a range of products to that buyer who belongs to a large and ill-defined target market (there are thousands of small businesses, in every kind of activity and market, and geographically widespread) and who makes such small-value purchases. At best, personal selling should be targeted at the stationer's or the office supplies retailer.

The two examples above serve as a warning that some B2B products behave more like consumer products and vice versa.

■ The product life-cycle stage

One further product characteristic that may affect the approach to communication is the product life-cycle stage reached (see pp. 195 *et seq.*). Since the overall marketing objectives tend to change as the product moves through each stage, it is likely that the specific communications objectives will also change. Different tasks need to be fulfilled and thus the balance of the promotional mix will alter.

Introduction. With the launch of a new consumer product, it is likely that there will be high initial expenditure on the promotional mix. Advertising will ensure that the product name and benefits become known and spread quickly among the target market, while sales promotions, perhaps based on coupons and sampling, help to generate trial of the product. Sales promotions will also be used in conjunction with intense personal selling effort to gain retailer acceptance of the product.

Growth. Communications activity is likely to be a little less intense as the product begins to find its own impetus and both retailers and consumers make repeat purchases. There might also be less emphasis on awareness generation and information giving, and more on long-term image and loyalty building. As competitors launch similar products, it is important to ensure that differential advantage is maintained, and that customers know exactly why they should continue to buy the original product rather than switching over to a competitor. This could mean a shift towards advertising as a prime means of image creation that works over a longer period.

Maturity. The maturity stage is likely to be a defensive or holding operation, since competitors with younger products may be threatening to take custom away from the product. Most people know about the product, most people (apart from a few laggards) who are likely to try it already have done so. Thus the role of communication is reminding (about the brand image and values) and reassurance (about having chosen the right product), probably through mass advertising. In B2B markets, this stage is likely to be about further developing and consolidating relationships with customers in preparation for newer products in your portfolio.

Decline. Marketing communication is not going to rescue a product that is clearly on its way out; it can only stave off the inevitable for a while. The majority of consumers and, for that matter, distributors, will have already moved on to other products, leaving only a few laggards. A certain level of reminder advertising and sales promotion might keep them in the market for this product for a while, but eventually even they will drift off. There is little point in diverting resources that could be better used on the next new product.

eg In launching T&T, a new fruit juice-based carbonated soft drink brand, in the UK the manufacturers wanted to gain retail support and to target the brand at teenagers, not only creating awareness of the brand, but taking the consumer right through to desire and action. In 2003 T&T developed and marketed the 'had enough of pop' campaign signalling a shift to move away from the plethora of imitation pop shows that started to appear on national television and embark on developing a new territory within the tweens/teens market that adopts a more unconventional, rebellious and 'cool' brand attitude to capitalise on the growing anti-mainstream pop music scene amongst this age group. Significant changes were made to packaging artwork, formulations and communications.

Source: T&T Beverages Ltd.

eg Sunny Delight was launched in the UK market in 1998. Within two years, it had become a firm favourite with £150m. of sales, second only to Coca-Cola in the UK soft drinks market. It was marketed as 'The great stuff kids love' and the label on the bottle presented it as a 'vitamin-enriched citrus drink'. Parents believed that somehow because it was a fruit-based drink it was healthier for their kids and therefore didn't mind how much of it they drank. During 2000, however, the brand began to attract adverse publicity as parents and food lobby groups cottoned on to the fact that Sunny Delight was only 5 per cent fruit juice and actually contained just as much sugar as Cola drinks. In the year to October 2001, sales fell by 38 per cent. In spring 2002, therefore, Procter and Gamble, Sunny Delight's owner, relaunched a reformulated Sunny Delight brand. New flavours, such as apple, blackcurrant and kiwi, were introduced and the amount of sugar has been cut by 84 per cent. The packaging has also been redesigned to make it look less like a fruit juice. The Original Sunny Delight is still sold alongside the new products. The total investment in the revitalisation of the brand is thought to be some £20m., including a £5m. advertising campaign and £7m. in direct marketing and sales promotion (Dignam, 2002; Poulter, 2002; Rogers, 2002).

The above analysis assumes that a product takes an unexceptional course through the classical stages of the life cycle. Many consumer goods, however, are revamped at some time during the maturity stage to extend their life cycle. In such a case, there is every reason to rethink the communications package and treat the process more like a new product launch. There is much to communicate both to the trade and to the consumer about the 'new improved' brand, the increased value for money, the enhanced performance, more stylish looks or whatever aspects are being emphasised. In a sense, this stage is even more difficult than the new product launch, as the marketer has to tread a fine line between overturning old preconceptions about the product, convincing the market that there is something new to consider and confusing and alienating existing users who might think that the familiar, comforting brand values have been thrown out.

The life-cycle concept, as discussed on pp. 198 *et seq.* does have its problems, and in the context of marketing communication, its unthinking, rigid application as a primary basis for communications planning is dangerous. If a product is assumed to be mature/declining, then the application of a communications package appropriate to that stage may well hasten its demise. There are other, more relevant factors, both internal and external, which should have a far greater bearing on the planning process. Some of the external factors will now be discussed.

■ Situation analysis (3): the environment

Again, some revision of an earlier chapter might stand you in good stead here. Chapter 2 analysed the marketing environment in some detail. This section will, therefore, only look at ways in which environmental elements specifically affect communications.

Social and cultural aspects of the environment will mostly have an impact on the message element of communication. What is said about the product and the scenario within which it is depicted in advertisements will reflect what is socially acceptable and culturally familiar to the target market. There must be something that they can recognise, identify with and/or wish to aspire to, if they are going to remember the message, and particularly if they are expected to act on it. This reinforces what was said on pp. 281 *et seq.* about the necessity of knowing the target market well.

Organisations are particularly keen to spot changes and shifts in social mores and then to capitalise on them, often creating a bandwagon effect. The 'green' issue is a good example of this. Many companies perceived that there was pressure on them to produce environmentally friendlier products, but rather than lose time in developing really new alternatives (and risk lagging behind their competitors), a few simply created new advertising messages and emphasised green-oriented product claims on their packaging to create the desired image. However, questionable approaches have been widely publicised, such as labelling washing-up liquid 'phosphate free', when that kind of product doesn't ever contain phosphate anyway, and emphasising that packaging can be recycled when the recycling facilities do not exist, leading to confusion and suspicion in the consumer's mind about all green claims.

eg During the 1990s the safety of silicone breast implants was publicly questioned on several occasions. Activated by anti-implant groups such as Silicone Support and Survivors of Silicone, stories in television documentaries and in the press linked the implants with silicone poisoning and sometimes deformity caused by poor surgery. The Conservatives (twice) and the Labour Party both instigated reviews in the UK that could have resulted in the banning or severe restriction of implant use. That would have been bad news for McGhan breast implants from the market leader Inner Medical. A successful PR campaign was mounted by McGhan to remind journalists, politicians and the wider public that breast implants were used not just for cosmetic reasons, but also for reconstruction after a mastectomy (*PR Week*, 1999).

The most recent governmental review was set up in 1997 and concluded on scientific grounds that silicone was as safe as any other material used in implants, although there were grounds for improving the information available to women so that they could make informed choices. The Independent Review Group consists of people with no vested interests in the subject, and its first report was published by the Chief Medical Officer in May 1998. The sources included implanted women, doctors, lawyers, women's support groups and Members of Parliament capable of studying the scientific evidence from the USA (http://www.silicone-review.gov.uk). Although the industry had a direct opportunity to put its case to the review group, the PR campaign helped to ensure that an alternative view was presented to a public that was starting to believe the negative publicity about implants.

A more general criticism of advertisers' influence in the social and cultural area is about their alleged use and reinforcement of stereotypes. The advertisers argue that they simply

The controversy continues, however. The European Commission is considering tightening up the rules on breast implants which would mean that implants would only be available for those aged 18 or over; there would have to be independent counselling before and after surgery; and there would be compulsory national registers of every implant operation carried out (Castle, 2001). For the manufacturers of silicone implants, this is still better than an outright ban, although that has not been ruled out as studies into their long-term safety are ongoing.

reflect society as it is, and that it is not their business to change it – they *respond* to the customer's changing attitudes and lifestyle. Should there, however, be concern that if people see stereotypes being constantly presented through advertising as the norm, and even as states to be aspired to, then maybe the impetus to question their validity and to break them will be less urgent? This is a complex 'chicken and egg' debate that you may want to pursue for yourself outside these pages. There are no easy answers.

To be fair to the advertisers, the whole area of stereotypes does perhaps present one of the great insoluble dilemmas of mass communication. In moving away from one stereotype, it is too easy to replace it with another. Because the advertiser is trying to appeal to a relatively large number of individuals (even in a niche market), it is impossible to create an image that reflects every member of the target market in detail. What emerges, therefore, is a superficial sketch of the essential characteristics of that group and its aspirations, i.e. a stereotype! Thus the stereotypical housewife who lives in the kitchen and is fulfilled through the quality of her cooking has been usurped at the opposite extreme by the equally unrealistic power-dressing, independent dragon of the boardroom with the slightest whiff of Chanel and femininity. It seems that the advertisers cannot win.

eg Stereotypes can provide a rich seam of humour in advertising. In a television advertisement for Bounty kitchen roll, two big, hairy, unshaven labourers dressed in pretty print frocks and dire wigs, 'Barbara' and 'Maureen', race each other to see whose kitchen roll can clean 'her' hob without disintegrating. It offers an ironic, self-deprecating twist on the well-established and well-understood housewife stereotype that appeals to the modern woman for whom cleaning a hob is not the single most satisfying experience in life. It has to be said too that the formula works: the message that Bounty is stronger and better is clearly stated and demonstrated by the advertisement and perhaps is made all the more memorable by the jokey execution. Another jokey execution ran into trouble over stereotyping, however. Retailer WH Smith ran a series of advertisements featuring a middle-class family from the south of England visiting their rather unsophisticated relatives in Newcastle upon Tyne who were all portrayed as extremely overweight and speaking in broad Geordie accents. All the characters were played by popular actor Nicholas Lyndhurst. The ITC received 129 complaints from people who saw the advertisements as offensive stereotypes of Newcastle people and/or overweight people. The ITC decided that the portrayal of overweight people was exaggerated and unreal and that it was just sufficient to reduce the risk of causing distress or harm. The Geordie stereotyping was felt to have remained within the boundaries of acceptable humour and was unlikely to have caused much offence. The complaints were not, therefore, upheld (http://www.itc.org.uk).

No communications plan can be shaped without some reference to what competitors are doing or are likely to do, given the necessity of emphasising the differential advantage and positioning of the product in relation to theirs. This could affect every stage of the planning, from the definition of objectives, through the creative strategy, to the setting of budgets. These themes will be taken up under the appropriate headings later in this chapter, and will also feature in the chapters on the individual tools of the promotional mix.

Another important factor to take into account is the political/regulatory environment, as discussed in Chapter 2. Some products are restricted as to where and when they can be advertised. In the UK, for instance, cigarette advertising is not permitted on television. Restrictions may also exist about what can or must be said or shown in relation to the product. Toy advertising cannot imply a social disadvantage through not owning a product, and must also indicate the price of the toy. More generally, advertising aimed at children cannot encourage them to pester their parents to purchase (not that they normally need encouragement). Some regulations are enshrined in law, while others are imposed and applied through monitoring watchdog bodies such as the Advertising Standards Authority. Professional bodies, such as the UK's Institute of Sales Promotion or the Direct Marketing Association, often develop codes of practice to which their members undertake to adhere. As yet, no unified codes have been developed that apply across Europe.

corporate social responsibility *in action*

Don't drink and advertise!

The advertising and promotion of certain product categories such as alcohol are very closely regulated in the UK. The ASA (Advertising Standards Authority) regulates print, cinema, outdoor and electronic media and sales promotions while the ITC (Independent Television Commission) and the RA (Radio Authority) regulate broadcast media, although the ASA and ITC codes on alcoholic drinks are very similar. The ASA code, *British Codes of Advertising and Sales Promotion*, allows humour in advertising, but says that advertisements should not lead people towards unwise drinking habits. They should be socially responsible and not encourage excessive drinking. The code also states that advertisements should not in any way target the under-18s in terms of their content, imagery or their use of real or fictional characters, nor should advertisements appear in any medium if more than 25 per cent of its audience is under 18. People in advertisements shown drinking alcohol cannot appear to be under 25 years old.

Advertisers also have to be careful of the claims they make for their products: they can give factual information about the strength of the drink, but cannot make strength or the drink's capacity to get you drunk the major theme of the advertisement; they cannot claim that the drink will make you more popular, more sexy, or more successful; and they cannot

claim that people who drink are brave, tough or daring for doing so. Advertisements cannot show alcohol being consumed in situations in which it would be dangerous or in which concentration is essential, for example driving or operating machinery.

These rules inevitably lead to complaints to the ITC and the ASA as advertisers strive to understand where the boundaries of acceptability lie, and as consumers put their own interpretations on messages (the invisible penis – see below – being a prime example of an advertiser being criticised for something that isn't actually in the advertisement at all!). In 2000, complaints were made to the ASA over a poster campaign for the brand Red Square. One poster featured the boxer Lennox Lewis and the words 'energising Red Square and Lennox Lewis – a winning combination'. The ASA felt that the association between sport and alcohol implied that alcohol was healthy, and furthermore, that the use of the word 'energising' could encourage people to consume the product before sport or exercise. 'Energising' was also criticised as misleading because alcohol is essentially a depressant. Nor did the ASA like the use of 'winning combination' as it suggests a link between alcohol and sporting achievement. The company was asked to drop the energising claim altogether and to change its overall approach in future.

Posters for Smirnoff Vodka have also been the subject of ASA scrutiny. One poster showed a naked man (and

complainants believed that his penis was actually visible) sliding down a banister with a large round finial at the bottom. The slogan was 'If Smirnoff made painkillers'. While the advertiser made it clear that the man had actually been wearing flesh-coloured pants, the ASA felt that the public belief that there was a visible penis in the picture was sufficient to render the poster offensive and therefore that complaint was upheld. Not so much above-the-line as below-the-belt advertising. Perhaps more seriously, the ASA also decided that although the poster was clearly meant to be humorous and surreal, it did depict drunken activity and could encourage excessive drinking, and therefore the advertiser should change the approach in future.

By no means are all complaints upheld. The ITC looked into complaints that a television advertisement for Miller Genuine Draft condoned and encouraged drinking and driving. The advertisement showed members of the rock band Fun Lovin' Criminals getting bored in a traffic jam, drinking their Miller Genuine Draft and then performing an impromptu concert at the side of the road. The complaints were not upheld because, the ITC felt, the band were clearly shown only as passengers in a stationary car. There was no implication that any of those seen drinking were or had been doing any driving.

Sources: http://www.asa.org.uk; http://www.itc.org.uk

■ Objectives

Now that the background is in place and there exists a detailed profile of the customer, the product and the environment, it is possible to define detailed objectives for the communications campaign.

eg Research undertaken by GlaxoSmithKline, maker of the Ribena range of concentrated blackcurrant juice, showed that consumers tended to use more squash if they kept it ready-diluted in the fridge. The company wanted, therefore, to find a way of persuading mums to make up bulk quantities of Ribena and store it in the fridge. A sales promotion was run in which a free jug was attached to 2 litre bottles of Ribena. The jug would fit either on to a shelf or into a fridge door compartment. The promotion was run over July and August in the major supermarket chains and over 1 million jugs were given away. The impact on brand sales was significant: a 37 per cent increase over the equivalent period in the previous year (http://www.spca.org.uk).

To encourage greater use of Ribena concentrated blackcurrant juice, the company offered a jug which would allow larger quantities of diluted juice to be kept in the fridge.

Source: GlaxoSmithKline.

Table 9.2, based on the work of DeLozier (1975), summarises and categorises possible communications objectives. The first group relates to awareness, information and attitude generation, while the second group is about affecting behaviour. The final group consists of corporate objectives, a timely reminder that marketing communications planning is not only about achieving the goals of brand managers or marketing managers, but also about the contribution of marketing activity to the wider strategic good of the organisation.

What Table 9.2 does not do is to distinguish between short-, medium- and long-term objectives. Obviously, the short-term activities are the most pressing and are going to demand more detailed planning, but there does still need to be an appreciation of what happens next. The nature and character of medium- and longer-term objectives will inevitably be shaped by short-term activity (and its degree of success), but it is also true that short-term activity can only be fully justified when it is put into the context of the wider picture.

Finally, Table 9.2 also stresses the importance of precision, practicality and measurability in setting objectives. Vague, open objectives such as 'to increase awareness of the product' are insufficient. Who do you want to become aware of the product: the retail trade, the general public, or a specific target segment? How much awareness are you aiming to generate within the defined group and within what time scale? A more useful objective might therefore be 'to generate 75 per cent awareness of the product within three months among A, B and C1 home-owners aged between 25 and 40 with incomes in excess of £25,000 per annum who are interested in opera and the environment'.

Table 9.2 Possible communications objectives	
Area	*Objective*
Cognitive	Clarify customer needs
	Increase brand awareness
	Increase product knowledge
Affective	Improve brand image
	Improve company image
	Increase brand preference
Behaviour	Stimulate search behaviour
	Increase trial purchases
	Increase repurchase rate
	Increase word-of-mouth recommendation
Corporate	Improved financial position
	Increase flexibility of corporate image
	Increase cooperation from the trade
	Enhance reputation with key publics
	Build up management ego

Source: Copyright © 1975 The Estate of the late Professor M. Wayne DeLozier.

Until such precise definitions of objectives have been made, the rest of the planning process cannot really go ahead – how can decisions be made if you don't really know what it is you are aiming for? Precise objectives also provide the foundation for monitoring, feedback and assessment of the success of the communications mix. There is at least something against which to measure actual performance.

■ Strategies

Having defined objectives, it is now necessary to devise strategies for achieving them. The analysis done so far may already have established the broad balance of the promotional mix, but there is still the task of developing the fine detail of what the actual message is to be, how best to frame it and what medium or media can be used to communicate it most efficiently and effectively.

eg With the average viewer being exposed to 290 commercials per week and a barrage of alternative brands in the stores, interactive television (iTV) can make the advertiser stand out. The technology means that the product is exposed to the potential customer in real time and a transaction, whether a purchase or a request for more information, can be completed before a competitor gets a chance to present an alternative. That is especially important when over 40 per cent of the advertisements to which we are exposed are forgotten within one week (Turznski, 1999). Dedicated home shopping, banking and holiday channels can be ready for consumer action at the touch of a button. As Knight (2002) points out, companies are starting to use iTV to generate quality sales leads, provide further information and to generate customer feedback. Nissan, for example, used iTV to allow interested consumers to see a video of the vehicle, order brochures and/or request a test drive. The company claimed that a large number of brochures and test drives were generated and that the quality of sales leads generated was very high. Procter and Gamble too has found iTV a good medium for developing closer relationships with its customers. Using the Sky digital channels, during Pampers advertisements, consumers could access the Pampers iTV Baby World Service offering advice and information for mothers, a newsletter and a baby picture gallery so that you could upload a photo of your little darling and see him or her on the telly (*Marketing*, 2001). With the continued growth of digital television and the further development of the technology, and as targeting becomes ever more sophisticated, iTV looks set to become a mainstream part of integrated communications strategies.

Designing the message content, structure and format poses questions for managing any element of the promotional mix. Message content is about what the sender wants to say, while message structure is about how to say it in terms of propositions and arguments.

eg The ITC received 125 complaints about a television advertisement for Pampers Total Care nappies. The advertisement claimed that the product could not only 'handle pee but also soft poo'. Complainants found these words rather offensive and furthermore felt that the graphics used to demonstrate the product in action had put them off their food! In its judgement, the ITC felt that the words simply represented the way many mothers describe babies' bodily functions and thus were not offensive and that the graphics were innocuous. The complaints were not, therefore, upheld. Seventeen complaints against Curry's, the electrical goods retailer were, however, upheld. The retailer had advertised a sale featuring a number of specific products with the words 'Tomorrow only. Limited stock' superimposed. Complainants had found, however, that when they went to the store, they found that 'limited stock' meant that only the first 10 customers purchasing each featured item were actually offered the advertised sale price. Everyone else was expected to pay the full retail price. The ITC's decision hinged on the interpretation of the term 'limited stock' and the view that most people would think it meant the absolute number of items available rather than just the (rather more limited) number available at the reduced price. The ITC decided that the advertising had been misleading and ordered it not to be reshown (http://www.itc.org.uk).

The message format depends on the choice of media used for transmitting or transferring the message. This will determine whether sight, sound, colour or other stimuli can be used effectively. These are important themes, which will be further addressed in the context of each element of the promotional mix in the following five chapters. A money-off sales promotion, for example, is certainly appropriate for stimulating short-term sales of a product, but will it cheapen the product's quality image in the eyes of the target market? Is the target market likely to respond to a cash saving, or would they be more appreciative of a charity tie-in where a donation is made to a specific charity for every unit sold? The latter suggestion has the added benefit of enhancing corporate as well as brand image, and is also less easy for the competition to copy.

With advertising in particular, the organisation might use a character or a celebrity to communicate a message on its behalf to give it source credibility. The audience will see the spokesperson as the source of the message and thus might pay more attention to it or interpret it as having more credibility (Hirschman, 1987).

marketing *in action*

Would you buy anything from these people?

Using celebrities in advertising can make a big impact. The charity Respect for Animals made a 60-second film called *Fur and Against*, attacking the use of fur in the fashion industry to coincide with the 2002 London Fashion Week. The film featured actors Jude Law and Sadie Frost, singers Sir Paul McCartney, George Michael, Moby, Chrissy Hynde and Mel C., fashion designer Stella McCartney and model Helena Christensen. The advertising agency that made the film argued that 'The use of celebrity works on three levels: to create a powerful anti-fur message to the general public; as a celebrity-to-celebrity message to the fashion industry; and on a craft level' (as quoted by Benady, A., 2002). There is also a view, however, that the use of celebrities can be dangerous, especially for a charity, because it could trivialise the message or even

▶

sabotage it. There should be a clear link between the celebrity and the cause. Thus Michael J. Fox makes sense as a spokesperson for Parkinson's disease, but David Ginola and landmines is a more problematic linkage. Sabotage may be inadvertent: the use of Geri Halliwell in a breast cancer campaign created concern among younger women rather than raising awareness among the real at-risk target group of older women. There is also a risk that celebrities will fail to live up to the high ethical standards they endorse. Naomi Campbell appeared in a PR stunt on behalf of PETA, 'I'd rather go naked than wear fur', yet not long afterwards was back on the catwalk . . . modelling fur.

Even for mainstream FMCG goods, experts constantly stress the need to achieve a good fit between the celebrity and the product. Coca-Cola is endorsed by teen pop star Christina Aguilera, while Britney Spears represents Pepsi. She fits the young profile of customers that Pepsi is trying to attract and as she grows up from 'kid star to broad based pop star', as Pepsi puts it, Pepsi's marketing will evolve accordingly. Her contract with Pepsi is estimated to be worth around $2m. per year. Once a celebrity has been associated with a product, their every appearance in the media acts as a reminder. And yet, 'Success depends on the personality of the celebrity and how well they fit with the brand and the advertising idea. Spurious celebrity campaigns don't work', said one agency. A series of John Cleese advertisements for

Sainsbury's failed partly because the agency assumed that his Basil Fawlty character per se would sell the product and forgot the core advertising skills of engaging the audience and creating a believable scenario and claims for the product. 'Where a celebrity is used for celebrity's sake they rarely have the power to motivate consumption and purchase. When they are used in a way that's relevant to the product advertised, in an engaging, believable manner, then the ad has a lot of power' (Don Dillon, European Regional Director, McCann Erickson, as quoted by Cowen, 2000).

There is a need, therefore, to find a celebrity who sums up the values that you want to associate with the product and then spend a lot of time and money building up the association between celebrity and product. There is a risk of 'promiscuous' celebrities diluting the effect of the association by endorsing so many products that nobody knows what they really stand for. There is also a risk that a celebrity will 'misbehave', courting bad publicity, or that they will be caught doing something that questions their endorsement of the brand. In October 2001, for example, Pepsi's Britney Spears was caught drinking Coke by an Australian newspaper. Oops I did it again, as the diva herself might say.

While not quite in the same league as Britney, Gary Lineker, ex-England football captain turned television presenter, signed a £1.5m. five-year deal with Walker's Crisps in 2000. His contract also has an exclusivity clause preventing him from endorsing any

other product during that time to avoid any confusion about what brand Lineker represents. Walker's is running a bit of a risk, however. It has been using Lineker since 1994 and over the years, the brand has become almost inseparable from Lineker, thus the size of the new contract's fee is perhaps not so surprising. If this five-year association with Lineker is equally successful, what will it cost Walker's to renew it again? Meanwhile, in the run-up to the 2002 World Cup, England captain David Beckham signed a (reportedly) £100,000 deal to promote Golden Wonder snack brands, including Wotsits Goalden Balls. This could cause some interesting debate in the Beckham household, as David's wife Victoria 'Posh' Beckham is endorsing Walker's upmarket crisps, Sensations.

The actual cost of using a celebrity can vary widely. According to Hampton (2001), it can cost anything up to £3m. to get a celebrity to endorse a product; £100,000 or more if they are to star in a television advertisement; and up to £50,000 for a voice-over in a television advertisement. Is the cost justified, however? Bashford (2001) cites research showing that 91 per cent of UK consumers say that celebrity endorsement makes no difference to whether or not they purchase a product, and 4 per cent said that it would make them less likely to buy. The 16–24-year-olds, however, are more likely to be swayed: 13 per cent of them said that celebrity endorsement would make them more likely to buy.

Sources: Bashford (2001), Benady, A. (2002), Bruss (2001), Conlan (2002), Cowen (2000), Hampton (2001), Kleinman (2002).

The marketing manager might also have to decide whether or not to use personal or impersonal media. Table 9.3 compares the marketing advantages and disadvantages of a range of media, from informal word-of-mouth contact such as friends recommending products to each other through to a formal professional face-to-face pitch from a sales representative.

Whichever element of the communications mix is being used, the important consideration is to match the message and media with both the target audience and the defined objectives. These issues are covered in further detail for each element of the mix in the following chapters.

■ Budgeting

Controlled communication is rarely free. The marketer has to develop campaigns within (often) tight budgets, or fight for a larger share of available resources. It is important, therefore, to develop a budgeting method that produces a realistic figure for the marketer to

Table 9.3 Comparison of personal and impersonal media for communications

	Word of mouth	Sales representative	Personalised mail shot	Mass media advertising
Accuracy and consistency of delivery	Questionable	Good	Excellent	Excellent
Likely completeness of message	Questionable	Good	Excellent	Excellent
Controllability of content	None	Good	Excellent	Excellent
Ability to convey complexity	Questionable	Excellent	Good	Relatively poor
Flexibility and tailoring of message	Good	Excellent	Good	None
Ability to target	None	Excellent	Good	Relatively poor
Reach	Patchy	Relatively poor	Excellent	Excellent
Feedback collection	None	Excellent – immediate	Possible – depends on response mechanism	Difficult – costly and time consuming
	Personal			**Impersonal**

work with in order to achieve objectives. Even in the same sector, the spend on advertising can vary considerably. In the chicken and burger fast food sector, for example, in 2000, McDonald's spent around £42.3m. on advertising, while its biggest-spending rivals, KFC and Burger King, spent £12.9m. and £11.3m. respectively (Mintel, 2002b). Similarly, in laundry products, Lever Fabergé spent £20m. advertising Persil, while Procter and Gamble (P&G) spent only £8.5m. advertising the Ariel brand in 2000. The 2001 figures look very different, however: in the first 10 months of 2001, P&G spent £16.7m. on Ariel while Lever Fabergé spent £17.4m. on Persil (Mintel, 2002a).

There are six main methods of budget setting, some of which are better suited to predictable, static markets, rather than dynamic, fast-changing situations.

Judgemental budget setting

The first group of methods of determining budgets are called judgemental budget setting because they all involve some degree of guesswork.

Arbitrary budgets. Arbitrary budgets are based on what has always been spent in the past or, for a new product, on what is usually spent on that kind of thing.

Affordable method. The affordable budget, closely linked to the arbitrary budget, is one which, as its name implies, imposes a limit based either on what is left over after other more important expenses have been met or on what the company accountant feels to be the maximum allowable. Hooley and Lynch (1985) suggest that this method is used in product-led rather than in marketing-led organisations because it is not actually linked with what is to be achieved in the marketplace.

Percentage of past sales method. The percentage of past sales method is at least better, in that it acknowledges some link between communication and sales, even though the link is illogical. The chief assumptions here are that sales precede communication, and that future activities should be entirely dependent on past performance. Taken to its extreme, it is easy to imagine a situation in which a product has a bad year, therefore its communication budget is cut, causing it to perform even more poorly, continuing in a downward spiral until it dies completely. The judgemental element here is deciding what percentage to apply. There are industry norms for various markets; for example in the pharmaceutical industry, 10–20 per cent is a typical advertising/sales ratio, but this drops to less than 1 per cent in clothing and footwear. For industrial equipment the advertising/sales ratio is often lower than 1 per cent although the sales force cost/sales ratio is often considerably higher in such industries. However, this is only part of the picture. The industrial equipment manufacturer might well invest much more in its sales force. Such percentages might simply be the cumulative habits of many organisations and thus might be questionable when considered in the context of the organisation's own position and ambitions within the market.

Percentage of future sales method. None of the budgeting methods so far considered takes any account of the future needs of the product itself. However, the percentage of future sales method is an improvement, in that communication and sales are in the right order, but again there is the question of what percentage to apply. There is also an underlying assumption about there being a direct relationship between next year's expenditure and next year's sales.

Data-based budget setting.

None of the methods examined so far has taken account of communications objectives – a reminder/reinforcement operation is much cheaper than a major attitude change exercise – or indeed of the quality or cost-effectiveness of the communication activities undertaken. There is a grave risk that the money allocated will be insufficient to achieve any real progress, in which case it will have been wasted. This then paves the way for the second group of techniques, called data-based budget-setting methods, which eliminate the worst of the judgemental aspects of budgeting.

Competitive parity. The competitive parity method involves discovering what the competition is spending and then matching or exceeding it. It has some logic, in that if you are shouting as loudly as someone else, then you have a better chance of being heard than if you are whispering. In marketing, however, it is not necessarily the volume of noise so much as the quality of noise that determines whether the message gets across and is acted on.

If it is to have any credibility at all, then the competitive parity method must take into account competitors' own communications objectives, how they compare with yours and how efficiently and effectively they are spending their money. For all you know, the competitors have set their budgets by looking at how much you spent last year, which takes you all back into a stalemate similar to that of the arbitrary budget method.

Objective and task budgeting. The final method of budgeting, arguably the best, is objective and task budgeting. This is naturally the most difficult to implement successfully. It does, however, solve many of the dilemmas posed so far and makes most commercial sense. It requires the organisation to work backwards. First define the communications objectives, then work out exactly what has to be done to achieve them. This can be costed to provide a budget that is directly linked to the product's needs and is neither more nor less than that required. A new product, for example, will need substantial investment in integrated marketing communication in order to gain acceptance within distribution channels, and then to generate awareness and trial among consumers. A mature product, in contrast, might need only 'maintenance' support, which will clearly cost much less. The only danger with objective and task budgeting, however, is that ambition overtakes common sense, leading to a budget that simply will not be accepted.

The art of making this technique work lies in refining the objectives and the ensuing budget in the light of what the organisation can bear. It may mean taking a little longer than you would like to establish the product, or finding cheaper, more creative ways of achieving objectives, but at least the problems to be faced will be known in advance and can be strategically managed.

The European Central Bank (ECB) was faced with a huge challenge in planning a large pan-European campaign to launch the euro on 1 January 2002. A mix of PR, direct marketing and above-the-line advertising was required to inform individuals and organisations about the changeover arrangements in the Eurozone countries as well as ensuring that the look, feel, size, denominations and security features of the new currency would be recognisable to everyone. A PR campaign running throughout 2001 constantly disseminated information through the media, while a mass media campaign with broadcast and print advertising began in September 2001 along with a public information leaflet drop to 300 million Europeans. The mass media campaign centred around the slogan 'The Euro. Our Money', and a single campaign was translated into 11 languages rather than trying to develop a different campaign for each country. Publicis was the agency which developed the campaign in liaison with the ECB, national central banks, government finance ministries and other bodies. The agency had 70 staff working on the project, including 30 at a specially opened 'Euro Buro' office near the ECB headquarters coordinating teams at other Publicis offices across Europe. The objectives of this integrated campaign were non-negotiable and had to be achieved if the euro launch was going to run smoothly. The campaign was designed around those objectives, and the cost is reported to have been between £50 and £80m. (*Financial Times*, 2001; Garrett, 1999; http://www.euro.ecb.int).

Mitchell (1993), as reported by Fill (2002), suggested that 40 per cent of companies use the objective and task method, while 27 per cent use a percentage of future sales, 8 per cent use a percentage of past sales, and 19 per cent use their own methods. Overall, across the whole promotional mix, organisations are likely to use some kind of composite method that includes elements of judgemental and data-based techniques (Fill, 2002).

Positioning the budgeting element so late in the planning flow does imply that the objective and task method is the preferred one. To reiterate, there is no point in throwing more money at the communication problem than is strictly necessary or justifiable in terms of future aims, and equally, spending too little to make an impact is just as wasteful.

■ Implementation and evaluation

The aim of planning is *not* to create an impressive, aesthetically pleasing document that promptly gets locked in a filing cabinet for a year. It is too easy for the planning process to become an isolated activity, undertaken as an end in itself with too little thought about the realities of the world and the practical problems of making things happen as you want them to. Throughout the planning stages, there must be due consideration given to 'what if . . .' scenarios and due respect given to what is practicable and manageable. That is not to say that an organisation should be timid in what it aims to achieve, but rather that risks should be well calculated.

Planning also helps to establish priorities, allocate responsibilities and ensure a fully integrated, consistent approach, maximising the benefits gained from all elements of the communications mix. In reality, budgets are never big enough to do everything, and something has to be sacrificed. Inevitably, different activities will be championed by different managers and these tensions have to be resolved within the planning framework. For example, many organisations are reappraising the cost-effectiveness of personal selling in the light of developments in the field of direct marketing.

An equally important activity is collecting feedback. You have been communicating with a purpose and you need to know at least whether that purpose is being fulfilled. Monitoring during the campaign helps to assess early on whether or not the objectives are being met as expected. If it is really necessary, corrective action can thus be taken before too much time and money are wasted or, even worse, before too much damage is done to the product's image.

It is not enough, however, to say that the promotional mix was designed to generate sales and we have sold this much product, and therefore it was a success. The analysis needs to be deeper than this – after all, a great deal of time and money has been invested in this communication programme. What aspects of the promotional mix worked best and most cost-effectively? Was there sufficient synergy between them? Do we have the right balance within each element of the mix, for example choice of advertising media? Are consumers' attitudes and beliefs about our product the ones we expected and wanted them to develop? Have we generated the required long-term loyalty to the product?

It is only through persistent and painstaking research effort that these sorts of question are going to be answered. Such answers not only help to analyse how perceptive past planning efforts were, but also provide the basis for future planning activity. They begin to shape the nature and objectives of the continued communication task ahead and, through helping managers to learn from successes and mistakes, lead to a more efficient use of skills and resources. The following chapters will discuss some of the techniques and problems of collecting feedback on specific elements of the promotional mix, and Chapter 5 is also relevant in a more general sense.

Communications planning model: review

Rothschild's (1987) model of the communications planning process (see Figure 9.2) is an invaluable framework, as it includes all the main issues to be considered in balancing the promotional mix. In reality, however, the process cannot be as clear-cut or neatly divided as the model suggests. Planning has to be an iterative and dynamic process, producing plans that are sufficiently flexible and open to allow adaptation in the light of emerging experience, opportunities and threats.

It is also easy, when presented with a flow-chart type of model like this one, to make assumptions about cause and effect. There is a great deal of logic and sense in the sequencing of decisions indicated by this model – definition of target market defines objectives; objectives determine strategies; strategies determine budgets and so on – but in reality there have to be feedback loops between the later and earlier elements of the model. Budgets, for instance, are likely to become a limiting factor that may cause revision of strategies and/or objectives and/or target market detail. Objective and task is the preferred approach to budget setting, but it still has to be operated within the framework of the resources that the organisation can reasonably and justifiably be expected to marshal, as discussed earlier.

The concluding messages are, therefore, that the planning process:

1 is very important for achieving commercial objectives effectively and efficiently;
2 should not be viewed as a series of discrete steps in a rigid sequence;
3 should not be an end in itself, but should be regarded as only a beginning;
4 should produce plans that are open to review and revision as appropriate;
5 should be undertaken in the light of what is reasonably achievable and practicable for the organisation;
6 should be assessed with the benefit of hindsight and feedback so that next year it will work even better.

Chapter 12 looks at marketing planning more generally, and will further discuss the techniques and problems of implementing plans within the organisational culture.

Chapter summary

■ An integrated approach to marketing communications planning is vital, given the importance of effective communication to the success of products and given the level of investment often required for integrated marketing communication activity. The main stages in the planning flow include analysing the situation, defining objectives, defining strategies, setting budgets and implementation and evaluation.

■ Communications objectives must be precise, practical and measurable. They can be cognitive (e.g. creating awareness and disseminating knowledge), affective (e.g. creating and manipulating brand images), behavioural (e.g. stimulating the consumer to purchase action) or corporate (e.g. building and enhancing corporate image).

■ Different promotional tools are effective for different types of objective. While advertising might be more appropriate for cognitive objectives, personal selling and sales promotions could be better for behavioural objectives, for example. Direct marketing can be very useful in creating and enhancing longer-term relationships with customers.

■ Communications budgets can be set in a number of ways. Judgemental methods involve a degree of guesswork, for example being set arbitrarily or on the basis of what can be afforded. They can also be set on the basis of expected future sales, or made dependent on historical sales figures. Data-based methods are more closely related to what is actually happening in the marketplace and include competitive parity and the objective and task method.

questions for *review and discussion*

9.1 What are the five main elements of the *promotional mix*?

9.2 What are the stages in the *marketing communications planning flow*?

9.3 What are the three broad stages of *buyer readiness*, and how might the balance of the promotional mix vary between them?

9.4 What are the main categories of *marketing communication objectives*?

9.5 What are the main advantages and disadvantages of *objective and task* budget setting compared with the other methods?

9.6 How and why might the balance of the promotional mix differ between:

(a) the sale of a car to a private individual; and

(b) the sale of a fleet of cars to an organisation for its sales representatives?

case study 9.1

Xbox: the mean green machine

I don't think the gaming industry has ever had as much energy as it has now. We're entering the golden age of gaming. Whatever happens, there will be better games on every platform because Microsoft have come in and set a new standard and, when Sony or Nintendo release their next machines, they're going to be completely different. Why? Because of Xbox. (Richard Teversham, Xbox's Head of UK Marketing as quoted on http://www.gamesradar.com)

So what is the Xbox? It is Microsoft's first foray into the fast-moving world of computer games consoles. It's a highly competitive world too, dominated by Sony (PlayStation2) and Nintendo (Gameboy Advance), but a lucrative one. The global video game market is said to be worth $20bn and analysts estimate that by 2005, the annual market for games consoles alone will be worth £28bn. In the UK alone, it is forecast that the computer games market in 2002 will be worth £2bn, up from £1.6bn in 2001. Microsoft itself believes that while 30 per cent of UK households currently have a games console, in the future, they'll be as common as video recorders are now. It is hardly surprising, therefore, that Microsoft has been tempted to enter this market.

Having decided to enter, Microsoft moved fast, taking only 18 months from initial brainstorming to product launch, and from 20 people working on the project to 2,000. The Xbox is different from its competitors and has been described as being more like a cheap PC with a powerful graphics chip rather than a traditional console. It is currently the only console with built-in broadband capability so that eventually gamers will be able to download new levels, characters, and games, and online multiplayer gaming is due to start in the summer of 2002 in the Japanese market.

The Xbox was launched first in the USA on 15 November 2001, followed in Japan in February 2002 and Europe in March 2002 with a $500m. worldwide advertising campaign. Its global target was to sell between 4.5 and 6 million Xbox consoles by June 2002. In the USA alone, Microsoft had sold 1.4 million consoles by the end of 2001. The Japanese launch was a little less promising, however. In the first week after its launch, Xbox had sold only 150,000 units (although 250,000 units had been shipped to Japan). In comparison, when Sony launched the PlayStation2 in Japan in 2000, it sold 720,000 within three days and 1 million within a week. There was also a technical problem that caused some bad publicity: nearly 600 complaints were received about the consoles damaging DVD and CD games. Microsoft's response to these complaints was said to be hesitant – it took nearly two weeks. This alienated early buyers and tarnished its image. Three Japanese retailers suspended sales of the Xbox for two weeks until Microsoft confirmed that it would replace or repair offending consoles. Sandy Duncan, Microsoft's Vice-president of Xbox Europe, blamed adverse publicity that ▶

turned a few technical glitches into 'Xbox ate my DVD' headlines. In Microsoft's opinion it was a very minor problem that certainly hadn't been an issue in the US market.

Meanwhile, the simultaneous launch in 16 European countries was scheduled for 14 March 2002 and a lot of preparation went into it. 'Europe as a console market is as important as the US in terms of volume – if we are going to be successful we have to be successful over here' said Sandy Duncan. Microsoft invited the top two retailers from each country to an Xbox event in Milan in 2001, and in October 2001, Xbox hosted the X01 event experience ('more than a press conference or trade show') in Cannes providing details on the European price, availability and shipment quantities (1.5 million consoles for the first three months to the end of June). X01 ran over two days and around 1,000 journalists and representatives of the video games industry attended. There was as much emphasis on the games and future development plans for games as on the hardware.

Advertising broke in the games and consumer press on 7 February 2002 followed by a television campaign nearer to the launch date. Retailers also had an important role to play and 7,000 pre-launch demo units were installed in European retail outlets. The weekend of 9–11 March was the final opportunity to pre-order an Xbox in the UK before the official launch. Sony wasn't prepared to let Microsoft have it all its own way, however, and chose that same weekend to promote the launch of *Metal Gear Solid 2: Sons of Liberty*, what Sony describes as 'the biggest games launch the industry has ever seen'. That game had taken 550,000 pre-orders and was expected to turnover £9m. in its first weekend on sale.

Around 300 stores across the UK started selling the machines at midnight on 13 March. Electronics Boutique opened 168 of its 330 UK stores at midnight and this retailer claimed to have received 'tens of thousands' of pre-orders. Virgin Megastores (official retail partner for the launch) had all-night parties running in London, Birmingham, Glasgow and Manchester, themed as Xmas Eve – mince pies, prezzies from Santa (including Xbox merchandise), entertainment and a gaming area where punters could play on demo machines. Thus several hundred people were in the queue for the launch at the Virgin Megastore in Oxford Street. A student who bought his console just after midnight said, 'I love my PlayStation 2 but the Xbox is even better. The games are more advanced and more exciting. Besides, it's something to spend my student loan on' (ever heard of books, mate?). To heighten the excitement, the person at the head of the queue in London to buy his Xbox after midnight was whisked home in a limo with an escort of six motorbikes. A poll of 3,000 people who pre-ordered Xbox from Amazon found that 75 per cent of them intended to take a day off work to play with their new toy. The desirable status of the Xbox was perhaps finally confirmed not long after midnight when the first one had been stolen from someone waiting for a bus home!

The launch itself was not the end of the campaign, however. From the 29 March to 1 April, Xbox was at Multiplay UK's i10 event, the UK's largest LAN gaming event. A thousand UK gamers attended and the Xbox Experience featured 8 networked Xboxes to allow 16 people to compete at Halo all at the same time. Other demo machines were also available. Also, once customers have bought Xbox games, they can be entered into a customer database, built through registration cards distributed in the game boxes and through http://www.playmore.com, Xbox's 'brand experience' website.

Xbox is also supported by http://www.xbox.com which has information about the Xbox and its games, news updates, competitions, and a chat room. Visitors can also sign up to receive a newsletter or take out an Xbox magazine subscription. The site also features Xbox TV: 'the place to take a sneaky look at games before you buy 'em'. It shows video clips of the games so you can see the graphics, hear the sound effects and see the action, and also get background information on how the games were created. The quality and desirability of the games are obviously important influences in selling the console. The Xbox launched with 20 games, costing about £45 each (claimed to be the strongest portfolio of games ever for a console launch) but 60 are planned by the end of June. Halo is one of only a handful of games to get a 10 out of 10 rating from Edge, an influential European games magazine. The hardware and software are extensively covered and reviewed in games magazines and on gaming websites such as: http://www.gamesdomain.com, http://www.gamespot.co.uk, http://www.gamesradar.com and http://www.computerandvideogames.com.

Sales of games are also important financially as Microsoft earns approximately 30 per cent royalty on every game sold for the Xbox. In the USA, nearly 4 games are being sold with every Xbox while early indications show that on average 2.5 games are sold with a European Xbox. This is especially important as analysts' estimates suggest that Microsoft could be losing as much as $125 on each console sold and will not break even for five years, despite the royalties earned on games. As it is, the Xbox console cost around £300 at its launch, compared with around £200 for a PlayStation2.

According to http://www.computerandvideogames.com (20 March 2002), Xbox sold 48,000 units in its first three days in the UK market. Trade speculation is that Microsoft shipped 80,000 units for the launch (cf. PlayStation2 selling c. 70,000 in the UK in two days), although Microsoft claims that Xbox was 'a near sell-out' on its first day. In the longer term, competitor Nintendo's GameCube is due for its European launch on 3 May 2002 with a £60m. launch budget and a target of selling 1 million consoles by July. Analysts forecast that by 2006, PlayStation will have sold between 90 and 110 million consoles with Xbox and GameCube selling between 25 and 35 million each. Then gamers will be looking to the next generation of consoles.

Sources: Abrahams (2002), Chandiramani (2002), Cope (2002), *Daily Post* (2002), *Daily Record* (2002), Grande (2002), Harney (2002), Islam (2002), Lambeth (2002), Nakamoto (2002a, b), Rowan (2002), Uhlig (2002), Wray (2002), http://www.computerandvideogames.com, http://www.gamesradar.com, http://www.xbox.com

Questions

1 Categorise the various communications activities mentioned in the case according to whether they represent push or pull tools.

2 To what extent do you feel that the negative publicity received in the Japanese market is likely to have been a problem?

3 Why do you think advertising alone was not considered sufficient for the European launch?

4 Analyse the likely role of xbox.com in the future marketing communications strategy of Xbox.

References for chapter 9

Abrahams, P. (2002), 'Microsoft Urged to Play by the Rules', *Financial Times*, 13 March, p. 20.

Bashford, S. (2001), 'A Famous Face is Not Sufficient to Lure Customers', *Marketing*, 12 July, p. 5.

Benady, A. (2002), 'For and against Celebrity Endorsement', *The Times*, 22 February, p. 21.

Benady, D. (2002), 'Sugar the Pill', *Marketing Week*, 14 February, pp. 37–41.

Bruss, J. (2001), 'Star Power', *Beverage Industry*, November, p. 34.

Castle, S. (2001), 'Europe Planning Tough Rules for Breast Implants', *The Independent*, 16 November, p. 11.

Chandiramani, R. (2002), 'Microsoft's Xbox Adopts "Positive" Brand Positioning', *Marketing*, 24 January, p. 1.

Conlan, T. (2002), 'Posh v Becks: in the Battle of the His 'n' Hers Crisps', *Daily Mail*, 7 March, p. 11.

Cope, N. (2002), 'All-American Game Boy Wins Through in War of the Consoles', *The Independent*, 4 March, p. 15.

Cowen, M. (2000), '£1.5 m Buys a Lot More of Mr Nice Guy', *The Independent*, 10 December, p. 19.

Daily Post (2002), 'New Xbox Stolen within Hours', *Daily Post*, 15 March, p. 2.

Daily Record (2002), 'Gamers' Midnight Rush for the Xbox', *Daily Record*, 14 March, p. 3.

DeLozier, M. (1975), *The Marketing Communications Process*, McGraw-Hill.

Dignam, C. (2002), 'The Comeback of Sunny Delight', *The Times*, 27 February, p. 32.

Fill, C. (2002), *Marketing Communications: Contexts, Strategies and Applications* (3rd edn), Financial Times Prentice Hall.

Financial Times, (2001), 'The Euro Campaign', *Financial Times* 19 June, p. 8.

Garrett, J. (1999), 'Agencies Contest £80mn "Euro" Brief', *Campaign*, 30 April, p. 1.

Grande, C. (2002), 'Plug and Play Broadband Gaming Promises Valuable New Revenue Streams', *Financial Times*, 26 March, p. 4.

Hampton, N. (2001), 'How Stars Earn Those Astronomical Fees', *Evening Standard*, 18 June, p. 6.

Harney, A. (2002), 'Microsoft Fired Up for Console Wars', *Financial Times*, 7 February, p. 28.

Hirschman, E. (1987), 'People as Products: Analysis of a Complex Marketing Exchange', *Journal of Marketing*, 51 (1), pp. 98–108.

Hooley, G. and Lynch, J. (1985), 'How UK Advertisers Set Budgets', *International Journal of Advertising*, 3, pp. 223–31.

Islam, F. (2002), 'Gates' Baby Plays Catch-up', *The Observer*, 17 March, p. 6.

Jones, J. (1991), 'Over Promise and under Delivery', *Marketing and Research Today*, 19 (November), pp. 195–203.

Kleinman, M. (2002), 'Beckhams Go Head-to-head in Snacks Ad Drive', *Marketing*, 7 March, p. 1.

Knight, P. (2002), 'Let's Not Miss a Chance to Make iTV a Big Winner', *Marketing*, 21 February, p. 20.

Lambeth, J. (2002), 'Microsoft's Black Box Squares Up to its Rivals', *The Daily Telegraph*, 12 March, p. 33.

Marketing (2001), 'Best Use of Interactive TV', *The Marketing Awards: Connections 2001* supplement to *Marketing*, November, p. 20.

Marketing Week (1999), 'IDM Silver Award Winner', *Marketing Week*, 20 May, p. 62.

Mintel (2002a), 'Clothes Washing Detergents and Laundry Aids', 29 January (accessed via http://www.mintel.com).

Mintel (2002b), 'Chicken and Burger Bars', 13 March (accessed via http://www.mintel.com).

Mitchell, L. (1993), 'An Examination of Methods of Setting Advertising Budgets: Practice and Literature', *European Journal of Advertising*, 27 (5), pp. 5–21.

Nakamoto, M. (2002a), 'Xbox Flaw Blights Microsoft in Japan', *Financial Times*, 8 March, p. 21.

Nakamoto, M. (2002b), 'Microsoft Shows Slow Reactions', *Financial Times*, 12 March, p. 22.

Oliver, J. and Farris, P. (1989), 'Push and Pull: a One-Two Punch for Packaged Products', *Sloan Management Review*, 31 (Fall), pp. 53–61.

Pickton, D. and Broderick, A. (2001), *Integrated Marketing Communications*, Financial Times Prentice Hall.

Poulter, S. (2002), '£12mn 'Healthy' Makeover for Sunny Delight', *Daily Mail*, 21 February, p. 39.

PR Week (1999), 'Breast Implants', *PR Week*, 4 December, p. 11.

Rogers, D. (2002), 'P&G in £12mn Relaunch of Sunny Delight', *Marketing*, 14 February, p. 2.

Rothschild, M. (1987), *Marketing Communications: From Fundamentals to Strategies*, Heath.

Rowan, D. (2002), 'Video Game Giants Roll Out Big Guns for Marketing War', *The Times*, 9 March, p. 9.

Strong, E. (1925), *The Psychology of Selling*, McGraw-Hill.

Thurtle, G. (2002), 'Balloting Blair's Babies', *Marketing Week*, 28 February, pp. 25–7.

Turznski, G. (1999), 'Will Interactive Media Bring Advertisers Relief?', *Marketing Week*, 10 June, p. 16.

Uhlig, R. (2002), 'Games Fans Lured by the X-factor', *The Daily Telegraph*, 15 March, p. 3.

Wray, R. (2002), 'Xboxed Up and Nowhere to Go', *The Guardian*, 12 March, p. 21.

chapter 10

promotion: advertising and personal selling

LEARNING OBJECTIVES

This chapter will help you to:

1 define advertising and its role within the promotional mix;

2 appreciate the complexities of formulating advertising messages and how they are presented for both print and broadcast media;

3 differentiate between types of advertising media and understand their relative strengths and weaknesses;

4 appreciate the role played by advertising agencies and understand the stages in the management process of managing advertising activities;

5 appreciate the role that personal selling plays in the overall marketing effort of the organisation and define the tasks undertaken by sales representatives; and

6 analyse the stages involved in the personal selling process and appreciate the responsibilities involved in sales management.

Introduction

This chapter discusses advertising, an indirect form of communication, and personal selling, a very direct way of getting a marketing message across.

This chapter examines the role of advertising in the promotional mix and the important aspects of message design and media selection in the development of successful campaigns. The stages in developing an advertising campaign are then presented, along with the main management decisions at each stage. Sometimes these decisions are made in conjunction with the support of an external advertising agency, while in other organisations the campaign process is controlled almost exclusively in-house. The decision to use an agency and the importance of the client–agency relationship are thus also considered within the chapter.

While advertising tends to target a mass audience, personal selling in contrast tends to focus on one-to-one communication. As Chapter 9 suggested, personal selling will thus probably play a much bigger role in the promotional mix of a high-priced, infrequently purchased industrial good, for example, than in that of a routinely purchased consumer product.

Nevertheless, personal selling is important in some consumer markets. Car manufacturers spend many millions on advertising, but the purchase decision is made and the final deal negotiated at the showroom. The sales assistants thus play a very important role, particularly in guiding, persuading and converting the wavering customer without being too pushy. In the car industry, failure at this stage lets the whole glossy marketing process down.

Regardless of whether a sales force is selling capital machinery into manufacturing businesses, FMCG products into the retail trade, or cars or financial services to individual consumers, the principles behind personal selling remain largely the same. This chapter, therefore, will define what personal selling is, and look at the different roles it can play and the objectives it can achieve. From this, the chapter moves on to look at some of the skills and techniques involved in selling, using a framework that traces the selling process through from identifying likely prospects to making the sale and following it up. Having looked at selling from such a practical point of view, it is important to round off the picture by considering some of the managerial issues surrounding personal selling.

 In 2001, Orange, a subsidiary of France Telecom, was confirmed as the UK's number one mobile phone operator, with a customer base that had grown by 65 per cent over the first half of the year. By the end of 2001 it had 12.4 million subscribers. Advertising had a large part to play in that success, but becoming number one does not mean that the company can sit back and slacken off on the communications front. Orange has continued to use high profile advertising campaigns to maintain its hard-won status. Orange used television advertising in its £4m. campaign in January 2002, for instance, to promote text messaging among 'light users'. The advertisement showed how text messaging could play an important emotional role in staying in touch with friends and loved ones. Then, in March 2002, Orange UK launched a multimedia campaign to persuade high-value customers from other networks to switch to Orange. The campaign included radio, TV, outdoor and online media. Orange's advertising spend in 2001 amounted to just over £51m., with £18m. spent on television advertising, £12.4m. on press advertising, £3.5m. on cinema advertising, £2.5m. on outdoor media and the rest on direct mail. Clearly, with this level of budget, it is vitally important to make the right strategic decisions not only about the campaign objectives, but also about the message itself, the media to be used and the creative approach. It is also important to monitor carefully and evaluate the impact and cost-effectiveness of campaigns (Cowen, 2001; Grant, 2002; *Marketing*, 2002; White, 2002).

The role of advertising

■ Within the promotional mix

Advertising can be defined as any paid form of non-personal promotion transmitted through a mass medium. The sponsor should be clearly identified and the advertisement may relate to an organisation, a product or a service. The key difference, therefore, between advertising and other forms of promotion is that it is impersonal and communicates with large numbers of people through paid media channels. Although the term 'mass media' is often used, it has to be interpreted carefully. The proliferation of satellite and cable television channels, along with the increasing number of more tightly targeted special interest magazines and the use of the Internet, means that on the one hand advertising audiences are generally smaller, but on the other the audiences are 'better quality'. This implies that they are far more likely to be interested in the subject matter of the advertising carried by their chosen medium. Advertising normally conforms to one of two basic types: product oriented or institutional (Berkowitz *et al.*, 1992), as shown in Figure 10.1. A product-oriented advertisement focuses, as the term suggests, on the product or service being offered, whether for profit or not. Its prime task is to support the product in achieving its marketing goals.

Product-oriented advertising can itself take one of three alternative forms: pioneering, competitive, or reminder and reinforcement advertising.

Pioneering advertising

Pioneering advertising is used in the early stages of the life cycle when it is necessary to explain just what the product will do and the benefits it can offer. The more innovative, technically complex and expensive the product is, the more essential this explanation becomes. Depending on the product's newness, the prime emphasis might well be on stimu-

Figure 10.1 Types of advertising

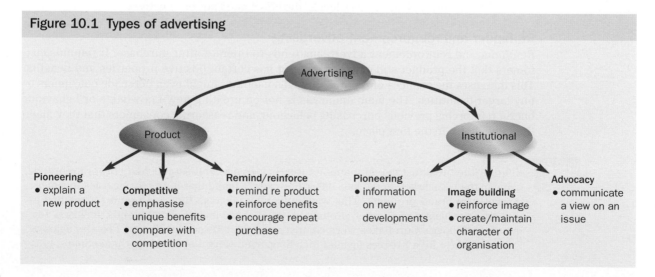

lating basic generic demand rather than attempting to beat competition. In these cases, the prime emphasis in the advertising is to provide enough information to allow potential buyers to see how this product might relate to them, and thus to stimulate enough interest to encourage further investigation and possibly trial.

Competitive advertising

Competitive advertising is concerned with emphasising the special features of the product or brand as a means of outselling the competition. Usually the seller seeks to communicate the unique benefits, real or imaginary, that distinguish the product and give it its competitive edge. Given that most markets are mature and often crowded, this type of advertising is very common and very important.

eg   The ale sector within the UK beer market is struggling to maintain its share, given the aggressive competition it faces from lagers and pre-packaged spirits, such as Bacardi Breezers, in particular. Advertising thus plays an important role in establishing distinctive brand images and trying to create differential advantage. Boddingtons 'Cream of Manchester' campaign during the 1990s, starring sexy model Melanie Sykes, really put the brand on the map, in more ways than one, as a down-to-earth northern product with a sense of humour. This was reinforced by the subsequent 'Chilled Cream' campaign featuring cartoon character Graham the Cow who represented the brand for over two years. The £4m. 2002 campaign, however, dropped the cream theme and returned to sexy female models using the slogan 'It's a bit gorgeous'. In one advertisement, for example, an actress finds her co-star such a turn-off that she has to pretend he's a pint of Boddingtons in order to produce a convincing screen kiss. Smith (2002) does, however, raise the concern that dropping the creaminess means dropping an essential differentiating characteristic of the brand which was at the heart of its positioning. As Smith's article puts it, 'There are any number of merely "gorgeous" beers out there', so what is there to distinguish Boddingtons from its direct competitors in the ale sector and from the strongly positioned lager brands?

At least with beers consumers can try the different brands and then decide which one they like.

A form of competitive advertising that has grown in significance in recent years is comparative advertising. This means making a direct comparison between one product and another, showing the advertiser's product in a much more favourable light, of course (Muehling *et al.*, 1990). Alternatively, the comparison may be more subtle, referring to 'other leading brands' and leaving it up to the target audience to decide which rival product is intended. Initially, it was thought unwise to use a direct comparison approach as it gave a free mention to competitors and was likely to bring about a 'knocking copy' reaction. However, advertisers have now realised that in a competitive world even if they do make a comparison with a market leader with already high awareness levels, the effect need not be negative.

Reminder and reinforcement advertising

Reminder and reinforcement advertising tends to operate after purchase. It reminds customers that the product still exists and that it has certain positive properties and benefits. This increases the chances of repurchase and sometimes might even persuade consumers to buy larger quantities. The main emphasis is not on creating new knowledge or behaviour but on reinforcing previous purchasing behaviour, and reassuring consumers that they made the right choice in the first place.

eg   Kellogg, the breakfast cereal manufacturer, has a very well-established corporate brand name in the UK market. In the late 1990s, however, it found that it was losing sales to supermarket own-brand products. This was happening because the own-brand ranges had a directly equivalent, but cheaper, product for each of the main Kellogg brands. In Tesco, for instance, Kellogg's Cornflakes were competing against Tesco Cornflakes; Frosties against Frosted Flakes; Rice Krispies against Rice Snaps and Coco Pops against Choco Snaps, etc.

Kellogg responded to this by targeting lapsed buyers and users of its Cornflakes with a reminder advertising campaign designed subtly to reinforce the brand heritage and quality. Most adults are aware of the existence of Kellogg's Cornflakes and what they are, and so do not need information, just a gentle reminder. The slogan 'Remember How Good They Taste?' took adults back to the last time they tried Kellogg's Cornflakes, encouraging them to recall their own experience of the brand and how much they liked it. A small price cut, prominently marked on the box, also helped to encourage retrial.

This kind of advertising clearly relates to established products in the mature stage of the product life cycle where the emphasis is on maintaining market share at a time of major competition.

Institutional advertising

In contrast, institutional advertising is not product specific. It aims to build a sound reputation and image for the whole organisation to achieve a wide range of objectives with different target audiences. These could include the local community, financial stakeholders, government and customers, to name but a few.

Institutional advertising may be undertaken for many reasons, as shown in Figure 10.1, for example pioneering, in the sense of presenting new developments within the organisation, image building, or advocacy in the sense of presenting the organisation's point of view on an issue. Some institutional advertising might be linked with presenting the organisation as a caring, responsible and progressive company. These advertisements are designed to inform or reinforce positive images with target audiences. Others may adopt an advocacy perspective, indicating the organisation's view on a particular issue for political, social responsibility or self-interest reasons.

■ Within the marketing mix

The above categorisation of product and institutional advertising broadly describes the direct uses of advertising. Within the marketing mix, advertising also plays a less direct but equally important role in supporting other areas of marketing activity. In B2B markets, advertising often directly supports the selling efforts of the sales team by generating leads, providing information on new developments to a wider audience more quickly and creating a generally more receptive climate prior to the sales visit.

Similarly, with sales promotion, a short-term incentive offer may be actively advertised to encourage increased traffic. For example, airlines offering 'two for one' deals or a free ticket competition frequently support their promotions with media advertising. Furniture stores also make frequent use of television and press advertising to inform the public of short-term promotional price cuts or low/no interest financing deals to stimulate interest in furnishing and to draw people into stores that they might not otherwise have thought of visiting at that particular time.

More strategically, advertising may be used to reposition a product for defensive or aggressive reasons in order to improve its competitive position. This may be achieved by demonstrating new uses for the product or to open up new segments, either geographically or benefit based.

corporate social responsibility *in action*

Laughing all the way to a successful CRM partnership

Cause-related marketing (CRM), a promotional link-up between a brand and a cause or charity, can provide an interesting focus for an advertising campaign, as well as generating publicity. Lever Fabergé's Persil brand, for example, was associated with Comic Relief's Red Nose Day 2001, raising money to fund programmes helping disadvantaged people both in the UK and in Africa. Comic Relief's 2001 theme, 'Say Pants to Poverty', was a perfect match for a laundry brand and Persil's packs were temporarily and prominently

▶

emblazoned with all kinds of underwear reflecting the theme. A donation was made to Comic Relief for each pack sold and the packs effectively used their space to advertise Comic Relief, with fundraising ideas and information. Persil's own advertising also reflected the 'Pants' theme. Television, print, poster and other outdoor media were all used to display images of white boxer shorts with a nice red nose print and the slogan, 'Saying Nice Clean Bright Pants to Poverty'. Over six weeks, Persil raised over £300,000.

Manor Bakeries' Mr Kipling brand, which produces 'exceedingly good cakes' also joined in with the fun. Mr Kipling's cherry bakewell became the official Red Nose Cake with a

donation made for each pack sold, and again, this featured heavily in television advertising. The cakes raised over £50,000.

For both companies, the incorporation of advertising into the CRM effort served a number of purposes, beyond the normal objectives of promoting their brands. Obviously, the advertising helped to emphasise the companies' involvement with Comic Relief, reinforcing their other PR and promotional efforts on behalf of the charity, and this in turn could contribute to that elusive but desirable goal of generating 'emotional engagement' among consumers. The CRM link reinforces the integrity of the brand and its manufacturer, adding another dimension to the brand

proposition. Comic Relief in particular is quite a powerful CRM linkage, as a lot of excitement is generated through PR and other marketing communications efforts in the build-up to Red Nose Day, and a lot of individuals get involved in fundraising events. Seeing a big-name advertiser also 'doing its bit' gives the company a more human face and reinforces a sense of the company pulling with the wider community for a common, altruistic motive. Comic Relief benefits, of course, not only from the donations from the packs sold, but also from the free exposure it gets through the prime advertising slots and sites purchased by its CRM partners.

Sources: Arnold (2001a); http://www.bitc.org.uk; http://www.comicrelief.com; http://www.elida.co.uk

In other situations, advertising may support other marketing mix activities to spread demand or to reduce sales fluctuations. The problems of seasonality are well known in the services field, whether in relation to holidays, restaurants or cinemas. Combined with pricing, advertising may seek to spread or even out demand patterns, saving the service provider from having to accept periods of marked underutilisation of capacity. The various cross-channel ferry companies, for example, advertise low-priced deals to France during the winter to boost passenger numbers.

Overall, advertising's role within an organisation depends on a range of contexts, environments and competitive challenges, and may even change within the same organisation over time. The detailed role of advertising will be specified in the marketing plan, which will clearly specify objectives, resources, activities and results expected. These issues will be revisited on pp. 320 *et seq.*, where the stages in developing an advertising campaign are considered.

Formulating the advertising message

The essence of communication, as outlined in the previous chapter, is to decide what to say, to whom, by what means and with what results. This section centres on the very demanding decision area of designing an appropriate message, with the emphasis on the message content, its tone and how it can then be presented for either print or broadcast communication.

■ Message

Before producing an advertisement, you need to know who the target audience is and give careful consideration to what you want to say to them. This requires a sound understanding of the targets, their interests, needs, motivations, lifestyles, etc. In addition, there needs to be an honest appraisal of the product or service to determine the differential characteristics or benefits that are worth highlighting to achieve the desired results.

eg Even the charity Age Concern has attempted to grab attention using sexual imagery to help get its message across. As part of its remit to break down negative stereotypes of older people and to become more relevant to the 40- and 50-something generation, it used a poster campaign which echoed the imagery and style of the Wonderbra series of advertisements. The poster showed an attractive 56-year-old model wearing a black bra with the heading 'The first thing some people notice is her age' (Chandiramani, 2001).

Breaking stereotypes, Age Concern used an older model unexpectedly wearing a black bra to catch the attention of the public.

Source: Age Concern UK.

Clearly, marketing and promotional objectives are at the heart of message formulation. If the prime objective is to generate awareness, then the message must offer clear information to alert the audience to what is on offer. If the objective is to stimulate enquiries, then the focus would need to be on moving the customer through to action, making sure that the response mechanism is clear and easy to use. There also needs to be consistency between the product positioning (see pp. 203 *et seq*.) desired and the content and style of the advertisement.

The main aim in message design and execution is to prepare an informative and persuasive message in terms of words, symbols and illustrations that will not only attract attention but retain interest through its presentation so that the target audience responds as desired. Grabbing and holding attention may mean making someone watch an entire 30-second television advertisement, read a long, wordy print advertisement, or simply dwell long enough on a non-verbal graphic image to start thinking about what it means. Whatever the medium or the style of communication, it is therefore essential that the message is understandable and relevant to the audience.

Sometimes the message may be sent out through both broadcast and print media using the same theme. In other cases, a number of different messages may be communicated in different ways over the length of the campaign.

eg As Murphy (1999) points out, 'Strong advertising may help drive the product, but the retail environment is where the purchasing decision is actually made.' He argues that it makes sense to extend the themes and images developed in advertising campaigns into other marketing activities such as point-of-purchase (POP) materials. This reminds customers of the advertising messages when and where they are making serious purchasing decisions and provides an opportunity to influence that decision. John Smith's Extra Smooth Bitter, for example, is represented by the six-feet-tall cardboard cut-out 'No Nonsense Man', both in pubs and in broadcast advertising. He looks like a typical young casual drinker with a glass of beer in his hand and a tee-shirt saying 'John Smith's doesn't need any nonsense to help sell it (that's why I'm here)'. A similar cut-out of Lara Croft appeared in and around retail outlets to advertise Lucozade, although one poor Lara outside a certain campus shop had been artistically defaced in the tee-shirt department with a marker pen to make her look like a convincing Miss Wet Tee-shirt 2002 candidate!

POP is very much a tool of integrated marketing communications. In 2001, for example, Shell developed a sales promotion across nine European markets to increase customer loyalty. Customers picked up a game card and then were given a sticker with a letter on it with every subsequent petrol purchase. The objective was to collect the right stickers to spell out 'Shell' to win a prize. The success of the promotion depended on the support of radio and outdoor media advertising to raise awareness, and perhaps to encourage drivers to seek out Shell stations specifically so that they could participate, and also good POP advertising to remind them about it at the point of sale and to reinforce excitement about the potential prizes (Middleton, 2002).

■ Creative appeals

After the marketing issues of message content have been considered, the creative task can proceed. It is here that agencies can play a particularly major role in the conceptualisation and design of messages that appeal effectively.

Rational appeals centre on some kind of logical argument persuading the consumer to think or act in a certain way. However, often it is not just a case of *what* is said, but also *how* it is said. The bald logic in itself may not be enough to grab and hold the consumers' attention sufficiently to make the message stick. How it is said can introduce an *emotional appeal* into the advertisement to reinforce the underlying logic of the message. The concern here is not just with facts but also with the customer's feelings and emotions towards what is on offer. It is often the emotional element that gives the advertisement an extra appeal.

eg Many advertisements that feature scientists in white coats have rational appeals at their core. Your toilet is full of germs, but our laboratory tests (enter white-coated bespectacled boffin clutching test tube) have shown that our product kills more germs more quickly with longer-lasting effect than our rival's product (split screen shot: on left sparkling white spotless porcelain, on right dubious-looking, murky, streaky porcelain), so buy our product (end with reassuring contented smile from boffin clutching pack). A nice twist on the boffin theme was used when Henkel launched Glist 3-in-1 automatic dishwashing tablets in the UK. The £6m. campaign featured actress Julie Walters extolling the virtues of Glist surrounded by white-coated boffins. Her view is that if the boffins from the Good Housekeeping Institute say the product is good, then it must be because 'you can't beat a good boffin' (Arnold, 2001b).

Fear is not, of course, the only kind of emotional appeal. Positive emotions can be equally effective in creating memorable and persuasive messages, which do not necessarily need any solid rational basis in order to be effective. Humour and sex are particularly powerful tools for the advertiser, particularly in appealing to people's needs for escapism and fantasy.

It may be argued that television is better at creating emotional appeals, as it is more life-like, with sight, sound and motion to aid the presentation, whereas print is better for more rational, factually based appeals.

Product-oriented appeals

Product-oriented appeals centre on product features or attributes and seek to emphasise their importance to the target audience. The appeals may be based on product specification (air bags or side impact protection bars in cars, for example), price (actual price level, payment terms or extras), service (availability) or any part of the offering that creates a potential competitive edge in the eyes of the target market. With a product-oriented appeal, there are several options for specific message design strategy. These include, for example, showing the audience how the product provides the solution to a problem. The message could also centre on a 'slice of life', demonstrating how the product fits into a lifestyle that either approximates that of the target market or is one with which they can identify or to which they can aspire.

Getting closer to real life, news, facts and testimonials offer hard information about the product or proof through 'satisfied customers' that the product is all it is claimed to be. Magazine advertisements trying to sell goods that the target market might perceive to be more expensive, or goods that sound too good to be true, or goods that a customer would eg Since 2000, grocery retailer Sainsbury's has very successfully used a slice of aspirational celebrity life in its advertising. Jamie Oliver, known as 'The Naked Chef', is a popular, down-to-earth, cheeky young Essex guy without any of the pretensions often associated with top chefs. The series of television advertisements show him in a whirl of activity throwing meals together from Sainsbury's ingredients in his home for visiting friends and family. One advertisement shows Jamie sneaking off to his mum's house and begging for a curry, complaining that his wife, Jules, is into 'all that low fat malarkey'. While he lounges on the sofa, the viewer sees his mum make a curry – out of low fat ingredients – which he then wolfs down. After he has gone, the advertisement ends with mum on the telephone to Jules telling her that Jamie never suspected a thing. The slice of life theme was nearly jeopardised, however, when Jules hit the headlines after being photographed coming out of rival supermarket, Waitrose, with a huge amount of grocery shopping. A few weeks later, she made sure she was photographed with lots of Sainsbury's shopping instead (Adamson, 2002; Watson, 2001)!

Nevertheless, research has shown that his character really appeals to the target audience of female 30-something shoppers and his first two years with Sainsbury's were so successful in increasing sales that he was given a four-year extension to his contract, at a cost of about £500,000 per year (Beard, 2002).

normally want to see or try before purchase, often use testimonials from satisfied customers. These might help to alleviate some of the doubt or risk and encourage the reader to respond to the advertisement.

In magazines and trade publications, news and fact-based approaches can also take the form of advertorials. These are designed to fit in with the style, tone and presentation of the publication so that the reader tends to think of them as extensions to the magazine rather than advertisements. The overall objective is that the reader's attention should be able to flow naturally from the magazine's normal editorial content into and through the advertorial and out the other side, maintaining interest and retention. This is particularly effective where the advertorial is short.

eg Print media advertorials are very popular and can appear in newspapers as well as magazines, of course. NFU Mutual, an insurance company specialising in rural areas, for example, occasionally runs advertorials in *The Western Mail*, a regional newspaper based in Cardiff. One of its advertorials contained two pieces, one focused on the potential hazards of country driving, and the other on pension planning. In a journalistic style, the 'article' on road safety gave a lot of practical tips to help motorists drive more safely (and presumably, therefore, make fewer insurance claims!) and the format meant that the points could be expanded in detail and there was no sense of any selling going on. At the end of the piece is a single sentence pointing out the main benefit offered by NFU Mutual motor insurance. In a similar vein, a later advertorial covered the topic of rural crime against farms with lots of suitably scary statistics (NFU Mutual, 2001, 2002).

Customer-oriented appeals

Customer-oriented appeals are focused on what the consumer personally gains through using this product. Such appeals encourage the consumer by association to think about the benefits that may be realisable through the rational or emotional content of the advertisement. Typically, they include the following.

Saving or making money. Bold 2-in-1, for example, could sell itself simply on the product-oriented appeal that it incorporates both a washing powder and fabric conditioner in its formulation. In fact, its advertising takes the argument further into a customer-oriented appeal, demonstrating how this two-in-one product is cheaper than buying the two components separately, thus putting money back in the purchaser's pocket.

Fear avoidance. The use of fear avoidance appeals is a powerful one in message generation and has been extensively used in public, non-profit-making promotions, for example AIDS prevention, anti-drinking and driving, anti-smoking and other health-awareness programmes. Getting the right level of fear is a challenge: too high and it will be regarded as too threatening and thus be screened out, too low and it will not be considered compelling enough to act on.

Security enhancement. A wide range of insurance products aimed at the over-50s are advertised not only on the rational basis that they are a sensible financial investment, but also on the emotional basis that they provide peace of mind. This is a customer-oriented appeal in that it works on self-interest and a craving for security. Stairlifts are also sold on the basis of security enhancement, with the implication that they make going up and down stairs easier for the elderly. The advertisements also suggest that with a stairlift, the elderly will be able to retain their independence and remain in their own homes longer, a great concern to many older people.

Self-esteem and image. Sometimes, when it is difficult to differentiate between competing products on a functional basis, consumers may choose the one that they think will best improve their self-esteem or enhance their image among social or peer groups. Advertisers recognise this and can produce advertisements in which the product and its function play a very secondary role to the portrayal of these psychological and social benefits. Perfumes, cosmetics and toiletries clearly exploit this, but even an expensive technical product such as a car can focus on self-esteem and image.

eg Alfa Romeo (http://www.alfaromeo.com) advertises its Alfa 156 model to French executives with macho promises in the headline of 'Power and mastery at your fingertips'. The body copy of the print advertisements starts by emphasising the Formula 1 technology in the car, then goes on to talk about cornering and overtaking abilities and finally implies a certain relaxed superiority, whatever the traffic or road conditions. All of this clearly appeals to a male ego that likes to have its status and dominance reflected in its choice of car and driving style, rather than just being one of the crowd.

Usage benefits – time, effort, accuracy etc. An approach stressing usage benefits is very similar to a rational, product-oriented appeal, but shows how the consumer benefits from saving time, or gains the satisfaction of producing consistently good results through using this product. Such savings or satisfactions are often translated into emotional benefits such as spending more time with the family or winning other people's admiration. They even work in B2B advertising.

eg Gulfstream sells its executive jets to companies, not on sexiness or status, but on usage benefits. Its advertisements in trade and business publications (for example that appearing in *EuroBusiness*, March 2002, p. 93) emphasise comfort, quality, performance and reliability as well as customer service and after-sales product support. Similarly, Executive Airlines, a private-flight airline, offers executives flexibility, privacy and fewer delays: 'our company makes travel time-productive' (*EuroBusiness*, March 2002, p. 88).

Advertising media

Advertising media are called on to perform the task of delivering the message to the consumer. The advertiser needs, therefore, to select the medium or media most appropriate to the task in hand, given their relative effectiveness and the budget available. Most organisations either cannot afford expensive television advertising or find it inappropriate. Print media, such as local and national newspapers, special interest magazines and trade publications, have thus become the primary focus for most organisations' advertising efforts. This section will look further at each advertising medium's relative merits, strengths and weaknesses, but first defines some of the terms commonly used in connection with advertising media.

■ Some definitions

Before we examine the advertising media themselves, several basic terms need to be defined, based on Fill (2002).

Reach

Reach is the percentage of the target market that is exposed to the message at least once during the relevant period. If the advertisement is estimated to reach 65 per cent of the target market, then that would be classified as 65. Note that reach is not concerned with the entire population, but only with a clearly defined target audience. Reach can be measured by newspaper or magazine circulation figures, television viewing statistics or analysis of flows past advertising boarding sites, and is normally measured over a four-week period.

Ratings

Ratings, otherwise known as TVRs, measure the percentage of all households owning a television that are viewing at a particular time. Ratings are a prime determinant of the fees charged for the various advertising slots on television.

> **eg**   The most expensive regular advertising slots in UK television occur during the soap opera *Coronation Street* which is screened four times per week. A 30-second slot can cost around £100,000. Some one-off television advertising opportunities can cost even more: a 30-second slot during the England vs Portugal match during the Euro 2000 soccer tournament cost £340,000 (http://www.ipa.co.uk).

Frequency

Frequency is the average number of times that a member of the target audience will have been exposed to a media vehicle during the specified time period. Poster advertising space, for example, can be bought in packages that deliver specified reach and frequency objectives for a target audience.

Opportunity to see

Opportunity to see (OTS) describes how many times a member of the target audience will have an opportunity to see the advertisement. Thus, for example, a magazine might be said to offer 75 per cent coverage with an average OTS of 3. This means that within a given time period, the magazine will reach 75 per cent of the target market, each of whom will have three opportunities to see the advertisement. According to White (1988), it is generally accepted that an OTS of $2\frac{1}{2}$–3 is average for a television advertising campaign, whereas a press campaign needs 5 or more. As Fill (2002) points out, an OTS figure of 10 is probably a waste of money, as the extra OTSs are not likely to improve reach by very much and might even risk alienating the audience with overkill!

Ideally, advertisers set targets to be achieved on both reach and frequency. Sometimes, however, because of financial constraints, they have to compromise. They can either spend on achieving breadth of coverage, that is, have a high reach figure, or go for depth, that is, have a high level of frequency, but they cannot afford both. Whether reach or frequency is better depends entirely on what the advertisement's objectives are. Where awareness generation is the prime objective, then the focus may be on reach, getting a basic message to as many of the target market as possible at least once. If, however, the objective is to communicate complex information or to affect attitudes, then frequency may be more appropriate.

Of course, when measuring reach, the wider the range of media used, the greater the chances of overlap. If, for instance, a campaign uses both television and magazine advertising, some members of the target market will see neither, some will see only the television advertisement, some will see only the print advertisement, but some will see both. Although the overall reach is actually likely to be greater than if just one medium was used, the degree of overlap must enter into the calculation, since as a campaign develops the tendency is towards duplicated reach.

■ Broadcast media

Television

Television's impact can be high, as it not only intrudes into the consumer's home but also offers a combination of sound, colour, motion and entertainment that has a strong chance of grabbing attention and getting a message across. Television advertising does present a tremendous communication opportunity, enabling a seller to communicate to a broad range of potentially large audiences. This means that television has a relatively low cost per thousand (the cost of reaching a thousand viewers) and that it has a high reach, but to largely undifferentiated audiences. Some differentiation is possible, depending on the audience profile of the programmes broadcast, and thus an advertiser can select spots to reach specific audiences, for example during sports broadcasts, but the advertising is still far from being narrowly targeted.

The problem, therefore, with television is that its wide coverage means high wastage. The cost per thousand may be low, and the number of thousands reached may be very high, but the relevance and quality of those contacts must be questioned. Television advertising time can be very expensive, especially if the advertisement is networked nationally. Actual costs will vary according to such factors as the time of day, the predicted audience profile and size, the geographic area to be covered, the length of time and number of slots purchased and the timing of negotiation. All of this means that very large bills are soon incurred.

A new product launch in the FMCG sector is almost guaranteed to be an expensive undertaking. When Kellogg launched its cereal bars in the UK, for example, it spent £8.6m., including £3.3m. on outdoor media and £3.9m. on television advertising. Companies and brand managers not only have to think of media costs but also of production costs for advertisements. Guinness's 'surfer' ad, featuring surfers riding huge waves with giant white horses leaping out of them, cost £1m. just for production and took a year to make. Although using a celebrity in an advertisement might cause fewer production problems than creating white horse effects, it still costs a lot of money (see pp. 295–6).

Quite apart from the cost involved, television is a low-involvement medium. This means that although the advertisers control the message content and broadcasting, they cannot check the audience's level of attention and understanding, because the recipient is a passive participant in what is essentially one-way communication. There is no guarantee that the recipient is even watching the advertisement, never mind following the message, learning from it and remembering it positively. Retention rates tend to be low, and therefore repetition is needed, which in turn means high costs.

The growth of internationally broadcast cable and satellite television channels is changing the shape of television advertising by creating pan-European segment interest groups. MTV, for example, has opened up communication with a huge youth market linked by a common music culture.

Radio

Radio has always provided an important means of broadcast communication for smaller companies operating within a restricted geographic area. It is now, however, beginning to emerge as a valuable national medium in the UK because of the growth in the number of local commercial radio stations and the creation of national commercial stations such as Classic FM, Virgin Radio and talkSPORT.

While still not as important as television and print, in general terms radio can play a valuable supportive role in extending reach and increasing frequency. Despite being restricted to sound only, radio still offers wide creative and imaginative advertising possibilities and, like television, can deliver to fairly specific target audiences. Narrow segments can be attractive for specialist products or services.

Classic FM, with its programming of classical music, has created a new radio-listening segment of older, affluent, potential customers who otherwise would be difficult and expensive to contact as a group. Advertisers of financial products, home furnishings and other 'exclusive' products have found a very cost-effective medium.

Compared with television, radio normally offers a low cost per time slot. However, as a low-involvement medium, it is often not closely attended to, being used just as background rather than for detailed listening. More attention might be paid, however, to the car radio during the morning and evening journey to and from work. Nevertheless, learning often only takes place slowly, again requiring a high level of repetition, carrying with it the danger of counterproductive audience irritation at hearing the same advertisements again and again. Radio is, therefore, a high-frequency medium. Television for the same budget will provide more reach, but far less frequency. The choice between them depends on objectives, and brings us back to the earlier 'reach vs frequency' discussion. Large advertisers can, however, use the two media in conjunction with each other, with radio as a means of reminding listeners of the television advertisements and reinforcing that message.

■ Cinema

Cinema can be used to reach selected audiences, especially younger ones. In the UK, for example, nearly 80 per cent of cinema-goers are in the 15–34 age group. The improvement in the quality of cinema facilities through the development and marketing of multiplexes has led to something of a resurgence in cinema audiences over the last 10 years or so.

Cinema-goers are a captive audience, sitting there with the intention of being entertained. Thus the advertiser has an increased chance of gaining the audience's attention. The quality and impact of cinema advertising can be much greater than that of television, because of the size of the screen and the quality of the sound system. Cinema is often used as a secondary medium rather than as a main medium in an advertising campaign. It can also screen advertisements, rated consistently with the film's classification, that would not necessarily be allowed on television.

■ Print media

Magazines

The main advantage of a printed medium is that information can be presented and then examined selectively at the reader's leisure. A copy of a magazine tends to be passed around among a number of people and kept for quite a long time. Add to that the fact that magazines can be very closely targeted to a tightly defined audience, and the attraction of print media starts to become clear. Advertisers also have an enormous range of types and titles to choose from. There exists an enormous number of special-interest magazines, each tailored to a specific segment. As well as broad segmentation, by sex (*Freundin* for women in Germany; *Playboy* for men anywhere), age (*J-17* and *Mizz* for teenage girls; *The Oldie* for the over-50s in the UK) and geography (*The Dalesman* for Yorkshire and its expatriates), there are many narrower criteria applied. These usually relate to lifestyle, hobbies and leisure pursuits, and enable a specialist advertiser to achieve a very high reach within those segments.

Trade and technical journals are targeted at specific occupations, professions or industries. *Industrial Equipment News*, *The Farmer*, *Accountancy Age* and *Chemistry in Britain* each provide a very cost-effective means of communication with groups of people who have very little in common other than their jobs.

Whatever the type of publication, the key is its ability to reach the specific target audience. New technology has created this diversity of magazines to suit a very wide range of targets.

Magazines have other benefits. Some may have a long life, especially special-interest magazines that may be collected for many years, although the advertising may lose relevance. Normally, though, an edition usually lasts as long as the timing between issues. The regular publication and the stable readership can allow advertisers to build up a campaign with a series of sequential advertisements over time to reinforce the message. An advertiser may also choose to take the same slot – for example the back page, which is a prime spot – to build familiarity. The advertiser may even buy several pages in the same issue, to gain a short burst of intense frequency to reinforce a message, or to present a more complex, detailed informational campaign that a single- or double-page spread could not achieve.

There has been an interesting growth in international rather than purely national magazines. *Vogue*, for instance, is a recognised name across the world, yet produces different editions to suit the different tastes of various geographic regions. Airlines also have to cater for international readerships with their in-flight magazines. BA issues *Business Life* to frequent flyers, *High Life* on certain routes and *Sinbad* for Middle Eastern routes. These magazines carry advertising not only for the airline, but also for hotels, car rentals, computers and business services, etc. Long-haul flight magazines also include direct response advertising (see Chapter 11), capitalising on the bored captive audience. Although these in-flight magazines conform to high standards in production, their circulation and readership can obviously vary considerably.

Magazines also have one potentially powerful advantage over broadcast media, which is that the mood of the reader is likely to be more receptive. People often save a magazine until they have time to look at it properly, and because they are inherently interested in the magazine's editorial content, they do pay attention and absorb what they read. This has a knock-on effect on the advertising content too. People also tend to keep magazines for reference purposes. Thus the advertising may not prompt immediate action, but if readers suddenly come back into the market, then they know where to look for suppliers.

Newspapers

The main role of newspapers for advertisers is to communicate quickly and flexibly to a large audience. National daily papers, national Sunday papers and local daily or weekly papers between them offer a wide range of advertising opportunities and audiences.

Classified advertisements are usually small, factual and often grouped under such headings as furniture, home and garden, lonely hearts, etc. This is the kind of advertising used by individuals selling their personal property, or by very small businesses (for example a one-woman home hairdressing service). Such advertisements are a major feature of local and regional newspapers. *Display advertising* has wider variations in size, shape and location within the newspaper, and uses a range of graphics, copy and photography. Display advertisements may be grouped under special features and pages: for instance, if a local newspaper runs a weddings feature it brings together advertisers providing the various goods and services that the bride-to-be would be interested in. Such groupings offer the individual advertisers a degree of synergy. Local newspapers are an important advertising medium, not only for small businesses, but for national chains of retailers supporting local stores and car manufacturers supporting local dealerships.

The main problem with newspaper advertising is related to its cost efficiency – if the advertiser wants to be more selective in targeting. Wastage rates can be high, as newspapers can appeal to very broad segments of the population. Furthermore, compared with magazines, newspapers have a much shorter lifespan and can have problems with the quality of reproduction. Although colour and photographic reproduction quality in newspapers is rapidly improving, it is still inferior to that offered by magazines, and can be inconsistent. The same advertisement, for instance, published in different newspapers or on different days can take on varying colour values and intensities, and be more or less grainy or focused.

■ Outdoor and ambient media

The last group of advertising media includes posters and hoardings, ambient media (such as advertising on bus tickets, toilet walls and store floors) as well as transport-oriented advertising media (advertising in and on buses, taxis and trains and in stations). It can be very cost-effective. According to Ray (2002), it can cost £30 to reach 1,000 through television but only £2.80 through outdoor media.

Advertising posters range from small home-made advertisements placed on a noticeboard to those for giant hoardings. This section concentrates on the latter group. Hoarding sites are normally sold by the month. Being in a static location, they may easily be seen 20–40 times in a month by people on their way to and from work or school, etc. In the UK, over one-third of poster sites are taken by car or drink advertisers. The reach may be small, but the frequency can be quite intense. They can, however, be affected by some unpredictable elements, out of the control of the advertiser. Bad weather means that people will spend less time out of doors, and are certainly not going to be positively receptive to out-door advertising. Hoardings and posters are also vulnerable to the attentions of those who think they can improve on the existing message with some graffiti or fly posting.

Size is one of the greatest assets of the advertising hoarding, creating impact. Over 80 per cent of hoarding space in the UK is taken by 4-, 6- or 48-sheet sites (a 48-sheet hoarding is 10 feet by 20 feet). Also, sites can be selected, if available, according to the match between traffic flows and target audience. However, in appealing to a mobile audience, the message needs to be simple and thus usually links with other elements of a wider campaign, either for generating initial awareness or on a reminder and reinforcement basis.

marketing *in action*

The great outdoors

Almost anything can be used as an advertising medium: bus tickets, tube tickets, hot air balloons, airships, supermarket trolleys, shops' floors, airline meal trays, sandwich bags, even cows and toilet walls. Campaigns using these 'ambient media' can be very creative and their value to the advertiser is reflected in the fact that around £90m. is spent every year on this kind of advertising.

Some campaigns are particularly memorable. Cows were recruited to wear coats advertising vegetarian cookery courses, for instance. Toyota used petrol pumps to advertise its fuel-efficient Prius model. This targeted motorists at a time when they are thinking about how much it costs to fill up their cars, and when they have nothing better to do than read and consider the advertisement on the pump. Toyota's commercial director said, 'You're never going to mass-market a product with ambient, but it's a valuable filler.' Similarly, an online recruitment company advertised on sandwich bags to target people when they were taking time out during the working day and likely to be thinking about how lousy their current jobs are. The bags might even be taken back to the office and left lying around for other people to see.

High-flying advertisers might like the idea of doing business with bmi media which sells all kinds of advertising associated with bmi British Midland aircraft. Around 350,000 passengers per month can be targeted through the in-flight magazine, cards placed on meal trays, advertisements on seat backs, and through advertising in airport business lounges. A more down-to-earth form of ambient medium is the taxi cab. Taxi Media is a company

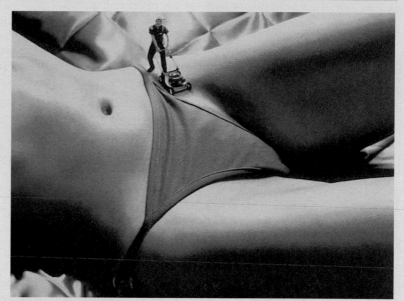

It's a lot more fun than waxing.
Source: Kookaï/CLM/BBDO.

selling advertising space in and out of taxi cabs in London and across the UK. Taxis can be branded both inside and out and drivers can participate by handing out freebies or advertising messages. Similarly, PhoneSites sells advertising space on and in telephone boxes. Research suggests that 30 per cent of the UK population uses a payphone every month and that increases to 73 per cent of 16–24-year-olds. PhoneSites also offers to set up 'hot buttons', automatic direct dialling through to the advertiser. Research has shown that this generates 40 per cent higher response rates than just printing a full telephone number for the consumer to dial.

Even traditional outdoor media such as posters can also attract attention through controversy. A poster by French fashion retailer Kookaï showing a tiny

man pushing a lawnmower down a woman's bikini line ran on French poster sites and in women's magazines with no problems. Kookaï then wanted to use the same image in a £100,000 campaign in the UK featuring the advertisement on buses in Manchester, London and Leeds. Just before it was due to be launched in London, however, TDI, the agency responsible for selling London Transport bus advertising space, decided to ban the ad as being in poor taste. Kookaï's response was to develop a new advertisement showing a portion of the original advertisement with 'censored' slashed across it. The new caption read, 'They say our ad is too risqué . . . we don't.' The new advertisement duly appeared on the buses.

Sources: Croft (2001), *Marketing* (1999), Ray (2001), Woolgar (1999).

Finally, there are the *transport-oriented media*. These include advertisements in rail or bus stations, which capture and occupy the attention of waiting passengers who have nothing better to do for a while than read the advertisements. Similarly, advertising inside trains, taxis and buses has a captive audience for as long as the journey takes. Advertising on the outside of vehicles, perhaps even going so as far as to repaint an entire bus with an advertisement, extends the reach of the advertisement to anyone who happens to be around the vehicle's route.

Using advertising agencies

It is not surprising, given the complexity and expense involved, that many organisations employ an agency to handle the development and implementation of advertising programmes. It is important, however, to select the right kind of agency, and in this section we will examine briefly the criteria for selecting an agency, and finally, there will be a few thoughts on client–agency relationships.

Clearly, selecting an agency is very important since its work can potentially make or break a product. Different writers suggest different checklists against which to measure the appropriateness of any given agency. The following list has been compiled from the work of Fill (2002), Pickton and Broderick (2001), Smith and Taylor (2002) and White (1988), and is also shown in Figure 10.2.

■ Relative size of agency and client

It might be useful to try to match the relative sizes of the client and the agency, certainly in terms of the proposed advertising spend. This is to ensure the right level of mutual respect, attention and importance. The client might also want to think ahead strategically, and choose an agency that will either grow with the client or be able to meet increased future needs. This might mean coping with a bigger account, coping with integrated communications, or coping with international advertising.

■ Location and accessibility

A smaller business with a limited geographic market might prefer to work with a small agency that has deep local knowledge and understanding. A larger business, wishing to

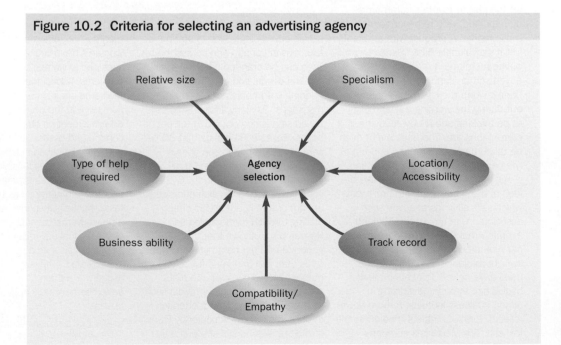

Figure 10.2 Criteria for selecting an advertising agency

keep a close eye on what the agency is doing and thus wanting frequent face-to-face meetings with the account team, might also find it more convenient to use an agency located near by.

Type of help required

Clearly, a client wants an agency that can supply the kinds of services and expertise required. The client might want a full service agency, or just specialised help in media buying, for example. The client might also want an integrated service, covering a wide range of communications techniques, not just advertising. Any prospective agency thus needs to be measured against its ability to deliver an appropriate package.

Specialism

Some agencies have a reputation for specialising in particular products or services, for example higher education advertising or financial services advertising. Some clients might find this attractive on the basis that they can be sure that the agency has detailed knowledge of the relevant marketing and competitive environments. Others, however, might find it off-putting. They might feel that the agency works for the client's competitors or that they are 'stale' from doing too much work in one field. Nevertheless, a degree of relevant experience in some related area might be a good indicator of an agency's ability to handle this new account.

Track record

Regardless of whether the agency specialises in particular types of advertising or not, a new client is going to be interested in its track record. How has the agency grown? Who is on its client list? How creative is its work? How effective is its work? Does it seem able to retain its clients, generate repeat business from them and build strong relationships?

Compatibility, empathy and personal chemistry

Compatibility and empathy are about corporate culture and outlook and about individual personalities. Clearly, a client wants an agency that is sympathetic to what the client is trying to achieve and can find the right way of talking to the target audience. A great deal of this depends on client–agency communication and the ability of the agency personnel who will be working on the account to get on well with the individuals from the client company with whom they will be liaising. It is quite legitimate, therefore, for the client to ask just who will be working on the account.

Business ability

Advertising is extremely expensive and so a client wants to be reassured that the agency can work within budget, cost-effectively, efficiently and within deadlines. This might, therefore, mean looking at their research and planning capabilities. Furthermore, a client should make sure that they understand the basis on which they will be charged by the agency and precisely what is and is not included.

The client–agency relationship

Whatever the type of agency used, a good relationship is essential. With sound briefing, mutual understanding and an agreed system of remuneration, the agency becomes an extension of the organisation's own marketing team. Cooperation may depend on mutual importance. For instance, a large client working with a large agency is fine, but a small client dealing with a large agency may become lost. There may be other constraints affecting agency choice. If an agency deals with a competitor, for example, then the conflict of interest needs to be avoided.

It is clear that the ability to deliver the goods, in terms of timing, creative content and within budget, is crucial to success. Communication and developing deeper mutual understanding and trust are also important if the agency is going to diagnose, understand and solve the client's advertising problem. If these points are taken out of the advertising agency context, they can be seen to be the fundamental criteria for any good buyer–supplier relationship.

Developing an advertising campaign

It is almost impossible that one free-standing advertisement in the press or on television would be sufficient to achieve the results expected, in terms of the impact on the target audience. Normally, advertisers think about a campaign that involves a predetermined theme but is communicated through a series of messages placed in selected media chosen for their expected cumulative impact on the specified target audience over time.

There are a number of stages in the development of an advertising campaign. Although the emphasis will vary from situation to situation, each stage at least acknowledges a need for careful management assessment and decision-making. The stages are shown in Figure 10.3 and are discussed in turn below.

■ Deciding on campaign responsibilities

This is an important question of organisational structure and 'ownership' of the campaign. If management is devolved on a product basis, then overall responsibility may rest with the brand or product manager. This certainly helps to ensure that the campaign integrates with sales promotion, selling, production planning, etc., since the brand manager is very well versed in all aspects of the product's life. If, however, management is devolved on a functional basis, then the responsibility for an advertising campaign will lie with the advertising

Figure 10.3 Stages in developing an advertising campaign

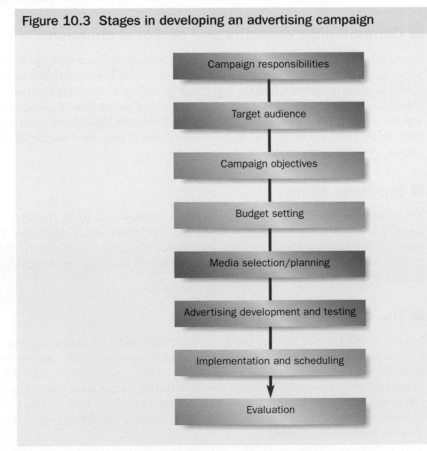

and promotion manager. This means that the campaign benefits from depth of advertising expertise, but lacks the involvement with the product that a brand manager would supply. Whatever the arrangement, it is essential to define who is ultimately responsible for what tasks and what elements of the budget.

■ Selecting the target audience

As discussed on pp. 281 *et seq.*, knowing who you are talking to is the foundation of good communication. Based on segmentation strategy, the target audience represents the group at whom the communication is aimed within the market. In some cases, the segment and the target audience may be one and the same. Sometimes, however, the target audience may be a subdivision of the segment. If, for instance, an organisation served a particular hobby segment, different approaches to advertising would be taken depending on whether they wanted to talk to serious, casual, high spenders, low spenders, general-interest or specific-interest subgroups. This underlines the need to understand the market and the range of target audiences within it.

A profile of the target audience increases the chances of successful promotion and communication. Any details, such as location, media viewing (or listening or reading) habits, geodemographics, attitudes and values, can be used to shape the propositions contained within the campaign or to direct the creative approach and media choice.

> **eg** An advertising agency thinking about advertising a brand of watches in different European countries found from research that in general, Italians treat watches like fashion accessories and might own several to coordinate with different outfits. In contrast, Germans assess watches according to the sophistication of their technology and the number of different functions built in, whereas the British just want a functional and reliable way of telling the time. Clearly, these differences in target market attitudes towards watches will lead to fundamentally different advertising approaches for the brand in those countries.

Whatever the type of product, if the assessment of the target audience is incomplete or woolly, there may be problems in directing campaign efforts later.

■ Campaign objectives

Communication objectives were considered on pp. 293 *et seq.*, and provide a clear view of what the advertising should accomplish. These objectives need to be specific, measurable and time related. They must also indicate the level of change sought, defining a specific outcome from the advertising task. If there are no measurable objectives, how can achievements be recognised and success or failure judged?

Most advertising is focused on some stage of a response hierarchy model, such as those presented in Figure 9.5 (p. 284). These models highlight the stages in the process of consumer decision-making from initial exposure and awareness through to post-purchase review. Issues such as liking, awareness or knowledge, preference and conviction are important parts of that process, and advertising can aim to influence any one of them. These can thus be translated into advertising objectives with measurable targets for awareness generation, product trial and/or repurchase, attitude creation or shifts, or positioning or preferences in comparison with the competition.

These objectives should be driven by the agreed marketing strategy and plan. Note the difference between marketing and advertising objectives. Sales and market share targets are legitimate marketing objectives as they represent the outcomes of a range of marketing mix decisions. Advertising, however, is just one element contributing to that process, and is designed to achieve specific tasks, but not necessarily exclusively sales.

■ Campaign budgets

Developing a communication budget was considered on pp. 296 *et seq.* Look back to these pages to refresh your memory on the methods of budget setting. Remember that there is no one right or wrong sum to allocate to a campaign, and often a combination of the methods proposed earlier acts as a guide.

Often the setting of budgets is an iterative process, developing and being modified as the campaign takes shape. There is a direct link between budgets and objectives such that a modification in one area is almost certainly likely to have an impact in the other. Even if the underlying philosophy of the budget is the 'objective and task' approach, practicality still means that most budgets are constrained in some way by the cash available. This forces managers to plan carefully and to consider a range of options in order to be as cost-effective as possible in the achievement of the specified objectives.

The first job is to link marketing objectives with the tasks expected of advertising and promotion. Targets may be set, for example, in relation to awareness levels, trial and repeat purchases. Not all these targets would be achieved by advertising alone. Sales promotion, and of course product formulation, may play a big part in repeat purchase behaviour.

■ Media selection and planning

The various media options were considered individually on pp. 312 *et seq.* The large range of alternative media needs to be reduced to manageable options and then scheduling (discussed on p. 323–4) planned to achieve the desired results. The resultant media plan must be detailed and specific. Actual media vehicles must be specified, as well as when, where, how much and how often. The important aim is to ensure a reasonable fit between the media vehicles considered and the target audience so that sufficient reach and frequency are achieved to allow the real objectives of the advertising a fighting chance of success. This is becoming more difficult as audience profiles and markets change (Mueller-Heumann, 1992). The media plan has an important role to play in integrating the campaign effort into the rest of the marketing plan and in communicating requirements clearly to any support agencies.

A number of considerations guide the selection of media. First, the media selected must ensure consistency with the overall *campaign objectives* for the campaign in terms of awareness, reach, etc. The *target audience* is also, however, critical to guiding the detailed media selection. As close a fit as possible is required between medium and audience. A consideration of the *competitive factors* includes examining what they have been doing, where they have been doing it, and with what outcomes. A decision may have to be made whether to use the same media as the competition or to innovate. The *geographic focus* may be relevant depending on whether the target audience is international, national or regional, and sometimes a selection of media or vehicles may have to be used to reach dispersed groups within the target audience. As discussed on pp. 296 *et seq.* *budget constraints* mean that practicality and affordability usually enter into the planning at some stage. A proposal of 20 prime-time slots on television might well give the chief accountant apoplexy and have to be replaced with a more modest print campaign that makes its impact through stunning creativity. *Timing* too is an issue, as the plan needs to take into account any lead-in or build-up time, particularly if the product's sales have a strong element of seasonality. Perfumes and aftershaves, for example, look to Christmas as a strong selling period. Advertisers of these products use glossy magazine advertising all year round, but in the weeks up to Christmas, add intensive and expensive television campaigns to coincide with consumers' decision-making for gifts. Similarly, timing is important in launching a new product, to make sure that the right level of awareness, understanding and desire have been generated by the time the product is actually available.

As with any plan, it should provide the reader with a clear justification of the rationale behind the decisions, and should act as a guide as to how it integrates with other marketing activities.

■ Advertising development and testing

At this stage, the advertisements themselves are designed and made, ready for broadcasting or printing. As the advertisement evolves, pre-testing is often used to check that the content, message and impact are as expected. This is particularly important with television advertising, which is relatively expensive to produce and broadcast, and also would represent an extremely public embarrassment if it failed.

Tests are, therefore, built in at various stages of the advertisement's development. Initial concepts and storyboards can be discussed with a sample of members of the target audience to see if they can understand the message and relate to the scenario or images in the proposed advertisement. Slightly further on in the process, a rough video of the advertisement (not the full production – just enough to give a flavour of the finished piece) can also be tested. This allows final adjustments to be made before the finished advertisement is produced. Even then, further testing can reassure the agency and the client that the advertisement is absolutely ready for release. Print advertisements can similarly be tested at various stages of their development, using rough sketches, mock-ups and then the finished advertisement.

Pre-testing is a valuable exercise, but its outcomes should be approached with some caution. The testing conditions are rather artificial, by necessity, and audiences (assuming even that the testers can assemble a truly representative audience) who react in certain ways to seeing an advertisement in a theatre or church hall might respond very differently if they saw that same advertisement in their own homes under 'normal' viewing conditions.

■ Implementation and scheduling

In the implementation phase, a number of professional experts may be needed to develop and deliver the advertising campaign. These will include graphic designers, photographers, commercial artists, copywriters, research specialists and, not least, media and production companies. The role of the advertising manager is to coordinate and select these professionals within a budget to achieve the planned objectives.

A key part of the implementation phase is the scheduling of the campaign. This describes the frequency and intensity of effort and guides all production decisions. There are many different scheduling patterns (Sissors and Bumba, 1989). Sometimes, advertising takes place in *bursts*, as shown in Figure 10.4. This means short-term, intense advertising activity, such as that often found with new product launches. Most organisations do not have the resources (or the inclination) to keep up such intense advertising activity indefinitely, and thus the bursts are few and far between. The alternative is to spread the advertising budget out more evenly, by advertising in *drips*, also shown in Figure 10.4. The advertising activity is less intense, but more persistent. Reminder advertising for a frequently purchased mature product might take place in drips rather than bursts.

A number of factors will help to determine the overall schedule. *Marketing factors* might influence the speed of the impact required. An organisation launching a new product or responding to a competitor's comparative advertising might want to make a quick impact, for example. If *turnover of customers* is high, then there is a need to advertise more frequently to keep the message available for new entrants into the market. Similarly, *purchase frequency and volatility* could be relevant factors. If demand is highly seasonal or perishable, then the scheduling might provide for a short period of high-frequency advertising. The peak time for advertising perfumes and toys, for example, is in the run-up to Christmas. Similarly, various chocolate products peak at Easter or Mother's Day, for example. Alternatively, there may be a

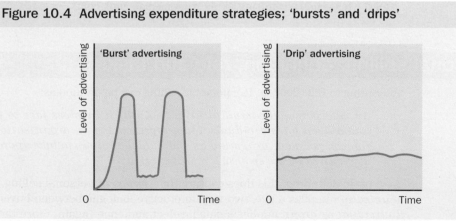

Figure 10.4 Advertising expenditure strategies; 'bursts' and 'drips'

link with brand loyalty. Higher loyalty may need less frequency, provided that the product is not under competitive attack. This is, however, a dangerous assumption.

If the danger of forgetting is high, then the advertiser is likely to need a more active campaign implemented at regular intervals. Different groups learn and forget at different rates. Therefore these *retention and attrition rates* of the target audience are yet another assessment that needs to be made. *Message factors* relate to the complexity and novelty of the message. A campaign for a new product may need more repetition than one for an established product, because of the newness of the message. More generally, simple messages or those that stand out from the crowd demand less repetition. Similarly, smaller advertisements or those placed in less noticeable spots within a print medium may need more frequency to make sure they are seen.

Media factors relate to the choice of media. The fewer media or advertising vehicles in the plan, the fewer OTSs are likely to be needed. This smaller limit may be important for a smaller business with a limited budget or for a major business seeking to dominate a particular medium by means of monopolising the best slots or positions. Such dominance increases the repetition to those in the target audience. The more congested the medium, the more OTSs there need to be, to cut through the background 'noise'.

None of this makes one media plan better than another. It depends on objectives and the particular market circumstances prevailing. If the product is new or seasonal, a more intensive effort may be appropriate. The scheduling plan may, of course, evolve over time. During the introduction stage of the product life cycle an intensive burst of advertising will launch the product, and this may then be followed by a more spread-out campaign as the growth stage finishes. Creating awareness in the first place is expensive, but critical to a product's success.

■ Campaign evaluation

The evaluation is perhaps the most critical part of the whole campaign process. This stage exists not only to assess the effectiveness of the campaign mounted, but also to provide valuable learning for the future.

There are two stages in evaluation. *Interim evaluation* enables a campaign to be revised and adjusted before completion to improve its effectiveness. It enables a closer match to be achieved between advertising objectives and the emerging campaign results. Alternatively or additionally, *exit evaluation* is undertaken at the end of the campaign. Post-testing can check whether the target audience has received, understood, interpreted and remembered the message as the advertiser wished, and whether they have acted upon it.

> **eg** World Books, a book club, was worried about falling response rates to its door-to-door and direct mail campaigns. In certain television regions, therefore, an advertising campaign was developed to tell people that a mailshot or door drop was on its way, and encouraging them to respond to it. Analysis showed that response rates increased by over 25 per cent in areas where the advertising was shown and that the 6,000 extra responses generated virtually paid for the television advertising (http://www.mediacomuk.com).

Personal selling: definition, role and tasks

According to Fill (2002, p. 16), personal selling can be defined as:

> *An interpersonal communication tool which involves face to face activities undertaken by individuals, often representing an organisation, in order to inform, persuade or remind an individual or group to take appropriate action, as required by the sponsor's representative.*

As a basic definition, this does capture the essence of personal selling. *Interpersonal communication* implies a live, two-way, interactive dialogue between buyer and seller; *with an individual or group* implies a small, select audience (again, more targeted than with the other elements); *to inform, persuade or remind . . . to take appropriate action* implies a planned activity with a specific purpose.

Note that the definition does not imply that personal selling is only about making sales. It may well ultimately be about making a sale, but that is not its only function. It can contribute considerably to the organisation both before and, indeed, after a sale has been made. As a means of making sales, personal selling is about finding, informing, persuading and at times servicing customers through the personal, two-way communication that is its strength. It means helping customers to articulate their needs, tailoring persuasive selling messages to answer those needs, and then handling customers' responses or concerns in order to arrive at a mutually valued exchange. As a background to that, personal selling is also a crucial element in ensuring customers' post-purchase satisfaction, and in building profitable long-term buyer–seller relationships built on trust and understanding (Miller and Heinman, 1991).

eg Avon, the cosmetics company, employs over 160,000 representatives in the UK (3 million worldwide) and 500 area sales managers for its direct selling operation, which is the largest in the world. The representatives have a key role in providing advice, demonstrating products, allowing sampling and relationship-building in their territories. Changes are starting to happen, however. Although the catalogue and door-to-door approach is still used, in the USA e-representatives are an alternative type of service provider. In the UK, IT is helping the company to manage the sales process better. The area managers are increasingly being provided with PCs so that orders can be placed online and monitored. It will be interesting to see whether this is the start of a process that could eventually change the whole nature of selling within Avon as Internet usage develops (Ashworth, 2001; http://www.avon.com).

Chapter 9 has already offered some insights into where personal selling fits best into the promotional mix. We discussed how personal selling is more appropriate in B2B than consumer markets on p. 281, while pp. 287 *et seq.* looked at its advantages in promoting and selling high-cost, complex products. The discussion on p. 286 also notes that personal selling operates most effectively when customers are on the verge of making a final decision and committing themselves, but still need that last little bit of tailored persuasion.

■ Advantages of personal selling

By looking at the main characteristics of personal selling, it is possible to compare it in more detail with the other elements of the promotional mix, highlighting its complementary strengths and weaknesses. The characteristics to be examined are impact, precision, cultivation and cost.

Impact

If you do not like the look of a TV advertisement, you can turn it off, or ignore it. If a glance at a print advertisement fails to capture your further attention, you can turn the page. If an envelope on the doormat looks like a mailshot, you can put it in the bin unopened. If a sales representative appears on your doorstep or in your office, it is a little more difficult to switch off. A person has to be dealt with in some way, and since most of us subscribe to the common rules of politeness, we will at least listen to what the person wants before shepherding them out of the door. The sales representative, therefore, has a much greater chance of engaging your initial attention than an advertisement does.

It is also true, of course, that an advertisement has no means of knowing or caring that you have ignored it. Sales representatives, on the other hand, have the ability to respond to the situations in which they find themselves, and can take steps to prevent themselves from being shut off completely. This could be, for instance, by pressing for another appointment at a more convenient time, or by at least leaving sales literature for the potential customer to read and think about at their leisure. Overall, you are far more likely to remember a person you have met or spoken to (and to respond to what they said) than you are to remember an advertisement. In that respect, personal selling is very powerful indeed, particularly if it capitalises on the elements of precision and cultivation (see below) as well.

Precision

Precision represents one of the great advantages of personal selling over any of the other promotional mix elements, and explains why it is so effective at the customer's point of decision-making. There are two facets of precision that should be acknowledged: targeting precision and message precision. Targeting precision arises from the fact that personal selling is not a mass medium. As this chapter has already shown, advertising can be targeted within broad parameters, but even so, there will still be many wasted contacts (people who are not even in the target market; people who are not currently interested in the product; people who have recently purchased already; people who cannot currently afford to purchase, etc.), and each of those wasted contacts costs money. Personal selling can weed out the inappropriate contacts early on, and concentrate its efforts on those who offer a real prospect of making a sale.

Message precision arises from the interactive two-way dialogue that personal selling encourages. An advertisement cannot tell what impact it is having on you. It cannot discern whether you are paying attention to it, whether you understand it or whether you think it is relevant to you. Furthermore, once the advertisement has been presented to you, that is it. It is a fixed, inflexible message, and if you did not understand it, or if you felt that it did not tell you what you wanted to know, then you have no opportunity to do anything about it other than wait for another advertisement to come along that might clarify these things. Because personal selling involves live interaction, however, these problems should not occur. The sales representative can tell, for example, that your attention is wandering, and therefore can change track, exploring other avenues until something seems to capture you again. The representative can also make sure that you understand what you are being told and go over it again from a different angle if you are having difficulty with the first approach. Similarly, the representative can see if something has particularly caught your imagination and tailor the message to emphasise that feature or benefit. Thus, by listening and watching, the sales representative should be able to create a unique approach that exactly matches the mood and the needs of each prospective customer. This too is a very potent capability.

Cultivation

As Chapter 3 implied, the creation of long-term, mutually beneficial buyer–seller relationships is now recognised as extremely important to the health and profitability of organisations in many industries. The sales force has a crucial role to play in both creating and maintaining such relationships. Sales representatives are often the public face of an organisation, and their ability to carry the organisation's message professionally and confidently can affect judgement of that organisation and what it stands for. When Avon, the cosmetics company, decided to target the teenage beauty business, they realised that to build and maintain customer relationships it had to reconsider whether the direct sales force employed was suitable for the different customer group. The new range 'exclusively for teens' (called 'mark') was launched in the USA in 2003 with global launch due in the second quarter of 2004, but instead of using an army of 'Avon ladies', the company intends to recruit teenagers who are better placed to demonstrate and promote the products to that audience (Singh, 2001).

Cost

All the advantages and benefits discussed above come at a very high cost, as personal selling is extremely labour intensive. In addition, costs of travel (and time spent travelling), accommodation and other expenses have to be accounted for. It can cost well over £50,000 to keep a sales representative on the road, and for the more demanding roles, a cost in excess of £100,000 can be expected. Generally, the salary paid is only around 50 per cent of the total cost of keeping a sales representative mobile and connected. The actual time spent selling to a customer can vary considerably, and estimates of 50 per cent of time spent on travelling, 20 per cent on administration, 20 per cent on call planning and 10 per cent on actual face-to-face contact are not uncommon (McDonald, 1984; Abberton Associates, 1997). IBM found that whereas telemarketing sellers could handle 50 calls in a day, the typical sales representative is often hard pressed to manage 5 sales calls per day (Blackwood, 1995). This emphasises the importance of call effectiveness and achieving better personal interrelationships, as only then can the high cost of personal selling be justified.

Selling cosmetics and toiletries to friends and neighbours in the comfort of your own home is the way in which Avon works very successfully.

Source: Avon Cosmetics.

■ Tasks of personal selling

There is a tendency to think of the sales representative in a one-off selling situation. What the discussion in the previous sections has shown is that in reality, the representative is likely to be handling a relationship with any specific customer over a long period of time. The representative will be looking to build up close personal ties because much depends on repeat sales. In some cases, the representative might even be involved in helping to negotiate and handle joint product development. All of this suggests a range of tasks beyond the straight selling situation.

Figure 10.5 summarises the range of typical tasks of the sales representative, each of which is defined below.

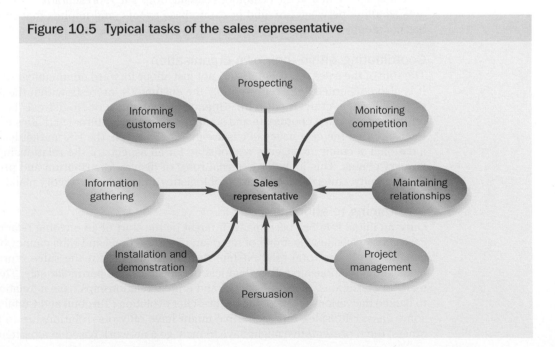

Figure 10.5 Typical tasks of the sales representative

Prospecting

Prospecting is finding new potential customers who have the willingness and ability to purchase. For Rentokil Tropical Plants, for example, the role of the sales representative is to contact a range of potential clients including offices, hotels, shopping centres and restaurants to design and recommend individual displays of tropical plants on a supply and maintenance basis. Prospecting is an important task, particularly for organisations entering a new market segment or for those offering a new product line with no established customer base.

> **eg** When Pennine Telecom was appointed as a major Dolphin Telecommunications service provider, it had to employ a sales team to launch a new communications technology for businesses. The new communication system offered two-way radio, cellular phone, paging and large volume data transfer within one system. Most of the early work of the sales team was to find potential customers through cold calling and by appointment and then to convince them of the usage benefits of the system compared with its existing one.

Informing

Informing is giving prospective customers adequate, detailed and relevant information about products and services on offer. In B2B markets, once contact has been made with prospects, the sales representative needs to stimulate sufficient information exchange to ensure a technical and commercial match that is better than the competition.

Persuading

Persuading is helping the prospective customer to analyse the information provided, in the light of their needs, in order to come to the conclusion that the product being offered is the best solution to their problem. Sometimes, presenting the main product benefits is sufficient to convince the buyer of the wisdom of selecting that supplier. On other occasions, especially with purchases that are technically or commercially more complex, the persuasion might have to be very subtle and varied, according to the concerns of the different members of the buying team.

Installing and demonstrating

Particularly with technical, B2B purchases, the buyer may need considerable support and help to get the equipment installed and to train staff in its use. The sales representative may join a wider team of support personnel to ensure that all this takes place according to whatever was agreed and to the customer's satisfaction. The representative's continued presence acts as a link between pre- and post-purchase events, and implies that the representative has not stopped caring about the customer just because the sale has been made.

Coordinating within their own organisation

The role of the sales representative is not just about forward communication with the buyer. It is also concerned with 'representing' the customer's interests within the selling organisation. Whether concerned with financial, technical or logistical issues, the sales representative must coordinate and sometimes organise internal activities on a project basis to ensure that the customer's needs are met. At Duracell, the UK market leader in batteries, a national account manager is responsible for all aspects of the relationship with the large grocery chains. This includes external roles of display, distribution and promotional planning as well as internal coordination of logistics and product category management.

Maintaining relationships

Once an initial sale has been made, it might be the start of an ongoing relationship. In many cases, a single sale is just one of a stream of transactions and thus cannot be considered in isolation from the total relationship. An important role for the sales representative is to manage the relationship rather than just the specifics of a particular sale. This means that in many organisations, more substantial and critical relationships have a 'relationship manager' to handle the various facets of the buyer–seller evolution (Turnbull and Cunningham, 1981). In some cases, the sales representative might have only one relationship to manage, but in others, the representative might have to manage a network based in a particular sector.

eg The prime responsibility of an account manager at Colgate-Palmolive is to maintain and develop business relationships with major multiple retailer accounts. These relationships in some cases go back over many years. In order to achieve this, the emphasis is on cooperation and customer development through working together in such areas as category management, logistics and merchandising. There is a need to ensure a close fit between retail requirements and Colgate-Palmolive's brand strategies. This means that the account manager must be able to analyse brand and category information in order to develop plans that will help sales of Colgate's personal and household care products. Any account manager who sought short-term sales gains at the expense of customer trust and goodwill would not benefit Colgate-Palmolive's long-term plans for the account.

Information and feedback gathering

The gathering of information and the provision of feedback emphasise the need for representatives to keep their eyes and ears open, and to indulge in two-way communication with the customers they deal with. 'Grapevine' gossip about what is happening in the industry might, for example, give valuable early warning about big planned purchases in the future, or about potential customers who are dissatisfied with their current supplier. Both of these situations would offer opportunities to the organisation that heard about them early enough to make strategic plans about how to capitalise on them. In terms of relationships with existing customers, sales representatives are more likely than anyone to hear about the things that the customer is unhappy about. This feedback role is even more important when developing business in export markets, where the base of accumulated knowledge might not be very strong. Personal contacts can help to add to that knowledge over time (Johanson and Vahlne, 1977).

Monitoring competitor action

The representative works out in the field, meeting customers and, in all probability, competitors. As well as picking up snippets about what competitors are planning and who they are doing business with, the representative can provide valuable information about how his or her organisation's products compare with those of the competition in the eyes of the purchasers. During the course of sales presentations, prospective customers can be subtly probed to find out what they think are the relative strengths and weaknesses of competing products, what they consider to be the important features and benefits in that kind of product, and how the available offerings score relative to each other (Lambert *et al.*, 1990).

---

marketing *in action*

The sales rep: on the endangered list?

A sales representative is an expensive asset for an organisation to maintain. Representatives need cars, computers, mobile phones, samples, presentation equipment and administrative support. They also run up bills for hotel accommodation and entertaining clients. When economic times are hard, therefore, many organisations cut their sales forces or rationalise them to save on costs. Other factors have also led to a reduction in the number of sales representatives. In consumer goods markets, for instance, there has been a reduction in the number of small independent retailers and a corresponding increase in the share of business taken by the big multiples. The bigger retailers tend to have computerised stock control systems with online ordering, so that there is no need for a representative to visit individual branches so often (if at all). HP Foods, for example, had between 70 and 100 sales representatives in the 1970s. By the millennium, the number had been slimmed down to 12 business development executives who each manage a portfolio of national and regional accounts. The largest proportion of HP's orders, however, comes in via computers or the telephone.

There is, of course, still a role for the representative in consumer goods markets in visiting smaller retailers, both to take orders and to help with promotional events or point-of-sale displays. Many organisations, however, find it cheaper and more efficient to use contract sales staff

▶

from field marketing agencies for such tasks. When Mars launched Celebrations, for example, a field marketing agency was used rather than Mars' own sales force to work with cash and carry and other wholesalers to provide free samples, provide product information and to negotiate special point-of-sale displays. The benefit of contract staff is that the organisation only has to pay for them when they want them, and can have as large or small a 'sales force' as a particular task or project requires. Contract sales staff tend to work in small territories and thus have established close relationships with the retailers and other customers that they regularly visit.

Field marketing (FM) has grown in popularity over the last 10 years as an effective substitute for client-owned sales forces where the emphasis is on the more routine tasks of order taking and in-store demonstrations. FM has been defined as 'the business of creating, directing and managing full-time merchandising, sales and training teams to influence change at the point of purchase' (Gary MacManus, Aspen Field Marketing, as quoted by Middleton, 2001). The main activities are sales, i.e. acting as a client's sales team or supplementing the activities of the client's sales team or meeting specific coverage or time requirements; merchandising; auditing; and mystery shopping. As a sector it is expanding fast, with growth rates in 1999 and 2000 of between 30 and 35 per cent in sales.

Some organisations might worry, however, that because contract sales staff are not employed by them full time, there might be questions about their loyalty and motivation. Agencies are well aware of this and try to overcome it by setting up quality control systems to monitor the performance of their staff in the field, and ensuring that staff are fully and properly briefed at the start of an assignment. To try to engender 'loyalty' to the task in hand, the agency will also ensure that a member of staff is only working for one client in a particular product market at a time. Because of the amount of time contract staff spend in the field and because of the wide range of customers and product types they deal with, these agencies can amass a wealth of data about what is going on in the market that a company's own sales force would not have either the time or the resources to collect. Agencies can thus feed information back to clients, providing an additional benefit to their service.

As FM has grown in popularity, so its role has expanded from just being point-of-sale merchandising. The contract sellers' sales forces are becoming better trained, more IT literate and skilled in providing useful market information back to the contracting company. There are two broad areas in which contract sales staff are currently used: in FMCG, dealing with retailers, and in door-to-door selling, covering a wide range of products and services including cable television, utilities and financial services. High pressure selling and misselling were exposed in the utilities sector, where untrained and unscrupulous sales people made a wide range of promises that could not be honoured to encourage consumers to change energy suppliers. Most reputable field marketing agencies seek to avoid such problems through careful recruitment, appropriate training and local control. For example, it has been suggested that the ratio of sales representatives to managers should be 10 : 1 in FMCG and 6 : 1 in door-to-door selling.

Thus, although the grocery trade still dominates the use of FM agencies, other sectors have now started to realise the benefits of more flexible sales force arrangements. The major credit card companies recruit new card holders through direct selling using agencies, and car manufacturers such as Honda, BMW and Volvo use FM to encourage sampling and test drives. Some smaller companies have found that using FM agencies can provide them with a dedicated sales team they could never previously have afforded. The next stage of development is likely to be closer integration of FM into pan-European promotional campaigns. According to FM agency CPM, however, few truly pan-European FM campaigns are being run, with companies such as Mars and Disney preferring to run separate country-by-country FM campaigns. Some larger companies are seeking to find one agency to handle all their different campaigns across Europe. So Momentum, with 33 offices across Europe, has organised a test drive campaign for Saab in six European countries and P&G has operated similar activities in 11 EU states. The need to address local market situations and culture will for some time act as a brake on genuine pan-European FM campaigns.

So, the sales representative might not be about to become extinct. What is certain is that organisations are rethinking how they manage and organise their sales forces and their selling processes. Thus the role and the tasks of representatives will change, and how they are employed might change, but they will always be needed in some capacity.

Sources: Gofton (2002), McLuhan (2001a, b), Middleton (2001), Miles (1998); http://www.ukfm.co.uk

Thus while selling remains the central activity for a sales representative, the roles of prospecting for new customers, maintaining communication links with customers, servicing customers' needs before and after sale and information gathering are no less important in enhancing the selling process and maximising the investment in such a labour-intensive promotional element.

The personal selling process

At the heart of the sales process is the sales representative's ability to build a relationship with the buyer that is sufficiently strong to achieve a deal that benefits both parties. In many situations the main decision relates to *supplier choice* rather than whether or not to buy. The sales representative's role is to highlight the attractions of the specification, support, service and commercial package on offer. Differences between products, markets, organisational philosophies and even individuals will all have a bearing on the style and effectiveness of the selling activity.

In reality, personal selling does not lend itself to a prescribed formula: there is no one approach that is right for all situations, nor is there any one approach that is right for all types of sales representative. It is possible, however, to define a number of broad stages through which most selling episodes will pass (Russell *et al.*, 1977). Depending on the product, the market, the organisations and individuals involved, the length of time spent in any one of the stages will vary, as will the way in which each stage is implemented (Pedersen *et al.*, 1986). Nevertheless, the generalised analysis offered here provides a useful basis for beginning to understand what contributes to successful personal selling.

Figure 10.6 shows the flow of stages through a personal selling process and each stage is discussed in full below.

■ Prospecting

Before sales representatives can get down to the real job of selling something, they have to have someone to sell to. In some organisations, perhaps those selling an industrial product with a specific application to a relatively small number of easily defined B2B customers, this will be a highly structured activity, involving sales representatives and support staff, and will lead to the representative going out on a call knowing that the prospect is potentially fruitful. In contrast, double glazing companies often employ canvassers to walk the

Figure 10.6 The personal selling process

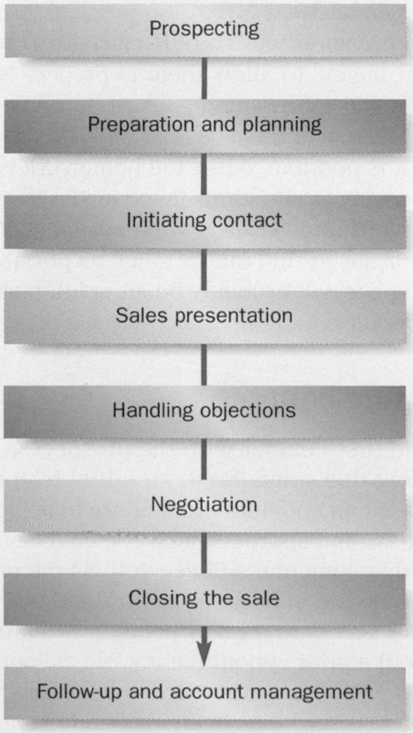

streets knocking on doors to see if householders are likely prospects. This is not a particularly efficient use of the representatives' time, as most people will say that they are not interested, but in promoting an infrequently purchased, high-priced product, yet in a mass market, it is difficult to see what else in the way of prospecting they can do.

In a B2B rather than a consumer market, the sales representative needs a prospect bank, a pool of potential customers to be drawn on as appropriate. This bank could include potential customers who have made enquiries or responded to advertising, but not been followed up already. Second, there are those who have already been approached in an exploratory way, for example through telemarketing, and look promising enough to deserve further encouragement. Third, and most problematic, are the lists of names. These lists might be purchased from a list broker or be compiled from a trade directory or a list of organisations attending a particular trade exhibition. Sales representatives may have to develop their own prospect banks from referrals, either from word of mouth from contacts outside the organisation, or from telemarketing support staff discussed above. They can also compile lists from directories, or from scanning the media for relevant company news that might open up an opportunity. This might lead to a session of preliminary cold calling (by phone or in person) to establish whether this person or organisation really is a viable prospect.

■ Preparation and planning

Identifying a qualified prospect is only the beginning of the process. Before the real selling begins, it is very important to obtain further information on the prospect in order to prepare the best and most relevant sales approach and to plan tactics.

In selling to a B2B customer, this may mean scanning a number of company reports, assessing the norms for that industry in relation to likely buying criteria and needs. Analysing the prospect's company report might promise indications of the strategic direction in which it is moving, as well as revealing its financial situation. It is also necessary to think about the kind of purchasing structures that the representative is going to have to work through, identifying the most likely influencers and decision makers. In addition, it is also useful to find out as much as possible about the application of the product and the features and benefits required. This allows the representative to construct a sales presentation that will be relevant to the buyer and thus will have more chance of engaging their attention and being persuasive.

Sales representatives in B2B markets are fortunate that sufficient information exists about their buyers to allow them to prepare so well in advance. In consumer markets, it is more likely that representatives have to think on their feet, analysing customers while they are face to face with them.

Where it is possible, doing the homework is essential, and it often needs to be very thorough, especially in situations involving large, complex projects with stiff competition. Also, if the competition is already well entrenched in doing business with a prospect, it is even more important to find out as much as possible in advance, since getting that customer to switch supplier will probably be an uphill task unless you can find the right approach with the right people.

■ Initiating contact

Making the first contact with the prospect is a delicate operation. There are two ways of approaching this stage. First, an initial telephone call that qualifies the prospect may be used to solicit an appointment. Failure to achieve that means that the selling process cannot begin. The second approach is to use cold calling. This means turning up on the doorstep in the hope that someone will see you, as the double glazing sales representative does. This can be very wasteful in terms of time and travel. There is no guarantee that the representative will get access to the key people, who probably would not in any case be able to spare time without a prior appointment. Cold callers are often seen as time wasters, and do not do themselves or their organisations any favours in the eyes of the prospects.

Once an approach has been made and an appointment secured, the next stage is the initial call. This helps the representative to discover whether the initial assessment of the customer's likely need is borne out in practice. In these early meetings, it is important to build up rapport, mutual respect and trust between buyer and seller before the more serious business discussion gets under way. The time spent in establishing this relationship is well spent. It helps to build a solid foundation for the later stages of discussion.

■ The sales presentation

At last, the representative has enough insight and information to allow the preparation of the sales presentation itself that lies at the heart of the selling process. The ease of its preparation and its effectiveness in practice owe a great deal to the thoroughness and quality of the work done in the earlier stages. The objective of the sales presentation is to show how the product offering and the customer's needs match. The presentation must not be product oriented, but be concerned with what the product can do for that particular customer. In other words, do not sell the features, sell the benefits.

There may be some practicalities to be handled as part of the presentation. The representative may have to demonstrate the product, for example. The product or sample used must look right, and will need to be explained, not in technical terms, necessarily, but in terms of how it offers particular benefits and solutions. A demonstration is a powerful element of a sales presentation, because it gets the prospect involved and encourages conversation and questions. It provides a focus that can dispel any lingering awkwardness between buyer and seller. Also, in getting their hands on the product itself, or a sample, the prospect is brought very close to the reality of the product and can begin to see for themselves what it can do for them.

> **eg** When a 61-year-old man enquired about a £5,000 spa bath at a Merlin Timber Products showroom, it allegedly led to his death. Although the prospective customer just wanted a brochure, the keen salesman invited him and his wife to witness a demonstration of the water turbulence created by high-powered air pumps, blowers and jets. Unfortunately, as the customer was invited to feel the therapeutic turbulence, the jets of air also sprayed the unsuspecting customer with a fine mist. Two days later he complained of flu-like symptoms and just 17 days later died of multiple organ failure from legionnaires' disease. Samples taken from the water confirmed that the bacteria were present three weeks after the incident. The Surrey Health Council, under whose environmental responsibility the showroom came, found that the ozoneator was not working properly and if it had been, the bacteria would have been killed. The Council also found that sales staff had not been properly trained about the health risks associated with demonstrating spa baths, so the accident that happened was, to some, entirely predictable. The coroner recorded a verdict of accidental death on the poor customer (Payne, 2002).

Handling objections

It is indeed a rare and skilful sales representative who can complete an entire sales presentation without the prospect coming out with words to the effect of 'that's all very well, but …'. At any stage in the selling process that involves the customer, objections can and probably will be made. These may arise for various reasons: lack of understanding; lack of interest; misinformation; a need for reassurance; or genuine concern. The sales representative must be prepared to overcome objections where possible, as otherwise the sale is likely to be lost completely. If the customer is concerned enough to raise an objection, then the representative must have the courtesy to answer it in some way. Homespun wisdom among seasoned sales representatives argues that the real selling does not begin until the customer raises an objection.

Organisations that do not subscribe to the formula approach to selling often do train their sales staff to handle specific objections that commonly arise in their field in a set way. If a buyer says, for example 'I think your product is not as good as product x', the sales representative should explore what is meant by the use of the word 'good'. This could cover a whole range of different areas in the competitive offering. The representative's response may therefore be designed to explore in more detail the underlying problem by asking 'In what way is it not as good?' Agreeing with the objection and countering it is often called the 'yes, but' technique. Where the objection is founded in fact, all the representative can legitimately do is agree with the substance of it, then find a compensating factor to outweigh it. Thus if the prospect argues that the product being sold is more expensive than the competition's, the representative can reply with 'Yes, I agree that value for money is important. Although our product is more expensive initially, you will find that the day-to-day running costs and the annual maintenance add up to a lot less …'. Such a technique avoids creating excessive tension and argument, because the customer feels that their objection has been acknowledged and satisfactorily answered.

All in all, handling objections requires a very careful response from representatives. They must not see objections as a call for them to say just anything to clinch the sale, since doing so will only lead to legal or relationship problems later. The representative must assess the situation, the type of objection and the mood of the customer and then choose the most appropriate style of response, without overstepping any ethical boundaries in terms of content. It is critical that winning the argument used to overcome the objection does not lead to a lost sale. Objections may interrupt the flow of the sales process either temporarily or permanently, and unless they are overcome, the final stages of the selling process cannot be achieved.

Negotiation

Once the main body of the sales presentation is drawing to a close, with all the prospect's questions and objections answered for the time being, the selling process may move into a negotiation phase. Negotiation is a 'give and take' activity in which both parties try to shape a deal that satisfies both of them. Negotiation assumes a basic willingness to trade, but does not necessarily lead to a final deal. The danger for the sales representative, of course, is that a deadlocked or delayed negotiation phase may allow a competitor to enter the fray.

Despite the fact that deals are becoming more complex, sales staff are still expected to be able to negotiate. If they are going to be given the power to negotiate on behalf of the organisation, then they need clear guidelines on how far they are permitted to go in terms of concessions, and what the implications of those concessions would be. An extra month's credit, for example, could be quite expensive, particularly for an organisation with short-term cash-flow problems, unless it is traded for another prized concession. This effectively means that the sales representative needs financial as well as behavioural training in order to handle complex and sometimes lengthy negotiations.

As a final point, it must be said that negotiation need not be a separate and discrete stage of the selling process. Negotiation may emerge implicitly during the process of handling objections, or may be an integral part of the next stage to be discussed, closing the sale.

Closing the sale

The closing stage of the personal selling process is concerned with reaching the point where the customer agrees to purchase. In most cases, it is the sales representative's responsibility to close the sale, to ask for the order. Where the prospect still seems to have doubts, the timing of the closure and the way in which it is done could affect whether a sale is made. Try to close the sale too soon, and the buyer might be frightened off; leave it too long, and the buyer might become irritated by the prolonged process and all the good work done earlier in the sales presentation will start to dissipate.

Watching the buyer's behaviour and listening to what they are saying might indicate that closure is near. The buyer's questions, for example, may become very trivial or the objections might dry up. The buyer might go quiet and start examining the product intently, waiting for the representative to make a move. The buyer's comments or questions might begin to relate to the post-purchase period, with a strong assumption that the deal has already been done. A representative who thinks that the time to close is near, but is uncertain, might have to test the buyer's readiness to commit to a purchase. Also, if the prospect seems to be teetering on the edge of making a decision, then the representative might have to give the buyer a gentle nudge in the direction of closure, for example by offering the buyer a number of alternatives, each of which implies an agreement to purchase. The buyer's response gives an insight into how ready they are to commit themselves. Thus if the representative says, 'Would you like delivery to each of your stores or to the central distribution point?', there are two ways in which the buyer might respond. One way would be to choose one of the alternatives offered, in which case the sale must be very close, since the buyer is willing to get down to such fine detail. The other response would be something like, 'Wait a minute, before we get down to that, what about . . .', showing that the buyer has not yet heard enough and may still have objections to be answered.

■ Follow-up and account management

The sales representative's responsibility does not end once a sale has been agreed. As implied earlier on pp. 327 *et seq.*, the sales representative, as the customer's key contact point with the selling organisation, needs to ensure that the product is delivered on time and in good condition, that any installation or training promises are fulfilled and that the customer is absolutely satisfied with the purchase and is getting the best out of it.

At a more general level, the relationship with the customer still needs to be cultivated and managed. Where the sale has resulted in an ongoing supply situation, this may mean ensuring continued satisfaction with quality and service levels. Even with infrequently purchased items, ongoing positive contact helps to ensure that when new business develops, that supplier will be well placed. In the case of the consumer buying a car, the sales representative will make sure in the early stages that the customer is happy with the car, and work to resolve any problems quickly and efficiently. In the longer term, direct responsibility usually passes from the representative to a customer care manager who will ensure that the buyer is regularly sent product information and things like invitations to new product launches in the showrooms.

In the B2B market, an important role for the sales representative is to manage the customer's account internally within the selling organisation, ensuring that appropriate support is available as needed. Thus the representative is continuing to liaise between the customer and the accounts department, engineering, R&D, service and anyone else with whom the customer needs to deal.

Sales management

The previous section concentrated on the mechanics of selling something to a prospective buyer. That is important, certainly, because if the selling process does not work well, then there will be no sales and no revenue. Equally important, however, is the management of the sales force. Whether in a multinational organisation or a small company, the selling effort needs to be planned and managed, and sales management provides an essential link between the organisation's strategic marketing plans and the achievement of sales objectives by the representatives in the field.

eg Procter and Gamble decided to reorganise its sales force away from a retail focused strategy to more specific brand-selling activities. Although the large retailers would still be serviced by account teams, each individual sales representative was to be given a more specific remit. Instead of having responsibility for the whole paper category from nappies to toilet rolls, for example, under the new structure an individual representative would take responsibility for a specific area within the category such as paper tissues. Through the reorganisation, it is expected that higher levels of expertise will be developed in advising retailers on merchandising and in-store marketing activities (Bittar, 2001).

■ Planning and strategy

The sales plan outlines the objectives for the selling effort and the details of how the plan should be implemented. This plan itself arises from, and must fit closely with, the marketing objectives set for products and market share, etc. These marketing objectives need to be translated into sales objectives, both for the sales force as a whole and for individuals or groups within the sales force. Setting sales objectives provides an essential yardstick against which to measure progress and to motivate and influence the selling effort. Normally, quantitative measures are used to specify exactly what is required, such as sales value and/or volume. Setting objectives in sales and profit terms is often necessary either to avoid the dangers of chasing low profit sales or to lessen the temptation to reduce margins to generate more sales volume but less gross profit. Targets for individual sales representatives need not only relate to selling quantities of products. Performance targets might be agreed in terms of the number of sales calls, the number of new accounts recruited, the call frequency, call conversion rates (i.e. turning prospects into buyers) or selling expenses.

Assuming that the selling effort is to be managed internally, the sales manager also has to decide how the sales force will be organised: by geography (e.g. each sales representative is allocated a geographic region as their sales territory); by product (e.g. each sales representative is allocated a particular brand or family of product lines to sell); by customer type (e.g. each sales representative concentrates on a particular industry within which to sell); or by customer importance (e.g. the most important customers, perhaps in terms of sales, are identified and allocated their own sales representative or account team).

> **eg** Philips (http://www.philips.com) has structured its selling effort around the main divisions of the company. Therefore the consumer electronics division sales force is responsible for sales of such products as DVD players, digital televisions and CD players to retailers. In contrast, the business electronics division would handle such items as digital transmission systems and sell direct to business users. Similar sales teams have been organised around other divisions such as lighting and medical. However, although the company is organised around distinct product types, geographic territories are still used to allocate the defined areas to sales staff.

There is clearly no one universally applicable and appropriate organisational structure. Sometimes a mixed structure may be best, combining geographic and major customer specialisation. Johnson & Johnson, for example, employs regionally based territory sales managers for its UK consumer products, but with specific responsibility for certain types of customer, such as independent pharmacies and wholesale cash and carries. This allows the organisation to benefit from the advantages of both types of allocation, while reducing the effect of their disadvantages. The chosen structure will be the right one as long as it reflects the objectives and marketing strategy of the firm.

A further decision has to be made on the ideal size of the sales force. A number of factors need to be considered, such as the calling frequency required for each customer, the number of calls possible each day, and the relative division of the representative's time between administration, selling and repeat calls (Cravens and LaForge, 1983). All these matters will have an impact on the ability of the sales force to achieve the expected sales results from the number of accounts served. For a smaller business, the issue may be further constrained by just how many representatives can be afforded!

■ Recruitment and selection

As with any recruitment exercise, it is important to begin by developing a profile of who the organisation is looking for. A detailed analysis of the selling tasks should lead to a list of the ideal skills and characteristics of the representative to be recruited. Table 10.1 lists the attributes of sales representatives typically appreciated by buyers.

A common dilemma is whether previous experience is an essential requirement. Some organisations prefer to take on recruits new to selling, then train them in their own methods rather than recruit experienced representatives who come with bad habits and other organisations' weaknesses. Others, especially smaller organisations, may deliberately seek experienced staff, wishing to benefit from training programmes that they themselves could not afford to provide.

Table 10.1 Sales representative attributes typically appreciated by buyers

- Thoroughness and follow-up
- Knowledge of seller's products
- Representing the buyer's interests within the selling organisation
- Market knowledge
- Understanding the buyer's problems
- Knowledge of the buyer's product and markets
- Diplomacy and tact
- Good preparation before sales calls
- Regular sales calls
- Technical education

The actual selection process needs to be designed to draw out evidence of the ability of each candidate to perform the specified tasks, so that an informed choice can be made. The cost of a poor selection can be very high, not just in terms of recruitment costs and salary, but also, and perhaps more seriously, in terms of lost sales opportunities or damage to the organisation's reputation. In view of the importance of making the right choice, in addition to normal interview and reference procedures, a number of firms employ psychological tests to assess personality and some will not confirm the appointment until the successful completion of the initial training period.

■ Training

The recruitment process generally only provides the raw material. Although the new recruit might already have appropriate skills and a good attitudinal profile, training will help to sharpen both areas so that better performance within the sales philosophy of the employing organisation can be developed. Sales force training applies not just to new recruits, however. Both new and existing staff, even well-established staff, may need skills refinement and upgrading.

Training may be formal or informal. Some organisations invest in and develop their own high-quality training facilities and run a regular series of introductory and refresher courses in-house. This has the advantage of ensuring that the training is relevant to the organisation and its business, as well as signifying an ongoing commitment to staff development.

Other organisations adopt a more ad hoc approach, using outside specialists as required. This means that the organisation only pays for what it uses, but the approach carries two serious risks. The first problem is that the training may be too generalised and thus insufficiently tailored to the organisation's needs. The second problem is that it is too easy for the organisation to put off training or, even worse, to delete it altogether in times of financial stringency.

Finally, a third group uses informal or semi-formal 'sitting with Nelly', on-the-job coaching. This involves the trainee observing other representatives in the field, and then being observed themselves by experienced sales representatives and/or the sales manager. There is nothing quite like seeing the job being done, but with this approach the organisation needs to take great care to deal with a number of points. One concern is to ensure that such training is comprehensive, covering all aspects of the job. Another is to ensure that bad habits or questionable techniques are not passed on. The main problem with this kind of on-the-job training is that the training is not usually done by professional trainers. Therefore the quality can be variable, and there is no opportunity for fresh ideas to be introduced to the sales force.

■ Motivation and compensation

An organisation will not only want to motivate new recruits to join its sales force, but also have an interest in making sure that they are sufficiently well rewarded for their achievements that they will not easily be poached by the competition (Cron *et al.*, 1988). There are many ways in which the sales team can be motivated to achieve outstanding results and rewarded, and not all are financially based. Opportunities for self-development through training, well-defined career progression routes, and a feeling of being valued as an individual within a team can all increase job satisfaction.

> **eg** Rentokil Initial with interests in hygiene, tropical plants, office solutions and medical services offers a package of financial and non-financial benefits to attract and retain staff. Part of the compensation comes in the form of benefits for a mobile phone, pension scheme, company car, regular training and promotion prospects. The salary package includes a basic salary and monthly commission potentially leading to on-target earnings of £29,000–£35,000 (with top earners on £50,000), and an incentive scheme based on quarterly and annual performance. This comprehensive range of benefits is part of a culture that values the sales force and believes that there is a direct link between motivated sales representatives and additional sales.

Nevertheless, pay still remains a vital ingredient in attracting and retaining a committed sales force. Three main methods of compensation exist: straight salary, straight commission, and a combination of salary and commission. Each method implies a number of advantages and disadvantages, listed in Table 10.2. The straight salary compensation plan is where a fixed amount is paid on a salary basis. The straight commission compensation plan means that earnings are directly related to the sales and profit generated. Finally, the most popular method is the combination plan, involving part salary and part commission. The selection of the most appropriate method will partly be determined by the nature of the selling tasks, and the degree of staff turnover that can be tolerated given the training and recruiting costs.

Table 10.2 Comparison of compensation plans

	Commission only	Salary only	Part salary/part commission
Motivation for rep. to generate sales	High	Low	Medium
Motivation for rep. to build customer relationship	Low	High	Medium
Motivation for rep. to participate in training	Low	High	Medium
Cost effectiveness for organisation	High	Potentially low	Medium
Predictability of cost to organisation	Low	High	Medium
Predictability of income for rep.	Low	High	Medium
Ease of administration for organisation	Low	High	Low
Organisation's control over rep.	Low	High	Medium
Organisation's flexibility to push sales of particular products	High	Low	High
Overall, best where …	• Aggressive selling is needed • There are few non-selling tasks	• Training new reps • Difficult sales territories exist • Developing new territories • There are many non-selling tasks	• Organisation wants both incentive and control • Sales territories all have similar profiles

■ Performance evaluation

Given that many sales representatives work away from an office base, the monitoring and control of individual selling activity are vital functions in the sales management role. The sales representative's performance can be measured in both quantitative and qualitative terms. Quantitative assessments can be related to either input or output measures, usually with reference to targets and benchmarks (Good and Stone, 1991). Input measures assess activities such as the number of calls and account coverage. Output measures focus on the end rather than the means, and include measurement of sales volume, sales development, number of new accounts and specific product sales.

To create a rounded picture of the sales representative's performance, qualitative measures that tend to be informal and subjective are also used. These could include attitude, product knowledge, appearance and communication skills. Using them in conjunction with quantitative measures, the sales manager may be able to find explanations for any particularly good or bad performance underlying the quantitative evidence of the formal results achieved (Churchill *et al.*, 2000).

Either way, the assessment can form the basis of a deeper analysis to encourage a proactive rather than reactive approach to sales management. The analysis might indicate that action needs to be taken on call policy, training or motivation, or even that problems may lie not with the sales force, but with the product or its marketing strategies.

Chapter summary

- Advertising is a non-personal form of communication with an identified sponsor, using any form of mass media. Advertising can help to create awareness, build image and attitudes and then reinforce those attitudes through reminders. It is an invaluable support for other elements of the promotional mix, for example by creating awareness and positive attitudes towards an organisation in preparation for a sales team, or by communicating sales promotions. Advertising also has strategic uses within the wider marketing mix. It can contribute to product positioning, thus supporting a premium price, or it could help to even out seasonal fluctuations in demand.

- The advertising message is extremely important. It has to be informative, persuasive and attention grabbing. It has to be appropriate for the target audience and thus speak to them in terms to which they can relate. There are several types of creative appeal that advertisers can use: rational, emotional and product centred. The appeal has to be relevant to the target audience, making a sufficient impact to get the desired message across and to get the audience to act on it.

- The advertiser has a wide choice of media. Broadcast media have a wide reach across the whole population, but it can be difficult to target a specific market segment precisely. Cinema is a relatively minor medium delivering captive, well-profiled audiences. It can make a big impact on the audience because of the quality of the sound and the size of the screen. Print media broadly consist of magazines and newspapers. Magazines tend to have well-defined readerships who are receptive to the content of advertisements relevant to the magazine's theme. Newspapers, on the other hand, have a very short life-span and are often skimmed rather than read properly. Outdoor media includes advertising hoardings, posters, ambient and transport-related media. They can provide easily digested messages that attract the attention of bored passengers or passers-by. They can generate high frequency as people tend to pass the same sites regularly, but can be spoiled by the weather and the ambience of their location.

- Advertising agencies are often used to provide expertise. Choosing an agency is an important task, and an organisation needs to think carefully about the relevant criteria for choice. Once the client has signed up an agency, it is then important to continue to communicate and to build a strong mutual understanding, with both sides contributing to advertising management according to expectations. First, campaign responsibilities need to be decided so that the process and the budget are kept under proper control. Once the target market and their broad communication needs have been defined, specific campaign objectives can be developed. Next, the budget can be set in the light of the desired objectives. Media choices, based on the habits of the target audience, the requirements of the planned message and the desired reach and frequency, can then be made. Meanwhile, the advertisements themselves are developed. Testing can be built in at various stages of this development to ensure that the right message is getting across in the right kind of way with the right kind of effect. Once the advertising has been fully developed, it can be implemented. Both during and after the campaign, managers will assess the advertising's effectiveness against the original objectives.

■ Although personal selling can be an expensive and labour-intensive marketing communication activity, it has a number of advantages over other forms of communication. It makes an impact, because it involves face-to-face contact and is less likely to be ignored; it can deliver a precise and tailored message to a target customer who has already been checked out to ensure that they fit the right profile; it helps in the cultivation of long-term buyer–seller relationships.

■ The personal selling process can be a long and complicated marketing activity to implement. The process starts with the identification of prospective customers, and then the representative has to do as much background work on the prospect as possible in order to prepare an initial approach and a relevant sales presentation. Initial contact breaks the ice between buyer and seller, allowing an appointment to be made for the real selling to begin. The sales presentation will give the representative the opportunity to present the product in the best possible light, while allowing the customer to ask questions and to raise any objections they may have. Negotiating the fine details of the deal may lead naturally to closing the sale, and then all that remains is for the representative to ensure the customer's post-purchase satisfaction and work towards building a long-term relationship leading to repeat business and further purchases.

■ Sales management is an important area of marketing, and involves a number of issues. Sales planning and strategy means making decisions about sales objectives, both for the organisation as a whole and for individual sales representatives or teams. Recruitment and training are also both important aspects of sales management. Apart from benefiting from training programmes, sales representatives have to be properly motivated and compensated for their efforts. A natural part of all this is performance evaluation. Sales managers need to ensure that representatives are achieving their targets and, if not, why not.

questions for *review and discussion*

10.1 In what ways can advertising support the other elements of the promotional mix?

10.2 Find examples of advertising that use:

(a) a rational appeal; and
(b) a fear appeal.

Why do you think the advertisers have chosen these approaches?

10.3 Find a current advertising campaign that uses both television and print media. Why do you think both media are being used? To what extent is each medium contributing something different to the overall message?

10.4 Develop a checklist of criteria against which a prospective client could assess advertising agencies. Which criterion would you say is the most important, and why?

10.5 What are the stages in the personal selling process?

10.6 Find 20 job advertisements for sales representatives and summarise the range of characteristics and skills sought. Which are the most commonly required and to what extent do you think that they are essential for a successful sales representative?

case study 10.1

Driving a sober message home

Every year around Christmas, the UK government sponsors an advertising campaign to prevent drinking and driving. Over the years, the messages, based around fear of the consequences of drinking and driving, succeeded in raising public awareness generally but were not making the desired impact on the core target audience of young males. The problem was that the audience felt that for such horrible things to happen, the driver had to be absolutely blind drunk, and since they themselves were never in that state, the message did not apply to them. From 1992 onwards, therefore, the tone of the fear campaign was altered.

The 1994 campaign, for example, pointed out that 'even great blokes can kill', featuring a driver who had only 'had a quick one' and then been responsible for killing the parents of two young children. In 1995, the campaign changed direction slightly by showing the damage that 'a quick one' can do to the driver himself. The television advertisement showed a young man, clearly paralysed and brain damaged, being spoon-fed liquidised food by his worn-out mother. With each spoonful, she is encouraging him with 'Come on, Dave, just one more'. In the background as a ghostly echo, pub noises can be heard, specifically a group of lads having a good time and encouraging each other with 'Come on, Dave, just one more'. The message made all the more impact by focusing on what could happen to me (i.e. a largely selfish concern) rather than on what I could do to an unknown third party (i.e. appealing to a sense of responsibility or duty).

The 1998 campaign changed direction again. The series of 15 advertisements reconstructed police videos of real fatal accidents with police radio messages talking of dead bodies smelling of alcohol. There was no voice-over, allowing the reality of the video and the messages and conversations between members of the emergency services to speak for themselves. The end shot is of a black screen with the message 'Don't drink and drive' fading to 'Don't drink and die'. Although no bodies are actually seen, some of the advertisements were still graphic enough to have to be shown only after 9 p.m.

Accident scenes featured strongly again in the 2000 campaign. The £1.9m. campaign used television, radio, outdoor media and point-of-sale media (posters and postcards) in pubs and clubs on the theme of 'Drinking and driving is one Christmas tradition we can all do without. THINK'. The television advertise-

How hard can it be to say no to a drink?

DRINKING AND DRIVING WRECKS LIVES.

1995 drink/drive campaign

Source: Department for Transport Film Images (London).

ments showed real accident scenes accompanied by favourite Christmas songs, 'Silent Night', 'Mistletoe and Wine', and 'I Wish it could be Christmas Every Day' but no voice-over. The radio advertisements featured extracts from pop tracks with verbal endorsements of the anti-drink-drive message from the artists. In 2001, £1m. was spent on repeating the same television campaign, but supported by new radio advertisements.

All these campaigns have made an impact and raised awareness, but the difficulty lies in actually challenging and changing people's attitudes and behaviour without seeming to preach or lecture at them. The Department for Transport, says, 'We want people to sit up and take notice, whatever approach we take, whether hard-hitting or more subtle. We are constantly looking at new ways of making advertising ▶

work and keeping a freshness to it so people don't look at the ad and think "oh no not again" (as quoted by Hedberg, 2001).

Government research seems to suggest that while it has been a slow process, the series of campaigns since 1976 have succeeded in changing attitudes to drink driving. Research among men who drive and who also drink outside the home has shown that the percentage who had driven after drinking on at least one occasion in the previous week had fallen from 51 per cent in 1979 to 23 per cent in 1997. The percentage claiming to 'leave the car at home' when going drinking had risen from 54 per cent in 1979 to 79 per cent in 1997. Social attitudes also seem to have changed for the better: the percentage agreeing with the statement 'it is difficult to avoid drinking and driving in the social context' had fallen from 61 per cent in 1979 to a mere 19 per cent in 1997. Nevertheless, as Clarke (2000) says, 'It's one thing to say your behaviour has changed, another to change your behaviour, and still another to measure that change.' The measurable statistics look promising, however. In 1979, the number of fatalities in collisions in which one or more driver was over the legal drink–drive limit was, 1,640. By 2000 that had fallen to 520, and over the same period, the percentage of drivers killed who were over the legal limit dropped from 32 to 19 per cent.

2001 drink/drive campaign

Source: Department for Transport.

The correlation between the advertising and the falling death rate may not be as clear as it seems, however. Shock-tactic drink–drive advertising that left absolutely nothing to the imagination was used in the state of Victoria, Australia, between 1990 and 1997. The number of alcohol-related road deaths halved, but as Clarke (2000) points out, that was as much to do with a police crackdown on enforcing the relevant laws as with advertising. Experts interviewed by Roberts (2001) also take the view that the only real way to cut the carnage is zero-tolerance of drink-driving and heavy penalties. Ireland has used similar shock advertising, but there has been no appreciable change in the numbers of fatalities. Similarly, in New Zealand where shock advertising was not supported by other activities, the change in the death rate was minimal. A 1998 study in New Zealand found little evidence to suggest that the advertising had had any effect on the behaviour of drivers who drink. Australian research found that the more graphic the gory scenes in an advertisement, the more likely it is that the viewer will attribute the crash to non-drink related causes beyond the driver's control.

1998 drink/drive campaign

Source: Department for Transport.

There are also concerns that 17–24-year-old men are overrepresented in terms of both the number of positive breath tests and the casualty figures, probably because young drivers overestimate their own abilities and tend to be less responsible than older ones. This poses a particularly tough communications task because of the well-entrenched role that alcohol seems to play in young people's lives, even by the age of 17. A study into adolescent drinking behaviour by MacKintosh *et al.* (1997) found that for

GUESS WHAT THOUSANDS OF DRUNK DRIVERS AND BUGS HAVE IN COMMON EACH YEAR?

Gradually campaigns to encourage people to not mix drinking and driving have become more hard hitting, showing the reality of the death and destruction it causes.

14- and 15-year-olds, drinking is a 'normal' part of their social lives and drinking to excess for the sake of getting drunk is quite common. While 16- and 17-year-olds drink more in total than the younger age group, they are more mature in their attitudes.

Although this age group may still drink to get drunk, they are learning their own limits and are more likely to see drinking as enhancing their social activities rather than as being their social activity. They enjoy both the process and outcome of drinking. . . . Alcohol was a 'social lubricant' for most and they talked about its ability to relax them, to increase their confidence and to lower their inhibitions (MacKintosh *et al.*, 1997).

Given these social attitudes, and in the face of a drinks industry that spends some £227m. per year on advertising to tell young people in the sexiest ways permissible that alcohol is sophisticated, fun, enjoyable and an essential 'social lubricant', can the Department for Transport really win with its essentially gloomy messages?

Sources: Campaign (1998), Clarke (2000), DMB&B (1995), Hedberg (2001), MacKintosh *et al.* (1997), Roberts (2001), http://www.alcoholconcern.org.uk, http://www.dtlr.gov.uk

Questions

1 Why is this kind of campaign much more difficult to design in advertising terms than a 'normal' FMCG campaign?

2 What types of appeal have been used in the campaigns outlined in this case? To what extent and why do you think they might have worked?

3 What are the advantages and disadvantages of the different main types of advertising media for a campaign like this?

4 The government has pinpointed 17–24-year-old males as a particularly vulnerable group. How could this group be targeted better?

References for chapter 10

Abberton Associates (1997), *Balancing the Selling Equation: Revisited* (accessed via http://www.cpm-int.com).

Adamson, C. (2002), 'Jules Back On Message at the Shops', *Evening Standard*, 22 February, p. 18.

Arnold, M. (2001a), 'CRM Shows its Winning Ways', *Marketing*, 19 July, p. 19.

Arnold, M. (2001b), 'Bringing Henkel Home', *Marketing*, 11 October, p. 4.

Ashworth, J. (2001), 'The Avon Lady Takes High-tech to Doorsteps', *The Times*, 24 September, p. 22.

Beard, M. (2002), 'Sainsbury Signs Jamie Oliver in £2mn Deal', *The Independent*, 17 January, p. 11.

Berkowitz, E. *et al.* (1992), *Marketing*, Irwin.

Bittar, C. (2001), 'P&G Eyes Sales Force Revamp amid Slump', *Brandweek*, 1 October, p. 32.

Blackwood, F. (1995), 'Did You Sell $5 Million Last Year?', *Selling*, October, p. 47.

Campaign (1998), 'AMV Unveils Graphic Anti-drink-drive Xmas Campaign', *Campaign*, 4 December, p. 2.

Chandiramani, R. (2001), 'Is Age Concern Wise to Target Younger Market?', *Marketing*, 20 September, p. 15.

Churchill, G., Ford, N., Walker, O., Johnston, M. and Tanner, J. (2000), *Sales Force Management* (6th edn), Richard D. Irwin Inc.

Clarke, M. (2000), 'Advertising with Plenty of Body', *Sunday Times*, 17 December, p. 28.

Cowen, M. (2001), 'Cowen on . . . Orange', *Campaign*, 12 October, p. 19.

Cravens, D. and LaForge, R. (1983), 'Salesforce Deployment Analysis', *Industrial Marketing Management*, July, pp. 179–92.

Croft, M. (2001), 'A Flash in the Pan', *Marketing Week*, 16 August, pp. 37–9.

Cron, W. *et al.* (1988), 'The Influence of Career Stages on Components of Salesperson Motivation', *Journal of Marketing*, 52 (July), pp. 179–92.

DMB&B (1995), *A DMB&B Case Study: Drink–Drive*, DMB&B.

Fill, C. (2002), *Marketing Communications: Contexts, Strategies and Applications* (3rd edn), Financial Times Prentice Hall.

Gofton, K. (2002), 'Field Marketing Grows Up', *Campaign*, 25 January, p. 22.

Good, D. and Stone, R. (1991), 'How Sales Quotas are Developed', *Industrial Marketing Management*, 20 (1), pp. 51–6.

Grant, J. (2002), 'Orange Ad Highlights Emotional Value of Text Messages', *Marketing*, 17 January, p. 20.

Hedberg, A. (2001), 'Government Exchanges Preaching for Teaching', *Marketing Week*, 13 December, p. 20.

Johanson, J. and Vahlne, J. (1977), 'The Internationalisation Process of the Firm: a Model of Knowledge Development and Increasing Foreign Market Commitment', *Journal of International Business Studies*, 8 (1), pp. 23–32.

Lambert, D. *et al.* (1990), 'Industrial Salespeople as a Source of Market Information', *Industrial Marketing Management*, 19, pp. 141–5.

McDonald, M. (1984), *Marketing Plans*, Butterworth-Heinemann.

MacKintosh, A., Hastings, G., Hughes, K., Wheeler, C., Watson, J. and Inglis, J. (1997), 'Adolescent Drinking: the Role of Designer Drinks', *Health Education*, 97 (6), pp. 213–24.

McLuhan, R. (2001a), 'Food Remains Top for Field Activities', *Marketing*, 30 August, p. 37.

McLuhan, R. (2001b), 'UK Agencies Focus on European Arena', *Marketing*, 30 August, p. 42.

Marketing (2002), 'Company CV: Orange', *Marketing*, 7 March, p. 50.

Marketing (1999), 'Hair Today, Gone Tomorrow', *Marketing*, 21 April, p. 80.

Middleton, T. (2001), 'Field Questions', *Marketing Week*, 22 November, pp. 51–3.

Middleton, T. (2002), 'Global POP', *Marketing Week*, 11 April, pp. 36–7.

Miles, L. (1998), 'Discipline on the Doorstep', *Marketing*, 19 November, pp. 37–40.

Miller, R. and Heinman, S. (1991), *Successful Large Account Management*, Holt.

Muehling, D. *et al.* (1990), 'The Impact of Comparative Advertising on Levels of Message Involvement', *Journal of Advertising*, 19 (4), pp. 41–50.

Mueller-Heumann, G. (1992), 'Markets and Technology Shifts in the 1990s: Market Fragmentation and Mass Customisation', *Journal of Marketing Management*, 8 (4), pp. 303–14.

Murphy, D. (1999), 'Taking Your Ads In-store', *Marketing*, 18 March, pp. 35–6.

NFU Mutual (2001), 'Time to Check Out Your Security Measures', *Western Mail*, 13 October, p. 21.

NFU Mutual (2002), 'Hidden Hazards of the Country Road', *Western Mail*, 5 January, p. 21.

Payne, S. (2002), 'Shopper at Garden Centre Died after Testing Spa Bath', *The Daily Telegraph*, 15 February, p. 8.

Pedersen, C. *et al.* (1986), *Selling: Principles and Methods*, Irwin.

Pickton, D. and Broderick, A. (2001), *Integrated Marketing Communications*, Financial Times Prentice Hall.

Ray, A. (2001), 'Ambient Enters the Mainstream Arena', *Marketing*, 21 June, p. 31.

Ray, A. (2002), 'Using Outdoor to Target the Young', *Marketing*, 31 January, p. 25.

Roberts, R. (2001), 'Get Tough on Drink-drivers', *Western Mail*, 7 December, p. 2.

Russell, F. *et al.* (1977), *Textbook of Salesmanship* (10th edn), McGraw-Hill.

Singh, S. (2001), 'Avon Plans Global Teen Assault', *Marketing Week*, 16 August, p. 5.

Sissors, J. and Bumba, L. (1989), *Advertising Media Planning* (3rd edn), NTC Business Books.

Smith, P. and Taylor, J. (2002), *Marketing Communications: an Integrated Approach* (3rd edn), Kogan Page.

Smith, R. (2002), 'Boddingtons Braves Cream-free Strategy', *Marketing*, 28 February, p. 15.

Turnbull, P. and Cunningham, M. (1981), *International Marketing and Purchasing: a Survey among Marketing and Purchasing Executives in Five European Countries*, Macmillan.

Watson, S. (2001), 'Posh and Becks Modelling for M&S?', *The Guardian*, 16 November, p. 2.12.

White, J. (2002), 'Lowe Unveils Orange Ads Targeting Users from Rival Networks', *Campaign*, 1 March, p. 6.

White, R. (1988), *Advertising: What It Is and How To Do It*, McGraw-Hill.

Woolgar, T. (1999), 'Outdoor Answers Back', *Campaign*, 16 April, p. 29.

promotion: other tools of marketing communication

LEARNING OBJECTIVES

This chapter will help you to:

1 define sales promotion and appreciate its role in the communications mix through the objectives it can achieve and the methods it uses in targeting consumers, retailers and B2B customers;

2 understand what direct marketing is and appreciate its role in the communications mix through the objectives it can achieve and the various methods it employs;

3 appreciate the importance of creating and maintaining a database of customers and understand the importance of using the database as a direct marketing tool;

4 appreciate the contribution that trade shows and exhibitions can make to achieving B2B marketing objectives;

5 define PR and understand its role in supporting the organisation's activities and outline the techniques of PR and their appropriateness for different kinds of public;

6 understand the role of sponsorship in the marketing communications mix and the benefits and problems of different types of sponsorship; and

7 understand the nature of cause-related marketing and the benefits it offers to all parties involved.

Introduction

This chapter discusses a wide range of marketing communications tools. First, we shall explore sales promotion. Traditionally the poor cousin of advertising, sales promotion actually covers a fascinating range of short-term tactical tools that can play a vital complementary role in long-term promotional strategy. Its aim is to add extra value to the product or service, over and above the normal product offering, thus creating an extra inducement to buy or try it. Although individual sales promotions are usually regarded as short-term tactical measures, sales promotion generally, as an element of the promotional mix, is increasingly being recognised as a valid strategic tool, working alongside and supporting other promotional elements. This chapter will define more clearly what sales promotion is, the techniques it employs and what strategic role it can play within the promotional mix.

eg Extra excitement can be added to sales promotions by linking them with current events. The 2002 soccer World Cup, for example, generated a lot of linked promotional activity as brands sought to exploit public interest. Nestlé's 'Know your football, know your chocolate' campaign, fronted by Terry Venables, for example, ran across five different Nestlé confectionery brands. The promotion featured on 55 million product wrappers and included an instant win element, with thousands of £10 prizes at stake, while 10 winning wrappers gave consumers the chance to win up to £10,000. The ten winners were telephoned by Terry Venables, who asked them two easy questions, one on football and one on chocolate. Each question answered correctly won £5,000. The promotion was integrated with television, radio and print advertising, which informed consumers about the promotion and generated interest and excitement around it.

Planning and executing a promotion like this is no easy matter, however. First of all, with five different brands involved, Nestlé had to ensure that all the relevant brand managers were happy with the concept and that the promotion fitted well with the individual brand strategies. A lot of market research then went into deciding the fine details of the promotion and ensuring that it would stand out in what is a very competitive market. Eight focus groups were held involving both men and women aged between 16 and 34, and including people with varying levels of interest in football. The results of the research helped to determine the prize structure, the POS support for the promotion, the way in which the promotion was delivered, and the scripts of the advertisements, as well as the choice of Terry Venables. The research showed that cash delivered through instant wins would be the most effective motivator (Kleinman, 2002; Pemble, 2002).

> Nestlé clearly takes its promotions seriously, and rightly. Promotion has an important role to play in the integrated marketing communications mix and can generate interest and excitement around a brand, as well as giving consumers a real reason to try it and buy it.

The next area considered is direct marketing. Direct marketing is more than just 'junk mail'. It encompasses a wide range of commonly used techniques, not only direct mail but also telemarketing, direct response mechanisms, mail order, and Internet marketing. The chapter will look at each of those areas, although Internet and new media issues will be covered in more detail later in Chapter 14.

eg Saab is positioned in the tough premium sector of the car market in which sales have been declining in recent years. The difficulty for Saab was that although advertising and direct marketing had succeeded in raising awareness levels from 5 to 29 per cent, only 17 per cent of those responding to the campaign had requested a test drive. Experience has taught most motor manufacturers that the test drive is an important stage in the buying process and provides a great opportunity to showcase the product and to close the sale afterwards. Saab had found that the conversion rate was 1 in 4 after test drives. In 2000, therefore, Saab decided on a direct marketing campaign to make test drives more appealing by offering a 24-hour test drive (without the car salesperson!), the first such offer in the sector. A mailshot developed around the creative theme of 'Letting Go' supported by the promise that 'after 24 hours you won't want to give it back' was sent to potential customers, supported by mail and online response mechanisms. Further campaigns, using the same theme on various products, were run throughout the year, supported by outdoor posters and press advertising. The campaign increased the number of leads from 3,469 in 1999 to 19,744 in 2000 and response rates rose to 3.1 per cent, well above the previous 0.6 per cent (*Marketing Week*, 2001).

Trade shows and exhibitions are also briefly considered, as a useful part of the B2B communications mix in particular. We examine their role and value to organisations, not least their ability to generate qualified sales leads and to reinforce the organisation's presence and image in the marketplace as a basis for future direct marketing campaigns.

Public relations (PR) is the area of marketing communications that specifically deals with the quality and nature of the relationship between an organisation and its publics, such as its financial backers, its employees and trade unions, its suppliers, the legal and regulatory bodies to which it is answerable, interested pressure groups, the media, and many other groups or 'publics' which have the ability to affect the way in which the organisation does business. Its prime concern is to generate a sound, effective and understandable flow of communication between the organisation and these groups so that shared understanding is possible. While publicity or press relations can make a significant contribution, PR utilises a much wider range of activities, which this chapter will cover.

The final sections of this chapter consider sponsorship and cause-related marketing (CRM). Sponsorship of sport, television programmes and the arts will be discussed in terms of the benefits gained by both parties. CRM is loosely related to sponsorship, in that part of its remit is looking at how corporate donors or sponsors can help charities and other non-profit organisations. It also covers PR and sales promotion activities that link companies with non-profit organisations and examines the benefits gained by all those involved.

Sales promotion

■ Sales promotion: definition and role

According to the Institute of Sales Promotion, sales promotion is:

> . . . a range of tactical marketing techniques designed within a strategic marketing framework to add value to a product or service in order to achieve specific sales and marketing objectives.

The word 'tactical' implies a short, sharp burst of activity that is expected to be effective as soon as it is implemented. The fact that this activity is *designed within a strategic marketing framework* means, however, that it is not a panic measure, not just something to wheel out when you do not know what else to do. On the contrary, sales promotion should be planned into an integrated communications mix, to make the most of its ability to complement other areas such as advertising and its unique capacity to achieve certain objectives, mostly tactical, but sometimes strategic (Davies, 1992).

The key element of this definition, however, is that the sales promotion should *add value to a product or service*. This is something over and above the normal product offering that might make buyers stop and think about whether to change their usual buying behaviour, or revise their buying criteria. This takes the form of something tangible that is of value to the buyer, whether it is extra product free, money, a gift or the opportunity to win a prize, that under normal circumstances they would not get.

Perhaps the main problem with the definition is that the area of sales promotion has almost developed beyond it. The idea of the short-term tactical shock to the market is very well established and understood, and will be seen to be at the heart of many of the specific techniques outlined in this chapter. With the development of relationship marketing, that is, the necessity for building long-term buyer–seller relationships, marketers have been looking for ways of developing the scope of traditional sales promotion to encourage long-term customer loyalty and repeat purchasing behaviour. Loyalty schemes, such as frequent flyer programmes, are sales promotions in the sense that they offer added value over and above the normal product offering, but they are certainly not short-term tactical measures – quite the opposite. Wilmshurst (1993) clearly states that creatively designed sales promotions can be just as effective as advertising in affecting consumers' attitudes to brands. This means, perhaps, that the definition of sales promotion needs to be revised to account for those strategic, franchise-building promotional techniques:

> . . . *a range of marketing techniques designed within a strategic marketing framework to add extra value to a product or service over and above the 'normal' offering in order to achieve specific sales and marketing objectives. This extra value may be of a short-term tactical nature or it may be part of a longer-term franchise-building programme.*

Sales promotion objectives: overview

Sales promotion objectives all fall into three broad categories: communication, incentive and invitation. Sales promotion has a capacity to communicate with the buyer in ways that advertising would find hard to emulate. Advertising can tell people that a product is 'new, improved', or that it offers certain features and benefits, but this is conceptual information, which people may not fully understand or accept. Sales promotion can, for instance, put product samples into people's hands so that they can judge for themselves whether the claims are true. Learning by one's own experience is so much more powerful and convincing than taking the advertiser's word for it.

The incentive is usually the central pillar of a sales promotion campaign. The potential buyer has to be given encouragement to behave in certain ways, through an agreed bargain between seller and buyer: if you do this, then I will *reward* you with that.

eg   In common with many airlines, SAS operates a loyalty scheme whereby travellers earn points for each flight they take, with the number of points awarded varying according to the length of the flight. Points can be exchanged for free flights or other rewards. In March 2001, however, the Swedish Competition Authority decided that SAS's EuroBonus scheme distorted competition and banned SAS from awarding points that can be used for free flights on domestic routes where there is a competitor. According to the Authority, many scheme members are regular business travellers, and thus their companies pay for their flights, but the individuals get the points and the resulting free flights for their personal use. Individuals naturally tend to join the scheme of the airline that offers the most flights, and with a 70 per cent share of the domestic market, that puts SAS in a very strong position. All of this means

▶

that choice of airline for a domestic flight is more likely to be made on the attractiveness of its benefits package rather than on price or service quality, and in the Authority's view, this leads to unfair competition and higher prices. The Authority claims that 10 per cent of the price of an SAS ticket goes towards the cost of the EuroBonus scheme, although SAS dispute this and say that it is only 1 per cent (Nicholas, 2001).

Through its incentive, the promoted product is saying, 'Buy ME, and buy me NOW'. The promotion is, therefore, an invitation to consider this product, to think about your buying decision, and to do it quickly. The ephemeral nature of most sales promotions reinforces the urgency of taking up the invitation immediately. It prevents the buyer from putting off trial of the product, because the 'extra something' will not be around for long. For the consumer, in particular, the point of sale represents the crucial decision-making time. A product that is jumping up and down, shouting 'Hey, look at me!' through its sales promotion is offering the clearest possible invitation to do business.

The rest of this section will focus further on the objectives that sales promotion can achieve within the context of the relationship within which they are used.

Manufacturer–intermediary (trade promotion)

The intermediary provides a vital service for the manufacturer in displaying goods to their best advantage and making them easily available to the consumer. In a competitive market, however, a manufacturer might wish to use trade sales promotion techniques to encourage the intermediary to take a particular interest in particular products for various purposes. Intermediaries might even expect or insist on sales promotions before they will cooperate with what the manufacturer wants.

As shown in Figure 11.1, and discussed below, trade promotions revolve around gaining more product penetration, more display and more intermediary promotional effort. As Fill (2002) points out, however, this might cause conflict between the manufacturer and the intermediary, since the intermediary's prime objective is to increase store traffic. The level of incentive might thus have to be extremely attractive!

Increase stock levels. The more stock of a particular product that an intermediary holds, the more committed they will be to put effort into selling it quickly. Furthermore, intermedi-

Figure 11.1 Manufacturer–intermediary sales promotion objectives

aries have limited stockholding space, so the more space that your product takes up, the less room there is for the competition. Money-based or extra-product-based incentives might encourage intermediaries to increase their orders, although the effect might be short-lived and in the longer term might even reduce orders as intermediaries work through the extra stock they acquired during the promotion.

Gain more and better shelf space. There is intense competition between manufacturers to secure shelf space within retail outlets. Intermediaries are often willing to accept incentives to help them to allocate this scarce resource to particular products or manufacturers. Again, this may link with money- or product-based trade promotions, but could also be part of a joint promotion agreement or a point-of-sale promotion, for instance. The quality of the shelf space acquired is also important. If a product is to capture the consumer's attention, then it needs to be prominent. This means that it must be displayed either at the customer's eye level or at the end of the aisles in a supermarket where the customer is turning the corner and all the trolley traffic jams occur. There is keen competition for these highly desirable display sites, also called *golden zones*, and again, intermediary-oriented sales promotion may help a manufacturer to make its case more strongly.

New product launch. The launch period is a delicate time in any new product's life, and if the distribution aspects of the marketing strategy are weak, then it could be fatal. A new product needs to be accepted by the appropriate intermediaries so that it is available for all those consumers eager to try it. To the trade, however, a new product is a potential risk. What if it doesn't sell? Trade promotions (particularly with a push strategy – see pp. 282 *et seq.*) can reduce some of that risk. Money-based promotions reduce the potential financial losses of a product failure, while 'sale or return' promotions remove the fear of being left with unsaleable stock. Sales force support, meanwhile, can reassure the intermediary that staff are ready, willing and able to sell the product and fully understand its features and benefits. This is particularly appropriate with more complex, infrequently purchased items, such as electrical goods.

Even out fluctuating sales. Some products, such as lawnmowers, ice cream and holidays, suffer from seasonality. While the design of the product offering or the pricing policies adopted can help to overcome these problems, sales promotion can also play a part. If manufacturers are able to encourage intermediaries to take on more stock or to push the product harder during the 'quieter' periods, sales can be spread a little more evenly throughout the year. This process can also be enhanced by a related consumer-oriented promotion, so that the manufacturer is gaining extra synergy through simultaneous push and pull activity.

Counter the competition. It has already been indicated that a manufacturer is competing with every other manufacturer for an intermediary's attention. Sales promotions, therefore, make very useful tactical weapons to spoil or dilute the effects of a competitor's actions. If, for instance, you are aware that the competition is about to launch a new product, you might use a trade sales promotion to load up a key intermediary with your related products, so that at best they will be reluctant to take on the competition's goods, or at worst, they will drive a much harder bargain with the competitor.

Retailer–consumer (retailer promotion)

In the same way that manufacturers compete among themselves for the intermediary's attention, retailers compete for the consumer's patronage. Store-specific sales promotions, whether jointly prepared with a manufacturer or originating solely from the retailer, can help differentiate one store from another, and entice the public in. Retailers also try to use sales promotions in a longer-term strategic way to create store loyalty, for example through card schemes that allow the shopper to collect points over time that can be redeemed for gifts or money-off vouchers. Retailers use sales promotion for many reasons and these are summarised in Figure 11.2.

Figure 11.2 Retailer–consumer sales promotion objectives

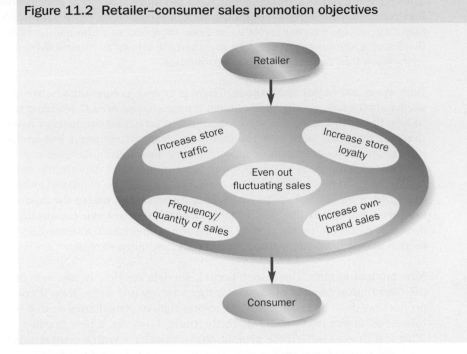

Increase store traffic. A prime objective for a retailer is to get the public in through the shop door. Any kind of retailer-specific sales promotion has a chance of doing that. Money-off coupons delivered from door to door or printed in the local newspaper, for example, might bring in people who do not usually shop in a particular store. Such promotions might also encourage retail substitution, giving shoppers an incentive to patronise one retailer rather than another. An electrical retailer might advertise a one-day sale with a few carefully chosen items offered on promotion at rock-bottom prices. This bait brings potential customers to the store, and even if the real bargains have gone early, they will still look at other goods.

Increase frequency and amount of purchases. Even if a customer already shops at one retailer's outlets, the retailer would prefer them to shop there more often and to spend more.

eg Short-term promotions are often used by retailers to increase store traffic. Supermarket chain Safeway, for instance, uses price-based offers to draw shoppers into its stores. By advertising rock-bottom bargains on a selected number of big-name brands in the local press and through door-to-door leafleting within a store's catchment area, shoppers are tempted to pay a visit. The range of offers changes week by week, thus keeping the shopper's interest fresh. The hope is that the shopper will keep returning every week and that once in the store, they will buy far more than just a limited range of discounted brands.

Increase store loyalty. Supermarkets in particular use sales promotion as a means of generating store loyalty. The kinds of activities outlined in relation to increasing the frequency and amount of purchases help towards this, as does a rolling programme of couponing and money-off offers. The problem with this type of promotion, however, is that it risks creating a 'deal-prone' promiscuous customer who will switch to whichever retailer is currently offering the best package of short-term promotions. To counteract this, some retailers have introduced loyalty schemes using swipe cards.

eg In the UK, Tesco's Clubcard was the first major supermarket loyalty scheme. Shoppers have an incentive to shop regularly at a particular retailer in order to accumulate points. Using the customer database, coupons and money-off vouchers can be regularly issued and delivered to the customer's own home, thus creating a stronger, more personal retailer–customer link (see also Case Study 11.1, pp. 384–5).

Increase own-brand sales. Retailers are increasingly investing in their own-brand ranges. These are, therefore, legitimate subjects for a whole range of consumer-oriented promotions. These promotions do not have to be overtly price or product based.

eg In-store free recipe cards can help to promote the store's fresh foods or own-label products by giving the shopper meal ideas and encouraging them to buy the ingredients. This can be linked with other promotions so that, for instance, one of the own-label ingredients could feature a price reduction to encourage purchase further. The magazines sent out with loyalty card statements and vouchers can also promote own-label goods, again through recipes, through editorial copy explaining how products can be used and their benefits, or through the more obvious mechanism of extra money-off vouchers.

Even out busy periods. In the same way that manufacturers face seasonal demand for some products, retailers have to cope with fluctuations between the very busy periods of the week or year, and the very quiet times. Offering sales promotions that apply only on certain days or within certain trading hours might divert some customers away from the busier periods.

eg A one-day sale on a Wednesday or Thursday can be a good way for a retailer to divert shoppers away from the busier weekend, especially if it is well advertised in the local area. One DIY retailer also instituted Wednesday afternoon discounts for senior citizens, presumably because that is an easily defined group who can change their shopping day because they are not likely to be working.

Manufacturer–consumer (manufacturer promotion)

While it is obviously important for manufacturers to have the distribution channels working in their favour, there is still much work to be done with the consumer to help ensure continued product success. After all, if consumer demand for a product is buoyant, that in itself acts as an incentive to the retail trade to stock it, effectively acting as a pull strategy. There are many reasons for manufacturers to use sales promotions to woo the consumer, and some of these are outlined below and summarised in Figure 11.3.

Figure 11.3 Manufacturer–consumer sales promotion objectives

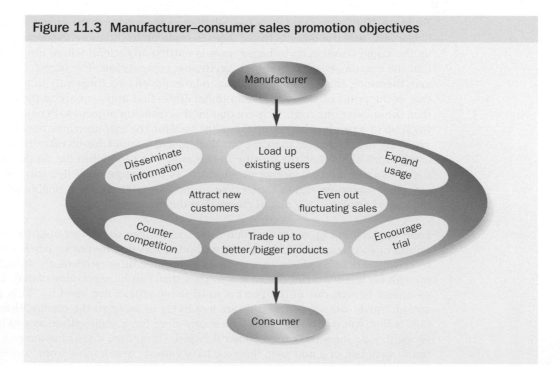

Encourage trial. The rationale in encouraging trial is similar to that discussed earlier in relation to the intermediary and new product launches. New products face the problem of being unknown, and therefore consumers may need incentives to encourage trial of the product. Samples help consumers to judge a product for themselves, while coupons, money off and gifts reduce the financial penalty of a 'wrong' purchase. Sales promotions thus play an important role in the early stages of a product's life.

Expand usage. Expanding usage involves using sales promotion to encourage people to find different ways of using more of the product so that, of course, they purchase more.

eg Mayonnaise brand Hellmann's offered consumers a free recipe book when they purchased jars of its various mayonnaise products. The book, with 12 recipes, could be obtained by calling a telephone number on the label. The jars themselves carried special edition labels with pictures encouraging consumers to use Hellmann's in different ways (*Promotions and Incentives*, 2002). This promotion integrated well with the theme of Hellmann's television advertising which also showed imaginative ways of using the product with a broad range of different foods and meal occasions.

Disseminate information. Sales promotions can be used effectively as a means of getting information across to consumers. Even a small sample pack distributed door to door, for example, not only lets the consumer experience the product, but also gives the manufacturer a chance to tell that consumer quite a lot about the product's features and benefits, where to buy it, and related products in the range. While advertising can do the same sort of information dissemination, it is easily ignored. If the consumer is tempted to try the sample, then they may take more notice of the information with it, and only then pay attention to the advertising.

Attracting new customers. An established product may be striving to acquire new customers, either by converting non-users or by turning irregular customers or brand switchers into regular buyers. Advertising can only go so far in creating a positive image of the product, and sales promotion may be necessary to generate that first trial, or that repeat purchase. The kind of promotion that depends on collecting tokens over time to qualify for a mail-in offer might be sufficient, if it is backed up with strong advertising, to set up regular purchasing habits and brand preference.

Trade up. There are two facets to trading up. One is getting the consumer to trade up to a bigger size, and the other is to get them to trade up to the more expensive products further up the range. Trading up to bigger sizes is particularly useful where the manufacturer feels that the customer is vulnerable to aggressive competition. The bigger size will last longer and, therefore, that consumer is going to be exposed less frequently to competitive temptation at the point of sale. Any promotional effort that applies only to the bigger size rather than the smaller one might achieve that kind of trade-up objective. Persuading consumers to trade up to a product higher up the range benefits the manufacturer because such products are likely to earn higher margins. Car dealers and manufacturers often try to do this. Again, using promotions that are specific to one model or product in the range, or using increasingly valuable and attractive promotions as the range goes up, can help to focus the customer's mind on higher things. Price-based promotions are probably not a good idea in this case, because of the risk of cheapening the product's image.

Load up. Loading up is partly a defensive mechanism to protect your customers from the efforts of the competition. A customer who is collecting tokens or labels towards a mail-in offer with a tight deadline, or who finds a cut-price offer particularly seductive, might end up with far greater quantities of the product than can be used immediately. Effectively, that customer is now out of the market until those stocks are used up. This is a two-edged sword: the advantage is that they are less likely to listen to the competition; the disadvantage is that you will not be selling them any more for a while either, as you have effectively brought your sales to that customer forward. Of course, if that customer was originally a brand switcher, or a non-user, then you have gained considerably from loading them up.

Even out fluctuating sales. Evening out fluctuating sales links with the comments made above in relation to manufacturer–intermediary sales promotions. If seasonality is a problem, then sales promotion aimed at the consumer could help to even out the peaks and troughs a little.

Countering the competition. Again, the concept of countering or spoiling competitors' activities was introduced in the discussion of manufacturer–intermediary sales promotions. Diverting the consumer's attention through your own promotion can dampen the effects of the competitors' efforts, particularly if what they are doing is not particularly creative in its own right.

Within these main categories of sales promotion (consumer, retail trade and organisation-oriented sales promotions), there are a number of possible techniques for achieving defined objectives. The techniques in each area are not mutually exclusive; ideas can be drawn from any one area and applied in another. The techniques selected will not only depend on the objectives and target audience of the sales promotion campaign, but also be influenced by a range of factors. These typically are market characteristics, competitive levels and activities, promotional objectives and the relevance of each technique to the product and its cost profile. The following sections outline a number of sales promotion methods, classified by target audience.

■ Methods of sales promotion to consumers

Money-based

Money-based sales promotions are a very popular group of techniques used by manufacturers or intermediaries. Sometimes they work on a 'cash-back' basis (collect a certain number of tokens then send away for a cash rebate), but more often they are immediate price reductions, offered either at the point of sale or on the pack itself, designed as a short-term measure either to gain competitive advantage or to defend against competitive actions. Such price reductions must be seen to be temporary or else the consumer will not view them as incentives. Furthermore, if money-based methods are used too often, consumers will begin to think of the promotional price as being the real price. They will then think of the product as being cheaper than it really is, and adjust their perceptions of positioning and quality accordingly (Gupta and Cooper, 1992).

> **eg** The major supermarket chains are keen to give the impression that they offer better value for money than their competitors and short-term reduced price promotions are one way of reinforcing this stance. All the major chains have their generic ranges at the bottom of the price range and occasionally these are used to make attention-grabbing price statements. Thus at various times shoppers have found washing-up liquid at 7p per bottle, tins of beans at 3p per can and other products selling at approximately 10 per cent of the price of their premium branded competitors. These are in addition to a day-to-day selection of less drastic short-term price cuts on other own-label and premium brands.

Coupons (printed vouchers that the consumer takes to a retail outlet and uses to claim a set amount of money off a product) are a form of money-based sales promotion that do not look like a price cut, mainly because the price quoted at the shelf or on the product remains intact. The coupon is also a little more selective than a straight price cut, in that only those who collect a coupon and remember to redeem it qualify for the discount. However, to counter that, coupons are very common, and consumers are overexposed to them. Unless a coupon carries a significant discount on the product, or applies to something intrinsically new and exciting, it is difficult as a consumer to be enthusiastic about them.

Coupons are distributed using a variety of means. They are printed within advertisements, on leaflets delivered from door to door, on inserts within magazines and newspapers, through direct mail, at the point of sale and on packs. The technology is also now available to allow retailers to issue coupons at the checkout, as an integral part of the bill issued to the customer.

For manufacturers, coupons act as a kind of pull strategy, creating an upturn in consumer demand for the product, thus encouraging retailers to stock and prominently display the brand. Coupon redemption rates are crucial and can vary from just over 1 per cent with coupons in magazines to over 25 per cent with coupons appearing on or in packs. Not surprisingly, it has been found that the higher the coupon value, the greater the interest and redemption. According to NCH's analysis of the UK coupon market, it has also been found that using personalised coupons can improve redemption rates by between 3 and 6 percentage points. Personalised coupons also allow the issuer to track exactly who is responding, when and where, which is useful data for planning future campaigns. The main problem for manufacturers, however, is misredemption. Some supermarkets, overtly or covertly, will accept any coupon at the checkout, regardless of whether the consumer has actually bought the coupon's product or not. Preventing this from happening is difficult.

A big drawback of money-based sales promotions is that because they are so common among consumer goods, it is very difficult to raise much enthusiasm about them in the market. The main problem is the lack of creativity that usually accompanies these methods. It is also far too easy for a competitor to copy or match a money-based promotion, and thus any competitive advantage may be short-lived.

It is also important to remember that money-based promotion can be an expensive way of putting money back in the pockets of people who would have bought the product anyway. If an organisation offers 10p off a product, then that costs the organisation 10p per unit sold in addition to the overhead costs of implementing the offer. In other words, in most cases money-based sales promotions cost the organisation their full cash value, unlike many of the merchandise offers, yet the long-term effect (especially if the technique is overused) may be to cheapen the value of the product in the consumer's eyes (Jones, 1990).

In their favour, however, money-based promotions are relatively easy to implement, they can be developed and mobilised quickly, and they are readily understood by the consumer. They appeal to many consumers' basic instincts about saving money, and the value of 10p off a price, or £1 cash back, is easy for the consumer to assess. If the objective of the exercise is to attract price-sensitive brand switchers, or to make a quick and easy response to a competitor's recent or imminent actions, then this group of methods has a part to play.

Product-based

One of the risks of money-based promotions is the ease with which consumers can relate the promotion to price cutting, and thus the image of the product can, in their eyes, be cheapened. One way of overcoming that problem is to opt for a promotion centred on the product itself.

The 'extra free' technique involves offers such as an own-label can of tomatoes with '20% extra free' or a pack of own-label kitchen roll offering three rolls for the price of two, proclaiming 'ONE ROLL EXTRA FREE'.

A money-based promotion might put 20p back in the consumer's hand; a product-based promotion might give them 20p's worth of extra product free. To the manufacturer, either option rewards the buyer with 20p, but the buyer's perceptions of the two are very different: 20p in the hand is 'giving something back', whereas extra product free is clearly 'giving something in addition' and in the consumer's mind, might be valued at a good deal more than 20p. These product-based promotions, therefore, break the link between promotion and price. This method may be especially attractive as a response to a competitor's price attack, as it can shape the value image of a product without a direct price war.

In contrast to offering extra free product within a single package, the BIGIF (Buy 1 Get 1 Free) or the BOGOFF (Buy One Get One For Free) offers centre on bigger rewards, and are aimed primarily at loading up the customer. Effectively, the offer is saying '100% EXTRA FREE'. Retailers are increasingly using a variation on this method, based around bulk purchasing, making the offer, 'Buy two and get a third one free'.

These offers may need shorter lead times than the 20 per cent extra free type, because they do not involve significant changes to the packaging. Two ordinary packs can be banded together away from the main production line if necessary. In the case of the retailers' B2G3F offers, no banding is needed at all. The offer is made through notices at the shelf, and the computerised checkout is programmed to make the discount automatically when the required number of items have been scanned through.

eg Procter and Gamble launched Ariel Futur Alpine by offering a 1 litre refill free with every 1.5 litre bottle bought. The two packs were presented together in a cardboard box with the word FREE prominently displayed in red on a yellow background. The promotional boxes were also placed in an end of aisle 'golden zone' in Tesco, for example, and extra loyalty card points offered with them. All of this made the new Alpine variant attractive to the consumer, not only to generate awareness and trial, but also to load up customers to protect them from the competition. Supermarkets also regularly offer discounts for bulk purchases with varying conditions, anything from 'buy one get one free' to 'buy six get a seventh free'.

A variation on the 'free product' technique is sampling, used when the main objective is to persuade people to try a product. People can experience the product for themselves at little or no financial risk and decide on their own evidence whether to adopt the product and buy the full-sized pack or not. Samples are thus popular and effective. Seventy per cent of households claim to use the free samples that come through the letterbox. The added bonus, particularly with those samples distributed away from the point of sale, is that the sample's packaging can teach the consumer about the product's benefits, and through graphics that relate directly to the full sized pack, aid brand recognition in the store.

marketing *in action*

Bringing the product to consumers – wherever they are

Sampling is a powerful promotional tool: a survey showed that over 70 per cent of consumers believed that free samples received through door-to-door distribution were 'very useful', and even people who claim they do not like unaddressed mail still welcome samples, coupons and special offers. Using the sophisticated techniques offered by geodemographic profiling systems (see pp. 113 *et seq.*) it is now possible to target door-to-door sampling and other drops to specific households. As one agency put it, 'Client companies know exactly who they want to target from their databases and they only want to deliver their message to those people. All the tools are there. We now have the potential to understand every postcode in the country' (as quoted by Miller, 2001). Door-to-door specialists, Circular Distributors, launched Personal Placement in 2000, a door-to-door service that delivers targeted messages to selected households, i.e. it only delivers to households that match specified profiles. According to Circular Distributors, 'We can deliver to specific households based on a range of criteria – everything from whether they own a cat or have a home computer or have children between the ages of five and 16.' This cuts out wastage and reduces the

cost of a door-to-door sampling exercise. One client was a large ISP that wanted to distribute CD-ROMs to households with a PC. Circular Distributors was able to deliver to 500,000 computer-owning addresses. 'It is a precise and low-cost method of placing a tangible item directly into the hands of this hard-to-reach, but very valuable, audience.'

Even with this precision, door-to-door sampling has to work hard to grab attention and to ensure safe delivery of the sample, however. When Philips wanted to tell consumers about its Softone light bulbs, it dropped a bag through the door with a brochure about the product and a money-off voucher. If the consumer was interested, they left the bag outside the door the next day after ticking a box to say which colour bulb they wanted and the sample was left in the bag for them. This allowed the company to deliver a fragile object safely and allowed consumers to opt out of the sampling exercise if they wanted to, thus making it more cost-effective and better targeted.

Home is not the only place where marketers can offer samples to consumers. An airport delivers a captive audience, often with time to kill while waiting for a flight, often in a spending frame of mind, and often

A bright idea for distributing light bulb samples.

Source: Circular Distributors Ltd.

looking to airport stores for new experiences. Nestlé offered samples of its Polo Supermints to travellers at Gatwick airport and then directed them to the shops where they were on sale. Similarly, samples of alcoholic drinks can be offered just a short distance away from the duty-free stores that sell those brands. World Duty Free offers drink, cosmetic and fragrance samples in both departure and arrivals areas at airports near to its retail stores. The company has found that sampling is much more effective than money-off vouchers or gifts in stimulating sales.

▶

Ferry terminals and railway station concourses can also be good places to carry out a sampling exercise. Concourse Initiatives, a company that markets and manages concourse space, claims that rail commuters tend to be affluent ABC1s aged under 45, and that 70 per cent of them are primary grocery buyers, in broad terms an attractive target group for many manufacturers. Around 2.4 million people pass through London Liverpool Street station every week, and outside London, stations in Birmingham, Leeds and Glasgow can deliver 0.5 million passengers or more per week. Given that passengers have, on average, 7 minutes of 'dwell time' to kill while waiting for trains, stations offer a wonderful sampling opportunity. For one client, a walk-in freezer was built on a concourse and 25,000 ice-cream samples per day handed out. Over three years, Häagen Dazs handed out over 1 million samples in this way. Similarly, samples of draught Guinness have been handed out on a concourse, with a follow-up leaflet giving the consumer money off a Guinness four-pack as well as the opportunity to phone in for a free Guinness glass. Interestingly, alcohol sampling is allowed in small measures on concourses but the drink cannot be handed out in bottles or in large quantities. It cannot be given to station staff or consumers aged under 18 and a security guard must be present at all times.

For many manufacturers, the numbers of consumers that concourses deliver are attractive, but there are potential problems. First, size isn't everything. It might be a large audience, but it is a broad one and it is difficult to identify and select a more specific sub-group out of it. Second, consumers on concourses, especially commuters, are often rushing to be somewhere else and, unless they have time to kill waiting for a train, are not likely to be receptive to messages, especially if they are stressed. Nevertheless, leaflets can be handed out quickly for consumers to look at later (on the train?) and incorporating competitions on them is a good way of generating responses and thus leads.

Sources: Fletcher (1999), Gray (1999), McLuhan (2000), Miller (2001), Wilson (2001), http://www.initgroup.com

Gift, prize or merchandise based

A wide range of activities depend on the offer of prizes, low-cost goods or free gifts to stimulate the consumer's buying behaviour. Holidays, brand-related cookery books, mugs or clothing featuring product logos and small plastic novelty toys are among the vast range of incentives used to complement the main product sale.

Gifts or merchandise. Self-liquidating offers invite the consumer to pay a small amount of money, and usually to submit specified proofs of purchase, in return for goods that are not necessarily directly related to the main product purchase. The money paid is usually just enough to cover the cost price of the goods and a contribution to postage and handling, and thus these promotions become self-financing if the expected number of customers takes them up. Often, such a promotion is used to reinforce the brand name and identity of the products featuring the scheme.

eg A link-up between Disney and Britvic showed good synergy between the partners in the promotion, the premium offered and the target market. A promotion featured on bottles of Robinsons fruit juice concentrates offered a *Monsters, Inc.* alarm clock with a detachable cuddly Sully character. The 12-week promotion was timed to coincide with the build-up to the release of the film in February 2002 and the period immediately after its release. To get the clock, consumers had to send in four bottle caps and £6.99. The number of caps required gives at least short-term brand loyalty, while the £6.99 covers the basic costs of providing the clock and administering the offer. The tie-in with the film ensures extra consumer excitement about the promotion as it benefits from synergy with the film's own marketing efforts. As well as featuring prominently on the packs, the promotion was supported with a £2m. advertising campaign on children's television and in the press (*The Grocer*, 2002b). In the first month of the campaign the brand achieved its highest ever four-weekly volume share of 49 per cent, and highest ever household penetration of 54 per cent (Derrick, 2002).

In the case of a free mail-in, the consumer can claim a gift, free of charge, in return for proofs of purchase and perhaps the actual cost of postage (but not handling charges or the cost of the gift itself). The free goods attract the consumer and encourage a higher response rate than self-liquidating offers, and the responses potentially provide the organisation with direct marketing opportunities. Of course, the promotion is only free to the consumer. The promoter has to consider carefully the merchandise costs, postage, packing, processing and even VAT. All of this has to be put into the context of the likely response rate, so that the total cost of the promotion can be forecast and an appropriate quantity of merchandise can be ordered and available when the promotion begins.

Offering free gifts contained inside or banded on to the outside of the pack can make a big impact at the point of sale because the reward is instant, and the purchaser does not have to make any special effort to claim it. One-off gifts are designed to bring the consumer's attention to a product and to encourage them to try it. The offer might shake them out of a routine response purchase and make them think about trying a different brand.

eg Rather than offering a separate free gift, the packaging itself can be used as an incentive. Twinings tea, for example, offered a free tea caddy with its 50-teabag packs of Earl Grey and English Breakfast teas. The bags were packed inside metal caddies replicating the Twinings logo and packaging images (*The Grocer*, 2002c). Similarly, Oxo stock cubes have been sold (with no increase in price) in attractive tins, plastic money boxes and pencil cases instead of the usual cardboard box. All of these items are kept for a long time and are heavily branded, thus providing the constant reminder. Obviously the costs of such sales promotions are high in terms of product and handling, but the rewards are often very recognisable and tempting to the consumer at the point of sale, as the consumer's attention is attracted to the fact that there is clearly something different about the packs.

'Free with product' is similar to an on-pack offer, except that the gift is not attached to the product but has to be claimed at the checkout. The consumer, for example, might be invited at the point of sale to buy a jar of coffee and claim a free packet of biscuits. The computerised checkout can tell whether the conditions of the promotion have been met and automatically deducts the price of the biscuits from the final total.

Customer loyalty schemes. Given the increasingly high cost of creating new customers, organisations have turned their attention to ways of retaining the loyalty of current customers. Major international airlines have their frequent flyer schemes, many different retail and service organisations give away air miles with purchases, and petrol stations and supermarkets issue swipe cards through which customers can accumulate points as mentioned earlier. All of these schemes are designed to encourage repeat buying, especially where switching is easy and generic brand loyalty is low. Price promotions can be dangerous in that they encourage consumers to become price sensitive, and are easily copied by competitors. Tokens, points and stamps that can be traded in for other goods are all ways of adding value to a product, while avoiding costly price competition. They are thus known as alternative currencies.

One of the problems with loyalty schemes, however, is the sheer number of them. When every airline has a frequent flyer scheme and when every supermarket has a loyalty club, then the competitive edge is lost. Furthermore, there is evidence that the loyalty generated by such schemes is questionable, as will be seen in Case Study 11.1 (see pp. 384–5). Nevertheless, loyalty schemes are fast becoming an established part of the marketing scene.

Contests and sweepstakes. Gifts given free to all purchasers of a product necessarily are limited to relatively cheap and cheerful items. Contests and sweepstakes, however, allow organisations to offer very attractive and valuable incentives, such as cars, holidays and large amounts of cash, to very small numbers of purchasers who happen to be lucky enough to win. Such promotions might be seen as rather boring by consumers, unless there is something really special about them.

Contests have to involve a demonstration of knowledge, or of analytical or creative skills to produce a winner. Setting a number of multiple choice questions, or requiring the competitor to uncover three matching symbols on a scratch card, or asking them to create a slogan, are all legitimate contest activities.

'Get there before the moles do' was the advertising slogan used by petrol company Texaco to support its Treasure Hunt sales promotion. The company buried five Mercedes SLK convertibles in secret locations across the UK, then gave out clues to their locations on cards given away with petrol purchases. Each site was marked with a Texaco hub cap under which was a spade, instructions and a flag. A hotline was also set up so that treasure hunters could check that they had indeed found the right site before they put in any digging effort. One vehicle was dug up in Kelso, Scotland, but the three people who found it said that they wouldn't be able to drive it because they couldn't afford the insurance! Around 3.6 million people took part in the hunt and 400,000 people called the hotline. The promotion was supported by broadcast, print, POS and poster advertising, and the PR coverage generated was estimated to be worth £3m. (Brabbs, 2000; *Daily Record*, 2000; Middleton, 2002).

Texaco customers were teased with clues as to the location of a buried car when they bought fuel. Large numbers were encouraged to choose Texaco for their next refuel in the hope of a further clue.

Source: Texaco HACL & Partners.

Sweepstakes do not involve skill, but offer every entrant an equal chance of winning through the luck of the draw. Additionally, they must ensure that entry is open to anyone, regardless of whether they have purchased a product or not. Thus *Reader's Digest* prize draws have to be equally open to those not taking up the organisation's kind offer of a subscription.

Such activities are popular with both consumers and organisations. The consumer gets the chance to win something really worthwhile, and the organisation can hope to generate many extra sales for a fixed outlay. With price or gift-based promotions, the more you sell, the more successful the promotion, the more it costs you because you have to pay out on every sale. With competitions and sweepstakes, the more successful the activity, the more entries it attracts, yet the prizes remain fixed. The only losers with a popular contest or sweepstake are the consumers, whose chances of winning become slimmer! However, at some stage consumers may become bored with such activities, especially if they do not think they have any reasonable chance of winning. At that point, a more immediate but less valuable incentive might be more appropriate.

Store-based

This section looks more generally at what can be done within a retail outlet to stimulate consumer interest in products, leading perhaps to trial or purchase.

Sales promotion at the point of sale (POS) is critical in situations where the customer enters the store undecided or is prepared to switch brands fairly readily. Many different POS materials and methods can be used. These include posters, displays, dispensers, dump bins and other containers to display products. New technology has further changed POS promotion with flashing signs, videos, message screens and other such attention-seeking display material. Interactive POS systems can help customers to select the most appropriate offering for their needs, or can direct them to other promotional offers.

In-store demonstrations are a very powerful means of gaining interest and trial. Food product cooking demonstrations and tasters are used by retailer and manufacturer alike, especially if the product is a little unusual and would benefit from exposure (i.e. new cheeses, meats, drinks). Other demonstrations include cosmetic preparation and application, electrical appliances, especially if they are new and unusual, and cars. These demonstrations may take place within the retail environment, but the growth of shopping centre display areas provides a more flexible means for direct selling via a demonstration.

eg Linking back to sampling, Birds Eye Wall's believes that providing potential customers with cooked samples of product at the point of sale is extremely effective for stimulating sales. Using a mobile kitchen, 10,000 cooked samples a day can be produced in a supermarket car park. In 2001, Sainsbury's had 250 mobile sampling units set up in its car parks, available for any advertiser to use. In 2002, it decided to use 12 of them for itself, to promote its 'Be Good to Yourself' healthy-eating product range (*Marketing Week*, 2002a). If shoppers sample and like the products then they are more likely to go to look for them in the store and buy them.

■ Methods of sales promotion to the retail trade

Manufacturers of consumer goods are dependent on the retail trade to sell their product for them. Just as consumers sometimes need that extra incentive to try a product or to become committed to it, retailers too need encouragement to push a particular product into the distribution system and to facilitate its movement to the customer. Of course, many of the consumer-oriented activities considered in previous sections help that process through pull strategies. Some trade promotions are tightly linked with consumer promotions to create a synergy between push and pull strategies.

eg Powerade is an isotonic sports drink owned by Coca-Cola. When three new flavours were launched early in 2002, trade advertising was undertaken to convince retailers that they should stock the product. The advertising highlighted the £7m. allocated as brand support for the launch period and during 2002, as well as reiterating the product benefits. A trade-oriented promotion consisting of '12 bottles for the price of 9' through participating wholesalers was prominently featured in the advertisements. A hotline telephone number was also given so that retailers could call to request a point-of-sale promotional pack.

The main push promotions are variations on price promotions and direct assistance with selling to the final customer. These will now be looked at in turn.

Allowances and discounts

Allowances and discounts aim to maintain or increase the volume of stock moving through the channel of distribution. The first priority is to get the stock into the retailer, and then to influence ordering patterns by the offer of a price advantage. These techniques encourage retailers to increase the amount of stock held over a period, and thus might also encourage them to sell the product more aggressively. This may be especially important where there is severe competition between manufacturers' brands.

Retailers can thus be offered discounts on every case ordered or a bulk discount if they fulfil a condition relating to volume purchased. A version of BIGIF (for example buy 10 cases and get another 2 free) is also commonly used. A more complex technique is the discount overrider, a longer-term, retrospective discount awarded on a quarterly or annual basis, depending on the achievement of agreed volumes or sales targets. These may be applicable to an industrial distributor selling components as a retail outlet. Although the additional discount may be low, perhaps 0.5 per cent, on a turnover of £500,000 this would still be an attractive £2,500. Count and recount is also a retrospective method in that it offers a rebate for each case (or whatever the stock unit is) sold during a specified period. Thus on the first day of the period, all existing stock is counted and any inward shipments received during the period are added to that total. At the end of the period, all remaining unsold cases are deducted. The difference represents the amount of stock actually shifted, forming the basis on which a rebate is paid.

eg Bendicks offered a free merchandise promotion to smaller retailers through special cases bought from selected wholesalers and cash and carries. The cases contained rolls of Werther's Original and Campino sweets and offered 120 rolls for the price of 98. The 22 free rolls, the equivalent of a 20 per cent discount on the price of the merchandise, were worth £6.60 at the recommended retail price, thus giving the retailer £6.60 extra profit. In addition, the case converted to a display unit to be put on the store's counter. The retailer had the choice of offering a further consumer-oriented promotion of 'buy any two for 49p' to encourage brisk sales, or could sell the rolls at the usual price of 30p each (*The Grocer*, 2002a).

Price-based promotions aimed at the trade are less risky than those aimed at consumers, as the organisational buyer will view them as legitimate competitive tactics rather than using them judgementally to make emotive evaluations of the product. Price promotions appeal to the trade because they make a direct and measurable impact on the retailer's cost structure, and the retailer has the flexibility to choose whether to keep those cost savings or to pass them on to the end consumer. However, in common with price promotions offered to the consumer, trade-oriented price promotions do have the disadvantage of being quickly and easily copied by the competition, leading to the risk of mutually destructive price wars.

Selling and marketing assistance

A number of manufacturer-supported sales and marketing activities assist the reseller by means of promotion at both local and national level.

In cooperative advertising a manufacturer agrees to fund a percentage of a retailer's local advertising, as long as the manufacturer's products are featured in at least part of the advertisement. Cooperative advertising support can be very costly, and thus the manufacturer needs to think very carefully before offering it, as it can potentially put far greater pressure on the manufacturer's own promotional budget than some of the methods previously discussed.

Although in theory manufacturer support may result in better advertising, attempts by resellers to crowd a print advertisement with products, often with price promotions, tend to undermine the position and value of some goods – FMCG brands in particular. Rather than leaving the control of the advertisement in the hands of an individual reseller, therefore, some manufacturers prefer to develop dealer listings. These are advertisements, controlled by the manufacturer, which feature the product and then list those resellers from whom it can be purchased. These are particularly common with cars, higher-value household appliances, and top of the range designer clothing, for example.

Using money to provide merchandising allowances rather than for funding advertising may have a more direct benefit to the manufacturer. Payment is made to the retailer for special promotional efforts in terms of displays and in-store promotions such as sampling or demonstrations. This is especially attractive if the product moves quickly and can sustain additional promotional costs.

A manufacturer might also wish to offer training or support for a retailer's sales representatives who deal directly with the public. Such assistance is most likely to be found in connection with higher-priced products of some complexity, for which the purchaser needs considerable assistance at the point of sale. Cars, hi-fi equipment and bigger kitchen appliances are obvious examples of products with substantial technical qualities that need to be explained.

Various prizes, such as cash, goods or holidays, may be used in sales contests to raise the profile of a product and create a short-term incentive. Unfortunately, the prizes often need to be significant and clearly within the reach of all sales assistants if they are to make any real difference to the selling effort. This is especially true when other competitors may adopt similar methods.

Other more direct incentives than those already mentioned are also possible. Additional bonuses, i.e. premium money, may be made available to sales assistants who achieve targets. These are useful where personal selling effort may make all the difference to whether or not a sale is made. However, the manufacturer needs to be sure that the cost is outweighed by the additional sales revenues generated.

■ Sales promotion to B2B markets

As the introduction to this chapter made clear, sales promotion in its strictest sense is inappropriate to many B2B markets. Discounts and incentives are applicable in situations where the buyer and seller are in direct contact and there is room for negotiation of supply conditions. Of course, where B2B marketing starts to resemble consumer marketing, for example in the case of a small business buying a range of standard supplies from a wholesaler, much of what has already been said about manufacturer–consumer or retailer–consumer sales promotions applies with a little adaptation.

In industrial distribution situations, however, it is even more important than in consumer markets for the distributor's sales representatives to have full product knowledge and commitment. As the distributor is likely to carry many product lines, the sales representative is unlikely to be knowledgeable about all products and applications, and thus training through manuals and briefings funded by the manufacturer are likely to assist in selling to the end customer. That takes care of the knowledge base, but even that might not be enough, and the provision of sales aids and a formal sales training programme might need to be introduced for the distributor's sales force. As well as providing detailed training, the manufacturer's own sales force may undertake joint visits with the distributor's representatives to raise the profile of the product in selected areas. Not only does this directly support the selling effort and provide valuable feedback on customer problems, it also enables informal advice to be given on the best methods of presenting the product and service.

Direct marketing

There are a number of reasons for the rapid growth of direct marketing, connected with the changing nature of the customer, the marketing environment and, in particular, technological development. Direct marketing is being used increasingly across a wide range of both consumer and B2B markets. Even in the relatively conservative financial services industry, there has been a marked increase in the direct selling and direct marketing of a wide range of banking facilities and insurance. This next section of the chapter, therefore, looks more closely at what direct marketing is and how it is being used as an element of integrated marketing communications.

■ Direct marketing: definition and role

Definition

The US Direct Marketing Association has defined direct marketing as:

> *An interactive system of marketing which uses one or more advertising media to effect a measurable response at any location.*

This is quite a broad definition which does, however, capture some basic characteristics of direct marketing. Interactive implies two-way communication between buyer and seller, while *effect a measurable response* implies quantifiable objectives for the exercise. *At any location* implies the flexibility and pervasiveness of direct marketing, in that it is not inextricably linked with any one medium of communication, but can utilise anything (mail, phone, Internet, broadcast or print media) to reach anyone anywhere. What this definition does not do, however, is to emphasise the potential of direct marketing as a primary means of building and sustaining long-term buyer–seller relationships.

It is, therefore, proposed to extend this definition to form the basis of the content of the rest of this section:

> *An interactive system of marketing which uses one or more advertising media to effect a measurable response at any location, forming a basis for creating and further developing an ongoing direct relationship between an organisation and its customers.*

The key added value of this definition is the phrase *ongoing direct relationship*, which implies continuity and seems to contradict the impersonal approach traditionally offered by mass media advertising. Is it really possible to use mass media in a mass market to create a relationship with a single customer? Is it really possible to capitalise on the advantages of personal selling that arise from one-to-one dialogue to build and sustain that relationship without the need for face-to-face contact?

If the answer to those two questions is to be 'yes', then the problem becomes one of information gathering and management. To create and sustain *quality* relationships with hundreds, thousands or even millions of individual customers, an organisation needs to know as much as possible about each one, and needs to be able to access, manipulate and analyse that information. The database, therefore, is crucial to the process of building the relationship. We will look in some detail at the issues of creating, maintaining and exploiting the database on pp. 370 *et seq.*

Objectives

There are a number of tasks that direct marketing can perform, depending on whether it is used for direct selling or supporting product promotion. The tasks may be related to ongoing transactions and relationships with customers. At its most basic, therefore, direct marketing can fulfil the following objectives.

Direct ordering. Direct marketing aims to enable direct ordering, whether by telephone, mail or, increasingly, by direct computer linkage. The use of credit cards, passwords and specific account numbers makes this possible. All kinds of direct marketing techniques can be used to achieve this, but the example of online ordering of CDs is particularly interesting because sellers can both take the order and deliver the product immediately.

Information giving. Direct marketing aims to open a channel of communication to enable potential customers to ask for further information. Information may be given verbally by a sales person, downloaded via the Internet or distributed as printed literature.

Visit generation. Direct marketing aims to invite a potential customer to call in and visit a store, show or event with or without prior notification. Nissan, for example, used direct mailshots targeted at fleet buyers to encourage them to visit the Nissan stand at the UK Motor Show.

Trial generation. Direct marketing aims to enable a potential customer to request a demonstration or product trial in the home, office or factory.

Loyalty creation. Direct marketing offers organisations the opportunity to create loyal customers. If customers have entered into dialogue with an organisation, and have had their needs and wants met through a series of tailored offerings, then it is going to be quite difficult for the competition to poach those customers. Furthermore, using techniques such as direct mail, an organisation can communicate at length and in depth with its customers personally and privately (certainly when compared with advertising).

The big benefit of using direct marketing to build an ongoing relationship with an individual customer is that as time goes on, the customer's trust and confidence in the organisation build up. The hardest job is to get the initial purchase, but once customers have had one successful and satisfactory experience, they will be much more receptive and willing to try again. A shrewd direct marketer can capitalise on this by analysing a customer's purchasing habits in order to tailor future offerings to fit that customer's profile, and by gently nudging the customer upmarket into more expensive purchases.

How and when to use direct marketing

Initiation. An important decision in direct marketing is how best to use it at various stages of the relationship with the customer. The earliest stage, *initiation*, can be very difficult, as it involves creating the initial contact and making the first sale. A combination of appealing advertising and sales promotion techniques may be used, for example, to overcome the potential customer's initial apprehension and risk aversion. Thus in its introductory offer, a book club may reduce the customer's perceived risk through drastic price reductions on the first order (any four books for 99p each), and further specifying a period within which the books may be returned and membership cancelled without obligation. Alternatively, a sale on credit or even a free trial may ease the customer's initial fears, despite the high administration costs. Any of these methods makes it easier for customers to part with their cash on the first order, thus opening the opportunity for a longer-term relationship.

Relationship building. Most direct marketing is in fact aimed at the *relationship stage* customer. This is when the seller has started to build a buying profile, supported by more widely available non-purchase specific data. This enables a steady flow of offers to be made, whether by telephone, mailshot or catalogue update. Customers are also likely to be more responsive at this stage, as they have established confidence in product quality and service performance.

Combination selling. Finally, combination selling results from using contacts gained from one medium, such as a trade exhibition, for regular contact by direct marketing means. This could be the mailing of special offers, price lists, catalogues or telephone calls to gain a face-to-face meeting, etc. The direct marketing activity is therefore used in combination with other methods.

---

corporate social responsibility *in action*

Anyone for spam?

No, not the much revered spam of Monty Python, school dinners and spam fritters fame, but the modern version that is fast becoming the most irritating side of direct marketing. Spam is the unsolicited e-mail messages sent to consumers from listings acquired without the receiver's permission. Although the EU Council of Ministers wants spam e-mail to be banned, with a preference for an opt-in scheme, the European Parliament has taken the position that spam should be outlawed only according to the wishes of individual member states (Boyarski *et al.*, 2002). The opt-in scheme already exists in

Germany, Austria, Italy, Denmark and Sweden and others are likely to follow soon. In the case of Germany, where consumer protection is especially tough, sending unsolicited e-mails, although not illegal, does violate the country's competition laws. The direct marketing industry favours an opt-out approach, so if you forget to tick the box you can expect a flood of unwanted mail (Meller, 2001).

Although relevant laws and directives are in place, for example a 1999 privacy directive issued by the EU requiring marketers to tell consumers what data they will collect and retain, exactly how it will be used

in the future, and then giving them the option of opting in or out of the process, spam e-mails and even some junk mail is still being sent that flouts the law (Dirskovski, 2001; Bertagnoli, 2001). In the UK, the 1998 Data Protection Act also prohibits spamming. Although junk mail has been progressively legislated against, through tighter controls on the resale of mailing lists and the obligation on direct marketers to allow consumers to opt in for additional mailings, it is not the same for direct e-mail campaigns in which everything from financial services to 'herbal Viagra' and outright pornography has been

▶

promoted on an unsolicited basis. If a reply is made, even to tell them to get lost, your existence is confirmed and another batch of e-mails will soon arrive, some of which may contain viruses. It is also a problem if you want to let children near the computer.

There are some interesting variants to spamming. In the UK, viral campaigns are regarded as entirely legitimate, where you can relay a web page and message on to a friend in return for a small incentive. Handbag.com, for example, a London-based women's portal covering relationships, health, careers and beauty, has a list of 150,000 users and logged a 48 per cent response rate with a recent viral campaign (Bertagnoli, 2001). By sending on messages, the list is expanded without significant effort from the marketer.

Unlike junk mail, it is much harder to legislate against spamming because junk e-mail originating from Russia or the Far East is not under local jurisdiction and it is difficult for the ISPs to track down and stop it. Spammers have little regard for the law or the impact on the DM industry as a whole and will move their operations to places whence it is not illegal to send spam e-mail. The annual cost of handling this number one source of customer complaints has been estimated at £17m. (Otley, 2002). Although filtering software can help by picking up keywords and phrases such as sex, Viagra and 'xxx action', the only real solution is never to reply to any spammed e-mails and never to give out your e-mail address. Word screening can be especially difficult if you are in the erection

business, whether in steel or concrete! All of this unwanted activity could have a knock-on effect on other areas of direct marketing such as direct mail and telemarketing, if consumers become more resentful of unwanted intrusion. It will also affect legitimate direct marketing organisations, as the opt-in approach will reduce the power of listings. Spam is not synonymous with direct marketing, and indeed it is not good practice for many organisations as it does not involve accurate targeting. It is, however, giving the industry a bad name and it will, if not stopped, make legitimate e-mail marketing campaigns such as those considered in Chapter 14, more difficult.

Sources: Bertagnoli (2001), Boyarski *et al*. (2002), Dirskovski (2001), Meller (2001), Otley (2002).

The discussion so far has talked generally about the concept of direct marketing, with passing reference to specific areas such as direct mail and direct response, among others. The next section looks more closely at each of these areas and their individual characteristics. Figure 11.4 gives an overview of the range of direct marketing areas.

■ Techniques of direct marketing

The scope of direct marketing is very wide. It utilises what might be called the more traditional means of marketing communication, such as print and broadcast advertising media, but it has also developed its own media, through mail, telecommunications and modem. Each of the main techniques in direct marketing will now be considered in turn.

Figure 11.4 The range of direct marketing techniques

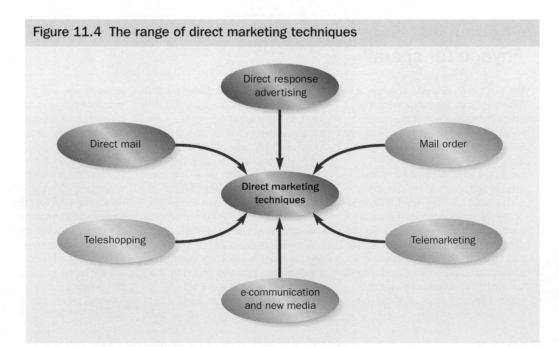

Direct mail

Direct mail is material distributed through the postal service to the recipient's home or business address to promote a product or service. What is mailed can vary from a simple letter introducing a company or product through to a comprehensive catalogue or sample. Many mailshots incorporate involvement devices to increase the chances of their being opened and read, through stimulating curiosity.

Most direct mail is unsolicited. Organisations compile or buy lists of names and addresses, and then send out the mailshot. The mailing list used may be cold, that is, where there has been no previous contact between the organisation and the addressee, or may reflect various selection criteria based on data held about previous or existing customers. It can, however, be very precisely targeted. The London Herb and Spice Company, for example, wanted to create awareness of its fruit teas and so used a mailshot aimed at 90,000 users of competitive products.

Direct mail has the problem that it has suffered from bad PR. All of us as consumers can probably think of a couple of examples of direct mail we have received that have been completely inappropriate, and misconceptions about direct mail's effectiveness are often based on such personal experiences of receiving 'junk'. Historically, this has arisen partly from the lack of flexibility and detail within databases, and partly from poor marketing thinking. Increasingly, though, marketers are using the information at their disposal more intelligently, and mailing smaller groups of well-defined prospective customers, using better-designed creative material. They are also keeping their databases more current, and so a household should not receive direct mail addressed to people who moved away or died over a year ago. In theory, then, an individual should be receiving less direct mail, but what they do receive should be of prime relevance and interest.

eg Boots ran into trouble with the Advertising Standards Authority (ASA) for sending mailings to customers who had specifically asked not to be contacted. The letter said 'When you joined the Advantage card scheme, you expressed a preference not to receive mail from us. However, we thought you might like to know that you are missing out on . . .'. Unfortunately for Boots, some of its cardholders did not want to know and the one complaint was upheld by the ASA. Under the Data Protection Act of 1998, which came into force in 2001, it is illegal to mail consumers with further offers if they have opted out. In this case, Boots apologised and indicated that it would refrain from further mailings (Brabbs, 2001).

Although the information in Table 11.1 is heartening, it may not be enough. Think about the hierarchy of effects models shown in Figure 9.5, and how direct mail fits into those. Using the AIDA model as an example, opening the envelope begins the *awareness* stage, reading the content generates *interest* and *desire* and, finally, the mailshot clearly defines what subsequent *action* is expected. The main objective is to move the recipient quickly through all the stages from awareness to action. The key is not simply the opening of the envelope, but whether the content can pull the reader right through to the completion of action. As a consolation prize, if the recipient reads the content but chooses not to respond, there may still be an awareness or interest effect that may 'soften up' the customer for subsequent mailings or, in B2B markets, a sales visit.

Direct response advertising

Direct response advertising appears in the standard broadcast and print media. It differs from 'normal' advertising because it is designed to generate a direct response, whether an order, an enquiry for further information or a personal visit. The response mechanism may be a coupon to cut out in a print advertisement, or a phone number in any type of advertisement. This area has grown in popularity in recent years as advertisers seek to get their increasingly expensive advertising to work harder for them.

By using advertising media, direct response advertising's initial targeting, unlike that of some of the other forms of direct marketing, relies much more on an assessment of the medium's reader or viewer profile than on a pre-prepared mailing list. Responses to such advertising, however, can then be used as a database for other forms of direct marketing in the future.

Table 11.1 Some facts about direct mail in the UK

1 The average UK household receives 13.1 items of direct mail every four weeks (17 for the AB socioeconomic group)

2 Business managers are sent an average of 14 direct mail items per week

3 4,939 million items of direct mail were sent out in 2001. These were split: 75 per cent B2C mailing and 25 per cent B2B mailings

4 Direct mail volume has increased by over 100 per cent in the last 10 years

5 In 2001, £2,228 m. was spent on direct mail advertising compared with £895 m. in 1991

6 On average, 68 per cent of B2C direct mail is opened and 43 per cent read. The lowest is household insurance (16 per cent) and the highest is travel (81 per cent)

7 Response rates overall average 10 per cent. They range from 3.5 per cent for credit cards to over 22 per cent for brown goods (TVs, hi-fis, etc.)

8 38 per cent of consumers find direct mail intrusive compared with 81 per cent for telesales

9 In B2B markets opinion on the value of direct mail is almost equally divided between 'useful' and 'not useful'

10 Business managers open 83 per cent of their direct mail, 9 per cent is re-directed to a colleague and 16 per cent is filed or responded to

11 The average consumer spends £514 per year on average through direct mail

12 More than £23.4 billion of consumer business is generated every year by the direct mail industry

Source: adapted from http://www.dmis.co.uk reproduced by kind permission of Direct Mail Information Service (DMIS).

eg Slendertone UK became the market leader in the body-toning market within three years of its launch and much of this was attributed to its successful use of direct response media. Market share grew from 6 to 49 per cent. While sales went up sixteenfold, the cost per sale reduced by 40 per cent in just two years. How do they do it? After building a profile of target customers, the company is able to match it with the reader and viewer profiles of different media. The full range of direct response media are used, including television, press and radio as well as direct mail, catalogues and point-of-sale materials in selected retail outlets. Over 40 titles are used and each is tracked for the number and nature of responses. The campaigns are well integrated with the emphasis on creating impact. Potentially the world's largest bottom featured on a billboard advertisement with the headline 'Does my bum look big in this?' at the junction of Oxford Street and Tottenham Court Road to announce the launch of the Slendertone Flex Bottom and Thigh System. Worth a trip to London to see it? (http://www.slendertone.com).

By using an eye-catching large bottom and making the viewer think of the common question 'Does my bum look big in this?', Slendertone managed to attract the attention of passers by.

Source: Slendertone.

There is a range of types of direct response mechanisms that can be used in advertising. Advertisers can provide an address to write to, a coupon to fill in and send off for more information, telephone numbers or website addresses. Either the advertiser or the customer can pay for any postal or telephone charges. The ones who expect the consumer to pay for a phone call or postage, or who expect the consumer to compose a letter rather than filling in a coupon, are immediately putting up barriers to response. Why should consumers make any undue effort, or even pay directly, to give an organisation the privilege of trying to sell them something? In the light of that view, organisations either need to have incredibly compelling direct response advertising that makes any effort or cost worthwhile or, more realistically, they need to minimise the effort and cost to the potential customer. Schofield (1994) confirms that certainly in B2B markets, response should be as easy as possible. The easier the response, the greater the number of enquiries and the greater the conversion rate and revenue per enquiry.

eg Sight Savers International, the international blindness charity, uses DRTV to recruit more donors so that it can continue its work in the developing nations. The two main areas of its marketing budget are DRTV and direct mail. The advantage of television is the powerful images that can be presented, such as a young mother in Malawi suffering from trachoma, with the camera seeing through her eyes. The television can communicate not only the misery of those who are suffering, but also the immense relief and joy that comes as a result of treatment funded by SSI. It has used fragmented media to its advantage by targeting niche segments through satellite and cable, whereas terrestrial advertising costs would have been prohibitive (Kleinman, 2000).

McAlevey (2001) identified a number of principles to follow to enable more effective direct response. Although generated in a North American cultural context, a number of them are relevant to European DR users seeking greater impact and higher response rates. The principles are:

- the focus should always be on what sells;
- don't always reinvent the wheel when designing campaigns;
- make the 'offer' the central theme of the creative execution;
- long copy can sell if the reader is engaged;
- select creativity that sells, not that which just looks good;
- always test and measure response;
- select and retain media not on their ratings, but on their ability to sell for you;
- always ask for the order or for further action. It must be loud, clear, easy to understand and easy to execute.

To McAlevey, success is 40 per cent the offer, 40 per cent the media/lists used and 20 per cent the message creativity. Perhaps that is why some of the hard-hitting direct response television advertisements for double glazing (no names!) are such a turn off.

Telemarketing

While direct response advertising and direct mail both imply the use of an impersonal initial approach through some kind of written or visual material, telemarketing makes a direct personal, verbal approach to the potential customer. However, although this brings benefits from direct and interactive communication, it is seen by some as extremely intrusive. If the telephone rings, people feel obliged to answer it there and then, and tend to feel annoyed and disappointed if it turns out to be a sales pitch rather than a friend wanting a good gossip. The Henley Centre found that only 16 per cent of consumers actually welcome calls and the rest are basically not interested (McLuhan, 2001).

Telemarketing, therefore, can be defined as any planned and controlled activity that creates and exploits a direct relationship between customer and seller, using the telephone.

Hertz Lease is an example of outbound telemarketing, where the organisation contacts the potential customer. Inbound telemarketing, where the potential customer is encouraged to contact the organisation, is also popular. This is used not only in direct response advertising, but also for customer care lines, competitions and other sales promotions.

Hertz Lease is a leading vehicle leasing and management service provider in the UK and European B2B markets. Rather than the sales force using cold calling and prospecting techniques, Hertz Lease decided that it would prefer them to use their time more effectively by following up qualified sales leads. For over five years HSM, a telemarketing company, has been assigned to generate around 200 sales appointments per month for the sales force to follow up. As part of the exercise, HSM was contracted to build a database on company and fleet information for research purposes and to guide telemarketing campaign planning. Over time, the role of telemarketing has changed and as the internal staff have become better trained and sufficiently experienced to take dialogue further with senior staff in the buying organisation, now all inbound enquiries are handled by the HSM team.

There have been a number of benefits from the relationship between Hertz Lease and HSM, not only by generating sales leads and databases, but also helping to improve the productivity of the sales force. They can now concentrate on the hottest clients, with whom their higher-level sales and negotiation skills can be used to best advantage. In addition, regular contact can be maintained with the target prospect base using direct mail, telemarketing and e-mail marketing contact. This enables a more timely response, should a customer seriously consider changing or developing its vehicle management system. The sales team could not maintain such a presence cost-effectively (http://www.hsm.co.uk).

Telephone rental or ownership is high across Europe, averaging over 80 per cent of households, and thus if an appropriate role can be defined for telemarketing within the planned promotional mix, it represents a powerful communication tool. As with personal selling (see pp. 324 *et seq.*), there is direct contact and so dialogue problems can be addressed. Similarly, the customer's state of readiness to commit themselves to a course of action can be assessed and improved through personal persuasion, and efforts made to move towards a positive outcome. Telemarketing can also be used to support customer service initiatives. A carefully designed and managed inbound telemarketing operation can provide an important, sometimes 24-hour, point of contact for customers. This is an important part of maintaining an ongoing relationship with the customer.

Nevertheless, outbound telemarketing in particular is still not widely accepted by consumers and is often seen as intrusive. Where customers have an existing relationship with an organisation, however, and where the purpose of the call is not hard selling, they are less suspicious. Research by Datamonitor, reported by Bird (1998), found that 75 per cent of respondents like receiving calls that check their satisfaction with the product or service or that simply thank them for their custom. The figure drops to less than half if the call is linked to information gathering and a sales pitch. If the outbound calls are badly handled, research by Outbound Teleculture has indicated that 70 per cent of customers become annoyed and in some cases this damages the reputation and prospects for future business for that company.

Seeboard sells energy to approximately 2 million households and businesses in the UK, mainly selling gas and electricity in the Kent, Sussex and Surrey areas. Although it had a strong brand awareness and customer base within its home territory, when it decided to expand beyond that to elsewhere in the UK it was faced with trying to reach a potentially large number of consumers with a limited marketing infrastructure, little existing brand awareness, and heavy competition. It contracted Telegen to provide an outbound telemarketing service to target the residential and business sectors outside its home patch. Telegen established a dedicated outbound call centre to include dialling technology, digital call recording capability and tailored telesales training modules dedicated to Seeboard's requirements. Using prepared IT technology, the operators had access to scripts, tariffs and payment mechanisms to help with a smooth conversion.

Despite it being a tough marketing challenge, the operation has, according to Telegen, exceeded Seeboard's expected telesales performance, including improved hourly agent performance, acquisition cost reduction and shorter than expected lead-in times for system development and set up. Within a 6-month period Telegen has expanded the Seeboard team to over 100 full-time staff, suggesting that conversion effectiveness is moving in the right direction (http://www.seeboard.com; http://www.telegenuk.com).

Mail order, e-communication and teleshopping

E-communication. The rapidly growing area of e-communications and new media will be considered in depth in Chapter 14. It is probably too early to appreciate the full potential impact of some of the recent developments, but the growth of web and online marketing, texting and e-marketing gives marketers the ability to reach large audiences cost-effectively while retaining the targeting power of direct marketing. The challenge for planning an integrated marketing communications programme is to understand the potential of these relatively new and fast-changing areas, consider how they will fit into the mix, and execute them effectively. Whether it is web, WAP, SMS (and increasingly EMS), or e-mail communication, each information delivery gateway needs to be considered and exploited to its full advantage. At present, they are largely supplementing other communication elements, but substitution over time is inevitable. What is certain, however, is that as bandwidth speeds improve dramatically, third-generation (3G) technology becomes widely accepted, and users become fully adapted to new media, there will be many more creative opportunities open to the marketer.

Mail order. Mail order, as the name suggests, involves the purchase of products featured in advertising or selected from a catalogue. The goods are not examined before ordering, and thus the advertisement or the catalogue has to do a good sales job. Mail order companies promote themselves through any media, and receive orders through the mail, by telephone or via an agent. Direct selling through one-off, product-specific advertisements has largely been covered on pp. 365 *et seq.* under direct response advertising. This section will therefore concentrate on the mail order catalogue sector.

The home shopping market is now going through a period of rapid growth, as much as 20 per cent per year according to Smith, P. (2001), and it is now worth £15bn in the UK. Although that figure covers all forms of home shopping, including online purchasing, it is dominated by mail order catalogue sellers. Modern mail order catalogues have abandoned the large, comprehensive catalogues and are now more varied, better quality, and niche targeted. Developments in database-building techniques, customer acquisition, promotion, fulfilment, postal services and logistics have all helped the shift towards speciality catalogue selling. An average specialty catalogue in the UK might have a listing of around 1 million names, compared with only 150,000 nine years ago (Metcalfe, 2000). Now, approximately one in 10 households in Europe receives one or more shopping catalogues each year.

eg Lands' End is an international mail order catalogue seller. Although it does have 16 stores in the USA, two factory stores in the UK and a store in Japan, the bulk of its business is mail order and online selling. In 2001 in the USA, it distributed 269 million catalogues and on its website it claims that it gets between 40,000 and 50,000 calls on a typical day, but during the Christmas period this can rise to 100,000 calls a day on 1,100 phone lines. Eight catalogues are available, although in Europe the catalogue choice is more limited. It has 6.7 million customers who have made at least one purchase in the previous year. Its US mailing list has 31 million names.

The catalogue came to the UK in 1991 and with a 24-hour, 7-day-a-week operation, carefully selected merchandise, a full guarantee that merchandise can be returned at any time for any reason, the operation has grown to make Lands' End one of the dominant players in the mail order market. Although telephone ordering still predominates, the online ordering facility is rapidly growing in popularity. In addition, with the wider acceptance of websites, it is becoming much easier to enter markets than in the era when everything depended upon the catalogue.

The website increases the speed with which a database can be developed in a new market. From registrations on the web, it is far easier now to ensure that the catalogues reach people who are interested rather than having to rent a list of names. When Lands' End entered the French market, it used only PR and some limited media advertising to attract customers to its website. As the list builds, it plans to introduce a paper catalogue (Sliwa, 2001; http://www.landsend.co.uk).

This kind of catalogue is really a form of distribution channel, in that the operator performs the tasks of merchandise assembly, marketing and customer service. The important thing is to find the selection of merchandise appropriate to the market niche served, and to design an appealing kind of service package (in terms of ordering mechanisms, delivery, returns, etc.). Table 11.2 shows the perceived advantages and disadvantages of mail order over retailing from the consumer's perspective.

Table 11.2 Typical advantages of mail order over retail outlets

Advantages of shops over mail order	Advantages of mail order over shops
Can see/touch goods	Delay payment
Can try on/test goods	Choose at leisure
No delay in acquiring purchases	Choose at convenience
Easy to return goods	Easy to return goods
Easy to compare prices	Saves time
Cheaper	No pestering
Shopping is enjoyable	Shopping is not enjoyable
Advice/service available	Home delivery of purchases

Teleshopping. Developments in communications technology in telephone, cable and satellite television are enabling significant growth in home-based shopping or teleshopping even before the impact of the Internet is considered. Direct marketing through these media can vary from fairly standard one-off advertisements screened during a normal commercial break, to slots featured in dedicated home shopping programmes or channels, usually involving product demonstration, often to a live audience. The main problem with developments in this area is not the capability of the technology, but the willingness of consumers to participate. Digital television has opened up further sales channels for companies such as QVC, which specialises in selling via the television and has 10,000 products on offer. There are also new opportunities for travel agencies and other retailers, a trend that is likely to continue.

■ Database creation and management

Any organisation with a serious intention of utilising direct marketing needs to think very carefully about how best to store, analyse and use the data captured about its customers. This means developing a database with as detailed a profile as possible about each customer in terms of geodemographics, lifestyle, purchase frequency and spend patterns. In B2B markets, information might also be held about decision makers and buying centres. Whatever the kind of market, the deeper the understanding of the customer, the easier it is to create effective messages and products. However, if database usage goes wrong, it can cause some unfortunate errors, for example offering maternity wear or prams to pensioners. When the database works well, it can help to offer products that will appeal to the target audience and generate a response, enabling relationships to build and prosper.

This section looks at some of the issues connected with database creation and management, as summarised in Figure 11.5. Note that the end of the first cycle, customer recruitment and retention, is the start of a stronger second cycle, based on better, recorded information and subsequent targeting.

Customer information. The customer and sales database is a most valuable source of information for relationship management and campaign planning. Having the software to edit, sort, filter and retrieve data is essential (Lewis, 1999). Typical information contained in a database describes customer profiles (certainly their demographic profiles and perhaps their psychographic profile as well) and their purchasing and relationship history with the company. Through analysis and model building, its predictive potential can be exploited.

Figure 11.5 Database creation and management

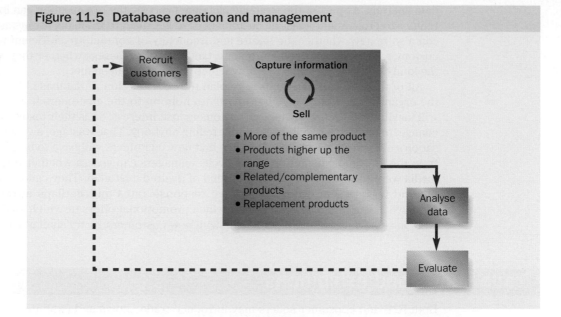

Keeping customers and reselling to them. As with any marketing effort, the continuation of exchanges will depend on how well needs have been satisfied, service provided and value offered. However, the real challenge for direct marketing is to continue to communicate actively with the customer and win further orders after the initial contact has been made. It is always more cost-effective to retain customers than to win new ones, so careful use of direct marketing can assist the overall promotional programme.

There are five stages in a retention and customer development programme. These are considered in turn.

1 *Welcome*. The obvious first stage applies shortly after the customer has become active. An early contact can be reassuring, and assists in engendering receptivity to further communication. When *Next Directory's* called new customers to welcome them after receiving their first orders, a much higher proportion of new customers were retained and they spent 30 per cent more than 'non-welcomed' customers.

2 *Selling up*. Apart from normal repeat business, such as occurs with customers of a book club, organisations should encourage the customer to adopt a better or higher valued model. This approach would be appropriate for a wide range of products and services including cars, cameras and credit cards. American Express, for example, used direct mail to encourage green Amex cardholders to trade up to gold card status. The timing of contact will depend on the expected replacement period for the product.

3 *Selling across*. The selling across or cross-selling stage is where an organisation tries to sell a wider range of products than those in the area originally selected. A customer who purchases car insurance from a particular company might subsequently receive mailings about house insurance or private health cover, for example.

4 *Renewal*. With products that involve annual or regular renewal, such as motor insurance, the timing of appropriate and personalised communication around the renewal date can reinforce repeat purchases.

5 *Lapsed customers*. Customers may be temporarily dormant or permanently lost. A continuation of communication may be appropriate for a period of time so as not to lose contact, especially if reorder frequencies are high.

Review and recycle

As implied above, once a database is up and running it should be monitored, reviewed and evaluated periodically to make sure that it is working well and achieving its full potential. This is not just about 'cleaning' the database (i.e. making sure that it is up to date and that any individuals who have disappeared without trace are deleted from it), but also about data analysis. As part of the strategic planning process, the organisation can look for opportunities to cross-sell to existing customers or to get them to trade up, for instance. Managers can also review whether the nature and frequency of contact are sufficient to achieve full customer potential. Perhaps more importantly, they can assess whether they have recruited the kind of customer expected and whether targets have been met.

All of this analysis can be used to plan the continuation of database building. Although the organisation will be trying primarily to hold on to the customers it already has, there will inevitably be some wastage as customers lose interest, or as their tastes and aspirations change, or as they move house without telling anybody. That wastage, as well as the organisation's own growth aspirations, means that new customers will have to be sought. Learning from the first implementation of the cycle, managers can assess whether the 'right' kind of media were used to attract the 'right' kind of desired customer. They can refine their profiling and targeting in order to improve response rates and perhaps attract even more lucrative customers. They can review which promotional offers or which kinds of approach were most successful and repeat those with new customers, or try similar activities again.

Trade shows and exhibitions

Both B2B and consumer sellers may introduce trade shows and exhibitions into their promotional mixes. Such events range from small-scale local involvement, for example a specialist bookseller taking a stall at a model railway exhibition, to an annual national trade show serving a specific industry, such as the DIY and Home Improvement Show, or Pakex for the packaging industry. In either case, the exhibition may become an important element of the year's marketing activities, as this section will show. Even those who specialise in organising and supporting exhibitions have their own exhibitions!

eg Allison Transmissions, a subsidiary of General Motors, has successfully used exhibitions to re-establish itself in the European market. As a supplier of automatic transmissions for commercial vehicles, it was having difficulty in getting specified by the vehicle manufacturers. To do so meant a two-pronged approach, influencing users as well as the manufacturers. Unlike in the USA, automatic transmission is not widely used across Europe so part of the job was to convince users that it could be better than manual transmission.

Exhibitions were used to present a unified corporate image and message across Europe. Through product demonstrations, including 'ride and drive', it was possible to show potential customers the benefits of specifying automatic when renewing the vehicle fleet. The company particularly targeted uses where the vehicle is constantly stopping and starting, such as refuse vehicles, buses and fire engines. The national truck and bus exhibitions were targeted, such as the IAA (Hanover) in Germany. Despite having relatively few customers, the power of the exhibition is in the face-to-face contact and high visual impact. Allison now spends 30 per cent of its marketing budget on exhibitions, more than on any other element in the promotional mix (Rines, 1999).

Exhibitions and shows can be of particular importance to the smaller business that may not have the resources to fund an expensive marketing communications programme or to support a large sales force. The exhibition can be used as a cost-effective means of building more 'presence' and reputation with the trade, and to generate potential sales leads. For any sized organisation, international exhibitions can be particularly valuable because they bring together participants from all over the world who might otherwise never meet, and can thus lead to export deals. The Nuremberg International Toy Fair has been running for 50 years. It represents an opportunity for the trade to present new products to retail buyers from across Europe. New product launches are often planned to coincide with the fair to maximise both the impact to visitors and the subsequent coverage in the trade and hobby press.

For the manufacturer, attending exhibitions provides a formal opportunity to display the product range and to discuss applications and needs with prospective customers in a neutral environment. Depending on the type of show and the care that an organisation puts into planning its presence there, an exhibition provides a powerful and cost-effective way of getting the message across and making new contacts that may subsequently turn into sales.

> **eg** Sunny Delight is one of the best selling drinks in the UK. When it was launched, the brand owner Procter and Gamble (P&G) decided that an exhibition presence was necessary to encourage retailers to stock the product. The stand itself was colourful and exciting in order to attract visitors to an unknown brand. An island site was chosen so that visitors could access it from all sides. P&G was particularly keen to establish a database of independent retailers for follow-up contact. With plenty of free samples, television monitors showing the brand advertising and stands to explain the trade and consumer promotions, the short-term series of exhibitions was a great success. Whereas a typical stand at a retail exhibition attracts between 10 and 15 per cent of visitors, P&G attracted 35–40 per cent and 2,106 visitor contacts were made at the Birmingham Convenience Retailing Show (http://www.exhibitionswork.co.uk).

Public relations

■ Public relations: definitions and role

Stanley (1982, p. 40) defined public relations as:

> *A management function that determines the attitudes and opinions of the organisation's publics, identifies its policies with the interests of its publics, and formulates and executes a programme of action to earn the understanding and goodwill of its publics.*

The Institute of Public Relations (IPR) is rather more succinct in its definition:

> *The deliberate, planned and sustained effort to institute and maintain mutual understanding between an organisation and its publics.*

The latter is, nevertheless, a more useful definition that gets close to the core concern of PR, which is *mutual understanding.* The implication is that the organisation needs to understand how it is perceived in the wider world, and then work hard to make sure, through PR, that those perceptions match its desired image. Two-way communication is essential to this process. Another interesting element of this definition is the specific use of the word 'publics'. Advertising, in its commonest usage, is usually about talking to customers or potential customers. Public relations defines a much broader range of target audiences, some of whom have no direct trading relationship with the organisation, and thus PR encompasses a wide variety of communication needs and objectives not necessarily geared towards an eventual sale. Finally, the definition emphasises that PR is *deliberate, planned and sustained.* This is important for two reasons. First, it implies that PR is just as much of a strategically thought out, long-term commitment as any other marketing activity, and second, it counters any preconceptions about PR simply being the ad hoc seizing of any free publicity opportunity that happens to come along.

A public is any group, with some common characteristic, with which an organisation needs to communicate. Each public poses a different communication problem, as each has different information needs and a different kind of relationship with the organisation, and may start with different perceptions of what the organisation stands for (Marston, 1979).

> **eg** A university has to develop relationships with a wide range of publics. Obviously, there are the students and potential students and the schools and colleges that provide them, both nationally and internationally. The university also has to consider, however, its staff and the wider academic community. Then there are the sources of funding, such as local authorities, the government, the EU and research bodies. Industry might also be a potential source of

▶

All areas of the mass media can be used for publicity purposes. Within the broadcast media, apart from news and current affairs programmes, a great deal of publicity is disseminated through chat shows (authors plugging their latest books, for instance), consumer shows (featuring dangerous products or publicising companies' questionable personal selling practices, for instance) and special interest programmes (motoring, books, clothing, etc.). Print media also offer wide scope for publicity. National and local newspapers cover general interest stories, but there are many special interest, trade and professional publications that give extensive coverage to stories of specific interest to particular publics. It must also be remembered that sections of the media feed each other. National newspapers and television stations may pick up stories from local media or the specialist media and present them to a much greater mass audience.

Publicity may be unsought, as when the media get the smell of scandal or malpractice and decide to publicise matters which perhaps the organisation would rather not have publicised. To reduce the risk of bad publicity, however, most organisations cultivate good press relations, and try to feed the media's voracious appetite with 'good news' stories that will benefit the organisation. This can be done through written press releases or verbal press conferences or briefings.

eg When P. J. Holloway became the sole UK distributor for fans made by the German firm Rosenberg Ventilation, if it had simply issued a press release, it might have gained limited coverage in the trade press. Instead, it invited key journalists to visit Rosenberg's manufacturing facility in Germany. As a result of this extra investment in press relations, it found that its coverage was considerable and many more complimentary comments than they could otherwise have expected were made about the product benefits.

The media are obviously very powerful, not only as a public in their own right, but also as a third-party channel of communication with other publics. It may be argued that advertising can do just as good a communication job, in spreading good news to mass audiences, but publicity has a few advantages. Advertising is paid for, and therefore publics have a certain cynicism about the bias within the message. Publicity, on the other hand, is seen as free, coming from a neutral third party, and therefore has more credibility. Also, a good PR story that captures the imagination so that it gets wide coverage across both print and broadcast media can achieve an incredible level of reach (see p. 313) at a fraction of the cost, and might even make an impact on sections of the audience who wouldn't normally see or absorb advertising.

These advantages do, however, need to be balanced against the big disadvantage, *uncontrollability*. Whereas advertising gives the advertiser complete control over what is said, when it is said, how it is said and where it is said, the control of publicity is in the hands of the media. The organisation can feed material to the media, but cannot guarantee that the media will adopt the story or influence how they will present it (Fill, 2002). The outcome of this might be, at worst, no coverage at all, or patchy coverage that might not reach the desired target publics. Another potential risk is distortion of the story. It is not true to say that there is no such thing as bad publicity. The risks of negative coverage can, however, be minimised by the maintenance of ongoing, good press relations, and by setting up a crisis management plan so that if disaster strikes, the damage from bad publicity can be limited and even turned to advantage.

Other external communication

Other forms of external communication are also used for PR. Advertising can be used as a tool of PR, although it is something of a grey area. The kind of advertising to which we are referring here is not the selling or promoting of a specific product or range of products, but the type that concentrates on the organisation's name and characteristics. As previously suggested, although this sort of advertising lacks the impartiality of publicity, it makes up for it in terms of controllability. As a means of helping to establish and reinforce corporate image, it is certainly effective, and as a mass medium will reach members of most publics.

An organisation can host or participate in various events for PR purposes. As well as press conferences, mentioned above, the organisation may host other social events. If it has just opened a new factory, for instance, it may hold a party on the premises for key shareholders, employees, customers and suppliers. Such one-off events will also, of course, create media interest.

An important public is the one with a financial interest in the organisation. The organisation's annual general meeting is an important forum for both shareholders and the financial media. Efficient administration and confident presentation can help to increase credibility (although none of that can disguise a poor financial position). A well-presented annual report is also an important PR tool. Like the annual general meeting, it is an opportunity to present the organisation in the best possible positive light and to make public statements about the organisation's achievements and its future directions.

Lobbying is a very specialised area, designed to develop and influence relationships with 'authority', particularly national and EU governmental bodies. Lobbying is a way of getting an organisation's views known to the decision makers, and trying to influence the development and implementation of policy.

Internal communication

Although employees and other internal publics are exposed to much of the PR that is directed to the external world, they do need their own dedicated communication so that they know what is going on in more detail, and they know it before it hits the wider media (Bailey, 1991). This emphasis on keeping people informed rather than in the dark reflects quite a major change in employers' attitudes towards their employees. It is important for motivation, as well as being a means of preparing people for change and strengthening corporate culture. The two main types of communication are written (house journals, intranet pages or newsletters) and verbal (management briefings, for instance). Few people would want to read a long working paper written by the managing director on quality management or production targets, but most would at least glance at a well-illustrated, short, clearly written summary of the important points presented in journalistic style. Briefings provide a good mechanism for face-to-face contact between management and staff, and for increasing staff involvement and empowerment. Frequent, regular departmental or section meetings can be used to thrash out operational problems and to pass communication downwards through the organisation. Less frequently, once a year perhaps, more senior management can address staff, presenting results and strategic plans, and directly answering questions.

Sponsorship

■ Sponsorship: definition and role

Sponsorship is defined by BDS Sponsorship (http://www.sponsorship.co.uk) as:

> *... a business relationship between a provider of funds, resources or services and an individual, event or organisation which offers in return some rights and association that may be used for commercial advantage.*

While some sponsorship certainly does have altruistic motives behind it, its main purpose is to generate positive attitudes through associating the corporate name with sport, the arts, charitable enterprise or some other activity. That is why so many companies use sponsorship, including familiar names such as Coca-Cola, JVC, McEwan's lager, Carlsberg, Opel, Lloyds TSB and the Nationwide building society.

eg   Mobile telephone operators have been active in using sponsorship to carry their brand names to large audiences. Vodafone's sponsorship portfolio includes Manchester United, the Australian Rugby Union team and Ferrari, all suggesting global excellence through association. Sponsoring champions also means a lot of media coverage, nationally, on a pan-European basis and sometimes further afield, as when Manchester United toured Asia.

▶

Vodafone approaches sponsorship deals not as a fan or supporter, but in terms of what the association can do for corporate communications. It has a centralised sponsorship strategy team in Germany which guides local market decisions and ensures that all the spin-off benefits arising from sponsorship are realised (Fry, 2001).

Vizzavi, the Internet portal owned by Vodafone and Vivendi, took a chance when it agreed to sponsor the 2002 Pop Idol Contest to the tune of some £2m. It could not have known what an outstanding success the show would become with a sponsorship package which included on-air credits, online support and promotional and merchandising rights. The peak time exposure before, during and after every commercial break would have cost Vizzavi far more in advertising expenditure and probably would have made a lot less impact (Brech, 2001).

Sponsorship grew in popularity during the 1980s, partly because of its attractiveness as a supporting element in the promotional mix, and partly because of the growing cost of media advertising compared with the potentially greater coverage of various sports and arts activities (Meenaghan, 1998). Sponsorship has also become more global and has fitted well with the increased trend towards brand globalisation (Grimes and Meenaghan, 1998). Its growth was also helped by the tobacco companies using it as a means of achieving exposure in spite of the ban on television advertising.

■ Types of sponsorship

Sports sponsorship

With the widespread appeal of sport across all ages, areas and lifestyles, it is perhaps not surprising that sports sponsorship has grown in popularity. This is especially true when it is linked to the televising of the events. The mass audiences possible through television, even for some minority sports, enable the widespread showing of the sponsor's name.

eg Flora has been sponsoring the London Marathon since the mid-1990s, as part of its commitment to a healthier Britain, as it claims. There is a clear link between the brand values and the nature of the event. As a bonus, television viewing figures often exceed 6 million, there is a website which clearly links the event to Flora and it has resulted in spontaneous awareness increasing to above 50 per cent. It now even has an international dimension, with the Flora Sydney marathon in 2002 (http://www.london-marathon.co.uk).

Paula Radcliffe crossing the finishing line to win the 2002 Flora London Marathon.

Source: Flora London Marathon.

Many sports attract heavy television coverage and so although the typical sponsoring costs may be high, in comparison with the cost of direct television advertising, such sponsorship can actually be very cost-effective. Sponsorship of sport has the added benefit that although people may ignore commercial breaks, they do pay attention when a 'real' programme is on, and therefore may be more likely to absorb the sponsor's name.

Soccer has been one of the major sports to attract sponsorship because of its large-scale media coverage in all kinds of media. This has attracted sponsors at player, club, national league and international levels throughout the world.

At league level, Barclaycard committed £48m. to be the English Premier League sponsor for the 2001–4 period, taking over from Carling which sponsored the league for nine years. It sought to follow an integrated approach by using sponsorship alongside its television advertising campaign; it planned a football-related credit card; and will invest a further £4m. on a grass-roots football programme. An additional attraction was the opportunity to feature in named broadcasts to 142 countries with a cumulative audience over the sponsorship period of 500 million people in the UK alone (White, 2001). Even for that price, it still did not get complete soccer coverage, however. Coca-Cola also supports the ITV highlights programme and Ford is supporting Sky's live coverage, all of whom will be competing for the public's 'sponsor awareness' (Smith, C., 2001).

International soccer sponsorship is often too big a challenge for individual organisations, however large they are. For the World Cup in France 1998 there were 12 official sponsors paying as much as £250m. each to FIFA for the privilege. Mastercard has been a major main sponsor of the World Cup since 1990, and although no official disclosure has been made on the sums involved, it is thought to be in excess of $20m. per cup. The 2002 tournament was especially attractive in terms of global reach and appeal to advertisers as it was being held for the first time in the Asian market (Matthew, 2001).

If the sponsorship of tournaments does not appeal, then there is always the option of sponsoring individual athletes or players, although some sportsmen and women come at a high price. An Olympic medal winner should be able to net around £1m. in sports endorsements and sponsorship. On a more limited basis, companies can sponsor match programmes, balls or even the corner flags. Smaller or non-league clubs are appealing for local businesses who want to reinforce their role in the community, and even large organisations can value this.

All of this works well as long as the sport and the individual clubs continue to maintain a 'clean' image. A riot in the stands or a punch-up on the pitch generates the kind of publicity and media coverage of the type 'What kind of depths has the game sunk to?' that sponsors will not want to be associated with. Every time a player is sent off for violent conduct with the sponsor's name on his chest, an F1 vehicle breaks down, a player becomes embroiled in a scandal in his or her personal life, there is a risk to the sponsoring organisation. It has also been suggested that sponsors are becoming concerned over the commercial risks associated with ethical problems such as the drug testing that has featured in some high-profile cases (O'Sullivan, 2001).

Broadcast sponsorship

Broadcast sponsorship, sponsoring programmes or series on television or the radio, is a relatively new area in the UK. Television sponsorship forms the largest part of broadcast sponsorship, but it still comprises a minor proportion of a channel's commercial income compared with advertising revenue.

eg Domino's Pizza uses broadcast sponsorship as it wants us to watch more television. Research indicated that we are more likely to order a home-delivered pizza if we are glued to our favourite programme. Domino's sponsored *The Simpsons* on BSkyB, believing that the programme's viewers reflected its target customers, as well as, of course, its sponsorship being entirely appropriate given Homer Simpson's special relationship with pizza (Mmmm, pizza). Through television credits, special promotions and hyperlinks from the Sky and Simpson's web pages to the Domino's site, brand share has risen from 15 to 19 per cent and sales of Domino's Pizza increased by 29 per cent in 1998 (*Marketing Week*, 1999).

Television broadcasters have started to exploit the potential of gaining sponsorship for major sports coverage such as the soccer World Cup, league action and other major events. The broadcasters gain much needed additional revenue and the sponsors are clearly linked to the show in all screenings and associated promotional coverage. Even within the current, fairly restrictive regulatory framework, broadcast sponsorship still has much to offer. As with advertising, of course, it is reaching potentially large audiences and creating product awareness. Further than that, however, it also has the potential to help enhance the product's image and message by association. *London's Burning*, a drama series about fire fighters, for example, was sponsored by Commercial Union, an insurance company. To get the best out of broadcast sponsorship, however, it should be integrated into a wider package of marketing and promotional activities. This might mean using characters or themes from the programme in promotional materials.

Sponsorship of the arts

Arts sponsorship is a growing area, second only to sport in terms of its value in the UK, and the art forms covered range widely from music, including rock, classical and opera, to festivals, theatre, film and literature.

> **eg** Barbie featured in her own movie in 2001, displaying her prowess as a ballet dancer. It was therefore an obvious link for Mattel, the owner of the Barbie brand name, to sponsor the English National Ballet's Christmas run of *The Nutcracker*. The £85,000 sponsorship was important for the ENB, struggling with a large deficit, and fitted the needs of Mattel. The ENB's chief executive was quoted as saying, 'Ballet is all about fantasy and taking people into an imaginary world. So is Barbie. The deal will also help us get new people into the theatre to see the production.' Other sponsors of the ENB have included Herbert Smith and Harrods. Herbert Smith is an international law firm and was a major sponsor of ENB in 2001, providing support for *Double Concerto*, a new ballet by the talented young choreographer Christopher Hampson. This was the only new production the Company was able to present during the financial year 2001–2, largely due to the sponsorship. Herbert Smith benefited from the programme of national activities by having corporate entertainment facilities, both at the world premiere and the London premiere of its sponsored production. It also received recognition through branding and joint publicity campaigns to enhance its corporate profile and raise awareness of its support of the arts in Britain (Branigan, 2001; http://www.ballet.org.uk).

To arts organisations, at a time of declining state funding, private sponsorship has become critical for survival. The state subsidy of the Berlin Philharmonic Orchestra, for example, reduced from 57 per cent of its budget in 1997 to 48.4 per cent in 2000, while that of the Teatro alla Scala in Milan has been cut from well over 50 per cent to 44.3 per cent (*The Economist*, 2001). The theatres, opera houses, orchestras and galleries are not, however, able to sit back and wait for the sponsorship income to roll in. They have to be proactive and approach potential sponsors and donors for money.

Arts sponsorship isn't just about trying to reach an audience that is older, more affluent, and more highly educated than the typical sports audience, through opera, ballet and fine art exhibitions. A wider, if perhaps somewhat less discerning, youth audience can be reached through rock music. A number of companies have sought to appear target-audience-friendly by sponsoring events for individual artists, such as the Lloyds TSB Live Tour of The Corrs and the Celine Dion tour sponsored by Avon Cosmetics.

The important consideration for marketers in deciding whether to sponsor these events is understanding the link between the product and the music. To gain maximum value, it is necessary to ensure that the event features in all aspects of the communications mix, including packaging, advertising and sales promotion. This means exploiting the association before, during and after the music event.

With arts sponsorship there are a number of opportunities to present the sponsoring organisation, including on stage, in programmes, through associated merchandise including videos and CDs, around venues, and even on tickets. There are also advantages in hosting key customers and suppliers at high-profile events, by offering the best seats and perhaps hosting a reception during the interval or after the show.

Cause-related marketing

Linkages between organisations and charities benefit both parties. If, for example, a company runs a sales promotion along the lines of 'We'll donate 10p to this charity for every token you send in', the charity gains from the cash raised and from an increased public profile. Consumers feel that their purchase has greater significance than simple self-gratification and feel good about having 'given', while the company benefits from the increased sales generated by the promotion and from the extra goodwill created from associating its brands with a good cause. Murphy (1999) argues that companies are taking a longer-term view of cause-related marketing because of the positive image associated with a good and caring cause.

eg J&B Rare Scotch Whisky associated itself with raising money to help endangered species such as the black rhino by making a donation for each promotional bottle sold. The impact of such activities is greater if there is a clear synergy between the brand and the charity, or at least if the charity has a particular appeal to the same target audience as the brand. A scheme to save rare plant and animal species through sponsorship support was not well subscribed. Tesco did support the skylark with £100,000 and the water vole raised £150,000 from Norsk Hydro, a Norwegian chemical and oil company. Even the dung beetle raised a few thousand pounds and Glaxo Wellcome decided to back a medicinal leech with £18,000. However, around 100 species that still need saving have no backers, including the red squirrel. The issue for a potential sponsor is that there is little direct link between the brands and the animals and the audiences are very specialised, so the only real benefit is a feeling of good citizenship (Nuttall, 1998).

Not all cause-related marketing is linked with sales promotions, however. Many large organisations set up charitable foundations or donate cash directly to community or charitable causes. Others might pay for advertising space for charities, whether on television, radio, press or posters. This is important at a time when consumers are becoming more conscious of the ethical and 'corporate citizenship' records of the companies they patronise.

eg While most sponsorship activities are usually related to the wider integrated marketing mix, cause-related activities often tend to be part of the PR activity of an organisation and may be treated as free-standing. Thus although Nationwide has paid large sums for sponsoring the football league, it also supports a number of community projects and causes that it considers to be appropriate and worthy of support. Its flagship charity is the Macmillan Cancer Trust to which it has donated £2m. since 1993. In part, the support has been financial but it also involves Nationwide's staff as, for example, in the 'World's Biggest Coffee Morning' allowing staff at the branch level to raise further funds. Over £3m. has been raised for the cause in this way (*Marketing Week*, 2002b; http://www.nationwide.co.uk).

Organisations clearly do not just take an altruistic view of their charity involvement. As with any other marketing activity, it should be planned with clear objectives and expected outcomes. Criteria such as the scale of the impact, the opportunity for spin-off on-site sales, the fit with the core business, target customers and values and the link with the wider media are important considerations.

Schools have become the latest type of organisation to become alert to the possibilities of local fund raising and sponsorship. With budgets tight, finding organisational and private donors is becoming a valuable way of providing the extra facilities and resources that would otherwise not be invested in. Although for some such activities are not regarded as mainstream to the work of a head teacher, the opportunities for small-scale sponsorship from local organisations are potentially great if they are approached in the right way on projects that capture the imagination and offer a spin-off benefit to the sponsor (Smithers, 2002).

Computers for schools

When supermarket chain Tesco decided to undertake a cause-related community sponsorship programme, it wanted an idea that would give it a high profile and a uniqueness that were not readily available from many traditional community-based sponsorship activities. The outcome, the Tesco Computers for Schools annual event, has now been running very successfully since 1992 and has even attracted its own sponsors, such as Nestlé Ice Cream, Coca-Cola and Pringles with the brands linked to the promotion. In 2001, over 4,000 computers and 66,000 other items of equipment were given to the schools, making the grand total of new computers since the scheme was launched in excess of 40,000 and the total equipment worth over £70m.

The scheme allows shoppers to collect vouchers, normally over a 10-week period, with one voucher given for every £10 spent in a Tesco store. Programme sponsors, such as Coca-Cola, might fund an extra voucher for the purchase of their brands. The local schools collect the vouchers from willing donor shoppers to cash them in for computer equipment and software from a special 50-page catalogue. The initiative is especially valuable to schools as it provides much needed access to equipment that may not otherwise be available from their hard-pressed budgets. Over 60 per cent of UK schools now take part in the scheme.

Tesco has worked hard to ensure that it receives considerable public relations benefit from the scheme. Not only does it generate increased store traffic, it also enhances Tesco's reputation as a good corporate citizen that is responsible and caring in its community. The chief executive of Tesco stated, 'Education remains a high priority at Tesco. Tesco believes that one of the most important contributions it can make to the community is to help equip schools with resources that will give children the skills they need for the future.' In order to emphasise the community orientation, regionally based launches, alongside the national launch each year, provide an excellent media opportunity. The local launches often feature schoolchildren, Tesco staff and local celebrities and dignitaries. In 2001, spin-off events were undertaken to raise the profile of the scheme. Stores cut and shared a Tesco Computer for Schools birthday cake with local schools and celebrities. On other occasions balloons have been let loose at stores to create additional photo opportunities. The awards events themselves have become 'must attend' high-profile events for local MPs, MSPs and other local politicians and dignitaries.

Tesco has now become the leading schools-based promotion organisation. The coordinated approach between stores, schools and the media has been highly effective. In order to maintain its position, Tesco has extended its involvement in education. It now sponsors three other awards:

The Every Little Helps Award: to recognise the special contribution to school or community life by an individual who is a help to others and makes a difference.

The Working Together Award: for a group of young people who have worked as a team to improve their school or community.

The Young Scientist Award: for young people who have used their knowledge of science to explore new ideas in an innovative way.

Tesco is also a co-sponsor of the Green Code Programme for Schools, a £1m. computer-based programme to encourage children to explore environmental issues and the importance of sustainability. All of these sponsored activities work closely in the communities surrounding the growing number of Tesco stores and are designed to demonstrate its commitment to the enhancement of education as part of its wider values, described as, 'treating people how we like to be treated. As such, we recognise our responsibilities to communities and to the environment, wherever we operate. Our philosophy of "Every Little Helps" underpins these wide-ranging responsibilities' (http://www.tesco.co.uk).

Although other companies have also become involved with school-based promotions, the Tesco scheme remains the one to emulate. It creates a lot of goodwill where it matters – in the community. That, of course, is no bad thing as an appeal to shoppers and also for the planning authorities as finding new sites becomes increasingly problematic.

Sources: Tesco Computers for Schools press information, kindly provided by Bell-Pottinger.

Chapter summary

■ Sales promotion is part of a planned integrated marketing communications strategy that is mainly used in a short-term tactical sense, but can also contribute something to longer-term strategic and image-building objectives. Sales promotions offer something over and above the normal product offering that can act as an incentive to stimulate the target audience into behaving in a certain way. Manufacturers use promotions to stimulate intermediaries and their sales staff, both manufacturers and retailers use them to stimulate individual consumers and manufacturers might use them to stimulate other manufacturers. The methods of sales promotion are many and varied. In consumer markets they can be classed as money-based, product-based, or gift-, prize- or merchandise-based. Customer loyalty

use of Clubcard Deals helped Tesco customers to save over £25m. on a wide range of offers. One in three UK households has a Clubcard and they play a part in 8 out of 10 sales. In May 2002, Tesco entered into an agreement to allow jewellery chain H. Samuel to award Clubcard points. As in the Tesco stores, one point is given for every £1 spent and accumulated points can be redeemed for Tesco vouchers, Air Miles or Clubcard Deals. It is likely that other partnerships with other retailers will soon follow.

More interesting partnerships with suppliers are also on the cards. Tesco is looking to exploit the links between its Clubcard and its home shopping service, Tesco.com. Using Clubcard data, Tesco can develop lists of customers to be targeted with personalised e-mails jointly with a particular supplier. It could, for example, develop a list of customers who buy a rival brand and then e-mail an incentive to switch including a link back to the Tesco.com site. Unilever was the first supplier to participate.

It is also true that questions have been raised about the ability of such schemes to influence loyalty. A MORI poll showed that over half of UK shoppers hold one or more loyalty cards. Nearly 70 per cent of cardholders claimed that the cards did not influence their choice of where to shop. The problem is that many people hold cards for more than one retailer and therefore the card itself is not likely to be the prime store choice criterion. Nearly 90 per cent said that they were more concerned with getting lower prices than points. More than 25 per cent said that they rarely or never redeem the points they collect. Nevertheless, an NOP poll showed that 73 per cent of card holders use them as often as possible to save money, and 73 per cent prefer saving money on their shopping bills rather than using points for Air Miles or for buying or gaining discounts on other goods and services such as Clubcard Deals.

Because of findings like these, not all retailers are convinced about the value of a loyalty card scheme, and some have had their fingers burned. Safeway discontinued its ABC card in May 2000 after five years of operation and a £250m. investment because it was felt that the scheme was not paying for itself through increased sales or increased customer value. ASDA spent £32m. and five years testing a scheme in the mid 1990s but abandoned it soon after the Wal-Mart takeover. Both ASDA and Safeway are now EDLP-oriented (every day low price). It is interesting to note that the two supermarkets with the most loyal customers are ASDA and Morrisons, neither of which has a loyalty card scheme.

Thus Tesco and Sainsbury's, the two market leaders, have been left in head-to-head competition in loyalty card terms. The schemes provide a flexible mechanism through which other promotional activities can take place. The retailer can, for instance, link with a brand and offer a double or treble points promotion very quickly. Through the Tesco Clubcard magazine, mailed out regularly to customers along with their vouchers, tailored offers relevant to the recipient's shopping habits can be made. Thus money-off coupons relating to specific brands or product categories can be used to reinforce brand loyalty or to increase the volume or frequency of purchase.

The biggest advantage of a loyalty card, however, is the quantity and quality of data it generates on customer purchasing preferences and habits, thus providing the basis for measuring the response to various types of promotional offer so that better targeted and better designed promotions can be developed in the future. The use of data is starting to go further than that, however, and what started off as a humble promotional tool is starting to play a pivotal role in retail strategy, and even in manufacturer strategy. Tesco is using its Clubcard data to determine the layout and product assortment carried by individual stores. The company sees this as a 'pull' strategy with customers essentially driving decisions. Tesco is extending this 'pull' up the distribution channel to manufacturers by sharing its knowledge with them, collaborating on promotional deals, and selling advertising space to them in its Clubcard magazine mailings. Such is the value of these services that Procter and Gamble decided to launch its new hair care brand, Physique, exclusively through Tesco stores and advertising exclusively through Tesco media. As Mitchell (2002) puts it, 'Loyalty cards (and the internet) make mass "bottom up" signalling from consumers economically viable – for the first time. . . .The Tesco experience . . . shows that when marketing initiatives are shaped by signals coming from the consumer . . . then targeting costs plummet and responses soar.'

Whatever fancy plans they have for their loyalty schemes, retailers would perhaps do well to remind themselves of a fundamental marketing truth: 'The best way to establish loyalty is to give people what they want at a price they are prepared to pay' (Brian Roberts, senior European retail analyst for Mintel as quoted by Thurtle, 2001). ASDA, Safeway and Morrisons already have this at the core of their offering, and only time will tell whether Tesco's pull strategy will succeed in implementing it in the most powerful way yet.

Sources: Goodman (2002), The Grocer (2002d), Hemsley (2002), Mitchell (2002), Swengley (2001), Tesco (2002a, b), Thurtle (2001), Tomlinson (2001), Williams (2001).

Questions

1 What factors have led the supermarkets towards these kinds of loyalty scheme and what do they hope to achieve from them?

2 What are the practical problems of setting up, managing and maintaining a promotion like this?

3 In what ways do you think suppliers could benefit from loyalty card schemes?

4 In the longer term, do you think that retailers such as Safeway, ASDA and Morrisons are right to reject the loyalty card concept?

References for chapter 11

Bailey, J. N. (1991), 'Employee Publications' in P. Lesly (ed.), *The Handbook of Public Relations and Communication* (4th edn), McGraw-Hill.

Bertagnoli, L. (2001), 'E-marketing Tricky in Europe', *Marketing News*, 16 July, p. 19.

Bird, J. (1998), 'Dial 0 for Opportunity', *Marketing*, 29 October, pp. 31–3.

Boyarski, J., Fishman, R., Josephberg, K. and Linn, J. (2002), 'European Authorities Consider "Cookies" and "Spam"', *Intellectual Property & Technology Law Journal*, 14 (3), p. 31.

Branigan, T. (2001), 'Barbie to Support the Ballet', *The Guardian*, 10 September, p. 1.4.

Brabbs, C. (2000), 'Texaco Entombs Cars for Treasure Hunt Promotion', *Marketing*, 6 July, p. 4.

Brabbs, C. (2001), 'ASA Slams Boots for Unsolicited Customer Mailing', *Marketing*, 20 September, p. 3.

Brech, P. (2001), 'Vizzavi Ties with Pop Idols in £2m Sponsorship First', *Marketing*, 26 July, p. 1.

Cutlip, S. *et al.* (1985), *Effective Public Relations*, Prentice Hall.

Daily Record (2000), 'Buried Merc Found by Trio', *Daily Record*, 18 July, p. 13.

Davies, M. (1992), 'Sales Promotion as a Competitive Strategy', *Management Decision*, 30 (7), pp. 5–10.

Derrick, S. (2002), 'Making Money from Movies' (accessed via http://www.pandionline.com).

Dirskovski, R. (2001), 'EU Cannot Hope to Halt Spam via the Statute Book', *Marketing Week*, 6 December, p. 14.

The Economist (2001), 'Hands in Their Pockets – Private Money for the Arts', *The Economist*, 18 August, pp. 67–9.

Fill, C. (2002), *Marketing Communications: Contexts, Strategies and Applications* (3rd edn), Financial Times Prentice Hall.

Fletcher, K. (1999), 'Getting the Most out of Mailshots', *Marketing*, 13 May, pp. 38–9.

Fry, A. (2001), 'How to Profit from Sponsoring Sport', *Marketing*, 16 August, pp. 25-6.

Goodman, M. (2002), 'Supermarket Cards Fail to Keep Shoppers Loyal', *Sunday Times*, 3 February, p. 3.

Gray, R. (1999), 'Targeting Results', *Marketing*, 13 May, p. 37.

Grimes, E. and Meenaghan, T. (1998), 'Focusing Commercial Sponsorship on the Internal Corporate Audience', *International Journal of Advertising*, 17 (1), pp. 51–74.

The Grocer (2002a), 'Bendicks Offers Savings to Retailers', *The Grocer*, 19 January, p. 65.

The Grocer (2002b), 'Robinsons Aims to Clock Up Monster Sales with Disney', *The Grocer*, 26 January, p. 64.

The Grocer (2002c), 'Twinings Aims to Stimulate Sales with Caddy Offer', *The Grocer*, 26 January, p. 64.

The Grocer (2002d), 'Tesco Link with Suppliers for Personalised Online Appeal', *The Grocer*, 16 February, p. 4.

Gupta, S. and Cooper, L. (1992), 'The Discounting of Discount and Promotion Brands', *Journal of Consumer Research*, 19 (December), pp. 401–11.

Hemsley, S. (2002), 'Loyalty in the Aisles', *Promotions and Incentives* supplement to *Marketing Week*, 21 February, pp. 9–10.

Jones, P. (1990), 'The Double Jeopardy of Sales Promotions', *Harvard Business Review*, September/October, pp. 141–52.

Kleinman, M. (2000), 'Sight Savers Builds with DRTV', *Marketing*, 7 December, p. 16.

Kleinman, M. (2002), 'Venables to Front Nestlé World Cup Work', *Marketing*, 4 April, p. 2.

Lewis, M. (1999), 'Counting On It', *Database Marketing*, May, pp. 34–7.

McAlevey, T. (2001), 'The Principles of Effective Direct Response', *Direct Marketing*, April, pp. 44–7.

McLuhan, R. (2000), 'Promoting Sales in Departure Lounges', *Marketing*, 7 December, pp. 39–40.

McLuhan, R. (2001), 'How DM Can Build Consumer Loyalty', *Marketing*, 3 May, pp. 45–6.

Marketing (2001), 'Public Relations Agency of the Year: Cohn & Wolfe', *Marketing*, 13 December, pp. 17–18.

Marketing Week (1999), 'Brand Sponsorship', *Marketing Week*, 15 April, p. 57.

Marketing Week (2001), 'IDM Gold Award Winner', *Marketing Week*, 17 May, p. 47.

Marketing Week (2002a), 'Sainsbury's Promotes Own Brand with TMV', *Marketing Week*, 24 January, p. 8.

Marketing Week (2002b), 'Hollis Sponsorship Awards: Charity and Community Sponsorship', *Marketing Week*, 25 April, p. 45.

Marston, J. (1979), *Modern Public Relations*, McGraw-Hill.

Matthew, G. (2001), 'Sponsor Hopes to Score at World Cup', *Financial Times*, 3 December, p. 10.

Meenaghan, T. (1998), 'Current Developments and Future Directions in Sponsorship', *International Journal of Advertising*, 17 (1), pp. 3–28.

Meller, P. (2001), 'DM Industry Welcomes EU Spam Decision', *Marketing Week*, 15 November, p. 8.

Metcalfe, J. (2000), 'The New European Market', *Catalog Age*, February, pp. 51–3.

Middleton, T. (2002), 'A Winning Formula', *Promotions and Incentives* supplement to *Marketing Week*, 21 February, pp. 3–6.

Miller, R. (2001), 'Marketers Pinpoint their Targets', *Marketing*, 18 January, pp. 40–1.

Mitchell, A. (2002), 'Consumer Power is on the Cards in Tesco's Plan', *Marketing Week*, 2 May, pp. 30–1.

Murphy, C. (1999), 'Brand Values Can Build on Charity Ties', *Marketing*, 25 March, p. 41.

Nicholas, G. (2001), 'Swedes Miss the Points as Free Flights are Grounded', *Financial Times*, 20 March, p. 18.

Nuttall, N. (1998), 'Big Business Shuns Call of Wild in Animal Rescue Flop', *The Times*, 6 January, p. 5.

O'Sullivan, T. (2001), 'A Leap in the Dark for Sponsors Facing Drugs Tests', *Marketing Week*, 30 August, p. 25.

Otley, T. (2002), 'Flooded Out by Junk e-mails', *The Times*, 1 March, p. 2.5.

Pemble, A. (2002), 'Nestlé Targets Football Fans with Cash Quiz' (accessed via http://www.pandionline.com).

Promotions and Incentives (2002), 'Hellmann's Runs Free Cook Book Recipe Incentive' (accessed via http://www.pandionline.com).

Rines, S. (1999), 'Point of Contact', *Marketing Week*, 25 February, pp. 63–4.

Schofield, A. (1994), 'Alternative Reply Vehicles in Direct Response Advertising', *Journal of Advertising Research*, 34 (5), pp. 28–34.

Sliwa, C. (2001), 'Clothing Retailer Finds Worldwide Business on the Web', *Computerworld*, 30 April, p. 40.

Smith, C. (2001), 'Is Barclaycard on the Way to Glory in the Premiership?', *Marketing*, 16 August, p. 17.

Smith, P. (2001), *Keynote Report: Home Shopping*, May.

Smithers, R. (2002), 'Special Pleading', *The Guardian*, 22 January.

Stanley, R. (1982), *Promotion: Advertising, Publicity, Personal Selling, Sales Promotion*, Prentice Hall.

Stone, N. (1991), *How to Manage Public Relations*, McGraw-Hill.

Swengley, N. (2001), 'Shop Loyalty Cards Buy Cupboard Love', *Evening Standard*, 22 May, p. 5.

Tesco (2002a), 'Air Travel Set to Soar as Tesco Team Up with Air Miles', press release dated 15 March (accessed via http://www.tesco.com).

Tesco (2002b), 'H Samuel Joins Clubcard Scheme', press release dated 29 April (accessed via http://www.tesco.com).

Thurtle, G. (2001), 'M&S Card Will Need a Strong Hand', *Marketing Week*, 13 December, pp. 19–20.

Tomlinson, H. (2001), 'Yes, I Do Have a Card, But is There a Loo?', *The Independent*, 25 March, p. 5.

White, D. (2001), 'Big-name Signings for All Seasons', *The Daily Telegraph*, 4 October, p. 65.

Williams, C. (2001), 'A Revolution in the Way We Shop', *Western Mail*, 14 September, p. 18.

Wilmshurst, J. (1993), *Below the Line Promotion*, Butterworth-Heinemann.

Wilson, R. (2001), 'Tried and Tested', *Promotions and Incentives* supplement to *Marketing Week*, 6 September, pp. 15–18.

chapter 12

marketing management, planning and control

LEARNING OBJECTIVES

This chapter will help you to:

1 define marketing planning and the internal and external influences affecting it;

2 understand the different types of plan found within organisations and the importance of formal planning processes;

3 define the stages in the marketing planning process and their contribution to sound, integrated plans;

4 outline alternative ways of structuring a marketing department and their advantages and disadvantages; and

5 understand the need for evaluation and control of marketing plans and their implementation, and the ways in which this can be achieved.

Introduction

So far, this book has looked at the practical aspects of marketing, from identifying consumer needs and wants through to designing and delivering a product package that aims to meet those needs and wants, and maintains customer loyalty despite the efforts of the competition. The tools that make up the marketing mix are, of course, critical for implementing the marketing concept, but so far, the focus has largely been operational and oriented to the short term. Managers must, however, think of their operational marketing mixes in the context of wider, more strategic questions, such as:

- Which markets should we be in?
- What does our organisation have that will give it a competitive edge? (This need not necessarily come directly from marketing.)
- Do we have the resources, skills and assets within the organisation to enable planned objectives to be achieved?
- Where do we want to be in five or even 25 years' time?
- What will our competitors be doing in three or five years' time?
- Can we assume that our current modus operandi will be good enough for the future?

These concerns are strategic, not operational, in that they affect the whole organisation and provide a framework for subsequent operational decisions. The focus is on the future, aligning the whole organisation to new opportunities and challenges within the changing marketing environment, as discussed in Chapter 2. The questions suggested above seem deceptively simple, but finding answers to them is, in fact, a highly skilled and demanding task and the whole focus of the marketing planning process. The future welfare of the whole organisation depends on finding the 'right' answers.

eg Marketing planning is important to car rental companies if they are to remain competitive in a market dominated by global organisations such as Hertz, Budget and Avis. A company like Holiday Autos (http://www.holidayautos.co.uk) has created and defended a niche, as the name suggests, targeting holidaymakers. It does not actually rent the cars out, leaving that to the experts, but it acts as an intermediary, agreeing bulk prices with the rental companies and then aggressively marketing and passing on some of the discounts. It has, therefore, access to 750,000 cars, ranging from budget cars to luxury and off-road vehicles, in 4,000 locations.

The marketing plan and strategy are carefully developed. They seek to play to their strengths, i.e. no insurance excess charged; the wide choice of vehicles offered; the number of locations; straightforward booking through its call centre and online; discounted prices; and even a travel information section on the web covering route planners, health advice and other useful information (Wall, 2001). Because of its intermediary role, innovation has revolved around the service package featuring no-nonsense benefits such as no insurance excess, fully inclusive prices and late deal offers. Before the launch of Holiday Autos, it was always wise to check for the hidden and not-so-hidden extras, and with some car rental companies that is still the case.

It is a fast-moving business and an MIS is employed to give daily feedback on prices and sales so that rapid adjustments can be made in any of the 40 countries in which it operates. Close monitoring takes place during any promotional campaigns or where special discounts are being offered direct or through tour companies. It also watches what the demand generators, such as low-cost airlines and holiday companies, are doing. Holiday Autos realised, for instance, that as the low-cost airlines started to increase promotion and gain sales after September 11th 2001, it would be an opportunity for Holiday Autos itself to increase its promotional spend similarly when others were cutting back (Hoare, 2002).

To achieve a nimble response in the market, a management structure that enables quick and effective decisions is needed. To remain just ahead of the market curve requires managers to be empowered but well coordinated within the framework of an agreed strategy and plan. The company may have longer-term aims and objectives, but the priority is making the most of the opportunities presenting themselves in the present.

This chapter first introduces strategic marketing planning issues by defining some of the commonly used terms and showing how they fit together. It examines some of the issues associated with designing a planning system for marketing and how it fits into the organisational planning process. Then, the various stages of the marketing planning process are discussed in detail. Although the implementation of the planning process may vary from situation to situation, the outline given here at least demonstrates the interrelated nature of many planning decisions.

The chapter then moves on to examine other managerial issues associated with managing marketing. Making sure that the organisational structure of the marketing function is appropriate, for example, is essential to the achievement of the tasks specified in the plans. Issues of marketing control and analysis are also considered because without adequate and timely control systems, even the best-laid plans may be blown off course without managers realising the seriousness of the situation until it is too late to do anything about it.

The role and importance of marketing planning and strategy

Planning can be defined as a systematic process of forecasting the future business environment, and then deciding on the most appropriate goals, objectives and positions for best exploiting that environment. All organisations need to plan, otherwise both strategic and operational activities would at best be uncoordinated, badly focused and poorly executed. At worst, the organisation would muddle through from crisis to crisis with little sense of purpose, until eventually competition would gain such an advantage and demand reach such a low level that continuation would just not be viable.

The marketing plan provides a clear and unambiguous statement concerning what strategies and actions will be implemented, by whom, when and with what outcomes. Marketing strategy cannot, however, be formulated in isolation. It has to reflect the objectives of the organisation and be compatible with the strategies pursued elsewhere in the organisation. This means that marketers must refer back to corporate goals and objectives before formulating their own strategy and plans, to ensure consistency, coherence and relevance. The two-way process between marketing and corporate strategy is shown in Figure 12.1.

To help to clarify the two-way interaction, we shall first provide an overview and definitions of some of the different, and often overlapping, internal strategic perspectives, both corporate and marketing specific, that marketers have to consider in their strategic thinking. We then examine some of the broader factors that affect the formulation of marketing strategy in practice.

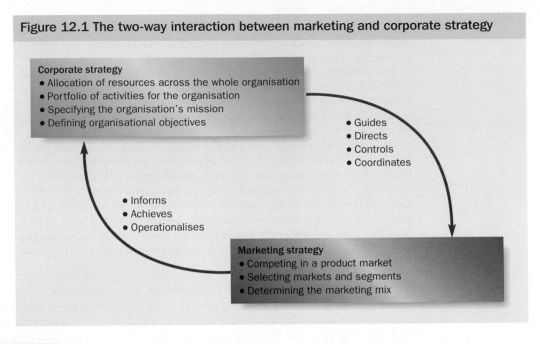

Figure 12.1 The two-way interaction between marketing and corporate strategy

■ Definitions

This subsection outlines some of the strategic perspectives of the organisation, starting with the broad picture required by corporate strategy, then gradually focusing down towards the very specific detail of marketing programmes.

Corporate strategy

Corporate strategy concerns the allocation of resources within the organisation to achieve the business direction and scope specified within corporate objectives. Although the marketing department is primarily responsible for responding to perceived marketing opportunities and favourable competitive environments, it cannot act without the involvement of all other areas of the organisation too. Corporate strategy, therefore, helps to control and coordinate the different areas of the organisation, finance, marketing, production, R&D, etc., to ensure that they are all working towards the same objectives, and that those objectives are consistent with the desired direction of the business as a whole. Typical issues of concern to corporate planners might thus be market expansion, product development priorities, acquisition, divestment, diversification and maintaining a competitive edge.

marketing **in action**

A sound strategy

Linn Products is a Scottish manufacturer of high quality hi-fi equipment that targets the high-performance, top end of the worldwide market. It made its mark with its first product in 1972, the Linn Sondek LP12, a transcription turntable that became the benchmark against which all the others are judged. The company applied the same standards and positioning to Linn speakers and the first solid state pitch accurate amplifiers. Linn now

has over 50 products including CD players, tuners, amplifiers and speakers that it sells in 30 countries. In just under 30 years, Linn has become a world leader in sound technology, innovative design and precision engineering. It operates a policy of continuous improvement to ensure that it stays at the cutting edge of its niche.

More recently, Linn diversified into the home theatre market, a growing

sector at the top end of the hi-fi market. In 1994 the Knekt system was launched, an advanced multi-room sound distribution and control system. It is powerful stuff. A 16-source system, for example, could distribute to 128 rooms. This was followed in 1995 by entry into the digital multi-channel sound market with the Linn AV51, a new home cinema and multimedia high-fidelity sound system. This means that buyers can have a designed-in system in a number of rooms and, because it is multi-channel, they can both watch a movie and listen to audio in the same room from the same entertainment system. People are now taking for granted that they can access all their entertainment needs throughout the home and the Knekt system allows this kind of multi-use. It attracts attention at the top end of the market. When Harrods' furniture department decided to design a new display area, it featured Linn custom-installed home entertainment products. Linn was also selected to design a new audio system for the Aston Martin V12 Vanquish, one of the most technologically advanced Aston Martins ever built. Linn products were considered ideal for its discriminating and demanding customers and the products enhanced the exclusive image of the car.

Linn's mission is 'to thrill customers who want the most out of life from music, information and entertainment systems that benefit from quality sound by working together to supply them what they want when they want it'. Each product has the signature of the product builder. One product builder is responsible for the assembly, testing and packaging of an item. An old-fashioned attention to detail does not mean old-fashioned inefficient production processes, however. Linn claims to have one of the smallest plants in the world with automated materials handling right up to the assembly point. Within that, 'real-time' manufacturing is practised, meaning that each day's production is

made to order for specific customers. The product designers too are close to the customer and are committed to continuous improvement.

Linn's customer care philosophy extends from the manufacturing process through to the distribution channel. The company is selective about appointing dealers because it sees the key to selling its products as the expertise and product demonstration offered by the retailer. Linn is looking for those retailers that are the best in their area and have a quality reputation that fits with Linn's own. It wants retailers that want to sell quality products and are prepared to spend time with customers demonstrating and installing them. Retailers should be able to:

- work with customers to discover what kind of musical expectations and sound needs they have
- appreciate the cost–value relationship inherent in Linn systems, if necessary comparing them with the competition
- show customers how best to use and accommodate equipment
- help customers consider system expandability.

Linn is very reluctant to supply retailers that are not trained or are unable or unwilling to stock the range for demonstration purposes.

Overall, Linn is an excellent example of how the vision and values of the leader of a business are translated into marketing strategy. Although one might expect the customer to be at the heart of a business from which a compact disc player could set you back £12,000 and to which a rock star paid

£200,000 for a sound system for each room of his house, Mr Tiefenbrun, the owner, is controversially quoted as saying, 'the customer comes third, the supplier comes first and the employee second. It was only by working with suppliers that the company got the components that worked in the way that customers wanted. Satisfied customers follow on from satisfied suppliers and employees' (as quoted by Murden, 2001).

Sources: Murden (2001), http://www.linn.co.uk

Linn speakers are quality products sold to customers by knowledgeable retailers with time to discuss individual needs.

Source: Linn Products Ltd.

To help to make the corporate planning process more manageable, larger organisations often divide their activities into strategic business units (SBUs). An SBU is a part of the organisation that has become sufficiently significant to allow it to develop its own strategies and plans, although still within the context of the overall corporate picture. SBUs can be based on products, markets or operating divisions that are profit centres in their own right.

Competitive strategy

Competitive strategy determines how an organisation chooses to compete within a market, with particular regard to the relative positioning of competitors. Unless an organisation can create and maintain a competitive advantage, it is unlikely to achieve a strong market position. In any market, there tend to be those who dominate or lead, followed by a number of progressively smaller players, some of whom might be close enough to mount a serious challenge. Others, however, are content to follow or niche themselves (i.e. dominate a small, specialist corner of the market).

eg   Andrew Barber and Robin Hall, both graduates in their 30s, both believed that the best rewards are gained from working for oneself and that they could design a better sports car than most, and so they decided to cut loose to design, produce and sell their own car. They spent many weekends and evenings building prototypes, but lacked the capital to take them into production. After seeking external advice, they decided to create a niche product and came up with a £26,000 V6 sports car concept, 'Census'. In 2000, this enabled them to attract £240,000 from two business angels, despite having no orders, to set up a factory in Brackley under the name FBS Engineering. The individual design and high performance made a big impact in motor shows and motoring trials and the Census was described by *Top Gear's* Tiff Needell as 'a real driver's car'.

The Census was positioned at a relatively moderate price against the BMW Z3, Alfa Spider V6 and Honda S2000 as a roadster that could achieve 0–60 mph in 5.8 seconds. To make acceptable profit levels, it was thought that around 50 cars per year would have to be made, but by 2002 output was just one per month. The first sales boosted confidence, even though it had taken eight years from the initial idea to the first revenues being generated. Because of the company's size, the aim was to sell direct, either online or through motor shows and events. One of the advantages of being a niche player in the motor industry is that journalists tend to be interested in writing about something different, and in the case of the Census a steady flow of praise was received from the specialist press. This also avoided the need to spend heavily on advertising and to create a dealer network, although the owners recognised that dealers might become necessary as sales build up.

By mid-2002, breakeven had not been reached. There was, however, a waiting list for at least three cars and the first delivery took place in mid-2002. It seems, though, that the company was not able to convert interest into sales at a rate that compensated for the steady outflows of cash. Despite the completion and sale of five customer cars between April 2000 and March 2003, an administrative receiver was appointed in August 2003. This is not the end of Census, however. The physical and intellectual assets associated with the car have been bought by another company which is undertaking a stratgic review with a view to relaunching the Census. (Derrick, 2001; O'Donnell, 2001; *Warwickshire Choice*, 2001; http://www.fbs-eng.co.uk).

The Census: 'A real driver's car'.

Source: FBS Cars/Matt 1 600.

Marketing strategy

The marketing strategy defines target markets, what direction needs to be taken and what needs to be done in broad terms to create a defensible competitive position compatible with overall corporate and competitive strategy within those markets. Marketing mix programmes can then be designed to best match organisational capabilities with target market opportunities.

Marketing plan

It is in the marketing plan that the operational detail, turning strategies into implementable actions, is developed. The marketing plan is a detailed, written statement specifying target markets, marketing programmes, responsibilities, timescales and resources to be used, within defined budgets. An overall corporate marketing plan in a large organisation might well bring together and integrate a number of plans specific to individual SBUs. Planning at SBU level and then consolidating all the plans ensure that the corporate picture has enough detail, and allow overall implementation and control to be managed.

Marketing programmes

Marketing programmes are actions, often of a tactical nature, involving the use of the marketing mix variables to gain an advantage within the target market. These programmes are normally detailed in the annual marketing plan, and are the means of implementing the chosen marketing strategy. Linn hi-fi systems, mentioned earlier in this chapter, found that an advertising campaign of £250,000 using quality journals, a direct mail programme, an annual brochure and a biannual magazine was appropriate for stimulating trial and maintaining customer relationships. Programmes provide clear guidelines, schedules and budgets for the range of actions proposed for achieving the overall objectives. These are determined within the framework of the overall marketing plan to ensure that activities are properly integrated and that appropriate resources are allocated to them.

■ Influences on planning and strategy

There are various influences on an organisation's marketing strategy, each of which is now discussed in turn.

Organisational objectives and resources

Marketing strategists need to be guided by what the organisation as a whole is striving for – what its objectives are and what resources it has to implement them. Some organisations might have very ambitious growth plans, while others might be content with fairly steady growth or even no growth at all, that is, consolidation. Clearly, each of these alternatives implies different approaches to marketing.

Resources are not only financial. They also include skills and expertise, in other words any area of the organisation that can help to add value and give a competitive edge. The exploitation, through marketing, of things that the organisation does well, such as manufacturing, technical innovation, product development or customer service, might help to create non-financial assets such as reputation and image, which are difficult for competitors to copy.

eg Swiss Company Holcim, formerly Holderbank, is one of the world's largest suppliers of cement, aggregates and concrete with sales of CHF13.6 bn in 2001. For any company of this nature to survive, there have to be economies of scale in production, consistent supplies of raw material and low transport costs. Holcim has established three fundamental strategic principles to guide its competitive position: cost leadership in its many overseas markets, market leadership to achieve volume sales, and strong vision and firm control over central strategy yet still allowing local autonomy.

To achieve cost leadership, Holcim invests heavily in technology to reduce unit costs and often locates plants either near to raw materials or near to customers. Through a process of acquisition and new plant openings, it now has interests in cement plants in 70 countries, giving the company over 630 ready-mix concrete plants, many of which operate under different names. Wherever Holcim decides to expand, largely driven by construction opportunities because of demographic development or infrastructure renewal, the formula is the same: large volumes, efficient operations and local service. The strategic risk is spread by its involvement in many different markets, each at different stages of growth, decline and maturity, and this allows it to concentrate on its core business, to the point of divesting more marginal activities. Although Europe is still its strongest market, Latin America is a high priority. Most of its investment is now in emerging markets, but it is facing increasing international competition from France's Lafarge and Mexico's Cemex and the change of name to Holcim was part of a strategy to start building a global brand. That may also help with pricing. In Thailand more than 40 per cent of cement is bought over the Internet, and brand names are considered important in achieving premium prices. In any case, in Asia generally the 'better' the brand name the higher the prices (*Financial Times*, 2001).

Attitude to change and risk

The corporate view on change and risk often depends on the approach of top management. Risk tolerance varies widely from individual to individual, and from management team to management team. Managers will also, of course, be guided by the nature of the organisation and their interpretation of its business environment. The managing director of a small business may not want to take on high-risk projects, feeling that the firm's size makes it more vulnerable to failure through its lack of resources. A larger firm might be able to absorb any losses, and therefore feel that the risk is worth taking.

eg In the pharmaceutical and biotech sectors particularly, some small businesses take a very positive approach to risk. The biotech sector is experiencing rapid growth through a steady stream of technological breakthroughs, many coming from smaller companies. Being a smaller organisation can help to create a culture that encourages flexibility and inventiveness, as long as there is sufficient capital to see it through the leaner start-up period. Venture capitalists do absorb some of that risk on the promise of future returns. Specialist bioinformatics companies such as Lion Biosciences of Germany, GeneData of Switzerland and NetGenics of the USA, for example, have all been supported that way (Cookson, 2001). Due in part to its well-developed science park network, the UK has 5 of the top 10 European biotech companies and has twice as many products in clinical or pre-clinical trials as the rest of Europe put together (Swann, 2002). Often, just one new product breakthrough can generate multi-million pound revenues, transforming the prospects of a small company. The challenge is then to move on to spread the risk by becoming a multi-product organisation. Amgen has managed that transition with three medicines on the market; its first has been out for 12 years and the second for 10, yet it still maintains a 20 per cent annual growth rate (Taylor, 2001).

The giant pharmaceutical companies, by contrast, invest far more heavily, perhaps two or three times the level of smaller biotech companies, as they need to record global product sales in the billions rather than millions to sustain growth. This can sometimes increase the development period and stifle some inventions that do not meet that criterion. Often, the large pharmaceutical companies could learn from the enterprise and drive of the smaller biotech companies, while the smaller companies could learn from the expertise of the big manufacturers in achieving success in getting ideas to the marketplace. These differences have led some to suggest that the pharmaceutical and biotech sectors are working closer together, with one, biotech, almost becoming the breeding ground for new ideas which are then capitalised upon by the pharmaceutical companies through alliances and takeovers (Dyer, 2001).

Market structure and opportunities

Markets vary considerably in their structure and dynamics. Some are fairly stable and not a great deal happens in them unless one of the major players decides to become aggressive and seeks to improve its competitive position. Some markets are simply too complacent. A good example would be the Dutch agriculture sector, which has been criticised for failing to keep up with market changes and increased levels of European competitiveness. Although competitiveness has been maintained in cut flowers and seeds, ground has been lost in the dairy, vegetable and pork sectors. The real problem has arisen from changes in the marketing environment, as consumers have sought a wider variety of products and higher product specifications, and European supermarket buyers have sought greater efficiency.

eg Ribena, the blackcurrant drink, dates back to the 1930s and has become a well-established brand. In recent years, however, it has experienced the need for change to keep up with increased turbulence in the marketplace. For nearly a decade, the soft drinks market has grown significantly, fuelled by new flavours, ingredients, formats, packaging, and usage occasions backed by increased marketing budgets (Hardcastle, 2002). Ribena is number four of all soft drinks in the UK, but the sector is still being squeezed by new areas such as energy and sports drinks. Ribena is up against Proctor & Gamble's Sunny Delight and Britvic's Robinsons brands all of which have equally powerful marketing support. In recent years, after a period of growth in the late 1990s, Ribena's sales have started to slip and in an effort to retain its position, Ribena's owner GlaxoSmithKline has had to revitalise its marketing effort. It introduced a number of new variants such as 'Ribena Light', but not all have been successful.

To reverse the trend, the relaunch will cost £27m. and will include new packaging, a focus on taste, and a doubling of advertising spend to £10m., as well as sponsorship of the FA Premier League (Arnold, 2002). The brand is, at its core, a good one, but although it is a difficult product to challenge head-on, the markets it sells into are highly competitive and not so secure. The target market is mothers with children, including the competitive children's lunchbox sector, but Ribena has resisted calls to reposition itself towards an older audience capitalising on brand loyalty that goes back to adults' own dim and distant lunchbox days! Nevertheless, Ribena is now having to find ways of dealing with far more market turbulence than ever before.

Competitor strategies

The competitive structure in different product markets will vary to create conditions of strong or weak competition. In markets such as computer chips, the dominant competitor has a major influence over the level and nature of competition. Challenges can still arise, but nevertheless, within constraints set by governmental competition policy and public pressure, a dominant competitor is effectively able to decide when and how to compete. The dominant competitor is likely to be confident that it has sufficient strength through its market position, volume sales, and thus perhaps through its cost base to fight any serious challenger successfully.

■ Types of plan

It is important to distinguish between *plans*, the outcomes of the planning process, and *planning*, the process from which plans are derived. While the process of planning is fairly standard and can be transferred across functions and organisations, there are often wide variations in the actual use of plans to guide strategy and operations. This is partly because there are several different types of plan that can emerge from a planning process. Plans may be differentiated in terms of a number of features. These are as follows.

Organisational level

Managers are involved with planning at all levels of an organisation. The concerns of managers, however, change at higher levels of the organisation, and the complexities affecting planning also change. The more senior the manager, the more long term and strategic becomes the focus. At the highest level, the concern is for the whole organisation and how to allocate resources across its various functions or units. At lower levels, the focus is on implementation within a shorter-term horizon, and on operating within clearly specified parameters. The marketing director may thus have a particular concern with developing and positioning innovative products and opening new segments, while the sales representative may have to focus on sales territory planning to achieve predetermined sales and call objectives.

Timescale

Plans may be short, medium or long term in focus. *Short term* normally means the shortest period of time appropriate to the operations of the organisation. Normally this is one year, or in some industries, such as fashion, one season. *Medium-term* plans are more likely to cover a one to three year period. The focus is not so much on day-to-day operations and detailed tactical achievement as on renewal. This could include the opening up of a new market, a product innovation, or a strategic alliance to improve market position, for example. *Long-term* plans can be anything from 3 to 20 years, with the timescale often dictated by capital investment periods. Long-term plans are nearly always strategic in focus and concerned with resource allocation and return.

Regularity

Most longer-term plans have annual reviews to monitor progress. Shorter-term plans are often part of a hierarchy linking strategy with operations. Some plans, however, are not produced regularly as part of an annual cycle, but are campaign, project or situation specific. A *campaign plan*, for example for a specific advertising campaign, might have a limited duration to achieve defined objectives. *Project plans* are specific to particular activities, perhaps a new product launch, a change in distribution channels, or a packaging innovation. These activities are of fixed duration and are not necessarily repeated.

Focus

Plans will vary in their focus across the organisation. *Corporate plans* refer to the longer-term plans of the organisation, specifying the type of business scope desired and the strategies for achieving it across all areas of the business. The focus is on the technology, products, markets and resources that define the framework within which the individual parts of the organisation can develop more detailed strategies and plans. *Functional or operational plans* are, therefore, developed within the context of the organisational corporate plan but focus on the implementation of day-to-day or annual activities within the various parts of the organisation.

Contingency plans are efforts to cater for the 'what if?' questions that emerge in more turbulent environments. Planned responses to any possible scenarios that might occur are prepared. A major new competitor entering the market, a supply shortage or a radical product innovation from a competitor could all affect the best-laid plans. By thinking through the implications and alternatives before the crisis arises, a number of options can be identified to support management if the scenario really materialises.

Organisational focus

Plans will vary according to the nature of the organisation itself. A number of alternative ways of organising marketing are considered later (see pp. 420 *et seq.*). If the organisational focus is on products, then plans will also take that focus, while if markets or functional areas are emphasised, plans will reflect that structure. For example, a functional organisational marketing plan will have distinct elements of pricing, advertising, distribution, etc. If SBUs are formed, then there is immediately a requirement for a two-tier planning structure: (a) considering the portfolio of SBUs at a corporate level, and (b) for each SBU, looking at the more detailed organisational design. Similarly divisional, regional, branch or company plans may all be used in different circumstances.

There are several benefits to be gained from taking a more organised approach to planning marketing activity. In summary, the benefits can be classified as relating to the development, coordination or control of marketing activity, as shown in Figure 12.2.

Despite the obvious benefits, we cannot assume that all organisations practise planning, and even those that do might not achieve all the results they expect. Planning in itself does not guarantee success. Much depends on the quality of the planning, its acceptance as a fundamental driving force within the organisation, and the perceived relevance of the resulting plans. There is no room for a weak link in the chain, since the plans are only as good as the process that generated them, and the process is pointless if it does not result in acceptable, implementable plans.

Figure 12.2 Benefits of planning

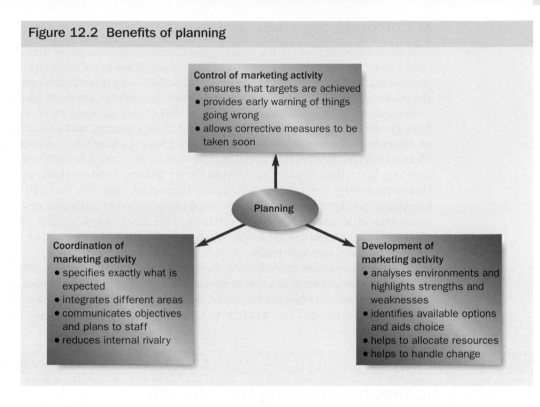

The marketing planning process

The purpose of marketing planning has been defined as:

> *to find a systematic way of identifying a range of options, to choose one or more of them, then to schedule and cost out what has to be done to achieve the objectives.*   (McDonald, 1989, p. 13)

Although the structure of a marketing plan will vary according to the complexity and variability of the organisation, and the emphasis may vary according to the turbulence in the environment and the resultant challenges facing the organisation, a number of broad phases in the planning process are likely to operate in any case. The main stages in the planning process are shown in Figure 12.3 and each stage is considered in turn.

Figure 12.3 Stages in the planning process

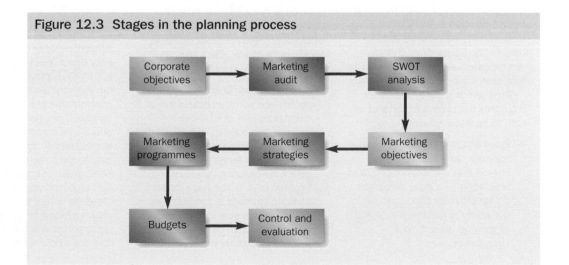

■ Corporate objectives and values

Corporate objectives are at the heart of the planning process, since they describe the direction, priorities and relative position of the organisation in its market(s). Some objectives, such as market share (by value), sales, profit and ROI are quantitative, while others, such as the philosophies reflected in mission and values statements, are more qualitative in nature.

Philosophical targets, often called vision and values statements, or mission statements, have grown in popularity in recent years as a more enduring and all-embracing perspective of where an organisation seeks to journey and how it intends to conduct itself on the way. McDonald's has the vision of providing the world's best quick service restaurant experience and to achieve that, it seeks to provide a level quality, good service, cleanliness and value that makes every customer in a restaurant smile. In contrast, Vivendi, the entertainment company, has the vision of being the world's preferred creator and provider of entertainment, education and personalised service to consumers anywhere, at any time and across all distribution platforms. Qualitative targets also include things such as service levels, CSR performance and innovativeness.

Whether quantitative or qualitative, these objectives help to create guidelines for marketing plans, since the output of the corporate planning process acts as an input into the marketing planning process. All objectives must be realistic, achievable within a specific timescale, and cited in order of priority. This will lead to a hierarchy of interlinking objectives.

corporate social responsibility *in action*

Cadbury Schweppes: walking the CSR talk

Cadbury has developed from a small family business established on Quaker values into an international company that still upholds the importance of taking a socially responsible approach to all facets of its work, despite being a commercial enterprise. Quakers have strong beliefs that are carried through into campaigns for justice, equality and social reform, reflected in Cadbury's original ideal of helping to end poverty and deprivation in Victorian Britain. The foundations for a corporately socially responsible organisation were, therefore, laid over 100 years ago and have endured and been embodied in the social responsibility programme of today, despite the tremendous change, diversification and internationalisation that have happened in the company.

The overriding policy statement highlights the central importance of CSR to business strategy:

Good ethics and good business go together naturally. We firmly believe that our responsibility and reputation as a good corporate citizen plays an important role in our ability to achieve our objective of growing value for our shareowners.

Keeping a watch over all aspects of the company's activities is a Corporate and Social Responsibility Committee at board level and chaired by a high-profile non-executive director, Baroness Wilcox, a former head of the National Consumer Council.

The CSR policy at Cadbury Schweppes breaks down into five areas: corporate governance; human rights; community and social investment; environment; and employment practices. Not all these areas are examined in detail in this book, but each, individually and collectively, has helped to build a strong reputation, confidence and a record of achievement that could be considered a model. Each area is considered briefly in turn:

■ *Corporate governance*: A corporate governance policy embraces the broad principles of business dealings and conduct with all Cadbury's publics in terms of ethics, openness and honesty. These reflect the enduring values inherited from the past. It also has a code of conduct approved by the board to which all employees are expected to adhere. This code embraces more practical issues, for example legal

and compliance issues, handling of conflicts of interests, gifts, dealing with competition, whistleblowing, confidentiality and political contributions. Each employee is provided with their own copy of the code and compliance to the code is enforced through the management process. To Cadbury, good ethics and good business go together.

■ *Human rights*: Cadbury is particularly sensitive to the dangers of operating in cultures where different norms and practices may apply. The reports of slave child labour in the cocoa industry in West Africa were of particular concern (see p. 43). Although the allegations were made about the Ivory Coast where Cadbury does not buy, it is playing a full part in the industry, along with governments and NGOs, to ensure that such practices are stamped out. It fully contributes to surveys of child labour practices, independent monitoring and the certification of cocoa to ensure that all conditions have been met. Closer to home, the company has also published its own human rights and ethical trading policy covering labour rights, dignity at work, health and safety, fair remuneration, diversity, a respect for differences and the need for personal development. Progress measurement in each of these areas is assessed by a working group reporting to the CSR Committee. This will increasingly also apply to the supply chains feeding into the company. A programme of education and implementation is now under way in all its businesses around the world.

■ *Community and social investment*: Cadbury also recognises the role and responsibilities it has in the communities in which it operates. The policy is not about handouts and high-profile gift giving but takes a longer-term integrated approach as part of a 'managing for Community value' programme. This means carefully selecting the initiatives to encourage and taking on a longer-term approach to achieving agreed objectives. It has a Foundation that makes grants to projects and partner organisations, especially in the fields of education and employment, focusing on social exclusion and deprivation in places such as Birmingham, Sheffield, Bristol and London.

■ *Environment*: Sustainability is central to the policies in this area. The 'Environmental Report' outlines the programmes the company has undertaken in developing long-term sustainability, protecting the environment and assessing the environmental impact of its prime activities. The policy itself is still evolving to include transportation, supply chain management and raw material sourcing. The report also considers a number of areas such as waste management, water conservation and energy use to demonstrate the company's efforts to improve the environment. The beverages plant in Carcagente in Spain, for example, recycles all of its organic waste. Packaging is more problematic, but the PET, glass bottles and aluminium cans can all be reprocessed in-house or with specialist recyclers. Even broken pallets are repaired and reused. Between 1997 and 1999, the percentage of waste that was recycled improved from 75 to 82 per cent.

■ *Employment practices*: This area of CSR covers a variety of human resource issues such as personal development, the working environment and equal

opportunities, all of which are beyond the scope of this text.

By adopting such a comprehensive approach to CSR, the values embodied within Cadbury and the business principles espoused are put into practice. Care has to be taken, however. One attempt to undertake cause-related marketing in Kenya led to a blurring of objectives. When sponsoring the Mediae Trust which produces radio programmes for rural communities focusing on social and environmental themes such as animal husbandry and child abuse, the distinction between education and advertising became confused. Cadbury paid for the air time for Mediae broadcasts in return for some advertising space, so although it helped product sales, it also contributed to broader rural social development policies. However, one audience member is quoted as saying, 'I like the show because it educates us, like what to do if your child is mistreated, it also teaches us how useful Cadbury's is; that it builds healthy bodies' (as quoted by Turner, 2002). Overall, though, Cadbury has 'walked the talk' and presents a good example to other companies.

Sources: Turner (2002), http://www.cadburyschweppes.com

■ The marketing audit

A marketing audit systematically takes stock of an organisation's marketing health, as the formal definition implies:

> *[The audit] is the means by which a company can understand how it relates to the environment in which it operates. It is the means by which a company can identify its own strengths and weaknesses as they relate to external opportunities and threats. It is thus a way of helping management to select a position in that environment based on known factors.* (McDonald, 1989, p. 21)

It is really the launching pad for the marketing plan, as it encourages management to reflect systematically on the environment and the organisation's ability to respond, given its actual and planned capabilities. The marketing audit is first and foremost about developing a shared, agreed and objective understanding of the organisation. Table 12.1 summarises the issues that a marketing audit should consider.

The audit should be undertaken as part of the planning cycle, usually on an annual basis, rather than as a desperate response to a problem. To help the audit process, it is critical to have a sound marketing information system covering the marketing environment, customers, competitors, etc., as well as detail on all areas of the internal organisational marketing effort. In order to complete an audit, managers thus have to look at both operational variables (i.e. an internal audit) and environmental variables (i.e. an external audit).

Table 12.1 Marketing audit issues

- Macro environment: STEP factors (see Chapter 2)
- Task environment: *competition, channels, customers* (see Chapters 3–4)
- Markets (see Chapter 12)
- Strategic issues: *segmentation, positioning, competitive advantage* (see Chapters 4 and 12)
- Marketing mix (see Chapters 6–11)
- Marketing organisational structure and organisation (see Chapter 12)

Internal audit

The internal audit focuses on many of the decision areas discussed in Chapters 3–11 and their effectiveness in achieving their specified objectives. It is not just, however, a post mortem on the 4Ps. Auditors will also be interested in how smoothly and synergistically the 4Ps fit together, and whether the marketing actions, organisation and allocated resources are appropriate to the environmental opportunities and constraints.

Portfolio analysis. In assessing the marketing health of the organisation, it is not enough to look simply at the performance of individual products. Although products may be managed as individual entities on an operational basis, strategically they should be viewed as a product portfolio, that is, a set of products, each of which makes a unique contribution to the corporate picture. The strategist needs to look at that corporate picture and decide whether, for example, there are enough strong products to support the weak ones, whether the weak ones have development potential or whether there are appropriate new products in development to take over from declining ones. The various portfolio models outlined below can be applied either to SBUs or to individual products, and thus the use of the word 'product' throughout the discussion should be taken to mean either.

The BCG matrix. Sometimes referred to as the Boston Box, or the BCG matrix, the Boston Consulting Group (BCG) market growth–relative market share model, shown in Figure 12.4, assesses products on two dimensions. The first dimension looks at the general level of growth in the product's market, while the second measures the product's market share relative to the largest competitor in the industry. This type of analysis provides a useful insight into the likely opportunities and problems associated with a particular product.

Market growth reflects opportunities and buoyancy in different markets. It also indicates the likely competitive atmosphere, because in high-growth markets there is plenty of room for expansion and all players can make gains, while in low-growth markets competition will be more intense, since growth can only be achieved by taking share away from the competition.

Figure 12.4 BCG matrix

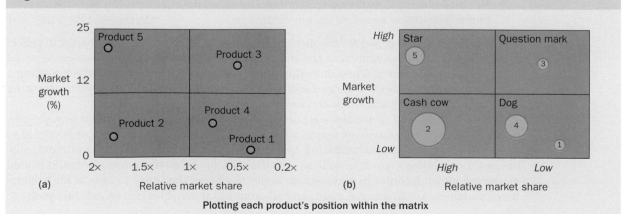

Plotting each product's position within the matrix

Market share position is measured on a logarithmic scale against the product's largest competitor. Thus a relative share figure of 0.2 means that the product only achieves 20 per cent of the market leader's sales volume, a potentially weak competitive position. Similarly, a share figure of 2 would mean that the product has twice the market share of its nearest rival. A share figure of 1 means roughly equal shares, and therefore joint leadership.

Figure 12.4(a) gives an example of the resultant matrix after all the products of an organisation have been thus analysed. The next stage is to plot the products within a four-cell matrix that reflects the differing competitive positions, as shown in Fig. 12.4(b). Each cell offers different types of business opportunities and imposes different resource demands. The general labelling of the cells as 'high' and 'low' gives an instant and sufficient feel for each product's situation, and the circle that represents each SBU's contribution to the organisation's total sales volume provides a further indication of the relative importance of different products. In Figure 12.4(b), for example, Product 2 can be seen to be the biggest contributor to overall sales volume, whereas Product 1 contributes very little. The 'ideal picture' is one where the portfolio is reasonably balanced between existing strength and emerging opportunity. We now look in turn at each cell of the matrix.

Dog (low share, low growth): A dog holds a weak market share in a low-growth market, and is likely to be making a loss, or a low profit at best. It is unlikely that its share can be increased at a reasonable cost, because of the low market growth. A dog can be a drain on management time and resources.

eg

Liptonice, a cold, fizzy, canned lemon tea, and other products like it had proved to be successful in continental Europe and its owners were confident that it could succeed in the UK market too. What they had not taken into account, however, was the nature of the British consumer's love affair with tea and the perception of it among younger consumers. In the British mind, tea should be drunk hot and milky – even drinking it hot and black with lemon is considered a bit risqué. The ritual of making tea 'properly' is also deeply culturally ingrained. Add to that the young person's view that tea is for grannies, and the prospects for canned, cold, fizzy lemon tea start to look less promising. A £6m. product launch and later a £4m. relaunch failed between them to achieve the product's target of £20m. sales per year and the product quietly disappeared from UK stores. The initial failure has not, however, deterred further attempts. In 2002, Lipton Ice Tea was relaunched with a £5m. marketing campaign in the growing cold soft drinks market. Initial trials suggested that the drink was especially popular with students and an extensive outdoor sampling campaign is planned to persuade the British consumer to acquire a European taste. Sixty students have been hired as student brand managers to develop brand credibility and a merchandising campaign for 5,000 retail outlets. Time will tell whether the relaunched drink will become an outright dog or at least enable a breakthrough in encouraging consumers to try a new soft drink product and maybe even adopt it (*The Grocer*, 2002b; *Marketing*, 2002).

The question, therefore, is whether or not to shoot the dog, that is, withdraw the product. Much depends on the strategic role that the dog is fulfilling and its future prospects. It may, for example, be blocking a competitor (a guard dog?), or it may be complementing the company's own activities, for example creating customers at the bottom of the range who will then trade up to one of the organisation's better products (a guide dog, or a sheepdog?).

Question mark (low share, high growth): The high market growth of a question mark is good news, but the low share is worrying. Why is relative market share so low? What is the organisation doing wrong, or what is the competition doing right? It may simply be that the question mark (also sometimes called a problem child or a wild cat) is a relatively new product that is still in the process of establishing its position in the market. If it is not a new product, then it might just need far more investment in plant, equipment and marketing to keep up with the market growth rate. There is also a risk, however, that a question mark with problems might absorb a great deal of cash just to retain its position.

Some of the alternatives for question marks, such as dropping or repositioning, are the same as for the dogs, but there are some more creative options. If the product is felt to have potential, then management might commit significant investment towards building market share, as mentioned above. Alternatively, if the organisation is cash rich, it might seek to take over competitors to strengthen its market position, effectively buying market share.

Star (high share, high growth): A star product is a market leader in a growth market. It needs a great deal of cash to retain its position, to support further growth and to maintain its lead. It does, however, also generate cash, because of its strength, and so it is likely to be self-sufficient. Stars could be the cash cows of the future.

Cash cow (high share, low growth): As market growth starts to tail off, stars can become cash cows. These products no longer need the same level of support as before since there are no new customers to be had, and there is less competitive pressure. Cash cows enjoy a dominant position generated from economies of scale, given their relative market share.

eg Kodak is in the fortunate position of having a cash cow in a consumer film business that is at best mature, but more likely to be declining, given the impact of digital photography. In 2001, Kodak generated $1bn in free cash flow, a considerable percentage from consumer film. Such large cash flows are enabling Kodak to generate new business sectors such as the health imaging unit, new digital imaging and screen technologies. Kodak cannot be complacent, however. Fuji and others are trying to get a bigger share of the profitable consumer film business, and digital photography has the potential to change the storage and display of traditional photographs. Why bother to print when digital storage and retrieval is so straightforward? Sales of digital cameras reached 30 per cent of all camera sales in 2001 and although Kodak makes digital cameras, it is not yet a profitable business unit and every sale takes a customer away from the high margin film business. Margins on high quality paper and digital processing are considerably lower than on film. Cash cows don't live for ever – get the picture (Carter, 2002; Serwer, 2002)?

The management focus here is on retention and maintenance, rather than on seeking growth. Management might be looking to keep price leadership, and any investment will be geared towards lowering costs rather than increasing volumes. Any excess cash can be diverted to new areas needing support, perhaps helping to develop dogs and question marks into stars.

Once the BCG matrix has been developed for an organisation, it can be used to assess the strength of the company and its product portfolio. Ideally, a strong mix of cash cows and stars is desirable, although there may be embryonic stars among the dogs and question marks. The situation and the portfolio become unbalanced where there are too many dogs and question marks and not enough cash cows to fund new developments to allow them to break out of those cells. There is also a risk dimension to all this. The organisation as a whole is vulnerable if there are too many products with an uncertain future (question marks).

Abell and Hammond (1979), however, identified a number of weaknesses in the BCG model and its assumptions, for instance that cash flow and cash richness are influenced by far more than market share and industry growth, and that return on investment (ROI) is a more widely used yardstick of investment attractiveness than cash flow. Although it is conceptually neat, the BCG matrix does not adequately assess alternative investment opportunities when there is competition for funds, as for example when it is necessary to decide whether it is better to support a star or a question mark.

eg Dr Oetker, the large German food company, was more confident that it could quickly gain a leadership position in the declining UK frozen pizza market. Consumer taste is switching towards chilled pizzas and the frozen sector declined by 3 per cent in 2001. The 10 inch frozen pizza, thin and crispy, will initially come in four varieties, retailing at £1.99 each. A £5m. advertising budget has been allocated to support the brand. To gain the top spot, it will have to overcome market leaders Schwan and McCain and some experts believe that far from creating a cash cow, Dr Oetker could be dealing with a dog within a few months of launch (*The Grocer*, 2002a; Mowbray, 2002).

Market attractiveness model: the GE matrix. Developed first by General Electric (GE), the market attractiveness–business position portfolio assessment model was designed to overcome some of the problems of models such as the BCG matrix.

The GE matrix adds more variables to aid investment decision appraisal. It uses two principal dimensions, as seen in Figure 12.5: *industry attractiveness* (the vertical axis) and *business strengths* (the horizontal axis). Within the matrix, the circle size represents the size of the market and the shaded part the share of the market held by the SBU.

The first dimension, industry attractiveness, is a composite index determined by market size, rate of growth, degree of competition, pace of technological change, new legislation and profit margins achieved, among others. The second dimension, business position, is another composite index, comprising a range of factors that help to build stronger relative market share, such as relative product quality and performance, brand image, distribution strength, price competition, loyalty, production efficiency, etc. Both dimensions need to work positively together, since there is little point in having a strong position in an unattractive market, or a weak position in a strong market.

Within the matrix, there are three zones, each implying a different marketing and management strategy:

1 *Zone 1 (high attractiveness, strong position).* The strategy here should be investment for further growth.
2 *Zone 2 (medium attractiveness).* Because there is a weakness on one dimension, the strategy here should be one of selective investment, without overcommitting.
3 *Zone 3 (least attractive).* Either make short-term gains or proceed to pull out.

The main areas of concern with this model are linked to methodology and the lack of clear guidelines for implementing strategies.

Shell's directional policy matrix. Shown in Figure 12.6, the Shell directional policy matrix has two dimensions, competitive capabilities and prospects for sector profitability. The nine cells of the matrix offer different opportunities and challenges, so that placing each product in an appropriate cell provides a guide to its strategic development.

Review of models. Portfolio models have been criticised, but they have, nevertheless, been useful in forcing managers, especially in large complex organisations, to think more strategically. The great advantage of the models is that they force managers to reflect on current and projected performance, and to ask important questions about the continued viability of products, their strategic role and the potential for performance improvement. These models do not, however, give solutions about what strategies should be adopted, and they need to be supported by clear action plans. The main problem with them is the rather simplistic use of variables that contribute to the axes and the decision rules sought from the models. The preoccupation with market share is of particular concern, since it might be just as valid to

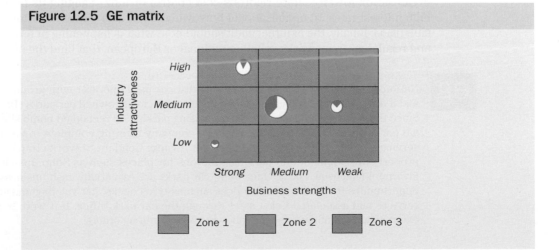

Figure 12.5 GE matrix

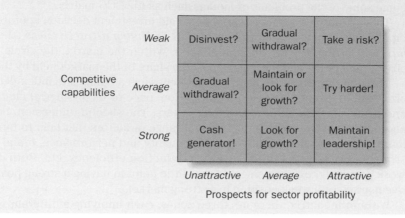

Figure 12.6 Shell directional policy matrix

consolidate and perform better as to pursue high-growth, high-share business. The models also fail to consider the synergies between businesses, where one may support another.

In some situations, it might be more appropriate to focus on a small number of areas and perform really well in these than to overextend in the pursuit of market share or market growth. In many markets, a set of businesses survive with little reference to market share as niche operators. They might, therefore, develop attractive returns without necessarily seeking market share for its own sake or incurring the costs and risks associated with the pursuit of relative sales volume. This is also true in situations where technological change and obsolescence can quickly erode any significant advantage gained.

Although these models are commonly described in textbooks, they are not so widely used in practice. They are conceptually easy to design, but very difficult to implement effectively. They require considerable management skill and judgement, because of their focus on the identification of variables, weighting decisions and future changes, rather than just on present, tangible, measurable factors.

External audit

The external audit systematically looks at the kinds of issues covered extensively in Chapter 2 as the STEP factors. Sociocultural changes, such as in the demographic make-up of a market or in public concerns or attitudes, may well influence the future strategic direction of an organisation. The early identification of technological change might also change strategic direction, as the organisation plans ways of exploiting it to make cheaper, better or different products ahead of the competition. Economic and competitive factors are both, of course, very important. Low disposable incomes among target customers may force the organisation towards more rigorous cost control or into changing its product mix, while high interest rates on organisational borrowing might delay diversification or other expansion plans. Finally, the external audit should note what is happening in terms of the political and regulatory frameworks, whether national or European, that bind the organisation.

eg National Car Parks (NCP) is Europe's largest car park operator with around 530 car parks and it also provides management services for municipally owned car parks (Batchelor, 2001). Since the 1950s, it has evolved from organising parking on reclaimed bomb sites to property-led parking and finally to being a service company offering complete town centre parking services. Increasingly, through its current owners Cendant, it works to pursue combined property development and parking solutions for places such as Soho, Ipswich, Leeds and Liverpool (Jameson, 2002). Once built, car parks are essentially cash businesses. There are opportunities for added-value services such as tyre checks, car valeting and servicing, fleet services and associated ticket sales through the car park office. If it were to undertake an external audit, it might raise the following issues, among others:

1   *Competition*. A number of rivals from mainland Europe and the USA have entered the UK market.

2   *Negotiating for sites*. Increased competition means that acquiring new sites or even renewing the leases on existing ones is more difficult. On the other hand, competitors who are struggling provide an opportunity for NCP to pick up sites and contracts.

3   *Management contracts*. Many site owners (local authorities, airports, hotels, shopping centres, etc.) now prefer to award management contracts to car park operators, rather than giving them complete autonomy over the car park operation. NCP's traditional approach has been one of autonomy, and its competitors have been faster to accept management contracts.

4   *Service*. Direct parking is now available from operators such as Interlink (http://www.webworld.co.uk/mall/inter-link). These competitors offer lower prices and collect customers from their hotels.

5   *Government policy for transport*. The government's drive to get cars off the road could have an adverse effect on demand for parking. On the other hand, city centre traffic restrictions and proposed tolls to get into centres could lead to an increase in demand for 'park and ride' schemes and thus edge-of-town parking. Any move to invest in light rail options such as those running in Manchester, Birmingham, London Docklands and Croydon could depress city centre demand for regular parkers and season ticket holders, especially given the UK government's aim to double the use of trams by 2010 (Harper, 2000). In the first six weeks of light rail operation, the demand for car parking in the centre of Croydon dropped by nearly 10 per cent.

6   *Security*. Both the general public and the police are pressurising car park operators to install increasingly sophisticated security systems.

7   *Shopping habits*. The rise of out-of-town shopping with ample free parking not only pulls shoppers away from town centres, NCP's traditional territory, but also highlights the high cost of town centre parking. 'Park and ride' schemes operated from edge-of-town sites into the centres might provide an opportunity for NCP in cooperation with local authorities.

8   *Property development opportunities*. These opportunities might become available on a partnership basis.

Sources: Batchelor (2001), Foster (1996), Jameson (2002), Harper (2000), http://www.ncp.co.uk

Competitor analysis. As part of the external audit, competition also has to be analysed very carefully on all aspects of its marketing activities, including its response to STEP factors and its choice of target markets. Competitors are an important factor that will influence the eventual success or failure of a business in any market. Ignore competition, and the likelihood of being taken by surprise or of being caught out by a strong new product or a major attack on a loyal customer base is very great and can create severe problems.

At the macro level, Porter (1979) in his Five Forces Model, defined the competitive forces that operate in an industry and shape the characteristics of a market. They are:

- the bargaining power of suppliers
- the bargaining power of customers
- the threat of new entrants
- the threat of substitute products and services
- the rivalry among current competitors.

Porter's five forces form a useful starting point for undertaking a competitive analysis, in particular because they encourage a very wide definition of competition. Competition is not just about established, direct competitors at end-product level, but also about indirect and future competitors and about competition for suppliers. Before the development of the Channel Tunnel, the cross-channel ferry companies felt little need to compete aggressively with each other. Once the concept of the tunnel became a reality, however, they were shaken into action because of the perceived competitive threat.

The Porter model gives a sound foundation, but there are still several areas that should be analysed, if there is to be a full appreciation of competitors.

Competitor identification. As the Porter model implies, the identification of competitors is often broader than it first appears. The exercise should look at potential competitors, focus on the extent to which market needs are being satisfied and look at the needs that are emerging, as well as evaluating the activities and capabilities of the obvious competition. Latent or new competitors can take a market by surprise. An organisation needs to decide with whom it is really competing and not just assume that it is companies or brands that are very similar to its own. Small local shops discovered the hard way that they were competing with the supermarket multiples.

In a large market, once competitors are identified, it might be possible to group them into clusters, depending on their focus and strategy in terms of cost structures, products, markets amd segments served, quality, distribution channels utilised, etc. This can provide a useful framework for identifying opportunities, but remember that in order to implement the technique, the organisation needs detailed competitor information, not just on financial performance but also on segments served and marketing strategies, etc.

Competitive strengths and weaknesses. Examining a competitor's strengths and weaknesses provides a valuable insight into its strategic thinking and actions. A full range of areas should be examined, for example manufacturing, technical and financial strengths, relationships with suppliers and customers and markets and segments served, as well as the usual gamut of marketing activity. It is particularly worth undertaking a detailed review of the product range, identifying where volume, profits and cash come from, where the competitor is the market leader, where it is weak and where it seems to be heading.

eg Airbus and Boeing are global rivals for the passenger aircraft market. As rivals for virtually every major contract from national airlines, each has a detailed insight into the strengths and weaknesses of the other. Of critical importance is getting the basic aircraft design right in the first place and each has taken a radically different view of future air passenger demand. Airbus is planning the A380, the world's biggest airliner with 555 seats and due for a maiden flight in 2004, whereas Boeing is going for the sonic cruiser, with 250 seats, in an aircraft built to travel at 98 per cent of the speed of sound. One is built for volume hub-to-hub traffic, the other for fast point-to-point services. These polarised alternatives reflect radically different views on the future of passenger demand over the next 20 years. There might, however, be no loser, as both could serve different niches with neither dominating the global market. What will be clear, however, is that both will know exactly how to argue against the other when trying to close a deal (*The Economist*, 2002).

Competitive reaction. It is very important to be able to assess competitors' responses to general changes in the marketing environment and to moves in major battles within the market. These responses could range from matching a price cut or an increase in promotional spend, through to ignoring events or shifting the ground completely. An organisation can learn from experience how competitors are likely to behave. Some will always react swiftly and decisively to what is seen as a threat, others may be more selective depending on the perceived magnitude of the threat.

Competitive information system. The above discussion of competitor analysis demonstrates the need for a well-organised and comprehensive competitor information system. This would be part of the MIS discussed in Chapter 5. Often, data need to be deliberately sourced on an ongoing basis, collated, analysed, disseminated and discussed. Then, management at all levels can learn what is happening. They may dispute the findings or the data may provide a basis for seeking further insights.

Market potential and sales forecasting. The extent to which plans can be successfully implemented depends not only on managers' abilities in setting and implementing strategies, but more fundamentally on their ability to predict the market accurately. This means two things: first, assessing the market potential, that is, working out how big the total cake is, and second, forecasting sales, that is, calculating how big a slice of that cake our organisation can get for itself. The following subsections will look at both of these areas.

Market and sales potential. The concept of market potential is very simple, but in practice it is very difficult to estimate. Market potential is the maximum level of demand available within the total market over a given period, assuming a certain level of competitive marketing activity and certain conditions and trends in the marketing environment. This definition immediately raises problems in calculating a figure for market potential, as it involves many assumptions about competitors and the environment, needs a precise definition of 'the market' and requires methods of quantifying the variables concerned.

eg There is a well-known story of the shoe sales representative arriving in a remote Amazon jungle community to find that none of the locals are wearing shoes. Is this a hopeless market with no potential, or a prime market for development? A similar problem faced Kooshies Baby Products from Canada when it sought to launch non-disposable nappies on to the Chinese market as part of a joint venture with a flannel cotton products company in China. Unlike Kooshies' other international markets, China was not used to non-disposable, flannel nappies, and has a preference for brushed cotton. Flannel is considered inferior and the Chinese are less interested in the environmental aspects of nappy use. Just 20 Kooshies non-disposable nappies can replace up to 7,000 disposable ones. Other product adaptations were necessary: white waistbands were associated with funerals and animal patterns on nappies were not appreciated. So, just what is the Chinese market potential? Twenty million babies are born in China each year, but how many of those can be considered as representing real market potential given the environment described? What is the sales potential for Kooshies and is it worth the risk and the investment required to develop it (Gamble, 2001)?

Even after the potential has been estimated for the market as a whole, an organisation will then need to determine its own sales potential, that is, the share of the market that it could reasonably expect to capture. Obviously, sales potential is partly a result of the organisation's marketing effort and its success in attracting and holding on to customers. Although the level of total market potential will create a ceiling for an organisation's individual sales potential, in reality sales potential should be based on a clear understanding of the relative success of individual organisations' marketing efforts.

Having a clear idea of market and sales potential provides a useful input to the marketing planning process. It is especially important for planning selling efforts and allocating resources. The allocation of sales force effort, and the establishment of distribution points and service support centres, for example, can reflect sales potential rather than actual sales, thus allowing scope for expansion. Similarly, sales potential can also be used to plan sales territories, quotas, sales force compensation and targets for prospecting.

Sales forecasting. Marketing often plays a central role in preparing and disseminating forecasts. This is perhaps one of its most important functions, as the sales and market forecasts provided are the basis of all subsequent planning and decision-making within most areas of the organisation. Get it wrong and the whole organisation can be caught out by major capacity or cash flow problems. In fashion markets, for example, it can be very difficult to forecast what styles are going to sell in what quantities, hence the popularity of 'end of

eg Earlier (see p. 406), we considered the rivalry for global dominance of the skies between Airbus and Boeing. Both companies accept the view that the market for air travel will triple over the next 20 years, but they disagree on the structure of that demand. Boeing believes that the total demand will be for 18,120 new aircraft, of which only one-third will be large Jumbo-type models. Airbus, however, believes that the market will only be for 14,670 aircraft, but around half of those will be large variants such as the A380. With such a different view of the market, it is perhaps not surprising that each company is pushing forward different design options (*The Economist*, 2002). The differences are based on the assumptions that underpin the models for demand forecasting. The world's airline fleet was about 20,500 in 2001, but short-term changes are hard to predict, especially given the impact of September 11th 2001. In terms of world fleets, Boeing has over 10,000 planes flying (51.7 per cent) and Airbus around 2,550 (12.5 per cent) (Kingsley-Jones and Duffy, 2001).

season' sales as retailers try to sell off surplus stock. Holiday companies also find forecasting difficult, and again find themselves selling off surplus holidays at a discount right up to departure dates.

There is no such thing as a rigid or absolute forecast. Different forecasters using different forecasting methods are almost certain to come up with different results. Genna (1997) in a study of purchasing managers found that only 59 per cent of them believed that the sales forecasts they received from sales and marketing areas were only 'somewhat accurate'. This calls into question the usefulness of those forecasts in guiding production planning. Another study by Mentzer and Bienstock (1998) found that 55 per cent of forecasters do not access market information when developing sales forecasts, so the problems of inaccurate and unrealistic forecasting are perhaps not surprising.

eg Just how many viewers would the new BBC3 digital channel for young adults attract and what impact would it have on the other channels, especially Channel 4? These were important questions for the service providers and for the government which had to approve the plans. Channel 4 claimed that it would attract millions of viewers and thus Channel 4 would lose substantial advertising revenue. In the longer term, that could strengthen still further the power of the BBC in broadcasting. The BBC claimed, however, that it needed a channel like BBC3 to win back lost audiences. At the heart of the question was the nature and quality of the assumptions behind management judgements as to the likely level of viewer switching and new viewer attraction. Although forecasting models can be built to demonstrate interactions under various assumptions, it would still come down to executive and political judgement as to which forecast should be accepted (Douglas, 2002).

■ SWOT analysis

The marketing audit is a major exercise which ranges widely over all the internal and external factors influencing an organisation's marketing activity. It generates, therefore, a huge amount of material that has to be analysed and summarised to sift out the critical issues that will drive the marketing plan forward. The commonest mechanism for structuring audit information to provide a critical analysis is the SWOT analysis (strengths, weaknesses, opportunities, threats).

Strengths and weaknesses

Strengths and weaknesses tend to focus on the present and past, and on internally controlled factors, such as the 4Ps and the overall marketing package (including customer service) offered to the target market. The external environment is not totally ignored, however, and many strengths and weaknesses can only be defined as such in a competitive context. Thus, for example, our low prices may be seen as a strength if we are pricing well below our nearest competitor in a price-sensitive market. Low prices may, however, be a weakness if we have been forced into them by a price war and cannot really sustain them, or if the market is less price-sensitive and our price is associated with inferior quality when compared with higher-priced competitors in the minds of the target market.

eg Teuscher (http://www.teuscher.com) truffle shops claim to offer a fairy-tale experience to all their visitors. Top quality chocolate surrounded by elaborate design in over 25 stores worldwide helps Teuscher to differentiate itself significantly from its competitors. The designs are deliberately themed and changed simultaneously in all shops four or five times per year. Examples have included autumn pheasants, pink flamingos and bears, to name but a few, all set amid plants and flowers. Attention to detail also extends to the products themselves. The raw material is carefully selected couverture that has been specially tempered and has a high cocoa content and low melting point. Such delights as champagne truffles, chewy florentines, candied orange slices, hearts and fish shapes, golf balls, trains and pianos are all offered – in chocolate, of course. This attention to detail, a high level of creativity and an emphasis on premier class make Teuscher shops very special places (Style, 1999).

Teuscher chocolates offer the customer many different varieties of their truffles aimed at chocolate connoisseurs.

Source: Teuscher Chocolates of Switzerland.

Opportunities and threats

Opportunities and threats tend to focus on the present and the future, taking a more outward-looking, strategic view of likely developments and options. Thus the organisation that is the price leader in a price-sensitive market might see the opportunity to get its costs down even further as a means of maintaining its position and pressurising any challengers. The challenger's SWOT analysis would define that same scenario as a threat, but might see an opportunity in opening up a new, non-price-sensitive segment. Many opportunities and threats emerge from the marketing environment, when shifts in demographic and cultural factors are taken into account; when developments in emerging markets, such as China, are analysed; when, in fact, the implications of anything included in Chapter 2's STEP factors are considered.

eg   WH Smith has become an international player in the book and stationery retail market, with around 530 stores in the UK and a further 575 in the USA, Australia and Asia. If it were doing a SWOT analysis, it might identify the rise in online commerce and learning as both a threat and an opportunity. It is a threat in the sense that it has generated new competitors such as http://www.amazon.co.uk focusing on the UK as well as making it relatively easy for UK consumers to buy from the USA or anywhere else. The threat is intensified with the evidence that there is a significant shift towards online book buying.

Related opportunities for a High Street retailer could be that the online market is young enough to support more providers and a retailer could open a parallel distribution channel to sell online to compete directly with the likes of Amazon. WH Smith has, in fact used its strengths as an established retail name and as a distributor to open its own e-commerce website, but it has not yet made a significant impact. WH Smith has also identified a trend in consumer preferences, accelerated by the online revolution and the associated fragmentation of mass markets, towards more focused retailers rather than generalists. One way that

▶

WH Smith has tried to capitalise on this is by acquiring Hodder Headline, which is involved in children's and educational publishing. This backward integration could improve WH Smith's expertise and focus in those areas as well as strengthening any online offer (Hollinger and Rawsthorn, 1999). WH Smith must not, however, lose sight of its core retailing business and will have to pay greater attention to making its retail stores more amenable, to encourage browsing and impulse buying as well as giving people a reason to visit 'real' shops rather than online ones (Hirst, 2001).

Understanding the SWOT analysis

The SWOT analysis, therefore, helps to sort information systematically and to classify it, but still needs further creative analysis to make sense of it. The magnitude of opportunities and threats, and the feasibility of the potential courses of action implied by them, can only really be understood in terms of the organisation's strengths and weaknesses. If strengths and weaknesses represent 'where we are now' and opportunities and threats represent 'where we want (or don't want) to be' or 'where we could be', then the gap, representing 'what we have to do to get there', has to be filled by managerial imagination, as justified and formalised in the body of the marketing plan.

■ Marketing objectives

Objectives are essential for clearly defining what must be achieved through the marketing strategies implemented, and also provide a benchmark against which to measure the extent of their success. Marketing objectives do, however, have to be wide ranging as well as precise, as they have to link closely with corporate objectives on a higher level but also descend to the fine detail of products, segments, etc. They must, therefore, be *consistent*, with each other and with corporate goals, *attainable*, in that they can be achieved in practice and their progress can be measured, and *compatible* with both the internal and external environments in which they are to be implemented. These criteria are generally applicable, despite the fact that marketing objectives can vary over time and between organisations.

eg

Ryanair, the Ireland-based low-cost airline, continued to expand despite the problems that the major scheduled airlines faced after September 11th 2001. The core theme underlying its marketing objectives is to offer a no-frills, price-oriented proposition that few other airlines can match. Expansion has been progressive since the company started in 1985. Initially, it broke the high price levels operated by British Airways and Aer Lingus on the Dublin–London route by offering fares at half their rates. New aircraft were bought and new services established by the early 1990s, and services were expanded from Dublin to Glasgow, Birmingham, Manchester and Gatwick. By 1995, Ryanair was carrying over 1.5 million passengers, double the figure for 1989. At that stage, prices were reduced further, with some fares as low as €30 (Edwards, 2001).

The service package has to be worked out backwards from the low price and expected capacity on each flight. Onboard services such as meals cost extra, online booking cuts out commission to travel agents; and lowest cost airport services are used. Sometimes, for example, the gates used are well away from the main terminal and even the choice of airport has led to some criticism. For instance, Copenhagen was the advertised destination, but Malmo (Sweden) was the destination airport, some 45 minutes' bus ride away. Similarly, the Frankfürt Hahn destination airport is actually 60 miles west of the commercial centre (Peachey, 2002). These less popular airports not only make it easier to get take-off and landing slots, but also mean lower landing charges. Price is always the main feature in any advertising and it is normally compared directly with the main scheduled carriers' prices.

Even as Ryanair expands and develops its hubs at Stanstead and Hahn, the marketing formula remains with tactics designed to beat off the competition. The Hahn expansion takes Ryanair head to head with Lufthansa with the declared intention to 'break its high fares monopoly in the German market' (as quoted by Done, 2001), as it did to Aer Lingus nearly 20 years ago. Ryanair might not have it all its own way, however, as Lufthansa is planning to launch its own low-cost airline (Harnischfeger, 2002).

Whatever the basis of the objectives, they cannot be left at such a descriptive level. It is not enough to say that our objective is to increase our market share. It is essential to quantify and make explicit precisely what is intended. Even then, the objective is still quite general, and a number of detailed sub-objectives, which will perhaps relate to constraints or parameters within which the main objective is to be achieved, should also be defined. The main objective of increasing market share, for example, may have sub-objectives relating to pricing. Thus the marketing manager might have to find a way of increasing market share without compromising the organisation's premium price position.

■ Marketing strategies

A marketing strategy is the means by which an organisation sets out to achieve its marketing objectives. In reality, an organisation will find that it has a range of strategic options, relating to its defined objectives. Some will be related to increasing volume, while others relate to improving profitability and holding on to what the organisation already has (reducing costs, increasing prices, changing the product mix, streamlining operations, etc.).

The Ansoff matrix

This section examines a number of different strategies that organisations might adopt if their priority is growth. It is important to remember, however, that growth is not always a priority. In many small firms, for example, survival or sustaining the status quo might be the main objective. In other situations, standing still might be the right strategy if the market is starting to tighten up. The preoccupation with growth, therefore, should not be assumed to be relevant to all organisations all the time.

The product–market matrix proposed by Ansoff (1957) provides a useful framework for considering the relationship between strategic direction and marketing strategy. The four-cell matrix shown in Figure 12.7 considers various combinations of product–market options. Each cell in the Ansoff matrix presents distinct opportunities, threats, resource requirements, returns and risks, and will be discussed below.

Figure 12.7 Ansoff's growth matrix

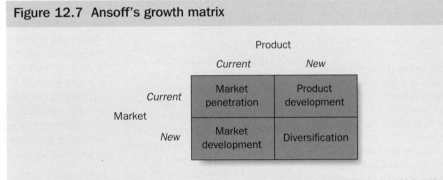

Source: Ansoff (1957). Adapted and reprinted by permission of *Harvard Business Review*. Exhibit 1 on p. 114 from '*Strategies of Diversification*' by Ansoff, H.I. Issue No. 25 (5), Sept/Oct 1957, pp. 113–25, Copyright © 1957 the Harvard Busness School Publishing Corporation; all rights reserved.

marketing *in action*

Unilever goes for growth

Unilever, the large FMCG multinational, is going for growth. Under the heading 'Path to Growth' it has been fundamentally reviewing and changing its product portfolio to achieve sales growth of between 5 and 6 per cent overall on a turnover of €53.4bn. It has been carefully managing its product portfolio in recent years to guide investment and divestment decisions. In the late 1990s it classified its brands into categories A and B (Campbell, 1999). At that time it had around 1,800 brands in its portfolio and believed that it could not achieve category dominance with such a large range and thus pruning was needed to release resources to support growth. Category A brands such as Dove, Lynx, Lipton, Hellmann's, Magnum, Omo

▶

and Cif were deemed central to future plans whereas category B brands such as Pears Shampoo, Timotei and Brut were up for review. The criteria used to differentiate the brands were based on the planning models presented in this chapter, adapted to the Unilever context and environment. The criteria were:

- Size of the brand: volume share, value share, number of customers
- Loyalty: strength of loyalty
- Potential: new market segments, brand extension, etc.
- Trends: at market and product levels.

The overall aim was to reduce the portfolio to 400 leading brands which would then become the focus of product innovation, brand extension and increased marketing support. There would also be associated benefits in logistics and service levels with less variety and higher volumes on the remaining brands. The change could not happen overnight, but the expectation was that by 2004 the leading brands would account for 95 per cent of Unilever's turnover, compared with 84 per cent in 2002 and 75 per cent at the start of the programme in 1999. By 2002, around 97 per cent of all advertising expenditure was concentrated on the top 400 brands.

In the analysis, Unilever did not take a country-by-country view but considered the global competition in its main markets and the position of its global brands in each. In some cases, product development was used to strengthen its position, for example the Dove range of soaps has experienced considerable extension into shampoo, deodorant and skincare products in all regions as well as being

rolled out to new regions such as Asia. As part of the renewed effort, Dove sales increased by 29 per cent in 2001. Pro Activ, Cuilese and Brunch spreads have been launched in Europe as well as new formats for Cornetto. Cornetto sales grew by 21 per cent during 2001.

When it considers that a faster track can be employed through acquisition, which of course is also a means of removing a potential competitor, Unilever has been very active. In 2000 it made 20 acquisitions to the value of €30.5m. including:

- Bestfoods: foods (international)
- Amora Maille: culinary products (France)
- Ben & Jerry's: ice cream (primarily in the United States)
- Codepar/SPCD: home and personal care (Tunisia)
- Cressida: foods, home and personal care (Central America)
- Jaboneria: foods, home and personal care (Ecuador)
- Slim Fast: nutritional bars and beverage products (United States).

The Bestfoods acquisition was especially challenging as it had a large portfolio of brands and employed 33,000 people in 63 countries in 120 factories. The priority was thus on rationalisation and integration. This involved selling off some duplicate or poor fit brands such as Campbell, combining the sales forces, grouping media buying and ensuring a unified effort in segments in which one was stronger than the other. It gave Unilever control, however, over strong brands in adjacent categories such as Hellman's and Knorr which it could build on a global scale. Unilever has already been

able to achieve global leadership in tea, ice cream and spreads as a result of the Bestfoods takeover.

At the same time, however, the disposal programme has also been very active, some for strategic reasons and others as part of any competition agreements associated with an acquisition. Over 50 brands have already been divested. Minor brands and those with no long-term future or fit have gone already: Elizabeth Arden fragrances was sold for €244m.; its Unilever's North American seafood business was sold to Nippon Suisan; its refinery business at Unimills in the Netherlands was sold, and so was Johnson Wax professional, to name but a few. At the same time, other brands have been harvested prior to disposal or termination.

To help the focus, Unilever concentrated its brands into two global divisions: Unilever Bestfoods, and Home and Personal Care. Both divisions have an executive board, responsible for divisional strategy and for implementation across the world. This has helped to overcome one of the main difficulties often facing organisations when disposing of products, i.e. local management who are resistant to terminating 'their' brands and who prefer to argue that repositioning will rejuvenate sales. In Unilever, the clear sense of purpose and strategy right through the organisation enables an almost ruthless approach to product portfolio management that regards acquiring and building brands as the other side of the disposal coin.

Sources: Campbell (1999); http://www.unilever.com.

■ Intensive growth

Three cells of the Ansoff matrix offer opportunity for sustained growth, although each one has different potential according to the market situation.

Market penetration. The aim of market penetration is to increase sales volume in current markets, usually by more aggressive marketing. This means using the full range of the marketing mix to achieve greater leverage.

A number of continental European brands have significantly penetrated the UK market. Müller has established a 40 per cent share of the yogurt market and has become the second largest food brand in the country since its 1987 UK launch. The German company swept aside UK competitors, St Ivel, part of Unigate, and Eden Vale which have both fallen back from their comfortable 1987 market shares of 40 per cent each. Müller has achieved this dramatic turnaround through strong product development and by using price to outcompete the local rivals. Its main advantage was the split-pot yogurt, with plain yogurt in one half and fruit in the other allowing consumers to choose how they mix and eat their yogurt. Prices were set low to achieve economies of scale and an annual $10m. advertising budget is normally allocated to the brand. The UK competitors did not think that a split-pot format would catch on, and by the time they found out that it had succeeded, it was too late and they were unable to claw market share back. The combination of regular innovation, value for money promotions, widespread distribution and national advertising has been a powerful force for building and retaining Müller's market lead. The 'three for 99p' type of offer characterises Müller and between 80 and 85 per cent of sales are made that way (Carmichael, 2002; Hardcastle, 2001; Urry, 2001).

Market development. Market development means selling more of the existing product to new markets, which could be based on new geographic segments or could be created by opening up other new segments (based, for example, on age, product usage, lifestyle or any other segmentation variable). Danish firms control nearly half of the world's market for wind turbine machines. Companies such as Vestas Wind Systems depend heavily on achieving growth by developing new markets.

eg The prime objective of these companies is to grow by opening up new markets around the world. Vestas Wind Systems (http://www.vestas.com) is the world's leading manufacturer of wind turbines. The world market for wind turbine systems is expected to continue growing over the next 10 years due to greater energy consumption, more environmental awareness and greater efficiency as technology continues to lower unit costs. From its origins in Scandinavia, Vestas now has a 24 per cent share of the global market for wind power, which itself grew by over 50 per cent in 2001. European markets have been opened up, especially in Germany and Spain, and other markets being developed include Japan, the USA, China and Australia. In 2000, it agreed a new dealership in Japan to form Vestech Japan Corporation, which is owned by a number of large Japanese corporations including Toyota and Kawasaki. This has enabled a fast entry into an otherwise difficult market. Additionally, contracts were signed for the first time in Costa Rica and Iran while the less well cultivated markets in Poland and Portugal showed positive signs. By opening up new markets, Vestas is able to retain and build its global position.

Part of the market development strategy is to establish local production facilities through acquisition or direct investment. In addition to Denmark, factories exist in Germany, Spain and India and sales offices are also being opened to support the development of a market, as it may take some time to achieve regulatory approval and to negotiate with power providers. Despite the international coverage, the success of Vestas has been built on the platform of product development, occupying 9 per cent of the workforce, quality, pre- and post-sales service, efficient production and competitive pricing. Although still primarily a wind turbine producer, Vestas' sales had grown from DK2830m. in 1996 to DK9521m. by 2001, helped by a market that continues to grow.

Product development. Product development means selling completely new or improved products into existing markets.

eg Bloomsbury Publishing is one of Europe's leading independent publishing houses and it requires a steady flow of new authors and desirable titles to grow. Formed in 1986, its core competence is its ability to identify new authors and then use its marketing skills to ensure that the books are launched successfully. Its authors include Michael Ondaatje (*The English Patient*), David Guterson (*Snow Falling on Cedars*) and not least J. K. Rowling. In 2001, 6 of its books were in the *Daily Telegraph* top 10 list and although the Harry Potter *Goblet of Fire* went straight to the number one position in paperback, the number of top 10 successes indicates the wider strength of having an active approach to new product development either by author or title. Few would have predicted the success of the Harry Potter series at its launch. The initial print run was 1.5 million copies, but worldwide sales now far exceed 100 million. The series takes over 19 per cent of the £140m. children's book market, with the next nearest series taking just 3.9 per cent. In addition, clever merchandising and the sale of film rights opens up even more profitable opportunities for author and publisher. Even the Harry Potter website receives 15 million hits per month. With further books planned in the series, Bloomsbury is thus well placed to reap further benefit from its ability to spot winners from the hundreds of manuscripts and proposals it receives (*Marketing Week/CIM*, 2001; http://www.bloomsbury.co.uk).

Diversification. Diversification, the final cell in the Ansoff Matrix, happens when an organisation decides to move beyond its current boundaries to exploit new opportunities. It means entering unfamiliar territory in both product and market terms. One of the main attractions of this option is that it spreads risk, moving the organisation away from being too reliant on one product or one market. It also allows expertise and resources to be allocated synergistically, for example theme parks diversifying into hotel accommodation, or airlines diversifying into tour packages. The danger is, of course, that the organisation spreads its effort too widely into areas of low expertise, and tries to position itself against more specialist providers.

There are two main types of growth through diversification as follows.

Concentric diversification. Concentric diversification happens where there is a link, either technological or commercial, between the old and the new sets of activities. The benefit is, therefore, gained from a synergy with current activities. An organisation could, for example, add new, unrelated product lines to its portfolio, but still use the same sales and distribution network.

eg Video distributor Contender established a successful £6.8m. video distribution business from scratch. That is still small, however, by industry standards. The UK market for videos is dominated by large US distributors such as Warner, Universal, Buena Vista and Twentieth Century Fox, between them accounting for 65 per cent of the market. Contender holds a share of less than 1 per cent. As an intermediary, it buys the rights to a programme, typically for around £100,000, and then sells it on to retail outlets. Contender found its niche by distributing programmes with adult appeal such as the TV series *The Avengers* and *Bad Girls*. A typical title will sell between 25,000 and 50,000 copies over 12 months with profit of around £3 per sale. The key to success is buying the right programme rights and then being able to sell them on. That is getting harder as the larger organisations have increasing power over the production as well as the distribution of videos.

Contender decided, therefore, to diversify into video production and publishing, using the core competencies and industry appreciation acquired in the original business. The fragmentation of media and new television channels increasingly allows for specialist and more personalised video material. It typically costs £100,000 to produce a relatively low budget programme such as the Helen Adams Dance Workout video, a series looking at British waterways or children's videos. Original programmes now account for around 15 per cent of Contender's sales and a further 10 per cent is expected to come from spin-off merchandising and books, especially in the children's programmes area. Although the company has the industry skills and market contacts necessary to expand into video production, mistakes are made with programmes that simply fail, and then the upfront costs invested before any sales revenue is generated cannot be recouped. This eventually could lead to a loss of independence because when video production companies get to a certain size, around £15m. sales, they become attractive acquisition targets for larger, better capitalised industry players (Sumner-Smith, 2002).

Conglomerate diversification. The conglomerate diversification route is taken when an organisation undertakes new activities in markets that are also new. This involves risks in both the product development area and gaining acceptance in the marketplace.

eg   American Express decided to become a multi-product business, building on its image and experience with certain lifestyle segments gained through its credit cards. Not only was direct banking piloted in Germany, but consideration was also given to mobile phone services, travel products and private health care. The common thread for the diversification was the use of the Amex name.

'No growth' options

Not all strategies have to be growth-oriented. *Harvesting* is a deliberate strategy of not seeking growth, but looking for the best returns from the product, even if the action taken may actually speed up any decline or reinforce the no growth situation. The objective is, however, to make short-term profit while it is possible. Typically, products subjected to harvesting are likely to be cash cows in the mature stage of their life cycles (see pp. 195 *et seq.*), in a market that is stable or declining, as considered on pp. 400 *et seq.* Harvesting strategies could involve minimal promotional expenditure, premium pricing strategies where possible, reducing product variability and controlling costs rigidly. Implementing such strategies helps to ensure that maximum returns are made over a short period, despite the potential loss of longer-term future sales. Effectively, the company is relying on the short-term loyalty of customers to cushion the effect of declining sales.

In more extreme cases, where prospects really are poor or bleak, *entrenchment* or *withdrawal* might be the only option. A timetable for withdrawal or closure would be developed and every effort made to maximise returns on the remaining output, in the full knowledge that harm will be done to sales volume in the short term. Some care should, however, be exercised when considering withdrawal, as although the profit potential may be poor and the costs of turnaround prohibitive, the loss of a product in a range may affect other parts of the range adversely. Thus entrenchment, protecting the product's position as best you can without wasting too many resources on it, might be the most appropriate course of action.

Competitive positions and postures

A final stage in the determination of a competitive strategy is to decide how to compete, given the market realities, and how to either defend or disturb that position. This means that the organisation has to consider its own behaviour in the context of how competitors are behaving, and select the most appropriate strategy that will enable overall objectives to be achieved. Two aspects need to be considered, competitive position and competitive posture. Competitive position refers to the impact of the organisation's market position on marketing strategies, whereas competitive postures are the strategies implemented by organisations in different positions who want to disturb the status quo.

Competitive positions. An organisation's competitive position usually falls into one of four categories, according to its relative market share. The four categories, and the kinds of marketing strategies that go with them, are shown in Figure 12.8 and are now considered in turn.

Market leader. In many industries, one organisation is recognised as being ahead of the rest in terms of market share. Its share might only be 20–25 per cent, but that could still give it a dominant position. The market leader tends to determine the pace and ways of competing in the market. It sets the price standard, the promotional intensity, the rate of product change and the quality and quantity of the distribution effort. Effectively, the market leader provides a benchmark for others to follow or emulate.

Market leadership can be at company, product group or brand level. Hellmans claims over 50 per cent of the UK mayonnaise market, just ahead of a series of own-brand products. Chivers Hartley is the market leader in jams and marmalades, and Otto Versand is Germany's market leader in mail order. In each case there are a number of rivals, so the power associated with being a leader might not necessarily be very great, especially if markets are defined from a European rather than a domestic perspective.

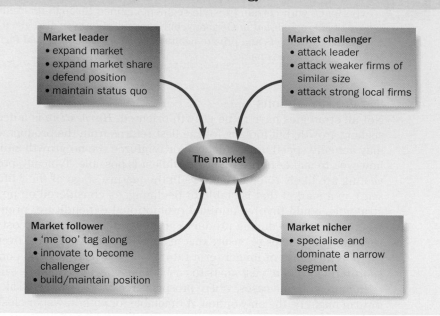

Figure 12.8 Competitive position and strategy

Market challengers. Market challengers are organisations with a smaller market share, but who are close enough to pose a serious threat to the leader. However, an aggressive strategy can be costly, if the challenger is thinking of attacking where there is uncertainty over winning. Before making a concerted effort to steal share, therefore, the challenger needs to ask itself whether market share really matters so much, or whether there would be greater benefit from working on getting a good ROI from existing share.

Assuming that the decision is made to attack, there are two key questions: where to attack, and what the likely reaction will be. It is never easy to attack leaders, who tend to retaliate through cutting prices or by investing in heavy promotion, etc. It is, therefore, a high-risk but high-return route if it works. The challenger needs a clear competitive advantage to exploit to be able to neutralise the leader.

When Quaker Petfoods challenged Pedigree Petfood's Whiskas' dominance of the catfood market, it did it by product improvement to create a high-quality brand with premium packaging, supported by appealing press and television advertising. Despite Whiskas' £10m. spend (compared with Felix's £3m.), its market share fell within three years from 50 to 35 per cent. The challenger might also have to be prepared to absorb short-term losses as a result of defending against the leader's retaliation. Again, Felix had to increase its advertising spend considerably to attack the leader. The moral of this story is not to enter the fight unless you are really convinced that you can win and are prepared to invest in the battle.

Market followers. Given the resources needed, the threat of retaliation and the uncertainty of winning, many organisations favour a far less aggressive stance, acting as market followers. There are two types of follower. First, there are those who lack the resources to mount a serious challenge and prefer to remain innovative and forward thinking, without disturbing the overall competitive structure in the market by encouraging open warfare. Often, any lead from the market leader is willingly followed. This might mean adopting a 'me too' strategy, thus avoiding direct confrontation and competition.

The second type of follower is the organisation that is simply not capable of challenging and is content just to survive, offering little competitive advantage. Often, smaller car rental firms operate in this category by being prepared to offer a lower price, but not offering the same standard of rental vehicle or even peace of mind should things go wrong. A recession can easily eliminate the weaker members of this category.

Market nichers. Some organisations, often small, specialise in areas of the market that are too small, too costly or too vulnerable for the larger organisation to contemplate. Niching is not exclusively a small organisation strategy, as some larger firms may have divisions that specialise. The key to niching is the close matching between the needs of the market and the capabilities and strengths of the company. The specialisation offered can relate to product type, customer group, geographic area or any aspect of product/service differentiation.

eg Dwr y Cwm sells bottled water from the heart of Snowdonia in Wales. Using natural water from underground sources, a supply of 5,500 gallons per hour can be achieved, enough to meet the expected demand for the new business. Rather than competing head-on with the national brands in the retail sector, Dwr y Cwm will be concentrating on hotels, restaurants and conference venues for distribution throughout the UK. The brand trades on the purity and freshness qualities of natural water from Snowdonia, and by concentrating on a niche that has received less attention it hopes to build a defendable position (Jones, 2001).

Competitive postures. The previous section considered the underlying rationale for defending, attacking or ignoring what is going on in the market from the point of view of an organisation's relative market position. This section examines *how to attack* or *how to defend* a position and the possibilities of alliances with competitors.

Aggressive strategies. Aggressive strategies are implemented when one or more players in a market decide to challenge the status quo. Again, the question of who to attack, when to attack and where to attack all need to be answered carefully in the context of the resources needed, the competitive reaction and the returns to be gained – and at what cost. Even in warfare, head-on assaults can be costly and do not always succeed.

eg The wet shaving market has seen many upheavals since Bic (http://www.bic.fr) took the market by storm in the 1960s with the disposable razor. The Bic attack was full frontal, offering convenience, low prices and ease of repurchase supported by heavy advertising and mass distribution. Gillette and Wilkinson Sword retaliated within three years with their own versions, but a third of the market had already been lost. Since then there have been many other shaver wars as one party seeks to gain a product or market advantage over the other. In the early 1990s, for example, innovation took place in the premium wet shaving sector with the launch of the Sensor and Protector close shave systems. In 1999, the battle continued as Wilkinson Sword launched a high-tech response, the FX Diamond, to the Gillette Mach 3 triple-blade razor.

This razor enabled it to capture 69 per cent of the razor market, well ahead of the number two, Wilkinson Sword, with just 15 per cent. The battle has continued into the new millennium and has been joined by a potentially powerful third brand. Unilever, with its Lynx brand, hopes to exploit the established brand name through extending into the shaving market with a youth-oriented product that also has a triple blade. Despite Unilever's £5m. television advertising spend, however, the power of Gillette in that market will still present a tough challenge for Lynx's attack (Oldfield, 2000). Furthermore, Gillette responded by launching its own upgraded Mach 3 Turbo version in 2002 using 'antifriction blade technology'. The launch was to be supported by a £140m. worldwide advertising campaign. To avoid any replication by competitors, it is covered by 35 different patents (Mazur, 2002; Singh, 2001).

Defensive strategies. Defensive strategies might be adopted by a market leader under attack, or by a market follower or nicher put under pressure by competitive activity. Even a challenger needs to reflect on likely competitive retaliation before committing itself to aggressive acts. One option is to sit tight and defend the current position. This can be risky, in that such defences might then be bypassed rather than attacked directly.

Selective withdrawal, to delay or even offset the attacking force, is also a form of defence. In commercial terms, that could mean withdrawing from marginal segments and areas where the presence is small and cannot be defended. This might mean that in areas where strengths do exist a better, more concentrated fight can take place.

Travel agents have been accused of being too complacent about the threat of direct links between supplier and customer that are made possible by the Internet. Although the power of the Internet is recognised, travel agents tend to believe that it is an alternative distribution channel, not a force that could radically reshape the industry. This has allowed the online travel agency sector to grow at a rapid rate alongside the websites of airlines offering direct bookings. For the High Street travel agent, both are eating into the traditional travel booking business. GetThere, a computer reservations system company, found that 800 of its large corporate clients used online booking services for 13.5 per cent of all travel in 2001, nearly double the previous year. Barclaycard reported that 71 per cent of business travellers had booked via the Internet in the past year and even more intended to do so in the future (Bray, 2002). Ignoring these trends could be dangerous for UK travel agents, who have argued that customers prefer direct contact with sales staff and value the expertise of travel agents in finding the best deals.

The phrase 'the best form of defence is to attack' is now a recognised business strategy. If an organisation feels that it might soon be under attack, rather than wait for that to happen it takes deliberate aggressive actions. Alternatively, signals can be sent that any attack would be vigorously defended.

Cooperation. It would be incorrect to assume that all competitive behaviour is challenging and confrontational. Many situations are characterised by peaceful coexistence and at times by cooperative alliances between competitors. Strategic alliances occur when organisations seek to work together on projects, pooling expertise and resources. This could include R&D, joint ventures or licensing arrangements, sometimes on a worldwide scale. Many large construction projects demand that different firms work together to provide a turnkey package. The alliance can be general, on many fronts or specific to a certain project (Gulati, 1998).

eg Philips forged a strategic alliance with Dell to bring about collaboration on a range of electronics projects, including computer monitors. The arrangement includes cross-supply of components to be incorporated into each other's products, sharing knowledge and building joint computing architecture, for example for Philips' medical systems division. The deal also allowed Philips' products to appear on the Dell website in the USA, a market it had had trouble developing. The deal was anticipated to be worth $5bn over five years (Cramb, 2002). Meanwhile, Hino Motors, the Japanese lorry manufacturer, and Scania, the Swedish equivalent, also decided to form a strategic business alliance. Scania would provide heavy trucks for Hino to sell in Japan under its own brand name and dealer network. It was not an equity deal, but based on contractual agreement. In return, Hino would provide light and medium trucks to Scania. This enables both companies to enter markets that otherwise would be very difficult in terms of establishing brand awareness and dealer networks (Burt and Ibison, 2002).

There are many forms of alliance that can be created for mutual benefit. A number of non-competing organisations in the consumer goods area are forming marketing alliances to reduce costs and improve market impact. Coca-Cola uses marketing alliances to dominate the non-carbonated juice beverage market. It is working with Walt Disney to market its Minute Maid juices under the Disney brand, using containers featuring Mickey Mouse and Winnie the Pooh, etc. The alliance was expected to generate $200m. over four years (Liu, 2001).

Finally, *collusion* is where firms come to an 'understanding' about how to compete in the market. Legislation prevents this from extending to deliberate price fixing: neither retailers nor manufacturers can openly collude to set retail or supply prices between them, although they can, of course, watch each other's pricing policies carefully and choose to match them if they wish. Although collusion is the unacceptable side of cooperation, the scale of investment and rate of change in technology, accompanied by increasingly global markets, is likely to generate more alliances and ventures in future.

■ Marketing programmes

Whereas the previous stage was about designing marketing strategies, this one is about their detailed implementation. The marketing programme will precisely specify actions, responsibilities and timescales. It is the detailed statement that managers have to follow if strategies are to be put into operation, as it outlines required actions by market segment, product and functional area. Within the marketing programme, each mix element is considered individually. This is in contrast to the marketing strategy itself, which stresses the interdependency between elements of the mix for achieving the best synergy between them. Now, the individual strands that make up that strategy can be picked out, and for each functional area, such as pricing, managers can go through planning processes, audits, objectives, strategies, programmes and controls.

On the basis of the overall marketing strategy, managers can emphasise those areas of comparative strength where a competitive edge can be gained, strengthen those areas where the organisation is comparable with its competition, and work to develop further or overcome those where the organisation is more vulnerable. The key challenge at the end of it all, however, is to ensure that the marketing mix is affordable, implementable and appropriate for the target segment. With that in mind, and given the dynamic nature of most markets, managers will also have to review the mix on a regular basis to make sure that it is still fresh and still serving the purposes intended.

■ Marketing budgets

The marketing plan must specify and schedule all financial and other resource requirements, otherwise managers might not be able to accomplish the tasks set. This is partly about costs, such as those of the sales force which include their associated expenditures, advertising campaigns, dealer support, market research, etc., and partly about forecasting expected revenues from products and markets. In determining budgets, managers need to balance precision against flexibility. A budget should be precise and detailed enough to justify the resources requested and to permit detailed control and evaluation of the cost-effectiveness of various marketing activities, yet it also needs the flexibility to cope with changing circumstances.

eg When Cadbury Schweppes introduced its Managing For Value (MFV) programmes, it had far-reaching effects on marketing planning and budgeting. The underlying concept of MFV is that all existing and proposed products have to be profitable to survive. This means assessing a brand's impact, not just in terms of marketing returns, but also in terms of the total capital investment, such as in production machinery and logistics. To assess the return, marketing managers were expected to consider a variety of cost equations and schedules on different marketing and production options. The MFV also focused more attention on the effectiveness of the marketing budget and its contribution to market share, volume and earnings growth. Cadbury has a total marketing expenditure of over £1.1bn, representing nearly 20 per cent of sales revenue, which is steadily increasing year on year. The marketing plan must thus ensure that spend follows the various brands' strategic priorities and focuses appropriately on markets highlighted for development.

We discussed budget setting, and some of the issues surrounding it, in Chapter 9 in a marketing communications context (see pp. 296 *et seq.*). Many of the points made there are more widely applicable, particularly the relative strengths and weaknesses of objective and task budgeting compared with methods based on historical performance (for example basing this year's budget on last year's with an arbitrary 5 per cent added on).

■ Marketing controls and evaluation

Control and evaluation are both essential if managers are to ensure that the plans are being implemented properly and that the outcomes are those expected. Although the defined marketing objectives provide the ultimate goals against which performance and success can be measured, waiting until the end of the planning period to assess whether they have been achieved is risky. Instead, managers should evaluate progress regularly throughout the period against a series of benchmarks reflecting expected performance to date. At that point, managers can decide whether their strategies appear to be well on target for achieving objectives as planned or whether the deviation from expected performance is so great that alternative actions are called for.

Control and evaluation can take either a short- or a longer-term perspective. In the short term, control can be monitored on a daily basis through reviewing orders received, sales, stockturn or cash flow, for example. Longer-term strategic control focuses on monitoring wider issues, such as the emergence of trends and ambiguities in the marketing environment. This has strong links with the marketing audit, assessing the extent to which the organisation has matched its capabilities with the environment and indeed the extent to which it has correctly 'read' the environment.

This whole area of control and evaluation will be considered in greater detail on pp. 423 *et seq.*

Organising marketing activities

Effective marketing management does not happen by itself. It has to have the right kind of infrastructure and place within the organisation in order to develop and work efficiently and effectively. Central to the marketing philosophy is a focus on customer needs, and by understanding markets, customers' needs and wants and the ways in which they are changing and why, the marketer is providing essential information for planning corporate direction and the activities of other functions within the organisation.

It is important to distinguish between a functional marketing department and marketing orientation as a management philosophy. Any organisation can have a marketing department, yet not be truly marketing-oriented. If that marketing department is isolated from other functional areas, if it is just there to 'do advertising', then its potential is wasted. Marketing orientation permeates the whole organisation and *requires* marketing's involvement in all areas of the organisation.

Whether or not there is a marketing department, and how it is structured, depends on a number of factors. These might include the size of the organisation, the size and complexity of the markets served, the product and process technology and the rate of change in the marketing environment. There are several ways of incorporating and structuring marketing within the organisation, and these are discussed below.

■ Organisational alternatives

There are four main choices for structuring marketing management within a department, focusing on function, products, regions or segments. The marketing department might also choose to develop a matrix structure, allowing an equal focus on both function and products, for example. These are all shown in Figure 12.9. The organisation might, of course, choose not to have a formal marketing department at all. Each of these choices is discussed below.

Functional organisation

A functional department is structured along the lines of specific marketing activities. This means there are very specialised roles and responsibilities, and that individual managers have to build expertise. Such a department might have, for example, a market research manager, an advertising and promotions manager and a new product development manager, each of whom will report to the organisation's marketing director.

This system works well in organisations where the various business functions are centralised, but problems can arise where they are decentralised. Then, functional marketing tasks have to be coordinated across diverse areas, with greater or lesser degrees of cooperation and acceptance.

Figure 12.9 Forms of marketing organisation

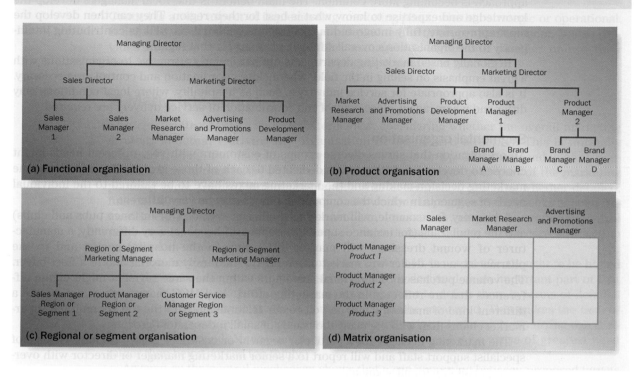

(a) Functional organisation

(b) Product organisation

(c) Regional or segment organisation

(d) Matrix organisation

Product organisation

Giving managers responsibility for specific products, brands or categories of product might suit a larger company with major brands or with diverse and very different product interests. The manager, reporting to a product group manager or a marketing director, builds expertise around the product, and is responsible for all aspects of its development, its strategic and marketing mix planning and its day-to-day welfare. Other specialist staff, such as market researchers, might be involved as necessary to help the product manager.

> **eg** Cadbury Schweppes organises its marketing effort around its leading brands. Titles such as assistant product manager, product manager, senior product manager and group product manager are all used to signify different responsibility levels within the marketing department. The product managers are responsible for the brands and their marketing mix planning. Ultimately, all these positions report through to a marketing director at board level (http://www.cadburyschweppes.com).

The product, brand or category management approach is very popular in FMCG markets. It gives clear lines of management responsibility, but there is still a need for a central function to coordinate the overall portfolio. The main problem with product organisation is working with other functions, such as production, finance, etc. to get the resources, attention and effort that the product needs. There is also the risk that too many management layers will be introduced, hence the move towards category management (i.e. responsibility for a group of brands) rather than individual brand management.

Regional organisation

An organisation with its activities spread over a wide geographic area, or one operating in markets with distinct regional differences, might find regionally based marketing responsibility attractive. The regional marketing manager, along with a support team, will make all marketing decisions relevant to planning and operations in that territory. There will then be some mechanism for coordinating regional efforts at a national or international level to

plan and its manager. It could be that targets were hopelessly optimistic, in the light of the emerging market conditions. Alternatively, other departments within the organisation, for example production or logistics, may have failed to achieve their targets.

Chapter summary

- Marketing planning is about developing the objectives, strategies and marketing mixes that best exploit the opportunities available to the organisation. Planning should itself be a planned and managed process. This process helps organisations to analyse themselves and their marketing environments more systematically and honestly. It also helps organisations to coordinate and control their marketing activities more effectively. Planning should be a flexible, dynamic activity that is fed with accurate, reliable and timely information, and is not divorced from the managers who have the day-to-day responsibility for implementing the plans. Marketing plans help to integrate activities, schedule resources, specify responsibilities and provide benchmarks for measuring progress.

- There are eight main stages in the planning process: corporate objectives, the marketing audit, marketing analysis, setting marketing objectives, marketing strategies, marketing programmes, controls and evaluation and budgeting. Techniques such as product portfolio analysis and competitor analysis can be used to help compile the marketing audit, the key points of which can then be summarised in the SWOT analysis, a snapshot of 'where are we now?' On the basis of the SWOT, objectives can be set and strategies defined with the help of tools such as the Ansoff matrix ('where do we want to be?' and 'how do we want to compete?'). These strategies are operationalised through marketing programmes ('how do we get there?'). Controls and evaluation help to monitor progress towards achieving objectives.

- In order to fulfil its function properly, the marketing department should have a central role within the organisation, with senior management of equal status to those in other functional areas. It is also important, however, that the marketing philosophy pervades the whole enterprise, regardless of the size or formality of the marketing department. There are several approaches to structuring the marketing department itself. These are the functional, product based, regional, segmental or matrix approaches.

- As marketing plans are being implemented, they have to be monitored and controlled. Strategic control concerns the longer-term direction of marketing strategy, whereas operational control assesses the day-to-day success of marketing activities. Using information gathered in the monitoring process, the actual achievements of marketing strategies can be compared with planned or expected outcomes. Managers can then analyse gaps and decide whether they are significant enough to warrant corrective action. Although this can be a quantitative analysis, it should still be looked at in the context of more qualitative issues concerning customer needs and synergies between customers, markets or products.

questions for *review and discussion*

12.1 Define the main factors influencing organisations' *marketing strategies*.

12.2 Define the stages in the *marketing planning process*.

12.3 What is a *product portfolio* and what are the problems of implementing portfolio models in practice?

12.4 Using whatever information you can find, develop a SWOT analysis for the organisation of your choice. What are the implications of your analysis for the organisation's short- and long-term priorities?

12.5 For each cell of the Ansoff matrix, find and discuss an example of an organisation that seems to have implemented that particular growth strategy.

12.6 What kind of marketing organisational structure would be appropriate for each of the following situations and why?

  (a) a small single product engineering company;
  (b) a large FMCG manufacturer selling a wide range of products into several different European markets;
  (c) a pharmaceutical company manufacturing both prescription and 'over the counter' medicines.

case study 12.1

Stopping the bottom falling out of the jeans market

The life cycle of the denim jeans market shows a series of peaks and troughs as jeans go in and out of fashion. In 1999 the market was definitely in a trough, with sales volumes falling at about 11 per cent per year, for a number of reasons. As denim moves through the fashion cycle and becomes 'uncool' again, other products take over. This time it was combat pants. Combat, cargo and carpenter pants became popular because opinion formers such as the band All Saints and clubbers wore them, and this style filtered through to the youth market generally which was bored with denims and the obvious marketing efforts that went with them. Combats were practical and, initially at least, unbranded and unmarketed. Some companies spotted the trend early and responded accordingly. Both The Gap and Wrangler, for instance, introduced combat ranges relatively early on, before companies like Levi's had probably even noticed that there was a trend to spot! The problem was summed up by Damian Mould, chief executive of integrated youth marketing agency Slice, thus:

> *The consumer market was once one where the tradition that Levi's relies on mattered. But it has become more aspirational and youth-focused. This meant that other denim brands, unencumbered by history, could quickly and easily define themselves within the new cultural currency and move in on the lucrative youth market* (as quoted by Grant, 2002).

Certain brands in the jeans market were not just losing out to the combat cult, however. Middle-of-the-road jeans, such as Levi's 501s, also found themselves stranded between the designer brands at the top end of the market and retailer own-brands, such as The Gap, at the mass market end, both taking sales away from them. Demographic factors have also made life a lot tougher. The core market, 18- to 25-year-olds, is declining in numbers in Europe as well as turning away from jeans as 'something dad wears'. In the UK, jeans sales overall fell by 14.3 per cent in 1998. In the UK and Europe Levi's suffered particularly badly, being so dependent on one brand, the 501s. Through the late 1980s and early 1990s, the 501s brand had shown rapid and satisfying growth and, unlike its competitors, Levi's had seen no reason to innovate or to spread its risk. It was so sure of its customers that it forgot to check how their needs and wants were changing as the market matured and to see how the competition was better meeting those needs and

wants. Effectively, Levi's was a one-product company offering no new or different 'looks' to its customers. In the UK market, Levi's further alienated some customers by refusing to supply 'non-approved' retailers such as supermarket chain Tesco with jeans. When Tesco started selling Levi's sourced on the grey market at reduced prices, this focused the consumer's attention on price and value for money.

In such a difficult environment, companies have to be alert to changes in the market and have strategies in place for dealing with them and even for survival. Part of Levi's problem was that it was not responsive enough. It was rather internally focused on 'doing very well what has always been done' (Heller, 1999). The US company, for instance, spent two years and $850m. reducing the time it took to get new products to the market from 15 months to 3 months and retail stock replenishment time down from three weeks to a target level of three days. The problem was that not only had nobody thought through the cost implications of offering that kind of service, but more fundamentally, while this systems development was going on, the company failed to pay due attention to the marketplace and sales just evaporated.

Once Levi's had identified its problems, it began to act, first with a restructuring. The post of UK marketing director was abolished and replaced with a regional marketing and development director for northern Europe (including the UK, Benelux countries, Norway and Sweden). In the UK, market research showed that lack of innovation was the key issue among the core 18- to 25-year-old market and furthermore that new products would bring back young customers.

Thus Levi Strauss began to take a more segmented approach. It introduced high-fashion hand-crafted jeans at the top end of the market to compete with the designer labels, retailing for about €300. In the middle of the market, innovations such as its 'Red Tab', 'Twisted' and 'Engineered' product ranges were designed to rekindle interest among fashionable youth. Early signs were promising. Grant (2002) reported that the Engineered range, as worn by opinion-leader Britney Spears, and the sponsorship of live music events had helped the brand to regain some street cred. At the bottom end of the market, it was planning to launch a low-priced product range retailing for about €45 (*c.* £27) in Europe, i.e. about 60 per cent of the price of the mainstream Levi's products, competing on price with competitors such as Lee and Wrangler. It might just bring back those customers who were buying the cut-price, grey market jeans from supermarkets. James Hobbs, account director at Taylor Nelson Sofres Fashion Trak, thinks that:

> *It's a smart move. Currently, sales of jeans at £45-plus account for only 8.5 per cent of the market, whereas £30-plus accounts for 24 per cent. So it triples their potential sales* (as quoted by Benady, 2002).

Overall, Levi Strauss hopes that by 2003 the combined effects of these moves will at least stabilise sales. It is a tall order: by June 2002, things were still looking gloomy. Over the previous 12 months, factory closures and job losses had continued in the interests of streamlining operations and cutting costs; the company had announced losses of some $80m.; and worldwide sales had fallen by a further 12 per cent. Whether it is doing enough still remains to be seen.

Sources: Barrett (1998), Benady (2002), Buckley (2002), Grant (2002), Heller (1999), Jardine (1999), Lee (1999), Munk (1999).

Questions

1 Into which cells of the Shell directional policy matrix would you place (a) Levi's 501s, (b) Levi's high-fashion hand-crafted jeans, and (c) The Gap's range of own-brand jeans? Justify your answer, stating clearly any assumptions that you are making.

2 What kind of aggressive or defensive strategy do you think the introduction of the low-priced €45 product range is? Why? What are the risks of this particular strategy?

3 What are the advantages and potential problems of replacing the UK marketing director with a regional marketing brand development director for northern Europe?

4 What can Levi's learn from its experiences and what impact might those lessons have on its future marketing strategies?

References for chapter 12

Abell, D. and Hammond, J. (1979), *Strategic Market Planning*, Prentice Hall.

Ansoff, H. (1957), 'Strategies for Diversification', *Harvard Business Review*, 25 (5), pp. 113–25.

Arnold, M. (2002), 'Is Taste the Weapon to See Off Ribena's Rivals?', *Marketing*, 21 March, p. 13.

Barrett, L. (1998), 'Hard-hit Levi's Cuts Top UK Role', *Marketing*, 22 October, p. 1.

Batchelor, C. (2001), 'Cendant May Sell NCP Arm for £1bn', *Financial Times*, 7 December, p. 27.

Benady, A. (2002), 'Jeans Group Unveils its Third Leg', *Financial Times*, 5 February, p. 18.

Bray, R. (2002), 'Internet Booking on the Increase', *Financial Times*, 12 February, p. 17.

Buckley, N. (2002), 'Levi Reports Loss of $80.9m', *Financial Times*, 21 June, p. 17.

Burt, T. and Ibison, D. (2002), 'Hino Motors Set for Alliance with Sweden's Scania', *Financial Times*, 19 March, p. 17.

Campbell, L. (1999), 'Why Unilever B Brands Must be Cast Aside', *Marketing*, 10 June, p. 13.

Carmichael, M. (2002), 'Move Over Britannia', *The Grocer*, 13 April, pp. 38–9.

Carter, A. (2002), 'Kodak's Promising Developments', *Money*, February, p. 39.

Cookson, C. (2001), 'Bioinformatics and Big Biology', *Financial Times*, 27 November, p. 2.

Cramb, G. (2002), 'Philips and Dell Agree on Global Alliance', *Financial Times*, 28 March, p. 32.

Derrick, S. (2001), 'Fast Company', *Growing Business*, December.

Done, K. (2001), 'Ryanair Plans Big Expansion at Frankfurt-Hahn', *Financial Times*, 23 November, p. 25.

Douglas, T. (2002), 'BBC3 – Are Many of Us Really Going to Watch it?', *Marketing Week*, 21 March, p. 17.

Dyer, G. (2001), 'The Power Shifts to Industry's Wunderkinds', *Financial Times*, 27 November, p. 5.

The Economist (2002), 'Towards the Wild Blue Yonder: Special Report', *The Economist*, 27 April, pp. 75–7.

Edwards, O. (2001), 'Flying High on the World Stage', *EuroBusiness*, November, pp. 62–3.

Financial Times (2001), 'Holderbank Lays New Foundations', *Financial Times*, 30 March, p. 20.

Foster, M. (1996), 'NCP Fights for its Space', *Management Today*, February, pp. 54–8.

Gamble, J. (2001), 'The Struggle to Get Nappies off the Ground', *Financial Times*, 31 May, p. 14.

Genna, A. (1997), 'What's Wrong with Sales Forecasts?', *Purchasing*, 5 June, pp. 20–1.

Grant, J. (2002), 'Can Levi's Engineer a Reversal of Fortunes?', *Marketing*, 18 April, p. 13.

The Grocer (2002a), 'Dr Oetker is Confident of Seizing Number One Spot in Frozen Pizza', *The Grocer*, 23 March, p. 8.

The Grocer (2002b), 'An Ice Cuppa Tea is Tickling the Tastebuds of the Iced Beverage Sector', *The Grocer*, 4 May, p. 64.

Gulati, R. (1998), 'Alliances and Networks', *Strategic Management Journal*, 19 (4), pp. 293–317.

Hardcastle, S. (2001), 'Yogurt and Pot Desserts', *The Grocer*, 21 April, pp. 33–6.

Hardcastle, S. (2002), 'Soft Drinks', *The Grocer*, 4 May, pp. 47–50.

Harnischfeger, U. (2002), 'Lufthansa Threatens to Start Budget Airline', *Financial Times*, 23 January, p. 29.

Harper, K. (2000), 'Labour's Transport Plan: Buses', *The Guardian*, 21 July, p. 1.4.

Heller, R. (1999), 'When Goliaths Start Wobbling', *Management Today*, June, p. 34.

Hirst, C. (2001), 'New Chapter at WH Smith', *The Independent*, 28 January, p. 7.

Hoare, S. (2002), 'The Man Who Went into Overdrive', *The Times*, 19 February, p. 9.

Hollinger, P. and Rawsthorn, A. (1999), 'WH Smith Books a Place in New Retailing Era', *Financial Times*, 25 May, p. 21.

Jameson, A. (2002), 'Venture Capitalists Set to Bet on Parking', *The Times*, 7 May, p. 37.

Jardine, A. (1999), 'Life for Denim in Combat Era', *Marketing*, 4 March, p. 19.

Jones, D. (2001), 'Family-run Snowdon Water Scheme Will Create 30 Jobs', *Daily Post*, 21 November, p. 2.

Kingsley-Jones, M. and Duffy, P. (2001), 'Over the Precipice', *Flight International*, 16–22 October, pp. 40–69.

Lee, J. (1999), 'Can Levi's Ever Be Cool Again?', *Marketing*, 15 April, pp. 28–9.

Liu, B. (2001), 'Coca-Cola and Disney Plan Drinks Venture', *Financial Times*, 1 March, p. 30.

McDonald, M. (1989), *Marketing Plans*, Butterworth-Heinemann.

Marketing (2002), 'Unilever Aims to Revamp Lipton Ice Tea for UK Market', *Marketing* 14 March, p. 3.

Marketing Week/CIM (2001), 'Harry Potter', *Marketing Week/CIM Effectiveness Awards 2001*, pp. 6–7.

Mazur, L. (2002), 'Innovation and Branding Make a Powerful Mix', *Marketing*, 28 March, p. 16.

Mentzer, J. and Bienstock, C. (1998), *Sales Forecasting Management*, Sage.

Mowbray, S. (2002), 'Dr Oetker Determined to be a Major UK Player', *The Grocer*, 9 March, p. 6.

Munk, N. (1999), 'How Levi's Trashed a Great American Brand', *Fortune*, 12 April, pp. 82–90.

Murden, T. (2001), 'Hi-fi Boss Who Strikes a Very Different Note', *Sunday Times*, 17 June, p. 7.

O'Donnell, J. (2001), 'Insiders Show How to Raise Venture Capital', *The Sunday Times*, 18 February, p. 3.16.

Oldfield, C. (2000), 'Unilever Goes for a Cut of Razor Market', *Sunday Times*, 10 September, p. 2.

Peachey, P. (2002), 'Ryanair "Misled" Public over Flight Destinations', *The Independent*, 13 March, p. 4.

Porter, M. (1979), 'How Competitive Forces Shape Strategy', *Harvard Business Review*, 57 (2), pp. 137–45.

Serwer, A. (2002), 'Kodak: In the Noose', *Fortune*, 4 February, pp. 147–8.

Singh, S. (2001), 'Gillette in $200m Mach3 Successor Launch', *Marketing Week*, 1 November, p. 5.

Style, S. (1999), 'Step Right in here for the Chocoholic's Dream Shop', *Greater Zurich supplement to Financial Times*, 29 June, p. IV.

Sumner-Smith, D. (2002), 'Video Minnow Must Take on the Industry Giants to Grow', *Sunday Times*, 17 February, p. 12.

Swann, C. (2002), 'Incubators Help Britain Keep Ahead', *Financial Times*, 1 May, p. 2.

Taylor, P. (2001), 'Two Cultures are Merging', *Financial Times*, 27 November, p. 5.

Turner, M. (2002), 'Cadbury's Clean Conscience', *Financial Times*, 18 February, p. 18.

Urry, M. (2001), 'Brand That Cornered the Market in Yoghurts', *Financial Times*, 13 October, p. 8.

Wall, M. (2001), 'www.holidayautos.com', *Sunday Times*, 8 July, p. 4.

Warwickshire Choice (2001), 'They Made it in Britain', *Warwickshire Choice*, July/August.

services and non-profit marketing

LEARNING OBJECTIVES

This chapter will help you to:

1 define the characteristics that differentiate services from other products and outline their impact on marketing;

2 develop an extended marketing mix of 7Ps that takes the characteristics of services into account and allows comprehensive marketing strategies to be developed for services;

3 understand the importance and impact of service quality and productivity issues;

4 understand the special characteristics of non-profit organisations within the service sector, and the implications for their marketing activities.

Introduction

The focus of this chapter is on the marketing of services, whether sold for profit or not. Service products cover a wide range of applications. In the profit-making sector, services marketing includes travel and tourism, banking and insurance, and personal and professional services ranging from accountancy, legal services and business consultancy through to hairdressing and garden planning and design. In the non-profit-making sector, services marketing applications include education, medicine and charities through to various aspects of government activity that need to be 'sold' to the public.

Marketing these kinds of intangible service products is somewhat different from marketing physical products. The major marketing principles discussed in this book, segmenting the market, the need for research, sensible design of the marketing mix and the need for creativity, strategic thinking and innovation, are, of course, universally applicable, regardless of the type of product involved. Where the difference arises is in the detailed design and implementation of the marketing mix. There are several special factors that provide additional challenges for the services marketer.

This chapter will, therefore, examine in detail the special aspects of services that differentiate them from physical products. It will then look at the issues involved in designing the services marketing mix and the marketing management challenges arising from its implementation. Finally, the whole area of marketing services in the non-profit sector will be considered.

eg Hoteliers want every visitor to thoroughly enjoy an overnight stay with them. If there is a mismatch between customers' expectations and their experiences, if they are unhappy with the room, service or choice in the hotel, they may not make a return visit. As discussed throughout this book, most businesses rely on repeat business. This requires a considerable attention to detail on the part of the hotelier, for example communicating the location of the hotel, providing car park security, levels of service in the front office, and not least creating the ambience and ensuring the functionality of the room itself.

Increasingly, the type of services offered are being targeted at specific customer groups. The Marriott chain is testing a facility where business travellers can use a central hotel printer from their room (Bray, 2002). The next major phase of development will include broadband and wireless connectivity to the bedroom, videoconferencing units, high-definition television, wireless smart-card keys, full corporate office systems, and two-way video devices (Moore, 2001). Others are investing in enhancing keep fit facilities, not just with a fitness suite, but with a fitness delivery service which allows a personal trainer to be delivered to your room along with any equipment for accompanied workouts. Others are offering 20-minute yoga sessions with leading instructors through cable television in their rooms. Yoga is said to be an especially effective treatment for jet lag (Lewis, 2002). Although there is a trade-off between price and the value offered, the experience must be up to scratch. Again, with the impact of IT and its ability to create and update a guest database, the accommodation experience will soon become far more personalised. Your preferred room temperature, a television that lists your favourite programmes and videos, a menu displayed on the television tailored to your tastes, a mini bar with your choice of drinks, a room with your preferred style and location (type of bed, floor covering, smoking etc.) are just some of the variables that a database could flag up to make your experience that bit more special. Oh yes, and all this would be in your native language (Warren, 1999)!

Perspectives on service markets

Services are not a homogeneous group of products. There is wide variety within the services category, in terms of both the degree of service involved and the type of service product offered. Nevertheless, there are some general characteristics, common to many service products, that differentiate them as a genre from physical goods. This section, therefore, explores the criteria by which service products can be classified, and then goes on to look at the special characteristics of services and their implications for marketing.

■ Classifying services

There are few pure services. In reality, many product 'packages' involve a greater or lesser level of service. Products can be placed along a spectrum, with virtually pure personal service involving few, if any, props at one end, and pure product that involves little or no service at the other. Most products do have some combination of physical good and service, as shown in Figure 13.1. The purchase of a chocolate bar, for example, involves little or no service other than the involvement of a checkout or till operator. The purchase of a gas appliance will involve professional fitting, and thus is a combination of physical and service product. A new office computer system could similarly involve installation and initial training. A visit to a theme park or theatre could involve some limited support products, such as guides and gifts, while the main product purchased is the experience itself. Finally, a visit to a psychiatrist or a hairdresser may involve a couch, a chair and some minor allied props such as an interview checklist or a hair-dryer. The real product purchased here, however, is the personal service manufactured by the service deliverer, the psychiatrist or the hairdresser.

■ Special characteristics of service markets

Five main characteristics have been identified as being unique to service markets (see e.g. Sasser *et al.*, 1978; Cowell, 1984).

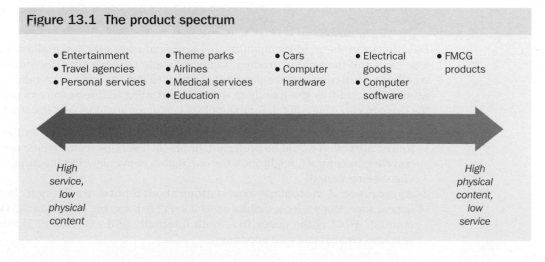

Figure 13.1 The product spectrum

- Entertainment
- Travel agencies
- Personal services

- Theme parks
- Airlines
- Medical services
- Education

- Cars
- Computer hardware

- Electrical goods
- Computer software

- FMCG products

High service, low physical content

High physical content, low service

Lack of ownership

Perhaps the most obvious aspect of a service product is that no goods change hands, as such, and therefore there is no transfer of ownership of anything. A legal transaction does still take place; an insurance company agrees to provide certain benefits as long as the premiums are paid and the terms and conditions of the policy are met. A car rental company allows the customer full use of a vehicle for an agreed length of time, subject to some restraints on named drivers and type of usage, but the ownership of the vehicle remains with the rental company. A train seat can be reserved for a journey, but it is not owned. A subscription to the National Trust provides rights of access free of charge but no actual share in the ownership of its properties. The access, use or experience of the service is, therefore, often time specific, usage specific and subject to contractual terms and conditions.

The lack of ownership raises the issue of the transient nature of the purchase. Most service products involve some kind of 'experience' for the customer. This might be surrounded by props, for example a stage, lighting and sound systems, a lecture theatre, an insurance policy, a vehicle or a room, but these only serve to enhance or degrade the experience of the service. The faulty fuel gauge which means that the hire car runs out of petrol in the most remote location, the hotel room next to the building site, the ineffective microphone at a concert all spoil the memory of the service consumed.

Intangibility

A visit to a retail store reveals an inviting display of products to purchase. These products can be examined, touched, tried on, sampled, smelt or listened to. All this can help the customer to examine what is on offer and to make choices between competing brands. The consumer regularly uses the whole range of senses to assist decision-making, enabling them to assess what is being offered, to weigh up value, and to develop the confidence to act. This is especially important before the purchase is made, but even after the sale the product can be assessed in terms of its use, its durability and whether it lives up to general expectations. If there is a fault with a physical product, it can be returned or exchanged.

With service products, it is far more difficult to use the senses in the same way as a means of making a purchase decision because the actual service experience can only take place after that decision has been made. The heart of a service is the experience created for the customer, whether individually as with a personal service such as dentistry or hairdressing, or as a group experience, such as a lecture, a show or a flight. In many cases, once the purchase decision has been made, all the customer will receive is a ticket, a confirmation of booking or some promise of future benefit. The service experience itself is intangible, and is only delivered after the customer is committed to the purchase.

> **eg** The Scottish Tourist Board ran a 'reawaken your senses' campaign to promote spring breaks. The campaign attempted to capture the intangible nature of the tourist experience by concentrating on visual imagery, such as fish, sea spray and scenery. The problem for this type of promotion is that it is difficult to distinguish the Scottish product offering from the many others available in equally scenic locations (http://www.visitscotland.com).

Despite the problem of intangibility, the potential customer can make some kind of prior assessment of the service product. Using available tangible cues, the customer can assess whether a particular service provider is likely to deliver what is wanted. The actual cues used and the priority given to them will vary according to the customer's particular needs at the time. In choosing a hotel, for example, a customer might look at the following:

1 *Location.* If the customer is on holiday, then perhaps a hotel near to the beach or other tourist attraction would be preferred, or one in a very peaceful scenic setting. A business traveller, in contrast, might look for one that is convenient for the airport or close to the client being visited.
2 *Appearance.* A customer's expectations about a hotel are likely to be affected by its appearance. Does it look shabby or well kept? Is it too big or too small? Does it look welcoming? What is the decor like, both internally and externally? Do the rooms seem spacious enough and well appointed?

3 *Additional services*. The customer might be concerned about the peripheral aspects of the service on offer. The tourist who will be spending two weeks in a hotel might be interested in the variety of bars and restaurants provided; hairdressing, laundry or crèche facilities; shopping and postal services; or the nightlife. The business traveller might be more concerned about car parking, shuttle buses to the airport, or fax and telephone provision.

4 *Customer handling*. If the potential customer contacts the hotel for further information or to make a reservation, the quality of the handling they receive might affect the purchase decision. Courtesy and friendliness will make a good impression, as will a prompt and accurate response to the query. This kind of efficiency implies a commitment to staff training and good operating systems to assist easy access to relevant information and the speedy processing of bookings.

marketing *in action*

The multiplex: Oscar winner or turkey?

A visit to the cinema has been revolutionised over recent years, and further changes are still expected as efforts continue to be made to upgrade the customer experience. It is not very long ago that going to the cinema meant a choice of one main feature and a 'B' film and that was all. Stern-faced usherettes guided you with their torches towards a seat (usually the one you did not want), then they doubled up as ice-cream sellers during the interval (until they ran out of stock). Parking was usually non-existent, as cinemas were located in town centres, and queuing was the norm for more popular shows as no advance booking was possible. The seating was not particularly comfortable, and the whole episode was not very customer friendly. It is perhaps not surprising that cinema audiences declined over many years as people switched to new leisure pursuits. In the late 1940s, around 1.6 billion tickets were sold each year, but this had shrunk to 54 million by 1984 (Rushe, 2001). Television and video were thought to be the culprits behind the dramatic decline.

Since the opening of the first multiplex in Milton Keynes in 1985, the decline has stopped as marketing strategies have become far more oriented towards the modern consumer's needs. Cinema entered a second golden age that is still with us. This is very evident from a visit to a multiplex cinema, a format which has been a major influence in the rise in cinema attendances in the UK. A multiplex is a large building containing

Multiscreen cinemas offer a variety of films for all age ranges along with opportunities to buy food, confectionery and drinks. Trailers and posters will encourage the customer to come back soon to see the next blockbuster.

Source: Odeon Cinemas/Red Consultancy.

a number of small, individual cinemas around a central circulation area. A multiplex can thus show 12 or more different films at any one time and can seat up to 3,500 customers in total. The size of the individual cinemas varies, so that, for example, blockbusting new releases can be put into bigger ones or even be shown in two cinemas at once, reflecting the expected popularity of the film. The seating in all the cinemas is invariably of a high standard.

Despite the undoubted success of the multiplex format in offering choice and an experience that cannot be

replicated on a small screen, there is growing concern over how long the rapid development of new sites can continue. Between 1988 and 1991 around 14 sites per year were added, stopped by the recession in the early 1990s. The period 1992–95 saw growth again, but at a rate of six sites per year. Since 1996, however, the number of new multiplexes has risen to 25 per year (Dodona, 2001). Warner Village, UGC (formerly Virgin) and Cine UK have added the most, followed by Odeon, UCI and Showcase. There are now 10 UK cities with more than 50 multiplex screens within a 15–20 minute drive

▶

of the city centres although some smaller towns still have no provision (Cox, 2002).

The impact of multiplex cinemas might not yet have been fully played out, as they have become part of the property development business. The concept has expanded into multi-leisure parks (MLPs) that are now taking prime edge-of-town sites with plenty of parking, with the multiplex as the anchor tenant, a bowling alley and a choice of restaurants making the sites 'one-stop shop entertainment experiences'. Following the US lead, there are 170 sites already in the UK and more are planned. Star City outside Birmingham, for example, has a 36-screen cinema, 12 restaurants and shops. These sites are attracting leisure trade that previously used the city centre. Town centres can attract between 15 and 20 per cent of their income from the night-time economy, so a competitive response is likely, probably through efforts to create a café, pub and club culture to draw people back (McCarthy, 2002).

There is an alternative view, however, that suggests that significant growth in demand for multiplex cinemas is over, and in 2001 four actually closed (in Dundee, Romford and two in Manchester). The cinema market is not in decline, but it may be oversupplied thus affecting individual site viability. This is paralleled in the United States where an oversupply led to rationalisation (Rushe, 2001). Estimates vary about how many seats are needed to make a profit, some suggesting that a seat must be sold between three and four hundred times a year to make money. Some multiplexes are struggling to reach 200 times. As most of the costs are fixed, an empty seat is lost revenue for ever but with the same cost of providing it. Dodona (2001) estimates that by 2005 there will be nearly 3,400 screens, a growth of 1,400 on current levels, so it is critical for the multiplex operators that audiences should continue to rise. The real victims could, however, be the remaining traditional cinemas and those multiplexes that either are poorly sited or not modernising further. Warner Village is building five new multiplexes across London and is giving priority to wider seats, better views and special effects in an effort to build brand loyalty (Rogers, 2001). Others are improving booking systems including online reservations and pre-booking seat allocations. The aim now is not just to attract customers, but also to build loyalty.

Sources: Cox (2002); Dodona (2001); McCarthy (2002); Rogers (2001); Rushe (2001).

In a wider sense, marketing and brand building are also important, of course. These help to raise awareness of a hotel chain's existence and positioning, and differentiate it from the competition. These communicate the key benefits on offer and thus help the customer to decide whether this is the kind of hotel they are looking for, developing their expectations. Advertising, glossy brochures and other marketing communications techniques can help to create and reinforce the potential customer's perception of location, appearance, additional services and customer handling, as well as the brand imagery. Strong marketing and branding also help to link a chain of hotels that might be spread worldwide, giving the customer some reassurance of consistency and familiarity. A business traveller in a strange city can seek out a known hotel name, such as Novotel, Holiday Inn or Campanile, and be fairly certain about what they are purchasing.

eg Pizza Hut's menu, decor, servers, order processing, equipment, cooking procedures, etc. are all standardised (or allow minor variations and adaptations for local conditions), creating a consistent and familiar experience for the customer all over the world. Customers thus have a strong tangible impression of the character of Pizza Hut, what to expect of it, and what it delivers.

One of the greatest problems of intangibility is that it is difficult to assess quality both during and after the service has been experienced. Customers will use a combination of criteria, both objective and subjective, to judge their level of satisfaction, although it is often based on impressions, memories and expectations. Different customers attach significance to different things. The frequent business traveller might be extremely annoyed by check-in delays or the noise from the Friday night jazz cabaret, while the holidaymaker might grumble about the beach being 20 minutes' walk away rather than the 5 minutes promised in the brochure. Memories fade over time, but some bad ones, such as a major service breakdown or a confrontation with service staff, will remain.

Perishability

Services are manufactured at the same time as they are consumed. A lecturer paces the lecture theatre creating a service experience that is immediately either consumed or slept through by the students. Manchester United, Real Madrid or AC Milan manufacture sporting entertainment that either thrills, bores or frustrates their fans as they watch the match live. Similarly, audiences at Covent Garden or La Scala absorb live opera as it unfolds before them. With both sport and entertainment, it is likely that the customer's enjoyment of the 'product' is heightened by the unpredictability of live performance and the audience's own emotional involvement in what is going on. This highlights another peculiarity of service products: customers are often directly involved in the production process and the synergy between them and the service provider affects the quality of the experience. A friend might tell you, 'Yes, it was a brilliant concert. The band were on top form and the atmosphere was great!' To create such a complete experience, the band and their equipment do have to perform to the expected standard, the lighting and sound crews have to get it right on the night, and the venue has to have adequate facilities and efficient customer-handling processes. The atmosphere, however, is created by the interaction between performer and audience and can inspire the performer to deliver a better experience. The customer therefore has to be prepared to give as well as take, and make their own contribution to the quality of the service product.

Perishability thus means that a service cannot be manufactured and stored either before or after the experience. Manufacture and consumption are simultaneous. While a hotel is, of course, a permanent structure with full-time staff, its service product is only being delivered when there is a customer present to purchase and receive it. The product is perishable in the sense that if a room is not taken on a particular night, then it is a completely lost opportunity. The same is true of most service products, for example if a dentist cannot fill the appointment book for a particular day, then that revenue-earning opportunity is lost for ever. In situations where demand is reasonably steady, it is relatively easy to plan capacity and adapt the organisation to meet the expected demand pattern.

eg The Tussauds group owns the Alton Towers theme park in Staffordshire. Predicting capacity and occupancy were essential elements of the analysis justifying a £40m. investment in a new hotel and water theme complex. The new 216-room hotel, Calypso Springs, and the first covered water amusement park in the UK will provide many new features to attract customers. The current 175-room hotel, however, finds that its occupancy fluctuates from 100 per cent in the high season to just 19 per cent in the low season. It is expected that an all-year-round facility will enable occupancy levels to be raised in the shoulder months and in the low season when the outdoor climate is less predictable (Reece, 2002).

Even where demand does fluctuate, as long as it is fairly predictable managers can plan to raise or reduce service capacity accordingly. A larger plane or an additional performance might be provided to cater for short-term demand increases. It can be more difficult, however, if there are very marked fluctuations in demand that might result in facilities lying idle for a long time or in severe overcapacity. The profitability of companies servicing peak-hour transport demands can be severely affected because vehicles and rolling stock are unused for the rest of the day. Airlines too face seasonal fluctuations in demand.

eg Balkanair mothballs a number of its holiday jets over the winter, as the Black Sea resorts in Bulgaria virtually close down and there is little demand from foreign tourists. Sports and entertainment can be hit by unpredictable demand fluctuations. A football team that hits a run of bad luck can see its crowd fall to 5,000 but still have to maintain a 50,000-seater stadium. More drastically, a West End show that gets universally bad reviews might have to end its run early because it cannot fill the theatre on a regular enough basis.

The concept of perishability means that a range of marketing strategies is needed to try to even out demand and bring capacity handling into line with it. These strategies might include pricing or product development to increase demand during quieter periods or to divert it from busier ones, or better scheduling and forecasting through the booking and reservation system. Similarly, the capacity and service delivery system can be adapted to meet peaks or troughs in demand through such strategies as part-time workers, increased mechanisation or cooperation with other service providers. These will be considered in more detail later (see pp. 446 *et seq.*).

Inseparability

Many physical products are produced well in advance of purchase and consumption, and production staff rarely come into direct contact with the customer. Often, production and consumption are distanced in both space and time, connected only by the physical distribution system. Sales forecasts provide important guidelines for production schedules. If demand rises unexpectedly, opportunities might well exist to increase production or to reduce stockholding to meet customer needs.

As has already been said, with service products, however, the involvement of the customer in the service experience means that there can be no prior production, no storage and that consumption takes place simultaneously with production. The service delivery, therefore, cannot be separated from the service providers and thus the fourth characteristic of service products is inseparability. This means that the customer often comes into direct contact with the service provider(s), either individually, as with a doctor, or as part of a team of providers, as with air travel. The team includes reservations clerks, check-in staff, aircrew and perhaps transfer staff. In an airline, the staff team has a dual purpose. Clearly, they have to deliver their aspect of the service efficiently, but they also have to interact with the customer in the delivery of the service. An uncooperative check-in clerk might not provide the customer's desired seat, but in contrast, friendly and empathic cabin crew can alleviate the fear of a first-time flyer. The service provider can thus affect the quality of the service delivered and the manner in which it is delivered.

> **eg** British Airways (BA) is training all of its 13,500 cabin staff to be more aware of other cultures. The airline carries people from many different nationalities (over 60 per cent of its passengers are not from the UK) and it feels that it is important for cabin crew to think about different cultures and how they might behave when on board. Handling sensitive issues around food and drink can be especially important for cabin crew, for instance. How different cultures handle conflict situations with other passengers or crew can also vary. In addition to training, BA is looking to employ more staff from ethnic minority backgrounds. The recruitment drive improved numbers by 14 per cent from an average of just 85 UK-based flight attendants and 3,000 extra staff worldwide from a diverse range of ethnic backgrounds (http://www.ba.com).

While the delivery of a personal service can be controlled, since there are fewer opportunities for outside interference, the situation becomes more complex when other customers are experiencing service at the same time. The 'mass service experience' means that other customers can potentially affect the perceived quality of that experience, positively or negatively. As mentioned earlier, the enjoyment of the atmosphere at a sporting event or a concert, for example, depends on the emotional charge generated by a large number of like-minded individuals. In other situations, however, the presence of many other customers can negatively affect aspects of the service experience. If the facility or the staff do not have the capacity or the ability to handle larger numbers than forecast, queues, overcrowding and dissatisfaction can soon result. Although reservation or prebooking can reduce the risk, service providers can still be caught out. Airlines, for instance, routinely overbook flights deliberately, on the basis that not all booked passengers will actually turn up. Sometimes, however, they miscalculate and end up with more passengers than the flight can actually accommodate and have to offer free air miles, cash or other benefits to encourage some passengers to switch to a later flight.

What the other customers are like also affects the quality of the experience. This reflects the segmentation policy of the service provider. If a relatively undifferentiated approach is offered, there are all sorts of potential conflicts (or benefits) from mixing customers who are perhaps looking for different benefits. A hotel, for example, might have problems if families with young children are mixed with guests on an over-50s holiday. Where possible, therefore, the marketer should carefully target segments to match the service product being offered.

Finally, the behaviour of other customers can be positive, leading to new friends, comradeship and enjoyable social interaction, or it can be negative if it is rowdy, disruptive or even threatening. Marketers prefer, of course, to try to develop the positive aspects. Social evenings for new package holiday arrivals, name badges on coach tours, and warm-up acts to build atmosphere at live shows all help to break the ice. To prevent disruptive behaviour, the service package might have to include security measures and clearly defined and enforced 'house rules' such as those found at soccer matches.

---

eg Following on from the cabin crew example earlier, anyone who has experienced rowdy behaviour on an aircraft or at a sports match will know how distressing the experience can be and how it can detract from the overall willingness to repeat purchase. With airlines, cabin crew are in the front line of handling abuse, yet it is surprising that over two-thirds of airlines do not train their crew in how to handle such behaviour (Fox, 2001). Hearts football club in Scotland wants to be regarded as a family club, so it takes a strong line on hooligans and on drunk and disorderly behaviour. Six so-called fans were banned for life for their misdemeanours. One shouted out Republican chants during a minute's silence and five were thrown out for abusive and drunken behaviour (Cameron, 2002). The lesson from these examples is clear. The selling organisation must take responsibility for countering disruptive customers through its policy and deeds, and staff must be trained to deal with the incidents that occur all too frequently.

The implications of inseparability for marketing strategy will be considered on pp. 443 *et seq.*

Heterogeneity

With simultaneous production and consumption and the involvement of service staff and other customers, it can be difficult to standardise the service experience as planned. Heterogeneity means that each service experience is likely to be different, depending on the interaction between the customer and other customers, service staff, and other factors such as time, location and the operating procedures. The problems of standardising the desired service experience are greater when there is finite capacity and the service provided is especially labour intensive. The maxim 'when the heat is on the service is gone' reflects the risk of service breakdown when demand puts the system under pressure, especially if it is unexpected. This might mean no seats available on the train, delays in serving meals on a short-haul flight, or a queue in the bank on a Friday afternoon.

---

eg Virgin Trains has been struggling to make a success of its rail service. It is a tough challenge, with one in five trains running late or cancelled, and yet 75 per cent of the problems are out of Virgin's control, resting with the railway infrastructure. If the track or signalling is not up to scratch, or the non-Virgin locomotive in front breaks down, then it is difficult to offer a reliable service. With 28 million passenger journeys a year, there is plenty of scope for the complaining passenger and ironically, although many other train operators are also failing in service reliability, the high profile of Virgin often means that it is subject to more complaints.

An internal report on a typical day on Connex South Central in 2001 was alleged to contain details of 49 cancelled trains, 276 missed stations, and only 30 per cent of trains running on time (Syal, 2001). Most of the problems were due to driver shortages, but broken signals, technical difficulties with the rolling stock, and even a fatality at Clapham Junction all played their part. Such is the nature of heterogeneity for the rail operators. As this example shows, not all service breakdowns are caused by the service provider. Technical problems with a train are the responsibility of a rail service operator, but not the fog, signal breakdowns or problems with catering services at stations.

Some of the heterogeneity in the service cannot be planned for or avoided, but quality assurance procedures can minimise the worst excesses of service breakdown. This can be done by designing in 'failsafes', creating mechanisms to spot problems quickly and to resolve them early before they cause a major service breakdown. Universities, for example, have numerous quality assurance procedures to cover academic programmes, staffing and support procedures that involve self-assessment, student evaluation and external subject and quality assessment.

eg Mystery shoppers are widely used to monitor service levels and the service experience provided. They eat at restaurants to check food, service and facilities, stay in hotels, drink in pubs, travel on planes, and visit cinemas, health clubs and garages. The lucky ones even get to go on expensive foreign holidays. The feedback provides front-line commentary and however revealing, often shows companies the difference between the service promise and the reality of what is delivered. Most of the time, the focus is on the overall experience rather than individual performance, although at times staff are also the focus of attention. Normally, the mystery shopper is given a checklist of points to watch out for and they have to be skilled in classifying and memorising elements of the delivered service. To be effective, the mystery shopper must be believable and natural and thus cannot go round with a checklist on a clipboard (McLuhan, 2002). So next time you are in Burger King or Pret à Manger, to name but two, you could be next to a shopper on a mission.

Management therefore has to develop ways of reducing the impact of heterogeneity. To help in that process, they need to focus on operating systems, procedures and staff training in order to ensure consistency. New lecturers, for example, might be required to undertake a special induction programme to help them learn teaching skills, preparing materials and handling some of the difficulties associated with disruptive students. Managers have to indicate clearly what they expect of staff in terms of the desired level of service. This must cover not only compliance with procedures in accordance with training, but also staff attitudes and the manner in which they deal with customers.

eg The Welsh Tourist Board (http://www.visitwales.com) operates a quality assurance scheme that establishes the minimum standards that a tourist might expect when visiting or holidaying in Wales. Inspectors examine all aspects of the accommodation before awarding a star category. These range from five stars for exceptional quality and exemplary service to one star for a fair to good standard of furnishings and adequate service and guest care. The scheme extends to activity holidays and self-catering accommodation, and is designed to provide some standardisation in an inherently non-standard holiday experience for tourists.

The next section looks in more detail at the impact of the particular characteristics of service products on the design and implementation of the marketing programme.

Services marketing management

So far, this chapter has looked at the characteristics of service products in a very general way. This section looks further at the implications of those characteristics for marketers in terms of formulating strategy, developing and measuring quality in the service product and issues of training and productivity.

■ Services marketing strategy

The traditional marketing mix, consisting of the 4Ps, forms the basis of the structure of this book. For service products, however, additional elements of the marketing mix are necessary to reflect the special characteristics of services marketing. Shown in Figure 13.2, these are:

■ *people*: whether service providers or customers who participate in the production and delivery of the service experience;

■ *physical evidence*: the tangible cues that support the main service product. These will include facilities, the infrastructure and the products used to deliver the service;

Figure 13.2 The services marketing mix

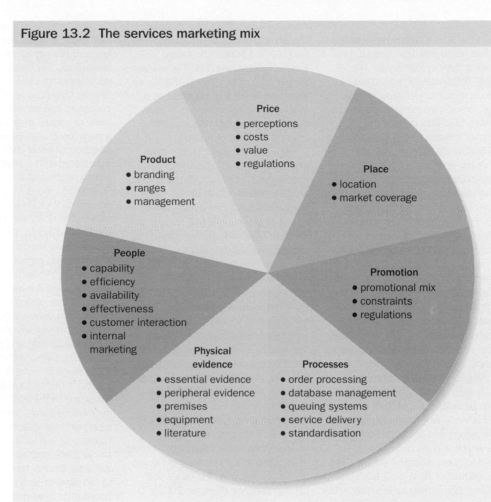

■ *processes*: the operating processes that take the customer through from ordering to the manufacture and delivery of the service.

Any of these extra marketing mix elements can enhance or detract from the customer's overall experience when consuming the service. However, despite the special considerations, the purpose of designing an effective marketing mix remains the same whether for services or physical products. The marketer is still trying to create a differentiated, attractive proposition for customers, ensuring that whatever is offered meets their needs and expectations.

All seven of the services marketing mix elements will now be considered in turn.

corporate social responsibility *in action*

A bloody theme park!

Taking measures to protect the environment is increasingly an area in which government and industry are expected to assume leadership and responsibility. From a government perspective, the needs of wider society, for employment, social stability and welfare, along with national prosperity have to be balanced against the preservation of a cultural and natural heritage and sustainable land use. Somehow it appears to be going wrong in Romania, where the government is actually promoting the destruction of an area of Transylvania renowned for its beauty, ancient oak forests and cultural heritage. And for what? A Dracula theme park experience in a country that has hardly been touched by the Hollywood legend.

Better-informed readers will know, of course, that Dracula never existed as such, but the character created by Bram Stoker was based on Vlad Tepes, a fifteenth-century ruler who shot to fame for impaling over 1,000

▶

Turks after a particularly nasty battle. His real name was Vlad Dracul, Dracul meaning Devil in Romanian. The 'Tepes' (impaler) was added later for obvious reasons. Hollywood added the fangs, blood drinking and associated niceties. Vlad was born in the medieval fortress city of Sighisoara, a UNESCO world heritage site which the Romanian government has undertaken to protect.

The project itself will initially develop 40 hectares of land, expanding to 60 in phase 2. It will cost around £30m. and should be ready for tourists by 2004. Castle Dracula will be the centrepiece, housing a judgement chamber, vampire den and alchemy laboratory. Included will be a mock torture room with stakes and knives, folk workshops for vampire protecting armour, a vampire fashion house and the rides will have vampire themes, bringing a whole new meaning to 'The House of Horror'. The restaurants will have such delicacies as 'blood pudding' and 'dish of brains' and for those who are brave enough, there are on-site motels. Linked to the park will be a golf course, campsite, 700-bed hotel, souvenir shops, beer halls and a ballroom for 2,000 dancers. Something for everybody, but not ecotourism (Moore Ede, 2002).

The park is expected to create around 3,000 jobs and is planned to generate $21m. per year from 1 million visitors. It is a poor region in a poor country with a quality of life that has been likened to Namibia and Libya (Douglas-Home, 2001). The theme park offers jobs in an area with 17 per cent unemployment, and the chance to buy shares in the venture, with 100 shares costing about £20, one-third the average monthly wage.

The company created to develop the park, Fondul Pentru Dezvoltare Turistica Sighisoara (FPDTS), will be 99 per cent owned by the Sighisoara municipality but it is intended as a profit-making enterprise. It is also argued that the city will be restored after many years of neglect.

From a government perspective, what better way for the Ministry of Tourism to start to rebuild the brand image of Romania, which for many Europeans is off the tourism scale? Although the Transylvania region has much to offer with fortified churches, castles, painted monasteries and unspoiled beauty, it is difficult to reach, about five hours by road from the capital Bucharest, it has little high standard tourism infrastructure such as hotels and restaurants, no effective waste disposal system and no service tradition as a result of the Communist era. Dracula could change all that, however, even though Dracula films were not legal until 1989 and the Stoker book was not published in Romanian until 1992. A 1973 'Dracula: Truth and Legend' tour disappointed many foreigners as most of the time was spent tracing the life of Vlad, rather than the fangs and cape experience (George, 2002). The planned theme park would address many of the issues of infrastructure over the next few years and give the tourists what they really want.

The more of an outcry there is in Western Europe, the less likely it is that the project will, at least in the short term, succeed. At least Walt Disney built on the outskirts of Los Angeles, not on the site of a rare medieval city that would all but be destroyed by the development under the banner of 'modernisation'. The

oak forest is protected by Romanian law and the city by its international obligations. For Western investors and developers it will be a dilemma. Should they pursue the development contracts and be associated with the park, or should they indicate that it is a park too many? Some may even question whether they want to be associated with a park that glorifies blood, death and the macabre. The Romanian view is clear, 'This is a government project. No one can tell us what to do in our own country' (as quoted by George, 2002).

Ultimately, economics could doom the park, and perhaps that is another reason why Western developers have been coy about investing. To succeed in any theme park a developer needs access to a constant flow of tourists, good infrastructure, an all-year-round congenial climate and proximity to a major city. Sighisoara meets none of these requirements. It also needs around 1 million tourists per year, and according to the business plan, 75 per cent will be living within 80 km. The local potential visitors are old, rurally based and few have a car or the money to pay the expected $25 entrance fee. Will international tourists flock in? It would have to be a very sophisticated package to draw people in, given the plethora of other theme park holidays available across Europe and beyond. The danger is that the low development budget will mean that it is tacky and cheap. Even allowing for the low cost of building in Romania, Castle Dracula has a budget of around $2m. compared with $200m. for some similar experiences in the USA. Perhaps Dracula should be left where he belongs after all – in Hollywood.

Sources: Douglas-Home (2001), George (2002), Moore Ede (2002).

Product

From a supplier's perspective, many services can be treated like any other physical product in a number of ways. The supplier develops a range of products, each of which represents profit-earning opportunities. A hotel company might treat each of its hotels as a separate product with its own unique product management requirements arising from its location, the state of the building and its facilities, local competition, and its strengths and weaknesses compared with others in the area. These products might, of course, be grouped into product lines and SBUs based on similarities and differences between them, just as physical products can be.

Many of the product concepts and the decisions concerning them that were discussed in Chapter 6 apply equally to services and physical products. Positioning, branding, developing a mix, designing new services and managing the product life cycle are all relevant.

Product development. Product development in some service situations can be complex as it involves 'packaging' otherwise separate elements into a service product. Therefore a holiday company may need to work with airlines, hotels and local tour companies to blend a package for the target segment. From a consumer perspective, any failure in any part of the system will be regarded as a criticism of the holiday company, even though air traffic delays or faulty plumbing may not be directly under the company's control. At a regional and national level, government and private companies may work together to develop new attractions and infrastructure for tourists.

eg

China is emerging as an international tourist destination, although there is still a need for considerable product development and many tourists' degree of prior knowledge is very limited. Many tourists' images are drawn from the media, from films such as *The Last Emperor* as well as the popular press, but beyond the Great Wall, the terracotta army, the Forbidden City and Tiananmen Square the level of knowledge is poor and the general impression is not favourable (Richards, 2001). Thus product development is needed to ensure that new visitor attractions are made accessible, that the transport infrastructure improves and that the hotels outside the main centres reach international standards. This will especially be a challenge in Tibet which is about to open its doors to an expected 5.6 million tourists over the next five years, attracted by the mountainous scenery and its 'spiritual' connotations (Barton, 2001).

Price

Because services are intangible, their pricing can be very difficult to set and to justify. The customer is not receiving anything that can be touched or otherwise physically experienced, so it can be hard for them to appreciate the benefits they have gained in return for their expenditure.

eg

A solicitor's bill or the labour charges added to a repair bill can seem to be incredibly high to customers, because they do not stop to think about the training that has gone into developing professional skills nor of the peace of mind gained by having the job done 'properly'. As with any product, therefore, the customer's perception is central to assessing value for money.

The prices of some services are controlled by bodies other than the service provider. The amount that dentists charge for work under the National Health Service or that pharmacists charge to dispense a prescription is imposed by central government. Similarly, the BBC is funded by licence fees determined by government and charged to television owners. Other services price on a commission basis. An estate agent, for example, might charge the vendor a fee of 2 per cent of the selling price of the house, plus any expenses such as advertising.

Other service providers are completely free to decide their own prices, with due respect to competition and the needs, wants and perceptions of customers. In setting prices, however, service providers can find it very difficult to determine the true cost of provision, perhaps because of the difficulty of costing professional or specialist skills, or because the time and effort required to deliver a service vary widely between different customers, yet a standard price is needed. Perishability might also affect the pricing of professional services. A training provider, for example, who has little work on at the moment might agree to charge less than the normal daily rate, just to generate some immediate income.

In service situations, price can play an important role in managing demand. By varying the price, depending on the time at which the service is delivered, service providers can try to discourage customers from purchasing at the busiest periods. Customers can also use price as a weapon. Passengers purchasing airline tickets shortly before the flight or visitors looking for a hotel room for the night might be able to negotiate a much lower price than that advertised. This is a result of the perishability of services: the airline would rather have a seat occupied and get something for it than let the flight take off with an empty one and, similarly, the hotel would rather have a room occupied than not.

The rail pricing system has changed considerably in the UK in recent years. Traditionally, the passenger bought a ticket, walked on to the train and found a seat. Few bothered to pay the additional charge for a seat reservation. The emphasis is now on encouraging advance booking so that capacity can be better planned. The price mechanism is used to achieve a spread of customers. Suitably indexed to give equivalents in today's prices, an 'ordinary return' from London to Manchester was £51 in 1949. In 1969, period returns, usually for return travel within a month, could bring the price down to £41. By 1989, 'savers' again gave a price of £41, and a low of £32 could be found in 1994 with advance booking. Virgin Rail now has three main Value fares depending upon whether the ticket is purchased 3, 7 or 14 days in advance. Generally the longer the period before travel, the lower the fare. Thus some tickets can be as cheap as £20 return for the V14, but £40 for the V3. Other walk-on fares and special offers are used from time to time. The customer needs to be highly aware of the different pricing schemes yet, contrary to popular opinion, rail travel really can be as cheap as it was 50 years ago (Doe, 1999; http://www.virgintrainfares.co.uk).

Place

According to Cowell (1984), services are often supplied direct from the provider to the customer because production and consumption are simultaneous. Direct supply allows the provider to control what is going on; to differentiate through personal service; and to get direct feedback and interaction with the customer. Direct supply can take place from business premises, such as a hairdresser's salon, a solicitor's office or a university campus. Some services can also be supplied by telephone or Internet, such as insurance and banking services. Others are supplied by the service provider visiting the customer's home or premises, such as cleaning, repair of large appliances, equipment installation and servicing, or home hairdressing services.

Direct supply can cause problems for the service provider. It limits the number of customers that can be dealt with and the geographic coverage of the service. For sole traders or small businesses who particularly value the rapport and personal relationships built up with regular clients, this might be perfectly acceptable. Businesses that want to expand might find that direct supply involving the original proprietor of the business is no longer feasible. Professional service businesses, such as accountants or solicitors, might employ additional qualified staff to expand the customer base or to expand geographic coverage.

A fitness-oriented society coupled with rising levels of obesity has been a major factor behind the rapid growth of the health and fitness sector since the mid-1990s. Participation among the adult population grew from 3.8 per cent in 1996 to 7 per cent in 2001, with an expected peak of around 17 per cent, while membership has grown by 88 per cent over the same period. As the supply of clubs has grown, however, membership numbers have tended to remain static at individual clubs and the challenge has been to find new members to compensate for those leaving. Holmes Place, an operator of 56 premium clubs with a membership overall of 228,000, has a retention rate of 60 per cent which is high compared with the rest of the industry (Mesure, 2001). In the UK alone there are over 2,500 clubs, a growth of 25 per cent in five years. The premium clubs are especially vulnerable as they need to invest in more and varied facilities such as swimming pools and indoor tennis courts. The main means of growth for most clubs has been to open branches designed to a standard package in more towns and cities. Fitness First has grown to 225 clubs in 14 countries, with 112 in the UK alone (Daneskhu, 2002). The question is whether the growth can continue as the market becomes saturated, with operators turning to increasingly smaller towns to attract new interest. Other marketing activities also involve extending the reach with, for example, tie-ins with local sports associations, corporate membership drives and joint initiatives such as LA Fitness' 'Wellness Centres' operated in conjunction with BUPA.

Other service businesses such as fast food outlets, domestic cleaners or debt collection agencies might opt to expand by franchising, while others will decide to move towards indirect supply through intermediaries paid on a commission basis. Thus the local pharmacist might act as an agent for a company that develops photographic film; a village shop might collect dry cleaning; insurance brokers distribute policies; travel agencies distribute holidays and business travel; and tourist information offices deal with hotel and guest house bookings. In some of these cases, the main benefit of using an intermediary is convenience for the customer and spreading the coverage of the service. In others, such as the travel agency and the insurance broker, the service provider gains the added benefit of having its product sold by a specialist alongside the competition.

Promotion

Marketing communication objectives, implementation and management for services are largely the same as for any other product. There are a few specific issues to point out, however. As with pricing, some professional services are ethically constrained in what marketing communication they are allowed to do. Solicitors in the UK, for example, are allowed to use print advertising, but only if it is restrained and factual. An advertisement can tell the reader what areas of the law the practice specialises in, but it cannot make emotive promises about winning vast amounts of compensation for you, for example.

Service products face a particularly difficult communications task because of the intangibility of the product. They cannot show you pretty pack shots, they cannot whet your appetite with promises of strawberry and chocolate-flavoured variants, they cannot show you how much of this amazing product you are getting for your money. They can, however, show the physical evidence, they can show people like you apparently enjoying the service, they can emphasise the benefits of purchasing this service. Testimonials from satisfied customers can be an extremely effective tool, because they reassure the potential customer that the service works and that the outcomes will be positive. Linked with this, word-of-mouth communication is incredibly important, especially for the smaller business working in a limited geographic area.

Finally, it must be remembered that many service providers are small businesses, who could not afford to invest in glossy advertising campaigns even if they could see the point of it. Many can generate enough work to keep them going through word-of-mouth recommendation, websites and advertisements in the *Yellow Pages*. Much depends on the level of competition and demand in the local market for the kind of service being offered. If the town's High Street supports four different restaurants, then perhaps a more concerted effort might be justified, including, for example, advertising in local newspapers, door-to-door leaflet drops and price promotions.

eg Jarvis Hotels (http://www.jarvis.co.uk) uses direct marketing to promote conference business in its 62 hotels in the UK. The information pack, which is targeted at potential business customers, includes a complete directory of locations, room configurations and prices along with a lot of visual imagery to show the standard of meeting rooms, food service and the range of staff who are employed to make the conference or meeting a success. The messages throughout stress quality and reliability.

It is important to remember, however, that customers are likely to use marketing communication messages to build their expectations of what the service is likely to deliver. This is true of any product but, as will be discussed on pp. 443 *et seq.*, because of intangibility, the judgement of service quality is much more subjective. It is based on a comparison of prior expectations with actual perceived outcomes. The wilder or more unrealistic the communication claims, therefore, the greater the chances of a mismatch that will lead to a dissatisfied customer in the end. The service provider does, of course, need to create a sufficiently alluring image to entice the customer, but not to the point where the customer undergoing the service experience begins to wonder if this is actually the same establishment as that advertised.

eg The Australian Tourist Commission also makes heavy use of imagery to portray the natural and cultural delights of Australia to European audiences. Whether it is kangaroos, Ayers Rock, the Great Barrier Reef or Sydney Opera House, the visual message is the same: vibrant, exciting and surprising. The media advertisements and PR usually reinforce these themes, making full use of holiday programmes and travel shows as well as supporting Australia-themed national supplements in some of the daily newspapers. 'Brand Australia' campaigns are, however, targeted to attract different audiences and a number of campaigns are run simultaneously in different geographical markets. In the UK, for example, the primary targets are younger travellers aged between 18 and 36 and older travellers, over 45, reflecting the reality that a 'full nest' family is more likely to stay nearer home. In Germany, three segments are targeted: Explorers (aged between 25 and 54), Third Age Independents (45–65) and Young Independents (18–29). There are unifying themes, however, such as overcoming the view that Australia is a remote, vast and 'once in a lifetime' destination to position it more as a 'liberating, civilised adventure' destination. A 'visiting journalist' programme, funded by the ATC, is especially important for stimulating more and better PR coverage, and around 1,000 print and broadcast journalists are invited each year. It also helps to show Australia as being more than scenery and sun, with coverage of urban culture, food, wine, arts and cultural themes (http://www.atc.australia.com; http://www.australia).

People

Services depend on people and interaction between people, including the service provider's staff, the customer and other customers. As the customer is often a participant in the creation and delivery of the service product, there are implications for service product quality, productivity and staff training. The ability of staff to cope with customers, to deliver the service reliably to the required standard and to present an image consistent with what the organisation would want is of vital concern to the service provider. This is known as *internal marketing*, and will be discussed later on pp. 446 *et seq*. The role of the customer in the service is known as *interactive marketing*, and will be discussed on pp. 443 *et seq*.

Physical evidence

Physical evidence comprises the tangible elements that support the service delivery, and offer clues about the positioning of the service product or give the customer something solid to take away with them to symbolise the intangible benefits they have received. Shostack (1977) differentiates between *essential evidence* and *peripheral evidence*. Essential evidence is central to the service and is an important contributor to the customer's purchase decision. Examples of this might be the type and newness of aircraft operated by an airline or of the car fleet belonging to a car hire firm, the layout and facilities offered by a supermarket, or a university's lecture theatres and their equipment as well as IT and library provision. Peripheral evidence is less central to the service delivery and is likely to consist of items that the customer can have to keep or use.

Processes

Because the creation and consumption of a service are usually simultaneous, the production of the service is an important part of its marketing as the customer either witnesses it or is directly involved in it. The service provider needs smooth, efficient customer-friendly procedures. Some processes work behind the scenes, for example administrative and data processing systems, processing paperwork and information relating to the service delivery and keeping track of customers.

eg United Parcel Service (UPS) regards itself as a leading global commerce facilitator. Best known for its parcel and freight service, it has to gear its operating processes and infrastructure to handle 13.6 million packages every day in 200 countries. To achieve the service levels promised, including time-definite, guaranteed delivery, it operates a large fleet of vans, has over 350,000 employees, operates over 600 aircraft and has spent over $12bn on technology to provide information processing, tracking and fulfilment. UPS uses a tracking number service not just for logistics but also as a selling point to customers. By having a tracking number assigned to the package the customer is able to track and verify arrival of any package (http://www.ups.com).

Systems that allow the service provider to send a postcard to remind customers that the next dental check-up or car service is due certainly help to generate repeat business, but also help in a small way to strengthen the relationship with the customer. Other processes are also 'invisible' to the customer, but form an essential part of the service package. The organisation of the kitchens in a fast food outlet, for example, ensures a steady supply of freshly cooked burgers available for counter staff to draw on as customers order. Well-designed processes are also needed as the service is delivered to ensure that the customer gets through with minimum fuss and delay and that all elements of the service are properly delivered. This might involve, for example, the design of forms and the information requested, payment procedures, queuing systems or even task allocation. At a hairdressing salon, for instance, a junior might wash your hair while the stylist finishes off the previous customer, and the receptionist will handle the payment at the end.

Banks have thought seriously about ways of making their services more accessible to their customers. Telephone and Internet banking, for example, with processes designed to protect customer security and to provide 24-hour coverage, allows customers easy access to their accounts from their own homes whenever they want it. Already in Scandinavia, electronic banking services have made a big impact. The regional banks are encouraging customers to use online services for retail transactions as well as share trading and foreign currency transactions. Svenska Handelsbanken has 140,000 Internet customers, including 15,000 small businesses in which the service flexibility has been especially well received. The banks are offering incentives for customers to use the Internet, including lower commission charges, and they believe that the next phase of competition between banks will be on customer service rather than price (Burt, 1999).

■ Interactive marketing: service quality

Central to the delivery of any service product is the *service encounter* between the provider and the customer. This is also known as interactive marketing. This aspect of services is an important determinant of quality because it brings together all the elements of the services marketing mix and is the point at which the product itself is created and delivered. The challenge for the service marketer is to bring quality, customer service and marketing together to build and maintain customer satisfaction (Christopher *et al.*, 1994). Quality issues are just as important for service products as they are for a physical product, but service quality is much more difficult to define and to control. Authors such as Lovelock *et al.* (1999), Devlin and Dong (1994) and Zeithaml *et al.* (1990), for example, stress the importance of customer perceptions and use them as the basis for frameworks for measuring service quality.

> **eg** Home delivery of pizzas is usually associated with supplier guarantees of free pizzas if delivered outside a certain period. This helps emphasise the speed of delivery and reinforces the convenience of home ordering services. A number of chains such as Domino's have added online ordering, with a central call centre directing orders to the nearest retail stores. The customer is then free to browse the menu at leisure and the site can be frequently updated with offers, etc. It has also gone further in ensuring improved service through the introduction of the Domino's Heat Wave hot bags with a patented electrically warmed heating mechanism. Once unplugged, it keeps the pizza hot during normal delivery times (http://www.dominos.co.uk).

Measuring service quality

Some aspects of the service product can, of course, be measured more objectively than others. Where tangible elements are involved, such as physical evidence and processes, quality can be defined and assessed more easily. In a fast food restaurant, for example, the cleanliness of the premises, the length of the queues, the consistency of the size of portions and their cooking, and the implementation and effectiveness of stock control systems can all be 'seen' and measured. Whether the customer actually *enjoyed* the burger, whether they *felt* that they had had to wait too long, or whether they *felt* that the premises were too busy, crowded or noisy are much more personal matters and thus far more difficult for managers to assess.

A particular group of researchers, Berry, Parasuraman and Zeithaml, have developed criteria for assessing service quality and a survey mechanism called SERVQUAL for collecting data relating to customer perceptions (see e.g. Parasuraman *et al.*, 1985; Zeithaml *et al.*, 1988, 1990). They cite 10 main criteria that, between them, cover the whole service experience from the customer's point of view:

1 *Access*. How easy is it for the customer to gain access to the service? Is there an outlet for the service close to the customer? Is there 24-hour access by telephone to a helpline?

2 *Reliability*. Are all the elements of the service performed and are they delivered to the expected standard? Does the repair engineer clean up after himself after mending the washing machine and does the machine then work properly? Does the supermarket that promises to open another checkout when the queues get too long actually do so?

3 *Credibility*. Is the service provider trustworthy and believable? Is the service provider a member of a reputable trade association? Does it give guarantees with its work? Does it seem to treat the customer fairly?

4 *Security*. Is the customer protected from risk or doubt? Is the customer safe while visiting and using a theme park? Does an insurance policy cover all eventualities? Will the bank respect the customer's confidentiality? Can the cellular telephone network provider prevent hackers from hijacking a customer's mobile phone number?

5 *Understanding the customer*. Does the service provider make an effort to understand and adapt to the customer's needs and wants? Will a repair engineer give a definite time of arrival? Will a financial adviser take the time to understand the customer's financial situation and needs and then plan a complete package? Do front-line service staff develop good relationships with regular customers?

Those first five criteria influence the quality of the *outcome* of the service experience. The next five influence the quality of the *inputs* to the process to provide a solid foundation for the outputs.

6 *Responsiveness*. Is the service provider quick to respond to the customer and willing to help? Can a repair engineer visit within 24 hours? Will a bank manager explain in detail what the small print in a loan agreement means? Are customer problems dealt with quickly and efficiently?

7 *Courtesy*. Are service staff polite, friendly and considerate? Do they smile and greet customers? Are they pleasant? Do they show good manners? Do service staff who have to visit a customer's home treat it with proper respect and minimise the sense of intrusion?

8 *Competence*. Are service staff suitably trained and able to deliver the service properly? Does a financial adviser have extensive knowledge of available financial products and their appropriateness for the customer? Does a librarian know how to access and use information databases? Do theme park staff know where the nearest toilets are, what to do in a medical emergency or what to do about a lost child?

9 *Communication*. Do service staff listen to customers and take time to explain things to them understandably? Do staff seem sympathetic to customer problems and try to suggest appropriate solutions? Do medical, legal, financial or other professional staff explain things in plain language?

10 *Tangibles*. Are the tangible and visible aspects of the service suitably impressive or otherwise appropriate to the situation? Does the appearance of staff inspire confidence in the customer? Are hotel rooms clean, tidy and well appointed? Do lecture theatres have good acoustics and lighting, a full range of audiovisual equipment and good visibility from every seat? Does the repair engineer have all the appropriate equipment available to do the job quickly and properly? Are contracts and invoices easy to read and understand?

It is easy to appreciate just how difficult it is to create and maintain quality in all 10 of these areas, integrating them into a coherent service package. In summary, Figure 13.3 shows the service experience and the factors that affect consumers' expectations of what they will receive. The criteria that influence their perception of what they actually did receive are also shown, as well as the reasons why there might be a mismatch between expectations and perceptions. This can have an important impact on the customer's perception of value and willingness to repeat purchase (Caruana *et al.*, 2000).

Smartcards keep queues moving smartish

The smartcard revolution is starting to impact upon European service provision, changing how we reserve, buy and use services and how we interact with service providers. Smartcards are a similar size to a credit card with an embedded microprocessor and a memory. Some cards are activated by physical contact with a reader, while others are 'contactless', activated by a signal-emitting device within the chip.

London Transport is planning to introduce an electronic fee collection system with contactless smartcards that can be used throughout the tube system and by the independent bus operators, thus overcoming the need for queues at ticket offices and platform barriers. Any reader who has waited 10 or 15 minutes in a ticket queue knows exactly how that impacts on perceptions of the service experience. Smartcards can be topped up via the Internet or through devices linked to a bank account, so finding change will become a thing of the past. Some technology can even read the card when it is firmly locked away in a case or wallet. The costs of introducing the system are, however, considerable, with around 16,500 pieces of equipment to install or modify, including gates, ticket machines and passenger ticket offices (Hibbert, 2000).

The cards are also very flexible in that they are not bounded by travel zones or time restrictions as are normal season tickets or travel cards. The card reader at the station will take account of the time of day and the distance travelled when calculating the fare to be deducted from the card. Discounts for frequent travellers, promotions or other concessions can also be implemented easily.

The good news is that smartcards can help to speed passenger flows and reduce the frustration factor.

Operationally, they also mean that there is less cash handling to be done at stations because most passengers will pay for and top up their smartcards using credit cards. The cards also should reduce fraud, in that the card reader can check that the right fare is paid for any specific journey. Mutual authentication techniques will be used between cards and readers to undertake integrity checks and to ensure that no tampering has taken place. From a strategic planning perspective, the new system will also collect accurate information about who is travelling, between what destinations and when, as well as helping to monitor the effects of promotions, discounts and differential pricing initiatives. The only potential disadvantage, however, is that smartcards do also reduce contact with staff and some of the personal touch of services marketing.

Other transport operators are also at different stages of development. In the USA, the Washington metro system claims 60 per cent usage of smartcards. Massachusetts rapid transit system is introducing a $120m. scheme to improve both customer service and efficiency in 2003. Currently the system operators have to produce and distribute, every month, 240,000 system-wide passes, plus 40,000 commuter rail, 100,000 subway, 35,000 bus, 50,000 bus–subway combination, and 15,000 extended travel range bus–subway combination passes. Inevitably, that all incurs costs that ultimately impact upon fares (RePass, 2002). Smartcards can be updated from simple vending machines in the station areas. Research has indicated, however, that not all of its customers have credit cards or bank accounts, so it still needs to sell cards with fixed values, rather like 'pay-as-you-go' mobile phone cards.

There are other applications of smartcards beyond transport. In banking, for instance, the UK, Finland and France are leading the way in chip-based credit cards to reduce fraud and to lower the cost of banking (Bansal, 2002). In Sweden, camping is now easier due to *Camping Card Scandinavia*. The credit-card-style £6 pre-purchased card makes registration and checkout much easier and in addition provides family accident insurance (Bryan-Brown, 2001). Hotels have been slow to adopt smartcards. As in banking, they are mainly used as an extra security device rather than a means of enhancing service and capturing valuable information on buyer behaviour. Nevertheless, they are beginning to be used by hotels to extend services to particular groups and to act as a charge card for additional in-hotel services and even for some services at nearby attractions.

The smartcard revolution is only just beginning. As technology and systems improve and there is more supplier and user confidence, the applications will grow. Along with the credit card and indeed as part of one integrated card, a significant step is being taken towards a cashless society and one in which service is enhanced in the process. There is always a downside, however. Under some transport plans, congestion charging, peak rate charging and zonal charging are all possible via smartcards fitted to cars (Winnett, 2002). Even children may not be immune from the 'big brother' effect as in Queensland, primary schools are piloting a smartcard that can be controlled by parents to prevent certain foods being purchased (chips!) and to prevent children making purchases in certain stores (*Retail World*, 2002).

Sources: Adams (2000), Bansal (2002), Bryan-Brown (2001), Glover (1999), Hibbert (2000), RePass (2002), *Retail World* (2002), Winnett (2002).

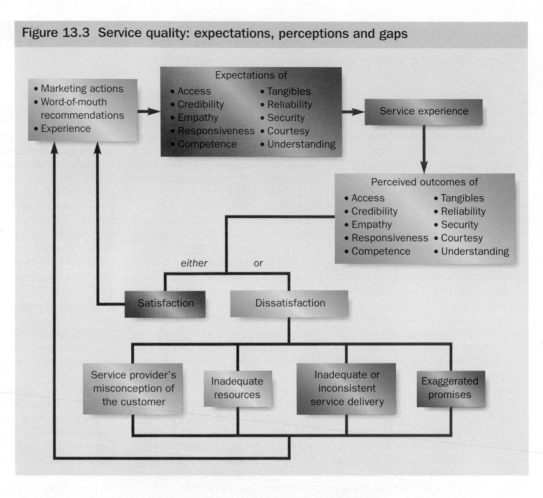

Figure 13.3 Service quality: expectations, perceptions and gaps

■ Internal marketing: training and productivity

Because of the interaction between customers and staff in the creation and delivery of a service, it is particularly important to focus on developing staff to deliver high levels of functional and service quality. The pay and rewards system employed can also help to boost staff morale and encourage them to take a positive approach to service delivery. Heskett *et al.* (1997) highlighted the connection between employee and customer satisfaction within services. The 'satisfaction mirror' can actually enhance the customer's experience if the service personnel are approaching service delivery in a positive way. They suggested that employees feeling enthusiastic about their job communicate this to customers both verbally and non-verbally and are also more eager to serve the customer. Similarly, employees who remain in the job longer reach higher capability levels and often a better understanding of customers, which again can enhance customers' feelings of satisfaction. Defining the ideal profile and right remuneration package for staff is not easy.

eg

Recent research from MORI suggested that staff attitude was more important than quality or price in influencing consumer choice when buying a service. It would appear that the young (aged between 15 and 34) and the more affluent are especially sensitive. Whether it is poor advice, indifferent attitudes, a failure to keep promises or just poor attention to detail, the message is clear to service providers. Many readers will almost certainly recall situations where poor staff attitude has had a bearing on the quality of the experience. This creates pressure to ensure that staff are well trained, not just about the products but also in how to deal sensitively with customers. Faced with increased difficulty in attracting the right calibre of younger staff, retailers such as Sainsbury's and B&Q have scrapped the upper age limit for their workers and actively seek older staff. Carphone Warehouse and Eagle Star are also employing older sales staff to attract the grey market (Buckley, 2002).

Staff training

Many service failures actually do stem from staffing problems. As Table 13.1 shows, some staff have direct or indirect involvement in the creation of the service product, and some staff are visible, whereas others are invisible to customers.

Staff who have direct involvement are those who come into contact with a customer as a key part of service delivery. In an airline, these might be air hostesses and stewards, check-in staff, and those at the enquiries desk. Indirect involvement covers all staff who enable the service to be delivered, but do not normally come into contact with the customer. They affect the quality of the service delivery through their impact on the efficiency and effectiveness of the operating system and the standards and performance possible from the facilities and infrastructure. Examples might include aircraft catering staff, cleaning and maintenance staff, ground staff at sports venues, banks' computer systems staff and railway signalmen.

Table 13.1 Staff in the service function

	Visible to the customer	Invisible to the customer

Direct involvement	■ Airline cabin crew
	■ Cashiers
	■ Sales assistants
	■ Medical staff
	■ Receptionists
		■ Telephone based services
		  – order takers
		  – customer helplines
		  – telephone banking

Indirect involvement	■ Hotel chamber maids ■ Supermarket shelf fillers	■ Office cleaners ■ Airline caterers ■ Administrative staff

Jarvis Hotels (mentioned earlier on p. 441), places special emphasis on its staff training in its promotional material. Entitled 'Summit Quality Signature', its brochure outlines the various dimensions of training and the phased approach to awarding the quality signature to all members of staff. The first stage concentrates on core values and considers such issues as service delivery, clear merchandising, first impressions, introductions, cleanliness, freshness and how to encourage extra sales. The second stage is concerned with consistency. Quality standards are set for each core value and both self-checking and regular external 'flight tests' are organised to ensure that standards are being maintained and that, where necessary, corrective action is being taken (Jarvis Hotels corporate literature).

Jarvis Hotels are designed to give customers quality and reliability wherever they are.

Source: Jarvis Hotels EPC.

Visible staff (both those with direct involvement and those with indirect involvement with the customer) are in the front line of service delivery. Not only are they concerned with the practical aspects of service delivery to the required standards, but their appearance, interpersonal behaviour and mannerisms will also make an impression on the customer. Airlines, for example, will pay particular attention to a cabin attendant's personal grooming and dress standardisation to ensure a consistent visual impact. Dress is often used to help the customer identify visible staff, both those directly involved in the service, such as air-craft cabin crew, and those who are indirectly involved, such as stewards at soccer matches or security staff.

Indirect visible staff also include people such as the cleaners at McDonald's, chambermaids in hotels, or staff supporting the cashiers in banks. Invisible staff might or might not have direct contact with customers. Staff who take telephone bookings or those who deal with customer queries on the telephone are heard, but not seen. In some cases, these staff might be the only major point of contact for the customer, and thus although their visibility is limited, their ability to interact well with customers is still extremely important.

The organisation's strategy for internal marketing will vary, depending on the different categories of staff employed. Staff who are in the front line of service delivery, with a high level of customer contact, will have to be trained to deliver the standards expected. Staff who do not have direct contact still have to be motivated to perform their tasks effectively and efficiently. They have to understand that what they do affects the quality of the service delivered and the ability of the front-line staff to perform to expected standards. All of this strongly implies, however, that the different groups of staff have to work closely and efficiently together, and deliver a quality service to each other, which in turn will affect the quality of service delivered to the end customer (Mathews and Clark, 1996). An Institute of Employment Studies survey of staff and customer attitudes in a major retailer found a direct and strong link between employee commitment and customer satisfaction. The importance of creating a positive organisational culture and good-quality line management all contribute to enhancing the service experience (Bevan and Barber, 1999).

Staff productivity

Staff productivity within services is also a difficult issue for managers. According to Cowell (1984), there are several reasons for service productivity being difficult to measure. The main reason is that services are 'performed' not 'produced' and there are too many external factors influencing this live creation of a product. The service production process simply cannot be controlled and replicated as reliably and consistently as a mechanised factory line. Service productivity particularly suffers from the involvement of the customer. If customers do not fill forms in properly, if they are not familiar with procedures or they do not really know what they want, if they turn up late for appointments, if they want to spend time in idle chatter rather than getting on with the business in hand, then it will take service staff much longer to deliver the product. Where productivity is measured in terms of the number of transactions handled, the amount of revenue generated, or the number of customers processed, such delays essentially caused by the customer can reflect unfairly on service staff. This raises the whole question, however, of what constitutes appropriate and fair measures of service productivity. A customer who is given a great deal of individual help or who feels that service staff have taken time for a friendly chat with them might well feel that they have received a much better-quality service and appreciate not being treated with cold, bureaucratic efficiency. It might be worth tolerating a slightly longer queue if you feel that you will be treated with care, respect and humanity when you get to the front of it. Definitions and measures of productivity therefore need to be flexible and sympathetic, striking a fine balance between the customer's needs and the business's need to work efficiently.

None of this absolves managers from looking at ways in which service productivity can be improved. There are several possibilities for delivering services more efficiently without necessarily detracting too much from their quality.

Staff. Through improved recruitment and training, staff can be given better skills and knowledge for dealing with customers. A clerk in a travel agency, for example, can develop a better knowledge of which tour operators offer which resorts so that the key brochures can be immediately pulled out in response to a customer query. Library staff can be fully trained in the use and potential of databases and online search mechanisms so that customers can have their problems solved immediately without having to wait for a 'specialist' to return from a lunchbreak. Improving the staff profile might also allow more delegation or empowerment of front-line service staff. A customer does not want to be told 'I can't do that without checking with my supervisor' and then have to wait while this happens. Staff should be given the responsibility and flexibility to deal with the real needs of customers as they arise.

Systems and technology. The design of the service process and the introduction of more advanced technology can both help to improve service productivity and the service experience for the customer (Bitner *et al.*, 2000).

eg Onboard catering on trains has always posed an operational nightmare for operators, yet in airlines the problem has been largely solved through a combination of systems and technology. Whereas most airline food is standardised, precooked, paid for in advance and delivered to a programmed schedule to passengers in predetermined seats, on some rail services it was not unusual to find a cook frying eggs or cooking vegetables at 80 mph in a confined space and waiters taking orders from an albeit limited menu. Meals were not part of the ticket price, so likely demand per journey had to be forecast. On some occasions, the restaurant on wheels would even break down or supplies would not be forthcoming. Train catering became the butt of many jokes, even though the quality of food, when available, probably exceeded airline levels.

Some of the problem rested in the ambience of on-train facilities. For many years the layout was fixed: a 20-seat dining area, a kitchen in the middle and a take-away bar at the other end of the carriage. There was little space for passengers to mingle and socialise and the counters were far too small so that produce could not be displayed, an essential part of any food operation. Queues became excessive and often extended back into the adjacent carriage. Eating was functional and rarely pleasurable.

The new generation of operators are trying to change things. In France on the Atlantique TGV, a whole coach is allocated to catering with a small bar at one end and a large social area for eating and drinking at the other, all separate from the restaurant facilities. On German trains (DBAG), a bistro facility has been incorporated to offer light meals, snacks and drinks, again in a social environment. The focus has been on enhancing the experience for the traveller. In the UK, efforts have been made by operators such as Virgin and GNER to improve restaurant service to enhance the overall service experience. On the seven former inter-city routes, five provide classic restaurant cars with meals cooked on board by a trained chef. In some cases, such as Virgin and Midland Mainline, the meals and drinks are included in the First Class ticket price. The buffet bar service experience is still variable, however. The ambience is often poor, the trolleys unreliable and the food choice limited. Microwaved burgers still remain the most popular food. Virgin's new trains will, however, feature shops offering food, drinks, newspapers, CDs and some stationery to a potentially captive audience. Nevertheless, to some train operators, catering remains a cost and a necessary evil (and perhaps to some customers too!), rather than a means of adding value (Perren, 1999a, b; Perren and Pyke, 2000).

Technology combined with well-designed systems can be very powerful in creating market transactions where no interpersonal contact is required between buyer and seller (Rayport and Sviokla, 1994). Libraries, for example, have used technology to improve their productivity. Laser scanning barcodes in books make it far quicker to issue or receive returned items than with the old manual ticketing systems. This has also allowed them to improve the quality of their service. The librarian can immediately tell you, for instance, which books you have on loan, whether or not another reader has reserved a book you have, and which other reader has borrowed the book you want. Some technology means that the service provider need not provide human interaction at all. In the financial sector, 'hole in the wall' cash machines, for instance, give customers 24-hour, 7-day-a-week access to their bank accounts, usually without long queues, and because of the way these machines are networked they provide hundreds of convenient access points.

Reduce service levels. Reducing service levels to increase productivity can be dangerous if it leads to a perception of reduced quality in the customer's mind, especially if customers have become used to high levels of service. Reducing the number of staff available to deliver the service might lead to longer queues or undue pressure on the customer to move through the system more quickly.

eg If a busy doctor's surgery introduces a system that schedules appointments at five-minute intervals, one of two things might happen. A doctor who wants to maintain the schedule might hurry patients through consultations without listening to them properly or allowing them time to relax enough to be able to say what is really worrying them. Patients might then feel that they have not got what they came for and that the doctor does not actually care about them. Alternatively, the doctor may put the patient first, and regardless of the five-minute rule take as long as is needed to sort out the individual patient. The patient emerges satisfied, but those still in the waiting room whose appointments are up to half an hour late might not feel quite so happy.

Reducing service levels also opens up opportunities for competitors to create a new differential advantage. Discount supermarkets such as Aldi, Netto and Lidl keep their prices low partly through minimising service. Thus there are few checkout operators, no enquiries desk, and nobody to help customers pack their bags. The more mainstream supermarkets have been able to use this as a way of emphasising the quality of their service, and have deliberately invested in higher levels of service to differentiate themselves further. Thus Tesco, for example, promised its customers that if there were more than three people in a checkout queue, another checkout would be opened if possible. Tesco also announced that it was taking on extra staff in most of its branches, simply to help customers. These staff might help to unload your trolley on to the conveyor belt or pack your bags, or if you get to the checkout and realise that you have forgotten the milk, they will go and get it for you.

Customer interaction. Productivity might be improved by changing the way the customer interacts with the service provider and its staff. It might also mean developing or changing the role of the customer in the service delivery itself. The role of technology in assisting self-service through cash machines has already been mentioned. The whole philosophy of the supermarket is based on the idea of increasing the customer's involvement in the shopping process through self-service.

Customers might also have to get used to dealing with a range of different staff members, depending on their needs or the pressures on the service provider. Medical practices now commonly operate on a group basis, for example, and a patient might be asked to see any one of three or four doctors. If the patient only wants a repeat prescription then the receptionist might be able to handle it, or if a routine procedure is necessary, such as a blood test or a cervical smear, then the practice nurse might do it.

If any measures are taken that relate to the nature of customer involvement and interaction, the service provider might have a problem convincing customers that these are for their benefit and that they should cooperate. Careful use of marketing communications is needed, through both personal and non-personal media, to inform customers of the benefits, to persuade them of the value of what is being done and to reassure them that their cooperation will not make too many heavy demands on them.

Reduce mismatch between supply and demand. Sometimes demand exceeds supply. Productivity might well then be high, but it could be higher still if the excess demand could be accommodated. Some customers will not want to wait and might decide either to take their business to an alternative service provider or not to purchase at all. At other times, supply will exceed demand and productivity will be low because resources are lying idle. If the service provider can even out some of these fluctuations, then perhaps overall productivity can be improved.

The service provider might be able to control aspects of supply and demand through fairly simple measures. Pricing, for example, as discussed earlier, might help to divert demand away from busy periods or to create extra demand at quiet times. An appointment booking system might also help to ensure a steady trickle of customers at intervals that suit the service provider. The danger is, though, that if the customer cannot get the appointment slot that they want, they might not bother at all. Finding alternative uses for staff and facilities during quiet times can also create more demand and increase productivity. Universities, for instance, have long had the problem of facilities lying idle at weekends and during vacations. They have solved this by turning halls of residence into conference accommodation or cheap and cheerful holiday lets in the vacations, or hiring out their more attractive and historic buildings for weddings and other functions at weekends, with catering provided.

If the service provider cannot or does not wish to divert demand away from busy times, then the ability to supply the service to the maximum number of customers will have to be examined. If the peaks in demand are fairly predictable, then many service providers will bring in part-time staff to increase available supply. There might be limits to their ability to do so, however, which are imposed by constraints of physical space and facilities. A supermarket has only so many checkouts, a bank has only so many tills, a barber's shop has only so many chairs, a restaurant has only so many tables. Nevertheless, part-time staff can still be useful behind the scenes, easing the burden on front-line staff and speeding up the throughput of customers.

eg A business school operating a modular scheme might find that there are substantial numbers of students wanting to take marketing options. This might not put too much pressure on the weekly lecture programme, since as long as a large enough lecture theatre is available, a lecturer can talk to 200 students as easily as to 50. The problems arise with the number of seminar groups to be serviced and part-time staff might be brought in to take some of the burden off full-time staff. Physical facilities are not likely to pose too many problems in this case, especially if staff and students are prepared to tolerate less popular timetable slots such as 4 p.m. on a Friday!

Non-profit marketing

The main focus of this section is the charities aspect of non-profit marketing, reflecting the growth of cause-related marketing (CRM) and the radical changes in the ways in which charities generate revenue, their attitudes to their 'businesses' and their increasingly professional approaches to marketing. Cause-related organisations form an important part of the non-profit sector. According to the Charities Association, in 2000 in the UK, over £28bn was generated by over 161,000 charities. Many are very small and just 393 of them generate over 43 per cent of all income. Two-thirds of charities raise less than £10,000 in income (http://www.fundraising.co.uk). Increasingly, charities are becoming brands with attributes, emotive appeals and value statements that are designed to appeal to the population of interest. Research by BRMB, for example, indicates that 20 per cent of the population intends to leave money to charities in their wills, 39 per cent support children's charities and 29 per cent will support illness/research charities (Singh, 2001).

Like many other organisations, charities have found that the environment within which they operate has changed. There are many more charities competing for attention and donations, and the attitudes of both individual and corporate donors have changed. Thus all sorts of organisations that have not traditionally seen themselves as 'being in business' have had to become more businesslike, fighting for and justifying resources and funding.

 The National Missing Persons Helpline (NMPH) was registered as a charity in the UK in 1993. It was set up because at any one time there are up to 250,000 people 'missing' in the UK, yet there was no central body to offer advice and support to missing persons' families, to coordinate information on missing people, or for missing people to contact for help. Although many people do 'go missing' on purpose and do not wish to be found, others disappear because they are distressed, ill or confused and need help and reassurance to solve their problems. A few are the victims of abduction.

▶

The NMPH therefore offers a number of services, including:

- a national 24-hour telephone helpline for families of missing people;
- a confidential 'Free Call Message Home' 24-hour freefone telephone helpline so that missing people who do not want to be 'found' can at least leave a message to reassure their families that they are all right;
- a national computerised database of missing people;
- searching for missing people, using contacts among the homeless population, and advertising and publicity;
- an image-enhancing 'age progression' computer that can create a photograph of what someone who has been missing for several years might look like now.

The charity's 'customers' are not just missing people and their families. The police find the NMPH and its database invaluable in assisting with identifying corpses and helping with missing persons cases generally.

In marketing terms, the NMPH's main problem is generating a steady and reliable flow of income. NMPH does not charge commercial rates for its services, even to the police. It hopes, of course, that those who have benefited from the service will make a donation, but this is unlikely to cover the full cost. It thus relies heavily on cash donations, corporate donations of goods and services, fund raising and promotional events. The higher the profile of the event, the greater the opportunity to raise cash. In 2002 a sponsored Glasgow to London walk was organised and various celebrities and families of missing people joined the core walkers. It also runs a celebrity memorabilia web auction where celebrity items such as a signed photo of Michael Owen would fetch over £30. It is particularly dependent on some of the 'donations in kind', for example television airtime or print advertising space, in order to carry on its work effectively.

Sources: NMPH literature; briefing given by Elaine Quigley at Buckinghamshire Chilterns University College; http://www.missingpersons.org.uk

This section, therefore, discusses the characteristics that differentiate non-profit from profit-making organisations. Then, the implications for marketing will be explored.

■ Classifying non-profit organisations

As suggested above, non-profit organisations can exist in either the public or private sector, although the distinction between them is rather blurred in some cases. A hospital that treats both National Health patients and private patients, for example, is involved in both sectors.

Characteristics of non-profit organisations

Clearly, all non-profit organisations operate in different types of market and face different challenges, but they do have a number of characteristics in common that differentiate them from ordinary commercial businesses (Lovelock and Weinberg, 1984; Kotler, 1982). These are as follows.

Multiple publics. Most profit-making organisations focus their attention on their target market. Although they do depend on shareholders to provide capital, most day-to-day cash flow is generated from sales revenue. Effectively, therefore, the recipient of the product or service and the source of income are one and the same. Non-profit organisations, however, have to divide their attention much more equally between two important groups, as shown in Figure 13.4. First, there are the customers or clients who receive the product or service. They do not necessarily pay the full cost of it. A charity, for example, might offer advice or help free to those in need, whereas a museum might charge a nominal entry fee that is heavily subsidised from other sources. Thus clients or customers concern the non-profit organisation largely from a *resource allocation* point of view. The second important group is the funders, those who provide the income to allow the organisation to do its work. A charity, for example, might depend mainly on individuals making donations and corporate sponsors, a medical practice on government funding and a museum on government grants, lottery cash, individual donations and corporate sponsorship as well as entrance fees. Thus funders concern the organisation from a *resource attraction* point of view.

Figure 13.4 Non-profit organisations: multiple publics

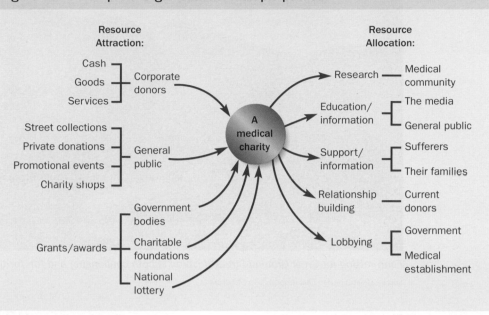

eg Great Ormond Street Hospital (http://www.gosh.nhs.uk) has the widest range of paediatric specialists in the UK, and welcomes over 13,000 inpatients and 131,000 outpatients every year, 50 per cent of whom are aged under two years. In order to provide care, to maintain its position at the frontier of medical research and to enhance its reputation for pioneering surgery, it needs to supplement the income it gets from the government via the National Health Service. Each year, the Great Ormond Street Hospital Children's Charity (GOSHCC) www.gosh.org, aims to raise £20m. from individuals and organisations to fund pioneering research into childhood diseases, buy vital new medical equipment and offer improved support services to families.

The hospital must therefore interact with a number of publics if it is to achieve its targets. Its core activities mean that it is working with patients, parents, local hospital consultants and doctors. Each has an interest in the paediatric care work of the hospital. The government and the National Health Service also have an interest in the hospital, given its role, profile and of course its prime funding source. However, the donor publics are critical to the future of GOSH and thus the hospital has an active fund raising programme through GOSHCC. Schemes include fund raising events, sponsorship, advertisements on the website, private donations, payroll covenants and legacies, company giving and joint sales promotions such as one undertaken with Baby Bio, which raised £20,000. Zoom.com supported GOSHCC by contributing 5p per card for the first 50,000 e-cards sent from its site. That was good for Zoom in terms of viral marketing as well as being good for GOSHCC. Employee fund raising through adopting GOSHCC for a month, a year or for a special event provides a further source of funds as well as raising the profile.

Employees at Ford went on a two-year fund raising programme to raise £100,000. Activities included a team of 12 cyclists undertaking a GOSHCC Anglo-Italian cycle challenge; 18 employees taking part in the London Marathon; and a further team undertaking the Three Peaks Challenge in Yorkshire. Perhaps the most exotic campaign was the Inca Challenge 2002, a 10-day expedition in the Peruvian mountains in search of a lost city. It attracted 44 people and raised over £60,000 for the charity through individual sponsorship. All of these events and programmes mean that GOSHCC has to plan its activities carefully to maintain good relations with individuals and organisations to attract resources and in return to ensure that the gratitude and goodwill from the well-being of its patients is fed back to the supporters.

Fund raising for Great Ormond Street Hospital is both challenging and fun for the participants.

Source: Great Ormond Street Hospital Children's Charity.

Multiple objectives. One definition of marketing offered earlier in this book is to create and hold a customer at a profit. As we have seen, there are many different ways of achieving this and many possible sub-objectives on the way, but in the end for most organisations it is all about profit. As a result, success criteria can be fairly easily defined and measured. In the non-profit sector, however, there might be multiple objectives, some of which could be difficult to define and quantify. They might concern fund raising, publicity generation, contacting customers or clients (or getting them to visit you), dispensing advice, increasing geographic coverage or giving grants to needy clients.

eg The Swanage Railway is a heritage line owned by its members in southern England and concentrates on running preserved locomotives, often steam, on a short stretch of track from Swanage to Norden, near Corfe Castle. It is primarily a line run by enthusiasts and supported by volunteers all intent on recreating scenes from bygone days. Members donate as much as they can afford and 'premier life membership' costs £350, which allows as much free travel as is wanted. General fund raising and special appeals to members are also operated from time to time, such as appeals to raise money to restore rolling stock or to help towards the cost of extending the line a few extra miles to Wareham. The main objective is to finish the complete reopening of the line and to run as wide a range of heritage stock on the line as possible. However, in order to achieve this objective a number of other objectives have to be realised first. Realistically, the line needs to become a tourist attraction, bringing in customers who may not be railway enthusiasts as such. This could mean some compromise of purist ideals, especially with the two Thomas the Tank Engine weekends in the shoulder months when Thomas himself and all the other working locos are adorned with faces, anathema to a real enthusiast. Nevertheless, even they would have to admit that Thomas weekends provide a significant source of additional revenues by attracting families with young children. The line runs 19 services per day in the summer season and the more passengers are on board, the higher the revenue and the sooner the main objectives can be realised. Grants and loans also have to be won, such as £500,000 funding from the Rural Development Commission for a 130-space car park at one of the stations. Similarly, the local authority has supported the line as it regards it as a valuable tourist feature. Therefore fund raising, membership and revenue-earning operations have to be undertaken successfully, even though they may conflict at times, if the core enthusiasts want to catch a whiff of steam and nostalgia (http://www.swanagerailway.co.uk).

Service rather than physical goods orientation. Most non-profit organisations are delivering a service product of some sort rather than manufacturing and selling a physical product. Many of the services marketing concepts already covered in this chapter therefore apply to them. In some non-profit bodies, the emphasis is on generating awareness about a cause, perhaps to generate funds, and giving information to allow people to help themselves solve a problem. Particularly where charities are concerned in generating funds, donors as a target audience are not directly benefiting from their participation in the production of this service, other than from the warm glow of satisfying their social conscience. This contrasts with the more commercial sector, where the customer who pays gets a specific service performed for their benefit (a haircut, a washing machine repaired, a bank account managed for them, etc.).

Oxfam International is not only delivering a service product, but one that is often directed at beneficiaries many thousands of kilometres away. Its many programmes vary from very high-profile activities such as dealing with humanitarian crises in Kosovo, Rwanda or Jenin, or helping in the aftermath of hurricanes, or participation in longer-term projects lasting many years. The River Basin Programme is one of Oxfam's largest projects aimed at helping poor people along the Ganges and Brahmaputra rivers and their hundreds of tributaries in Bangladesh and India. Areas more than 1,000 km wide are prone to severe flooding and Oxfam works on social and environmental aspects to help alleviate the worst effects.

Oxfam needs high-profile media coverage to make the suffering of people and the effective impact even of small donations more tangible. With natural disasters, much of the media coverage is done for Oxfam and the focus is on directing goodwill and sympathy to make donating easy. In other cases, more subtle lobbying and influence are required to achieve the mission of 'saving lives and restoring hope'. Reports highlighting, for example, that in the world there are 870 million illiterate people, that 70 per cent of them are women, that 125 million children do not start school and that another 150 million drop out after four years are designed to stimulate debate. Reports and briefing papers are published and sent to politicians alongside lobbying for change. One campaign is concentrated on fair trade by seeking to help poor producers to access international export markets and offering a protected, fair trade market during transition while they acquire new skills and competencies. Over the last 20 years, although international trade has tripled, the 48 least developed countries containing 10 per cent of the world's population, have seen their share of world exports decline to just 0.4 per cent over the period. Central to Oxfam's campaign are informing consumers about trade-related causes of poverty, promoting a consumer movement in favour of fair and ethical trade and lobbying for change in world trading systems where these cause poverty. The greater the publicity, the more tangible the problems and the more powerful the call for help (http://www.oxfam.org).

Public scrutiny and accountability. Where public money is concerned or where organisations rely on donations, there is greater public interest in the activities and efficiency of the organisation. To maintain the flow of donations, a charity has to be seen to be transparently honest, trustworthy and to be producing 'results'. The public wants to know how much money is going into administrative costs and how much into furthering the real work of the charity.

Greenpeace (http://www.greenpeace.org) relies exclusively on support from individuals and foundations. It makes a deliberate point in its publicity of stating that it does not seek funds from governments, corporations or political parties and will not take individual donations if they compromise its independence of action. It is proud to state that it has no permanent allies or enemies. Such a principled stand means that Greenpeace must be entirely transparent if it is to avoid criticism from parties who have suffered from its direct action, or even the wider publics that support its cause.

To achieve a policy of openness, Greenpeace must make public its campaigns, its governance arrangements and its financial affairs. The annual reports reveal detailed information in all areas. The campaigns in climate, toxins, nuclear, oceans, forests, ocean dumping and genetic engineering are all specified and details provided of the main achievements in each area. A number of the campaigns have already been considered in this book, such as the Amazon rainforest and the whaling industry. An important part of retaining public support is highlighting successes. In 2001, for example, it highlighted its success in lobbying the European Parliament to ban PVC-containing toxic substances. The substances, widely used in children's toys, had resulted in damage to the kidneys, liver and testicles in animal experiments.

The financial breakdown of income and expenditure revealed a net income of €103.1m., after €43 m. of fund-raising expenditure was deducted. Around 47 per cent of expenditure went on direct campaigns, 33 per cent on overhead support for those campaigns, and 20 per cent on organisational support. This indicates that around half of any donation is ploughed back into the campaigning for which it was intended. Finally, details of the 40 offices and the various boards of trustees are presented along with the respective roles of Greenpeace International in the Netherlands, the overall strategy group, and each local board is specified. With many powerful detractors and 2.4 million supporters on a global scale, Greenpeace must show the results and the methods used to reach them.

■ Marketing implications

In general terms, the same principles of marketing apply equally to a non-profit organisation as to any purely commercial concern (Sargeant, 1999). There are, however, a few specific points to note. A non-profit organisation might have quite a wide-ranging product portfolio, if the needs of both funders and customers or clients are taken into account. Their products might, for instance, vary from information, reassurance and advice to medical research and other practical help such as cash grants or equipment. Donors might be 'purchasing' association with a high-profile good cause or the knowledge that they have done a good deed by giving. Because the products vary so much, from the extremely intangible to the extremely tangible, and because there are so many different publics to serve, a strong corporate image and good marketing communication are particularly important to pull the whole organisation together.

If dispensing information and advice or increasing the profile of a cause are central objectives of the non-profit organisation, then marketing communication is an essential tool. This might mean using conventional advertising media, although that can be expensive for organisations such as smaller charities unless advertising agencies and media owners can be persuaded to offer their services cheap or free as a donation in kind.

Publicity can also be an invaluable tool for the non-profit organisation, not only because of its cost-effectiveness, but also because of its ability to reach a wide range of audiences. Publicity might encourage fund raising, help to educate people or generate clients or customers. Association with high-profile commercial sponsors can similarly help to spread the message, through publicity, sponsored fund-raising events or joint or sponsored promotions.

In sectors where a non-profit organisation offers a more clearly defined product to a specific target segment within a competitive market, then a more standard approach to marketing communication might be used. A university, for example, is offering degree courses to potential students. As discussed elsewhere in this book, it might use advertising media to tell potential students why this is the best place to study; printed material such as the prospectus, brochures and leaflets to give more detail about the institution, its location and the courses on offer; visits to schools and education fairs to meet potential recruits face to face; and publicity to increase awareness and improve its corporate image.

eg The RSPCA is the UK's best known animal welfare charity. It not only monitors animal welfare and rehomes animals, but also campaigns and lobbies on relevant issues, such as battery farming. Fund raising is vital to the RSPCA – its annual running costs are around £71m. per year and it gets no government or lottery funding. Marketing communication is clearly important in creating and retaining donors. Direct marketing is under strain with response rates dropping and thus it needs to be better targeted than ever and more creative than ever in finding mechanisms for asking for money. The charity has done a lot of work on its databases and their management in tracking the frequency of response, type of appeal responded to, size of donations, spontaneous donation rates, preferred ways of giving, etc. to help it plan its marketing better. The RSPCA makes five appeals per year through direct mail and appeals are tailored to suit different donor groups. One such group is people who give regularly via the 'payroll giving' scheme. Mailings to them are less focused on 'more money please' than on 'do you know about these other ways you can help us?' The RSPCA is looking to develop the most integrated marketing strategy it can in terms of creating donors and then maximising their value through getting them involved in as many other areas as possible. Thus a donor might sign up for an affinity card, for example, and then be persuaded to buy Christmas cards or set up a standing order for a regular direct donation.

Pricing is applied somewhat differently in the non-profit sector than in the commercial world. As mentioned earlier, those providing income might be totally different from those receiving the product. It is accepted in most areas of the non-profit sector that the recipient might not have to bear the full cost of the service or product provided. In other words, the recipient's need comes first rather than the ability to pay. In the profit-making sector it is more likely to be the other way around: if you can pay for it, you can have it. Non-profit pricing, therefore, might be very flexible and varied. Some customers will not be asked to pay at all, others will be asked to make whatever donation they can afford for the service they have received, others will be charged a full market price.

Issues of distribution, process and physical evidence, where applicable, are similar for non-profit organisations to those of other types of organisation. The organisation has to ensure that the product or service is available when and where the customer or client can conveniently access it. This might or might not involve physical premises. Clearly, non-profit institutions such as universities, hospitals, museums and the like do operate from premises. They face the same issues as any other service provider of making sure that those premises are sufficiently well equipped to allow a service to be delivered and to deal with likely demand. They also have to realise that the premises are part of the marketing effort and contribute to the customer's or client's perception of quality. Prospective students visiting a university on an open day might not be able to judge the quality of the courses very well, but they can certainly tell whether the campus would be a good place for them to live and work, whether the teaching rooms are pleasant and well equipped, and how well resourced the library and IT facilities seem to be.

Some non-profit organisations that focus mainly on giving information and advice by mail or by telephone do not, of course, need to invest in smart premises. Their priority is to ensure that customers or clients are aware of how to access the service and that enquiries are dealt with quickly, sympathetically and effectively.

eg The Samaritans (http://www.samaritans.org.uk) exists to provide a confidential counselling service to those in a desperate emotional state who are contemplating suicide. The service is offered 24 hours a day from 154 branches staffed by volunteers who answer the telephones and raise local donations. There is no move towards developing a central call centre as it would undermine the whole structure of the service. Volunteers are carefully selected and trained locally, and give of their time for no charge. In 2001, there were 12,800 volunteers across England on various shifts, normally giving no more than 180 hours per year each. Although the caller may not care where the Samaritan is located, the organisation insists that its volunteers should not have to travel more than 60 miles to an office. There were 3.8 million calls in 2000 in England and the operation had to be able to cope with that demand, especially during the recognised peaks between 10 p.m. and 2 a.m. Each volunteer takes over 250 calls per year, and some calls can last for a long time, depending on the needs of the caller. Each branch runs as an autonomous operation, generating its own funds to cover the *c.* £17,000 cost per phone line and office expenses.

Marketing in non-profit-making areas is rapidly evolving and the techniques used in commercial situations are being transferred, tested and evolved to cope better with the complexity of causes, ideas and attitude change in a wide range of situations. Marketing thinking is being applied to encouraging more 'users' and 'customers' to come forward to benefit from supportive contact for people or children at risk, such as that provided by the Samaritans and the NSPCC. It is also being applied backwards to attract resources into charitable organisations that often rely on voluntary staff and generous donations from individuals and corporations.

In addition, corporate sponsorship and affiliated programmes have been fast developing, as association with a number of the causes listed above does little harm to a corporate reputation. For example Tesco, Green Flag and Lindt all work with the RSPCA for their mutual benefit. Whether they take the form of joint promotions, supported advertising, or sponsored programmes and campaigns, the opportunities for cooperation are considerable.

Chapter summary

- Although the variety of service products is very wide, all of them share some common characteristics that differentiate them from other types of product. With service products, for instance, there is often no transfer of ownership of anything, because a service is intangible. Services are also perishable, because they are generally performed at a particular time and are consumed as they are produced. This means that they cannot be stored in advance of demand, nor can they be kept in stock until a customer comes along. The customer is often directly involved in the production of the service product and thus the manufacture and delivery of the product cannot be separated. It also means that there is extensive interaction between the customer and the service provider's staff. Finally, because of the 'live' nature of the service experience and the central role of human interaction, it is very difficult to standardise the service experience.

- The normal model of a marketing mix consisting of the 4Ps is useful but insufficient for describing services, and an additional 3Ps, people, processes and physical evidence, have been added to deal with the extra dimensions peculiar to services. *People* takes account of the human interactions involved in the service product; *physical evidence* looks at the tangible elements that contribute either directly or indirectly to the creation, delivery, quality or positioning of the service; and *processes* defines the systems that allow the service to be created and delivered efficiently, reliably and cost-effectively.

- Service quality is hard to define and measure. Judgement of quality arises largely from customers' comparisons of what they expected from various facets of the service with what they think they actually received. Management can ensure that the service product is designed with the customer's real needs and wants in mind; that it is adequately resourced; that it is delivered properly; and they can try not to raise unrealistic expectations in the mind of the customer, but in the end, quality is a subjective issue. Staff are an important element of service and its delivery and must be fully qualified and trained to deal with customers and their needs, and to deliver the service reliably and consistently. The emphasis that is put on this will vary depending on whether staff have direct or indirect involvement with customers, and whether they are visible to customers or not. Like quality, productivity is a difficult management issue because of the live nature of services and the involvement of the customer in the process. Managers have to think and plan carefully in terms of staff recruitment and training, systems and technology, the service levels offered and the way in which customers interact with the service, to try to maintain control and efficiency in the service delivery system. Trying to manage supply and demand can also help to streamline productivity.

- Non-profit organisations, which might be in the public or private sector, form a specialist area of services marketing. They differ because they are likely to serve multiple publics; they have multiple objectives that can often be difficult to quantify; they offer services, but the funder of the service is likely to be different from the recipient of it; and finally, they are subject to closer scrutiny and tighter accountability than many other organisations. It is also possible that where non-profit organisations are in receipt of government funding or where their existence or operation is subject to regulation, there will be limits placed on their freedom to use the marketing mix as they wish. Pricing or promotion, for example, might be prescribed or set within narrow constraints.

questions for *review and discussion*

13.1 What are the main characteristics that distinguish services from physical products?

13.2 What are the 10 criteria that affect customers' perceptions of service quality?

13.3 Design a short questionnaire for assessing the quality of service offered by a local dental practice.

13.4 In what ways might the following service organisations define and improve their productivity:

- a theme park;
- a university;
- a fast food outlet?

13.5 In what ways do non-profit organisations differ from other types of business?

13.6 What do you think might be the main sources of revenue for the following types of non-profit organisation and what revenue generation problems do you think each faces:

- a small local charity;
- a National Health Service hospital;
- a public museum?

case study 13.1

Full Stop

The NSPCC has one simple aim: to ensure that cruelty to children stops. However, it has to decide between many different, and sometimes conflicting, objectives to achieve its aim. The challenge is to ensure that the public is aware of the extent of the problem, when sometimes it is uncomfortable to think that such cruelty goes on in a modern society. The message has to be got across that, for example, every week in the UK one child dies at the hands of parents or carers and 600 children are added to the child protection registers.

The main objective of the charity is to end cruelty to children altogether, but as the figures above demonstrate, it is unfortunately a long way from that goal. It runs a series of programmes and campaigns to tackle child abuse, in the home, at work, at school, and in the community and in society. Since the campaign began, the NSPCC has been able to handle more calls on its National Child Protection Helpline, expand its schools service, produce parenting packs and work directly with over 10,000 children. To achieve its main objective, it must raise donations directly through fund raising from individuals and from corporate contributions. These sources provide 86 per cent of its income. It needs volunteers to raise funds, to run campaigns and to help with some of the core services. All of these contributors must believe they are doing a worthwhile thing in supporting the NSPCC rather than another charity. The NSPCC is therefore a prime lobbying and

pressure group on child welfare issues. Campaigns have been run to influence government to raise such issues on the political agenda, government spending priorities and in law and policy making.

The NSPCC actually ran into trouble for being too hard hitting with some advertisements as part of its Full Stop campaign. Overall, the campaign aimed to shake the reader out of complacency and to change public attitudes to enlist more support. The campaign's first stage was targeted at raising awareness of the brutality and types of child abuse that go on through a series of advertisements following a high-profile launch supported by Ewan McGregor and Madonna. The Prime Minister said at the launch, 'The private passion we feel for our own children should become a public passion we feel for all our children. I believe that ending cruelty is the right idea at the right time' (as quoted by Gray, 2001). The advertisements' imagery was very powerful and disturbing: 'Stop it, Daddy, stop it'. It featured well-known personalities such as pop group the Spice Girls, cartoon character Rupert Bear and footballer Alan Shearer covering their eyes as background voices focused on adults either physically abusing or just about to molest a child. Such an approach was considered necessary to shock readers and to bring home the reality of what sadly does go on for a small percentage of children. The first phase of the campaign was a great success, with independent research in 2001 confirming that the NSPCC generated the highest spontaneous awareness of any UK charity with a 12 per cent increase pre- and post-campaign. It also helped to raise over £90m. from donations.

This was followed by equally powerful imagery in the 'Real Children Don't Bounce Back' campaign. It featured a cartoon boy being beaten up by a human father against a background of canned laughter. It ends with the cartoon boy falling down the stairs and then transforming into a real, but unconscious – possibly lifeless – child lying at the foot of the stairs. The television advertisements generated over 100 complaints to the ITC, but the NSPCC's intention was to bring home the reality of abuse, a reality that we are sometimes keen to ignore. The advertising made its point: it doubled the number of calls to the child protection helpline and enabled public awareness to be raised further as well as carrying the message that whatever the emotional stresses on parents, it should never turn to violence and child abuse. The television campaign, only shown after the 9 p.m. watershed, was designed to leave the viewer in no doubt that 'together we can stop abuse', and that the helpline could be used by anyone who suspects child cruelty.

The NSPCC has also entered into partnerships with companies to provide corporate support and assistance with fund raising. Microsoft is a major supporter of the Full Stop campaign, directly sponsoring school fund-raising activities to provide £10m. for the NSPCC and also championing the cause within the IT industry to raise awareness and a further £5m. Meanwhile, retailer The Early Learning Centre gave out 50,000 leaflets on protecting babies and 25,000 'Have Fun and Be Safe' leaflets in-store. There is close synergy between the customer base targeted by ELC and child welfare. Finally, Mars agreed some joint on-pack promotions to raise donations for the charity.

A number of other more targeted campaigns are run by the NSPCC. The 2002 Annual Children's Day was themed around 'Hitting Children Must Stop. Full Stop. It's Simple Enough for a Child to Understand', highlighting the dangers of smacking and was supported by 2,000 billboard posters. One poster indicates again the power of the imagery used. Called 'She was hit because she wet herself. She wet herself because she was hit' highlighted the emotional scars left by physical punishment and how it can damage the child–parent relationship. Supported by Microsoft, a website, there4me, has been launched and targeted at 12–16-year-olds who may be suffering from abuse and who can access the Internet. Private 'inbox' facilities, confidential passwords and a chat line with a real counsellor supplement considerable information to enable young people to take matters further if appropriate. It also supports a team of educational advisers who work with teachers, schools and local education authorities to promote child protection.

Managing the media and PR is an important part of the marketing effort. The NSPCC actively lobbies Westminster, such as for the 'Tighten the Net' campaign which persuaded the Home Office to invest £1.5m. in a public awareness campaign to show the dangers to children from chatlines and the Internet. It also succeeded in arguing for the first Child Commissioner appointed in the UK, approved by the Welsh Assembly. Things do not always go to plan, however. Victoria Climbié was murdered by her great aunt and boyfriend in February 2000. It emerged that she had been referred to an NSPCC-run family centre seven months prior to her death. If someone had acted on this referral, they should have found out about and put a stop to the appalling abuse Victoria was being subjected to. The Director of the NSPCC at the inquiry did not seek to avoid responsibility, stating that 'It is clear that we had an opportunity to help Victoria. It is profoundly to my regret that we did not act in a timely, adequate and appropriate way and this opportunity was lost. We have taken the issues raised by this tragic case for all the agencies involved very seriously. At every stage crucial lessons that have come out of our review of Victoria's case have been acted upon' (as quoted by Chandiramani, 2002). By adopting an honest approach and accepting a degree of responsibility, the NSPCC was able to avoid the worst aspects of a media backlash that could have been harmful to the wider cause.

As the NSPCC relies on donations for 86 per cent of its income, it is essential that it gets its message across. With a plan to raise £250m. over five years in support of its revitalised action programmes, the NSPCC believes that it must use sometimes shocking promotional techniques to stir people out of complacency. Funds are also needed for the distribution of 1 million publications, to maintain the child protection helpline. The latter received 125,000 calls from people concerned about children's welfare. Faced with the reality, it is perhaps not surprising that it is prepared to push the frontiers of shock campaigning.

Sources: Chandiramani (2002), Gray (2001), http://www.nspcc.org

Questions

1 In what ways do the special characteristics of services and the 7Ps of the services marketing mix apply to a charity?

2 List the multiple publics for both resource attraction and resource allocation that an organisation like the NSPCC might be targeting. What kind of problems do you think might arise from having such diverse target audiences?

3 What benefits does a charity get from a promotional tie-in, such as the one between the NSPCC and The ELC?

4 To what extent can 'shock' campaigns such as those produced by the NSPCC be justified? What are the potential advantages and disadvantages of such a campaign?

References for chapter 13

Adams, B. (2000), 'A Few Hotels are Reaping Benefits from Smartcards', *Hotel and Motel Management*, 3 July, pp. 62–3.

Bansal, P. (2002), 'Smart Cards Spread across Europe', *The Banker*, March, pp. 122–3.

Barton, R. (2001), 'Tibet Smells a Rat in China's Decision to Embrace Tourism', *The Independent*, 27 May, p. 2.

Bevan, S. and Barber, L. (1999), 'The Benefits of Service with a Smile', *Financial Times*, 24 June, p. 15.

Bitner, M., Brown, S. and Meuter, M. (2000), 'Technology Infusion in Service Encounters', *Journal of the Academy of Marketing Science*, 28 (1), pp. 138–49.

Bray, R. (2002), 'Marriott Tests Central Printers', *Financial Times*, 26 March, p. 17.

Bryan-Brown, C. (2001), 'Sweden on Wheels', *The Times*, 15 December, p. 19.

Buckley, C. (2002), 'Will Retirement Become a Thing of the Past?', *The Times*, 18 January, p. 26.

Burt, T. (1999), 'The Northern Lights of Electronic Banking', *Financial Times*, 19 July, p. 17.

Cameron, N. (2002), 'Hearts Ban Rowdy Fans', *Daily Record*, 13 February, pp. 47, 52.

Caruana, A., Money, A. and Berthon, P. (2000), 'Service Quality and Satisfaction – the Moderating Role of Value', *European Journal of Marketing*, 34 (11/12), pp. 1338–53.

Chandiramani, R. (2002), 'Call to Action', *Marketing*, 28 March, p. 18.

Christopher, M. *et al.* (1994), *Relationship Marketing: Bringing Quality, Customer Service and Marketing Together* (2nd edn), Butterworth-Heinemann.

Cowell, D. (1984), *The Marketing of Services*, Butterworth-Heinemann.

Cox, J. (2002), 'Leisure Property Trends: Is it the End for Multiplex Anchors?', *Journal of Leisure Property*, 2 (1), pp. 83–93.

Daneskhu, S. (2002), 'Competition Puts Pressure on Once Healthy Bottom-lines', *Financial Times*, 15 March, p. 2.

Devlin, S. and Dong, H. (1994), 'Service Quality from the Customers' Perspective', *Marketing Research*, 6 (1), pp. 5–13.

Dodona (2001), Cinemagoing 9, *Dodona Research*, Leicester.

Doe, B. (1999), 'Service Please', *Modern Railways*, August, p. 597.

Douglas-Home, J. (2001), 'Dracula Goes Disney', *The Times*, 6 November, p. 2.5.

Fox, A. (2001), 'Unfriendly Skies', *HR Magazine*, September, p. 12.

George, R. (2002), 'Mickey Mouse with Fangs', *The Independent*, 27 January, pp. 18–21.

Glover, J. (1999), 'London Joins the Smartcard Set', *Modern Railways*, August, p. 585.

Gray, R. (2001), 'Partnerships for a Wider Awareness', *Marketing*, 3 May, pp. 31–2.

Heskett, J. *et al.* (1997), *The Service Profit Chain*, Free Press.

Hibbert, L. (2000), 'It's Easier by Card', *Professional Engineering*, 6 September, pp. 38–9.

Kotler, P. (1982), *Marketing for Non-Profit Organisations* (2nd edn), Prentice Hall.

Lewis, K. (2002), 'Fitness on Delivery', *Sunday Times*, 28 April, p. 44.

Lovelock, C., Vandermerwe, S. and Lewis, B. (1999), *Services Marketing*, Financial Times Prentice Hall.

Lovelock, C. and Weinberg, C. (1984), *Marketing for Public and Non-Profit Managers*, John Wiley & Sons.

McCarthy, M. (2002), 'Multiplex Cinemas Pose Threat to Town Centres', *The Independent*, 5 January, p. 8.

McLuhan, R. (2002), 'Brands Put Service under the Spotlight', *Marketing*, 21 February, p. 33.

Mathews, B. and Clark, M. (1996), 'Comparability of Quality Determinants in Internal and External Service Encounters', in *Proceedings: Workshop on Quality Management in Services VI*, Universidad Carlos III de Madrid: 15–16 April.

Mesure, S. (2001), 'As Economic Downturn Bites, Can Britain's Health Clubs Keep in Shape?', *The Independent*, 12 September, p. 19.

Moore, C. (2001), 'Hotels Open Doors to Wireless, Broadband', *InfoWorld*, 26 March, p. 34.

Moore Ede, P. (2002), 'Bloody Hell', *The Ecologist*, March, p. 47.

Parasuraman, A. *et al.* (1985), 'A Conceptual Model of Service Quality and its Implications for Future Research', *Journal of Marketing*, 49 (Fall), pp. 41–50.

Perren, B. (1999a), 'Service on Board', *Modern Railways*, May, p. 352.

Perren, B. (1999b), 'Service on Board', *Modern Railways*, August, p. 595.

Perren, B. and Pyke, N. (2000), 'Passenger Power: Joke Railway Sandwich Refuses to Die', *The Independent*, 27 August, p. 7.

Rayport, J. and Sviokla, J. (1994), 'Managing in the Marketspace', *Harvard Business Review*, 72 (November/December), pp. 2–11.

Reece, D. (2002), 'Tussauds Splashes Out', *The Sunday Telegraph*, 17 March, p. 2.

RePass, J. (2002), 'Smart and Smarter at the MBTA', *Railway Age*, February, pp. 20–1.

Retail World (2002), 'Smart Card Trial Pressures Ranging', *Retail World*, 15–26 April, p. 10.

Richards, G. (2001), 'Marketing China Overseas: the Role of Theme Parks and Tourist Attractions', *Journal of Vacation Marketing*, December, pp. 28–38.

Rogers, D. (2001), 'Cinema Bucks the Media Trend', *Marketing*, 29 November, p. 7.

Rushe, D. (2001), 'Multiplex Cinemas Close Their Doors', *Sunday Times*, 25 March, p. 6.

Sargeant, A. (1999), *Marketing Management for Nonprofit Organizations*, Oxford University Press.

Sasser, W. *et al.* (1978), *Management of Service Operations: Text, Cases and Readings*, Allyn & Bacon.

Shostack, L. (1977), 'Breaking Free from Product Marketing', *Journal of Marketing*, 41 (April), pp. 73–80.

Singh, S. (2001), 'Charity Begins in Your Pocket', *Marketing Week*, 1 November, pp. 36–7.

Syal, R. (2001), 'Secret Rail Dossier of Commuter Chaos', *The Sunday Telegraph*, 12 August, p. 8.

Warren, P. (1999), 'Welcome to the Hotel Room that Knows You Better than Your Mother', *The Express*, 17 January, p. 24.

Winnett, R. (2002), 'Road Tolls at Rush Hour Could Replace Car Tax', *Sunday Times*, 24 February, p. 28.

Zeithaml, V. *et al.* (1988), 'SERVQUAL: a Multiple Item Scale for Measuring Consumer Perceptions of Service Quality', *Journal of Retailing*, 64 (1), pp. 13–37.

Zeithaml, V. *et al.* (1990), *Delivering Quality Service: Balancing Customer Perceptions and Expectations*, The Free Press.

chapter 14

e-marketing and new media

LEARNING OBJECTIVES

This chapter will help you to:

1 understand the nature of Internet marketing;

2 appreciate the major trends in Internet penetration and usage in both consumer and B2B markets;

3 gain insight into the marketing uses of the Internet and its future development;

4 appreciate the nature and usage of the three main elements of new media: e-mail marketing, wireless marketing and interactive television marketing.

Introduction

With the net, a new way of conducting business is available, but it doesn't change the laws of business or most of what really creates a competitive advantage. The fundamentals of competition remain unchanged.

Professor Michael Porter (quoted by Newing, 2002)

Porter is absolutely right: the Internet does not change any of the fundamentals of doing 'good business' or 'good marketing'. Understanding the target customer's needs and wants and designing an integrated marketing package that delivers them remains critically important regardless of whether a company is a dotcom or a 'traditional' organisation. Porter goes on to say that the companies that will succeed and benefit from the Internet will be those that keep their core strategic objectives in view and then work out how to integrate, use and mould the Internet to help achieve those objectives and to create and sustain competitive advantage. Those that fail will be those that adopt a 'me too' attitude, jumping on the Internet bandwagon because 'our competitors are doing it' or that view Internet applications as a diversification, parallel and almost completely separate from their core traditional business.

To a lesser extent, the same can be said of the new marketing communications media, such as viral marketing, SMS and interactive television, that are emerging from technological innovation. Some companies are adopting them because they can see how they complement the use of traditional media within the context of the wider integrated communications strategy, and have defined a distinct 'fit' between the medium, the message and the target market (see, for instance, the 'Hey, Sexy!' Kiss 100 Marketing in Action vignette on pp. 487–8). Others, however, seem to be adopting them because they are the latest sexy thing that everyone else seems to be doing. No prizes for guessing which are likely to be the most successful campaigns!

eg Friends Reunited is a dotcom company with a difference. It is unashamedly in the nostalgia business and the number of users is growing at such a rapid rate that it is a challenge just to keep up with the necessary computer capacity to run it all. The site aims to link old school friends and work colleagues and has been responsible, if the press is to be believed, not just for reunions galore, but also marriages, divorces and even litigation from allegedly libelled teachers. Based on a similar idea in America (http://www.classmates.com), since its launch in October 2000 Friends Reunited has registered 7 million members, 45,500 schools and recorded 220 million page impressions in one month alone (http://www. friendsreunited.co.uk). It is one of the UK's most popular websites. On average, a user spends over 30 minutes per month on the site, 40 per cent of the users are female and 72 per cent are aged between 25 and 49 (Snoddy, 2001).

In the light of its high traffic levels and its phenomenal growth, the owners are very proud to admit that they have spent no money on advertising and promotion. That said, the human interest angle means that a steady stream of reunion stories keeps the press coverage high and it may, in time, come to be regarded as one of the best word-of-mouth campaigns in promotional history. Although accessing the site is free, it costs £5 to become a registered member so that you can use the e-mail service. The other main source of revenue is banner advertising on the site. With such high traffic levels, it is not surprising that profits are already starting to flow (*Financial Times*, 2001). Further expansion has already taken place in Australia, South Africa and New Zealand, as first-mover advantage is crucial for this type of operation.

Coors Brewers prefers to stick to traditional ways of selling beer rather than dabbling in dotcoms, but it does make creative use of new media opportunities. The 'Have You Seen My Sister?' campaign was a big hit, impressive in its simplicity but very effective. It involved an actor drinking bottles of Worthingtons in selected bars. Just before leaving a bar, he asks other consumers to call him on his mobile if his sister arrives. Not long after, the sister appears and when the consumers call the mobile number they receive a text message entitling them to two free bottles of Worthingtons, and of course the sister starts to hand out the samples on the spot. It created a lot of interest and proved to be an effective sales promotion (http://www.spca.org.uk).

Although generally using traditional marketing strategies to sell beer, Coors Brewers had a hit recently with the 'Have you seen my sister?' campaign. A text message followed by immediate free samples made sure drinkers remembered their beer.

Source: Coors Brewers/BD. BD originated the idea and implemented the sampling activity on the company's behalf.

The purpose of this chapter is to examine the ways in which the Internet and new media are providing new opportunities for marketers to get to know their customers better and to serve their needs and wants more effectively, and in some cases, a lot more engagingly. Throughout, we will be presenting examples and vignettes of organisations that are successfully using the Internet and new media with clear strategic purposes relating to the creation of competitive advantage in mind.

The first part of the chapter looks at that relatively well-established tool: the Internet. We examine its increasing penetration of both consumer and B2B markets and the ways in which markets are using and might use it in the future. The chapter then turns to the less familiar world of new media, focusing particularly on e-mail marketing (including viral marketing), wireless marketing and interactive television. Again, we consider how these techniques are being used and their potential for the future.

Internet marketing

■ The nature of Internet marketing

As more and more homes and businesses either get connected or develop their own websites, the Internet has become an increasingly important tool of marketing. Smith and Chaffey (2001) and Smith and Taylor (2002) summarise the main benefits of investing in e-marketing as the 5Ss:

■ *Sell*. Selling goods and services online, potentially to a global market.
■ *Serve*. Using the website as a way of providing additional customer service or of streamlining service delivery.
■ *Save*. Saving money in terms of the overheads associated with more traditional forms of doing business.
■ *Speak*. Websites offer companies a chance to enter into one-to-one dialogue with customers more easily than ever before. As well as providing valuable feedback, with good database management, that dialogue can be the basis for fruitful customer relationship management.
■ *Sizzle*. A website that is well designed, both in terms of its content and its visual impact, can add an extra 'something' to a brand or corporate image through engaging, educating and/or entertaining the visitor to the site. Increasingly, organisations are introducing an element of fun into their websites to grab and retain attention. Interactive games, webcam and video feeds, cartoons, free downloads and relaxed informality have all been introduced to keep the viewer's attention and to make company and product information more interesting.

Whatever its purpose, and however much is spent on it, a website should provide a powerful supplementary marketing tool. It should have all the creative flair of an advertisement, the style and information of a company brochure, the personal touch and tailored presentation of face-to-face interaction and, not least, always leave the visitor clear as to what action should be taken next.

For some small businesses, the Internet can become a valuable means of communicating with a potentially global audience easily and cost-effectively, freeing them from the constraints of geographic catchment areas. Cookson's, a builder's merchant, successfully extended its horizons (and its turnover) from serving a customer base largely restricted to a 7-mile radius of Stockport to a global reach through the Internet.

eg   Bluewave is a company that designs websites, describing itself as 'a global online solutions company, serving clients in the visualisation, development and ongoing enhancement of their online business' (http://www.bluewave.com). In conjunction with the Royal National Institute of the Blind (RNIB), Bluewave developed the first viral fund-raising application using Macromedia Flash MX that is fully accessible to blind and partially sighted Internet users. One objective was to encourage voluntary donations for RNIB's work with blind and partially sighted children, and another was to raise awareness of the RNIB's Campaign for Good Web Design, particularly among website designers.

The site (http://www.lookloud.bluewave.com) was linked with the RNIB's 'Look Loud Day' on 14 June 2002 when people all over the UK were asked to dress in their most garish and outrageous clothes and raise money for blind and partially sighted children. Julie Howell

▶

of the RNIB said, 'RNIB is really pleased that Bluewave has been able to use Macromedia Flash MX to produce a viral application that is fully usable by blind and partially sighted people. While we hope "Look Louder" will be an effective fund raising tool, we are also encouraging web designers to think about the needs of all potential users when designing viral applications. With the sophisticated web-design tools available today there really are no excuses for designing applications that people with disabilities can't use.' The site makes use of audio and visual techniques that guide the user experience and uses Flash MX's new accessibility features so that the application can be read by Windoweyes, a screenreading tool used by many blind internet users.

Visitors to the Look Loud website can choose a head, items of 'loud' clothing and accessories for a screen-based cartoon character which can then be sent on to friends and colleagues. The hope is that they too will visit the site and create their own badly dressed characters. The website also offers the visitor the chance to make an online donation to the RNIB Look Loud campaign (http://www.bluewave.com; http://www.rnib.org.uk; http://www.lookloud.bluewave.com).

The dotcom boom and bust

While traditional companies have largely sought to integrate and use the Internet and the 5Ss within the context of their existing businesses, the late 1990s also saw the rapid rise and equally rapid fall of many so-called dotcom businesses. These were businesses that came into being specifically to use the Internet as a platform for delivering goods and/or services in an innovative way. Many potential investors were carried away by the enthusiasm of the dotcom entrepreneurs and promises of mega-profits, pouring money into these businesses. It soon became clear, however, that many dotcoms were running into problems. Some ran into technical problems that made it difficult to deliver on their promises and others simply found that paying customers were a lot thinner on the ground than forecast.

eg Sports website Sportal was set up in July 1998 with about £4.8m. to offer action, information and links with sports clubs and events with a mission to 'create the first major sport brand of the 21st century'. It signed up for the Internet rights of the top European football clubs, allowing it to show any action involving those clubs on the Internet. Sportal earned revenue from showing football action and earned advertising revenue from running club websites. By the end of 1999, it had a number of offices in Europe and further afield, and was sufficiently well established to raise another £50m. in investment capital. This helped it to expand its services, for example supplying football content to Yahoo! and launching a WAP mobile phone service. The highlight of 2000 was winning the contract to design and produce the Euro 2000 website. While the website was very successful and helped to improve Sportal's brand image, it actually cost the company £5m. Overall, insufficient revenue was flowing in, but the deals were still being done. It is reported that Sportal spent a seven-figure sum to sponsor the shirts for Juventus' Champions League matches. In the last three months of 2000, Sportal made losses of more than £13m.

Part of the problem was that Sportal was not the only sports site on the Internet, and once Euro 2000 had finished, Sportal had nothing particularly distinctive to offer. Furthermore, people were not willing to pay for what it did offer, nor were the advertising revenues flowing. As one expert on online business said, 'Sport is about killer data – scores, tips and rumours. People will only visit a site regularly if they think they will find killer data' (as quoted by Barr, 2002).

In May 2001, redundancies were made, and Sportal, a company worth £270m. at its peak and employing 360 staff in 11 countries, limped on until November 2001 when it was sold for £1 (yes, that's £1 for the company itself, although its hardware was sold for £190,000) to UKBetting.com. The intention is that Sportal should be dedicated to the more light-hearted side of sport, featuring competitions, chat rooms and online games, complementing sister sites SportingLife.com (with a focus on news and information), bettingzone.co.uk (focus on independent betting news and statistics) and totalbet.com (focus on placing bets) which are also owned by UKBetting.com. Thus although the mission might have changed, at least the Sportal brand name has managed to survive.

Sources: Barr (2002), Doward (2002), *Marketing* (2002), Nichols (2001).

The dotcom boom was followed by the dotcom bust as businesses collapsed or were taken over by their more astute competitors. Those that have survived and established themselves as leaders in their marketplaces, such as lastminute.com (see Case Study 1.1), eBay and Amazon have done so not only by astute marketing and offering goods and services that people want and are prepared to pay for, but also by careful attention to defining and nurturing their competitive advantage along with some sober financial management. Investors have had to be patient, however: it took Amazon eight years before it was able to report its first small profits in January 2002.

■ The website

A US survey of 300 daily Internet users found that two-thirds of people said that if a website did not meet their expectations, they would never return to it again. According to the survey, the four essential characteristics of a 'good' website are that it must be continually updated, easy to navigate, have in-depth information on its subject and offer quick loading and response times (Gaudin, 2002).

The need for fast loading and response times is still a difficulty for marketers because of the technology driving website use. Once online, the quality of viewing can be reduced and the irritation level increased if graphics take a long time to load and in some cases crash the computer if they overload it. Better video plug-ins and ever more sophisticated browsers have enhanced quality and reduced loading times, but as yet for the average Internet user the experience can still be frustrating.

Apparel Industry Magazine (2000) set up a focus group to explore and assess four fashion e-tail sites. The results give an interesting insight into what people are looking for in terms of website design and facilities/services offered. Complexity of navigation was raised as a problem. On one site, users found they had to do a tutorial to learn how to use the site and make purchases. Even then it was easy to make mistakes. The user could have up to 10 windows open at a time and closing the wrong one would mean exiting the site altogether and having to start again. As Kolesar and Galbraith (2000) said, the customer is an integral part of the e-tail service experience and the role they play has to be in keeping with their knowledge and abilities as well as their self-image.

Users did like having the facility to dress a virtual mannequin and get her to 'do a twirl' so that they could see the effect of putting different garments together as an outfit. They also liked being able to ask for recommendations, for example to find some shoes to match a garment already chosen. Detailed product descriptions, including fabric care, and the ability to zoom in on garments to see fabric and styling detail were also appreciated, but the quality of photographs and colour reproduction was generally thought to be poor and inconsistent. Uncluttered pages were preferred rather than those trying to show nine or more garments per page. Users were frustrated by missing product photographs and messages such as 'unavailable in the size/colour requested'. When sites offer a very large assortment of goods, users liked being able to use menus or search facilities to specify product types, size ranges or price bands that they were interested in to narrow down the number of products shown.

All the sites examined were e-tail stores bringing together a number of brand names and designer labels on the one site. The focus group best liked the sites that gave them an 'aggregated shopping cart' so that they could select goods from lots of different labels and pay for them in one transaction. The group was less impressed with the fashion e-tailers that simply acted as portals, so that clicking on a label name took them through to that label's own site. This means that the shopper cannot have the facility to see what one label's sweater would look like with another label's jeans, for example. It also means the inconvenience of having to undertake individual transactions with individual sites. Also on the processing side, users wanted clear information about shipping costs and times and returns policies.

Interestingly, researchers have also found that the industries that tend to deliver the good websites are the ones that have faced the fiercest dotcom competition. Thus Amazon, for instance, has set the benchmark for any online bookseller in terms of the quality of the website that customers expect to see (Gaudin, 2002). Cap Gemini Ernst & Young (CGE&Y)

interviewed 6,000 consumers across nine European countries to find out what online shoppers felt to be important about the e-tailers they dealt with. Honesty, respect and reliability were all rated a lot more highly than having the highest quality merchandise or the lowest prices. These are not necessarily easy virtues to communicate or 'prove' and companies face a difficult task in winning the trust of a fundamentally suspicious public.

McKinsey has found a marked degree of mistrust among Internet users. Only about 4 per cent of online users routinely register at websites, and two-thirds of those who do not register say that it is because of lack of trust or protection of their privacy. If, therefore, companies want consumers to register, then they will have to make sure they are offering products, services, information and/or promotions that consumers really want and that will encourage them to overcome their misgivings about registering. McKinsey's research also suggests that companies that do get the consumer past this initial barrier and start to build relationships through well-targeted constant and interactive communication benefit from it. Amazon, for instance, generates 50 per cent of its sales from repeat customers against an average of 25 per cent for e-tailers generally (Saunders, 2001).

■ Consumer Internet penetration and spending

Clearly, the opportunities for Internet marketing are closely linked with a target market's ability to access the Internet. The Internet's penetration is still evolving and growing. According to Euromonitor (2002), in many EU countries, the percentage of households connected to the Internet is set to double between 2000 and 2006. The figures and predictions for online penetration among individuals are very similar. A UK survey found in 2002 that 45 per cent of UK adults use the Internet for personal use and another 10 per cent intended to go online within the next two years (Pastore, 2002). With many more people having access to the Internet at home, at school, college or university, at work, and at public libraries and cybercafés, its attraction to the marketer as a medium for communication, selling and other transactions is obvious.

Nevertheless, marketers need to exercise some caution. Euromonitor (2002)'s research also shows that, in 2002 in all EU countries, less than half of online users were actually using the Internet to buy things. In Belgium it was less than 20 per cent, while the best figures came from the UK with 41.6 per cent. Even by 2006, only a few countries are expected to have more than 60 per cent of users actually buying online. Of course, the Internet is not solely about e-tailing, but for many consumer goods companies it is a natural extension of their business, and it is important to them to see consumers becoming confident and accustomed to buying online to give them an opportunity to extend their customer base and generate extra revenues and economies of scale.

The good news for marketers is that the average spend per online buyer is rising. According to BMRB in 2002, 56 per cent of UK Internet users were shopping online. In May 2002, the average total online spend per shopper over the previous six months was £560. Extrapolating from these figures, BMRB estimated that the annual total value of consumer e-commerce in the UK is £11.9bn (Milsom, 2002). Euromonitor forecasts suggest that average spend will continue to rise. It is interesting to note that the UK buyer is spending much more on average than anyone else. UK consumers are spending far more than anyone else in Europe on online grocery shopping; more than twice as much as the Germans, who themselves are spending more than twice as much as their nearest rivals, the French (Euromonitor, 2002). The UK spend reflects the proactive and very competitive approaches taken to online grocery shopping by the dominant supermarket chains who have invested a lot of money in setting up and refining the infrastructure to allow online shopping and home deliveries, as well as investing in marketing efforts to develop an online customer base.

Another notable category in which UK and German consumers were spending much more freely than other Europeans in 2001 is books. Here, the influence of Amazon cannot be ignored. Amazon.co.uk and amazon.de have done a lot to encourage online book (and video and music) buying in the UK and Germany respectively, again, through proactive market-building strategies. The birth of amazon.fr will perhaps start to stimulate French spend on books, videos/DVDs and music similarly.

eg Tesco.com, offering over 40,000 product lines, has around 75 per cent share of the UK e-grocery market. It makes over 80,000 deliveries a week in its fleet of 800 vans, covering 96.6 per cent of the UK. Its customer base consists of well over 1 million households, mainly consisting of better-off families with both parents working. Nearly 94 per cent of its users are loyal to it and 30 per cent shop nowhere else online. The average spend per order is £85 (compared with £21 in-store) leading to sales in 2001 of £356m., up 50 per cent on the previous year. The potential for e-grocery shopping is huge: few people enjoy tramping round a busy store and lugging their shopping home afterwards. A survey by Barclays Bank has calculated that Internet users could save over 63 hours a year by using the Internet to buy what they need, the equivalent of 7 Saturdays or 25 evenings of late-night shopping.

While Tesco's success might make it look like an easy way to make money, other retailers have not fared so well with their online operations. Sainsbury's online business, Sainsbury's to You, is not performing as well as Tesco.com. Analysts estimate that it is generating less than £100m. in revenue and will make a loss of £50m. in 2002 and £35m. in 2003. In November 2001, Safeway analysed the results of a trial scheme and decided not to introduce a home-shopping operation at all because of the high level of investment required.

Sources: *Birmingham Post* (2002), Bruce (2002), Goodley (2002), Gregory (2002).

■ B2B Internet spending

According to eMarketer's 'E-Commerce Trade and B2B Exchanges' report (CyberAtlas, 2002), worldwide B2B e-commerce for 2002 was estimated to be worth $823.4bn, but by 2004, it is forecast that it will be worth nearly $2.4 trillion. The International Data Corp. is even more optimistic, quoting an estimate of $4.3 trillion by 2005 (http://www.idc.com). Much of this growth is being driven by companies recognising the advantages of moving to B2B e-commerce solutions, such as convenience, cost saving (up to 22 per cent in some supply chains), customer and competitor pressure as well as opportunities to generate new revenue.

Online procurement, pioneered by large, global organisations, represents a large part of B2B online commerce. Nearly 43 per cent of US large-volume purchasers said that the Internet was likely to be 'critical' or 'very important' in their future purchasing plans and a further 47 per cent said that it would be somewhat important. This could mean a lot of business. IBM, for example, spent over $43bn via e-procurement during 2000, and Boeing processes more than 20,000 daily transactions via its website (Pastore, 2001).

Some B2B online trading is being encouraged by the emergence of both independent and consortium-owned online 'marketplaces' or 'exchanges' that bring buyers and sellers together, facilitating transactions. They offer buyers access to a global network of suppliers and information on all aspects of their processes, practices, facilities and their marketing focus. Acting as an intermediary, the marketplace helps would-be buyers to prepare their 'request for quotation' which advertises their needs to potential suppliers, and helps would-be suppliers to prepare their bids. FreeMarkets is one of the leading online exchanges, and any bids that are made through it include a cost breakdown so that the buyer can assess how realistic it is. The Royal Bank Group in London uses FreeMarkets and while up to £70m. of its purchasing went through Freemarkets in 2001, the company can envisage an increasing proportion of its total annual spend of £2bn being spent through that channel in the future. This is perhaps not surprising, given that FreeMarkets estimates that its clients save between 2 and 25 per cent on their purchases (Anderson and Patel, 2001).

While online reverse auctions might be seen as a return to the bad old days of adversarial buyer–seller relationships, some companies and industries have thought in terms of 'e-collaboration' pooling information, data and resources online, often with direct competitors, and streamlining and integrating people, data and processes (Hewson, 2000). In October 2000, Covisint, an 'e-marketplace' or 'B2B exchange' serving the motor industry started trading. Covisint was set up collaboratively by General Motors, Ford, DaimlerChrysler, Renault and Nissan at a cost of $270m. with the intention of becoming the Internet focal point for the global motor industry, a portal to which every buyer and supplier goes in order to find and place business. Covisint would conduct auctions and also be used to help run collaborative product development projects, taking products through from the drawing board to development and testing and into production.

The buyer–supplier relationship under the hammer (or under the cosh?)

Through sites such as e-Bay, the idea of an Internet auction has become well established in consumer markets. The seller advertises the goods and the would-be buyer makes a bid. The highest bid made by the time the auction deadline passes gets to buy the goods. In B2B markets, the online reverse auction has started to become more common. The buyer advertises the specifications of what they want to buy and a starting price and then would-be suppliers make bids undercutting that price. All the bidders can see what others are bidding and can thus design their bids appropriately. Often, but by no means always, the lowest bid made by the close of the auction 'wins'.

Understandably, buyers and suppliers have very different views on the benefits and usefulness of reverse auctions, as well as on the ethics underlying them. Some see it as a cynical way of frightening existing suppliers into reducing their prices. They find themselves pitched into an auction against both obvious well-known competitors and a few unknown companies and although they don't make the lowest bid in the auction they still get to retain the business – but at a lower price than before. One existing supplier found that it did lose the business to an unknown competitor but later got a call asking it to continue to supply temporarily (at the new price, of course) because the auction winner had no experience of manufacturing that product and could not meet the delivery quantities required. Suppliers argue that if buyers were satisfied that all bidders could actually supply the quantities required to the specifications stated then the lowest

price would always win – but it doesn't. 'Auctions are not about getting the lowest price *per se* but getting the lowest price per supplier' as one manufacturer (as quoted by Watson, 2002b) put it.

Suppliers also feel that it is too impersonal a process with no room for old fashioned face-to-face negotiation. There is too much emphasis on price and not enough on issues of collaboration and longer-term business development for the benefit of both parties. Suppliers feel that buyers are damaging relationships built up over years for the sake of short-term cost savings that are often not reflected in retail prices to the end consumer. Some buyers, such as Cisco and Dell agree, and have said that they will not subject their suppliers to this kind of process.

Most buyers who use auctions do not see it like this, however. They see it as a much more transparent process that can work in the supplier's favour as they can see exactly what rival bidders are offering and decide whether to undercut it (or not) and by how much, rather than going all-out for the lowest possible bid they can manage. Some suppliers are, however, cynical about just how genuine some of the bids are. One supplier, claiming to be number one in its field, said that the opening price on a relevant auction was 25 per cent lower than its best price. But as one buyer (quoted by Watson, 2002b) said, 'At the end of the day, it's a pain in the arse to change a supplier. We're not going to hold an auction unless there is a chance of a significant price reduction. And if we set a ridiculous price to open, we just shoot ourselves in the foot. After all, no one has to bid.' That may well be true, but it

would be a brave supplier that would boycott an auction or would gamble on which rival bids should be taken seriously and which ignored.

Buyers also claim that they do not use auctions in product areas where they have strategic relationships with suppliers as they do not wish to damage those relationships, but suppliers are claiming that buyers work on the principle that 'As long as you can define the product and more than one supplier can make it, you can auction it' (as quoted by Watson, 2002a).

Overall, the appropriateness of online reverse auctions and their impact on the long-term quality of buyer–supplier relationships is debatable. What seems clear is that their use in an industry seems to depend on the relative power balance between the parties and the nature of the goods and services being traded. High-tech companies such as Cisco and Dell operating in industries where there are few alternative suppliers, where suppliers hold the bargaining power, and where long-term innovation and collaboration are paramount may well see little point in risking relationships for the sake of short-term cost savings. Where the buyers are few and powerful, where switching costs are relatively low, and where there are many alternative suppliers, then it seems that the reverse auction is here to stay. Rosenthal (2002) suggests that by 2006, it will account for 15 per cent of worldwide B2B e-commerce. It might not sound a lot, but in value terms it represents a significant amount of trade. What, however, does it contribute to the ethical treatment of suppliers?

Sources: Anderson and Patel (2001), Rosenthal (2002), Watson (2002a, b).

Sadly, it seems that this particular e-collaboration was a Utopian dream and that the motor manufacturers had underestimated the level of mistrust and cynicism among the 7,000 participating suppliers. The kind of objections outlined in the CSR in Action vignette above began to be voiced. Suppliers felt that it was all just a mechanism to squeeze their prices down and did not like the idea of sensitive pricing information about their businesses being so readily available to competitors (Grant, 2002).

■ The marketing uses of a website

There are many reasons for an organisation considering using the Internet, but they tend to group into three broad categories: as a research and planning tool; as a distribution channel; and for communication and promotion, as seen in Table 14.1.

Table 14.1 Marketing uses of the Internet

Research and planning tool
- Obtain market information
- Conduct primary research
- Analyse customer feedback and response

Distribution and customer service
- Take orders
- Update product offerings frequently
- Help the customer buy online
- Process payments securely
- Raise customer service levels
- Reduce marketing and distribution costs
- Distribute digital products

Communication and promotion
- Generate enquiries
- Enable low cost direct communication
- Reinforce corporate identity
- Produce and display product catalogues
- Entertain, amuse and build goodwill
- Inform investors
- Detail current and old press releases
- Provide basic product and location information
- Present company in a favourable light – history, mission, achievements, views, etc.
- Educate customers on the products, processes, etc.
- Inform suppliers of developments
- Communicate with employees
- Attract new job recruits
- Answer questions about the company and its products

Research and planning tool

The Internet provides direct access to a considerable amount of secondary marketing information. Some sources are free, but many can only be accessed through subscription. Increasingly, the need to visit the library or purchase bulky directories and reports is decreasing as the power, convenience and flexibility of online searching become better known. Most organisations offering subscription services, such as Mintel, *Financial Times*, and International Data Corp. will update their sites frequently by adding new and updated information and reports. Many of the secondary data sources considered in Chapter 5 can also be accessed online.

As Internet usage increases, the possibilities for primary research are also growing. Through online visitor books, feedback using structured questionnaires or via e-mail, web discussion groups and analysing visitor and online ordering traffic, useful information can be gathered for marketing planning purposes.

Distribution channel

The growth of Amazon shows just how the power of the Internet can have an impact on a conventional distribution channel. The impact will grow in the future as consumers gain more confidence in online purchasing. There are several advantages of online distribution:

eg

Market researchers undertook a survey of 50,000 people in the USA to see how effective banner advertising is in terms of affecting brand awareness, advertising recall and purchase intent. The research, on behalf of Nestlé Purina PetCare Co., showed that consumers exposed to Purina banner advertisements were nearly 50 per cent more likely to cite it as the first dog food brand that came to mind. The more times consumers were exposed to the advertising, the higher the awareness levels, thus among the group of respondents who had received 1–5 impressions, brand awareness rose from 22.3 to 28.2 per cent while among those who had received 6–20 impressions, it rose to 35.4 per cent. The number of impressions received also had an effect on purchase intent. Looking at one particular product in the range, Purina ONE, purchase intent rose from 23.6 to 34.7 per cent among those receiving 1–5 impressions, and to 38.4 per cent among those receiving 6–20.

The banner advertising performed well in advertising unaided recall tests too, although it is interesting to see that the number of impressions is less relevant here. Of those who had been exposed to 1–5 impressions, 5.5 per cent later recalled having seen a Purina advertisement, while only 5.1 per cent of those receiving 6–20 impressions did so. Among dog owners, the results were 6.3 per cent (1–5 impressions) and 6.4 per cent (6–20 impressions).

This research not only shows the important role that Internet advertising generally can play in brand building, but also the importance of the corporate or brand website itself in reinforcing brand loyalty, as existing Purina dog food buyers were far more likely to visit Purina.com than other Internet users (Saunders, 2002).

■ The viewer is actively searching for products and services, and so every site hit could gain a potential customer if interest can be maintained. Regular and loyal customers can take short cuts and skip all the general background information. 'Shopping baskets' help the customer to keep track of what they have bought on this visit and help give the impression of a store just like any other. In the late 1990s, four main sectors were considered to be at the forefront of online direct distribution: travel, books, music and software, but as mentioned earlier, however, groceries, clothing, and electrical goods, including PCs, have all become significant contributors to the e-tail economy. This is perhaps a sign that consumers are gaining enough confidence in online shopping to start making riskier purchases either in terms of financial risk (e.g. buying a high-priced PC or even a car and having sufficient faith that the online seller will deliver the goods in the first place and then be there to sort out any after-sales problems) or psychological risk (e.g. buying clothing on the basis of verbal descriptions and two-dimensional pictures).

■ Print and mailing costs are eliminated because no catalogue has to be produced and distributed each season. Although costs will be incurred in developing and maintaining an interesting website, they still represent a saving, especially because a website increases the seller's flexibility as it can be changed far more easily than the printed page with instant updates on prices, product availability and special offers. Amazon has well over 8 million users, yet the cost of communicating with them is a fraction of the cost that would have been incurred through direct mail or media advertising.

eg

Despite the fact that errors can be put right almost as soon as they are spotted, the fast-moving nature of the Internet means that a lot of damage can still be done in a very short space of time.

Kodak probably didn't feel like smiling for the camera in January 2002 after it made a slight mistake on its UK website. A digital camera was advertised for sale via the website for £100 for just 12 hours before Kodak realised that an error had been made and revised the price to £329. It was too late, however. Word of mouth had spread news of the bargain and thousands of orders had been placed before the error was rectified. Kodak's immediate response was to e-mail the 10,000 hopeful buyers and tell them that the orders would not be fulfilled at the £100 price. Its view was that when a potential customer places an order (s)he is simply making an offer to buy which the seller can then accept or reject. There is no binding contract until the offer to buy is accepted by the seller. Kodak intended to exercise its right to refuse the kind offers that its would-be customers were making.

Customers were not prepared to accept this, however, and threatened legal proceedings on the basis that Kodak had acknowledged receipt of the orders which legally is tantamount to accepting the customer's offer and creating a contract. Rather than pursue the matter through the courts, Kodak decided to honour the orders at a cost of £2m. (*The Daily Telegraph*, 2002; Eaglesham, 2002).

■ Order processing and handling costs are reduced with online ordering as everything is already in electronic form and the customer is handling all the order entry without assistance. McNutt (1998), however, has argued that it is important for organisations to realise that opening the front door to customers with a website providing ordering capability means that they have to ensure that all the 'behind the scenes' logistics operations can cope with changes in ordering patterns. Linking back into the organisational systems for stock control and order fulfilment is essential if customer service levels are to be maintained.

marketing *in action*

Fulfilling the customer's desires

Given the potential scale of online grocery shopping (see earlier example of Tesco.com), e-grocery services need to be sure that they have the right technological infrastructure and order processing and fulfilment design to ensure that they can deliver as promised. One ongoing debate is about the relative merits of warehouse versus store-based picking models, i.e. is it better to assemble and deliver a customer's order from a local store or to have dedicated regional warehouses that deal solely with e-shoppers?

Ocado is purely an e-grocer. Although it is 40 per cent owned by retailer Waitrose, it has no retail stores of its own. It thus uses the warehouse model. It has built a huge dedicated warehouse, the size of 20 normal supermarkets, in Hatfield and is confident that it can serve London and the whole of the south-east of England from that one site. Ocado's view is that it is a lot more cost-effective to operate like this than from individual stores. Other companies with dedicated warehouse facilities for e-grocery shopping are not so sure about the benefits. Sainsbury's has struggled with its dedicated warehouses and is running with a mixed model, using two dedicated facilities in Manchester and London supplemented from 41 stores in large cities. ASDA completely abandoned its attempt to operate from two dedicated warehouses. Tesco.com, however, Europe's biggest online grocer, does not use dedicated warehouses and manages to service over 80,000 deliveries a week from its store network profitably.

Whatever the models used, the infrastructure has to be able to tackle certain key issues that affect the service quality that the customer experiences. The biggest problems from the customer's perspective are lack of availability of products, substitution of products and mistimed deliveries (i.e. outside the specified time window). Ocado claims that its IT systems have solved the availability/substitution problems, with sophisticated software that integrates the orders that are in the system with stock levels in the warehouse so that stockouts are less likely to happen. If a product is not available, then the customer can be told at the time they place the order and can choose a substitute if they want. This is a lot more difficult under a store-based operating model because product availability depends on what is in stock in a particular store at the time when the order is assembled and that can be unpredictable because 'real' shoppers are continuously buying things and emptying the shelves! This means that substitution decisions are made by the member of staff who is assembling the order. Ocado claims that Tesco.com has to substitute about 15 per cent of items in any one order because of lack of availability in the local store, but Tesco claims that the substitution rate is a lot lower than that.

In terms of delivery times, Tesco.com may have the edge with local deliveries being made from local stores. With vans travelling relatively short distances, there is less scope for getting stuck in traffic and it is less likely that local van drivers will get lost! Ocado is serving a huge geographic area from one location and that involves negotiating the nightmare that passes for a road system in and around London and the South-East with the potentially long delays frequently caused by the sheer volume of traffic or accidents. While Ocado uses sophisticated route planning and navigation software, the long distances involved still make it difficult to predict exact delivery times.

Many improvements are being made to the service all the time, but there is still much to be done. *The Grocer* magazine regularly monitors online grocery services through mystery shopping. Sites are becoming easier to access and navigate but *The Grocer* has found that stockouts on very basic items, delivery errors (e.g. delivering someone else's order) and inconvenient delivery times are still major problems.

Sources: Birmingham Post (2002), Goodley (2002), The Grocer (2001, 2002), Patten (2002).

- The IT systems have to be able to offer real-time information flows between the customer, customer support, distribution and the supply chain. Only then can realistic claims be made for cost-efficient and effective customer service, whether a small parcel is delivered to Milan or Middlesbrough. Federal Express made a virtue of its integrated system by allowing customers to track the exact whereabouts of a particular parcel on the Internet as a means of reassurance. It also turned this service into an effective selling tool to differentiate itself from competitors.
- Better after-sales service can be provided online, not only because of cheaper and easier communication, but also through feedback links, usage information, newsflashes on any product changes and mechanisms for fault reporting.
- Digital products, in the form of magazines, music and video, are capable of being distributed via the Internet, without the need even to send a parcel through the post. The distribution of music products that can be downloaded on to a computer is causing concern to CD manufacturers for copyright and piracy reasons.

eg Online file-sharing services act as an intermediary, allowing people to contribute music or MP3 files or to download them. US research has indicated that 19 per cent of Americans aged 12 or over have downloaded files from such sites. Among 18- to 24-year-olds, the figures are even higher: 45 per cent. It is not an alien activity to older age groups, either. Fourteen per cent of US 35- to 54-year-olds have downloaded files from these sites. The interest in file-sharing has been driven to a large extent by technology, with PC manufacturers promoting music-focused packages including CD-R drives and appropriate software for downloading and recording music. This might look like bad news for the record companies, but in the research, 81 per cent of downloaders said that their CD purchases had stayed the same or increased since they began downloading music from the Internet. Furthermore, 84 per cent said that they did not just use the Internet for downloading music, they also used it to research bands and tour information, to listen to song clips and find out more about lyrics before actually buying a CD. Nearly half of them go on to say that they have purchased a particular band's or artist's CD purely because of something they first found on the Internet. Other global studies have reported similar findings, with about 41 per cent of teenage/young adult Internet users admitting to having downloaded music files in some format or another (Greenspan, 2002a).

- Manufacturers can get closer to the customer and potentially reduce costs through disintermediation, which simply means cutting one or more intermediaries out of the distribution channel (Rowley, 2002). Thus the package holiday company that sells online direct to the consumer rather than through a travel agent is bypassing an intermediary, as is the designer-label clothing manufacturer that sells direct rather than through a trendy Oxford Street retailer. There is a risk attached to this (quite apart from alienating the traditional intermediaries who are losing business), however. One of the roles of the intermediary is to bring assortments of products together and make them visible to the target market in one place. Online direct selling by a manufacturer loses this advantage and depends heavily on the consumer's ability to find the manufacturer's website. To overcome this, a new kind of intermediary, the cybermediary (Sarkar *et al.*, 1996), has developed including not only e-tail stores such as Amazon, but also virtual shopping malls (see Case Study 14.1), online directories and search engines, among others, to help guide the consumer to relevant sites or to sell goods to them as a retailer would.
- In time, however, the growth of powerful ISPs and the emergence of customers in full control of what they will and will not search for and purchase could mean that the most powerful intermediaries in the twenty-first century will be the ISPs and search engine providers who build a wealth of information on individual customer preferences and requirements (Mitchell, 1999).

Communication and promotion

The Internet is now as good as any other tool for communicating with customers and target audiences. Many of the principles discussed in Chapters 9–11 apply equally to the Internet. As well as operating a dedicated website, companies are also taking advertising space on other companies' websites as joint or paid promotions. As can be seen from Table 14.1, extensive use is made of the Internet for communications purposes. Many of the entries are self-explanatory. The main uses are as follows.

As an advertising medium. Table 14.2 shows the advantages and disadvantages of using the Internet as an advertising medium (Pickton and Broderick, 2001).

Table 14.2 The principal characteristics of the Internet as an advertising medium

Advantages	Disadvantages
■ Message can be changed quickly and easily	■ Limited visual presentation
■ Interactivity possible	■ Audience not guaranteed
■ Can create own pages cheaply	■ 'Hits' may not represent interest – casual browsers
■ Can advertise on others' web pages	■ Relies on browsers finding page
■ Very low cost possible	■ Can create irritation
■ Very large audience potential	■ Large numbers of target groups may not use Internet yet
■ Direct sales possible	■ Creative limitations
■ High information content possible on own web pages	

Source: Adapted from *Integrated Marketing Communications*, Financial Times Prentice-Hall, (Pickton, D and Broderick, A. 2001), Copyright © 2001 David Pickton and Amanda Broderick, reprinted by permission of Pearson Education Limited. Extracted from Exhibit 11.3, p. 210.

Table 14.2 demonstrates the Internet is not a perfect advertising medium by any means. Its limitations and disadvantages are no more 'fatal' than those of any other medium, however, and simply emphasise the importance of incorporating Internet activities fully into the wider marketing plan and using the medium within a coherent integrated communications strategy.

Advertising on the Internet is similar to advertising through any other medium. The message should be communicated simply, clearly and by creating interest that will move the viewer through to further action, whether that is an enquiry, an order or just getting better informed about what is available. Many of the free Internet access providers exploit this area to the full with comprehensive and sometimes intrusive display and banner advertising messages. Most of these messages are linked to the advertiser's website for further information and action. As the quality of information on web users improves, many of the ISPs have started to target advertising to their users, so for example a user with an interest in sport may receive banner advertisements on sports events and equipment. Amazon has gone further by creating a link with some search facilities, so if you want to know more about an organisation or market, you will be invited to allow Amazon to search for titles on that theme.

eg Choosing the right website upon which to advertise is obviously an important decision and there needs to be a close match between the brand's target audience and the profile of the audience delivered by the website. A number of brands targeting the 5- to 16-year-old age group have found the CiTV website (http://www.citv.co.uk) to be a successful medium for advertising and linked promotional activity. This website is connected with children's ITV and offers a fun, interactive environment with games, competitions, jokes, message boards, audio interviews, etc. Children are drawn to it not only because of its magazine-type content, but also because of its on-screen exposure during children's programming on the ITV channels and their desire to follow up links with specific programmes. The website regularly attracts over 170,000 page impressions a day.

McVities wanted to promote its Jaffa Cakes brand interactively online to children and to create a database. This was done successfully through a link up between McVities, Manchester

United and the CiTV website. A competition was run over six weeks on the website offering a main prize of a week's training at the Manchester United youth academy and runners-up prizes of signed footballs and photos every two weeks (24/7 Europe, 2002b, c).

Banner advertisements are still the main form of Internet advertising, and normally appear either on an ISP's pages while the customer is logging on to the Internet, alongside a search engine, or as part of a joint promotion on another organisation's website. Most banner and other display advertisements enable the viewer to access the main information or booking page for the product or company with one click. Despite their power and convenience, there is some evidence from the USA that banner advertisements are being ignored by viewers as wallpaper or background clutter, so their effect is wearing off, despite their intrusive capability. However, BMRB's Internet Monitor found that in spite of the fact that over half of Internet users agreed that 'all web advertising annoys me', 40 per cent had clicked a banner in the previous month. Only 20 per cent of Internet users agreed with positive statements such as 'I find web advertising interesting' and 'I find web advertising entertaining'. While Internet advertising does still seem to be driving people towards advertised websites, BMRB also found that television advertising was playing a role too. Internet users are noting website addresses from advertisements that interest them and then visiting the sites later (BMRB, 2000).

Loyalty reinforcement. The organisational website itself is also a powerful tool for increasing the level of interaction between the customer and the brand to reinforce loyalty. If the viewer can be entertained and informed, and enjoys coming back to the site, the brand values and image are enhanced.

eg Imperial Leather is long-established as a leading soap and bath/shower products brand in the UK. Cussons UK Ltd, the brand's owner, wanted to use online marketing communications to help increase brand awareness, educate the target market about the product range and the variants within the range, and to complement an advertising campaign running in more traditional media, such as television and posters. Since the target market mainly consisted of women from the ABC1 socio-economic groups, it was decided to use a banner advertisement on http://www.handbag.com, the leading UK women's portal. The banner, featuring the Cussons' duck logo, ran at the top of the health and beauty channel within handbag.com and allowed users to click through to Cussons' website. There was also a button on Handbag's make-up and skincare sub-channel taking users to an advertorial page. The banner advertisement achieved a click through rate of 3.4 per cent, and the button 1.92 per cent (24/7 Europe, 2002a).

Loyalty is clearly a big issue for e-tail sites too, trying to generate repeat business. As in any other form of marketing, it is cheaper and easier to sell to an existing online customer than to create a new one. Engendering loyalty through providing a trusted, quality product and service package is also important for e-tailers because it helps to deflect the consumer's attention away from pricing issues. One of the problems caused by the dotcom boom is that many e-tailers emphasised low price rather than service, product assortment or convenience as prime reasons to buy. This set up an unrealistic expectation in the minds of consumers that prices should be between 10 and 15 per cent lower on the Internet than elsewhere. This is a dangerous strategy because if the e-tailer cannot deliver lower prices, then the consumer will not buy from them, and if the e-tailer does deliver low prices, it is vulnerable to making losses or to losing business to leaner, meaner competitors who can undercut. Thus in the wake of the dotcom shake-out, companies are perhaps taking a more sensible approach to pricing and trying to develop and emphasise less tangible and less vulnerable sources of competitive advantage and customer loyalty.

Corporate communications. The Internet has been widely used by organisations to create goodwill, better understanding and provide important information to shareholders and the community alike. Many organisations detail their financial reports on the web and often provide considerable coverage of their community relations programmes.

Often press releases are automatically placed on the web and so regular updating is necessary. Not only does this service help the media, but it also enables the organisation to get its message across to a wider audience in a more direct manner. Even when full text is not available, contact details are provided to the press office for further enquiry.

eg Some web pages are designed to counter negative stories and views expressed by unofficial or even anti-lobbying group sites. Shell had to contend with a host of highly critical sites over its environmental record, particularly over its disposal of the Brent Spar oil rig, and its involvement in Nigeria. It now uses both special web-based discussion lines and campaigns, along with a free flow of information, to counter some of the wilder allegations that are not actionable.

From its home page on http://www.shell.com, the visitor can click on to Tell Shell, a series of open discussion forums that are uncensored, other than for legal necessity. At the time of writing, the featured topics were 'How much freedom should we trade for our security?', 'The environment: issues and comments', 'Society and multinationals', and 'Energy and technology: now and in the future'. Anyone can contribute anything, whether it is critical of Shell or not. Shell will also put its own point of view, entering into the debate as it evolves. As Bowen (2002) describes it, it is 'a clever way of being transparent while getting its own views across'.

Sometimes, though, such openness can be abused. Monbiot (2002) discusses a PR firm that specialises in Internet lobbying and claims that one of its methods is to create phantom individuals, apparently unconnected with any commercial interest, who infiltrate chat rooms and discussion forums to propagate or denigrate a particular point of view or organisation. While Monbiot focuses on a specific incident in the biotech industry, it is easy to see how Shell's hospitality could be similarly abused by a competitor or pressure group.

Sales promotion. Because of the relative ease of updating a web page and the flexibility it provides, it is possible to target offers on various products or over a defined period. Offers can be changed by the hour and the response of customers assessed (Wilson, 1999). Using price promotions, gifts and bonuses can all help increase short-term sales.

eg Games-related competitions seem to be a popular promotional feature of websites. Drinks brand T&T, for example, offered prizes to visitors who became adept at its Quencha game (similar to Pac Man), accessed via http://ttbeverages.com. The five people who were top of the highest scores list every week won two cases (48 cans) of T&T drinks. A competition like this not only keeps people making repeat visits to the site to try to better their performance but also encourages them to leave personal details that could be added (via an opt-in mechanism) to a database for future marketing purposes. Kellogg's similarly uses games-related prizes on its child-oriented Kellogg's World site (http://www.kelloggs.co.uk). The site offers a wide range of games, and over a certain period, everyone who made it on to a leader board for any of the games offered was put into a monthly prize draw. Kellogg's website is also used to draw the consumer's attention to its current on-pack offers across all its brands. Presumably, the consumer can then make a positive decision to participate in a promotion and consciously seek out the relevant brand in-store.

Personal selling. By its very nature, the web is impersonal and the Internet is designed more for sales support and generating enquiries rather than for making direct sales. The cost per potential customer hit can be very low, and because people who do visit a site are likely to be interested in what it has to offer, the potential for increasing the level of enquiries is very great as net usage expands. Even in highly routine order-taking roles, the Internet can be made more interactive if the customer database is able to personalise communication and relate it to offers that could appeal, based on a customer's previous enquiries and sales history.

Overall, the organisation should plan its use of the Internet carefully and be sure that it is integrated into the rest of the marketing mix. Sumner (1999) argues that as much consideration should be given to the offline use of the website as to its online use. By featuring a web address in other advertising and promotional media, the overall site visibility is increased and additional site traffic could be generated. A glance at much poster, print and television advertising will often show a mention of an Internet address for contact. It is important too that all of the Internet budget should not be spent on highly interactive, fun websites at the expense of the more mundane, but critical, job of responding to e-mail enquiries.

■ Broadband

The wider adoption of broadband links, as opposed to the current dominance of narrow band, is likely to revolutionise the potential for Internet usage. In the UK, in 2002 around 500,000 users had already switched to broadband and a further 20,000 a week were being connected according to Oftel (McLuhan, 2002). A US consultancy firm, ARC, suggested that by 2007 one-third of all Internet users will have broadband and that broadband business applications will grow significantly. Europe will account for one-third of the 300 million broadband users worldwide (Greenspan, 2002b; ARC Group, 2002).

Broadband not only means faster Internet connection, but because the bandwidth is greater it enables video and audio streaming rather than have the 'jerky' buffering and slower connections from normal line use. This means that live news and entertainment becomes a real possibility as a supplement, if not an alternative to television. The rate of broadband adoption will depend upon the interaction of supply and demand. At present, there are not that many streaming applications that merit the extra investment, after all why watch a film on a PC when there is top quality, high-definition digital television available? Until revenues and penetration pick up, it is not worth the broadcasters' while to consider producing dedicated content for broadband. It soon becomes a vicious circle, slowing the rate of growth.

What is needed is new applications that can compete with television. Watching sports or business highlights from work or on the move, accessing specialist material such as DIY or gardening information, or holiday brochures could all be enhanced by broadband. The challenge for marketers is to think through the applications where virtually real-time audio or visual would enhance the proposition or support to the customer. Although Tanner (2002) has suggested that people spend three times longer online each week (25 hours per week) when using broadband than narrow band, this may simply reflect the profile of heavier users and early adopters who would gain more from speed and flexibility. Just because using the Internet can be faster does not mean that the average user will spend more time online.

eg Would you like the experience of the car chase movie? BMWfilms' (http://www.bmwfilms.com) service 'The Hire' shows four films of car chases and claims to bring 'the power and quality of feature-length movies to a format designed for the internet'. Pure entertainment, but the idea is that you inform your friends about it and then of course there is a link to 'The Machines' featuring the BMW range. If all of that is too much for you, the Prudential's website shows its Chief Executive discussing various aspects of his company's performance, currently suited to narrow band using Real Player and Windows Media Players, but with broadband the interviews would be far more powerful if the picture fuzziness and delay could be avoided (http://www.prudential.co.uk).

Once broadband becomes more widely adopted, it will place the marketer in the role of broadcaster and empower the consumer to interact in real time. Suppliers, distributors, customers and field staff could all be contacted with news updates or other important information. In time, it would be possible to conduct some sales presentations in real time, especially for follow-up calls. Consumers can be empowered to choose what they want to see. A replay of a favourite advertisement, a virtual sightseeing tour or anything on demand is possible. This could be extended into virtual VCR, so that if a particular sports event or episode of a soap were missed, it would be possible to catch up on demand.

For broadband to achieve its full potential, technology, marketing and content need to be in line. A failure in any one can lead to delays and disappointment. As more material is compressed from video format, as new marketing applications are found and as broadband is installed, the power of the Internet will be demonstrated to an even greater degree than in the first wave revolution.

■ The future of Internet marketing?

So what of the future of the Internet in marketing? There are almost as many answers as there are pundits. What is certain is that more and more users will be attracted to the Internet; bandwidth increases will enable more powerful applications and real-time communication (Karakaya and Charlton, 2001); and finally the technologies will become more integrated, whether they are television-, PC-, or mobile-based and might even integrate some other home management systems such as hi-fi, security and climate control. To some, the Internet will become part of television entertainment (Duboff and Spaeth, 2000), and others argue for more mobile media through 3G and even 4G, but most consider the future role of the PC for Internet access to be limited in comparison (Feather, 2002).

For marketers this not only means greater opportunities for service provison, but also a more powerful medium for reaching consumers. It means more online research using chat-based focus groups, e-mail and Internet-based surveys, more secure online buying, more of a role for intermediaries to search, select and recommend buying options, as most organisations offer some form of electronic transaction facility (Tapp, 2002).

Finally, in a mobile, last-minute society, wireless Internet access will provide significant opportunities for attracting transient trade. Feather (2002) believes that there will be a move from 'www' to 'mmm' (mobile media mode), reflecting the increased use of access via mobiles. This will be considered later in this chapter. To Feather, the range of applications from mmm is very large indeed:

> *Appliances will sense when food stocks need replenishing and order replacements to be delivered automatically to the home. Cars will call home, turning on appliances, setting room temperatures, filling the jacuzzi, and starting dinner. Even physical health will be automatically monitored and appropriate steps taken on your behalf.*
>
> Feather (2002)

He then goes on to argue that by 2010, the Internet will account for 31 per cent of all retail spending and most bricks and mortar retailers will be in trouble if they have not embraced e-tailing, largely due to the fully integrated nature of Internet usage in individuals' lifestyles.

All of these exciting developments will depend less on technology, however; indeed in a number of cases the technology already exists. They will depend upon customer willingness to trust and participate with e-anything along with the suppliers of information and commerce services. With the service comes the loss of privacy when it is fully realised that virtually every click on the Internet can be recorded and analysed. So the power will shift to the consumer for as long the consumer is willing to use the low costs of switching and searching to full advantage. In part, that runs counter to many of the points mentioned earlier in this book about brand and company loyalty, buying inertia and risk aversion with some purchases.

Marketing and new media

Digitalisation has created new media opportunities to target messages better and to enable a far more effective personalised approach to acquiring and retaining customers. The advent of e-mail, wireless marketing and interactive television (iTV) has added a new dimension to integrated marketing communication and fragmented media usage to a degree not considered possible until a few years ago (Barwise, 2002). These new media opportunities have not replaced more traditional print and broadcast media, but are supplementing them as resources are reallocated to allow mass advertising and brand building and the more direct customer contact that is possible using new media.

This section examines the impact of three main elements of new media: e-mail marketing, wireless marketing and interactive television marketing.

■ E-mail marketing

More and more people use e-mail on a regular basis. A survey by Net Value estimated that in any one month we each send on average 12.3 e-mails and receive 39.1 from 13 million home computers. Overall, in January 2002 in the UK around 550 million e-mails were sent, over twice the number of letters sent over the same period and one-third more e-mails than in Germany or France (Dwek, 2002). E-mail has thus emerged as a powerful means of communication that marketers are increasingly adopting as part of their promotional activity. The trouble is, as with any medium, there are risks arising from bad practice and overcrowding. We primarily use e-mails to keep in touch with friends, colleagues and contacts, and occasionally we use them to search for information or to place an online order. We may even welcome an incoming e-mail from a company that we have done business with previously or where we have declared an interest in what they are offering. What we do not want is to be bombarded with offers of cheap financing deals, special travel discounts, get-rich-quick schemes, herbal viagra or pornography. Unsurprisingly, most recipients scan the list of incoming e-mails and a first selection is quickly made according to the subject or the sender. Many recipients are also wary of receiving viruses via e-mails from unrecognised sources and therefore tend to delete 'cold calling' e-mails without opening them, just to be safe.

> **eg** Love it or hate it, Chelsea FC has a loyal following of fans, including 30,000 who are more than happy to be contacted by the soccer club. When Chelsea decided to launch a television channel with Sky, it used those fans as targets for an e-mail campaign. Research indicated that 56 per cent of the fans accessed the club's website on a daily basis and most would be highly receptive to a direct offer. The campaign, part of a wider promotional exercise, featured three e-mails highlighting Chelsea TV, giving details of a subscription hotline, and offering the incentive of a competition, along with further information. The campaign was a great success. The Chelsea TV call centre experienced three times the volume of calls in the period just after the e-mails were sent out and 91 per cent of subscribers were familiar with the campaign before the TV channel launch (http://www.edesigns.co.uk).

Marketers are attracted to the potential of e-mail marketing as a communication tool that can target individuals rather than using mass media approaches. Carefully designed e-mail marketing can help to create initial contact as well as helping to develop an online relationship once transactions have taken place. The aim from a marketing perspective is primarily to encourage the reader to look at a website and to obtain permission to send more information to the recipient or to a third party. Typical uses of an e-mail marketing campaign are shown in Figure 14.1.

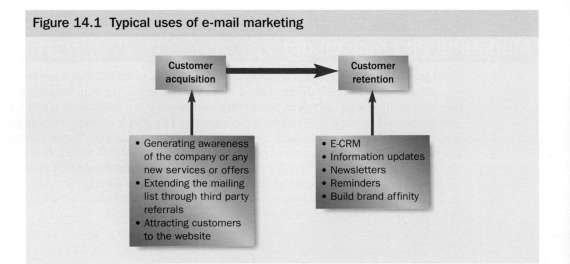

Figure 14.1 Typical uses of e-mail marketing

Rizzi (2001) argues that e-mail marketing has gone through three distinct phases since the first messages were sent through cyberspace in 1971, as shown in Figure 14.2. First there was the 'Broadcast/Spam Era' when e-mails were sent out indiscriminately, often with little attempt to target and tailor messages to the recipient. Consider sending out an e-mail message about Chelsea TV to an Arsenal supporter. Not only would response rates be very low, but it might actually generate (even more!) hostility to the sender. Some companies still operate this way, although European regulation is threatening to restrict spamming by moving from 'opt-out' to 'opt-in' schemes, thus assuming that people do not want to get e-mails unless they specifically request them. This has been prompted by the intrusive nature and sometimes dubious content of some spam e-mails.

The second generation represents the majority of e-mail marketers at present. Permission marketing offers the consumer the opportunity to volunteer to receive regular messages on special offers or new products (Dawe, 2002). Effectively it is an opt-in system but has been liable to some abuse as the low cost and higher response rates from e-mail have been interpreted by some senders as permission to bulk e-mail rather than to select messages relevant to recognised customer needs and interests (Rizzi, 2001). Permission is the starting point, not the objective, of an e-mail campaign so it is not, therefore, surprising that e-mail marketing is moving into a third phase, 'Precision Marketing'. This combines the power of e-mail with the power of IT to record and analyse responses to ensure even greater targeting and almost individual customer relationship management. In theory, each customer could receive slightly different mail.

Viral marketing

Viral marketing, or 'e-mail a friend', is word of mouth by e-mail. It is often deliberately stimulated by the marketer and is easy to achieve with use of a forwarding facility ('e-mail this page to a friend'). Alternatively, the customer could elect to provide details of friends who might like to receive information direct from the marketer. As considered in Chapter 10, word-of-mouth promotion and recommendation is often the most effective form of communication in terms of believability and trust.

Originally viral marketing was associated with youth brands to create a bit of excitement. If the material or the attachment is different and enjoyable, then there is more chance that it will be passed on. Lastminute.com (see Case Study 1.1), Budweiser and Levi's have all used viral marketing.

eg Sara Lee used viral marketing for Brylcreem as part of an integrated campaign. Press advertising featured an Easy Wash Wax hair product for men. The creative message was of a man in the middle of a car wash washing his hair, carrying the strap line 'Use your Head', implying that it is a lot easier to get wax out of your hair if you use this product. The viral campaign gave access to a 15-second video clip along the lines of a TV commercial, showing the man in the car with the sunroof open so that his hair could be washed in the car wash. This was sent to people on an e-mail database and to 2,500 highly viral people. Interested readers can download it from http://www.punchbaby.com, a viral factory site (*Marketing Week*, 2001).

Figure 14.2 E-mail marketing evolution

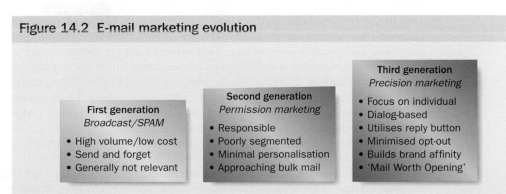

First generation
Broadcast/SPAM
- High volume/low cost
- Send and forget
- Generally not relevant

Second generation
Permission marketing
- Responsible
- Poorly segmented
- Minimal personalisation
- Approaching bulk mail

Third generation
Precision marketing
- Focus on individual
- Dialog-based
- Utilises reply button
- Minimised opt-out
- Builds brand affinity
- 'Mail Worth Opening'

Source: Rizzi (2001). Copyright © 2002 e-Dialog Inc.

There are, however, risks in using this approach. If the message is too promotional, smacks of unsolicited mail and is being spammed, the marketer might risk losing a customer or the customer might risk losing a friend. According to Carter (2002a), this is causing marketers to seek to add more value to their viral campaigns on the premise that it is becoming harder to get customers to listen, let alone act. This can be achieved through an interactive web facility, for example as used by men's toiletry brand Lynx and its 'zerogravity' campaign targeted at 18- to 24-year-old men. The www.lynxwhitelabel.com site enables the user to mix a dance track and create a personalised DJ name before sending it on to a third party. Response rates were high, with 45 per cent arriving at the site via an 'e-mail a friend' facility, and 20 per cent of them subsequently registered on the site (Ray, 2001).

Customer acquisition

Viral marketing is one way of building an e-mailing list, or lists can be purchased. Lists must, however, be based on permission, a willingness to receive e-mails acknowledged by an opt-in mechanism. It is risky to use large, cheap lists of people to whom your communication may be most unwelcome. Some list owners are taking particular care about how their lists are used to avoid inappropriate or overuse. Lifestyle data gatherers such as Claritas and Consodata often record e-mail addresses as do online list builders such as Bananalotto and My Offers which sell permission-based lists. Some website operators now offer lists as a sideline, gathered from the users of their sites. TheMutual.net and Another.com, for example, have developed lists of relatively affluent young users who may be an attractive target for an e-mailing. Despite the attraction of these lists, the click-through rate may however be low, and rarely does it exceed 10 per cent for cold mailings (http://www.emailvision.com).

Online lists depend heavily on the sender's ability to track contacts from within its website. Sources can include online surveys, website registrations and responses to competitions and offers over the website. Web forms vary in the degree of information required beyond the e-mail details. Some seek data to enable customer profiling to take place and better targeted messages to be sent before gathering the more specific information generated when/if clicks or orders are made. It is often advisable to seek only limited information at any one go, perhaps with three or four questions, rather than making the site visitor feel that they are being interrogated and delayed unnecessarily. If that happens, the visitor might lose patience or become uncomfortable about giving personal information away and fail to complete the registration process.

eg When Vodafone decided to adopt an e-mail marketing campaign to promote m-commerce in B2B markets, it established a list of existing and potential customers and then assessed them against predetermined qualifying criteria to ensure that they were appropriate decision makers. At that stage Vodafone gathered the appropriate opt-in permission to enable it to e-mail only willing recipients confidently.

Customer retention

One of the greatest benefits for e-mail marketing is its ability to create and build a relationship with a customer on an individual basis. It can, therefore, play an important part in any customer relationship programme. This requires a 'permission centre' (http:// www.email vision.com) comprising a list of opt-in respondents. Once the list has been developed, the response mechanism tracking can develop usable and powerful customer profiles. E-mails can be tracked for opening, clicks and purchases, so quite a detailed history, far superior to anything direct mail can achieve, can soon be built up. The more powerful and carefully designed the database, the easier it is to define small, well-focused subsegments for targeting. The trend now is towards smaller and smaller segments, *micro segments*, perhaps comprising a list of just 100 people (Trollinger, 2002).

Although recording customer use of websites is a valuable tool for targeting offers and messages, some organisations now use e-mail newsletters to keep in touch with current and previous customers. These newsletters can play an important part of a more general customer relationship management programme.

The British Museum runs an e-mail newsletter for its opt-in subscribers. The content varies but focuses primarily on featured books such as *Ming Ceramics in The British Museum* and *A Pocket Dictionary of Egyptian Gods and Goddesses*, along with information on new products in the store and up-to-date information on exhibitions and events. This enables it to maintain contact with customers who are sympathetic to the mission of the museum and who may be prepared to support it with online or store purchases of its specialised book and ancillary product collections (http://www.digivate.com).

Personalisation is the aim of most marketers when building customer relationships. When successful, it combines all the benefits of personal selling with the cost-effectiveness of technology-driven marketing. Personalisation can take many forms including:

- content;
- offer proposition;
- prefered frequency of contact;
- transmission format (text, flash, etc.);
- subjects of interest;
- personalisation by spend, product or interest.

The challenge for the e-mail marketer is to ensure that the database can facilitate data gathering and extraction to suit the particular purposes of a campaign.

Creative message design

Many of the principles of creative direct mail apply to e-mail messages. There is a need to make the right offer with a strong response-oriented copy (Friesen, 2002). This means careful targeting, a sound knowledge of customer clicking behaviour, personalisation wherever possible and tailored rather than bland messages for mass e-mailing. The type of message will depend on the e-mail format, plain text, graphical html or rich media. Given the speed of response to campaigns, with 90 per cent of responses within a 48-hour period, adjustment can be made after piloting (Rizzi, 2001).

Viewlondon.co.uk is a web-based guide to 11,500 restaurants, bars, pubs and clubs in London. In order to attract a greater number of hits on the site, given that its ultimate success lies in its effectiveness as an advertising medium, it ran a competition entitled 'Are you Cockney or Mockney?' testing the visitor's knowledge of London. Although anyone could play, to have a chance of a prize, such as CDs, free drinks and free tickets, full registration was required. During the campaign, there were over 500,000 page clicks, the game was played 98,000 times and most importantly for Viewlondon, 2,500 new registrations were made. To keep people interested, there are new games and quizzes each month (Murphy, 2002). So if you know whether it's the Taj Mahal, Eiffel Tower or Statue of Liberty that is in Paris, your name, postcode and e-mail address are all you need to enter. All these traffic builders support its aim to become the first point of reference for Londoners searching for entertainment in London.

Even small organisations can, with creative design, use e-mail marketing effectively. For them it can be a very powerful promotional tool, given the often low level of resources available for promotion.

The Fabulous Bakin' Boys from Witney near Oxford uses e-mail marketing. It created a database of jokes which could be downloaded from its website by registered users. The registration process asks basic questions such as gender, age, where you have seen the company's muffins for sale, and when you eat muffins. The prospect of some free samples is mentioned. It then introduced online games and cheeky advertisements are regularly mailed out to previous website respondents (http://www.bakinboys.co.uk). The games, such as Muffin Munchin' and Cake Invaders, are designed to attract repeat traffic and each can be 'mailed to a mate' as part of a viral campaign. Online ordering is possible and look out for the fly past (visit the site to see what we mean)! The theme 'Live fast, play hard and eat muffins' enabled the new company, which is growing at a rapid rate, to be less conventional than a larger company to stimulate interest in the site (Hunt, 2001).

As more organisations become familiar with using the Internet as more than just a brochure supplement, the use of e-mail linked website activity will also grow for smaller businesses. The fragmentation of high cost, national media and the availability of targeted media that are within the reach of small business marketing budgets mean that there is likely to be a lot greater use of e-mail marketing in the next few years.

Response and review

One of the major advantages of e-mail campaigns is the speed of response. Ray (2001) described the situation at a holiday auction company where a newsletter issued between 4 p.m. and 5.50 p.m. will generate a significant number of responses by 6.30 p.m. and the bulk of the responses are in within two days. This means that considerable care must be taken to have a system in place to handle the response traffic generated. In part, the technology infrastructure can help to handle 'bounced' e-mails, undeliverable e-mails and routine enquiries, but in some cases, it may be necessary to have an inbound e-mail answering service.

eg In the Vodafone example mentioned earlier, a real-time reporting and tracking engine was employed that could list how many e-mails were sent, how many opened and how many clicked through. Normally, only 50 e-mails at a time were sent to allow for tracking, primarily over a six-hour period. Of the e-mails sent, over 50 per cent were opened and read and 21 per cent clicked through to the appropriate section of the website. Many of the latter were then converted into leads by the telemarketing team (http://www.inbox.co.uk).

Overall, targeted permission-based mailing campaigns generate an average response rate of 10–15 per cent, but this can drop to 2 per cent for bought-in prospect e-mail addresses (Murphy, 2002). After all responses are in, the analysis of campaign effectiveness can begin. This often requires careful pre-planning to cross-check unsubscribers, assign codes to different target segments or different message types and to record the type of response generated, including where clicking has taken place but no formal response has followed. Data measured by campaign, customer or product on the number of openings and clicks, unsubscription rates, and bouncing, as well as responses, can be collected. This is an invaluable aid to updating records and further campaign planning.

■ Wireless marketing

If you are a Cahoot customer and about to go overdrawn you may receive a text message to warn you, and if you are on the Blue Arrow temps register you may be texted with information about vacancies as they become available (Middleton, 2002). Text messaging is becoming an ever popular form of wireless marketing. Wireless marketing, sometimes called m-marketing or mobile marketing, has emerged as another major opportunity to target customers more closely, and as with e-mail marketing, its application is expected to grow significantly over the next few years. With over 1 billion mobiles in the world and 8 billion text messages exchanged in Europe every month, it is not surprising that marketers are attracted to the possibility of being able to reach consumers when and where they want (http://www.flytxt.com). Wireless marketing can also include messages direct to PC via the Internet.

M-marketing provides the means to carry voice messages, but is primarily used for sending text messages to targeted individuals at any time. Because of its intrusiveness and because different customers will be more receptive at different times of day, however, the m-marketer must fully appreciate consumer lifestyles and be careful in setting the right tone of the communication to avoid damaging any trust in the sender's brand (Carter, 2002b). Consider, for example, your receptivity to a text message received as you dash for an important meeting compared with one received over a relaxing lunchtime meal.

As in e-marketing, compiling target lists and profiles is an essential starting point. Consumers must be able to choose whether they want to receive information and there is a responsibility to ensure that any information is relevant. Irritation will soon grow if a torrent of mortgage deal messages are sent to students struggling to find next week's rent. It also follows that it must be easy to opt out from receiving messages. Again, therefore, as with e-mail marketing, content selection should derive from customer profiling, but because of the medium, most text messages need to be short, alerting the individual to a special offer or promotion or engaging them with an interactive game that could direct them to a website.

> **eg** When Dunkin' Donuts opened its Rome franchise outlet it made heavy use of mobile technology. A press and poster campaign featured a telephone number that invited consumers to call to receive a text message voucher by return. The voucher could be presented at the new store when ordering donuts. Further questions were then asked of the voucher-holder at the point of purchase to build a database of mobile contact numbers and lifestyle information that could all be used for future promotions. The campaign, although difficult to administer, proved a successful traffic builder for store visits and has enabled an ongoing series of promotions to be considered (*Marketing Week*, 2002a).

Most text messaging, such as the one in the Dunkin' Donuts example above, is currently SMS (short messaging service), which, as the name implies, usually means short, sharp messages to remind or inform. Marks & Spencer, for example, used e-mail and text messaging vouchers to encourage shoppers to visit a new branch in London with the offer of a free lunch, while Diageo ran trials targeting 16- to 24-year-olds with SMS text information and money-off vouchers if they provided their mobile numbers on entering some shopping centres (Carter, 2002b).

The very strength of SMS could soon become its weakness, as more and more marketers are attracted to this new medium. One of the potential barriers to the development of text messaging is the continued bad practice of sending unsolicited text messages, along the lines of the earlier comments on e-mail spamming. One example that will surely become a classic was when an individual became alarmed at receiving a text message asking him to report to his local army recruitment centre after September 11th, 2001 only to find that it was an advertisement for a computer war game. Some other activities are scams designed to encourage premium rate telephone calls. There are computer programs that will generate random mobile numbers and send out SMS messages to all of them, whether there has been an opt-in or not, thus constant vigilance is needed from the service providers.

> **eg** HarperCollins targeted the readers of the teenage girls magazine *Sugar* as part of a promotion for two new book series under the Mary Kate and Ashley brand. The target was girls aged from 7 to 16 and the main objective of the campaign was to encourage them to seek the titles out instore. An opt-in system was used and an important consideration was not to destroy the trust in the Sugar brand by association with inappropriate advertising. With such campaigns, response rates can be as high as 30 per cent, compared with the 1 to 2 per cent from unsolicited, poorly targeted text messaging campaigns (Head, 2002; http://www.aerodeon.co.uk). HarperCollins has to be mindful, however, of the wider implications of text messaging to underage children and that some parents may not appreciate such approaches.

The alternative to SMS is interactive voice response (IVR), regarded by some as a lower-cost alternative to SMS that in addition can generate revenue from call charges. Virgin Mobile has introduced a 4321 service that enables diallers to access a voice-activated portal to gain information on sport, entertainment and news; to enter a virtual shopping mall; to buy CDs and DVDs; and even get a horoscope. Charged at 10p per minute, callers can, for example, find information on a good pub or restaurant in their vicinity, effectively making the service another media outlet for advertising (Jolley, 2002).

The main additional benefit of IVR is that by the inclusion of a voice, a human element is introduced and a less virtual experience is created. However, its continued progress will be determined by its effectiveness in generating traffic. Consumers are aware that calls cost money and there is a perception that text messaging is cheaper. In addition, the marketing organisation has to react to calls rather than being proactive (as with SMS) so the hit rates are a lot less certain.

Users

The target market for wireless marketing campaigns tends to be younger and more willing to try new ways of communicating (Barwise and Strong, 2002). Mobile usage has become an important part of our lifestyles; witness the scenes in any High Street or, more annoyingly, in a crowded commuter train. It has moved from being a status symbol to an essential communication device, and fits well with the rushed, high pressure and last-minute lifestyles of many younger people who leave decisions to the last minute and often make them 'on the run' (again, see Case Study 1.1 on Lastminute.com). That plays into the hands of the m-marketers.

Happy Dog, a wireless marketing consultancy, proposed three broad categories of prime customers for targeting in its Moby Study (reported in Carter 2002b):

- *Nomads*. Usually in the 18–24 age range, have few responsibilities, mainly live at home and tend towards last-minute decision-making rather than forward planning.
- *Gatherers*. Usually in the 25–40+ age range with the normal range of family responsibilities and career expectations. The mobile is used as an extension of the domestic phone as a matter of routine.
- *Hunters*. May be in the 20–35 age range, with few family responsibilities but enjoying to the full the stability and lifestyle that a career can bring.

These three groups may not represent all mobile users, but the profiles do suggest that the propensity to respond and the information sought will vary considerably between groups. This again highlights the importance of considering lifestyles as well as actual product usage behaviour when deciding on a particular campaign.

Systems and processes

Any successful wireless marketing campaign needs to be underpinned by an enabling technological infrastructure either established in-house or through the use of a specialist agency. The technological infrastructure enables reporting and tracking, personalisation, and the interactivity interface, and it must be capable of handling large numbers of outbound and inbound messages without crashing the system. Many organisations prefer to use established technology available from specialist agencies. Inbox (http://www.inbox.co.uk), for example, has a response management system that on receipt of an inbound message, sends a text message to the salesperson, orders a brochure to be sent to the sender by a fulfilment house, and e-mails an agent in a call centre. The priority then is to integrate the sophisticated technology that the specialist agency provides with the systems that individual marketers operate. MindMatics, for example, offers a 'Wireless Interactive Toolkit' that allows companies to start mobile marketing through standard applications without the need for any additional infrastructure. It uses a Windows-based application that connects directly with MindMatics' SMS gateway for sending and receiving.

The integration of these systems emphasises that it is dangerous to give too much attention to the creative and marketing application at the expense of the infrastructure that enables it to be adopted in the first place and to proceed effectively.

Next generation

SMS has limitations in that only relatively simple text messages can be sent, and it has been suggested that the number of text messages will soon start to plateau until the next generation of text services starts to become more widely available (Wray, 2002). The next innovation may incorporate wider use of EMS (enhanced messaging service) allowing small logos and icons to be sent over the air. A number of operators are, however, delaying major investment until MMS (multimedia messaging service) is introduced. MMS allows full colour pictures to be sent over the air and in conjunction with video has the power to bring a handset to life. This will enable pictures, melodies, animation and styled text to be fully exploited in message design. Currently, however, the mass launch of the necessary 3G technology has been delayed and only pilot schemes are in operation.

Despite uncertainty over the timing and scale of impact of MMS, Forrester Research concluded that by 2006, 37 per cent of all message traffic will be sent by MMS as long as the operators' focus shifts from the technology to customer usage (Forrester Research, 2002). Some companies are raring to go with MMS. Hasbro, which owns the board game Monopoly, tested a customised version using 2.5G rather than the 3G technology associated with MMS. By offering colour images, moving pictures and sound, it wanted to establish how effective mobile phones could be in drawing custom to its £95 MyMonopoly offer on http://www.mymonopoly.com (*Marketing Week*, 2002d).

marketing *in action*

Hey, sexy!

Kiss 100 is London's youth radio station. It started life as a pirate station but was legalised in 1990. Its success has come from the central role it has played in popularising dance music and pioneering the growth of genres such as House, Garage, Hip Hop Jungle, Ambient and Breakbeat. It is recognised as being at the cutting edge of dance music and therefore attracts a loyal band of listeners. It seeks to generate ratings by day, and a reputation for being 'hot and sexy' by night through its associated clubs. Every week, it reaches around 50 per cent of London's 15–24-year-olds who are among its 1.5 million listeners per week. It attracts a further 2 million viewers on its non-stop music channel on Sky Digital TV and the brand has been extended to holidays, clubs and network dance shows. Its Kiss CDs have sold 2 million.

Kiss is an experience brand that appeals to young people who enjoy fun and being sexy and has attracted an almost cult following. Kiss, therefore, wanted to use new media to create a strong customer relationship management programme for a generation that is unlikely to be responsive to direct mail and general mass media advertising. Kiss 100, with help from its retained creative agency, Angel Uplifting Marketing, and Flytxt, the wireless marketing expert, has thus used SMS effectively to promote greater listening and brand loyalty among its most loyal, committed listeners.

As part of a previous promotion, a database of 56,000 mobile phone numbers was created, called 'HeySexy' Club. This database of

Kiss 100 used its SMS database to send 'Hey Sexy' messages to 15–24-year-olds to encourage them to register their phones and possibly win prizes.

Source: http://www.flytxt.com.

listeners who had opted in to receive more information created a valuable marketing tool for maintaining regular contact with a willing audience, but it needed creativity and worthwhile ideas to keep them on the list and involved. Listeners initially registered by text message, via the website, or through a 0700HEYSEXY telephone line. Data captured included the registration medium, birth date and gender, as well as the obvious personal details. Flytxt and Angel Uplifting Marketing were then able to design a campaign to improve loyalty through games, competitions and promotions targeted primarily at the HeySexy members.

In all, over 20 different campaigns were designed to retain customer interest. These included:

■ The free 'Bamster' voicemail offer, whereby listeners could phone an IVR line and download a free Bamster voicemail for their mobiles.
■ The 'text to win' competition that invited listeners to text in to the station while a particular track was

being played, the track being repeated several times a day. Winners received a £100 prize, and there was evidence that listeners actually tuned in for longer periods to have a go at the competition.
■ 'The Birthday Greeting'. Every HeySexy member received a greeting from a Kiss DJ on their birthday, usually by the time the member woke up in the morning. The message is clear to the initiated 'HeySexy! Bam Bam here. Happy damn birthday from me and every1else here@Kiss100-have a blinder & keep listening! TXT STP2 unsub.'
■ 'The Anonymous Valentine Service'. Listeners could send anonymous Valentine's messages by texting a message along with the mobile number of loved ones to Kiss 100 for resending.
■ 'The Peach Party promotion' enabled listeners to sign up via text message for a £7 discount at the Peach Party guest list, a Kiss club at the Camden Palais.

The whole series of SMS promotions has been highly successful. Not only has the number of people on the HeySexy list grown, but an average of 13 per cent response rate for campaigns is normally achieved, which is well above what was expected. The response rate for the free Bamster voicemail was over 18 per cent. The Peach Party guest list contained over 16 per cent of all database members.

This example highlights the value of SMS in maintaining loyalty and developing a customer relationship management campaign using a medium that this particular age group is very familiar with and with content that is relevant to its lifestyle and language. Creating and retaining customer loyalty like this is very important to Kiss 100 as it seeks to attack Capital FM's dominant position among London's 15–to 24-year-olds (Marketing, 2001).

Sources: Marketing (2001), http://www.kiss100.com; and with grateful thanks to Lars Becker and Annabel Knight, Flytext.

■ iTV marketing

Interactive television (iTV) marketing is still in its infancy, but does have the potential to revolutionise marketing communications by allowing the user, rather than the advertiser, to tailor information content and actions to individual needs. iTV is two-way communication between the consumer and the service provider who is responsible for delivering the communication to a television set-top box via satellite, cable or aerial and then creating the technology for a 'back service' to allow the user to interact. Normally the back service is provided via a normal telephone line, wireless or, as in the case of NTL/Telewest, by special cable.

The problem with the development of iTV marketing relates to the overall take-up of digital television. According to Forrester Research (http://www.forrester.com), there are 7.9 million homes in the UK with iTV, well ahead of France, Spain and Germany combined. However, the majority of applications tend to be linked with live television formats, such as quiz shows, voting, sports action (for example the player cam on Sky Sports), and only to a much lesser extent with interactive advertising. The challenge is to convince advertising agencies and marketers that iTV offers a valuable addition to the media mix.

eg When Rimmel launched a new range of lipsticks, Exaggerate Hydracolour, it wanted to encourage product sampling among women aged between 16 and 44. It decided to experiment with iTV as part of a TV campaign, so that viewers of Sky could go interactive to request a free sample and have the opportunity to win one of 30 Rimmel cosmetic sets. The creative execution featured a traditional advertisement with a link to go interactive to a supporting advertisement, consistent in its use of voice-over, music and imagery. A single response page was used where viewers could answer a few questions, claim their lipstick, answer a simple question about Rimmel's competitors and then to opt in or out of future contact. The maximum on-time expected on the screen was 30 seconds. The campaign generated 52,000 responses, in line with the original objectives and double the normal interactive response rate, at 3.2 per cent. The resulting data were then analysed by lifestyle groups and with 68 per cent opting in, a list of over 30,000 new names was generated, useful for other promotions and offers (NetImperative, 2002).

For iTV to become an important part of the media mix it will have to be accepted by users and valued by advertisers and marketers. As many as 72 per cent of television viewers do not associate the TV with interactivity or commerce (Macklin, 2002). That means a consumer education task for service providers at a time when they are financially stretched building networks and customer bases. Just because the consumer can interact with the television, does not mean that they will. The growth of interactive programme guides (IPG) which help viewers to navigate the multitude of channels by genre, time and other criteria is an important first step in making the bewildering range of screen choices digestible, acting like an Internet portal on television. Given the early stage of consumer adoption of interactivity, there is a real risk that marketing initiatives will run ahead of consumer ability to understand how to work the system.

eg Egg, the Prudential's Internet bank, ran an iTV campaign 'Daisy goes to Russia to buy herself a husband (with her credit card)'. The main action point was to encourage credit card registration which could be achieved by pressing the red button on a television handset remote control to go interactive and then blue for registration. However, many consumers became confused, as there were then so many options that it was easy to get lost (http://www.broadbandbananas.com).

From the marketer's perspective the main benefits of iTV advertising and marketing are perceived to be (in order of importance) targeting niche audiences; personalisation and one-to-one dialogue; providing a new channel to market; deepening the brand; and revenue generation (http://www.emarketer.com).

Targeting and personalisation are well ahead of the other perceived benefits. The set-top box is a source of considerable information to the service provider and enables it to build up a user profile just like any other media publisher. For on-screen interactivity, the growing number of specialist television channels covering everything from holidays to music and sport to motoring, allows careful targeting and the profiling of subsequent replies by the box. There is some concern that the power of tracking that is possible from the set-top box raises issues of privacy. Once this is addressed, it may curtail some monitoring (http://www.broadbandbananas.com). In an era of greater personalisation rather than mass media advertising, iTV offers the potential to bring back some of the power of television advertising while also being able to follow through on a more tailored basis. Nissan used iTV to generate leads for its Primera. Viewers can link with full-screen video, explore the features of the car and request a brochure through the service. Such integration makes iTV a powerful complement to the mainstream advertising campaign.

Some organisations have also used iTV as a distribution channel to enable them to take orders on a similar basis to the Internet. The ability to respond to an instantaneous desire has been especially beneficial to Domino's Pizza. It uses iTV as a marketing channel to make it easier to order after its on-screen advertisements are broadcast. Although still only generating a small percentage of its total orders, interactive advertising, along with the website, has helped to drive up pizza orders, and this is expected to fuel further growth supported by wider strategies to ensure hot, fast and fresh home delivery (Macklin, 2002; *Marketing Week*, 2002c).

Despite some successes in the use of iTV, it is still early days for more widespread adoption. Even existing digital users regard the television as being for entertainment and the Internet for information searching, so with current adopters, the full range of interactive services are rarely activated. The service providers will have to promote the wider service benefits more positively, rather than focusing on the services at present that generate direct revenues. An advertising system that can show a standard car advertisement, for example, and with a press of the 'i button' can provide a menu of further information, show more footage, show the car in a selected colour and even allow a test drive to be organised, all from the comfort of an armchair, has many advantages over more conventional media that require telephone and mail responses. Its role for higher-involvement, high-priced, infrequently purchased items appears to be stronger than for more routine FMCG purchases.

All three forms of new media are still evolving, reflecting technological advances such as broadband, MMS messaging and two-way television. The opportunity to send personalised messages or to allow consumers opportunities to tailor the information they receive has been well received by marketers at a time of media fragmentation and greater difficulty in getting the message across. Coca-Cola, for example, has shifted some of its spend from television advertising into new media where it can target younger people with live music, sport and viral marketing (Day, 2001). As the technology improves, there will be more opportunities to create more complex campaigns to attract and retain attention, but only by encouraging interactivity will the real power of new media become evident.

Detica (reported by *Marketing Week*, 2002b) found that consumers feel frustrated with some self-service new media technology largely because of a lack of confidence or skill in using the technology and a feeling that such technology is there to benefit the organisation, not the consumer. Coupled with concern that as the volume of messages grows it will lead to a negative impact on the whole industry (Gander, 2001), the future of some of the new media platforms is far from certain. Marketers must not be blinded by technology ahead of customer adoption, understanding and acceptance, especially as the adoption process spreads away from more innovative age groups into the mainstream population, as text messaging has done. Mazur (2002) reminds us that viral marketing from the customer's perspective is not something that is done to them, but something they think they do, as happy or unhappy customers. Similarly with all interactive media, the majority of users believe that they control their own access to cyberspace and networks, rather than seeing themselves as the target of a marketer's strategy (Ellis, 2002). It is perhaps time to put the customer experience and usage back at the centre of new media strategies.

There are still important issues to overcome in all areas, especially concerning privacy and data protection. Although privacy does not always appear to be a major topic for consumers, that may reflect the low level of understanding of just how companies collect and manage data about individuals (Barwise, 2002). With legislative trends and industry standards being imposed, the question remains whether the impact of controls on spamming and poor targeting can come quickly enough to avoid consumer resentment at being bombarded with a series of unwanted messages. The last thing genuine marketers want is to have their brands devalued by being regarded as 'pushy', or by association with spammers.

Chapter summary

■ Internet marketing has a wide variety of uses within an organisation, including information dissemination, PR, selling, relationship management and market research, and is centred around the organisation's website which must be well designed to offer the user what they want in a form that is appealing and user-friendly. Internet marketing can be useful in any size and type of organisation, and can be very cost-effective in achieving marketing objectives when integrated with more traditional marketing tools and methods. The dotcom bust demonstrated that the 'traditional marketing values' of customer orientation, clear differential advantage and tightly controlled marketing planning and management and controls are still essential even for companies trading wholly on the Internet. Generating and maintaining consumer trust are also seen as major factors in Internet marketing success.

■ Internet marketing is increasing in importance as Internet penetration among the general population rises. As individuals gain experience of using the Internet and as their trust in it grows, they are likely to start spending more money via this channel on a much wider range of goods and services. The number of people buying via the Internet and their average spend is already increasing rapidly. Businesses too are spending more on e-procurement. B2B exchanges or e-marketplaces run by independent organisations have emerged to help match buyers, and sellers quickly and cost-effectively. Industry-specific exchanges, such as Covisint, dominated by large buyers have also arisen to streamline distribution chains and make them more cost-effective. E-collaboration on major projects is being experimented with, but so far has been disappointing.

■ The three main categories of Internet use for organisations are for research and planning, as a distribution channel, and as a communiucations medium. The Internet has opened up a vast wealth of information sources, both free and paid for, and has provided a new way of undertaking various types of market research. It has also become an additional cost-effective distribution channel with the emergence of e-tailers and cybermediaries alongside traditional companies using it in parallel with 'normal' retail channels. The Internet has also become an advertising medium in its own right to complement other media and is also a means of delivering imaginative sales promotions and other incentives. It can add a lot of value to customer service and customer relationship programmes. In the future as the technology underpinning the Internet improves (e.g. with the advent of broadband), its marketing uses are likely to become more sophisticated and consumers and businesses alike will come to regard it very much as a mainstream marketing tool.

■ The three main elements of the so-called 'new media' are e-mail marketing, wireless marketing and interactive television (iTV). E-mail marketing is primarily used as a means of customer relationship management, to create and nurture relationships with customers through regular, targeted, relevant contact. Imaginative and well-designed messages can be used in viral marketing campaigns, encouraging the recipient to pass the message on to a friend to exploit word-of-mouth advantages. Wireless marketing (m-marketing or mobile marketing) harnesses the power of the mobile telephone and mainly involves text messaging as a form of marketing communication. As with the Internet, advances in technology are likely to open up new applications for wireless marketing. iTV marketing provides the opportunity for two-way communication between the marketer and an individual via the television set. The consumer can use the interactive facility on the remote control to request further information about a product, or to interact in many ways as they would on the Internet. The main problems, however, are the costs of creating the necessary digital networks to deliver the iTV service, and consumer acceptance and adoption of the full range of iTV capabilities.

questions for *review and discussion*

14.1 What are the major advantages and disadvantages of reverse auctions from the B2B supplier's point of view?

14.2 Outline the three main categories of website usage for businesses.

14.3 What is viral marketing and why is it so useful to the marketer?

14.4 Compile a checklist of criteria against which a fashion e-tail website might be assessed. Visit three websites e-tailing clothing to a similar target audience. Compare and contrast those sites in terms of their performance on those criteria. How could each of them improve its offering?

14.5 'New media have nothing more to offer the marketer than the more traditional forms of marketing communications.' Discuss.

14.6 Draw up a table listing the advantages and disadvantages of e-mail marketing compared with more traditional approaches to direct marketing. In what kind of situations do you think e-mail marketing might work best?

case study 14.1

From dotcom to dotbomb to dotboom?

One of the most high-profile, not to mention stylish, dotcom failures was boo.com. It started trading in November 1999, and collapsed in May 2000, yet in principle, the idea seemed like a good one: Boo wanted to tap into the boom in online shopping and the popularity of branded sportswear to offer labels such as DKNY, Puma and Fubu to a global audience. Investors thought it was a good idea too. In 1998, Boo's two founders, Ernst Malmsten and Kajsa Leander, raised $135m. in venture capital to fund the start-up of the business. High-profile advertising began in May 1999, anticipating a June launch, but because of technical problems, the launch had to be postponed. A Boo employee said, 'There was an incredible buzz in the offices about establishing the brand, the technology came second. We thought we'd sort the gizmos later' (as quoted by Barr, 2002).

In truth, the brand was indeed the focal point. A crew of fashion consultants was even hired for $5,000 per day to perfect the look of Miss Boo, the virtual personal shopper. The company became famous (notorious?) for its PR activities. As one employee said, '[The founders'] secret was to overwhelm employees, investors and journalists with wild evenings at glamorous locations, providing them with a passport to outrageous people and places. There wasn't a newspaper or magazine they wouldn't pose for, spinning journalists a crazy tale of how a poetry critic and a model came to be running a multimillion-dollar business' (as quoted by Kanarek, 2001). Initially, the media fell for it, and Boo claimed that the positive coverage and its appearance on the front page of *Fortune* magazine persuaded its largest investor (worth $50m.) to make contact.

Meanwhile, the initial staff base of 30 people had expanded to 500, working in seven offices across the world, and money was flowing freely out of the business, but as yet no revenues were coming in. The launch plan was ambitious, but was backed by little in the way of sound planning, effective decision-making or attention to detail. Everything had to be built from scratch: financial systems, a pool of suppliers, warehousing, distribution and customer service, etc. Boo was to launch in 17 countries simultaneously, a complex and costly undertaking, and yet nobody was overseeing the detail to make it work in practical terms. The database of clothing sizes did not reflect variations between countries, and nobody had worked out how customers were to return goods from different countries or how credit card refunds were to be managed, for instance.

All the hype and the triumph of style over substance really came home to roost when boo.com started trading in October 1999. People were visiting the site, although less than 25 per cent of those who tried to access it actually succeeded. The number of visitors to the site on the first day of trading was 25,000 rather than the 1 million predicted. Of those who did get through to the site, few were buying anything. The site was technologically so complex that it was running very slowly and people were losing patience with it. In addition, consumers found that Boo's prices were no lower than those of more traditional retailers, so why bother buying from Boo? Sales were less than one-tenth of what had been promised.

An overhaul in early 2000 led to restructuring to cut costs and improvements in the technology. The business began to be managed more effectively and sensibly, and revenues began to flow. But it was too little too late. Boo had failed to 'get big fast' which was the only way it was ever going to succeed and survive. In April, the Nasdaq, the US technology stockmarket, suffered a huge drop and investors started to get jittery and more realistic in their expectations of dotcom companies. Boo began to lose its supporters and backers and the media coverage started to become hostile. One journalist who attempted to order a pair of trainers from boo.com wrote incredulously, 'Eighty-one minutes to pay too much money for a pair of shoes I'm still going to have to wait a week to get?' (as quoted by Woodward, 2002).

By May 2000, it was all over. Boo went bust and its investors and unsecured creditors, who were owed around $150m., got nothing back. The brand, the logo and the right to use the domain were bought for a mere $250,000 (estimated) by fashionmall.com, a US company that acts as a portal to other e-tail sites selling designer clothes, accessories, footwear and beauty products. Fashionmall generates its revenue by earning transaction fees on sales made on those sites and by selling advertising space on its own site to e-tailers.

By the end of October 2000, Boo was thus relaunched as a youth fashion portal. Miss Boo was back and she told website visitors, 'I've been off on holiday jetting the world and I've squandered a fortune! But I'm back with some yummy things for you to wear and do this season – not to mention a glorious sun-tan …' (as quoted by *The Independent*, 2000).

Fashionmall hoped to benefit from the enormous brand awareness that Boo had built up through its huge marketing budget, making it one of the top

10 most recognised brands on the Internet, and felt that although 'the business model of Boo has been discredited, the brand has not. Boo still stands for leading-edge fashion and style' (as quoted by Barker, 2000). Under Fashionmall's ownership, however, Boo was no longer selling goods directly from its own stock but introducing customers to relevant sites where they could buy what they want. 'The old Boo would have sold you a pair of Nike trainers from its warehouses. . . . Now the shopper will go straight to Nike. Our job is not to send you products. Our job is to introduce you to the person [who] has the product [and] can send it to you' (as quoted by Heavens and Kirchgaessner, 2000). As with Fashionmall's existing operation, revenue came from transactions fees and advertising. The plan was that on the basis of a $1m. marketing spend (compared with the $40m. the original Boo spent), the site would become profitable within two years.

Just over a year later, however, in December 2001, the headlines started to have a horribly familiar look with Boo reported as being 'poised to crash into oblivion for a second time' (Beaton, 2001). Fashionmall itself was said to be in difficulties with falling revenues and was also said to be considering abandoning online retailing because it could not make any money. While the Boo brand could be put up for sale, the reality was that very little business was being channelled through it.

As at July 2002, however, Fashionmall was still in business. The boo.com website was still operational, transferring the Internet user through to the Boo page on fashionmall.com. Other than the visibility of the Boo branding on the page, there does not appear to be anything particularly distinctive on offer: the page just offers a series of hyperlinks to various companies' websites. It seems that Miss Boo's heart just isn't in her job any more.

Sources: Barker (2000), Barr (2002), Barrow (2000), Beaton (2001), Heavens and Kirchgaessner (2000), *The Independent* (2000), Kanarek (2001), Mathieson (2000), Sliwa (2000), Snoddy (2000), Stockport *et al.* (2001), Woodward (2002).

Questions

1 Summarise the reasons why Boo originally failed.

2 If Fashionmall were to decide to sell the Boo brand, to what extent is it still likely to be attractive to a prospective purchaser?

3 Is clothing e-tailing ever likely to succeed in the same way that other product sectors such as books and CDs have? Why or why not?

References for chapter 14

24/7 Europe (2002a), 'Cussons Imperial Leather Advertorial and DHTML Banner' (accessed via http://www.247europe.com).

24/7 Europe (2002b), 'Kraft Foods "Lunchables" Integrated Online Promotion' (accessed via http://www.247europe.com).

24/7 Europe (2002c), 'Jaffa Cakes/Manchester United Campaign' (accessed via http://www.247europe.com).

Anderson, J. and Patel, P. (2001), 'B2B Makes Seller Suffer', *The Times*, 12 July, p. 2.9.

Apparel Industry Magazine (2000), 'Who Will e-tail Your Products Best?', *Apparel Industry Magazine*, February, pp. 40–1.

ARC Group (2002), 'Content and Applications for Broadband and Digital TV', *ARC Group Stratgeic Reports.2002* (accessed via http://www.arcgroup.com).

Barker, T. (2000), 'Miss Boo Makes Virtual Return at Fashionmall', *Financial Times*, 7 October, p. 16.

Barr, D. (2002), 'Whatever Happened to these Likely Fads?', *Evening Standard*, 11 June, p. 14.

Barrow, B. (2000), 'Boo Back in Business, This Time on a Budget', *The Daily Telegraph*, 30 October, p. 25.

Barwise, P. (2002), 'Great Ideas. Now Make Them Work', *Financial Times*, 28 May, p. 4.

Barwise, P. and Strong, C. (2002), 'Permission-based Mobile Advertising', *Journal of Interactive Marketing*, 16 (1), pp. 14–24.

Beaton, G. (2001), 'Boo on the Brink (Part 2)', *Mail on Sunday*, 2 December, p. 5.

Birmingham Post (2002), 'E-business: Tesco in Grocery Delivery Switch', *Birmingham Post*, 30 April, p. 20.

BMRB (2000), 'Users Ignore Banners, But Off-line Makes Up the Difference' (accessed via http://www.bmrb.co.uk).

Bowen, D. (2002), 'Handling the Bad News', *Financial Times*, 25 January, p. 11.

Bruce, A. (2002), 'Clubcard Takes to the Internet as Tesco.com Strives for Perfection', *The Grocer*, 4 May, p. 8.

Carter, M. (2002a), 'Branded "Viruses" Mutate to Entice Consumers', *Financial Times*, 7 January, p. 14.

Carter, M. (2002b), 'How to Hit a Moving Target', *The Guardian*, 27 May, p. 42.

CyberAtlas (2002), 'B2B E-commerce Headed for Trillions', 6 March (accessed via http://cyberatlas.internet.com).

The Daily Telegraph (2002), '$2m Bill over Camera Error', *The Daily Telegraph*, 2 February, p. 12.

Dawe, A. (2002), 'Hitting the Target', *Director*, February, p. 17.

Day, J. (2001), 'Hard Sell in Your Hand', *The Guardian*, 19 March, p. 50.

Doward, B. (2002), 'Sportal Bounces Back', *The Observer*, 3 March, p. 2.

Duboff, R. and Spaeth, J. (2000), 'Researching the Future Internet', *Direct Marketing*, 63 (3), pp. 42–54.

Dwek, R. (2002), 'E-mail in the UK Overtakes Snail', *Marketing Week*, 21 March, p. 44.

Eaglesham, J. (2002), 'A Troubled Deal on the Internet', *Financial Times*, 11 February, p. 18.

Ellis, J. (2002), 'Yahoo Kisses it All Good-bye', *Fast Company*, July, pp. 114–16.

Euromonitor (2002), *European Marketing Data and Statistics 2002*, Euromonitor (37th edn).

Feather, F. (2002), *FutureConsumer.Com: The Webolution of Shopping to 2010*, Warwick Publications.

Financial Times (2001), 'Friends Reunited', *Financial Times*, 9 October, p. 8.

Forrester Research (2002), 'Mobile Messaging's Next Generation' (accessed via http://www.forrester.com).

Friesen, P. (2002), 'How to Develop an Effective E-mail Creative Strategy', *Target Marketing*, February, pp. 46–50.

Gander, P. (2001), 'Mobile Options', *Marketing Week*, 6 September, p. 41.

Gaudin, S. (2002), 'The Site of No Return', 28 May (accessed via http://cyberatlas.internet.com).

Goodley, S. (2002), 'Yes, We Have No Bananas', *The Daily Telegraph*, 15 January, p. 27.

Grant, J. (2002), 'Covisint Fails to Move up into the Fast Lane', *Financial Times*, 4 July, p. 23.

Greenspan, R. (2002a), 'Making Money on Free Music', 12 June (accessed via http://cyberatlas.internet.com).

Greenspan, R. (2002b), 'Broadband Appeal', 16 April (accessed via http://www.cyberatlas.internet.com).

Gregory, H. (2002), 'Dotcom Driver', *The Grocer*, 16 February, pp. 36-8.

The Grocer (2001), 'Online Orders Grow at "Fantastic Rate"', *The Grocer*, 20 October, p. 8.

The Grocer (2002), 'Online Order Fulfilment Still Dogged by Delivery Glitches', *The Grocer*, 6 April, p. 5.

Head, J. (2002), 'Pandora's Inbox', *The Guardian*, 25 March, p. 40.

Heavens, A. and Kirchgaessner, S. (2000), 'US Portal Breathes Life into Boo.com', *Financial Times*, 2 June, p. 23.

Hewson, D. (2000), 'Firms Reap Net Profits by Learning to Work Together', *e-business* supplement to *Sunday Times*, 26 November, p. 2.

Hunt, J. (2001), 'Marketing's a Piece of Cake', *The Guardian*, 4 October, p. 7.

The Independent (2000), 'No Catcalls for the New Boo', *The Independent*, 22 October, p. 8.

Jolley, R. (2002), 'Marketers Warm to Voice Services', *Marketing*, 7 February, p. 23.

Kanarek, P. (2001), 'How We Went from Boo to Bust', *The Daily Telegraph*, 5 October, p. 23.

Karakaya, F. and Charlton, E. (2001), 'Electronic Commerce: Current and Future Practices', *Managerial Finance*, 27 (7), pp. 42–53.

Kolesar, M. and Galbraith, W. (2000), 'A Services Marketing Perspective on E-retailing: Implications for E-retailers and Directions for Further Research', *Internet Research*, 10 (5), pp. 424–38.

Macklin, B. (2002), 'What Every Marketer Needs to Know About iTV' (accessed via http://www.emarketer.com).

McLuhan, R. (2002), 'Using Streaming to Boost Brands', *Marketing*, 30 May, p. 25.

McNutt, B. (1998), 'A Matter of Priority', *Precision Marketing*, 21 December, p. 16.

Marketing (2001), 'Best Use of Technology: Customer Loyalty', *The Marketing Awards: Connections 2001* supplement to *Marketing*, November 2001.

Marketing (2002), 'Sportal Prepares to Relaunch with Agenda for "Fun"', *Marketing*, 17 January, p. 4.

Marketing Week (2001), 'First Brylcreem Viral Push Develops Press Ad Theme', *Marketing Week*, 6 December, p. 15.

Marketing Week (2002a), 'When in Rome, Eat as the Americans Do', *Marketing Week*, 28 February, p. 55.

Marketing Week (2002b), 'Self Service Fails to Impress Consumers', *Marketing Week*, 23 May, p. 39.

Marketing Week (2002c), 'Grabbing a Bigger Pizza the Online Action', *Marketing Week*, 23 May, p. 40.

Marketing Week (2002d), 'MyMonopoly', *Marketing Week*, 18 July, p. 12.

Mathieson, C. (2000), 'Investors Face Total Loss, Says Boo.com Liquidator', *The Times*, 3 June, p. 26.

Mazur, L. (2002), 'Firms Can't "Do" Viral Marketing: It is Done to You', *Marketing*, 27 June, p. 16.

Middleton, T. (2002), 'Sending Out the Winning Messages', *Marketing Week*, 16 May, pp. 43–5.

Milsom, P. (2002), 'Online Shoppers Exceed 10 Million for First Time in GB', *Revolution*, 2 July (accessed via http://www.bmrb.co.uk).

Mitchell, A. (1999), 'Online Markets Could See Brands Lose Control', *Marketing Week*, 15 April, pp. 24–5.

Monbiot, G. (2002), 'The Fake Persuaders', *The Guardian*, 14 May, p. 1.15.

Murphy, D. (2002), 'Marketers Put E-mail to the Test', *Marketing*, 6 June, pp. 19–20.

NetImperative (2002), 'Interactive TV Sector Report', June (accessed via http://www.broadbandbananas.com).

Newing, R. (2002), 'Crucial Importance of Clear Business Goals', *Financial Times*, 5 June, p. 4.

Nichols, P. (2001), 'Sport's Dot.com Meltdown', *The Guardian*, 10 November, p. 16.

Pastore, M. (2001), 'Global Companies Lead B2B Charge', 14 August (accessed via http://cyberatlas.internet.com).

Pastore, M. (2002), 'Britons Increase Use of Interactive Technologies', 15 March (accessed via http://cyberatlas.internet.com).

Patten, S. (2002), 'E-grocers Step up Battle of the Van Man', *The Times*, 26 March, p. 31.

Pickton, D. and Broderick, A. (2001), *Integrated Marketing Communications*, Financial Times Prentice Hall.

Ray, A. (2001), 'Profiting From the E-mail Grapevine', *Marketing*, 11 October, p. 27.

Rizzi, D. (2001), 'Precision E-mail Marketing', *Direct Marketing*, November, pp. 56–60.

Rosenthal, R. (2002), *Worldwide B2B Dynamic Pricing Forecast, 2002–2006: 'What Am I Bid for This . . .'*, March, Doc #26801 (accessed via http://www.idc.com).

Rowley, J. (2002), *E-business: Principles and Practice*, Palgrave.

Sarkar, M., Butler, B. and Steinfield, C. (1996), 'Intermediaries and Cybermediaries: a Continuing Role for Mediating Players in the Electronic Marketplace', *Journal of Computer Mediated Communication*, 1 (3) (accessed via http://www.ascusc.org/jcmc/vol1/issue3/sarkar.html).

Saunders, C. (2001), 'Trust Central to E-commerce, Online Marketing', 20 November (accessed via http://cyberatlas. internet.com).

Saunders, C. (2002), 'Branding Benefited by Banners', 17 April (accessed via http://www.cyberatlas.internet.com).

Sliwa, C. (2000), 'Boo.com To Rise Again, Run by Fashionmall', *Computerworld*, 21 August, p. 35.

Smith, P. and Chaffey, D. (2001), *eMarketing eXcellence: At the Heart of e-Business*, Butterworth Heinemann.

Smith, P. and Taylor, J. (2002), *Marketing Communications: An Integrated Approach* (3rd edn), Kogan Page.

Snoddy, J. (2000), 'Boo is Reborn in Confident Fashion', *The Guardian*, 27 October, p. 1.30.

Snoddy, J. (2001), 'Fallen for an Old Flame? Just Log on for Counselling', *The Independent*, 9 September, p. 8.

Stockport, G., Kunnath, G. and Sedick, R. (2001), 'Boo.com: the Path to Failure', *Journal of Interactive Marketing*, 15 (4), pp. 56–70.

Sumner, I. (1999), 'Web Site Novelties Can Bring PR Opportunities', *Marketing*, 17 June, p. 31.

Tanner, J. (2002), 'Broadband Vision', *America's Network*, 1 May.

Tapp, A. (2002), 'Proactive or Reactive Marketing? The Influence of the Internet on Direct Marketing, Part 3', *Journal of Database Marketing*, 9 (3), pp. 238–47.

Trollinger, S. (2002), 'The Role of E-mail in Micro-segmentation', *Target Marketing*, May, pp. 28–30.

Watson, E. (2002a), 'Online Auctions Come under Fire', *The Grocer*, 29 July, p. 4.

Watson, E. (2002b), 'Hitting the Floor', *The Grocer*, 6 July, pp. 34–5.

Wilson, R. (1999), 'Discerning Habits', *Marketing Week*, 1 July, pp. 45–7.

Woodward, D. (2002), 'Making a Drama out of a Crisis', *Director*, May, pp. 58–62.

Wray, R. (2002), 'Mobile Chiefs Get the Message', *The Guardian*, 14 May, p. 20.

Index

3G technology 486–7
4Ps 20–2, 52, 400, 436
5Ss 465
7Ps 22–3, 437–43
360 degree reporting 12

acceptability of brand names 188
accessibility
   advertising agencies 318–19
   market segments 128–9
   services 44
accessory goods 176
account management 335
accountability, non-profit organisations
     455–6
achievers 118
ACORN 116
Action on Smoking and Health (ASH) 44
activities, market segmentation 117
added value 249–54, 347
adjustments, prices 238–9
administered vertical marketing
     systems 268
administration 47
advertising
   advocacy 305, 307
   agencies 318–20
   broadcast presentation 314–15
   campaigns 320–4
   celebrities 295–6
   cinema 315
   comparative 306
   competitive 305, 306
   cooperative 360
   customer-oriented appeals 311–12
   creative appeals 310–12
   definition 305
   development 322–3
   direct response 365–7
   evaluation 324
   frequency 313
   green issues and 290–2
   image building 305
   institutional 307
   internet 475–6
   magazines 316–16
   in marketing mix 307–8
   media 47, 312–18, 322, 324
   messages 308–12, 324
   newspapers 316

outdoor 316–18
opportunity to see (OTS) 313, 324
pioneering 305–6
posters 316–17
print presentation 324
product-oriented 305–7, 310–11
promotional mix 279, 287, 305–7
public relations and 373, 376
publicity compared 376
radio 314–15
ratings 313
reach 313
regulation 58–60
reminder and reinforcement
     305, 306–7
role 305–8
source credibility 295–6
television 314
testing 322–3
Advertising Standards Authority (ASA)
     58–60, 292
advertorials 311
advocacy advertising 305, 307
affective attitudes 81
affective communications objectives
     283, 294
affordable budgets 297
age 37
agencies, advertising 318–20
agents 246, 247–8
aggressive strategies 417
agree and counter technique 334
agriculture 33–4
   Common Agricultural Policy (CAP)
     55–6
   farm produce 54
   intensive food production 41–2
AIDA response hierarchy model 122,
     201, 283, 365
aircraft 271, 312, 406, 407
airlines 50, 236–7
   business travellers 108–9
   catering 449
   comfor t 44–5
   inseparability 434–5
   visible staff 448
alcohol 49, 52, 60, 292, 341–3
   see also beer
alliances, strategic 418
allowances 239, 359–60

alternative closes of sales 334–5
alternative currencies 357
AMA (American Marketing Association)
     2, 4, 6
ambient advertising 316–18
American Marketing Association (AMA)
     2, 4, 6
analysis
   breakeven 235
   competitive 238
   competitors 405–6
   data 165
   marketing 408–10
   SWOT 408–10
animals 40, 41–2
annual reports 377
Ansoff matrix 411–12
anti-competitive practices 223–4
appraisal of suppliers 99
appropriate prices 102
arbitrary budgets 297
area sampling 158
arts 377, 380
ASA (Advertising Standards Authority)
     58–60, 292
ASH (Action on Smoking and Health) 44
aspirant groups 88
assessment of demand 230
assets, brands 182–3
associative brand names 187
assortment 251–2
attack strategies 417
attention, selective 77–8
attitudes 81–3, 121, 394, 446
attractiveness 403
attrition rates, advertising
     campaigns 324
auctions, internet 470
audits 140, 141, 399–408
augmented products 173, 174
Australia 441–2
Austria 190
authority publics 374
availability of brand names 188

B2B
   advertising, testimonials 310–11
   buying 96–103
   customers 92–3
   goods 26, 176–7, 246–8

internet spending 469–70
marketing 91–2
marketing research 136, 150, 153, 159
markets 93–6
    discounts 238–9
    Eurobrands 207
    geographic adjustments 239
    innovators 202
    pricing 237–9
    products 287–8
    purchases as investments 214
    sales promotion 361
    segmentation 110–12, 129
    target markets 281–2
personal selling 331–2, 335
purchasing policy 94–5
services 176–7
B2G3F 354
backward integration 267
bad publicity 376
bananas 51
banks and banking 110, 443
banner advertising 476
BCG matrix 400–2
beer 49, 56, 306, 464
behaviour
    buyer readiness stage 283–7
    buying 271
    communications objectives 293–4
    consumers see consumers
    organisational decision-making 96–9
    segmentation 119–22
belongingness needs 79, 80
benefits
    branding 181–3
    financing 253
    marketing planning 397
    products 213–15
    segmentation 120, 127
    usage, advertising appeals 312
BIGIF 354
biotech sector 394
birth 143
birth rate 37
BMRA (British Market Research
    Association) 166
BOGOFF 354–5
books 468
boomerang demand curves 220
Boston Box 400–2
brands and branding
    assets 182–3
    attitudes to 82–3
    benefits of branding 181–3
    definition of brand 180
    discreet branding 191
    Eurobrands 206–7
    extension 192–4
    generic brands 191
    lifecycles 200
    loyalty 121
    manufacturer brands 183
    meaning of branding 180–81
    names 180, 187–8
    own-label brands 184, 351

policy 191–2
retailer bands 184
strategy 184–95
values 182–3
wholesaler brands 184
bras 114
Brazil 41
breadth of range 257
breakeven analysis 235
breast implants 290–1
briefings 377
British Heart Foundation 44
British Market Research Association
    (BMRA) 166
broadband 478
broadcasting
    advertising 314–15
    sponsorship 379–80
    see also television
brokers 247
budgets and budgeting 296–9, 321–2, 419
bulk breaking 252
burst advertising 323
business ability, advertising agencies 319
business ethics see corporate social
    responsibility; ethics
business orientations 7–15
business services 177
business strengths 403
business-to-business see B2B
business travel 108–9
busy periods, evening out 351
buyer readiness 121–2, 283–7
buyer–seller relationships 5–6
buyer–supplier relationships 470
buyers 100
    see also consumers; customers
buying
    B2B 96–103
    behaviour 271
    complexity 94–6, 271
    locally 273
    situations 72–4
    see also purchasing

cable television 314
CAD (computer aided design) 47
CAM (computer aided manufacturing) 47
cameras 215
campaigns
    advertising 320–4
    plans 396
CAP (Common Agricultural Policy) 55–6
capabilities, organisational 270
CAPI (computer aided personal
    interviewing) 164
Capibus 140
capital goods 176
car rental 388–9
career security 103
case bonuses, promotions to
    retailers 360
cash cows 400, 402
catalogue showrooms 257, 262–3
catalogues, mail order 369–70

category killers 260
category management (CM) 150–1
CATI (computer aided telephone
    interviewing) 153, 164
causal research 138
cause-related marketing (CRM) 307–8,
    346, 381–2, 399, 451
CE marking 57
Central and Eastern Europe 8
CFC (chlorofluorocarbons) 61
challengers 416
changing environment 271–2
channels, distribution see distribution:
    channels
charities
    cause related marketing 381
    donations to 377
    non-profit marketing 451–8
Chartered Institute of Marketing
    (CIM) 2, 4, 6
children
    advertising 90–1, 475–6
    cruelty to 459–60
    marketing research 167
China 9, 244, 407, 439
chips 120
chlorofluorocarbons (CFC) 61
chocolate 43, 57–8, 408–9
CIM (Chartered Institute of Marketing)
    2, 4, 6
cinemas 315, 431–2
class 83–4
classification
    non-profit organisations 452–6
    products 174–7
    services 429
classified advertisements 316
client–agency relationships, advertising
    319–20
closed-loop verification 155
closed questions 160, 161
closing sales 334–5
clothing 39–40, 492–3
clusters, competitive 406
CM (category management) 150–1
cocoa 43
coding, questionnaires 163
coffee 43
cognitive attitudes 81
cognitive communications objectives
    283, 294
cognitive dissonance 71
cold calling 58, 264, 332
    see also outbound telemarketing
collection of data 147
collusion 418
combination selling 363
commercial enterprises 92–3
commercial publics 374
commission, sales representatives 338
commitment, suppliers 99
Common Agricultural Policy (CAP) 55–6
communication
    channel systems 274
    e-communication 369
    internal 377

communication (*continued*)
  internet marketing 471, 474–8
  models 280–300
  non-profit organisations 456
  promotional mix 279–80, 280–300
  sales promotion 347
  services 444
  theories 283–6
  see also advertising; information; integrated marketing communication
comparative advertising 306
compatibility 319
compensation, sales representatives 338
competence, services 444
competition 52
  in channels 266–7
  countering by sales promotions 349, 353
  monopolistic 54, 222–3
  perfect 54, 223
  segmentation benefits 127
  see also competitors
competition-based pricing 237–8
Competition Commission 52, 55, 58
competitive advantage 182
competitive advertising 305, 306
competitive analysis 238
competitive clusters 406
competitive edge 23, 25
competitive environment 34–5, 48–54
competitive factors 322
competitive information systems 406
competitive parity 298
competitive positions 415–17
competitive postures 415, 417–18
competitive reaction 406
competitive strategies 391, 416
competitive strengths and weaknesses 406
competitors 16, 222–3
  analysis 405–6
  communications planning and 291
  identification 406
  orientation 10
  price cuts 234
  sales representatives monitoring 329
  strategies 395
complexity 271
components 46, 177
computer aided design (CAD) 47
computer aided manufacturing (CAM) 47
computer aided personal interviewing (CAPI) 164
computer aided telephone interviewing (CATI) 153, 164
computerised kiosks 262
computers
  deep computing 46
  games 301–2
  pervasive computing 46
  schools 382
conative attitudes 81–2
concentrated targeting 124

concentration, geographic and industrial 94
concentric diversification 414
concessions 258–9
condoms 169–70
conflict 273–4
conglomerate diversification 414–15
consumer forces 42–5
consumer goods 21, 26, 175–7, 191, 244–6
consumer marketing 92
consumer markets
  innovators 202
  marketing research 136
  products 287–8
  sales force support 361–2
  target markets 281–2
consumer panels 139–40
consumer services 175–7
consumerism 42–5
consumers
  behaviour as buyers 66
    buying situations 72–4
    decision-making process 66–72, 89–90
    diffusion of innovation 201–3
    environmental influences 74–6
    psychological influences 77–83
    real-time recording 156
    sociocultural influences 83–91
  branding benefits perspective 181
  internet penetration and spending 468
  market segmentation 112–22
  pricing, influences on 218
  sales promotion 349–59
  spending 37–8
  see also customers
Consumers' Association 43, 61
contacts 332–3
contests 357, 361
contingency plans 396
continuous research 139–41
contractual systems 256
contractual vertical marketing systems 267–8
controls, marketing 419–20, 423–4
convenience goods 175
convenience stores 261–2
cooperation 273–4, 418
cooperative advertising 360
cooperatives, retail 268
coordination
  sales representatives, within own organisations 328
core products 173–4
corporate chains 256
corporate communications 294, 476–7
corporate governance 398
corporate internet communications 476–7
corporate objectives 398
corporate plans 396
corporate PR 374–5
corporate social responsibility (CSR)

11–12, 43, 398–9
corporate strategies 390–1
corporate values 398
corporate vertical marketing systems 267
cost-based pricing 235–6
cost of money 49–50
cost-plus pricing 235
costs 215–16, 226–7
  cost–volume–profit relationship 234–5
  definitions 234–5
  marginal 234
  personal selling 327
  savings 311
count and recount, promotions to retailers 360
coupons 350, 353–4, 365
courtesy, services 444
creative appeals, advertising 310–12
creative message design, e-mail marketing 483–4
credibility 376, 444
CRM (cause-related marketing) *see* cause-related marketing
CRM (customer relationship management) 487–8
cross-selling 371
CSR *see* corporate social responsibility
cultivation, personal selling 326
cultural aspects of environmen t 290
culture 85–7
current customers 16
customer-based structure, sales forces 336
customer importance structure, sales forces 336
customer-oriented appeals, advertising 311–12
customer relationship management (CRM) 487–8
customers
  acquisition, e-mail marketing 482
  B2B 92–3
  current 16
  information, databases 370
  interaction 450
  lapsed 371
  loyalty schemes *see* loyalty
  marketing and 47–8
  needs 3, 19–24
  new, attracting 352
  orientation 10
  perspectives on prices 213–15
  potential 16, 71
  pricing, influences on 218
  reselling to 371
  retention 371, 482–3
  segmentation benefits 127
  service 102, 471
  turnover, advertising campaigns 323
  understanding, services 444
  see also consumers
cuts in prices 234
cybermediaries 474

data
  analysis 165
  coding 163
  collection 147
  interpretation 165
  origins 138–9
  primary 147, 149–66
  protection 154–5, 365
  qualitative 165
  quantitative 165
  secondary 147, 148–9
data-based budget setting 298
databases 47, 75, 149, 370–2
dealers 254
debt 42
deciders 100
decision-making
  B2B buying process 96–9
  group 95
  organisational behaviour 96–9
  process 66–72, 89–90
  units (DMU) 99, 100
decision support systems (DSS) 144
decline of products 197–8, 289
deep computing 46
deep vein thrombosis (DVT) 44–5
defence 417–18
defendability, market segments 129
deforestation 40–1
deletion of products 194–5
delivery 99
  see also distribution
demand
  assessment 230
  curves 219–21
  derived 93
  determinants 219–20
  elasticity of 93, 220–1
  inelastic 93
  joint 93
  price elasticity 220–1
  pricing 236–7
  services 450-1-9
  structure of 93–4
demographics 37–9, 113, 117
demonstrations 328, 359
department stores 258–9
depth of range 257
derived demand 93
descriptive research 138
design, products 184–5, 186, 205, 206
desk research 147, 148–9
detergents 53
development
  advertising 322–3
  markets 413
  R&D 17, 45–6
  see also new products
dichotomous questions 161
diet products 60
diets 44
differential advantage 23
differentiated targeting 124
diffusion of innovation 201–3
digital television 232

direct mail 365, 366
direct marketing 6, 58, 279, 346, 361–70
Direct Marketing Association (DMA)
    60, 292
direct response advertising 365–7
direct response advertising on television
    (DRTV) 367
direct supply 244, 440
direct taxation 49
directional policy matrix 403
discount clubs 262
discount overriders, promotions to
    retailers 360
discounts 238–9, 360–1
discreet branding 191
disintermediation 474
dispersion 271
display advertising 316
dissociative groups 88
distance selling see direct marketing
distinctiveness 128, 188
distribution 4, 47
  chains 221–2
  channels 221–2, 243, 244
    channel strategies 265–74
    channel structures 244–8, 266–8
    intermediaries 249–65
    internet uses 471–4
    mail order catalogues 370
  exclusive 269, 270
  intensive 269
  non-profit organisations 457
  selective 269
distributors 254,
  channel structures 247–8
  sales representatives 361
  see also wholesalers
diversification 414–15
DMA (Direct Marketing Association)
    60, 292
DMU (decision-making units) 99, 100
dogs 400, 401, 402
dolphins 43
dominance, supermarkets 259
door-to-door selling 264
dotcoms 463, 466–7, 492–3
double glazing 287, 331–2
drinking and driving 314–3
drip advertising 323
'drive thru' grocery shopping 263
driving, drinking and 341–3
DRTV (direct response advertising on
    television) 367
DSS (decision support systems) 144
durability 175, 185
duties 49
DVD recorders 196–7
DVT (deep vein thrombosis) 44–5

e-business 45
e-commerce 45, 49, 265, 409
e-communication 369
e-mail
  marketing 480–1
    creative message design 483–4

  customer acquisition 482
  customer retention 482–3
  response and review 484
  viral 481–2, 490
surveys by 155
unsolicited 363–4
e-marketing 27
  e-mail marketing 480–4
  internet marketing 465–79
early adopters 202
early majority 202
Earth Island Institute 43
EAS (electronic article surveillance) 99
Eastern Europe 8
economic and competitive environment
    34–5, 48–54, 76
economic influences 76, 102
economic policy 48–51
EEA (European Economic Area) 51
EFTA (European Free Trade
    Association) 51
elasticity of demand 93, 220–1
elderly people 312
electricity industry 58, 98
electronic article surveillance (EAS) 99
electronic point-of-sale (EPOS) 143, 271
electronics 94
emergent marketing philosophies 11–14
emotional appeals, advertising 310
empathy, advertising agencies 319
EMS (enhanced messaging service) 486
end use 119
engineering 17
enhanced messaging service (EMS) 486
entrenchment 415
environment 40–1, 55
  consumer behaviour 74–6
  external 15–16, 34–5
  internal 16–17
  marketing 16, 34–5
  situation analysis 290–2
environmental scanning 35–6, 144
EPOS (electronic point-of-sale) 143, 271
essential evidence 442
esteem needs 7 9, 80
ethics
  business 40, 42
  marketing 11–12
  marketing research 167
  personal 40, 42
  see also corporate social
      responsibility
ethnic communities 86
euro 299
Eurobrands 206–7
Europe
  market segmentation 118–19
  marketing environment 33–61
  see also European Union
European Economic Area (EEA) 51
European Free Trade Association
    (EFTA) 51
European Parliament 54
European Union

Common Agricultural Policy (CAP) 55–6
    distribution by intermediaries 272
    duty-free access to markets 50
    e-mail spam 363–4
    harmonisation 57
    marketing environment 33–61
    monopolies 52
    political and regulatory environment 57–8
    product guarantees 186–7
    public procurement 93
    Single European Market (SEM) 50, 51, 57, 112, 118
    trade marks 180
evaluation
    advertising 324
    information 69–70
    integrated marketing communication 299–300
    marketing 419–20
    marketing research 166
    performance, sales representatives 339
    post-purchase 71–2
evening out fluctuating sales 349
events 377
evidence, physical 23, 442
evoked sets 70
exchange processes 4
exchange rates 50
exchange transactions 5
exclusive distribution 269, 270
exhibitions 346, 372–3
exit evaluation, advertising campaigns 324
expanding usage 352
experience curves 236
experimentation 156–7
exploratory research 137–8
extended problem solving 74
external environment 34–5
external influences on pricing decisions 36, 217–24
external marketing audits 404–8
external marketing information sources 142
external organisational environment 15–16
extra product promotions 354–5

face-to-face omnibus surveys 140
facilitating values 253–4
facts, advertising 310–11
fads 39, 199
failure 200, 394
families 88–91
farming see agriculture
fashion products 199
fashions 39–40
fast moving consumer goods (FMCG) 21, 191
fear 310, 311–12
feedback 254, 299–300, 329
feelings 310

field marketing 329–30
field research 147, 149–66
Fiji 126
file sharing services 474
filling product ranges 194
finance function 17
financial benefits of products 214
financial objectives 228–9
financial publics 374
financing benefits 253
fine fragrances 220, 269
Five Forces Model 405–6
fixed costs 234
fixed endorsed approach to branding 192
flexible endorsed approach to branding 192
flowers 3, 50
FMCG (fast moving consumer goods) 21, 191
focus 396
focus groups 151–2, 467
followers 416
food 33–4, 39, 41–2, 60, 51, 192
football 205, 240–1, 379, 380
forecasts 407–8
foreign exchange rates 50
Forest Stewardship Council (FSC) 40–1
forests 40–1
forward integration 267
franchising 255, 256, 268
free gifts 357
free mail-ins 356–7
free merchandise, promotions to retailers 360
free products 354
frequency, advertising 313
friendship 103
FSC (Forest Stewardship Council) 40–1
full service retailing 256
functional benefits of products 213–14
functional organisation 420, 421
functional packaging 189
functional plans 396

gas industry 58
gatekeepers 100, 101
gatherers 486
GATT (General Agreement on Tariffs and Trade) 51
gay market 131–2
GE matrix 403
General Agreement on Tariffs and Trade (GATT) 51
general public 374
generational marketing 37
generic brands 191
genetic modification 60
geodemographics 113–16, 122
geographic adjustments to prices 239
geographic concentration 94
geographic focus, advertising campaigns 322
geographic segmentation 112
geographic structure, sales forces 336
Germany 58, 190

gifts 356–8
    see also sponsorship
global sourcing 101–2
GM (genetic modification) 60
goals see objectives
golden zones 349
good publicity 376
goods 4
    consumer see consumer goods
    merchandise lines, retailing 257–8
    see also products
goodwill 182–3
governments
    bodies as purchasers 92–3
    economic policy 48–51
    political and regulatory environment 54–7
    spending 49
    see also local governments
grading 252
green issues 11–12, 290–2
    see also corporate social responsibility
grey market 37, 118
groceries 245, 256, 263, 473
groups
    decision-making 95
    interviews 151–2
    sociocultural influences 83–91
growth
    products 196–7, 202, 288
    strategies 411–15
guarantees 186–7

harmonisation 57
harvesting 415
health and fitness sector 440
health and safety 40
health concerns 42
heterogeneity, services 435–6
hi-fi equipment 390–1
hierarchy of needs 79–81
higher education see universities
hoardings 316–17
holidays 37, 126, 233, 268
    see also tourism
home audits 140
home deliveries 263
home shopping 369–70
horizontal competition 267
hotels 428–9, 430–1, 445, 447
house journals 377
human rights 398–9
hunters 486
hypermarkets 259–60

ideas 4
identification
    competitors 406
    customer needs 19–20
image 305, 307, 312
imitative products 199
impact, personal selling 325
implementation
    advertising campaigns 323–4

integrated marketing communication
299–300
imposition, distribution channels 254
in-home selling 264
in-pack promotions 357
inbound telemarketing 367
incentives 347–8
income 37–8
increasing frequency and amount of
purchases 350
independent retail outlets 255–6
Independent Television Commission
(ITC) 55, 60
indirect taxation 49
individuals, psychological influences
77–83
industrial concentration 94
industrial goods *see* B2B: goods
industrial marketing *see* B2B: marketing
industry attractiveness 403
inelastic demand 93
influencers 100
information 134
customer databases 370
direct marketing 362
dissemination 352
evaluation 69–70
overload 69
sales representatives gathering 329
searches 68–9
value added services 254
see also communication; data;
marketing information systems
informing, sales representatives 328
initiation, direct marketing 363
innovation 184
diffusion of 201–3
innovative products 199
innovators 202
inseparability, services 434–5
installing, sales representatives 328
Institute of Practitioners in Advertising
(IPA) 60
Institute of Public Relations (IPR) 60,
373
Institute of Sales Promotion (ISP) 60,
292
institutional advertising 307
institutions as purchasers 93
intangibility, services 430–2
integrated marketing communication
budgeting 296–9
definition 280
environment 290–2
evaluation 299–300
implementation 299–300
objectives 293–4
products 287–8
strategies 294–6
target markets 281–7
integration 267
integrative business function, marketing
as 17–19
intelligence 144
intensive distribution 269

interactive marketing 443–5
interactive programme guides (IPG) 489
interactive television (iTV) 295–6, 488–90
interactive voice response (IVR) 485–6
interest rates 49–50
interests, market segmentation 117
interface, marketing as 19
interfunctional orientation 10
interim evaluation, advertising cam
paigns 324
intermediaries 16
distribution channels 249–65
sales promotions to 348–9
internal communication 377
internal influences on pricing decisions
224–7
internal marketing
audits 400–4
information sources 142, 143–4
services 446–51
internal organisational environment
16–17
internal publics 374
international exhibitions 372
international marketing 27
international trading blocs 50–1
internet
auctions 470
B2B spending 469–70
banking 443
banner advertising 476
consumer penetration and spending
468
corporate communications 476–7
databases 149
file sharing services 474
lists 482
marketing 6
advertising 475–6
broadband 478
communication 474–8
future 479
loyalty reinforcement 476
nature 465–7
promotion 474–8
website uses 471–8
marketing research 154–5
omnibus surveys 140
ordering 47
reverse auctions 469
service providers (ISP) 237
shopping 187, 264–5
technologies 45
websites 47, 467–8
marketing uses 471–8
women, use by 75
interpretation of data 165
intertype competition 267
interviewers 163–4
interviews 149–53
introduction of products 195–6, 288
inventory 348–9
invitations, sales promotions 347
IPA (Institute of Practitioners in
Advertising) 60

IPG (interactive programme guides) 489
IPR (Institute of Public Relations) 60,
373
Iraq 96
ISP (Institute of Sales Promotion) 60,
292
ISP (internet service providers) 237
ITC (Independent Television
Commission) 55, 60
iTV (interactive television) 295–6, 488–90
IVR (interactive voice response) 485–6

Japan 14–15, 51
jeans 426–6
JIT (just-in-time) 102
joint demand 93
joint ventures 418
judgemental budget setting 297–8
judgemental sampling 159
just-in-time (JIT) 102

Kenya 3
kiosks, computerised 262

labelling 191
laggards 202
language 187
lapsed customers 371
late adopters 202
late majority 202
leading questions 162
leads 372
learning 78–9
legal environment 34–5, 292
buying process 96
pricing 223–4
less developed countries 50
licensing 418
lifecycles
families 88–91
products *see* products
lifestyles 44
segmentation 115, 117–19
slice-of-life advertising 310
Likert summated ratings 161, 162
limited problem solving 73
limited service retailing 257
lines *see* products
lists 365, 482
loading up 352,
lobbying 61, 377
local buying 273
local governments
political and regulatory environment
56
as purchasers 93
local procurement 101
location 110–11
advertising agencies 318–19
see also place
logging 40–1
logistical values 251–3
logistics *see* distribution
London Marathon 378
long channels 245

long-term plans 396
love needs 79, 80
loyalty 121
    brand 121
    cards 6, 122, 143, 350, 357, 384–5
    creation, direct marketing and 362
    reinforcement, internet marketing
        476
    schemes 347, 347–8, 350, 357, 384–5
luxuries 39

m-marketing 484–8
mackerel 219
macro segments 110–11
macroeconomic environment 48–51
magazines 113, 315–16
maggots 56
mail-ins 356–7
mail order 264, 369–70
mail questionnaires 153
mailing lists 365
maintenance
    products 185–6
    services 177
Malawi 3
management
    marketing see marketing management
    process, marketing as 2
    products see products: management
manufacturers
    branding benefits perspective 181–2
    brands 183
    channel structures 246–8
    concessions in department stores
        258–9
    consumer promotions 351–3
    intermediary sales promotions 348–9
mapping, perceptual 204
marginal costs 234
mark-up 235
market attractiveness model 403
market coverage 266, 268–70
market development 413
market followers 416
market forecasting 407–8
market leadership 415–16
market nichers 417
market opportunities 394–5
market penetration 412–13
market potential 406–8
market research 47, 134–5
Market Research Quality Standards
        Association 166
Market Research Society (MRS) 167
market segments see segmentation
market share 229, 415
market size 271
market structures 394
marketing
    concept 7, 15–19
    definitions 2–7
    development of 7
    transactional value 250
marketing alliances 418
marketing analysis 408–10

marketing audits 399–408
marketing budgets 419
market challengers 416
marketing channels see distribution:
        channels
marketing communication see
        communication
marketing controls 419–20, 423–4
marketing dynamics 1–32
marketing environment 16, 34–5
marketing evaluation 419–20
marketing factors, advertising campaigns
        323
marketing information systems (MIS)
        135, 141–4, 406
marketing management 19–25, 388–9,
        420–2, 436–51
marketing mix 20–4
    advertising in 307–8
    packaging in 189–90
    pricing and 216
    segmentation benefits 127
    services 436–43
marketing myopia 25
marketing objectives 225–6, 229–30,
        410–11
marketing orientation 7, 8, 10
marketing planning 388–9
    benefits 397
    importance 389–97
    internet uses 471
    market forecasting 407–8
    market potential 406–8
    organising marketing activities 420–2
    process 397–420
    purpose 397
    role 389–97
    sales forecasting 407–8
    sales potential 407
marketing plans 393, 397–420
marketing PR 374
marketing programmes 393, 419
marketing research
    briefs 146
    causal research 138
    conducting 163–4
    continuous research 139–40
    decision support systems 144
    definition 136–6
    descriptive research 138
    ethics 166
    evaluation 166
    exploratory research 137–8
    marketing information systems see
            marketing information systems
    objectives 145–6
    planning 146–7
    predictive research 138
    primary research 147, 149–66
    process 144–7
    qualitative research 138–9
    quantitative research 139
    reports 165–6
    role 136–7
    secondary research 147, 148–9

marketing scope 25–7
marketing strategies 40, 393, 411–18
    importance 389–97
    influences on 393–4
    role 389–97
    services 436–43
    see also strategic marketing
markets, street and indoor 262
Maslow's hierarchy of needs 79–81
materials
    handling 47
    technological environment 46
matrix organisation 421, 422
maturity 197, 289
media
    advertising 312–18, 322, 324
    ethnic communities 86
    involving 376
    new 369
    publics 374
    relationships 376
medium-term plans 396
membership groups 87–8
merchandise see goods; products
merchandise-based sales promotion
        methods 356–8
merchandising allowances 360
messages
    advertising 308–12, 324
    creative design 483–4
    precision 326
MFA (multi fibre arrangement) 51
micro segments 111–12, 482
microchips 46
microeconomic environment 51–4
middle class 84
milk 44
MIS see marketing information systems
mission statements 398
MLP (multi-leisure parks) 432
MMS (multimedia messaging service)
        486–7
mobile marketing 484–8
mobile phones
    product lifecycle 196
    sponsorship by operators 377–8
modifications to products 204–6
modified rebuys 96
money-based sales promotion methods
        353–4
money-off coupons see coupons
money saving or making, advertising
        appeals 311
monitoring 299
    see also evaluation
monolithic approach to branding 192
monopolies 52–3, 222
monopolistic competition 54, 222–3
MOSAIC 113–15
motivation 79–81, 338
motor industry
    advertising 312
    channel system competition 267
    marketing environment 36
    products 209–10, 200

MRS (Market Research Society) 167
multi fibre arrangement (MFA) 51
multi-leisure parks (MLP) 432
multimedia messaging service (MMS) 486–7
multiple-choice questions 161
multiple objectives, non-profit organisations 454
multiple publics 452
multiple sourcing 94
multivariable segmentation 122
music 251–2
mutual understanding 373
mystery shopping 156, 436

names, brands 180, 187–8
nappies 198, 407
Natural Resources Institute (NRI) 43
Ncompass 140
necessities 39
needs 3
    identifying 19–20
    Maslow's hierarchy 79–81
    satisfaction 20–4
    social 103
negotiation
    distribution channels 254
    personal selling 334
new media 479–90
new products
    development (NPD) 184, 413
        services 439
    introduction 195–6, 288
    launch 349
    pricing strategies 231–3
new task purchasing 96
news, advertising 310–11
newsletters 377
newspaper advertising 316
nichers 416
'no growth' options 415
nomads 486
non-durable products 175
non-economic influences 103
non-profit marketing 26–7, 451–8
non-random sampling 159
non-store retailing 263–5
NPD see new products: development
NRI (Natural Resources Institute) 43
nuclear industry 82

objections, handling 333–4
objective budgeting 298–9
objectives
    advertising campaigns 321, 322
    corporate 398
    direct marketing 362–3
    financial 228–9
    integrated marketing communication 293–4
    marketing 225–6, 229–30, 410–11
    marketing research 145–6
    multiple, non-profit organisations 454
    organisational 224–5, 270, 393–4
    pricing 228–30

questionnaires 159–60
    sales 229–30, 335–6
    sales promotion 347–8
observational research 155–6
OEM (original equipment manufacturers) 92
Office of Fair Trading (OFT) 55, 58
office supplies 288
Ofgem 58
Oflot 223
OFT see Office of Fair Trading
Oftel 58, 478
Ofwat 58
older people, grey market 37, 118
oligopolies 53, 222
olives 55–6
omnibus surveys 140–1
on-pack promotions 357
on-pack reduced prices 353
online see internet
open-ended questions 160–1
operating methods, retailers 258
operating supplies 177
operational benefits of products 214
operational control 423
operational plans 396
opinions, market segmentation 117
opportunities 409
opportunity to see (OTS) 313, 324
opt in schemes 481, 482
opt-out schemes 481
oranges 248
orders
    direct ordering 362
    online ordering 47
organisational alternatives 420–2
organisational behaviour, decision-making 96–9
organisational capabilities 270
organisational characteristics of macro segmentation 110–11
organisational focus 396
organisational level plans 395
organisational marketing see B2B
organisational objectives 224–5, 270, 393–4
organisational resources 270, 393–4
organising marketing activities 420–2
original equipment manufacturers (OEM) 92
origins of data 138–9
OTS (opportunity to see) 313, 324
out-of-town retail parks 260
out-of-town speciality stores 260
outbound telemarketing 367–8
outdoor advertising 316–18
own-label brands 184, 351
ownership
    retailing 255–6
    services and 430

packaging 46, 188–90
    functional 189
    labelling 191
    in marketing mix 189–90

promotional 189
    waste 190
parallel demand curves 221
partnerships, channel systems 274
parts 177
party plans 264
pay, sales representatives 338
penetration pricing 232–3
people 22–3, 442
    see also consumers; customers
perceived demand curves 219
percentage of sales budgeting methods 298
perception 77–8
perceptual mapping 204
perfect competition 54, 223
performance
    evaluation, sales representatives 339
    products 185, 205–206
peripheral evidence 442
perishability, services 432–4, 439
permission 480
permission-based e-mailing 484
permission marketing 481
personal benefits of products 214–15
personal chemistry, advertising agencies 319
personal ethics 40, 42
personal factors 103
personal interviews 149–50
personal selling 9
    definition 324
    internet 477–8
    process 331–5
    promotional mix 279, 324–43
    role 324–30
    sales management 335–9
    see also sales representatives
personalisation 483, 489
personalised registration plates 213
personality 77
persuading, sales representatives 328
pervasive computing 46
petrol 53, 125
petrol station forecourt retailing 262
pharmaceuticals 60, 283, 394
philosophical targets 398
PhoneBus 140
phones see mobile phones; telephones
physical evidence 23, 442
physiological needs 79–80
piloting 163
pioneering advertising 205–6
pizzas 228
place
    marketing mix 22
    services 440–1
    see also distribution; location; retailers; wholesalers
planned economies 9
planning
    definition 389
    marketing plans 393, 397–420
    marketing research 146–7
    personal selling 332

planning (*continued*)
  sales 335–6
  see also marketing planning
planning permission 56
PLC *see* products: lifecycles
PNS (Pre- and Post-Natal Survey) 139
point-of-purchase (POP) materials 309
point-of-sale (POS) displays 359
points, loyalty cards 357
Poland 85, 110
policies
  brands and branding 191–2
  pricing 231–4
political and regulatory environment
      34–5, 54–61, 76, 292
POP (point-of-purchase) materials 309
population definition 158
Porter's five forces 405–6
POS (point-of-sale) displays 359
positioning 203–6, 229
post-purchase evaluation 71–2
post-tests, advertising campaigns 324
posters, advertising 60, 316–17
potential customers 16, 71
potential products 173, 174
PPS (pre-packaged spirits) 104–5
PR *see* public relations
Pre- and Post-Natal Survey (PNS) 139
pre-packaged spirits (PPS) 104–5
pre-testing, advertising 323
precipitation 97–8
precision
  marketing 481
  personal selling 326
  targeting 326
predictive research 138
pregnancy 143
premium money 361
premium prices 216
press relations 376
press releases 376, 477
pressure groups 43–4, 61
prestige 103
price elasticity of demand 220–1
prices 4, 212–13
  adjustments 238–9
  appropriate 102
  changes 234
  competition-based pricing 237–8
  cost-based pricing 235–6
  customers' perspectives 213–15
  cuts 234
  demand-based pricing 236–7
  discounts 238–9
  external influences 36, 217–24
  fixing 224
  geographic adjustments 239
  internal influences on pricing
        decisions 224–7
  leadership 225
  legal and regulatory framework 223–4
  marketing mix 21–2, 216
  non-profit organisations 457
  objectives 228–30
  penetration pricing 232–3

perceptions 213–17
policies 231–4
premium prices 216
product mix pricing strategies 233–4
psychological pricing 237
range setting 234–8
reduced, offers 353
role 213–17
sellers' perspectives 215–16
services 439–40
setting 227–39
skimming 232
special adjustments 238–9
strategies 231–4
structures 238
tactics 238–9
pricing *see* prices
primary data 147, 149–66
primary research 147, 149–66
print presentation, advertising 324
privacy 490
privatisation 52
prize-based sales promotion methods
      356–8
PRiZM 115
probability sampling 158
problems
  definition, marketing research 145
  recognition 67–8
  solving 72–3
processes 23
  services 442–3
  wireless marketing 486
producers 244–6
product-based sales promotion methods
      354–6
product-based structure, sales forces 336
product champions 206
product managers 206
product–market matrix 411–12
product mix pricing strategies 233–4
product organisation 421
product-oriented advertising 305–7,
      310–11
production 17
  orientation 7, 8
  processes 46–7
productivity 448–51
products 172–3
  accumulation 252
  application, macro segmentation 111
  augmented 173, 174
  B2B markets 287–8
  benefits 213–15
  characteristics 271
  classification 174–7
  consumer markets 287–8
  core 173–4
  current needs 18
  customer needs 20–4
  definition 173
  deletion 194–5
  design 184–5, 186, 205, 206
  durability 175, 185
  failure 200

future needs 18
guarantees 186–7
integrated marketing communication
      287–8
items 178
lifecycles (PLC) 195
  communication 288–90
  decline 197–8, 289
  growth 196–7, 202, 288
  introduction 195–6
  maturity 107, 289
  pricing 225–6
  product levels, classes, forms and
        brands 200
  shape 198–200
  targeting 125
lines 178–9
maintenance 185–6
management
  brand creation 184–91
  brand development 191–5
  European strategy 206–7
  organisation 206
  product lifecycles *see* lifecycles
        above
marketing mix 20–4
meaning 173–4
mix 178, 179
modifications 204–6
non-durable 175
orientation 8–9
performance 185, 205–6
portfolios 400–4, 456
positioning 203–6
potential 173, 174
quality 185–6, 205, 206, 214
ranges 177–9, 191–2, 257–8
reliability 185–6
repositioning 204–6
services 175, 438–9
situation analysis 287–8
specification 98, 102
storage 252
style 186
tangible 173, 174
technological environment 46
see also brands and branding; goods;
      new products; packaging; services
professional purchasing 95
profits 215–16
  cost–volume–profit relationship
        234–5
project plans 396
promotion 4
  internet marketing 471, 474–8
  marketing mix 22
  services 442–3
      see also advertising; direct mar
        keting; exhibitions; integrated
        marketing communication; per
        sonal selling; public relations;
        sales promotion; sponsorship
promotional mix
  advertising 279, 287, 305–7
  communication 279–80, 280–300

direct marketing 279, 362–4
 personal selling 279, 324–43
 public relations 279, 373–7
 sales promotion 279, 346–61
promotional packaging 189
prospecting 328, 331–2
prospects 332
protectionism 51
psychographics 117–19
psychological discomfort 71
psychological influences, consumer
 behaviour 77–83
psychological pricing 237
public procurement 92–3
public relations 346
 advertising and 373, 376
 definition 373
 direct mail 365
 promotional mix 279, 373–7
 role 373–5
 techniques 375–7
public scrutiny, non-profit organisations
 455–6
public utilities 223
publicity 376–7
 non-profit organisations 456
publics 373–4, 452
pull strategies 282–3
purchase frequency and volatility,
 advertising campaigns 323
purchase significance 96
purchasing
 B2B policy 94–5
 see also buying
push strategies 282–3

qualitative data 165
qualitative research 138–9
qualitative targets 398
quality
 consistency 102
 Eurobrands 207
 products 185–6, 205, 206, 214
 services 443–6
quangos 58, 223
quantitative data 165
quantitative research 139
quantitative targets 398
question marks 400, 401–2
questionnaires 153, 159–63
quota sampling 159

R&D (research and development) 17,
 45–6
RA (Radio Authority) 60
radio advertising 314–15
Radio Authority (RA) 60
rail transport 435, 440, 449, 454
random sampling 158
range setting, prices 234–8
ranges, products see products
rating scales 161, 162
ratings, advertising 313
rational appeals, advertising 310
raw materials 177

rebuys 96
reach 313
recruitment, sales representatives 336–7
recycling 13–14, 46, 371–2
reduced prices 353
reduction on service levels 450
reference groups 87–8
regional organisation 421–2
registration plates, personalised 213
regularity of planning 396
regulatory environment 54–61
 buying process 96
 communication 292
 consumer behaviour 76
 distribution 272
 pricing 223–4
reinforcement advertising 305, 306–7
relationship managers 328–9
relationship marketing 5–6, 47
relationships
 building 363
 buyer–seller 5–6
 buyer–supplier 470
 media 376
 sales representatives maintaining
 328–9
reliability
 products 185–6
 services 444
 supply 102
reminder and reinforcement advertising
 305, 306–7
remoteness 271
renewal 371
repair services 177
reports, marketing research 165–6
repositioning 204–6
resale price maintenance 223
research
 internet uses 471–2
 see also marketing research
research and development (R&D) 17,
 45–6
resellers 92
reselling 371
resources 118
 allocation, non-profit organisations
 452
 attraction, non-profit organisations
 452
 Eurobrands 206
 organisational 270, 393–4
response hierarchy 122, 284–6
responsiveness 444
retail audits 141
retail cooperatives 268
retail parks 260
retailers
 branding benefits perspective 182–3
 brands 184
 channel structures 244–6
 non-store retailing 263–5
 sales force support for 360–1
 sales promotions by 349–51
 sales promotions to 359–61

selling and marketing assistance to
 360–1
 store types 258–65
retention 78, 324, 371
return on investment (ROI) 402
revenue 215–16
reverse auctions 469
reviewing databases 371–2
revitalisation products 200
rewards 347–8
risks
 attitudes to 394
 transactional value 250
road haulage 57
ROI (return on investment) 402
Romania 437–8
Rothschild's communications planning
 process model 280–1, 300
routine problem solving 72–3
routine rebuys 96
rules, questionnaires 163

safety 40, 79, 80
salaries, sales representatives 338
sale or return promotions 349
sales
 fluctuating, evening out 353
 forecasting 407–8
 potential 407
 objectives 229–30
 volume 229
sales branches 246
sales contests 361
sales-driven organisations 422
sales forces see sales representatives
sales management 335–9
sales offices 247
sales orientation 7, 8, 9–10
sales presentations 332, 333
sales promotion 58, 345
 B2B markets 361
 to consumers 353–9
 definition 346–7
 gift-, prize- or merchandise-based
 methods 356–8
 internet 477
 money-based methods 353–4
 objectives 347–8
 product-based methods 354–6
 promotional mix 279, 346–61
 to retail trade 359–61
 role 346–53
 store-based methods 359
sales representatives 325
 B2B markets 332
 sales management 335–9
 support 48, 360–1
 targets 336
 tasks 327–30
salt 125
samples 157–9, 355–6
satellite television 314
satisfaction of customer needs 20–4
sausages 216–17
SBU (strategic business units) 391

scheduling, advertising campaigns 323–4
schools 381–2
secondary data 147, 148–9
secondary research 147, 148–9
security 312, 444
segmental organisation 421, 422
segmentation 108–9
  B2B markets 110–12, 129
  benefits 127
  concept of 109
  consumer markets 112–22
  dangers 127–8
  implementation 123–6
  micro segments 482
  success criteria 128–9
selection
  channel members 272–4
  sales representatives 336–7
  suppliers 98–9
selective attention 77–8
selective distribution 269
selective perception 78
selective retention 78
self-actualisation needs 79, 80–1
self-esteem, advertising appeals 312
self-fulfilling prophecies 198
self-liquidating offers 356
self-orientation 118
self-service retailing 257
sellers
  perspectives on prices 215–16
  resellers 92
selling
  assistance to retailers 360–1
  combination 363
  cross selling 371
  orientation 7, 8, 9–10
  up 371
  see also personal selling; retailers;
    wholesalers
SEM (single European market) see
    European Union
semantic differential scales 161, 162
semi-finished goods 177
semi-structured interviews 150
senior market 37, 118
sensitivity, people 163
service goods 26
service orientation, non-profit
    organisations 455
services 4, 428–9
  application, macro segmentation 111
  characteristics 429–36
  classifying 429
  consumer 175–7
  internal marketing 446–51
  levels 256–7, 450
  marketing management 436–51
  people 442
  perspectives on markets 429–36
  physical evidence 442
  place 440–1
  price 439–40
  processes 442–3
  productivity 448–51

products 175, 438–9
  promotion 442–3
  quality 443–6
  training 447–8
SERVQUAL 444
shape of product lifecycles 198–200
shelf reduced prices 353
shelf space 349
Shell's directional policy matrix 403
shipbuilding industry 49
shopping
  goods 175
  home 369–70
  internet 187, 264–5
  see also retailers
short channels 244–5
short messaging service (SMS) 485, 486
short-term plans 396
SIC (standard industrial classification)
    111
silicone breast implants 290–1
single European market (SEM) see
    European Union
single sourcing 94
situation analysis 281–7
size
  markets 271
  organisations 110
  people 113
skimming 232
slice-of-life advertising 310
small businesses, marketing 27
smartcards 445
SMS (short messaging service) 485, 486
soccer see football
social class 83–4
social needs 103
societal attitudes on marketing strategy
    39–40
societal marketing 11–12
sociocultural environment 34–5, 36–45,
    290
  consumer behaviour 74, 83–91
socioeconomic groupings 84
sorting 252
soups 119
source credibility 295–6
South Africa 50, 248
Spain 55–6, 85
spam 363–4
special adjustments, prices 238–9
specialisms, advertising agencies 319
speciality goods 175–6
speciality stores 260–1
spending patterns 37–8
sponsorship 346
  arts 377, 378, 380
  broadcasting 379–80
  definition 377
  sport 377, 378–9
  see also cause related marketing
sport
  sponsorship 377, 378–9
  see also football
standard industrial classification (SIC)

    111
stars 400, 402
state-owned monopolies 52–3
status 117–18
status quo 229–30
STEP 34–6, 76, 404, 405
stereotypes 291
stock 348–9
storage 252
store-based sales promotion methods
    359
stores
  traffic 350
  types 258–63
strategic alliances 418
strategic business units (SBU) 391
strategic control 423
strategic marketing
  competitive positions and postures
    415–18
  growth strategies 411–18
  'no growth' options 415
  see also marketing strategies
strategic vision 24–5
strategies
  branding 184–95
  channels 265–74
  competitive 391, 416
  competitors 395
  corporate 390–1
  integrated marketing communication
    294–6
  marketing see marketing strategies;
    strategic marketing
  pricing 231–4
  sales 335–6
  services marketing 436–43
stratified sampling 158
strengths 408
strivers 118
Strong theory of communication 284–6
structured interviews 150
structures
  channel 244–8, 266–8
  market 394–5
  prices 238
strugglers 118
students 134–5, 451
style, products 186
subcultures 85–7
supermarkets 56
  dominance 259
  local buying 273
  loyalty cards 122, 384–5
  own brands 184
  sales promotion 353, 384–5
suppliers 16
  appraisal of 99
  B2B buying decision-making process
    96–9
  buyer–supplier relationships 470
  buying centres and 101–2
  choice 331
  commitment 99
  potential customers, attitudes to 71

selection 98–9
supply
    direct 244, 440
    reliability and continuity 102
    services 450–1
supportive brand names 188
surveys 140–1, 149–53
survival 230
sustainability 12–13
sustainable development 13
sustainable marketing 12–14
sweepstakes 357–8
switchers 121
Switzerland 86, 190
SWOT analysis 408–10
systems, services 449

tangibility, market segments 128
tangible products 173, 174
tangibles, services 444
Target Group Index (TGI) 139
targets
    advertising campaigns 321
    audiences, advertising 321, 322
    iTV marketing 489
    markets, integrated marketing
        communication 281–7
    philosophical 398
    precision, targeting 326
    qualitative 398
    quantitative 398
    segmentation 123–6
task budgeting 298–9
taxation 49
technological environment 34–5, 45–8,
        75–6
technology 271, 449
teenagers see young people
telecommunications 47, 52
telemarketing 332, 367–8
telephone banking 443
telephones
    industry 58
    interviews 152–3
    omnibus surveys 140
    see also mobile phones
teleshopping 264, 370
television
    advertising 314
    digital 232
    direct response advertising (DRTV)
        367
    interactive (iTV) 295–6, 488–90
    sponsorship 379–80
    sports sponsorship 379
    viewership panels 140
testimonials, advertising 310–11
testing, advertising 322–3
text messaging 484–8
textile industry 51
TGI (Target Group Index) 139
theme parks 433, 437–8
threats 409
time values 230
timing
    advertising campaigns 322
    Eurobrands 207

title 250
toasters 176
tobacco 49, 60
toilet tissue 203–4
tokens 357
total costs 235
total market 407
total quality management (TQM) 185
tourism 430, 436, 437–8, 439, 441–2
    see also holidays; hotels
town centre speciality stores 261
TQM (total quality management) 185
traceability 43
trade agreements 50–1
trade associations 61
trade marks 180
trade names 180
trade promotions 348–9, 360
trade shows 346, 372–3
trading blocs 50–1
trading stamps 357
trading standards officers 56
trading up 352
training
    retailers' sales forces 360
    sales representatives 337
    services staff 447–8
    value added services 254
trains see rail transport
transactional values 250–1
transport-oriented media 318
transportation 252–3
    see also delivery; distribution
travel
    agents 418
    business 108–9
    see also holidays; hotels; tourism
trial 352, 362
trust 103
tuna fishing 43

UK see United Kingdom
uncontrollability of publicity 376
undifferentiated targeting 124–6
United Kingdom
    monopolies 52
    sales promotion 58
    waste recycling 190
United States 118
universities 373–4, 422, 435–6
unsolicited e-mails 363–4
unsolicited mail 365
unsolicited text messaging 485
unsought goods 176
unstructured interviews 150
USA 118
usage
    benefits, advertising appeals 312
    expanding 352
    rates 111, 120
user-based product classifications 175–7
users 92, 100, 246–8, 486
utilities 223

VALS-2 (Values and Life Style) 118
value added 347
value added services 249–54

value added tax (VAT) 49
values
        brands 182–3
        corporate 398
        facilitating 253–4
        logistical 251–3
        statements 398
        transactional 250–1
Values and Life Style (VALS-2) 118
variable costs 234
variety stores 259
VAT (value added tax) 49
vending machines 71, 265
VER (voluntary export restraint) 51
vertical competition 266, 267
vertical marketing systems (VMS) 267
video games 301–2
videos 196
village grocery shops 256
viral marketing 481–2, 490
visible staff 448
vision
    statements 398
    strategic 24–5
visit generation 362
VMS (vertical marketing systems) 267
volumes
    allowances, promotions to retailers
        360
    cost–volume–profit relationship
        234–5
    sales 229
voluntary chains 268
voluntary export restraint (VER) 51
voting 284

waste 47
    packaging 190
    recycling see recycling
watches 321
water industry 58
weak theory of communication 284, 285
weaknesses 408
websites see internet
welcome calls 371
whales 14–15
whisky 197
wholesalers 255
    brands 184
    channel structures 245–6
    voluntary chains 268
wind power 413
wireless marketing 484–8
withdrawal 415
women, internet use 75
working patterns 272

yo-yos 200–1
yogurt 66
young people 37
    youth markets 87, 104–5
    see also students

Zimbabwe 3
zoned pricing 239

Index of company names

Note: Names are indexed under the first part of the name, eg John Lewis

A C Nielsen 139, 140, 156
AB Konstruktions-Bakelit 246
Abbey National 98, 134–5
Access Omnibus Surveys 140
Accountancy Age 315
Adidas 88
Aer Lingus 410
Age Concern 308–9
Ahold 243, 268, 277
Airbus 271, 406, 407
Albert Heijn 184, 243
Aldi 88, 225, 450
Alfa Laval 246
Alfa Romeo 312, 392
Alitalia 50
Allison Transmissions 372
Amazon 10, 280, 302, 409, 467, 468
American Express 371, 415
Amora Maille 195, 412
Andrex 203
Angel Uplifting 487
Ann Summers 264
Another.com 482
Apparel Industry Magazine 467
Apple 181
ARC 478
Argos 257, 263
Arsenal FC 180, 240
ASDA 56, 169, 223, 228, 260, 263, 385, 473
Aston Martin 391
Auchan 260
Audi 181, 209
Australian Tourist Commission 441–2
Austrian Airlines 50
Avantis 180
Avis 388
Avon 325, 380

B&Q 265, 446
Babcock Rosyth Defence 49
Bacardi 104–5
BAE 95
Bailey's 136–7
Balkanair 433
Bananalotto 482
Barbie 380
Barclaycard 379

Barclays Bank 469
BASF 13, 224
Batchelor's 119
Baxters 119
Bayer 375
Bayern Munich 205, 240
BBC 408, 439
Ben & Jerry's 412
Bendicks 360
Benetton 7, 256
Berlin Philharmonic Orchestra 380
Bestfoods 412
Bestway 274
bettingzone.co.uk 466
BhS 259
Bic 417
Bijenkorf 258
Bird's Eye 88
Bird's Eye Walls 359
Black & Decker 185, 186
Blackwells 264
Bloomsbury Publishing 413–14
Blue Arrow 484
Bluewater 259
Bluewave 465–6
bmi media 317
BMRB 139, 468, 476
BMW 174, 209–10, 214, 330, 392, 478
Boddingtons 306
The Body Shop 41, 42
Boeing 271, 406, 407
boo.com 492–3
Boots 75, 143, 169, 365
Borders 10–11
Bosch 178, 185, 186
Boston Consulting Group 400
Botton Village 285
Bounty 143, 291
BP 53
British Aerospace 95
British Airways 50, 109, 236, 316, 410, 434
British Museum 483
British Telecommunications *see* BT
Britvic 356, 395
BSkyB 379
BT 86, 225

BT Cellnet 146
Budget 388
Budweiser 481
Buena Vista 414
BUPA 440
Burger King 297, 436
Burmah Castrol 183
Business Life 316

Cadbury Schweppes 183, 398–9, 419, 421
Cadbury's 43, 192, 214
Cahoot 484
Campanile 432
Campbell 119, 412
Camphill Village Trust 285
Camping Card Scandinavia 445
Cap Gemini Ernst & Young 467–8
Cape Reefers 248
Capespan International 248
Carling 379
Carlsberg 377
Carphone Warehouse 446
Carrefour 244, 260, 277
Casino 3
Cemex 394
Census 392
Channel Tunnel 405
Chelsea TV 480, 481
Cheltenham & Gloucester 68–9
Chemistry in Britain 315
Chiquita Brands 51
Chivers Hartley 415
Chronos Publishing 131
Cine UK 431
Circular Distributors 355
Cisco 470
Citibank 183
CiTV 475–6
Claritas 482
Classic FM 314
Club 18–30: 59, 174
Cobblewood Mushrooms 273
Coca-Cola 87, 172, 181, 183, 289, 296, 359, 377, 379, 382, 418, 490
Codepar/SPCD 412
Colgate-Palmolive 207, 329
Colman 195

Comic Relief 307–8
Commercial Union 380
Concourse Initiatives 356
Condomania 169–70
Condomi 170
Connex South Central 435
Consodata 482
Contender 414
Coors Brewers 132, 464
Corus 26, 177
Costco 262
Covent Garden Soups 119
Covisint 469
Cressida 412
Cross & Blackwell 119
Curry's 295
Cussons 476

Daimler-Chrysler 469
Dairy Crest 174
The Dalesman 315
Danone 60
Datamonitor 368
Dell 418, 470
Diesel 60
Disney 183, 330, 356, 418, 438
Disneyland Paris 87
Dolphin Telecommunications 328
Domino's Pizza 379, 443, 489
Dr Oetker 402
Dresdner Kleinwort Benson 263
Drilcon 272
Dualit 176
Dun & Bradstreet 158
Dunkin' Donuts 485
Dunlop 26
Duracell 328
Durex 169–70
Dwr y Cwm 417

Eagle Star 446
Early Learning Centre 148, 460
easyJet 236
eBay 467, 470
Eden Vale 412
Egg 489
Electronics Boutique 302
Elior 73
Elizabeth Arden 412
Elo Pak 9
eMarketer 469
Eminem 173
English National Ballet 380
Entertainer Group 200
Esso 53
Euromonitor 149
European Central Bank 299
Evans 113
Executive Airlines 312
Experian 113–15

Fabulous Bakin' Boys 483–4
The Farmer 315
Fashionmall 492–3
FBS Engineering 392

FCUK 59, 87
Federal Express 474
Ferrari 377
Financial Times 471
Findus 177
Firestone 26, 267
Fisherman's Friend 63–4, 276–7
Fitness First 440
Flora 378
Florette 253
Flytxt 487
Fondul Pentru Dezvoltare Turistica
    Sighisoara 438
Ford 98, 124, 182, 192, 209, 267, 379, 469
Forrester Research 263, 487, 488
Foyles 10–11
France Telecom 304–5
FreeMarkets 469
French Connection 87
Fresh Produce Terminals 248
Freundin 315
Friends of the Earth 4, 41, 43, 61
Friends United 463–4
Fuji 402
Future Foundation 134, 154
Fyffes 248

Gallup 164
Gap 425
Gateshead Metro Centre 262
GeneData 394
General Electric 403
General Motors 372, 469
Gethal 40
GetThere 418
Gillette 207, 417
Glaxo Wellcome 381
GlaxoSmithKline 25, 293
GNER 449
Golden Wonder 296
Goodyear 26
Gossard 114, 257
Great Ormond Street Children's Hospital
    453–4
Green Flag 458
Greenpeace 4, 40–1, 43, 61, 455–6
Gucci 80
Guinness 314, 356
Gulfstream 312

H Samuel 385
Häagen Dazs 20, 356
Haburi.com 141
Hachette 73
Hamlin Electronics 24
handbag.com 75, 364, 476
Happy Dog 486
Harper Collins 485
Harris Research Centre 151
Harrods 203, 256, 380
Hasbro 487
Heinz 47, 112, 119, 177, 178, 184, 188,
    192, 194, 207, 214
Hellman's 352, 412, 415
Hema 258

Henkel 310
Henley Centre 230, 367
Hennes & Mauritz 257–8
Herbert Smith 380
Hermelin Research 153
Hershey 43
Hertz 388
Hertz Lease 367–8
High and Mighty 113
High Life 316
Hino Motors 418
HMV 251–2, 261
Hodder Headline 410
Holcim 393–4
Holiday Autos 388–9
Holiday Inn 432
Holmes Place 440
Honda 51, 267, 330, 392
Hoover 174, 182
Hotpoint 174
House of Fraser 259
HP Foods 329
HSM 368

Iberia 50
IBM 45–6, 91, 94, 266, 326
Iceland 60
Icelandair 229
ICI 183
IFAW (International Fund for Animal
    Welfare) 14–15
IKEA 238, 250–1
Impex 64, 276
Inbox 486
Indesit 174
Industrial Equipment News 315
Ingersoll-Rand 272
Inner Medical 290
Intel 94
Interbrand Newell & Sorrell 182
Intermarché 260
International Data Corp. 471
International Fund for Animal Welfare
    (IFAW) 14–15
iVillage.co.uk 75

J-17 315
J&B Rare Scotch Whisky 381
Jaboneria 412
Jaeger 259
Jaguar 182
Jarvis Hotels 441, 447
Jet 262
JJB Sports 241
John Lewis 176, 259
John Smith 309
Johnson & Johnson 207, 336
Johnson Wax 412
Jupiter MMXI 75
JVC 377

Kaufhalle 259
KEF 226
Kelda Group 12
Kellogg's 1–2, 91, 182, 192, 306–7, 314, 477

KFC 297
Kids 'a' Us 260
Kiss 100: 487–8
Kleenex 198, 203
Klemm 272
KLM 50, 236
Knorr 412
Kodak 187, 402, 472–3
Kompass 158
Kookaï 317
Kooshies Baby Products 407
Kruidvat 99
Kudos Group 132
Kwik Fit 152
Kwik Save 184, 225

LA Fitness 440
Lada 186
Lafarge 394
Lambourghini 186
Landmark 274
Land's End 187, 369
lastminute.com 29–31, 467, 481
Lazenby's 216–17
Lee 425
Lever Fabergé 178–9, 297, 307–8
Levi Strauss 182, 257, 425–6, 481
Lidl 225, 450
Lindt 458
Linn Products 390–1
Lion Biosciences 394
Lipton 401
Lloyds TSB 377, 380
Lofthouse of Fleetwood 63–4, 276–7
Londis 261
London Transport 12, 445
L'Oréal Elvive 116
Lowe Digital 75
Lucozade 309
Lufthansa 410
Lurpak 225
Lynx 178–9, 482

Mace 261
Macmillan Cancer Trust 381
Madonna 172
Madrange 39
Manchester United 205, 240–1, 377,
    475–6
Manor Bakeries 308
Manto Group 132
Marks & Spencer 3, 113, 182, 184, 256,
    259, 268, 485
Marriott 428
Mars 207, 330, 460
Mastercard 379
Mates Healthcare 169–70
Mattel 380
McCain 120, 402
McDonald's 42, 91, 93, 94, 181, 297, 398,
    448
McEwan's 377
McGhan 290
McQuillan Engineering Industries 271
McVities 475

Mediae Trust 399
Mercedes-Benz 209
Merck 25
Merlin Timber Products 333
Meto 99
Microsoft 196, 301–2, 460
Midland Mainline 449
Migros 3
Miller Genuine Draft 292
Millivres-Prowler Group 131
MindMatics 486
Mini 209–10
Mintel 471
Mizz 315
Momentum 330
Monoprix 259
MORI 140
Morrisons 385
Moser GmbH 247
Motorola 94
MRSL 149
Müller 66, 412–13
Mustang 270
My Offers 482

National Car Parks 404–5
National Health Service 439
National Lottery 223, 261
National Missing Persons Helpline 451–2
National Trust 430
Nationwide 155, 377, 381
Nedan Zoetwaren BV 276–7
Nederman 24
Nekermann 264
Nestlé 16, 33, 43, 178, 179, 207, 345–6,
    355, 382, 472
NetGenics 394
Netto 88, 225, 450
NetValue 480
Next 256, 257, 261
Next Directory 371
NFU Mutual 311
Nike 88, 108, 180, 182, 241, 493
Nintendo 301–2
Nippon Suisan 412
Nissan 51, 294, 362, 469, 489
Nokia 94, 101–2
NOP 75
Norsk Hydro 381
Novotel 432
NSPCC 95, 458, 459–60

Ocado 473
Odeon 431
Office World 246
O'Hagan 217
The Oldie 315
Olivetti 46
Olympic 50
Olympus 215
Opel 377
Orange 180, 182, 304–5
Otto Versand 264, 415
Our Price 170
Outbound Teleculture 368

Oxfam 27, 455
Oxo 357

P. J. Holloway 376
Pampers 198, 294, 295
Pedigree 416
Pennine Telecom 328
Pepe Jeans 87
Pepsi 4, 87, 296
PhoneSites 317
Pizza Hut 432
Playboy 315
Polaroid 198
Porsche 176
Post Office 256
Precious Woods Amazon 40–1
Pret à Manger 436
Preussag 268
Princes 42
Pringle 193
Pringles 382
Procter & Gamble 53, 53, 181, 207, 289,
    294, 297, 335, 355, 385, 395
Promodès 3
Prudential 478

Quaker 416
Quelle 264
QVC 370

Radion 68
Rank Hovis McDougall 181, 183
Reader's Digest 358
Real Madrid 205
Reckitt and Benckiser 192–3
Red Square 292
Reebok 88, 108, 257
Renault 209, 267, 469
Rentokil Initial 338
Rentokil Tropical Plants 328
Respect for Animals 295
Rey & Co 60
RHM 181, 183
Ribena 293, 395
Rimmel 488–9
Robinsons 356, 395
Roche 224
Rolex 80
Rolls-Royce 80
Rosenberg Ventilation 376
Royal Bank Group 469
Royal National Institute for the Blind
    465–6
Royal Vendex KBB 258
RSGB Omnibus 140
RSPCA 456–7, 458
Rural Shops Alliance 256
Rutland Gilts 185
Ryanair 236–7, 410
Rymans 246

Saab 246, 271, 330
Sabena 50, 236
Safeway 243, 273, 350, 385

Saga 37, 118
Sainsbury's 53, 184, 263, 273, 296, 311, 385, 446, 469, 473
Samaritans 457–8
Sandoz 25
Sara Lee 481
SAS 347–8
Scania 418
Schwan 402
Scott Worldwide 207
Scottish & Newcastle 132, 183
Scottish Tourist Board 430
Seeboard 368
Severn Trent 12–13
Shaw's 263
Shell 53, 262, 309–10, 477
Showcase 431
Siemens 94
Sierex BV 3
Sight Savers International 367
Sinbad 316
Skelair 272
Skoda 82–3, 174
Sky 379, 480, 488
Slendertone UK 366
Slim Fast 412
Smirnoff 105, 292
SNCF 52–3
Soleco 253
Sony 182, 199, 301–2
Spar 261
Sportal 466
SportingLife.com 466
Sports Marketing Surveys 148
SSL International 169
St Ivel 412
Staples 246
Star City 432
Strongbow 105
Sugro UK 245
Sun Microsystems 75
Sunny Delight 289
Superdrug 170, 261, 269
Svenska Handelsbanken 443
Swanage Railway 454

Swissair 236
Systembolaget 52

T&T 288–9, 477
talkSPORT 314
Tango 200
Taxi Media 317
Taylor Nelson Sofres 139
TDI 317
Teijo Pesukoneet 247
Telder 153
Telegen 368
Tengelmann 260
Tennents Caledonian Breweries 155
Tesco 6, 56, 75, 98, 143, 191, 263, 273, 277, 306, 350, 355, 384–5, 381, 382, 425, 450, 458, 469, 473
Tetra Pak 9
Teuscher 408–9
Texaco 358
TheMutual.net 482
Thorntons 261
Tie Rack 257
Today's 261
Top Man 170
totalbet.com 466
Tottenham Hotspur 240
Toyota 51, 317
Toys 'a' Us 260, 264
Tupperware 264
Turtle Island 126
Tussauds 433
Twentieth Century Fox 414
Twinings 357

UCI 431
UGC 431
UKBetting.com 466
Umbro 241
Unigate 412
Unilever 16, 53, 195, 411–12, 417
United Parcel Services 442
Universal 414

Valio 225

Van den Bergh 151
Van Dyck 178
Vendex 258
Vestas Wind Systems 413
Vestech Japan Corporation 413
Video Net 185
viewlondon.co.uk 483
Virgin 183
Virgin Megastores 170, 302
Virgin Mobile 485
Virgin Radio 314
Virgin Trains 435, 440, 449
Vivendi 378, 398
Vizzavi 378
Vodafone 182, 377–8, 482, 484
Vogue 316
Volvo 6, 36, 246, 330
Vroom & Dressman 258
VW 82, 209–10

Waitrose 263, 311, 473
Wal-Mart 385
Walker's Crisps 296
Warner Brothers 414
Warner Village 431, 432
Welsh Tourist Board 436
Werther's 360
WH Smith 131, 291, 409–10
Whitworths 231
Wilkinson Sword 417
World Books 324
World Duty Free 355
Wrangler 425
WWF 41

Xbox 301–2

Yahoo! 466
Yellow Pages 70, 441
Yomega 201
yorg.com 167
Yves St Laurent 189

Zanussi 174
Zara 267